EXPLAINING IT TO SOMEONE

Learning From the Arts

ROBERT HAGELSTEIN

LACUNAE MUSING
North Palm Beach, Florida
2020

Library of Congress Control Number: 2020934196

ISBN: 978-0-578-65465-2

First published in 2020
Lacunae Musing, North Palm Beach, FL
http://lacunaemusing.blogspot.com

The Cover:
Posters of Palm Beach Dramaworks' 'A Streetcar Named Desire,' 'Indecent,' 'Long Day's Journey Into Night,' 'Satchmo at the Waldorf,' and 'The Spitfire Grill' were designed by Frank 'Fraver' Verlizzo and are used with his and PBD's permission on the cover of this book
They have all been manipulated, resized or rearranged for artistic expression by Cover Designer S.M.Savoy

Printed in the United States of America

Digital books produced by Booknook.Biz

*There comes a time when you
realize that everything is a dream,
and only those things preserved in writing
have any possibility of being real.*

James Salter, *All That Is*

CONTENTS

INTRODUCTION

Published last year, *Waiting for Someone to Explain It: The Rise of Contempt and the Decline of Sense* is a collection of writings over more than a decade from my blog lacunaemusing.blogspot.com. Those entries attempted to document and understand the economic and political morass we found ourselves in at the beginning of the 21st century.

While writing about those issues, it was also a space where I could write about and analyze what I was personally experiencing in my cultural life, particularly the literature, music, and theatre of the same period. If I was seeking "answers" in my previous work from politicians or economists, perhaps better clues can be found in the works of some of our most creative people. I think of them as our greatest philosophers.

The present book focuses on those cultural experiences. For me they are beacons of insight into our frailties, leading us into a deeper understanding of the world and ourselves: they show us what it means to be human. Unlike most other works of literary or theatrical examination, this is an idiosyncratic one. I make no pretense that there is a central theme other than the works I cover are tied together by the unique thread of my own life and times. Sometimes I wonder whether I chose these works, or they chose me.

As such the plays and the books and the music I reviewed are a heterogeneous lot that I read or experienced mostly during the years I've been publishing the blog. For instance, I don't have any entries on Dickens or Hardy, both of whom I enjoyed reading in college and into my 20's. If they were alive today, imagine what they would be writing! But I sought out what I read and saw for a reason during the first two decades of the new millennium.

Our writers of fiction and drama drill down to the inner world of their characters, trying to make sense of life from within. Other artists, those in the performing or visual arts are doing the same thing, though perhaps more abstractly. What they have to say about our world matters as much as what the journalists and non-fiction writers offer us, perhaps more so. The writers of non-fiction are filtering information, even though it is purported to be fact. The filters of fiction are more intangible, leaving the reader without neat conclusions, provoking thought.

In this era of "fake" news, what is really fake? Many of us rely on our contemporary comedians such as Stephen Colbert, Bill Maher, and John Oliver for our "news." Interviews with elected officials don't rise to the bar of truth that even our comics transcend. Our artists whose works are considered "fiction" now similarly tilt the fiction / non-fiction scale the other way. Thus, what I hope emerges from this book is simply one person's reporting on contemporary theatre, literature and the performing arts, works that seem to point the way to understanding the anomalous world we live in.

While editing this work, I noted the occurrence of certain motivating influences or themes that need some explanation here. First and foremost among these influences is my wife, Ann. Throughout this book I seem to mention her as if the reader knows who I'm talking about. Probably by the time this book is published, we will have celebrated our 50th wedding anniversary. She has ever been my loving partner and supporter. She is also my best editor and critic. Without her there would be no book. So, when I mention Ann, think of her prodding me along.

You will also find aging a central and gathering theme in this book. About aging: I don't like it. I don't think of myself as "old" perhaps because during my publishing career, I was always the youngest guy in the conference room. It's hard to accept slowing down, and approaching what is now called "old, old age," not only fighting its attendant physical problems, but as is increasingly apparent in my writing, wrestling with the philosophical and psychological issues of my own mortality. This preoccupation seems to become more apparent in my later writings and I tend to latch onto quoting writers or playwrights I'm reviewing on that very subject.

In fact, being able to liberally quote is something I do often. As Alan Bennett says in his play *The History Boys*, "the best moments in reading are when you come across something – a thought, a feeling, a way of looking at things – which you had thought special and particular to you. Now here it is, set down by someone else, a person you have never met, someone even who is long dead. And it is as if a hand has come out and taken yours." I have experienced many such moments when writers and playwrights take my hand. And when they are particularly special, I have a tendency to quote them.

Also, while writing this over so many years Ann and I have been living a bifurcated existence, spending most of our time in our Florida home, and summers on our boat in Norwalk, Connecticut. So that would explain the many instances where I refer to "the boat" or "driving up I95" or "home again." Also, occasionally I refer to cruises we've been on. Besides sightseeing they are ideal platforms for reading. So when I reference cruises, I mostly eliminate the details of destinations and ship life and instead concentrate on the literature I read during those trips.

This is an edited collection, one where I have tried to minimize redundancies (inevitable when writing a book over such a long time period). *Waiting for Someone to Explain It* had a strictly chronological format. The present work is also chronological but is presented in three separate, distinct chapters. I retained the chronological order within these chapters as it shows my maturation as a writer, particularly as a critic. Such an organization also indirectly links the works I discuss or experiences I highlight to what was happening at the time.

Each chapter has its own introductory remarks, but here is an overview:

Chapter I examines the literature I read while writing my blog. Most are contemporary works that have evoked that special feeling when "a hand has come out and taken yours." This chapter, perhaps more than the other two, has entries that touch on personal commonalities which I did not hesitate to point out.

Chapter II presents reviews of the plays performed at Palm Beach Dramaworks, a renowned regional theatre company. It seemed fitting that one entire chapter should be devoted entirely to this one theatre company as I have reviewed every play they have performed in the past decade. Each production, in some way, has exhibited a gravitas that captures aspects of the human experience that helps to "explain it all."

Finally, Chapter III covers theatre works and musical performances other than those performed at Dramaworks, notably ones in the Florida area, Westport, Connecticut, New York City and its environs, and London's West End.

Ironically, in college so many years ago I took a course entitled "Theatre as Literature." Little did I know that in my retirement years I would be seeking theatre, for its content and consolation. Nonetheless, I do not claim any of my theatre or literature reviews to be professional criticism. These are my own personal points of view, expressing the impact these works have had on me. But if I am at all representative of "Everyman," perhaps they will resonate with you too.

In addition to my wife, I would like to acknowledge the helpful insight and suggestions made by dear friends, Ron Chambers, Bruce Rettman, and Betty Pessagno. Nonetheless, the responsibility for the contents is mine.

CHAPTER I

LITERATURE AND WRITING MUSINGS

There are readers who devour mostly fiction, and there are those who mostly read nonfiction. Although I enjoy the occasional nonfiction work, mostly biographies (and, even then, I tend to read biographies of writers or musicians), I most happily settle down with a novel as my window to the world.

Most of my "literary world" is now contemporary American literature. Why? Because, in short, to understand America, one must look to its literature. Yet, I introduce a few nonfiction works here that talked to me about American exceptionalism. Biography can also be as philosophically revealing as fiction. I've always found a malleable line between fiction and nonfiction. Being a good writer brings history to life.

Some of the works covered in this chapter came to my attention via serendipity, while others were recommended because of their importance. I gravitated to those that spoke to me personally, mostly because they shed light on our times, resonated with the themes of family and aging, or were deeply philosophical. At the time I started writing my blog, I "discovered" certain writers who particularly appealed to me, such as James Salter and Louis Begley. I then read and reviewed nearly everything they wrote. In the case of contemporary writers I was reading for years before writing my blog, such as Anne Tyler, I mostly cover their most recent works.

Some of my reviews are in depth, while others are more like post-it notes suggesting why I read them. Frequently, I quote liberally, allowing the writers to speak for themselves.

Philip Roth and John Updike are in the pantheon of the authors I've followed most closely; indeed, I have read nearly everything they've written. Both have been silenced now by death—a great loss—but their works are forever. Most of my reading of Updike took place before publishing my blog, but I reread some of Updike's books over the last few years and those are included here. I also took particular note of Roth's last few novels which were predominately focused on end-of-life issues.

Roth explains death best in his novel, *Sabbath*: "Mickey Sabbath doesn't live with his back turned to death the way normal people like us do. No one could have concurred more heartily with the judgment of Franz Kafka than would Sabbath, when Kafka wrote, 'The meaning of life is that it stops.'"

Friday, November 23, 2007 **Literature and Family**

I am reading Richard Russo's new novel, *Bridge of Sighs*. Russo is in one of the group of contemporary writers of which I have read nearly everything they've written and eagerly look forward to their next work and their next: Philip Roth, John Updike, Anne Tyler, John Irving, Russell Banks, Richard Ford, Richard Russo. To this list I could add recently deceased contemporaries such as Joseph Heller, John Cheever and Richard Yates.

What draws me to these writers is families, or more specifically, dysfunctional families. Strong mothers or weak fathers or weak mothers and strong fathers with borderline "crazy" behavior, dark humor and the unpredictable maturation of children from those families. Of course if art mirrors life, it may be that "dysfunctional" is merely normalcy in today's world. I am from one of those families, with parents who were quasi alcoholics. My mother thought she married into a family who would give her the love and the things she thought she was denied as a child. But when my father returned from WW II, with no other aspirations than running a family photography business that was established at the end of the Civil War in NYC, the realization that she will never move from her middle class roots in Richmond Hill, N.Y. became just one of the many rages that consumed her from within. Add to that mix extramarital affairs she hinted at, and my father's inability to "make" her "happy," and one has the ingredients of a novel, if I could only write it.

No wonder I am attracted to this literature and theatre such as *The Subject Was Roses*, which my wife and I recently saw at Dramaworks in West Palm Beach. This Pulitzer Prize-winning play by Frank Gilroy from the mid 60's chronicles a few nights and days in the life of the Cleary family, whose son has just returned from WW II, changed, but not changed enough not to fall into the fold of the old conflict between his controlling, driven, alcoholic father and his abused, emotionally depleted and disillusioned mother. The son is forced to take sides with one parent or the other – to "make nice" – entering into the dynamic trying to ameliorate his parents problems. His attempts, as were mine, are fruitless.

But I digress, so back to Richard Russo. I think his work has elements of the best of all the writers I most admire, the sardonic humor of some of Philip Roth (Russo's *Straight Man* is one of the funniest, laugh-aloud books I've ever read), the fragile characters of some of Anne Tyler's works, the great story-telling ability of John Irving, and the family / husband-wife relationships that resonate in Cheever and Updike.

One of the major issues in Russo is place, upstate NY mill towns that are in long-term decline, the characters caught in the maelstrom of such change, some trying to leave, but emotionally attached forever. Russell Banks touches some of the same bases. Richard Ford makes the New Jersey shore his place while Philip Roth has his Newark environs. Russo brings a gentle humanity to this change, documenting its subtleness and its impact on his characters, people who are not larger than life, but are ones we all know and grew up with.

Yes, many of his novels tend to repeat some of the same themes and settings, and one could easily see the similarities between *Nobody's Fool*, *Empire Falls*, and, now, *Bridge of Sighs*. But while you know you are reading a Richard Russo novel, the stories and characters are somehow different – like movements of a symphony are different, although they are the same work. So, I continue to take pleasure in the *Bridge of Sighs*, reading fewer pages as I reach the end. Like life, if it could only go on.

Russo once said "I think the place you grow up in is a lot like 'The Hotel California': you can check out any time you like, but you can never leave." And so it is with my roots as well as my parents. We are Richard Russo's people, with "everyman's" fragile dreams anchored in "anyplace, USA." People such as my father who returned from WW II with expectations of a family life depicted in the "Father Knows Best" TV series of the 50's only to be constantly disappointed.

Tuesday, January 27, 2009 **Updike at Rest**

John Updike passed away today. I deeply grieve. I've read most of his works, particularly his novels, except his most recent one, *The Widows of Eastwick*. Ironically, I just finished his penultimate novel, *Terrorist*.

Updike has been my companion since I began to read his work, starting with *Rabbit, Run* soon after it was published in 1960. The image of the young high school basketball star, Harry 'Rabbit' Angstrom, going up for a jump shot, "his hands like wild birds" as I recall Updike's description, is indelibly etched in my mind. I have followed Rabbit through cycles of life that seem to mirror mine. Those novels *Rabbit, Run, Rabbit Redux, Rabbit Is Rich*, and *Rabbit At Rest* were each published at the beginning of a new decade (as well as his briefer *Rabbit Remembered* published at the beginning of this decade). Each captures the Zeitgeist of those moments in time. Updike had an ear for language, the mores of the American suburbs, and wrote with an erudition befitting his Harvard education.

Although his sexually charged *Couples* published in 1968 might have put him in the mainstream of widely read contemporary American writers, I love some of his lesser-known works such as *Roger's Version* and *Toward the End of Time*.

But I was constantly drawn to Harry 'Rabbit' Angstrom who was about ten years older than I. When I read *Rabbit At Rest* I wondered whether there would be a similar fate, "escaping" to Florida, only to become lazy, flabby, and depressed. As it turns out, I did follow Harry to the sunshine state, and about ten years after him, but I would like to think that is the only similarity. After all, I always had Updike to keep me company, to help keep me engaged.

Updike increasingly ruminated about death in his later works, as one is prone to do as one ages: an acceptance that it happens to all of us – "no one gets out alive" – as we flippantly say. It's the singular part we must play in this birth/death comic tragedy that we wonder about. I found myself looking for clues of Updike's own feelings in his recent literature.

From *Terrorist* comes one of Updike's more poignant passages, describing the thoughts of Jack Levy (the novel's aging high school guidance counselor) in the dark of the early morning: *...Jack has personal misery, misery that he "owns," as people say now – the heaviness of the day to come, the day that will dawn through all this dark. As he lies there awake, fear and loathing squirm inside him like the components of a bad restaurant meal – twice as much food as you want, the way they serve it now. Dread slams shut the door back into sleep, an awareness, deepening each day, that all that is left on Earth for his body to do is to ready itself for death. He has done his courting and mating; he has fathered a child, he has worked to feed that child, little sensitive Mark with his shy cloudy eyes and slippery lower lip, and to furnish him with all the tawdry junk the culture of the time insisted he possess, to blend in with his peers. Now Jack Levy's sole remaining task is to die and thus contribute a little space, a little breathing room, to this overburdened planet. The task hangs in the air just above his insomniac face like a cobweb with a motionless spider in the center."*

What great writing. Just to keyboard these words makes me shudder with the knowledge that there will be no future Updike novels. We have lost a truly great American writer and, for me, a heartfelt companion.

Tuesday, February 3, 2009 *Aging and Writing*

Marking the passing of a great American novelist, *The New York Times Weekend Review* carried an outstanding essay "John Updike's Mighty Pen" by Charles McGrath.

Especially interesting was the Video *A Conversation with John Updike*, taped in October 2008, with Sam Tanenhaus, the editor of the Book Review, "about the craft of fiction and the art of writing." Disquieting to think he died only a few months later, but listening to the interview I was struck how much he ruminated about aging and writing. He said that he was currently working on an historical novel set in the 1st century, but not knowing much about the period he was trying to educate himself, lamenting, though, that "maybe I'm too old to be educated." He also said he was thrilled that the *New Yorker* had recently accepted two of his short stories as he was "trying to keep [his] name in the *New Yorker* after a long draught." "It makes me feel like a real person to get a short story in the *New Yorker*."

He went on to observe (and much of this is paraphrased here) that there comes a moment in a writer's life when you are full of material untouched in your mind and seemingly urgent and it merges with enough skill to get it down, but this skill tends to peak in an American writer's late 20s or early 30s. "In those years I could bring a naiveté and there-fore a sense of wonderment to my writing. I'm not ashamed of my later work, but feel there is an unforced energy in the earlier work." We never idolize anything beyond youth in this country. Consequently, we're all failed youths, as we don't believe in the wisdom of the ages especially now that so many people live forever in old age homes. "Some of our greatest writers were Hemingway and Fitzgerald; their idea of happiness is to be young." And those words concluded the interview.

I closely identify. In Florida that sense of aging, a feeling of irrelevancy, is particularly pervasive. As Updike says in his novel *Rabbit at Rest*: *there's a lot of death in Florida, if you look. The palms grow by the lower branches dying and dropping off. The hot sun hurries the life cycles along....Even friendship has a thin, provisional quality, since people might at any minute buy another condominium and move to it, or else up and die.*

I thought my feelings might be confined to those of a retired business-person living in the "sunshine state." This business of aging, still trying to stay productive, moving forward with learning as being the very essence of living, is something I would like to think we share with Updike.

Saturday, April 11, 2009 **A Bridge For the Ages**

Perhaps there is a time and place for every book. Some are instant successes while others are discovered and appreciated or even become classics long after the author is deceased. Similarly, there is a time or place for a particu-lar book in a reader's life. For me, I should have read the one I recently fin-ished, David McCullough's "biography" of the Brooklyn Bridge (*The Great Bridge*, 1972) when I lived in Brooklyn during the 1960's. I say "biography" rather than history as after reading his work, it feels like a living, breathing bulwark, a creation for the ages, one that was built while New York was just beginning to become a vertical city. When it was built, its 275-foot towers dwarfed everything in New York and Brooklyn, except Trinity Church, the tallest structure in Manhattan when it was built in 1846, at 281 feet. But the bridge's two towers are massive as well.

Over the years, New York, and Brooklyn, grew around the bridge, and by the time I lived in Brooklyn, to most New Yorkers it was just part of the skyline. Although I appreciated its architecture, particularly the few times I had crossed the bridge on its walkways, I confess I was somewhat oblivious to its extraordinary engineering (particularly for the time) and its intricate history. After college in Brooklyn, I lived mostly in downtown Brooklyn, at 175 Willoughby Street and also at 234 Lincoln Place in the Park Slope section. After my first son was born in 1965, a favorite destination for a Sunday walk was the Brooklyn Heights Promenade, the Brooklyn Bridge rising majestically at the north end.

Oh, had McCullough's magnificent history been written before then. I might have had a greater appreciation for how the bridge transformed the city and the engineering genius and architectural greatness of the structure. McCullough writes a biography as a novel, putting the reader into the times and the minds of the main characters. It is his later work, such as his Pulitzer Prize winning biography of John Adams that is leading me to his earlier histories. Here is his finely crafted description of the completed bridge, prose worthy of any novel: *The very shabbiness and stunted scale of the old neighborhood beneath the tower worked to the advantage of the bridge, which by contrast seemed an embodiment of the noblest aspirations, majestic, heaven-directed, lifting into the light above the racket, the shabbiness, and the confusion of the waterfront, the way a great cathedral rises over the hovels of the faithful. And the twin archways in the tower, seen from the street level, looked like vast vacant windows to the sky. For a child seeing it at night, the tower could have been the dark and mighty work of medieval giants. Where on earth could one see so many stars framed in granite?*

The building of the bridge is a microcosm of everything that is great and deplorable about mankind. John Roebling, a German born engineer and builder of The Roebling Suspension Bridge, spanning the Ohio at Cincinnati, completed plans for the Brooklyn Bridge but an accident led to his death before work commenced in 1869. His son, Washington Roebling, also an engineer, took over the plans and the responsibilities of the bridge, but during the construction of the massive foundations – to the depth of almost 45 feet on the Brooklyn side and 78 feet on the New York side – he suffered the effects of the bends from being in one of the huge caissons that had to be constructed and sunk for that purpose. As a consequence, he had a nervous condition and supervised the remaining construction from home on Brooklyn Heights. He did not even have the strength to attend the opening (his wife, Emily, was his steadfast emissary for such occasions). Meanwhile he had to contend with charges of kickbacks (his family owned one of the suppliers of steel cables) and a changing political scene ranging from Boss Tweed to various showdowns with politicians trying to grab headlines for themselves. He was even asked to resign at one point; he refused and insisted they (the Directors of the New York Bridge Company) fire him, which he knew they dared not. Throughout it all, he survived to build a bridge for the ages. It enjoyed its one-hundredth birthday anniversary in 1983. Engineers have estimated it could last another one hundred before the cables have to be replaced and if they are, perhaps the bridge will go on forever.

Although I still visit New York occasionally, I have no reason to go downtown, other than, now, traveling on the East River by boat. We brought our own boat up from the Chesapeake some fifteen years ago, passing under the Brooklyn Bridge with the World Trade Towers rising in the background. It would have been inconceivable that either landmark could be gone during my lifetime. But they both endure in my mind's eye, with wonder.

Thursday, May 21, 2009 **Updike, Roth, Dreiser**

This entry was really started by my blogger friend, Emily, who "tagged" me to name twenty-five writers who have "influenced" my life (not necessarily because they are great writers). Although I "answered" her with just their names, I had promised to explain why. To me, reading literature is to explore history and psychology, the human tapestry laid threadbare. Basically I am drawn to those writers I can personally relate to.

Before getting to my more detailed "answer" by writer, this is what I originally wrote to Emily: "Although I did come up with my 25 authors, there is a heavy bias to contemporary American fiction, with one biographer in the group. There are writers who have written, for me, their one-time classic (such as Jonathan Franzen's *The Corrections or Alan Lightman's The Diagnosis)*, not to mention some writers I studied in college (Franz Kafka for instance), who have had an impact on me. I could also add Pat Conroy whom you mention, but he didn't come up when I went through this mental exercise. One of the best works I read by him is a memoir, My Losing Season but you'd have to love basketball as much as I do to appreciate it. Also, I share your admiration for Russell Banks' *Continental Drift and Rule of the Bone* (which I think is his best work). But, as a start, here are the first three that came to mind:

John Updike. I once saw him at a Pen Writers meeting where he was the main speaker and wanted to go over to him to chat. He seemed so approachable and kindly, but I became involved in a discussion with Russell Baker whose book *All Things Considered* we had just reissued. So other people surrounded Updike and I thought there would be other opportunities, at the Frankfurt Bookfair or perhaps the American Booksellers Association meetings, or another Pen Writers conference, but our paths never crossed again, other than his speaking to me through his works. Updike's influence on me is he not only helped explain the American Zeitgeist, but he also explored issues relevant to my "maleness" ten years hence, as Updike was nearly exactly ten years older than I. The stages of Harry Angstrom's life as depicted in the Rabbit novels are neatly spaced out about a decade apart, so painstakingly capturing the times in America, his maturation and ultimate decline.

I am now reading his last novel, the *Widows of Eastwick*, with sadness and reverence for a great American writer. Only a man who has walked the walk can write words such as this: *Jim's illness drove her and Jim down from safe, arty Taos into the wider society, the valleys of the ailing, a vast herd moving like stampeded bison toward the killing cliff. The socialization forced upon her -- interviews with doctors, most of them unsettlingly young; encounters with nurses, demanded merciful attentions the hospitalized patient was too manly and depressed to ask for himself; commiseration with others in her condition, soon-to-be widows and widowers she would have shunned on the street but now, in these antiseptic hallways, embraced with shared tears -- prepared her for travel in the company of strangers.* Unfortunately, I've had similar "hospital experiences" and dread the inevitability of an encore.

Philip Roth. I think I respond in a similar way to Roth, a writer who seems to know me but in a different way. Where Updike awakens the Calvinist background of my early years and the suburban existence of my later life, Roth explores the "Jewishness" of my New York City years. I've long felt his *American Pastoral* is one of the great novels of the 20th century.

The novel made me relive those Vietnam years of the 60's and the social upheavals of the times. It is a novel in the negative universe of Updike's Rabbit, in that the main character is also a former high school star athlete, but from the inner city, one who in his attempt to create the "perfect life" of the American dream, an "American pastoral," finds his daughter caught up in Weather Underground violence as he also helplessly witnesses the destruction of his once beloved inner-city Newark in the 1970s. An American Dream turned American Nightmare, capturing exactly the way I felt at the time.

Roth's alter ego Nathan Zuckerman narrates the novel. It is through Zuckerman in many of Roth's other works that we have a window into Roth's view of writing itself. *The Anatomy Lesson* is one of the "Zuckerman" novels. In it Zuckerman is thinking about his writing and what it had become in his life:

It looked as though life had become bigger yet. Writing would intensify everything even further. Writing, as Mann had testified – not least by his own example – was the only worthwhile attainment, the surpassing experience, the exalted struggle, and there was no way to write other than like a fanatic. Without fanaticism, nothing great in fiction could ever be achieved. He had the highest possible conception of the gigantic capacities of literature to engulf and purify life. He would write more, publish more, and life would become colossal.

But what became colossal was the next page. He thought he had chosen life but what he had chosen was the next page. Stealing time to write stories, he never thought to wonder what time might be stealing from him. Only gradually did the perfecting of a writer's iron will begin to feel like the evasion of experience, and the means to imaginative release, to the exposure, revelation, and invention of life, like the sternest form of incarceration. He thought he'd chosen the intensification of everything and he'd chosen monasticism and retreat instead. Inherent in this choice was a paradox that he had never foreseen.

Of course in spite of all of Zuckerman's protestations, Roth has gone on to write at least a dozen novels after that one, and, thankfully, is still going strong. His more recent works are dark, clearly concerned with his physical decline and the future. But, writing is work, something that I have found, and few work as vigorously and focused as Roth.

Theodore Dreiser. I skip to a writer of my college years, having devoured everything he wrote during those years, either for assignments or just because I found his Darwinian philosophy of life a revelation at the time. I spent a harrowing week in the Brooklyn Hospital ward with pleurisy, the consequence of teenage stupidity because I had taken a lot of caffeine tablets while smoking up a storm of Chesterfields for a couple of all-nighters to study for exams and became exhausted. This led to my contracting that most painful condition. In the hospital I began to read Dreiser's "Cowperwood trilogy," the first two written before the 1920's and the last one some thirty years later after WW II, tracing the life of financier Frank Cowperwood. His life is built around an economically and socially hostile world, where the survival of the fittest reigns supreme. On his way to school as a ten year old, the future financier passes a store window which exhibits a lobster and a squid contained in a fish tank and one day he discovers the lobster had devoured the squid, Dreiser commenting: *The incident had a great impression on him. It answered in a rough way that riddle which had been annoying him so much in the past: How is life organized? Things lived on each other – that was it...Sure, men lived on men.* This social-Darwinian leitmotif runs through all of his writings and became a worldview that reverberated throughout my working life. My DNA, though, prevented me from doing the "eating" but I learned how not "to be eaten." In my very first job after college I was thrown to the wolves in a publishing company's production department. By "wolves" I mean coworkers who did not like my intense work ethic and would have eaten me alive except I learned how to deal with them from my Dreiser "education." That education would prove to be valuable right up to my retirement, helping me negotiate the labyrinths of corporate politics as well.

Thursday, June 11, 2009 **Serendipity**

Most books I read come to me because of my previous knowledge of the author's work or the recommendation of a review or by someone I respect. And such is the case with *Firmin* by Sam Savage but the way it came to me was through a chance chain of events befitting the role of chance in the book itself, a serendipitous journey of the book into my hands. My son, Jonathan, had recently been in Sardinia, quietly enjoying a cappuccino in a local café and a woman was nearby, tearfully finishing *Firmin* and they struck up a conversation. "Here," she said, "take the book and read it; you'll love it," offering him her worn paperback copy of a UK edition with a sticker on it, "Choose from any 3 for 2 at Waterstone's." At first Jonathan politely demurred thinking that it was probably some maudlin potboiler, but she was insistent and so he accepted. He read it on the plane when he left and suggested I read it when he last visited, so via happenstance the copy wound up with me.

Now, if I could imagine a Venn diagram of my 30-something son and my literary taste, there would be a majority overlap of books we both care deeply about, but the non-shaded area of books we do not mutually enjoy is meaningful enough to raise doubts regarding a book about "a well-read Rat" with a debonair soul who lives in the basement bookstore on Boston's Scollay Square in the 1960's. But Jonathan said: "trust me on this one" and as it is a book about books as well, I read it and I'm glad I did. It is quite a find under the proverbial radar.

Interestingly the subtitle of Sam Savage's work has morphed from "Adventures of a Metropolitan Lowlife" in the UK edition to "A Tale of Exile, Unrequited Love, and the Redemptive Power of Literature" in the American edition. Both are accurate but I suppose the latter makes it more marketable.

Like most novels narrated by a rat, it is a metaphor of life we human rats endure and bring upon ourselves, with themes of Hardy and Dickens running beneath the surface of lovable *Firmin's* narrative. It is a highly imaginative work, one you are doomed to compulsively read to the end in one sitting and at times finding yourself smiling.

And, for me, what is there not to love about a rat who is a voracious reader and plays the piano as well? But, *Firmin's* narration touches so many truths for me: *A rat's life is short and painful, painful but quickly over, and yet it*

*feels long while it lasts....I always think everything is going to last forever,
but nothing ever does. In fact nothing exists longer than an instant except
the things that we hold in memory. I always try to hold on to everything –
I would rather die than forget....One of the things I have observed is how
extremes coalesce. Great love becomes great hatred, quiet peace turns into
noisy war, vast boredom breeds huge excitement. Great intimacy spawns
huge estrangement.*

And that is but one of many.

Wednesday, July 8, 2009 **Do We Cry for the Sloth?**

Coffee House Press, the innovative US Publisher of *Firmin*, saw my blog
piece on their book and asked if I would like to review the author's forthcoming novel, *The Cry of the Sloth* (To be published Sept. 1). Sure, I said,
thinking that I might be graduating from reading about a lovable rat to
an equally lovable sloth, and sloths are much cuter to begin with, sort
of an upside down koala bear. The advance copy arrived as we were getting ready to leave for the summer so I looked forward to kicking off the
summer reading season with Sam Savage's new book. Not only did I love
Firmin, I was more than curious about the author as he is about my age
and it brings hope to us old guys; who knows, there might be a first book
in each of us still.

The Cry of the Sloth is an epistolary novel, set in a Midwestern town
during the 1970's, quite a departure from Firmin written in the first person
by a very literary rat. It is the first such novel I've read since *84 Charing
Cross Road*, which is actually not fiction but an exchange of letters between
a New York book buyer and an antiquarian bookseller in London. The one
thing all three books have in common is that they are about the literary
world, although the "Sloth's" world is faux literary.

The "action" mainly unfolds by following our protagonist, Andrew
Whittaker, over a four month period, through his letters and other miscellaneous writings, including his interpretations of his correspondents'
replies (in the rare cases when he received one), as well as just about
everything else he writes, including fragments of a novel ("meant to be
comic [but] it has acquired an overlay of desperation"), notices to his tenants of apartments he inherited ("Do Not Throw Cigarette Butts in Flower
Pots"), apartment ads ("Enjoy a Family Lifestyle!"), grocery lists ("t.p". –
toilet paper being prominent on each), fragments of ideas for stories, and
notes to himself.

Mainly, his letters are to the contributing writers of his failing literary magazine, *Soap, A Journal of the Arts*, of which he is the Editor, his
ex-wife, Jolie, to whom he owes alimony and on whom he was obviously

entirely dependent for keeping his life organized when *Soap* began, Vikki, a contributor and perhaps *Soap's* only donor, creditors who hound him for money, the Rapid Falls Current, the small town newspaper with which he is at war, and successful novelists, some old friends who obviously do not answer his pleas to participate in a spring literary festival. He obsesses on the festival as his salvation, much as Gogol's Akaky Akakievich saw his Overcoat.

It is a lonely, solitary journey, kaleidoscopic in nature so we, the reader, see only parts of the mosaic and always through the eyes of the 43 year old Andrew Whittaker. But through that prism we witness his slow slide, progressing through various states of mind, with his ranting and ravings, paranoia, even writing letters under pseudonyms to the local newspaper praising "That Andy is a quiet, dignified, private man," and then responding to his pseudonym under still another one.

His obsessive compulsive behavior leads him to perform all tasks, explain all his actions in minutiae and repetitively, sometimes hilariously but always to the point of sadness. He becomes fixated on why there are no photographs of him between the ages of seven and fifteen in the family album, pursuing an answer from his sister, from whom he is estranged (what else), and from his dying mother who is in a nursing home. *If everything we do not remember did not exist, where would we be?*

While packing up his books he finds an encyclopedia of mammals and it is there he comes across the "ai," a variety of a three-toed sloth which he sees as having a head too small for its body, *something I have thought about myself* obsessing to the point of having his head measured. But, he happily reports to his friend, Harold, that he moves his *...bowels once every day with clockwork regularity. I mention this because the ai shits and pisses only once a week.*

His wife has run off with an old novelist friend on a motorcycle who he remembers saying *she would never marry anybody as ambiguous as I am.* And there is an amorphous quality to Andrew and the novel itself, leaving the reader with more questions than answers, part of Savage's intent.

Towards the end of the novel, he writes to Vikki *I have sunk back into all my old vices – slovenliness, sloth, and gargantuan pettiness,* perhaps his most insightful introspective epiphany. In the Christian moral tradition "sloth" is also one of the seven deadly sins, characterized by wasting away and entropy, the essence of Andrew Whittaker. The punishment in hell for such a sin is to be thrown into snake pits and, interestingly, he finds a pair of snakeskin boots in his basement, ones someone had accused him of stealing.

Savage's writing is engaging, weaving satire and pathos. He portrays an inexorable path for our protagonist, a fascinating, tragicomic portrait of isolation and personal failure, in the tradition of Gogol and Kafka. *All around me things are in decay, or in revolt. If only I could walk out of myself the way one walks out of a house.*

As Andy says at the end of one very long letter: *Imagine a man in a room talking about himself, perhaps in a very boring way, while looking down at the floor. And while he goes on with his monologue, which as I said is of interest only to himself, one by one the other people in the room tiptoe away until he is all alone, the last one shutting the door silently behind him. Finally, the man looks up and sees what has happened, and of course he is overcome by feelings of ridicule and shame. Maybe this letter is now at the bottom of your wastepaper basket, a tiny trivial voice in the depths of a tin well, rattling on and on.*

Are we still in the room listening to Andy? Yes, or no, Savage has established himself, with *Cry of the Sloth*, and *Firmin*, as a "new" literary voice at the age of 67.

Sunday, July 26, 2009 **Richard Yates' Revolutionary Road**

A while ago I was "tagged" by a fellow blogger to name twenty-five writers who "influenced" my life. Although I began my reply by naming Updike, Roth and Dreiser, Richard Yates could have easily been among the first on my list.

He is certainly the only writer where I may have had some small reciprocal impact. Why? Because for almost ten years the only edition of his classic *Revolutionary Road* in print was the one I republished in 1971. Astonished to find it out of print at the time, we bought the rights from Yates' literary agent.

When our edition was published it was my intention to reread it, but career demands, other literary works, including all of Yates' later novels and short stories, encroached on my reading time, so on various bookshelves in the homes we've lived, this reprint edition nestled in waiting. The catalyst for recently rereading *Revolutionary Road* was the film of it, starring Leonardo DiCaprio and Kate Winslet. Reportedly, the book was "discovered" as a major American literary work by Kate Winslet and her husband, the film's director, Sam Mendes. The film seemed faithful to the novel so I finally read it again after so many years. In the process I was reminded why I was so taken with Yates' work in the first place.

Since I am an "old" production guy, I'll describe our edition, republished without a jacket but in a library binding, 88 point binder's boards, Arrestox "C" weight cloth with gold foil stamping on the spine, 5–1/2 x 8–1/2 trim size, headbands and footbands, printed on acid free, cream colored high-opacity 50 lb paper. It was probably printed in Ann Arbor, Michigan where we printed the majority of our books. It looked as new as the day it was republished. So, I have come full circle with the book, reading it soon after it was first published, reprinting it when it went out of print, seeing the movie, and now finally rereading my reprint edition of the novel, with more than 40 years intervening.

As I said I thought the movie closely followed the book but after rereading *Revolutionary Road*, I am struck by its *extreme* faithfulness. Maybe this is because Yates' elegantly developed plot moves chronologically and with an inevitability that drives the novel to its conclusion, making it so adaptable to the screen. But mostly, it is Yates' living dialogue and although I do not have the screenplay to compare, I am certain much of it was wisely lifted from the novel itself.

When I first read the novel I was going through a divorce, having been married at the end of my junior year in college. My ex-wife and I were two kids, not unlike Frank and April in *Revolutionary Road*. I take literature very personally and the novel spoke directly to me as my own marriage was disintegrating and I was looking for answers.

The relationship of Yates' men and women can be summed up by the titles of Yates' two terrific short story collections: *Eleven Kinds of Loneliness* and *Liars in Love*. I was struck by these two themes, loneliness and self deception, as depicted in *Revolutionary Road*, relating those to my own experience, not only in my first marriage but the failed marriage of my parents (although they continued the pretense of a marriage to their deaths). Yates' characters are perpetually struggling with one another, the men unsure of their masculinity, having to prove it in their work, their "need" to be loved by their wives, and to dominate women outside their marriages, while the women are highly neurotic and dependent but oddly headstrong and impulsive at the same time.

Towards the novel's dénouement, April, exhausted from her struggles with her husband Frank, determined to follow through on aborting their third child, sends Frank off to work with a little kiss. Frank is confused, astounded, but grateful as he goes off to catch his train. April thinks it was *...a perfectly fair, friendly kiss, a kiss for a boy you'd just met at a party. The only real mistake, the only wrong and dishonest thing, was ever to have seen him as anything more than that. Oh, for a month or two, just for fun, it might be all right to play a game like that with a boy; but all these years! And all because, in a sentimentally lonely time long ago, she had found it easy and agreeable to believe whatever this one particular boy felt like saying, and to repay him for that pleasure by telling easy, agreeable lies of her own, until each was saying what the other most wanted to hear – until he was saying 'I love you' and she was saying 'really, I mean it; you're the most interesting person I've ever met.'* Indeed, liars in love. It perfectly described my own experience and I've been hooked on Yates ever since.

Yates' characters wear different personas, playacting their way through their lives, with a natural capacity for self deception and disingenuousness. The book begins with a play in which April acts in a community theatre production. For a month after April finds she is pregnant with this third child, she and Frank go through their own elaborate play, she wanting an abortion (supposedly for Frank's sake) and Frank wanting the child (supposedly for moral reasons).

Subliminally he realizes that the pregnancy will put to rest April's impetuous desire to move to Paris and thus leave them with a "comfortable" suburban life.

Yates tackles the suburban landscape, reminiscent of Cheever and Updike, something that did not resonate particularly with me when I first read the book, but after having lived in the Westport, Connecticut area for some thirty years, now has a special meaning. Yates' portrayal is more scathing, depicting a desolate place where desperate people, lonely and unsure of themselves, toiling away in an era of placidity on the surface with deep anxiety running beneath. He describes the neighborhood as *invincibly cheerful, a toyland of white and pastel houses whose bright, uncurtained windows winked blandly through a dappling of green and yellow leaves.* The women raise the kids in their manicured homes and the men do battle in the city, snaking their way on the commuter railroad with their hats and their newspapers. Yates describes Frank, *...riding to work, one of the youngest and healthiest passengers on the train, he sat with the look of a man condemned to a very slow, painless death. He felt middle-aged.* This is as sad a depiction of the American dream's corruption as could have been conjured up by Fitzgerald.

Frank works at his father's old firm, a veneration of cynicism on his part. He gets a job in the Sales Promotion Department at Knox Business Machines, deciding "it would be more fun not to mention his father in the interview at all." *'The sales what? [April inquired]....What does that mean you're supposed to do?"Who the hell knows? They explained it to me for half an hour and I still don't know, and I don't think they do either. No, but it's pretty funny, isn't it? Old Knox Business Machines. Wait'll I tell the old man. Wait'll he hears I didn't even use his name." And so it started as a kind of joke. Others might fail to see the humor of it, but it filled Frank Wheeler with a secret, astringent delight as he discharged his lazy duties, walking around the office in a way that had lately become almost habitual with him, if not quite truly characteristic, since having been described by his wife as 'terrifically sexy' -- a slow catlike stride, proudly muscular but expressing a sleepy disdain of tension or hurry.* Work too, is nothing more than a performance, something without intrinsic meaning, like other aspects of their lives.

Paradoxically, the one character in the novel who does not suffer from self deception, is their real estate agent's son, John, who is an inmate in a mental institution, one who occasionally visits the Wheelers when he is released to his parents. When he learns that the Wheelers are not going to move to France and that April is pregnant, he says to them, first referring to Frank, *"Big man you got here, April...Big family man, solid citizen. I feel sorry for you. Still, maybe you deserve each other. Matter of fact, the way you look right now, I'm beginning to feel sorry for him too. I mean come to think of it, you must give him a pretty bad time, if making babies is the only way he can prove he's got a pair of balls....Hey, I'm glad of one thing, though? You know what I'm glad of? I'm glad I'm not gonna be that kid."*

Yates wrote six novels after *Revolutionary Road*. Among my favorites was *Easter Parade*, but *Revolutionary Road* stands on its own. He also had his short stories published in the two collections mentioned earlier, and, finally, he became more widely recognized with the publication of the *Collected Stories of Richard Yates* a few years ago. The wonderful introduction to that was written by Richard Russo who is yet another contemporary author influenced by Yates.

Thursday, August 27, 2009 "Typical American" and the Dream
Go west young man; that is, go so far west you find the opportunity for employment and pursue the promise of prosperity which is thought to be at the heart of the American Dream. For many recent graduates, that journey might now begin in China

Such are the ironies of life, a reversal of immigrants flocking to American shores in pursuit of employment and a richer, happier life.

For years Gish Jen's *Typical American* (Houghton Mifflin, 1991) had sat on my bookshelf waiting to be read. I first heard about the novel from a PBS program "Novel Reflections on the American Dream," but it was the recent extended stay of my son, Jonathan, in Shanghai that led me to finally read the novel, and to better understand the Chinese, and their assimilation into American culture. Also, I did business with the China National Publications Import Export Corporation and was impressed by their selection and importation of books we published over the years so I was curious about Jen's novel.

I expected a story about what it means to be a foreigner in a foreign land, especially the vicissitudes of being Asian in America soon after WW II, and while there are those elements, it reminded me more about the misinterpretation of the American dream, the illusion of prosperity being the definition of a meaningful life.

What does it mean to be, or become a "typical American?" The Chang family is at first derisive of their concept of the "typical American" until they begin to desert their traditional work ethic, moral groundings, and family loyalty as they become "typical Americans" themselves, enduring a tragedy to bring their values back into balance.

This is not a conventional story about immigrants, but, instead, is a very well written novel about what freedom and responsibility mean in relation to "life, liberty and the pursuit of happiness" in a land that "promises" no limits. Or as Ralph Chang discovers: *What escape was possible? It seemed to him...that a man was as doomed here as he was in China....He was not what he made up his mind to be. A man was the sum of his limits; freedom only made him see how much so. America was no America.*

And the writing is wonderful: *And then there was another pain too, quieter, weightier, its roots in what everybody knows – that one day a person looks back more than forward, that one day he'll have achieved as much as he was going to, loved as much as he was going to, been as happy as it was granted him to be. And that day, won't he have to wonder – was it enough, what he's lived? Can he call that a life and be satisfied?*

And isn't that the essence of the dream, and of any culture?

Wednesday, November 4, 2009 **Homer & Langley**

When we were recently in Asheville, we made our regular visit to Malaprop's, one of the great independent bookstores. They usually have a good selection of autographed copies and a couple of years ago I bought Russo's *Bridge of Sighs* there. I was looking for Russo's new novel *That Old Cape Magic.* Disappointed they didn't have one this time, I sought out the next on my list, E.L Doctorow's *Homer & Langley.* It is the best Doctorow novel I've read since *Ragtime* and the *World's Fair.*

Reading an autographed copy has its drawbacks. No turning back corners to be able to find favorite passages. No reading on the beach. Handle with care. After reading, it belongs under glass like a museum piece.

The book itself is beautiful, printed on antique eggshell paper with a deckle edge, set in the Caslon type face, an old style face in the same family as Garamond, the classic crispness of which almost cries out to the reader to savor every word. And Doctorow's writing is of museum quality too in its stark clarity and beauty. There are four main characters in the book, the brothers Homer and Langley Collyer, New York City, and Time (or the passage of the same).

Homer is blind but he is the one who can see truths as the book's narrator and in various parts of the book is the one who leads the sighted. *People my age are supposed to remember times long past though they can't recall what happened yesterday. My memories of our long-dead parents are considerably dimmed, as if having fallen further and further back in time has made them smaller, with less visible detail as if time has become space, become distance, and figures from the past, even your father and mother, are too far away to be recognized. They are fixed in their own time, which has rolled down behind the planetary horizon. They and their times and all its concerns have gone down together.*

A "Theory of Replacements" obsesses Langley, his older brother. *Everything in life gets replaced. We are our parents' replacements just as they were replacements of the previous generation. All these herds of bison they are slaughtering out west, you would think that was the end of them, but they won't all be slaughtered and the herds will fill back in with replacements that will be indistinguishable from the ones slaughtered.* Consequently, Langley lives his life collecting newspapers, categorizing stories, preparing what would be a "perpetual newspaper." *He wanted to fix American life finally in one edition, what he called Collyer's eternally current dateless newspaper, the only newspaper anyone would ever need. For five cents, Langley said, the reader will have a portrait in newsprint of our life on earth.... He will be assured that he reads of indisputable truths of the day including that of his own impending death, which will be dutifully recorded as a number in the blank box of the last page under the heading Obituaries.* Langley devolves into an antisocial eccentric, hoarding everything he finds, including his newspapers.

Doctorow's story is somewhat based on the real life of the Collyer brothers who lived in New York City but it only serves as a loose sketch for the canvas of this tour de force. An odyssey of people, representative of time's passing, drift in and out of their home, inherited from their parents, people from the depression, to WW II, to the Vietnam era, and the flower generation. While the brothers wage war with New York, the utility companies, and their neighbors, their home slowly degrades as time has its way and they withdraw from life itself.

Homer is a gifted pianist, the artist in the work, clearly Doctorow's voice and sensibility. Homer has had one true love in his life, Mary Elizabeth Riordan, who, like everyone else in the novel, transits through the Collyer home never to return. She was his "prompter" in a silent movie theatre, whispering the changing scenes on the screen in his ear so he could play the appropriate music, his only job when he was younger. Then, she becomes his piano student and finally she leaves, becoming a Sister and a missionary in far-away places, Homer occasionally receiving a letter. She is apparently murdered in Central America. Homer laments, *I am not a religious person. I prayed to be forgiven for having been jealous of her calling, for having longed for her, for having despoiled her in my dreams. But in truth I have to admit that I was numbed enough by this awful fate of the sister to be not quite able to connect it with my piano student Mary Elizabeth Riorden. Even now, I have the clean scent of her as we sit together on the piano bench. I can summon that up at will. She speaks softly in my ear as, night after night, the moving pictures roll by: Here it's a funny chase with people hanging out of cars...here the hero is riding a horse at a gallop...here firemen are sliding down a pole...and here (I feel her hand on my shoulder) the lovers embrace, they're looking into each other's eyes, and now the card says...'I love you.'*

And as at the end of a silent movie the lens slowly closes and Homer cannot "see to see."

Tuesday, December 1, 2009 *That Old Russo Magic*

Richard Russo's portrayal of fractured families marches to a similar drum beat as my own. I respond most strongly to works of art that strike a chord of intimacy such as his recently published, *That Old Cape Magic.*

It is pure Russo except he steps outside his usual upstate mill towns and makes Cape Cod, California, Maine, and *the mid-fucking West* his setting.

The heart of the novel (for me) can actually be found in the acknowledgments: *And finally, my gratitude to my mother, whose recent passing caused me to reflect more deeply on inheritance and all that the word implies. Not to mention love.*

Compare that to a quote from the novel: *The problem seemed to be that you could put a couple thousand miles between yourself and your parents, and make clear to them that in doing so you meant to reject their values, but how did you distance yourself from your own inheritance? You couldn't prevent your hair from thinning or your nose from taking over the center of your face. Even worse, what if he hadn't rejected his parents' values as completely as he'd imagined.* In fact, the protagonist, Jack Griffin, after a lifetime of trying to distance himself from his parents, says to his wife: *"Since yesterday, maybe for a while before that, I've been wondering..."* He stopped here, unsure how to continue, though what he'd been wondering couldn't have been simpler. *"I've been wondering if maybe I loved them. It's crazy, I know, but...do you think that's possible?"*

The novel is about taking responsibility for one's relationships, for one's life, reconciling the inner voices of one's parents. They haunt Griffin throughout the novel until he finally casts off his parents' ashes into the waters of Old Cape Cod.

Like Griffin, I too was *the reluctant witness to [my] parents' myriad quarrels and recriminations.* And like Griffin, I had to tip toe around my mother: *...even his most benign comments set his mother off, and once she was on a roll it was best just to let her finish. Their respect for his privacy had been, he knew all too well, mostly disinterest.*

As a young boy Griffin adopts a family, the Brownings, during one of his parents' vacations on the Cape. (*The Brownings had offered the refuge he needed, though any happy family would have probably served the same purpose...*) *During my childhood I sought out other families, any family, to escape from the oppression of my parents (and the humiliation they caused), who were locked in silent, and sometimes violent combat.* Griffin writes a short story "The Summer of the Brownings" later in life in an attempt to understand and exonerate his complicity in the relationship: *Far from resolving anything, the Browning story probably just explained how he'd come to be the husband and father he was instead of the one he meant to be.*

Russo develops a touching counterpoint story to Griffin's, that of Sunny Kim, a shy Korean boy who loves Griffin's daughter, Laura, from childhood and towards whom Laura has always shown kindness, even love, but not on a conscious level. Griffin worries about Sunny's awkwardness and about being somewhat ostracized at his daughter's birthday party as a child. It clearly reminded Griffin of his own childhood to which his wife, Joy, says *"Quit worrying. They're just kids. They have to figure these things out."* *"That's the problem,"* he said. *"They already have it all figured out. Who's cool, who's not, who's in, who's out."* *Nobody had to teach them either.*

And when Laura's best friend, Kelsey, is married more than a decade later, and Laura is there with her own husband-to-be, Andy, Griffin watches from afar again: *Back at the reception tent, when they finally decided to call it a night, Laura had detached herself from her friends, all of whom still crowded the dance floor, and came over to whisper in her mother's ear that Andy had proposed during that first dance while they'd been watching. It took Griffin's breath away to think that in the very moment of her great happiness, his daughter had remembered Sunny Kim and come to fetch him into the festivities. And he felt certain that he'd never in his entire life done anything so fine.*

And, finally, at Laura's wedding to Andy, Sunny comments that Laura seems to be happy and in love, and Russo leaves the reader with the aching truth: *LOVE Griffin thought, smiling. Only love made such a leap possible. Only love related one thing to all other things, putting all your eggs into a single basket – that dumbest yet most courageous and thrilling of economic and emotional strategies. 'I think she is,' he said, almost apologetically. His daughter was happy and deserved to be. Yet, sitting here in the dark, quiet bar with Sunny Kim, Griffin couldn't help wondering if the worm might already be in the apple. A decade from now, or a decade after that, would Laura suddenly see Sunny differently?*

Indeed, as with all relationships, which ones develop as planned? We are after all, at best, improvising as we tumble along life's journey, especially with our "inheritances" weighing upon us. *All families are fucked up*, observes Griffin at one point.

His relationship with his mother comes close to mine. He is forced to distance himself and his family from her and *when his mother suggested she be the one to accompany Laura on the....College Tour, he put his foot down. "I'm sorry Mom," he said, managing with great effort, not to raise his voice, but failing to keep the anger out of it, "but you don't get to infect my daughter with your snobbery and bitterness. All that ends here, with me." It had been a horrible thing to say, full of the very bitterness he was accusing her of. He regretted the words as soon as they were spoken, but there was no taking them back, nor could he quite bring himself to apologize.*

In fact, that was Griffin's plan all along: *With respect to their families, Griffin had hoped to invoke a simple, equitable policy: a plague on both their houses....He had no intention of inflicting his parents on Joy or, when the time came, on their children.*

When I remarried, my mother turned against my new wife (who she did not "approve" of as Griffin's mother disapproved of Joy). This devolved into a cold war, my having to keep my new family safe by trying to break off any contact with her. Still she pursued us with invectives, accusations, chronicling hurts I was not even aware of, such as when my two-year old son (from the unapproved second marriage), said something innocent about "a punch in the nose" and my mother was outraged that we did not correct his "misbehavior."

My father's death became a catalyst in the war's escalation. My "legal inheritance" was the contents of his desk and when I went back to my old childhood home, where my father had barricaded himself in my old bedroom in the attic, I went through the desk with my mother hovering over me to ensure that nothing "valuable" was taken for my younger son, the son of the "bad wife." One thing led to another and before I knew it she was screaming obscenities at me and I rushed to my car promising I would never see her again and would never return. I left with my father's penknife, my only "inheritance."

I made good on my promise for many years, avoiding any contact with her. Those were among the our most peaceful family years, not something I was particularly proud of, but necessary – as Griffin felt, protecting his family from bitterness and derision.

One day I received a Valentine card from her – at my office to avoid acknowledgment of my new family -- and began to get calls from her there as well, which always started off in a strained pleasant way and moved quickly to strident tirades. I was forced to write her a letter to put an end to that. Richard Russo, if you are reading this, feel free to incorporate any part in a future novel and thank you for understanding us Griffins of the world.

Towards the end I made an effort at some reconciliation. My sons were now grown so they no longer needed to be protected. When we saw each other, we tried to avoid discussions of the past. After she had suffered a stroke and then a broken hip, I went to see her, alone, in an assisted living home. She was despondent and subdued and I knew she felt that her life was near its end. I walked her wheel-chaired, frail body in the garden. She patted my hand and her last words to me were, "you were always a good boy." Three days later she was gone, almost exactly twenty years after my father. Since then *I've been wondering if maybe I loved them. It's crazy, I know, but...do you think that's possible?*

Tuesday, December 15, 2009 God, the Ninth, and Nine-Eleven

How does one reconcile the destructive events of 9/11 with the creative force of Beethoven's 9th Symphony both coming into being in the name of God? As Friedrich Shiller's *Ode to Joy* concludes -- the basis for Beethoven's massive choral addition to the symphonic form -- "Do you sense the Creator, world?/ Seek Him beyond the starry canopy!/Beyond the stars must He dwell." And no doubt the hijackers on that fated day believed they were performing a sacred duty for their "Creator."

I've been reading John Updike's last short story collection, *My Father's Tears*, interspersing those stories with other things I read, treating them like the little gems they are. Since 9/11 though I've made it a point to avoid anything about that horrible day, just because it is so raw in memory. We could see the columns of smoke 50 miles away in Connecticut on that crystal clear day.

So it was some trepidation when I realized that Updike's story "Varieties of Religious Experience" is about that very day; beginning with *THERE IS NO GOD: the revelation came to Dan Kellogg in the instant that he saw the World Trade Center South Tower fall. (He was from out of town, visiting his daughter and grandchild at their apartment in Brooklyn Heights.)* To get through this story, written from various perspectives (including a woman on the ill fated flight that crashed in PA), I had to continually take deep, slow breaths, just to control my anxiety. Not that Updike capitalized on gruesome details, but there is the constant unreal undercurrent of the lunacy of that day. One knows where it is all going, and if this is what God is all about, anyone's God, organized religion seems so hypocritical, a crutch or a means of justifying anything. One brief paragraph from the story encapsulates its essence:

Dan could not quite believe the tower had vanished. How could something so vast and intricate, an elaborately engineered upright hive teeming with people, mostly young, be dissolved by its own weight so quickly, so casually? The laws of matter had functioned, was the answer. The event was small beneath the calm dome of sky. No hand of God had intervened because there was none. God had no hands, no eyes, no heart, no anything. Thus was Dan, a sixty-four-year-old Episcopalian and probate lawyer, brought late to the realization that comes to children with the death of a pet, to women with the loss of a child, to millions caught in the implacable course of war and plague. His revelation of cosmic indifference thrilled him, though his own extinction was held within this new truth like one of the white rectangles weightlessly rising and spinning within the boiling column of smoke. He joined at last the run of mankind in its stoic atheism.

Thursday, March 11, 2010 **Irving Writes about Writing**

John Irving's *Last Night in Twisted River* characters are not ones I easily identify with so I follow them somewhat dislodged from the comfort zone I am normally within Anne Tyler's or Richard Russo's worlds.

And, indeed, *Twisted River* has a panoply of larger than life characters and Amazonian or Rubenesque women, the latter including Injun Jane, Six-Pack Pam, Carmella Del Popolo, and Lady Sky just to name a few of the colorful names. And then there are the men, who are often generically referred to as, "the cook" or "cookie" (Dominick), "the writer" (Daniel), "the riverman" or "the river driver" or the "logger" or the "woodsman from Coos County" (Ketchum), and the "constable" or the "crazy cowboy" or the "crazy cop" (Carl). In typical Irving fashion, there are scores and scores of supporting and minor characters.

Irving sometimes makes me feel as if I am entering a nightmare; so from the opening pages of *Twisted River* there is that sense of foreboding. His writing makes me stop here and there to figure out relationships, or potential relationships, as if I'm moving through molasses at times, but he is such a superior storyteller that you are drawn in and the story itself takes over.

He paints a portrait of three generations over the last fifty years and in a number of places, Colorado, Iowa, New Hampshire, Boston, Toronto, a twisted river of American life, Irving painting one part of the picture, jumping to another part of the canvas, temporally and geographically, circling and backfilling, bringing the story back to the beginning at the very end. It is an odyssey for the characters and for the reader. As Irving and I were born in the same year, the historical background of the novel is the one we've both lived at the same moment of our lives. The political history of "an empire in decline" is an omnipresent part of the novel's subliminal setting, the arrogance of power from the folly of Vietnam to the Iraqi invasion.

Many of the usual Irving themes or symbolism are here: the bears, wrestling, New England, hands (or lack of), tattoos, accidents and fate. But, of all his novels, this may be the most illuminating about Irving himself and the craft of his writing. He even describes his *Cider House Rules* as another work of fiction in this novel calling it *East of Bangor*.

The main character in *Twisted River* is Daniel Baciagalupo a.k.a. Danny Angel, his pen name for most of the novel. Danny is Irving's voice about writing, revealing his own tricks of the trade such as the following:

Maybe this moment of speechlessness helped to make Daniel Baciagalupo become a writer. All those moments when you know you should speak, but you can't think of what to say – as a writer, you can never give enough attention to those moments.

*All writers must know how to distance themselves, to **detach** themselves from this and that emotional moment, and Danny could do this – even at twelve.*

One day, the writer would recognize the near simultaneity of connected but dissimilar momentous events – these are what move a story forward.... (He was too young to know that, in any novel, with a reasonable amount of forethought, there were no coincidences.)

Childhood, and how it forms you – moreover, how your childhood is relived in your life as an adult – that was his subject (or his obsession), the writer Danny Angel daydreamed....

I particularly appreciated Irving's attention to Danny's experience at the Iowa Writers' Workshop. Some of my favorite writers have taught or have been taught there, luminaries such as John Cheever, Philip Roth, Richard Yates, Raymond Carver, Kurt Vonnegut and, of course, John Irving.

One of Danny's teachers there is Kurt Vonnegut *a kind man and a good teacher.* Describing Vonnegut's criticism of Danny's punctuation problem gives Irving the opportunity to reveal the major influences on his (both Danny's and Irving's) work: *Mr. Vonnegut didn't like all the semicolons. "People will probably figure out that you went to college – you don't have to try to prove it to them." [B]ut semicolons came from those old-fashioned nineteenth-century novels that had made Daniel Baciagalupo want to be a writer in the first place....Danny would be at Exeter before he actually read those books, but he'd paid special attention to those authors there – Nathaniel Hawthorne and Herman Melville...And English novelist Thomas Hardy naturally appealed to [him], who – even at twenty-five – had seen his share of what looked like fate to him.* Danny (and Irving), says of his former teacher: *Danny like[d] Kurt Vonnegut's writing, and he liked the man, too. Danny was lucky with teachers he had for his writing....*

Ketchum (the woodsman) is an idealized alter ego of Irving, perhaps the man he sees himself as being outside the world of writing, while Danny's father (the cook), a kindly man, protective of his son, is the idealized father who Irving never met. Irving loves these characters, and the stories of all three men are so tightly interwoven we mourn their aging in the novel as if they are one.

The reoccurring themes of Irving's novels, the vulnerability of childhood, and the inevitable loss of innocence, Irving's pessimistic distrust of human nature are evident here as well:

Danny Angel's novels had much to do with what the writer feared **might** *happen. The novels often indulged the nightmarish – namely, what every parent fears most: losing a child. There was always something or someone in a Danny Angel novel that was ominously threatening to children, or to a child. Young people were in peril – in part,* **because** *they were young!*

But what was political about [his] other five books? Dysfunctional families; damaging sexual experience; various losses of innocence, all leading to regret. These stories were small, domestic tragedies – none of them condemnations of society or government. In Danny Angel's novels, the villain – if there was one – was more often human nature than the United States.

It is well known that Irving works from the end of a story to the beginning and so does Danny: *As always, he began at the end of the story. He'd not only written what he believed was the last sentence, but Danny had a fairly evolved idea of the trajectory of the new novel....That was just the way he'd always worked: He plotted a story from back to front; hence he conceived of the first chapter* **last**. *By the time Danny got to the first sentence – meaning to that actual moment when he wrote the first sentence down – often a couple of years or more had passed, but by then he knew the whole story. From that first sentence, the book flowed forward – or, in Danny's case, back to where he'd begun.*

And so it is with *Twisted River*, a work that is a mirror within a mirror as it is Danny Baciagalupo who becomes its author in the end, Irving bringing together all the themes and characters in a coda so powerful that I found myself emotionally choked as I concluded the novel, especially relating to one of Irving's culminating thoughts: *Sometimes, people fall into our lives cleanly – as if out of the sky, or as if there were a direct flight from Heaven to Earth – the same sudden way we lose people, who once seemed they would always be part of our lives.* It left me bewildered as to how I could have been so unprepared for such a reaction, other than being in awe of Irving's gifts and the knowledge that we are all bobbing along on a twisted river, a circle of life.

Wednesday, May 12, 2010 **Confluence**

It is interesting how things come together, seemingly haphazardly, but connected in some way. Ann and I decided to celebrate our 40th wedding anniversary by taking a cruise in the Western Caribbean, places we've been before so we intended to spend most days on board, relaxing and reading.

I suppose that is the value of a Kindle or an iPad, being able to take a number of "books" with you, but for one week I figured one good novel and my half finished Library of America edition of Raymond Carver's short stories would do. So part of the fun planning the trip was selecting the novel, finally choosing one by a favorite author, Anne Tyler, her recently published *Noah's Compass*.

One review commented that she "plunges us into the troubled hearts of her characters and allows us to recognize in their confusions our own driven selves." Since at times I feel particularly driven, about the past, about my interests; I prepared to be plunged!

Tyler is a master of the tragic comedy, seeing the sadness and the humor in the minutiae of ordinary families and their relationships. The lives of Tyler's frequently quirky characters are compelling in their own way. And *Noah's Compass* is no exception to the winning Tyler formula. And as she moves into a later stage of her own life (we are about the same age), her writing reveals an increasing obsession with time, time spent (on what?) and time passing more quickly through the unrelenting hourglass.

So it is no surprise that Tyler pulled me into her novel immediately and although I am no Liam Pennywell (love her protagonist's name) in my demeanor, I am, like Liam, struggling with my memories and in fact just reading this novel, while celebrating our 40th anniversary, sparked a discussion while on the cruise as to what exactly happened that wedding day.

We remembered that I spent the night before in my apartment at 66 West 85th Street and Ann at hers at 33 West 63rd Street (although we were already living together on and off). We also recalled that we took a one-week trip to Puerto Rico a couple of weeks before we were married which, unknown to us at the time, was our honeymoon in advance. I was between my first job in publishing where we first met and the one I would occupy for the rest of my working career (like Tyler's characters I kept my shoulder to the wheel).

I returned to my new job in Westport, CT and shortly after, Ann placed a call to The Ethical Culture Society's leader, Jerome Nathanson, the man she wanted to marry us. He had only one date open in the next seven or eight months: a Sunday in April, exactly one week away. We looked at one another and said let's take it.

Consequently, Ann began hasty wedding arrangements, including ones to fly her mother and Aunt in from California, picking out a dress for herself and mother to wear, hiring a caterer and picking out flowers. We chose the list of attendees, mostly our immediate families and closest friends, including a few colleagues from work and of course, my young son from my previous marriage. Ann's brother and sister-in-law offered their home in Queens for the informal reception. Everything had to be done on a shoestring and obviously with a sense of urgency.

The ceremony itself was what one would expect from a humanist minister. A substantial part of the service captured our enthusiasm for the then victorious New York Knicks, with names such as Bill Bradley, Dave DeBusschere, Walt Frazier, and Willis Reed sprinkled throughout our wedding vows. Later that night we returned to my 85th Street apartment. We both had to go to work the next morning, my driving to Westport, while Ann took the subway downtown.

So the broad strokes were clearly remembered but for Liam Pennywell (back to Tyler's novel) much of his past is in a haze. He finds himself out of work in his early 60s, out of touch with his children and ex wife, and soon after downsizing to a smaller apartment comes the first twist in Tyler's plot, as Pennywell is knocked unconscious by an intruder during the night and wakes up in the hospital, banged up with no memory of the incident. He is intent on remembering (and in so doing conjuring up other memories of his past life as well) by pursuing someone he thinks can serve him as a "rememberer." This turns into a romance, something he clearly neither expected or even wanted. Liam is directionless, and explaining the Noah's Ark parable to his grandchild saying: *There was nowhere to go. He was just bobbing up and down, so he didn't need a compass, or a rudder, or a sextant.*

Later, Liam thinks, *We live such tangled, fraught lives...but in the end we die like all the other animals and we're buried in the ground and after a few more years we might as well not have existed.* But finally he realizes that *if the memory of his attack were handed to him today, he would just ask, Is that* **it**? *Where's the rest? Where's everything else I've forgotten: my childhood and my youth, my first marriage and my second marriage and the growing up of my daughters?* Tyler intercedes: *All along, it seemed, he had experienced only the most glancing relationship with his own life. He had dodged the tough issues, avoided the conflicts, gracefully skirted adventure.*

This wonderful story is told with Tyler's touching sense of humor, giving her characters the attributes and failures of us everyday folks. Unfortunately for me, while on this trip, the story was so compelling, I blew through the book in the first two days and I was concerned that I would also finish the

Carver short story collection I also brought. Then, I would go crazy not having anything to read!

So, before turning to the rest of the unread Carver short stories, I made a visit to the ship's library. There I found a well-stocked library of remainders, potboilers, mostly titles I never heard of, and certainly nothing I would choose to read. Consequently I was prepared to finish the Carver short story collection and start reading them all over again!

On my way out of the library, a large book caught my eye. What a shock to see one of the titles on my "must read" list, and how serendipitous it should be Carol Sklenicka's biography, *Raymond Carver: A Writer's Life*. I can't imagine why or how this magnificent work joined the pop culture potboilers that made up the ship's "library," but I resolved to devour its 500 pages for the remainder of the cruise.

The book reminded me of my introduction to the literary biography genre, Mark Schorer's *Sinclair Lewis: An American Life* (1961), a reading experience I never forgot because of Schorer's incredible attention to detail. And there are similarities between Lewis and Carver, their struggle with alcoholism and their keen observations of ordinary American life.

Equally impressive is the detail packed into Sklenicka's biography of Carver and her ability to integrate Carver's life and work, a biography by someone who clearly loves her subject. I particularly appreciated Sklenicka's relating specific poems and short stories to incidents in his life. Remarkably, Carver defined his career as "writer" while he was still in high school and never looked back. He was dependent on two women in his life, his first wife Maryann Burk and his second love, the writer Tess Gallagher who he married months before his death. They saw his genius and staunchly supported him, through his alcoholism and his early death from lung cancer (Carver was a militant smoker).

His inscription to his first wife in his last work, published only months before his death, but years after they had separated and divorced, says volumes about their relationship: *To: Maryann, my oldest friend, my youthful companion in derring-do, my mid-life companion in the same, my wife and helpmate for so long, my children's mother, this book is a token of love, and some have claimed obsession. In any event, this is with love always, no one knows, do they, just absolutely no one. Yours, Ray. May 1988*

Still, he was equally devoted to Tess Gallagher for the last years of his life and after he realized the tumors in his lungs had returned they were married in Reno in June 1988, as an expression of their mutual love and as a means of ensuring that she would manage his remaining literary rights as his survivor.

I called this entry "Confluence" as everything came together reading this biography, Sklenicka writing: *When Richard Yates came to Tucson to promote A Good School...Ray finagled the opportunity to spend most of a day with the writer who'd been his hero since he was stopped 'dead in his tracks' by Revolutionary Road in 1961. To mention that novel, Richard Ford writes, 'is to invoke a sort of cultural-literary secret handshake among its devotees.'* I am one of those devotees, not to mention a devotee to the works of Richard Ford (a life-long friend of Carver's), and John Cheever with whom Carver ran around at the University of Iowa's Writer's Workshop. Carver and Cheever had a mutual admiration society, two of our finest short story writers who were both, at the time of their closest association, serious alcoholics.

Thinking of Sklenicka's work, I wondered, if I were to write an autobiography, whether I could come up with the details of my *own* life. (*Where's everything else I've forgotten: my childhood and my youth?*) It is a testimony to Sklenicka's love of her subject and her prodigious research that *A Writer's Life* should emerge exactly as the subtitle promises.

In Carver's story *Blackbird Pie* a man's wife has left him (this wonderful story was greatly influenced by Carver's feelings towards his, then, ex-wife, Maryann). He's bewildered and is trying to make sense of it all, the first person narrator concluding: *It could be said, for instance, that to take a wife is to take a history. And if that's so, then I understand that I'm outside history now...Or you could say that my history has left me. Or that I'm having to go on without history. Or that history will now have to do without me – unless my wife writes more letters, or tells a friend who keeps a diary, say. Then, years later, someone can look back on this time, interpret it according to the record, its scraps and tirades, its silences and innuendos. That's when it dawns on me that autobiography is the poor man's history. And that I am saying good-bye to history. Good-bye, my darling.* Sklenicka is that "someone" who has looked back at that time and "interpreted" it according to the "record."

And for Carver, he "took another history," as did I, although mine can be explained only in autobiography and to the extent that memory serves.

Thursday, August 5, 2010 **Literary Concord**

Several years ago Ann cut out an article in the *Palm Beach Post* about Concord, Ma. and its rich literary and revolutionary war history. As we were visiting our son, Chris, in nearby Worcester, it was an ideal opportunity to push on to Concord for a couple of days, stay at a B&B (North Bridge Inn, highly recommended) and see for ourselves. We decided to concentrate on Concord's literary history, and its place at the crossroads of Transcendentalism with Emerson as the center of that universe. To walk where Emerson, Thoreau, Alcott, and Hawthorne walked is awe-inspiring.

They were all contemporaries, living near each other. This is indeed a sort of holy ground of American literary and intellectual history.

There is no better way to start such a trip than to visit the Concord Public Library, dedicated by Ralph Waldo Emerson when it opened in 1873. In this day of the Kindle and the iPad, it was refreshing to be in a traditional library, befitting the literary community which it is at the center. Inside one can find Daniel Chester French's sculpture of Ralph Waldo Emerson. French's tools were given to him by Louisa May Alcott.

In the Concord Museum Emerson's study is perfectly preserved, moved there after there was a fire in the Emerson home.

The Old Manse was home at one time or another to both Hawthorne and Emerson. Here Nathaniel Hawthorne and his bride Sophia rented for three years beginning in 1842. While on tour, we were able to see the following etching in one of the window panes using Sophia's diamond wedding ring:

Man's accidents are God's purposes. Sophia A. Hawthorne 1843 / Nath Hawthorne This is his study / The smallest twig leans clear against the sky / Composed by my wife and written with her diamond / Inscribed by my husband at sunset, April 3, 1843. In the Gold light.

One can still see the smallest twig leaning "clear against the sky." It would have been interesting to eavesdrop on conversations between Emerson and Hawthorne as Hawthorne was not a Transcendentalist. Henry David Thoreau (pronounced "Thorough" by the natives) is said to have planted the garden at the Old Manse as a wedding gift to the Hawthornes. The garden still blooms there. From the Old Manse Emerson's grandfather witnessed the "shot heard around the world," the opening volley of the American Revolution on the Old North Bridge.

The Old Manse also houses a 1864 Steinway piano and I was surprised when the docent invited anyone on the tour to try it. Most items on these house tours are of the "look-but-do-not-touch" nature. As no one volunteered I stepped forward to play a few bars of "Memories" by Andrew Lloyd Webber, my apologies to 19th century sensibilities. It was out of tune, but all keys functioned, more than 150 years after this piano was built.

This is how life was before the "conveniences" of modern life. Parlor games and music, plays written and performed by the residents, writing and philosophical discussions, and books read to the family by candlelight. (Hawthorne read the entire works of Sir Walter Scott to his children while living in Concord.)

The nearby Wayside is now a National Park property and tours of the home and the nearby North Bridge are conducted by Park Rangers. We were lucky enough to have had a private tour of this home. Louisa May Alcott spent her childhood there and many of the scenes from Little Women were set in her memory from that home. It is also the only home ever actually owned by Nathaniel Hawthorne who gave it the name, Wayside.

The tour of the Orchard House, where Louisa May Alcott actually wrote *Little Women* was inspired. The docent enacted several quotes from the novel, leaving one motivated not only to buy the book (once again) but others as well in the gift shop.

Alcott's father, an educator who struggled to make ends meet, was an enlightened man, encouraging his daughters to learn, building a small desk for Louisa May (unheard of at the time), and having the pleasure of watching his daughter become one of the best selling author's of her time, certainly making the family wealthy. That small, plain desk has been perfectly preserved. Father Alcott was devoted to Louisa May and she was devoted to him. Eerily, as the *New York Times* reported at the time in 1888, it is a noteworthy fact in connection with her life and death that Miss Alcott and her father were born on the same day of the month, and that they died within 24 hours of one another.

A couple years ago we had the pleasure of touring Emily Dickinson's home in Amherst. She is probably my favorite poet. I wonder whether her relative isolation in Amherst, while the literary hotbed of New England was not far away in Concord, but far enough to remove her from that scene, might have contributed to the quiet loneliness of her poetry. I am not aware of Dickinson ever meeting the Concord group.

Sleepy Hollow Cemetery is now the resting place of the Alcotts, Thoreau, Hawthorne and Emerson, Thoreau's grave just simply inscribed, "Henry." I cannot visit such a graveyard without thinking of Emily Dickinson's poem "I Died For Beauty" which I never forgot since reading it in college and in fact recited her words at Dickinson's gravesite in Amherst.

Our wonderful tour of Concord was concluded by having dinner at the Walden Grill with my best friend from college, Bruce, and his wife, Bonnie, residents of nearby Sudbury, and both dedicated teachers of literature. Perhaps learning, teaching and literature are in the water of Concord, Ma. and its environs!

Wednesday, October 6, 2010 **Freedom**

Jonathan Franzen's *Freedom* is a tour de force of our times covering the entire canvas of American culture, politics, and the forces that now shape our personal relationships and our society. It is stunningly and ingeniously written, with a fresh originality, a postmodern view of who we are and how we got here. In so doing, Franzen excoriates the worst aspects of American culture.

It is a story about the enmeshment of relationships, the extent to which we create our own hell (or heaven) having been dealt the hand of the families we are born into. Do we assume the roles of our parents or rebel against them? To what extent do we really have free will or become victims of abuse and misbehavior inflicted by prior generations? It is about competition and power, survival of the fittest, fathers vs. sons, almost echoing the Darwinian themes of Dreiser. It is about the conflict of personal freedoms and the need to protect the environment and control population growth. Will "the American bourgeoisie...voluntarily accept increasing restrictions on its personal freedoms"?

It is also a novel about a unique development in American life, new generations not having it better than previous ones, perhaps the consequence of having too many choices. As Franzen writes about the main character, Patty, *she was struck...by how much better off and more successful her parents were than any of their children, herself included. Her mother cursed her husband's genes for her kids' weirdness and ineffectuality.* At times the characters are "bludgeoned by depression," another leitmotif of the novel and certainly characteristic of our Prozac plagued times.

I couldn't help but think of Updike's *Rabbit* novels, written about every ten years, and Franzen, now, encapsulating the state of the first decade of the millennium. There is also the eerie coincidence of Patty being a basketball star in her youth, like Rabbit Angstrom. In many respects, there is a decidedly Updikian feel to the novel.

The novel is a shot across the bow of a society that values the culture of the American Idol and the worst aspects of capitalism more than the environment and intelligent political choices. At one point Patty's son, Joey, wishes *there were some different world he could belong to, some simpler world in which a good life could be had at nobody else's expense,* summing up the modern conundrum.

While it is a novel of social commentary, it is also a page-turner with memorable characters, ranking with the best in American literature. The writer who shared similar concerns in the early 20th century, Sinclair Lewis, said America is *the most contradictory, the most depressing, the most stirring, of any land in the world today.* I think Franzen would agree.

Thursday, February 10, 2011 **Marina Maiden Voyage**

I've been unable to post the past few weeks as we were on the maiden voyage of a beautiful new ship, Oceania's Marina, the first built by Oceania, whose current fleet is made up by the smaller ships of the Renaissance Line which ceased operations about ten years ago.

This ship was built to the exacting standards of adults who like some of the traditional touches reminiscent of what it was like to cruise in the halcyon days of trans Atlantic crossings, before jet travel almost destroyed the industry, and before Disney-like, mega ships made the cruise industry a mass market destination. (Think of the difference between Masterpiece Theater's recent *Downton Abbey* and the movie *Rambo*.)

So, during the languid afternoons, I'd find a quiet nook, or sit on the balcony of our room, watching the Ocean gently roll by, reading my books, almost finishing four novels during that period, two of which I brought and other two from the ship's library. So my literary friends for the journey were Canin, Shreve, Walter, and Casey.

America America by Ethan Canin was recommended by a good friend whose daughter knows the author, who teaches at Iowa writer's workshop, the same one where Carver, Cheever, and Irving have taught. Canin reminded me of some other favorite writers such as Richard Russo and Russell Banks, with upstate northeast small town and family dynamic themes. It is also a coming of age novel, with shadows of Fitzgerald's *Gatsby* and its American dream focus (from which the novel derives its bold title) -- glimpses into the upper classes with the hint that behind every great fortune is a great sin. Shifts in chronology make it interesting reading as well and sometimes I felt I was reading a novel that was indeed designed by a teacher, but a VERY good one, and I look forward to the future work of Ethan Canin.

I discovered Anita Shreve's *Rescue* in the ship's library and as I like her writing, in particular the *Weight of Water, Pilot's Wife, Sea Glass*, and *Body Surfing*, I snapped up the copy while I was finishing *America America*. *Rescue* comes uncomfortably close to my personal life, not that I was an EMT, but married early, "rescuing" not only my first wife, but myself. It is about codependency and dysfunctional families and alcoholism, it too a coming of age novel, the two main characters becoming what they were meant to be in the end. It is a very sparse prose, written in typical fluid Shreve style, with a sense of immediacy. This is not a novel to be read for the plot. It's all about the characters and the writing.

So, finishing that book I calculated that I'd finish the other novel I had brought (more on that later) so I panicked as the other novels I had seen in the ship's library -- at least those that I might have been interested in reading -- I had already read, but then I came across an unexpected treasure, *The Financial Lives of the Poets* by Jess Walter. I'm sometimes wary reading books by the "younger generation" although I have a high regard for Jonathan Franzen's works -- who was born when I was graduating from high school. Jess Walter is even younger than Franzen, a Generation Xer, but I was intrigued by the title and the fact that Richard Russo wrote a brief testimonial which was conspicuous on the jacket. I trust Russo: "When it comes to explaining to me my own too often baffling nation, there's no one writing today whom I trust as completely as Jess Walter. His intelligence and sympathy and great wit inform every page--indeed every sentence--of his terrific new novel, *The Financial Lives of the Poets*." That was enough for me to give it a try, and I am glad I did. (As I publisher, I was always dubious about the effectiveness of testimonial blurbs -- but they obviously work!)

This is a very funny but tragic book, a look at the financial debacle of the past few years and its impact on the main character, Matt Prior who had quit his job at the height of the financial boom to start a business web site that was to report news in verse, called Poetfolio.com. He had borrowed to start his business while his wife became a compulsive shopper on EBay trying to resell petty merchandise at a profit (*everyone else is doing it!*) and before they knew it their family, consisting of them, their two sons and Matt's increasingly senile father who is now living in their home, become embroiled in a financial nightmare. It is told, though, with the knack of Joseph Heller's *Catch 22*, updated for the dot.com world. Like *Rescue*, it is about some poor choices, but redemption is found at the end. It is a totally imaginative novel, one that seems so natural even though it is so satiric. In addition to Ethan Canin, I will be watching out for Jess Walter's future works.

Finally, I turned to the other novel I brought with me, John Casey's *Spartina*. I wanted to read this before Casey's sequel, *Compass Rose*, and also because it was a National Book Award–winning book. I was immediately drawn in because it is about the sea, and, in particular, an area we had regularly traversed in our own boat -- the waters off of Rhode Island. And it is about a commercial fishermen, one I might have met during my boating life, and the vicissitudes they endure because of their love of the sea (the main one, just trying to make a living). Dick Pierce is not only a fisherman but he is a boat-builder as well and he is building the boat of his dreams, one that is to provide for his family but also one that he views as a work of art. Casey brings his environment to life, whether it is in the cockpit of a fishing boat, heaving off the seas of Block Island, or the back marshes of the New England coast. Casey's writing is achingly heartfelt and even though I am not yet quite finished with the novel, I know this one will want to bring me to *Compass Rose* soon after.

Friday, April 29, 2011 **Conroy's Reading Life**

Our good friend Edie gave me *My Reading Life* by Pat Conroy when I recently entered the hospital, which was supposed to be for a more routine visit than it turned out to be. She knows I love good writing, and she thinks of me as a writer as well. It was a very thoughtful gift. Yes, I write, and I enjoy it, but to be a real writer means to forsake just about everything and dedicate yourself to the craft. It also helps to have an abundance of talent, an omniscient eye and an encyclopedic memory.

I cannot think of any great writer who is not obsessive compulsive about writing. In many ways, I wish I could roll back time and make that choice, but it would have been to the detriment of a publishing career I loved and other avocations such as the piano, studying the machinations of economic markets, politics, and a bunch of other things. Although I started Conroy's work in the hospital, I had difficulty concentrating on it or anything else after undergoing complicated open heart surgery. My recovery left me unable to do much but change channels watching awful TV which I can only describe as crap, and if that is emblematic of where American "culture" has migrated, there is no hope for our society.

Once I returned home, I picked up the book again. Conroy achingly cries out in poetic terms for an understanding as to why he writes, why he found refuge as a child in literature, first as a means of connecting with his mother (no, worshiping her) and as a means of escaping his father. I have a particular empathy for literature as a means to understand family.

It was heartbreaking, though, to read Conroy's dedication page. My Reading Life begins with: *This book is dedicated to my lost daughter, Susannah Ansley Conroy. Know this: I love you with my heart and always will. Your return to my life would be one of the happiest moments I could imagine.*

So, as in my family, succeeding generations are affected by the tribulations fostered by previous generations. I naturally tried to discover more, and found his comments about the dedication page in an NPR review: Apparently he has been estranged from his daughter since divorcing her mother in 1995: *She has a perfect right not to see me. She's 28 now. But I thought this [dedication] was going to be a last cry of the heart. I would at least try to get her attention and see if I could get her to come back. It has been one of the most soul-killing things to ever happen to me.*

Maybe his daughter will reconnect with her father if she has the opportunity to read this book and understand the undertow of Conroy's maturation as a man and as a writer. He covers a wide range of influences on his writing, first and foremost his mother, who became immersed in *Gone With the Wind,* continuously reading passages from the novel to her son, beginning when he was five years old. *I owe a personal debt to this novel that I find almost beyond reckoning. I became a novelist because of "Gone with the Wind," or more precisely, my mother raised me up to be a "Southern" novelist, with a strong emphasis on the word "Southern," because Gone with the Wind set my mother's imagination ablaze when she was a young girl in Atlanta, and it was the one fire of her bruised, fragmented youth that never went out....It was the first time I knew that literature had the power to change the world.*

Then there were the teachers, in particular Gene Norris's English class, and the "anti-teachers" in particular his father, Donald Conroy, the Marine who beat his family. Conroy bore much of this. *From an early age, I knew I didn't want to be anything like the man he was....I was on a lifelong search for the different kind of man. I wanted to attach my own moon of solitude to the strong attraction of a good man's gravitational pull.* Gene Norris was that man and he became a lifelong friend and mentor to Conroy and introduced Conroy to a wide range of classic literature.

Then there were people in his life who could have been negative influences, the librarian, Miss Hunter, at Beaufort High School, Cliff Grabart, the proprietor of the Old New York Book Shop in Atlanta, and the cantankerous, but lover of literature, a book representative, Norman Berg, who I myself met on several occasions at book conventions. Conroy even went out on sales calls with Berg. That was the foundation of the publishing business then.

From each of these people Conroy took away something and bonded with them in his own way. In fact, Conroy was sponge-like in his dealings with people and the literature he read, recording everything, the eyes and ears of a writer on duty at all times. This is what separates mediocre writers from great ones.

He did the ex-pat "thing" in Paris in the late 1970s. *Parisians... relish the xenophobic sport of stereotyping and love to offer an infinite variety of theories on the nature of Americans. To them, we as a people are shallow, criminally naive, reactionary, decadent, over-the-hill, uncultured, uneducable, and friendly to a fault....Whenever Parisians heard my execrable attempts at French, they would cover their ears with their hands and moan over the violation and butchery of their sweet tongue.* My own visits to France taught me a similar lesson, my high school French had to be left behind. But maybe the French are on to something, given my captivity by the mindless TV programming during my hospital stay.

Conroy was finishing *The Lords of Discipline* in Paris, staying at a hotel where he encountered a wide range of travelers, including other artists. As my son is an inveterate traveler, I was fascinated by Conroy's exquisite explanation as to what it is to be an ex-pat, meeting other people on similar journeys: *Because we were strangers who would know one another on this planet for a very short time, we could trade those essential secrets of our lives that defined us in absolute terms. Voyagers can remove the masks and those sinuous, intricate disguises we wear at home in the dangerous equilibrium of our common lives.*

But to this point, *My Reading Life* is merely a warm up for what is the main event and influence on Conroy's writing and he appropriately entitles the chapter "A Love Letter to Thomas Wolfe."

It was Gene Norris who gave him Wolfe's classic *Look Homeward, Angel* in 1961 as a Christmas present. *The book's impact on me was visceral that I mark the reading of "Look Homeward, Angel" as one of the pivotal events of my life....The beauty of the language, shaped in sentences as pretty as blue herons, brought me to my knees with pleasure....I was under the illusion that Thomas Wolfe had written his book solely because he knew that I would one day read it, that a boy in South Carolina would enter his house of art with his arms wide open, ready and waiting for everything that Thomas Wolfe could throw at him.*

I felt the same awe when I read the novel in college, probably at about the same time as Conroy. Never before had I felt that way when reading fiction. The only way to describe his writing is as being concurrently prodigious and poetic, an uncommon combination. And the novel was even larger before publication and luckily for Wolfe his editor was none other than the legendary Maxwell Perkins at Scribner's who also was Ernest Hemingway's and F. Scott Fitzgerald's. Wolfe was in good company.

The publication of *Look Homeward, Angel*, had, at its heart, detailed autobiographical elements, the same sort of autobiographical elements in which Conroy's own *The Great Santini* is grounded. Wolfe's work caused an uproar in his hometown, beautiful Asheville, North Carolina. For a while he was banished from the town, but he did return later to write *You Can't Go Home Again*.

Conroy has made the pilgrimage to Asheville, first with his teacher, Gene Morris, to visit Wolfe's "Old Kentucky Home," the boarding house maintained by Wolfe's mother. Conroy rocked on the chairs where the boarders gathered on the porch. He toured the home which has been so lovingly restored. I wonder whether Conroy has seen the wonderful play about Wolfe's return to Asheville, *Return of an Angel* which we were lucky enough to experience during one of our visits to Asheville. It brought Wolfe's return to Asheville alive.

We have been to the Wolfe home in Asheville twice and came away with the same feeling of time having been stopped during those years, before Wolfe's untimely death at the age of only 37. Imagine the great works he would have written if he had lived. As Conroy says, *I think the novels of his fifties and sixties would have been masterpieces. Time itself is a shaping, transfiguring force in any writer's life. Wolfe's best novels sleep in secret on a hillside in Asheville -- beside him forever, or at least, this is what I believe.*

Conroy's concluding chapter, "Why I Write" is probably one of the best I've ever read on the subject, setting the serious writer apart from the potboilers that weigh down today's best seller lists. *Stories are the vessels I use to interpret the world to myself...Good writing is the hardest form of thinking. It involves the agony of turning profoundly difficult thoughts into lucid form, then forcing them into the tight-fitting uniform of language, making them visible and clear.*

Also in that chapter, he returns to the overarching theme of literature and family, the role of literature explaining who we are and where we came from: *I've always wanted to write a letter to the boy I once was, lost and dismayed in the plainsong of a childhood he found all but unbearable. but I soon discovered that I've been writing voluptuous hymns to that boy my whole life, because somewhere along the line -- in the midst of breakdowns, disorder, and a malignant attraction to mayhem that's a home place for the beaten child -- I fell in love with that kid.* And I too fell in love, as much with Conroy's nonfiction as his novels, particularly with *My Reading Life*, as well as *My Losing Season*. Such truthfulness and beautiful writing. One can only hope his honesty will lead to a reconciliation with his daughter. It would be just.

Wednesday, June 1, 2011 **Shantaram**

It is rare to read literature outside of my "comfort zone" of contemporary American literature, and rarer still to read novels approaching 1,000 pages, so it was with some trepidation that I picked up *Shantaram*, recommended to me by my son, Jonathan, but within a few pages I was hooked. Really, a remarkable first novel, given its author, Gregory David Roberts, an Australian, was a convicted bank robber and heroin addict who spent ten years in an Australian prison before escaping and then fleeing to India. The novel is largely autobiographical. As he says in the Acknowledgements, it took him 13 years to write the novel and the first two drafts, "six years' work and six hundred pages were destroyed in prison."

He has a unique perspective on India, in particular Bombay which was to become Mumbai, but most people in India still call it Bombay, one of the most populous urban regions in the world. Dickens' London was such a city in the 19th century and in many ways Roberts' focus on the underbelly of the city reminds me of Dickens' concern with poverty, crime and imprisonment, and slum life. In fact, that is where real life can be found, in *Oliver Twist, Bleak House* and in *Shantaram.* They are also similar because of the multiplicity of characters. If you read *Shantaram,* develop a character list.

During many of my publishing years I worked through an agent for sales in India. Our business was not substantial enough to go there, but each year I met with our agent, Vinod, at the Frankfurt Bookfair, and we developed a good relationship. He was a tough negotiator, but he had a winning smile and in spite of other publishers' complaints about getting paid for sales to India, we shipped on open account and Vinod's word was always good. In reading this novel, Vinod kept coming to mind. Like Vinod, the first Indian, Prabaker, to befriend the novel's main character was a man with a winning smile. As another character in the novel says: *"This is India, man. This is India. This is the land of the heart. This is where the heart is king, man. The fuckin' heart!"*

India bestows the power of redemption upon our main character, Lindsay Ford, who escapes from an Australian prison and stops in Bombay on his way to another destination. But Bombay becomes his home and he plunges into the nadir of society, becoming a resident in its slums through his friendship with Prabaker. It is Prabaker's mother, Rukhmabai Kharre, who gives him the name, Shantaram: "Man of Peace, or man of God's peace" *I don't know if they found that name in the heart of the man they believed me to be, or if they planted it there, like a wishing tree, to bloom and grow. Whatever the case, whether they discovered that peace or created it, the truth is that the man I was born in those moments, as I stood near the flood sticks with my face lifted to the chrismal rain. Shantaram. The better man that, slowly, and much too late I began to be.* For much of the novel Shantaram is an ironic name as "Lin" or "Linbaba" as Prabaker names him, descends into familiar ways of violence and crime as the novel unfolds.

But there is a difference between his crimes in Australia and those in Bombay. He becomes a member of a mafia "family" and indeed, friendship, loyalty, and search for a spiritual father are also prevailing themes in the novel. There is honor among these thieves. As Abdel Khader Khan, his mafia boss and surrogate father says: *"We concentrate our laws, investigations, prosecutions, and punishments on how much crime is in the sin, rather than how much sin is in the crime....It is for this reason that I will not sell children, or women, or pornography, or drugs....In all of these things, the sin in the crime is so great that a man must give up his soul for the profit he makes."*

He adopts a "brother," Abdullah. *I learned that only one man in hundreds will stand with you, to the end, in friendship's name...Prison also taught me how to recognise those rare men when I met them. I knew that Abdullah was such a man. In my hunted exile, biting back the fear, ready to fight and die every haunted day, the strength and wildness and will that I found in him were more, and better than all the truth and goodness in the world.*

And the novel is about love, unrequited and requited, particularly his undying love for Karla, a Swiss-American woman who lives in the shadows. *One of the reasons why we crave love, and seek it so desperately, is that love is the only cure for loneliness, and shame, and sorrow. But some feelings sink so deep into the heart that only loneliness can help you find them again. Some truths about yourself are so painful that only shame can help you live with them. And some things are just so sad that only your soul can do the crying for you.*

Also central to this novel is the exile in society and literature. *When I'd climbed the wall of the prison all those years before, it was as if I'd climbed a wall on the rim of the world. When I slid down to freedom I lost the whole world that I knew, and all the love it held. In Bombay I'd tried, without realizing it, to make a new world of loving that could resemble the lost one, and even replace it.*

And in that "new world" he meets others like himself and those became his family. *If there was a bond between us, it was the bond exiles, the kinship of the lost, the lonely, and the dispossessed.*

There is a dancing bear in the novel, Kano, which Abdullah arranges to hug Linbaba and some 800 pages later Linbaba finds himself helping the bear to leave the same prison in Bombay where he also has spent some tortuous time. Then he helps the giant bear to escape the city disguised as a Genesha, on a trolley, at the end of an annual festival. *The elephant-headed god was known as the Lord of Obstacles and the Great Solver of Problems. People in trouble appealed to him with prayers....He was also the divine ministrant of writers.* Throughout the novel people turn to Linbaba. He served as ministrant to all, from learning to treat illness in the slums to helping friends, to serving his mafia family. Redemption and loyalty. That is the essence of the novel.

As a literary work, it labors at times and I thought it really was two novels, the main one in Bombay and another one in Afghanistan. Apparently, there is a sequel in the works which takes Linbaba to Sri Lanka. Also, not surprisingly, the movie rights to this epic novel were sold because of Johnny Depp's interest in the book and in starring in the movie. Ideal casting methinks, but the novel is sprawling and wrestling it into a manageable screenplay and Depp's schedule has delayed filming. One hopes it will see the light of day, even if the movie has to be truncated to include only the Bombay experience. By the way, part of the novel covers the Bollywood scene, as it does nearly everything else!

Friday, July 1, 2011 **A Meaningful Life**

We just returned from Sicily where we attended the wedding of the son of my wife's best friend, Maria. I packed my noise cancelling headphones with my iTouch and listened to music the entire flight while I read a recently reissued novel, *A Meaningful Life* by L.J. Davis originally published in 1971. This is a forgotten classic, the kind I used to seek when I was in the reprint business. Kudos to the *New York Review of Books* for discovering this one.

Two years ago I reviewed Sam Savage's *The Cry of the Sloth* and I have to wonder whether Savage had read Davis' *A Meaningful Life*. The two protagonists seem to be the same person confronting the dilemma of "a meaningless life." At the time, I said "Savage portrays an inexorable path for our protagonist, a fascinating, tragicomic portrait of isolation and personal failure, in the tradition of Gogol and Kafka." Davis did the same for his protagonist, Lowell Lake, more than thirty years earlier. *A Meaningful Life* is written in the finest tradition of the black comedy and I think if Woody Allen and Franz Kafka teamed up, this could have been their collaboration.

The novel is set in my familiar 1960's, the same decade I married my first wife while we were still in college and lived in Brooklyn. Lowell as well drifts into marriage in college, gives up his scholarship to graduate school, mostly to show his new wife that he is in charge of their lives and to prove it further, decides to move from California to New York City, where he will write a novel and she will work, over her objections (knowing Lowell to be unrealistic). His wife's mother also objects to Lowell right at the start (he's not Jewish; her daughter is). Her father simply entreats Lowell to call him Leo and that is about the extent of their relationship. Early in the novel Lowell fantasizes his future life as being a subject for the law and at the end this fear rears its head again. Davis' description of Lowell's wedding pretty much sets the timbre of the writing:

The moment Lowell took his place at the altar, a fog of terror blew into his mind and few things sufficiently penetrate its veil to be remembered with any clarity afterward. He hadn't been nervous that his voice would break or that he would fart loudly -- but he was scared now, and scared he remained. He was changing his status in the community of man. He was in the hopper of a great machine and he could no more get them to turn it off than a confessed and proven murderer could change his mind about his trial....He was going to be a grown up now, and there was no stopping it.

On their drive to New York, he makes a wrong turn and winds up in Brooklyn, foreshadowing Lowell's eventual involvement in the borough. But before that denouement they endure nine years of "marriage," Lowell at first "working" on his novel, which turns mostly to gibberish and both Lowell and his wife retreat to drinking when his wife daily returns from work. Their days are filled with the details of living, more like surviving, watching sitcoms, drinking, while Lowell slides down the vortex of a meaningless life, without any purpose. Why even dress?

At the end of six months his wife systematically began to throw away his clothes. True, his clothes were showing a few signs of wear; Lowell had never been particularly interested in clothing, bought it as seldom as possible, and wore it as long as he could, often developing a stubborn affection for certain items. It was also true that his underwear was a disgrace, his Jockey shorts hanging in soft tatters and his undershirts so full of holes that wearing them was nothing but a formality; on the other hand, it was kind of startling to go to the suitcase that served him in lieu of a bureau and find that his possessions had been weeded again, the supply growing shorter and shorter as the days wore on, the time fast approaching when he would go to his suitcase and it would be empty....If a kinder fate had not intervened, it was altogether possible that Lowell would soon have been totally naked, hovering thin and birdlike and obsessed above the typewriter like some kind of crackpot anchorite. Although this state of affairs

would have precluded ever leaving the apartment again, at least alive, that
would have been all right too.

Reaching the bottom, he symbolically fears he does not even exist. His
wife was to blame once again in his mind, a mind now totally disheveled and
lacking of purpose:

One day, in going over his papers, he discovered that his wife had
thrown out his birth certificate. There was no proof that she had done so,
but the damn thing was gone, and he knew instinctively what had hap-
pened to it. It was a blue piece of crackly paper with all of Lowell's statistics
arranged in graceful script above a gold medallion and the signatures of
the delivering physician, the resident, and the director of the hospital, just
like a diploma. It not only proved that he had been born, but the fact that he
possessed it proved that he was a grown-up.

Finally, Lowell admits to himself that his "novel" is nothing but a means
of passing time with booze. Through the shadowy connection of an "Uncle
Lester" -- his wife's uncle -- he gets a job as a copywriter for a plumbing
trade journal, neither knowing anything about plumbing, nor having any
interest in the subject. He took the job with the understanding (his, not his
employer's) that it would only be temporary (sort of like his life itself). As
soon as he got the job, *his wife settled down almost as if a wand had been*
waved over her, bought a black garter belt, and never chewed gum again.

But after nine years of marriage (Davis describes their marriage as a
cross between *Long Day's Journey Into the Night* and *Father Knows Best*),
his life amounted to *an endless chain of days, a rosary of months, each as*
smooth and round as the one before, flowing evenly through his mind. You
could count on the fingers of one hand the events and pauses of all that time:
two promotions; two changes of apartment (each time nearer the river); a
trip to Maine, where he realized that his wife's legs had gotten kind of fat--
five memories in nine years, each no more than a shallow design
scratched on a featureless bead. It was life turned inside out; some-
where the world's work was being done and men were laboring in
the vineyards of the Lord, Khrushchev was being faced down on the
high seas, and Negroes were being blown up and going to jail, but
all Lowell did was change his apartment twice, tell his wife to put on
some pants, and get promoted faster than anybody else on the paper --
a tiny, dim meteor in an empty matchbox.

But at this time Lowell discovers the biography of Darius Collingwood, a
tycoon and ruthless raconteur of the 19th century, a person as opposite of the
passive Lowell as one can be. He becomes mesmerized by his life, especially
by the discovery that Collingwood had built a mansion in Brooklyn, one
that was for sale in the Fort Green/Bedford Stuyvesant section of Brooklyn,

which in the 1960's looked more like Berlin at the end of WWII. Vagrants, bums, and all sorts of unsavory figures occupied empty disintegrating buildings. Lowell becomes fixated on buying the old Colingwood mansion and renovating it, not knowing anything about real estate, carpentry, plumbing, electrical repairs and with some savings he had secretly put aside from his "work" he plunges into a nightmarish version of *Mr. Blandings Builds His Dream House.*

The real estate closing with a "Mr. Grossman," the seller, reveals his ignorance:

[He never did]... get to see Mr. Grossman, who was represented at the closing by a lawyer of such intimidating respectability that he made Lowell feel like some kind of meek crook whenever he spoke to him. Sometimes Lowell wondered if Mr. Grossman existed at all, if he wasn't the creation of real-estate interests, doing voice imitations over the phone in order to collect rents and fight off city agencies and sell houses to people like Lowell. Anything seemed possible, even probable. Sitting there in the lawyer's office above Court Street with sleet rattling on the windows, money changing hands, and a great deal of incomprehensible but threatening nonsense going on all around him, he felt like a mental defective on trial for rape and witchcraft: he couldn't understand a word of it, but he had the distinct feeling that it would not end well. Papers were produced and signed; Lowell wrote checks, and they were taken from him; men conferred in glum, hushed voices with their heads close together, continually referring to Lowell as 'him."

So, with the first found enthusiasm of his life, Lowell begins work on his crumbling edifice. He evicts the squatters in the home. He buys tools. He has them stolen. He buys books about renovation and understands little. He seeks out a neighbor who had renovated a similar property (unsuccessfully) for suggestions. He is demonically watched by the so called residents in those slums. His wife helps for a while, but then goes to her mother's, but returns to their apartment where she lives a chaotic life. He finally gets to the point that he has to hire a contractor but only two show up to quote, the first of whom just walks out and the second, a Trinidadian by the name of Cyril P. Busterboy who agrees to take on the job with his crew. Lowell calls him Mr. Busterboy. Mr. Busterboy calls him Mr. Lake. Gradually Lake hangs around Busterboy and his crew, buying them beers and most of the work stops as they all get drunk during the day. Lowell is so drunk one night he sleeps in the remains of the building's master bedroom, on a tarp on the floor, hears a noise downstairs and confronts a shadowy figure. Lowell, with a crowbar in hand, and still in a drunken stupor, successfully bashes the intruder's head in like a crushed watermelon. He deposits the body in the dumpster and throws other trash over the body, leaving blood all over the room. The dumpster is picked up in the morning, Lowell convinced the police will come, but no one misses the intruder whose life was obviously as meaningful as Lowell's. Mr. Busterboy tells him not to worry, that his men will clean up the blood. This is covered over with sterile new plaster. He loses the house, but does not care, *contemplating a future much like his past, he realized that it was finally too late for him.*

Although a literary work, it is more a profoundly disturbing philosophical piece. How does one define a "meaningful life?" Lowell is a caricature in the extreme, simply being swept along by forces over which he has little control and when he does participate in the decision making, he inevitably makes the wrong ones, not realizing consequences. He simply has no interests, and therefore no real friends. Time erases all, but Davis' novel is a reminder to find one's passion -- and for most people that means meaningful work, or an avocation, something Lowell miserably fails at. Depressing? Yes, but Davis sees it as the modern dilemma.

Saturday, August 27, 2011 **Hurricane Irene and Jonathan Tropper**

We are hunkered down in a hotel awaiting Hurricane Irene, our boat secured to the best of our ability. So we wait, with our flashlights (as power will inevitably be lost) and enough bread, peanut butter and jelly to outlast the storm. The storm surge will be the key to our boat's survival, a sickening feeling having to wait out the next two days and hoping we can return to find minimal damage when the storm finally passes. Meanwhile, it is time to complete an entry concerning Jonathan Tropper which I had started to write before Irene dictated the turmoil of preparing for the storm.

I'm becoming a Jonathan Tropper admirer, a clever and talented writer. I had just finished Russell Bank's *The Reserve*, a beautifully written novel but humorless and needed a "pick me up" so I returned to Tropper, having liked his *Everything Changes*, and was curious whether one of his earlier ones would measure up. I chose *The Book of Joe* with some hesitancy as it seemed to have all its cultural references to the 1980s, where part of the novel is set. This is my younger son's generation, not mine.

But Tropper deals with such universal truths they transcend generational provincialism, certainly the mark of a good writer. My high school years of the 1950s had the same raw pulsating teenage angst, sexual urgency, and social vulnerability, the very ones portrayed by Tropper at Bush Falls High, their Cougar basketball players revered, and everyone else in a subordinate role. Teenagers can be the most sadistic humans on the face of the earth, something Tropper well understands about the high school caste system.

And Tropper poignantly captures that in *The Book of Joe*, using Thomas Wolfe's *Look Homeward Angel* experience as a very loose outline. Wolfe's novel outraged the residents of Asheville and had Wolfe returned, he, too, would have been vilified as is Tropper's Joe Goffman who leaves the small fictional town of Bush Falls, CT, somewhere north of New Haven. He writes a novel about the town and it becomes a sensational best-seller, thanks in part to his agent. He tells all in thinly veiled fiction, even his most private sexual fantasies concerning his best friend's mother. He finally returns 17 years later as his father has had a stroke and he now has to confront his family and former friends and high school hell raisers, the love of his life, and even the mother about whom he had fantasized.

Tropper writes terrifically believable dialogue and it is not surprising that he is also a screenwriter and a couple of his novels are in the process of being adapted for the screen. *The Book of Joe* is a fast read, poignantly tragicomic. Sometimes his writing reminds me of Joseph Heller's special gift for ironic humor.

I was surprised by how engaged I was in the world of this thirty-something protagonist, a world more inhabited by my sons, but universal truths never change.

Thursday, September 29, 2011 **Catching Up...**

The last few weeks went by in a whirlwind. During that period we took a two week cruise in the Baltic region, trans Atlantic flights to Holland and back, packing up from our summer on the boat, and then closing it up involving a myriad of operational chores best left unsaid and then driving the 1,250 miles home, 800 miles on the 2nd day -- made pleasurable by Stephen King's audio edition of *On Writing* read by the author himself -- arriving to assess all the work to be done in and around the house, particularly on the tropical overgrowth of landscaping, courtesy of the humid Florida summers.

Finally I can summarize my reading on the cruise, something for which there was little time. The first one I tackled, sort of an underground classic, J.L. Carr's *A Month in the Country*. This is written in the tradition of Thomas Hardy, a wonderful tale about a medieval mural of the apocalypse which was painted on the ceiling of a church in the countryside somewhere in England and whitewashed over. The man who is hired to restore the painting, in the process, resurrects his own soul in the bargain. He is separated from his wife, Vinny, and recovering from his experiences during WWI:*The marvelous thing was coming into this haven of calm water and, for a season, not having to worry my head with anything but uncovering their wall-painting for them. And, afterwards, perhaps I could make a new start, forget what the War and the rows with Vinny had*

done to me and begin where I'd left off. This is what I need, I thought --
a new start and, afterwards, maybe I won't be a casualty anymore. Well,
we live by hope. It is a little gem of a redemptive novel.

From the sublime to the entertaining I picked up another Jonathan
Tropper novel, *This is Where I Leave You.* Here is yet another clever novel
by him, the focal point of which is our hero, Judd Foxman, sitting a seven
day shiva with his dysfunctional family, as his marriage is falling apart.
Tropper is known for his smart witty dialogue and this novel delivers.
Although comic, Tropper is an observer of the manners and mores of modern times and I almost think of him as a Jane Austen type, delectable to
read, with stinging observations. For example, this is his riotous description of sitting shiva (sat on chairs lower than their visitors) on one particular day: *The parade of weathered flesh continues. Sitting in our shiva*
chairs, we develop a sad infatuation with the bared legs of our visitors.
Some of the men wear pants, and for that we are eternally grateful. But
this being late August, we get our fair share of men in shorts, showing off
pale, hairless legs with withered calves and thick, raised veins like earth-
worms trapped beneath their flesh who died burrowing their way out.
The more genetically gifted men still show some musculature in the calf
and thigh areas, but is more often than not marred by the surgical scars
of multiple knee operations or heart bypasses that appropriated veins
from the leg. And there's a special place in shiva hell reserved for men in
sandals, their cracked, hardened toenails, dark with fungus, proudly on
display. The women are more of a mixed bag. Some of them have managed
to hold it together, but on others, skin hangs loosely off the bone, crinkled
like cellophane, ankles disappear beneath mounds of flesh; and spider
veins stretch out like bruises just below the skin. There really should be a
dress code. A laugh a minute because it is so true.

My final novel for the cruise was one I've been saving for years for
the right moment, a mass market paperback edition, small and portable,
although some 500 pages, so ideal for carrying on a trip -- Pat Conroy's
The Lords of Discipline. I've read most of Conroy and when he writes autobiographical material, he is at his best. I'm sure many of the episodes he
chronicles in this book, one about a boy coming of age in a military college
in Charleston, SC, come right out of his own life experiences. It is powerful
and fast-moving, a page turner, beautifully written, Conroy being one of our
most lyrical writers today. It is about the true meaning of honor, a painful
lesson our protagonist, Will McLean, learns in the real world. Will is not
from the elite society of Charleston as are some of his classmates. He is on
scholarship as the point guard on the basketball team, as was Conroy himself when he went to school. Although Conroy's autobiographical *My Losing*
Season primarily deals with that subject (basketball), well worth reading,

this novel devotes only a dozen or so pages to the topic, but perhaps the most vivid, accurate ones I've ever read about playing the game. Still, it is the beauty of his writing that glued me to the pages of this novel: *The city of Charleston, in the green feathery modesty of its palms, in the certitude of its style, in the economy and stringency of its lines, and the serenity of its mansions South of Broad Street, is a feast for the human eye. But to me, Charleston is a dark city, a melancholy city, whose severe covenants and secrets are as powerful and beguiling as its elegance, whose demons dance their alley dances and compose their malign hymns to the far side of the moon I cannot see. I studied those demons closely once, and they helped kill off the boy in me.*

Thursday, November 3, 2011 **Home, Again**

After the round of obligatory medical appointments, and volunteering to be the pianist during visitors' hours at a West Palm Beach rehab center, and attend to work around the house after a Florida summer, it's been a busy period. Nonetheless, there is always time for some good literature and in that regard here are two I finished at the end of the days and while waiting for appointments.

Ethan Canin's *Carry Me Across the Water*, is a gem, beautifully crafted with multiple converging story lines. The child of a Jewish immigrant makes his way to America with his mother, leaving behind his father who stubbornly stays, not believing what was coming, when the Nazis finally prevail in the 1930's. His mother ultimately settles in Brooklyn, remarries the devout Hank Kleinman, from whom our protagonist August Kleinman derives his surname.

But the novel begins with Augie in his 78th year, a widower and father of three children, a man who pursued the American Dream through hard work, taking chances, and surviving WWII, the latter playing significantly in the novel. When Augie was a soldier he came across a Japanese soldier in a cave on one of the Japanese islands who has his own story, one that August becomes part of at the end. Meanwhile, after the war, August Kleinman becomes wealthy (a prevailing theme in Canin's work -- the juxtaposition of rags and riches).

Canin skillfully navigates multiple time lines, effortlessly leading the reader back and forth from Kleinman's childhood, to his long marriage to Ginger, often talking to her internally as he steers himself through those narrow cave passages when he was a GI, to his building a successful brewery in Pittsburg, and finally his declining years as he tries to make sense of his relationship to his middle child, Jimmy. During a visit with Jimmy and his wife and grandchild, he makes plans to go to Japan to find closure, for himself and for the family of the Japanese soldier. In the process, he is reconciling himself to his own mortality (*And the end is getting nearer. I know that. Don't think I can't feel it. But I don't give up. That's just Augie Kleinman. I always thought I had a secret that when the end came I would be ready for it -- that the grave would be a relief. But it turns out it's not that way.*)

As with all fine pieces of literature, the characters are real, and their conflicts familiar. It is the way of life and Canin captures it poignantly. *Carry Me Across The Water* is another example of a carefully executed piece of literature, a novella in length but packing meaning and emotion at every turn of the page.

I landed on *Carry Me* after more hilarity from the pen of Jonathan Tropper, enjoying his *How to Talk to a Widower*, cut out of the same mold of the others I've read by him, *Everything Changes*, *This is Where I Leave You*, and *The Book of Joe*. How many times can an author pretty much cover the same ground, the searching-thirty-something male adrift in a sea of Jewish family foibles and suburban females, married and unmarried and divorced or soon to be divorced, sexual predators at times. Here our protagonist is now Doug Parker who becomes a local newspaper celebrity writing a column about his status as a widower and his twin sister Claire's designs for him to snap out of his long-standing grief. Meanwhile he has to negotiate his younger sister's impending marriage, his father's erratic behavior from his stroke, a child from his deceased wife's first marriage, and his mother's matchmaking, not to mention the women who stalk him and, finally, the woman with whom he finally falls in love again.

In spite of Tropper covering well worn territory, he never seems to let it go stale and his humor never fails: *My parents may behave like they were abandoned in Greenwich and raised by WASPs, but when it comes to preparing meals, we are once again the chosen people.* And another gem: *I would come and sit on the lawn beside her grave and make halting attempts at one-sided conversation, but I just couldn't make myself believe there was anyone listening, and even if I could, talking to the grave never made any sense to me. If there's an afterlife, and they can hear you, shouldn't they be able to hear you from anywhere? What's the theory here, that talking to the dead requires range, like a cell phone, and if you go too far the call gets dropped?*

Besides the humor, there is Tropper the astute observer of human nature and of the suburban scene: *...moving out to New Radford [the suburban setting someplace in Westchester] had meant becoming friendly with a different sort of man than my younger, drunker, wilder single friends back in Manhattan.....[They] were all husbands and fathers either on the cusp or already descending into the tide pool of middle age. These men were all adrift in an alien landscape of mortgages and second mortgages, marriages and second marriages, children, child support, affairs, alimony,* *tuition, tutors, and an endless barrage of social functions. And all of their living had to be squeezed into those few hours on the weekends when they weren't working their asses off to pay for the whole mess. I'd always assumed that the people who lived in those fancy houses in the suburbs were financially better off then I was, and only once I'd joined them did I come to understand that it's all just a much more sophisticated and elaborate way of being broke.*

Furthermore, Tropper always finds a way to tug at your heart, and although he treads familiar ground, I say, bring it on.

Thursday, November 10, 2011 **Brooklyn**

I've written about my old "home town" before. I lived in downtown Brooklyn and in Park Slope for almost eight years before moving to Manhattan and finally Connecticut. But Brooklyn was a special place for me, where I went to college, met my first wife, and had a son.

So it was no wonder I picked up the novel *Brooklyn* by the Irish novelist, Colm Tóibín. It is a coming of age novel about a young Irish woman, Eilis Lacey, who immigrates to the US soon after WW II, settling in Brooklyn -- in fact near Fulton Street where I lived. There are similarities to the work of Henry James, contrasting the old world to the new, and written by a man about a female protagonist -- a remarkable novel well worth reading. One cannot help but contrast Brooklyn to James' *Portrait of a Lady*. Eilis having to make choices of suitors as did Isabel Archer.

Eilis finds work in a department store on Fulton Street called Bartocci's, but it might as well have been the old Abraham & Straus also on Fulton Street. What Eilis is told by the bosses' daughter the first day of work embodies the essence of the American immigrant experience: *"Brooklyn changes every day...New people arrive and they could be Jewish or Irish or Polish or even coloured. Our old customers are moving out to Long Island and we can't follow them, so we need new customers every week. We treat everyone the same. We welcome every single person who comes into this store. They all have money to spend...You give them a big Irish smile."*

Eilis is the reluctant immigrant at first, being sent to America by her mother and sister so she could have a better life and employment which was then so difficult to find in Ireland. She knows no one there except a Priest who sponsors her. Eilis finally embraces the experience (falling, she thinks, in love with an Italian boy, never being quite sure) before she finds that she has to return to her home for a few weeks (don't want a spoiler in this brief synopsis so will leave it at that). Her old home in Ireland now seems foreign to her but over the weeks she begins to feel that she cannot leave (thinking she is now in love with someone else). It is now Brooklyn that is feeling foreign although she has put down deep emotional roots there.

The resolution is somewhat surprising but Eilis is constantly reinventing herself for whatever situation. One can imagine what it must have been like for an immigrant, especially a young woman, to make her way in a strange land after WW II. It can stand with Gish Jen's novel about the Chinese immigrant, *Typical American.*

Tóibín skillfully takes the reader on Eilis' journey, a truly unforgettable portrait and lovingly rendered by the author.

Saturday, December 31, 2011 **King Time**

What better way of ringing in the New Year than writing about the past? In my case, there is much more of that than the future. Sounds like a downer, but it's one of those facts we all have to own up to. Nothing like a good book to get one thinking about such things.

So, it was about time that I read Stephen King's new book about time, *11/22/63.*

First, a full disclosure. I am one of the few people on the face of the earth who had never read a Stephen King anything. Maybe it is my abhorrence of the horror genre. So why turn to King, later in his career and late in my life?

It took one of our habitual long summer Florida/Connecticut commutes to change my mind. We usually pick up a few books on tape (well, now, on CD), swapping our used ones for "new" used ones at a local used-book. On a whim, as I am interested in the art of writing, I picked up Stephen King's *On Writing.* It was good, in fact spellbinding, King being able to weave memoir with mentoring -- a no nonsense guide to being a good writer (simply put, hard work). I thought it fascinating, maybe because I was a captive audience driving along I95 for hours and hours, but thinking, hey, if I had instead invested those mega hours of my publishing career into King's prescription for becoming a published writer....what if? It got me thinking about the past. But I've always lived with nostalgia on my brain.

A slight detour in King's usual genre finally brought me to his fiction. I liked science fiction as a kid. In high school, before my senior year when I discovered Thomas Hardy, I had thought, as a nascent reader, that the epitome of fiction was H. G. Well's *Time Machine.* So, after hearing King's *On Writing,* I thought I'd like to read something of his if only he would depart his horror / suspense thing. And as if my wishes were granted by a paranormal power, along came King's *11/22/63,* more historical and science fiction than anything else.

I ordered it so Ann could give it to me for Christmas, but it arrived on the 48th anniversary of *11/22/63,* soon after I had just posted a brief piece recounting my dark memory of Kennedy's assassination.

One of King's themes is that the past is harmonic -- that there are events that seem to reflect one another, or rhyme, in one's own life when juxtaposed to others. I guess I took the arrival of the book on that very day as a providential sign, an harmonic event, it was meant to be that I should start it immediately, even though I was in the middle of another book.

I will not dwell on plot here other than to say what any reader of the legion of book reviews already knows -- that the main character goes back in time with the intention of preventing Lee Harvey Oswald from assassinating President Kennedy and thus (he thinks) change history for the better. And I am not going to go into detail concerning the conceit he uses to rationalize the mechanics of Jake / George travelling back and forth from the present to sometime in 1958. Let's just call it a time portal.

King's writing is all about his characters and in *11/22/63* the tale is told as a first person account by our stalwart hero, Jake Epping (as he is named in the "Land of Ahead") AKA George Amberson (in the "Land of Ago"). It is as if Jake/George pulled up a chair and tapped the reader on the shoulder and said "I have a fascinating -- no unbelievable -- story to tell you, but it's true, so listen to every word" and you, the reader, feel thoroughly compelled to do so. King's tale is a page turner, moving along with an alacrity that makes the 900 or so pages fly by.

And while much of the book is almost conversational, there are those moments when King shows his mastery of suspense and horror, such as when George first returns to the past and decides, as an experiment which will ultimately lead to his main purpose of changing history, to prevent a murder that he knows is going to happen in the late 1950's. For me the most engaging invention of the novel was the invitation to live in the past once again. The scenes King paints are familiar ones, a land without cell phones, computers, color TVs (or any TVs at all in my case, remembering our first TV, a Dumont the size of Asia with a tiny screen, that arrived sometime in the late 40s in our household), seat belts, and when lyrics like "wop-bop-a-loo-mop alop-bam-boom" and "itsy, bitsy, teenie, weenie, yellow polka-dot bikini" wafted the radio airwaves. Or to put it another way, gas that was 20 cents a gallon, and a pack of cigarettes costing about the same.

When George first goes to 1958, he has to board a bus: *I let the working Joes go ahead of me, so I could watch how much money they put in the pole-mounted coin receptacle next to the driver's seat. I felt like an alien in a science fiction movie, one who's trying to masquerade as an earthling. It was stupid -- I wanted to ride the city bus, not blow up the White House with a death-ray -- but that didn't change the feeling.* While King's supernatural / horror themes may be more latent in this book, they are nonetheless subliminally there, reminding us that we're all in this ship of time together and none will get out alive. There is a foreboding feeling to *11/22/63*, all those moments of the past, all the choices that lead to the present, with the future becoming a smaller and smaller percentage of all of our lives.

King deals with several elements of what he thinks time travel might have involved, all interesting and plausible. Among these is his theory that time's "resistance to change is proportional to how much the future might be altered by any given act," something he mentions earlier in the novel and sort of foreshadows what eliminating Oswald might mean.

He also deals with the "butterfly effect." As his fellow time traveler, Al, puts it, *It means small events can have large, whatchamdingit, ramifications. The idea is that if some guy kills a butterfly in China, maybe forty years later -- or four hundred -- there's an earthquake in Peru.* (More foreshadowing.)

And the butterfly effect is the reason why, as George stalks Oswald, he decides to do nothing to even cross his path before it is time to act (that is, if he does act -- no spoiler here): *If there's a stupider metaphor than "a chain of events" in the English language, I don't know what it is. Chains... are strong. We use them to pull engine blocks out of trucks and to bind the arms and legs of dangerous prisoners. That was no longer reality as I understood it. Events are flimsy, I tell you, they are houses of cards, and by approaching Oswald -- let alone trying to warn him off a crime which he had not even conceived -- I would be giving away my only advantage. The butterfly would spread its wings, and Oswald's course would change. Little changes at first, maybe, but as the Bruce Springsteen song tells us, from small things, baby, big things one day come. They might be good changes, ones that would save the man who was now the junior senator from Massachusetts. But I didn't believe that. Because the past is obdurate.*

At his most eloquent, King philosophizes about the "harmonics" of time watching as Jake/George - teachers both past and present - observe two students, Mike and Bobbi, dance the Lindy as had George and Sadie (the gal he falls in love with in the past): *The night's harmonic came during the encore...It's all of a piece, I thought. It's an echo so close to perfect you can't tell which one is the living voice and which is the ghost-voice returning. For a moment everything was clear, and when that happens you see that the world is barely there at all. Don't we all secretly know this? It's a perfectly balanced mechanism of shouts and echoes pretending to be wheels and cogs, a dreamclock chiming beneath a mystery-glass we call life. Behind it? Below it and around it? Chaos, storms. Men with hammers, men with knives, men with guns. Women who twist what they cannot dominate and belittle what they cannot understand. A universe of horror and loss surrounding a single lighted stage where mortals dance in defiance of the dark.*

It is also a well researched historical novel, with King mostly playing down the conspiracy theories while nonetheless providing for the remote possibility. He makes his historical characters real -- this is a Lee Harvey

Oswald you get to know as a flesh and blood person (not someone most would want to know, but a real person). One especially feels sympathy for his wife, Marina, an abused woman in a strange land. In fact George draws a parallel (harmonics again) to his love, Sadie, thinking about taking Sadie to the future with him: *I could see her lost in 2011, eyeing every low-riding pair of pants and computer screen with awe and unease. I would never beat her or shout at her -- no not Sadie -- but she might still become my Marina Prusakova, living in a strange place and exiled from her homeland forever.*

And it was satisfying to hold the book itself, an impressive tome with a fabulous jacket, one side depicting the past as we know it and the other the past that might have been. In *On Writing*, King insists that writers must be readers. *11/22/63* is a book to be read.

Thursday, February 9, 2012 *Cruising and Reading*

Put me on a boat (a ship in this case) and give me a book and I am a happy man. And that about describes last week's cruise to many places we've been before, the ship being a destination onto itself So many of the days at sea, and even some of those in port, were spent in the solarium where I could dig into a good book. Before leaving, I went to the stack of books I sequester for future reading. Or, to use a baseball analogy, I went to the bench and called up three, the first being Jane Leavy's *The Last Boy; Mickey Mantle and the End of America's Childhood,* a work of great passion and meticulous scholarship.

How do you write an objective biography of a legend, one who you've worshiped as a kid? That was Leavy's challenge. But by telling the truth, Mantle with all his foibles, and there were many, she actually enhanced the legend.

Mantle's career in some ways is a real life version of Bernard Malamud's *The Natural*, published in 1952 only a year after Mantle's rookie season. Roy Hobbs is shot by a strange woman, while Mantle has his knee blown out by a drainage ditch in Yankee Stadium chasing a fly ball and trying to avoid running into the Yankee patrician, Joe DiMaggio, playing out his last year. Mantle and DiMaggio were never friends. Unlike Hobbs, Mantle did not have a "Wonderboy" bat, but his "Wonderboy" was a surfeit of guts. He played hurt when today's ballplayers would be seeking R&R. He played with a family history of illness and early death, and battled osteomyelitis throughout his career.

The book is as much a love affair as it is a scholarly biography, successful on both counts. And for me, it conjured up my own childhood, my own worship of Mantle, and my own indebtedness to baseball. Those names brought back memories of those glory days when the Yankees, the Giants, and the

Dodgers all played in NY and we argued about who was the greatest center-fielder, Mantle, Mays, or Snider. I think Leavy answers that question (read the book to find out!).

Leavy's work is more biography than a recounting of the great baseball moments of the Mick's life, although it is that too. Mantle came from a dysfunctional family, the father controlling his life (before and after his father's early death). What "Mutt," the Mick's father thought or would think became pivotal to Mantle and one of the factors of Mantle's alcoholism. And Mick was a real "good ole' boy" a carouser who felt most comfortable with the guys in the locker room and not with his family. Even after hanging them up, he spent more time on the road, frequently with other women leaving his wife at home. He paid. His family paid. But one thing about Mantle in addition to his baseball ability, he was loyal to his friends, fiercely loyal, and generous as well. Overall, you have to admire him, and hats off to Jane Leavy for a brilliant biography, walking the line between adulation and scholarly criticism. And Leavy went one step farther in analyzing her subject, by bringing in experts on the mechanics and the physics of the sport.

As a poor hitter in my brief baseball career (the reason I pitched), I always wondered how in the world anyone could hit a fast ball being thrown only sixty feet away, and downhill from a mound as well. And how could anyone hit it like Mantle. To answer that question, Leavy interviews experts, concluding that Mantle hit "with felonious intent:"

In an effort to pin down how Mantle generated such power, I asked Preston Peavy, a techno-savvy hitting coach, to analyze Mantle's form, using the visual motion-analysis system he created for his students at Peavy Baseball in Atlanta. He converted film and video clips of Mantle into a set of kinematics, moving digital stick figures that show the path of each part of the body as it moves through space... A 90-mile-per-hour fastball doesn't leave much time for thought. Traveling at a rate of 132 feet per second, it makes the sixty-foot, six-inch journey from pitcher to batter in four-tenths of a second. The ball is a quarter of the way to home plate by the time a hitter becomes fully aware of it. Because there is a 100-millisecond delay between the time the image of the ball hits the batter's retina and when he becomes conscious of it, it is physiologically impossible to track the ball from the pitcher's hand to the catcher's glove... that's where implicit memory comes in. The ability to infer the type of pitch and where it's headed with accuracy and speed is inextricably linked with stored experience-the hitter has seen that pitch before, even if he can't see it all the way. Add the reflexes to respond to that memory and a visual motor system that allows the batter to react on the fly to a change in the trajectory of a flying object, the right DNA, and Mutt and Grandpa Charlie out by the shed throwing tennis balls, and you have Mickey Mantle.

This deceptively simple act is an intricate biomechanical task requiring the coordinated mobilization of virtually every muscle in the body in less than a second. "Everything but the chewing muscles," said Dr. Benjamin Shaffer, a specialist in orthopedic sports medicine and head physician for the Washington Capitals. "Unless you grit your teeth."

Nobody gritted more than Mantle. Lefty or righty, he swung with felonious intent.

I just could not get enough of *The Last Boy*, and even read the Acknowledgements, Appendices, and Bibliography in detail. I did not want it to end, but it did, as did the last boy's life, riddled by cancer, and not long after he had successfully ridded himself of alcoholism. Moose Skowron, Hank Bauer, Whitey Ford, Johnny Blanchard, and Bobby Richardson (who was then a minister) were with him near the end, but he was with his son, David, and his wife Merlyn at the very end, dying on Aug. 13, 1995.

Such a downer, so I turned to a novel, *How To Be Good* by Nick Hornby, an English writer. I had picked this up because Jonathan Tropper is touted as "the American Hornby" and as I admire Tropper, I had to see/read for myself.

And I can see why there is the comparison: like some of Tropper's work it almost reads like a screenplay with a similar sardonic sense of humor. And like Tropper it is a fast read, a story of midlife crisis and its effect on the nuclear family. As the main character says: *We are the ideal nuclear family. We eat together, we play improving board games instead of watching television, we smile a lot. I fear that at any moment I may kill somebody.* Interestingly, it is written in the first person by the female protagonist. How Hornby can do that so effectively is a mark of a good writer, although at times I had the problem of thinking to myself, is this really how a man might think about how a woman thinks?

But it is the humor, or the truth in humor that is Hornby's strong point, such as his riff on organized religion, as expressed by our heroine, Katie, who in the midst of her crisis decides to go to a church, any church, with her daughter, Molly, although she has rarely gone to church and needs to pick one randomly. She describes her experience after arriving at a nearly empty service at a local Church of England ("C of A"):

It all feels a long way from God-no nearer than the bring-and-buy sale would be, and much farther away than I imagine Molly's friend Pauline is at this precise moment. It feels sad, exhausted, defeated; this may have been God's house once, you want to tell the handful of people here, but He's clearly moved, shut up shop, gone to a place where there's more of a demand for that sort of thing. And then you look around and wonder whether the sadness isn't part of the point: those who are able to drag themselves here once a week are clearly not social churchgoers, because there is nothing social happening here. This isn't a place to see and be seen, unless opera glasses are placed on the backs of the pews. You'd have to walk twenty yards to shake somebody's hand. No, these people are the hard-core, the last WASPs in Holloway, the beaten and the lonely and the bereaved, and if there is a place for them in the Kingdom of Heaven, they deserve it. I just hope that it's warmer there than here, and there is more hope, and youth, and there is no need for bring-and-buy sales, and the choir of angels isn't singing elsewhere that day, but you rather fear it might be; C of E heaven is in all probability a quarter-full of unhappy old ladies selling misshapen rock cakes and scratched Mantovani records.

Despair in humor. You get the point. As to the rest of the novel, a worthwhile read. I'll read another Hornby book again.

I finished my trifecta of books during our seven day cruise by going from the satiric to downright despair, the path of Philip Roth's most recent, novella length works, and in this instance his *The Humbling.* In a sense it completes the circle, the sunshine of youth as Mantle emerges from the playing fields of Oklahoma into the big leagues, the midlife struggles of the modern family in London, to the "loss of magic," decline at the end of life of Simon Axler, a famous stage actor who suddenly loses his acting abilities, a metaphor for life, and tries to resurrect a life with a woman twenty five years his junior, the daughter of one-time friends. As Axler's agent reasons with him, trying to convince him to see an acting coach:

"Look...everyone knows the feeling 'I can't do it,' everyone knows the feeling that they will be revealed to be false -- it's every actor's terror. 'They've found me out. I've been found out.' Let's face it, there's a panic that comes with age. I'm that much older than you, and I've been dealing with it for years. One, you get slower. In everything. Even in reading you get slower. If I go fast in reading now, too much goes away. My speech is slower, my memory is slower. All these things start to happen. In the process, you start to distrust yourself. You're not as quick as you used to be. And especially if you are an actor. You were a young actor and you memorized scripts one after the other after the other, and you never even thought about it. It was just easy to do. And then all of a sudden it's not as easy, and things don't happen so fast anymore....So you start to feel afraid, to feel soft, to feel that you don't have that raw live power anymore. It scares you. With the result...that you're not free anymore. There's nothing happening -- and that's terrifying."

So it is with aging and obviously a mordant fixation of Roth in his later works, something I understand. And I guess that is why I still appreciate Roth. I've "grown up" with him as I did with Updike. Roth fights desperately against the gravity of it all, Axler seeking respite in the arms of a younger woman, Pegeen, but as Roth beautifully and concisely writes: *A man's way is laid with a multitude of traps, and Pegeen had been the last. He'd stepped hungrily into it and then the bait like the most craven captive on earth.* Roth remains one of the great living American writers.

Tuesday, April 10, 2012 *About a Bear*

Here is a satiric fable, an extended parable for our times, making hilarity of the foibles of human nature, a change of pace from my usual reading fare, *The Bear Went over the Mountain* by William Kotzwinkle.

Simple story. Bear (who adopts the name of "Hal Jam" the last name coming off a jar of jam of course) finds a manuscript (intended to be the Great American Novel") written by an English professor who is on sabbatical in the woods of Maine, makes his way into the big city (the bear that is), poses as a human (you have to throw any sense of reality to the wind) to the extent that he can, and becomes the toast of the publishing world. He happily indulges in honey and other sweets, meeting important people, women pursuing him as if he is the reincarnation of Hemingway. The real author, meanwhile, in a fit of depression realizing he has lost his great novel, also loses his professorship, stays in the woods and, in fact, becomes bear-like, sleeping away part of the winter. I will not give the ending away, but who do you think Kotzwinkle thinks made the better trade of lives?

Meanwhile throughout the novel, the stage is set for some very funny moments. But one thing I cannot get out of my head while I read this is Jerzy Kosinski's novel, *Being There*, where the simple minded "Chauncey Gardiner" (the gardener at the estate of a well known man) is mistaken by the press to be a wise philosopher in his simplicity. "Plant the seeds and the garden will grow" -- Of course, if we make our investments and some tough decisions, the economy will revive! (Sort of like now.)

Here are but a few examples from *The Bear Went Over the Mountain*: Ms. Boykins, a literary agent pursuing Hal, says *"The sales forces will insist on a tour..."Hal Jam puts his paws over his ears as the din from the restaurant is overwhelming his "animality." The racing stream of human speech glistened as it curved around obstacles and glided on, relentless in its gradient, while he panted in animal stupidity And then his nose twitched, the olfactory bulb at its root a thousand times more sensitive than that of a human. He straightened and moved his head around to isolate the natural scent he'd found within the synthetic veil of perfumes. There it was, moist, cool. 'Salmon.'*

Boykins says: *"Yes, they do it skewered with tomatoes, mushroom, and green peppers."* ·

"Raw," said the bear with resurgence of primal authority."

"Raw?"

"Raw female. Lots of eggs. In my teeth." The bear tapped at his incisors.

"My god," thought Boykins, "he **is** another Hemingway."

Or when Hal Jam goes shopping in a supermarket... *The skyscrapers of Manhattan had astounded him, and now the endless amounts of honey that man had available to him had humbled him to the ground. The intelligence, the inventiveness, the time and courage, it took to lay in this much honey was the final proof that man wore the crown of creation. 'Bears are just along for the ride,' he said to himself as he filled his cart with honey....*

Or his meeting with a Hollywood agent, Ms. Zou Zou Sharr at whom the bear looked *from under the peak of his baseball cap. It was the first time he'd been this close to a human female for any length of time, and he liked the experience. If she had some fur on her face and the backs of her hands she might be good looking.*

Zou Zou misunderstands just about every brief phrase the bear utters as being a demand for a larger take from movie rights, saying *"'Believe me, Hal, your piece of the pie is just what it should be and so is CMC's.'"* "When I eat a pie, I eat it all," says the Bear. *Zou Zou replies: "Of course you do, and I understand. The book is yours, it's your creation, and you want your fair share."* Eventually, Zou Zou offers herself to the bear to get the contract. They "do it," the bear tossing her around the room. She's enthralled by being ravished -- he's an animal! Yes, another Hemingway! And they do it in a taxi -- *He'd passed a great human milestone. He'd done it more than once a year.*

Eventually, the bear meets the Vice President and the President, again, another hat tip to Kosinski's novel.

As a former publisher, I laughed at almost every page. Indeed, these are the trade publishing people I saw flitting around in Frankfurt every year absorbed by their self importance.

In many ways the book is also reminiscent of *Firmin* which is about a rat who lives in a bookstore. And a rat figures near the conclusion of this book as well. That Kotzwinkle can keep up the conceit of Hal Jam being part of the American literary, political, and New York scene for the entire length of the novel is a testimony to his satiric artistry. Lots of fun reading this one.

Thursday, June 21, 2012 *"Even if the Dream Isn't Real, the Dreamers Are"*

20th century American literature is awash in a particular version of the American Dream, the green light that always seems to be in grasp through the accumulation of wealth. But as Balzac purportedly opined, "behind every great fortune there is a great crime", be it to society or one's family or both. It plays out in our literature and one only has to read a newspaper to see it in life. Gatsby or Madoff, living the dream, for love or money or both, at least for a while.

In the last thirty years we have had two real estate busts, people pinning their hopes of wealth by buying and selling, flipping,the greater fool theory at work in its purist form, like a game of musical chairs, until the music stopped. And so it is for the protagonist in Eric Puchner's first novel, *Model Home,* as well as it was for the author's father. While the novel is in some ways autobiographical, in subtle or more transparent ways, so are most novels.

Here is a serious contemporary writer who knows how to tell a tale, paint a picture of American life through his characters, make us feel moved, walking the line through the comic-tragic, drawing us into something important about family relationships. It remains to be seen whether his first novel will be his best, a literary catharsis of his own life experiences, or whether this is setting him up for a truly great literary career.

The story itself, although set in the 1980s, is as relevant for today's economic times. It is about a family, the Zillers, who have moved to California for the "good life" -- a family which was close when they lived with more modest expectations in the Midwest -- but now find themselves being pulled apart. The father, Warren Ziller, hides his deteriorating economic circumstances from his family, which makes his wife, Camille, suspect him of having an affair. No such luck -- that would have been an easier road to travel.

In an ironic twist, the real estate development that Warren had been hawking, in the middle of the desert, but portrayed by him as an upcoming idyllic community (with the promise of a major shopping center which is actually being constructed as a waste treatment plant that stinks up the neighborhood literally, and their lives figuratively), ultimately becomes their own home, the only such residents, when Warren's secret comes out and his older son, Dustin, suffers disfigurement from the explosion and fire of their former home before it was repossessed. Meanwhile, his younger sister, Lyle, has had an affair with the security guard from their former community, Hector, who later becomes Dustin's caretaker (for reasons best explained by reading the novel). The younger child, Jonas, is neglected by his family, left to wander the desert outskirts.

This is a family that has been incinerated by the American Dream, and after a metaphorical climax, they are hurled in different directions. Puchner draws heavily on his own family history to portray the heartbreak of this devolution. Some of the author's feelings about his own childhood are endowed in Jonas.

Most great writers have a strong sense of place. Cheever had his NYC suburbs, Updike had New England and PA, Roth harkens back to Newark and its environs, Richard Ford's New Jersey, and Anne Tyler and Baltimore are peas in a pod. Puchner has staked out California to explain his version of the American dream. Ah, California, when as a publisher, I used to visit the American Film Institute and the Academy of Motion Picture Arts and Sciences, monuments to the documentation of the American dream itself. I felt LA, or at least that part of it, was unreal.

Puchner's particular focus is not California's glamorous Hollywood, it is the underbelly of the American dream as played out in the California desert. Like Theodore Dreiser's lobster and squid in mortal combat, in a scene from his *The Financier,* Dreiser writing: *It answered in a rough way that riddle which had been annoying him so much in the past: How is life organized? Things lived on each other – that was it...Sure, men lived on men.*

I couldn't help but think of that quote reading Puchner's description of Jonas' sojourns in the California desert: *Most days he spent roaming the desert. It was a relief to be free of school, that gloomy place where the teachers wore shorts and his locker was so hot he had to open it with a sock over his hand, where no one spoke to him except the garbled voice in his head and he'd somehow completed his transformation into a ghost. In the desert, at least, there were extraordinary things. There were scorpions eating each other. There were rats hopping around like kangaroos. There were wasps dragging tarantulas around by the leg. There were snake skins dried into paper, bird nests as small as contact lenses, lizard skeletons dangling from creosote bushes, delicate as ice. Once, not far from the house, he saw a roadrunner go after a rattlesnake, its right wing extended like a matador's cape, When the snake lunged, the roadrunner snapped up its tail and then cracked it like a whip, slamming its head against the ground - over and over - to bash its skull.*

And when one pursues dreams of riches, or in its more sanitized version, the better life, there are winners and losers. Even the material winners may find their dreams to be vapid. Warren's fall from grace is even harder, a once happy family, now grappling with his mismanagement and unfortunate economic circumstances. Like Madoff, Warren's life became one of lies and self deceit, convincing himself that even though they were rapidly running out of funds, the big payoff will come when he makes a success of his land development scheme (Auburn Fields, an ironic name for a place in the middle of the desert), all will be well: *He did not want to lie to her, but every time he considered telling her the truth-that he'd lost their retirement funds, the kids' college funds, and every fund in between-his tongue dried up like paper and he couldn't speak. When he managed to get Auburn Fields off the ground, he reminded himself, he'd be able to put the money back in.*

And dreams are not only Warren's. His wife, Camille, pursues appro-bation from her family and colleagues as a producer of educational films, without much success. Ultimately she has to leave him: *She could forgive him for moving them out to California, perhaps, for bankrupting them in pursuit of some fantasy of wealth, for falling victim to a malady of shame he could never pay off -- she could forgive Warren these things, but this was different from getting over them. In the end it was her disappoint-ment in him that had proved toxic.*

Dustin, the older son, sees a fabulous career for himself as a rock musi-cian but becomes a withdrawn malcontent after being disfigured in the explosion. Jonas who is mistakenly blamed (by himself as well) for Dustin's accident becomes the invisible child. Lyle, the daughter, has dreams of attending Columbia, but is convinced that hope is remote.

Each family member feels like he/she is on the outside, looking in, dazed by the events that profoundly change their individual lives and drive them apart. Puchner writes from Camille's perspective: *What had happened? How had they unraveled again, worse than before? The mystery of life was not how it started, Camille thought. "It was how people with every excuse to be close could grow distant as satellites."* Then, there is Warren's take on it: *"What an odd thing a family was,"* Warren thought. *"The permutations, like the patterns of a chess game, seemed endless."*

In fact, the forty-nine chapters of the novel constantly switch back and forth between the main characters, almost like a series of tightly woven short stories with the commonality of the Ziller family experience.

Thursday, July 19, 2012 **Richard Ford's CANADA -- a Classic**

Parents. You trust them and see the world through their eyes. They make plans and you follow, their logic not being completely clear, but you go along. Life metes out some choices but the accident of our parents meeting, marry-ing, and having children hurls us unrelentingly onto a path not of our choos-ing or, in most instances, not even theirs. Then in turn we make our own choices and in retrospect that is our life. These inexplicable choices, a form of accidental determinism, are what Richard Ford deals with in *Canada*, destined to become a classic American novel.

This is a coming of age novel, narrated by the fifteen year old protag-onist, Dell Parsons, but it is written by him some fifty years later. Thus, the voice in the novel is that of a somewhat naïve boy, but written with the knowledge of a mature man, one who we learn towards the end is the teacher of literature in high school. (How Ford walks this fine line is evidence of his writing skills.)

In fact, among the novels he teaches is *The Great Gatsby* and *The Mayor of Casterbridge* "that to me seem secretly about my young life." And, indeed,

Canada echoes some of our narrator's favorites, with a Gatsby like character one of the novel's centerpieces and Hardy's sense of place and dark fatalistic themes playing out in *Canada* as well.

Ford has long been one of my favorite authors, ever since reading *Sportswriter* and more recently *Lay of the Land*, both part of the Frank Bascombe trilogy, which also included *Independence Day*. *Canada* elevates his work further.

He gets right to the point in the few sentences of the first paragraph and if this isn't a sufficient "hook" to reel in the reader, then this book isn't for you: *First, I'll tell about the robbery our parents committed. Then about the murders, which happened later. The robbery is the more important part, since it served to set my and my sister's lives on the courses they eventually followed. Nothing would make complete sense without that being told first.*

This novel deals with themes about life, choices, and chance, and it is fittingly staged on the sprawling small towns and prairies of Montana and the Province of Saskatchewan in the late 1950's. There is a sense of isolation and solemnity of an Edward Hopper painting, a heaviness Dell Parsons has to deal with and in his innocence he goes forward, somehow ending up with a life more of his choosing than his less fortunate fraternal twin sister, Berner.

Poor Berner. Never even likes her name, but that was the one given to her by their father, ironically "Bev" Parsons. He is from Alabama, a fast talker, engaging, and able to turn on the southern charm. He wanted to be a pilot in the war but was a bombardier, dropping bombs on unknown victims. Dell thinks that it was his father's charm that attracted his mother to him and she had *unluckily gotten pregnant from their one hasty encounter after meeting at a party honoring returning airmen.* Their mother is Jewish, which complicates where they can live (the south is out of the question). Her name is Neeva Kamper, and she is as different from Bev as she could be: *His optimism, her alienated skepticism. His southernness, her immigrant Jewishness. His lack of education, her preoccupation with it and sense of unfulfillment. When they realized it... they each began to experience a tension and a foreboding peculiar to each of them and not shared by the other.*

After the Air Force Bev sells new and, then, used cars, while Neeva teachers 5th grade school, they having finally settled down in Great Falls, Montana (where people didn't even know what a Jew was). But Bev is a schemer and wants more and finds ways to make money selling stolen beef he acquires from local Indians, but this leads to a debt and he needs much more money, fast, the Indians threatening him and his family. He had always fantasized about robbing a bank, thinking his fast talking ability would enable him to do so smoothly, without much risk, and as long as he robbed less than

$10K, the government would pay the price and depositors wouldn't, and he wouldn't hurt anyone, so why not? His son could drive the getaway car. he thought. Neeva steps in to protect Dell and the inexorable fulcrum of the novel is set in motion.

Neeva has plans to use some of the money to go to her parents in Seattle with her children, leaving Bev. But she also has a contingency plan for the kids if they are caught – a friend has a brother, a very bright man, one who had once attended Harvard, but now lived in Saskatchewan where he owns a hotel, and this friend, Mildred, agrees to drive Berner and Dell there so they would not wind up in an orphanage. The parents are apprehended, but Berner flees to join a boyfriend, and Dell is left alone to accompany Mildred. Where they were going is unknown to him until they practically cross the Canadian border.

During the drive, Mildred offers advice to Dell: *"Don't spend time thinking old gloomy....Your life's going be a lot of exciting ways before you're dead. So just pay attention to the present. Don't rule parts out, and be sure you've always got something you don't mind losing. That's important... Does that make sense to you?" She reached across the seat and knocked her soft fist against my knee the way you'd knock on a door. "Does it? Knock, knock?" "I guess it does," I said. Though it didn't really seem to matter what I agreed with. That was the final time Mildred and I talked about my future.*

He is the perpetual optimist, and learns to adjust. One of his interests is chess, always carrying chess magazines and his chess pieces, hoping to find a game, but ending up playing against himself. His philosophy is expressed as the novel ends its "American segment," Dell thinking, *It's odd, though, what makes you think about the truth. It's so rarely involved in the events of your life. I quit thinking about the truth for a time then. Its finer points seemed impossible to find among the facts. If there was a hidden design, living almost never shed light on it. Much easier to think about chess – the true character of the men always staying the way they were intended, a higher power moving everything around. I wondered, for just that moment, if we – Berner and I – were like that: small, fixed figures being ordered around by forces greater than ourselves. I decided we weren't. Whether we liked it or even knew it, we were accountable only to ourselves now, not to some greater design. If our characters were truly fixed, they would have to be revealed later.*

While Hardy's characters always seem to come to crossroads, ones that inevitably lead to their downfall, most of the main characters in *Canada* seem to suffer the same negative fate, Dell's trusting, and childlike-innocence ironically enables him to escape similar misfortune.

His greatest challenge is dealing with the Gatsby-like character, the person to whom he has been abandoned, Mildred's brother, the mysterious

Arthur Remlinger. (*He wasn't consistent, the way I was used to people being.*) Dell had fantasized that he would befriend Remlinger, perhaps play chess with him, learn from him, but he rarely sees him and is assigned to a strange young scoundrel named Charley Quarters (a character straight out of Dickens) who works for Remlinger and serves as a guide to "Sports," men who visit the Remlinger's hotel to hunt geese. Charley sets up decoys and cleans the dead geese and this is the trade Dell learns for his keep. We find out that Remlinger has something on Charlie, something he could reveal, but Charlie has even more on Remlinger, a dark secret that becomes the denouement of the novel and one in which Remlinger involves Dell. To Charley's credit, he reveals that secret to Dell (one that Dell at first finds a way of doubting given his innocence) and warns Dell that he is merely a pawn to Remlinger,

As this terrible secret begins to be played out, Dell is at first caught off guard, thinking *I'd had plenty of time since the day before to route everything through my mind, and observe the things I needed to know, and be satisfied with not knowing all that was true, and to feel that probably not the worst was, and that in all likelihood nothing bad was going to happen....And in spite of believing what my father said about the importance of physical events, I'd come to think that what mattered more (this was my child's protected belief) was how you felt about things; what you assumed; what you thought and feared and remembered. That was what life mostly was to me – events that went on in my brain.* Until Remlinger reveals his true character.

But Dell befriends Remlinger's paramour Flo, who is an artist (whose style, fittingly, is Hopper's "Nighthawk" school of painting). *Her arrangement with Arthur Remlinger suited her because he had money and good manners and was handsome, in spite of being private and an American and younger than she was.* Flo arranges for Dell's ultimate escape to Winnipeg where her son and daughter-in-law live and they would put Dell in high school there. *She said I should consider becoming a Canadian.... This would fix everything. Canada was better than America, she said, and everyone knows that – except Americans. Canada had everything America ever had, but no one was mad about it. You could be normal in Canada, and Canada would love to have me.*

Ford's writing is sparse and compelling and the novel unfolds like a force of nature. He is finally reunited with his twin sister, but life has dealt her a harsher hand, she being more the pawn than a power piece in her own life. *Canada* is a haunting work of fine writing; my only regret is that its 400 some pages flew by so quickly.

Friday, August 3, 2012 **Summer Reading (Continued)**

It took a younger generation to introduce me to some fresh, intelligent and extremely moving literature, not only Eric Puchner's *Model Home* which I thought was a fabulous first novel, and now my son's second recommendation, another first novel, *The Miracle Life of Edgar Mint* by Brady Udall which was published in 2001 (Puchner's novel is more recent, 2010).

These are extraordinary first novels, major literary talent. Udall has published his follow up, widely praised as well, *The Lonely Polygamist* which I have yet to read. Interestingly, both the Puchner and Udall novels are set in the west and southwest, perhaps the new home of the American dream or the American nightmare. However, the two novels differ greatly in their perspectives and voice, Puchner reminding me somewhat of Updike, Cheever, and Yates, while Udall's *The Miracle Life of Edgar Mint* is a little *Huck Finn, Oliver Twist, Rule of the Bone and The Book of Mormon* – oh, and throw in the Paul Newman film, *Hombre,* about a half breed Apache.

Udall writes a genuine *Bildungsroman,* our lovable but struggling protagonist Edgar Mint living out an upside down life *(In many ways, it occurs to me now, I have lived my life in reverse. In the first half of my life I had to make all the hard choices and ride out the consequences, while in the second half I have lived the sheltered and uncluttered life of a child.)* He is an orphan but like Oliver Twist has to go through a horrific childhood before emerging into the sunshine of a loving caretaker.

Along the way we meet his friends and his Fagins, the story gathering force and momentum as it unfolds, beginning with his self-assessment: *If my life could be contained in a word it would be this one: "accident."* From there it is one finely written calamity to the next culminating in a complete circle, Edgar achieving peace and a kind of maturity that only hardship can teach.

He is a half breed, part white (a "cowboy" father from Connecticut of all places!) and an Apache mother who becomes an alcoholic and deserts Edgar, who ends up in an orphanage from hell, not unlike those in Dickens' novels. *(For the seven years my mother and I were together, I was nothing but an inconvenience to her, a burden, a source of pain, and her pregnancy with me was no exception.)*

Its first paragraph is spellbinding: *If I could tell you only one thing about my life it would be this: when I was seven years old the mailman ran over my head. As formative events go, nothing else comes close; my careening, zigzag existence, my wounded brain and faith in God, my collisions with joy and affliction, all of it has come, in one way or another, out of that moment on a summer morning when the left rear tire of a United States postal jeep ground my tiny head into the hot gravel of the San Carlos Apache Indian Reservation.*

He actually dies but a young doctor, Barry Pinkley (even the names give homage to Dickens) brings him back to life and Pinkley becomes obsessed with Edgar's well being afterwards *(Everyone agreed that my survival was either an absolute miracle or a freak happenstance...but there was also general agreement that simple survival was as far as the miracle would go: there was no chance on earth I was going to be anything but a mental and physical equivalent of a turnip.)* But Edgar befriends an older man in the hospital, Art, and when Edgar is diagnosed with "Dysgraphia," the "inability to write," Art insists that they get Edgar a typewriter. Even though Edgar confesses: *I have to say it was not love at first sight,* when he was given a Hermes Jubilee 2000 typewriter. It becomes his salvation and he carries the albatross of his enormous output in a trunk wherever he moves: great comic fiction with lots of dark humor driving the story.

Out of the hospital he is sent to the William Tecumseh Sherman School (*My first day of school at Willie Sherman and I was about to realize that I was no longer Saint Edgar the miracle-boy, hospital sweetheart, beloved by all, but a walking target, a chicken among the foxes. Not only was I the new kid...[and] not only was I a crossbreed.*)

But our hero survives and he is finally placed with a foster family in Utah, a Mormon family, the Madsens, as dysfunctional as any other American family, but at least a warm bed for Edgar, who thinks that this is the answer to his salvation, even receiving Baptismal and endeavoring to learn the Mormon religion. That too is not the answer for him, but he thinks he has developed a calling in life and that is to find the mailman and to forgive him (Edgar knows that the mailman thinks he had killed him).

While Barry Pinkley and his foster mother Lara Madsen figure prominently near the novel's conclusion, it is ultimately from this "calling" that the novel culminates into one of the finest written last chapters that I've read in years, gripping in its emotional power and a testimony to Udall's writing gifts by constructing the perfect coda.

As I am merely about ten years late in discovering this novel, there are plenty of other sources for more information, but both Udall and Puchner are on my radar screen for fine writing in the future.

Before posting this I also finished *Motherless Brooklyn*, by Jonathan Lethem, another recommendation made by my son. I do not mean to diminish its importance by not covering this novel with its own entry, but mysteries are not my usual reading fare and I feel a little off base reviewing the book. But while a mystery, this novel is a brilliant piece of writing, with the very clever conceit of the main character, Lionel Essrog, having Tourette's syndrome which gives Lethem a platform for demonstrating his writing skills. I'm also partial to *Motherless Brooklyn* as it is set not far from where I lived for almost ten years and through Lethem I could almost feel the macadam of the setting, Court Street, Carroll Gardens and Cobble Hill.

It shares some of the themes of Udall's novel as well, a novel about an orphan, Dickensian characters, a coming of age story but in the form of a detective novel, our erstwhile hero endeavoring to find the murderer of his mentor, an underworld character, Frank Minna, who has rounded up Lionel and other orphans from the "St. Vincent Home for Boys" to serve his nefarious ends, not unlike, again, Oliver Twist's upbringing.

The "language" of Tourette's is like a coiled spring throughout Lethem's tour de force: *I'm tightly wound. I'm a loose cannon. Both – I'm tightly wound loose cannon a tight loose. My whole life exists in the space between those words, tight, loose, and there isn't any space there – they should be one word, tightloose. I'm an air bag in a dashboard, packed up layer upon layer in readiness for that moment when I get to explode, expand all over you, fill every available space. Unlike an airbag, though, I'm repacked the moment I've exploded, am tensed and ready again to explode – like some safety-film footage cut into a loop, all I do is compress and release, over and over, never saving or satisfying anyone, least myself. Yet the tape plays on pointlessly, obsessive air bag exploding again and again while life itself goes on elsewhere, outside the range of these antic expenditures.*

There is one surprise after another in these pages, a labyrinth that the reader is compelled to negotiate to a fitting ending. Simply put: I loved reading *Motherless Brooklyn*. One is always rooting for Lionel, his eccentricities giving him a special place in literature and, no doubt, the mystery genre.

Wednesday, August 22, 2012 **We're All Beginners**

Raymond Carver's short story "The Beginners" was later published as his best known classic, the Gordon Lish edited version, "What We Talk About When We Talk About Love." As Mel says in the story, *It seems to me we're just beginners at love.* Carver's point; we're all "beginners." Anne Tyler takes this concept and also applies it to loving and then losing (and everything else in between) in her new novel, *The Beginner's Goodbye*.

I read the book soon after I finished Anita Shreve's *Light on Snow*. Anne Tyler and Anita Shreve are two of my favorite contemporary American female writers. They are different in so many ways, and their writing is so clearly unique to each. I make the gender distinction only because there is a feminine touch to their writing, making observations about matters normally invisible to their male counterparts.

Tyler has a special place in my heart as our very own Jane Austen, recording the foibles of society in that part of Baltimore I think of as Tylerville, where quirky dysfunctional men are portrayed along with their strange wives, mothers, and friends. Although these people live in Baltimore, as does the author, it is a Baltimore of Tyler's creation, more like a little city you'd find along a Lionel train board.

The Beginner's Goodbye particularly appeals to me as it is about a publisher, Aaron Woolcott, the narrator and protagonist. He works for a vanity
publishing company that he and his sister, Nandina, inherited from their
father (Nandina is more the grounded sibling and thus more in charge). It
is a vanity publisher in the old tradition, not the on-demand world of today
(although Woolcott Publishing is a contemporary firm in the novel). But
they also publish little guidebooks, slices of life they call "The Beginner's"
series. Just fill in the rest of the title. Hence, The Beginner's Goodbye is fittingly about loss and reclamation.

Aaron, like many other Tyler leading men, is damaged goods. Last time
in Noah's Compass it was Liam Pennywell. In this case, Aaron is in his late
30's, has a paralyzed arm, a stutter, and walks with a cane. His mother and
his sister have basically taken care of him and one would think bachelor-
hood would be his future, until he meets Dorothy, a plain speaking, but not
very compassionate doctor, some eight years Aaron's senior. The two most
unlikely people (for marriage) are married soon after they meet. Here is
Tyler's description of their courtship as expressed by Aaron: It makes me
sad now to think back on the early days of our courtship. We didn't know
anything at all. Dorothy didn't even know it was a courtship, at the beginning, and I was kind of like an overgrown puppy, at least as I picture myself
from this distance. I was romping around her all eager and panting, dying
to impress her, while for some time she remained stolidly oblivious.

Unfortunately, Dorothy is the victim of a tragic (almost comical) accident, and Aaron is now a widower. Here Tyler resorts to the contrivance of
Dorothy "coming back," Aaron catching glimpses of her and having imaginary conversations....until he can learn to say "goodbye."

Tyler's description of Dorothy is consummately written, viewed by
a woman of a woman, although the narrative is Aaron's: She was short
and plump and serious-looking. She had a broad, olive-skinned face,
appealingly flat-planed, and calm black eyes that were noticeably level,
with that perfect symmetry that makes the viewer feel rested. Her hair,
which she cut herself in a heedless, blunt, square style, was deeply absolutely black, and all of a piece. (Her family had come from Mexico two
generations before.) And yet I don't think other people recognized how
attractive she was, because she hid it. Or, no, not even that; she was
too unaware of it to hide it. She wore owlish, round-lensed glasses that
mocked the shape of her face. Her clothes made her figure seem squat –
wide, straight trousers and man-tailored shirts, chunky crepe-soled shoes
of a type that waitresses favored in diners. Only I noticed the creases as
fine as silk threads that encircled her wrists and her neck. Only I knew her
dear, pudgy feet, with the nails like tiny seashells. (Maybe a description to
some degree of the author?)

As for the publishing concept, the "Beginners" books: *These were something on the order of the Dummies books, but without the cheerleader tone of voice – more dignified. And far more classily designed, with deckle-edged pages [just like the book I'm holding] and uniform hard-backed bindings wrapped in expensive, glossy covers. Also, we were more focused – sometimes absurdly so, if you asked me. (Witness The Beginner's Spice Cabinet.) Anything is manageable if it's divided into small enough increments, was the theory; even life's most complicated lessons.* Indeed, maybe even saying "goodbye."

Fate and chance figure heavily in Tyler's work as does humor. A tree falls on their house, and a TV crushes Dorothy's chest: *Sony Trinitrons are known for their unusual weight....If we had had a flat-screen TV, would Dorothy still be alive? Or if her patient hadn't canceled. Then she wouldn't even have been home yet when the tree fell. Or if she had stayed in the kitchen instead of heading for the sunporch.*

Tyler describes most of her characters to a tee by defining the opposite, a "normal" character in Aaron's publishing company, Charles. *Generally we deferred to Charles in matters of public taste. He was the only one of us who led what I thought as a normal life – married to the same woman since forever, with triplet teenage daughters. He liked to tell little domestic-comedy, Brady Bunch –style anecdotes about the daughters, and the rest of us would hang around looking like a bunch of anthropologists studying foreign customs.*

Aaron moves in with his sister after he loses Dorothy and his house is partially destroyed. In fact, he painstakingly avoids going back to the house although it is being renovated. The contractor visits him at his sister's. Meanwhile, Dorothy begins to make unexpected appearances to Aaron, even having conversations (in his mind). Everyone, in particular his secretary, Peggy, tries to cater to him, bringing him food, trying to comfort him. But Aaron avoids the attention. This comes to a boil one day. Tyler's dialogue shines through Peggy:

"It's not fair, Aaron. You expect too much of us. We're not mind-readers. We're all just doing our best here; we don't know; we're just trying to get through life as best we can, like everybody else!"

Getting through life is what Tyler's characters seem to be struggling to do and in the process, finding some happiness along the way. Even straight-laced Nandina finds it and finally Aaron does in a perhaps contrived happy ending, that comically coincides with a new vanity title the firm publishes, one that goes on to be one of their best sellers, *Why I Have Decided to Go On Living.*

I've made this observation before concerning some of my favorite writers as they age. Tyler is one year older than I am, and thinking some of the same thoughts. Aaron is trying to piece together a photo album that was destroyed in the accident, frustrated that the photos were not labeled, having difficulty identifying subjects and years the photos were taken. *This business of not labeling photos reminded me of those antique cemeteries where the names have worn off the gravestones and you can't tell who is buried there. You see a little gray tablet with a melted-looking lamb on top, and you know it must have been somebody's child who died, but now you can't even make out her name or the words her parents chose to say how much they missed her. It's just so many random dents in the stone, and the parents are long gone themselves, and everything's been forgotten.*

Losing a child. Indeed, the worst. And in the annals of time, "random dents in stone." But from the tragic-comic we move to deadly serious, written on an entirely different plane, although it is also in the first person, and as in other Anita Shreve novels, written in the present tense (narrated by a 30 year old as seen through the eyes of her 12 year old self). Losing a child (and then saving another one) is central to this novel, *Light on Snow*. Consider some of Shreve's opening sentences that set the stage, both for the story and her style of writing:

The stillness of the forest is always a surprise, as if an audience had quieted for a performance. Beneath the hush I can hear the rustle of dead leaves, the snap of a twig, a brook running under a skin of ice. I am twelve on the mid-December afternoon (though I am thirty now), and I don't know yet that puberty is just around the corner or that the relentless narcissism of a teenage girl will make walking in the woods with my father just about the last think I'll want to do on any given day after school. Taking a hike together is a habit my father and I have grown into. My father spends too many hours bent to his work, and I know he needs to get outside.

A branch snaps and scratches my cheek. The sun sets. We have maybe twenty minutes left of decent light.

My father has lost the weight of a once sedentary man. His jeans are threadbare in the thighs and tinged with the rusty fur of sawdust. At best he shaves only every other day. His parka is beige, stained with spots of oil and grease and pine pitch. He cuts his hair himself, and his blue eyes are always a surprise.

The father in the story is Robert Dillon, former successful architect, who two years before lost his wife and their baby in an automobile accident and out of great despondency quits his job and takes his then ten year old daughter, Nicky, and simply drives north, settling in a remote town in New Hampshire where he (and she) become virtual hermits, he taking up furniture making, Nicky more or less being left to herself to go to a school where she knows no one.

Until, in the woods and in the snow, they come across a new born baby that had been abandoned only minutes before and from there the action begins, ultimately leading to their getting involved with the police, the town, and finally, the mother of the child. Chance and fate play roles in Shreve's novel as in Tylers'.

It is Shreve's spare prose and character development that gives the simple plot suspense and the feeling of loss and redemption. It is also a coming of age story for Nicky who is desperately seeking both a replacement for her lost mother and her lost sister. Perhaps the mother of the baby, Charlotte, can be both?

Robert, Nicky, and Charlotte are all changed by the time the tale is told, masterly by Shreve.

Tuesday, November 13, 2012 **Schmidtie**

Albert Schmidt, that is, but he prefers to be called "Schmidtie" and Louis Begley's trilogy captures the essence of a complex modern man. It bothered me that a movie had been made of the first novel, *About Schmidt* (1996), with Jack Nicholson playing the title role, and it took a while to get the image of good ole' Jack out of my mind. I also don't like seeing a film first and then reading the book, but years had intervened by the time I read the book last summer. Thus I had a hard time associating it with the film (other than Jack). But as it turns out the book is entirely different (it would be best to say the film was "suggested" by the novel) and in fact when I now think of what Schmidtie might look like, I see Louis Begley, a remarkable writer and with a remarkable personal history.

Begley came to writing late in life and like Joseph Conrad and Jerzy Kosinski, English is a second language, Polish being the language of their birth. The similarities to Kosinski are striking, Begley having to exorcise his demons about the Nazi occupation of Poland by writing *Wartime Lies*. It is a thinly autobiographical account of the protagonist's attempt to avoid persecution as a Jew . I remember reading Kosinski's *Painted Bird* when it was first published, a profoundly disturbing holocaust novel. I haven't read *Wartime Lies,* but it is now on my list.

After that novel, Begley felt he could move on as a writer, even though he remained a full-time attorney with the firm of Debevoise & Plimpton LLP, specializing in international corporate transactions. He has since retired and now devotes his full energies to writing at the tender age of 79!

I've dealt with enough attorneys in my career, mostly corporate ones and those specializing in intellectual property, to know that their work depends on the careful execution of language. Most of the attorneys I worked with thought that crafting a legal document was like building a fine piece of

furniture or even creating a work of art. No, that did not make them auto-
matically eligible to start a second career as a creative writer as one needs
something to say as well. In fact Begley, by his own admission, did not pursue a career as a writer at first for that very reason, although he enjoyed a
creative writing class at Harvard where he earned his AB in 1954. It took
him decades to find his voice, and now that he has, he is, thankfully, writing
full time.

Interestingly, his class of 1954 included none other than the late John
Updike. They both graduated summa cum laude and they must have known
each other. Whether they kept in touch over the years we will find out when
Begley's son, Adam Begley, is finished with the biography he is writing of
John Updike. I will be lining up for the first copy!

After finishing *All About Schmidt*, I promptly turned to the second novel
of the trilogy, *Schmidt Delivered* (2000) and now have finally finished the
third novel, *Schmidt Steps Back* (2012) and have been profoundly affected
by it. Although these were written years apart, I had the good fortune to
read all within a few months and, therefore, I almost think of them as one
work.

For me, Begley sort of picks up where Updike left off, following one
character and setting that character against the backdrop of the times in
which he lives. Updike updated us every ten years in the Rabbit tetrology
while Begley's trilogy is a more compressed time frame. Nonetheless, there
are many similarities, particularly the novel as memoir, a kind of history of
our times, and the intellectual level at which both Updike and Begley oper-
ate, their erudite prose befitting their excellent educations.

Rabbit is more of an "everyman" whereas Schmidtie is moving in the
upper echelon of society, certainly the upper 1% to borrow from the recent
election. And that should not be surprising as Begley's legal work put him
front and center in that stratum of society.

In terms of style, Begley writes like an attorney in many respects; his
sentences sometimes complex but finely crafted and I like his dispensing
with quotation marks for dialog. It takes a little getting used to, but it seems
so natural. I felt neutral to the protagonist in the first novel, moved a little
closer to him in the second, and by the third felt simpatico.

Rabbit and I shared many commonalities, and now I find myself in
Schmidtie's shoes, thinking similar thoughts and of course witnessing the
same events. It makes these novels living breathing documents.

Begley covers so many topics and themes in these novels, the ambiguity
of memory, Jewishness, moneyed privilege (consider this beautiful crafted
passage on that topic: *Tim had it all, every quality required to make him, as
the younger partners put it, the complete package. Handsome, imperially
slim, arrayed in discreet made-to-order suits and shirts that did not shout*

their *Savile Row and Jermyn Street provenance, he trailed an aura of old New York money.*), mental illness, homosexuality, the publishing industry and the legal establishment, the death of a spouse (his wife, Mary dies early on in the first novel), spring-winter romance, divorce and infidelity, the tragic relationship with his only child, Charlotte (*"His short-lived happiness had been added to the monstrous inventory of Charlotte's resentments. There was no doubt: the ever-deeper -- he was beginning to fear perma-nent -- estrangement from his daughter was his life's principal liability."*) and, finally, sex scenes worthy of Updike's *Couples*.

He throws down the gauntlet in the opening pages of *Schmidt Steps Back* (the best of the three novels), Schmidtie speculating as to how many years he has left (he guesses ten) and how death might come calling. Dr. Tang is his physician and Gil his best friend from college. I was fascinated by this long paragraph, as if Begley was listening in on my own private thoughts as they pertain to the inevitable. He also sets up some of the basic themes in the novel, the prospect of happiness (and his ability to have sex) with a woman he had romanced thirteen years before the opening of the novel, Alice, and the consequence and obligations of money:

Silly business, Schmidt thought, Dr. Tang's attention to his diet.... He had asked Dr. Tang whether she could foresee the form in which death would come for him. You won't scare me, he had said, everyone has an appointment in Samarra, and I own a cemetery plot with a view of Peconic Bay I rather like. She laughed gaily in reply and told him that with a patient in such good health it was impossible to predict. Schmidt's simultaneous translation was Don't ask stupid questions, leave it to team death, they'll figure it out. Ever polite, he had merely laughed back. In truth, he had his own hunches: stroke or cancer, demonic diseases that don't always go for the quick kill. But whatever it might turn out to be, no one, absolutely no one, would get him to move into a nursing home. If he was compos mentis, and not yet paralyzed, he would find his own way to the exit. Otherwise, the instructions left with Gil, naming him the sole arbiter of Schmidt's life and death, should do the job, with a little friendly nudge from Gil if need be. It was no more than he would do for Gil, who had made his own arrange-ments giving Schmidt the power of decision. Dementia, the illness most likely to cut off the means of escape, held more terror than any other. But he had not heard of a single ancestor, going back three generations, who had been so afflicted. The other side of the coin, the agreeable side, was his overall good health. Once he got going in the morning, he was still quite limber. In truth, he doubted there was much difference between his condi-tion thirteen years earlier, when he first called on Alice in Paris, to take an example that preoccupied him, and the way he was now. Not unless you wanted to fixate on the deep lines, running to the corners of his mouth, that had only gotten deeper or the hollow cheeks or the fold of skin sagging from his neck. Taken together, they gave him an expression so lugubrious that efforts to smile made him look like a gargoyle. The situation was less brilliant when it came to his libido and sexual performance. The grade he had given himself when last put to the test had been no higher than a pass, but as he had told Alice, he had not yet tried any of the miracle pills that old geezer-in-chief Bob Dole swore by on television. Besides, the test in question had been unfair: the lady whom he may have disappointed could not hold a candle to the incomparable Alice. Did his age and the ravages of time make it reprehensible to keep over- paying the Hampton mafia of gardeners, handymen, carpenters, and plumbers for the pleasure of having everything at his house just so? Or to pay the outrageous real estate taxes that financed town services, neatly itemized on the tax bill as though to taunt him by proving that he derived no personal benefit from them? Hell, there were lots of men unable to get a hard-on and lots of women who had faked orgasms until blessed moment when they could finally declare that at their age they'd given the whole thing up, living comfortably in houses much grander than his. Spending more money than he!

Then there is the notion of the novel as history. Begley gives witness to the manners and mores, the foibles, and the likes and dislikes of his times. Updike's characters are similarly entwined with their periods in American history. I would rather read a novel in this vein than any history book to get a sense of what people not only witnessed, but what they felt. Perhaps that is why I prefer fiction to nonfiction (although some of nonfiction could probably pass as fiction!). We all remember where we were on certain momentous days. My older relatives remember Pearl Harbor, while I remember where I was when Kennedy was assassinated that moment in time only to be surpassed by the events of September 11, 2001.

Begley flawlessly describes the horror and the incredulity of that infamous day in the third novel:

Tuesday, September 11, 2001. Perfect blue sky, perfect late-summer temperature. If it hadn't been for the foundation's board meeting, Schmidt would have stayed in Bridgehampton. As it was, he had driven in the evening before, got to the office early to prepare for the meeting, which was to start at ten. His secretary, Shirley, walked into his room shortly after nine to say good morning and ask whether he wanted coffee.

By the way, she added, one of those pesky little private planes has plowed into one of the World Trade Center towers. There's smoke coming out the building where it hit. If you come to reception you'll have a good view.

Schmidt glanced at his papers. For all practical purposes he was ready. He walked down the corridor to where a large number of Mansour

Industries employees already assembled in the forty-eighth-floor reception area were looking toward the southern tip of Manhattan, staring at the smoking tower, when the second plane hit. No one thought any longer that some neophyte aboard his Piper or Cessna was to blame. The traders who occupied two-thirds of the floor and had been glued to Madrid's El Mundo on their computers, unable to reach other sites, dashed in with the news; someone brought in a television set and connected to a German station. On the screen tiny-seeming figures, some of them holding hands, could be seen jumping from the vast height of the wounded buildings. Someone shouted, Look! Look! Schmidt turned away from the screen to look south, and before his eyes one tower crumbled and, not a half hour later, the second. Then came news of another plane that had hit the Pentagon and another still that had crashed in a field in Pennsylvania. And the passengers in those planes, men, women, children-their seat belts buckled-waiting for the moment of impact, knowing that they were to die in flames of burning jet fuel. Schmidt found that he could not detach his thoughts from them, as though it were his own nightmare from which he was unable to awake. Were they praying? Strangers embracing strangers next to whom they sat across armrests? Recollecting quickly all that had been good and beloved in their lives? Some of the children must have understood, but the others? The infants? Did the sound of their wailing fill the planes' cabins? Did it soften the murderers' hearts or was it their foretaste of paradise?

Perhaps he is working on his fourth Schmidt novel (one would hope!). He is a worthy writer to be added to my personal pantheon of "favorites.

Friday, December 28, 2012 **Went to a Garden Party**

Ann and I celebrated my 70th birthday on a cruise with our two sons, Chris and Jon, the first time we've been together for such an extended period since they were kids. But families find a way of settling into a familiar groove, wondering what the years have really done to us all (as a family) other than just growing older.

Twenty four hours after boarding, on my actual birthday, we were now attempting to move into full cruise mode and try to temporarily leave the world's troubles behind for a few days. After dinner and a celebratory birthday cake, too sinful for words, we decided to attend that evening's entertainment. What an ironic twist that on this night, my actual 70th birthday, the show in the ship's Theater, was "Ricky Nelson Remembered" performed by Ricky's twin sons, Gunnar and Matthew Nelson.

How appropriate, one of my boyhood idols, being honored by his two sons, on my birthday with my two sons.

I asked them whether they had ever heard of the *Ozzie and Harriet Show* (of course not) and I tried to explain something about that early TV feel-good sitcom -- covering a real family -- and the rise of the youngest son, Ricky, to become the first TV-made rock star. I was a teenager at the time, going through my "Elvis" stage, although the rockabilly songs of Carl Perkins and Gene Vincent appealed to me more. Ricky's songs were cut more from that mold and so he was put on my hit list for some precious 45's which I played in my attic bedroom to drown out my parents. I entitled this blog entry "Garden Party" as it is a song that resonates more for me in retirement than when he sang it for the simple reason that "you see, ya can't please everyone, so ya got to please yourself," one of the main reasons I write.

And what struck me from my reading as I was traveling with my family? Each family has its unique story. This cruise I devoured two biographies, *Hemingway's Boat* by Paul Hendrickson, and *Cheever, A Life*, by Blake Bailey who I think is emerging as the preeminent literary biographer. He brought Yates to life, and now Cheever.

Amazing to read about Hemingway and Cheever, so different in their writing and how they approached life and, yet again, such dysfunctional family lives (not as bad as Yates who led a depressed life in addition to being a drunk like Cheever). And for me amazing, the crisscrossing of aspects of their lives and mine, not that I'm a literary anything, but places and cultural commonalities galore.

The focus of Hendrikson's biography is indeed Hemingway's boat, a 1934 38 foot Wheeler named "Pilar' of Key West, made in my old stomping grounds of Brooklyn, NY. It had a 75 HP Chrysler reduction gear engine and a 40 HP Lycoming straight drive for trolling. He could run the boat at 16 knots with both engines (although that was rare). Ironically, the dimensions of his boat are about the same as mine. The 'Swept Away' is also 38 feet, holds about the same amount of fuel (330 gallons vs. 'Pilar's 300 gallons) and the same amount of fresh water, 100 gallons.

But "Hem" fished the boat and fished it hard, off of Cuba and Bimini in the Bahamas. The entire biography circles around the boat, the manufacturer, and the mates who ran the boat. It is more about his life and times than his writing.

The Cheever biography is as much about his writing as the man itself. His life was one of self doubt, always seeking approbation, unsure of his sexuality, and like Yates, one that gradually became consumed by alcoholism. During WW II he was in the infantry and was a week from being shipped off to Europe when he landed an assignment with the Signal Corps writing documentary films, ironically the same branch of the service as my father and Cheever's "office" was in Astoria, Queens, the same place my father's business landed before it was forced to close its doors. Most men from Cheever's unit were shipped off a week later and died on Utah beach, the same destiny that would have befallen him. Lucky for him and us or we would not have most of the short stories (and all of the novels) from one of most important writers.

Cheever is closely identified with the New Yorker school of writing as was his younger contemporary (and rival) John Updike, probably the most important American writer of the late 20th century along with Philip Roth. Updike and Cheever while respecting one another, kept an eye out for the other as well, especially Cheever who felt inferior in many ways to Updike, particularly because of his younger colleague's Harvard education (Cheever went to the school of hard knocks as did Richard Yates). While the careers of Cheever and Updike were constantly crisscrossing, Yates was an outsider, never achieving the distinction of a *New Yorker* published short story.

Between the two biographies, I read another novel by Louis Begley who is beginning to impress me as the next great American writer, but at the age of 79, he might not have enough time to establish an even greater reputation since switching his profession from the law to creative writing. After the *Schmidt* trilogy, I wanted to know more about the man, and chose his very autobiographical *Matters of Honor* in which his persona is occupied by two characters, Henry White, a Polish-Jewish refugee who was hidden as a child during World War II, with his mother and father, and therefore survived, who becomes an international attorney, and Sam Standish, the narrator, who becomes an author. Of course, Begley is both people and it is interesting how he orchestrates many characters in the novel in this coming of age story, from Henry and Sam being Harvard roommates in the 1950s and then their rise to the pinnacle of their careers later in life. Begley's struggle with anti-Semitism and the meaning of friendship constantly surfaces. This is the work of a mature novelist in every way.

So I shared my 70th birthday with my family and some of my favorite authors. My Garden Party was swell.

Monday, March 11, 2013 *Oh What A Paradise It Could Be*

I can't put *Oh What A Paradise It Seems* back onto our bookshelf, (reading it for a second time in my life), without saying something about it, what John Cheever has meant to me, and the catalyst the monumental biography by Blake Bailey, *Cheever: A Life,* has played in this mix.

It is unusual for us to have two copies of the same book and only one such title resides alongside our two different bedsides, here at our home in Florida and on our boat in Connecticut, *The Stories of John Cheever*. Before I retired, I used to carry it on any business trip that involved an airport or a hotel. It was my "get out of jail free" card. In case of any delay, that book was my reclamation, picking out a short story that was ideal to fill in the time, and as I had read them all before, nonetheless always finding some new meaning or just again enjoying Cheever's charmed lyricism. Cheever was the master short story writer and that is his genre. His novels, although a pleasure to read, never seemed to measure up to the "reread test." Until recently.

I had read his last novel *Oh What A Paradise It Seems* when it was first published in the early 1980s. At the time I was forty years old. I hadn't known of Cheever's illness then but probably thought of him as "old man" and the work seemed to me at the time to be disoriented and sad. But Bailey's biography led me to reread the work and today, from the prospective being not only an older man myself, even older than Cheever when he died, it seems prophetic and profound. It is a poignant work, clearly written by a man who knew he was dying and knew he would write little afterwards. And writing to Cheever was like breathing.

I feel Cheever's pain rereading the work, even his personal pain of being so conflicted over his bisexuality, and his failing sexual powers, and the macro-pain of his knowing he was leaving a planet that at times was such a paradise, but one which also seemed to be slouching towards a hellish environmental ruin.

The story is less important to me than the feeling it leaves me with -- almost one of regret. It is sad to bear witness, as does Cheever in the novel, to an overpopulated, hyperkinetic, media-obsessed society, seemingly hell-bent on environmental self destruction. This is a far cry from the suburbia normally associated with Cheever's work. Yet there is always hope and Cheever leaves us with that sense.

Cheever's favorite image, that of rain, begins the novel...*This is a story to be read in bed in an old house on a rainy night.*

The protagonist, Lemuel Sears is skating on the pond in his old village, where his daughter now lives. (Cheever was separated from his place of boyhood for most of his life, the Quincy, MA area, and he was returned there to be buried.) The setting of the mythical "sleepy village" of Janice of the novel must be very similar to where he was born. This beautiful passage denotes his "homecoming:" *Swinging down a long stretch of black ice gave Sears a sense of homecoming. at long last, at the end of a cold, long journey, he was returning to a place where his name was known and loved and lamps burned in the rooms and fires of the hearth. It seemed to Sears that all the skaters moved over the ice with the happy conviction that they were on their way home. Home might be an empty room and an empty bed to many of them, including Sears, but swinging over the black ice convinced Sears that he was on his way home. Someone more skeptical might point out that this illuminated how ephemeral is our illusion of homecoming.*

But the characters seem lost, homeless, nomads in the modern world. Harold Chisholm is one such character:

Nothing waited for him in his apartment. There was no woman, no man, no dog, no cat, and his answering tape would likely be empty and the neighborhood where he lived had become so anonymous and transient that there were no waiters or shopkeepers or bartenders who would greet him. He turned on the radio but all the music he seemed able to get was disco music, and disco music from those discos that had been closed the year before the year before last for drug pushing or nonpayment of income tax. He seemed to be searching for the memory of some place, some evidence of the fact that he had once been able to put himself into a supremely creative touch with his world and his kind. He longed for this as if it were some country which he had been forced to leave.

And in its 100 short pages we circle back to water and its primordial symbolism to Cheever:

Now and then the voice of the brook was louder than Chisholm's voice. A trout stream in a forest, a traverse of potable water, seemed for Sears to be the bridge that spans the mysterious abyss between our spiritual and our carnal selves. How contemptible this made his panic about his own contamination. When he was young, brooks had seemed to speak to him in the tongues of men and angels. Now that he was an old man who spoke five or six languages-all of them poorly-the sound of water seemed to be the language of his nativity, some tongue he had spoken before his birth. Soft and loud, high and low, the sound of water reminded him of eavesdropping in some other room than where the party was.

Cheever died only a few short months after its publication. Yet, his love of life always shines through as in the lyricism of one of the concluding paragraphs:

The sky was clear that morning and there might still have been stars although he saw none. The thought of stars contributed to the power of his feeling, What moved him was a sense of those worlds around us, our knowledge however imperfect of their nature, our sense of their possessing some grain of our past and of our lives to come, It was that most powerful sense of our being alive on the planet. It was that most powerful sense of how singular, in the vastness of creation, is the richness of our opportunity. The sense of that hour was of an exquisite privilege, the great benefice of living here and renewing ourselves with love, What a paradise it seemed!

I would like to remember Cheever for the beauty he captured in his writings, and as opening day approaches -- with the impending cry of "play ball!" -- I will revisit his short story, "National Pastime," of which I am fortunate enough to have a limited edition, signed by Cheever, something to be cherished. It tells a story, in a small way similar to my boyhood -- when I pursued baseball without much help of my own father who was either bogged down by his troubled marriage or by his photography business. As Cheever puts it, *the feeling that I could not assume my responsibilities as a baseball player without some help from him was deep, as if parental love and baseball were both national pastimes.*

Saturday, May 11, 2013 **Saturday**

Perhaps I am one of the last readers to discover Ian McEwan's *Saturday*, originally published some eight years ago. In my defense, the book has been sitting in my reading queue for some time -- the Jonathan Cape paperback edition -- and I finally picked it up and said it was about time I turn to this English novelist as I've heard so much praise about McEwan's work. (As a disclaimer, I had not read his best known work, *Atonement*, before it was made into a movie -- which I also have not seen, hoping to read the book first, but *Saturday* was already on my shelves by then.)

The protagonist, Henry Perowne is a very successful neurosurgeon, married to Rosalind who is an attorney for a newspaper. They have two children, both young adults, Daisy, a soon to be a published poet (like her maternal Grandfather) and Theo, a talented blues musician. All the action of the novel (mostly told as interior monologue) takes place on a Saturday (actually into early Sunday morning). It begins with Henry's early morning awakening, his watching the square over which his home looms, his thoughts about surgeries, past and future, and then finally noticing a plane, partially in flames, seemingly descending on London or perhaps trying to land at Heathrow. This is post 9/11, that early morning scene setting the tone for the entire novel, a sense of impending doom. Other things happen that day -- a mass demonstration protesting the, then, possible invasion of Iraq, a game of squash with Henry's highly competitive colleague, Strauss, for which he is delayed because of the demonstration and also because his Mercedes has had a run in with a BMW, occupied by a bunch of thugs, (the ring leader, Baxter, reminding me a little of a young Edward G. Robinson). Baxter is the catalyst for action later in the novel. It certainly changes Henry's day, although the novel almost ends as it began, making a full circle. McEwan's writing is in the tradition of Gustave Flaubert and Henry James, with some of the darkness of Joseph Conrad.

McEwan is as precise in his construction of the novel as is Perowne in the operating theatre, the place Perowne thinks of as "home" as much as the one on Fitzroy Square where he lives with his wife and son (Daisy has already gone, but as part of the plot, is coming home to London that Saturday as her book of poetry is about to be published).

Interestingly, Henry is juxtaposed to his daughter and her Grandfather, both poets, and to a lesser degree, to his son, Theo, the musician. He is a surgeon, one who believes in scientific inquiry, and although he appreciates classical music in the operating theatre, and jazz figures such as Bill Evans, Henry is first and foremost a man of science.

I quote several passages from the novel as they give not only a sense of McEwan's exceptional writing style, but they reveal some of the major themes as well. I mentioned that the novel unfolds in the shadow of 9/11, beginning with a possible airliner crash, perhaps an accident, or a terrorist act. McEwan writes about Henry's feelings on air travel: *Like most passengers, outwardly subdued by the monotony of air travel, he often lets his thoughts range across the possibilities while sitting, strapped down and docile, in front of a packaged meal. Outside, beyond a wall of thin steel and cheerful creaking plastic, it's minus sixty degrees and forty thousand feet to the ground. Flung across the Atlantic at five hundred feet a second, you submit to the folly because everyone else does. Your fellow passengers are reassured because you and the others around you appear calm....Air travel is a stock market, a trick of mirrored perceptions, a fragile alliance of pooled belief; so long as nerves hold steady and no bombs or wreckers are on board, everybody prospers. When there's failure....[t]he market could plunge.*

And what about a deity's role in all of this? *And if there are to be deaths, the very god who ordained them will soon be funereally petitioned for comfort. Perowne regards this as a matter for wonder, a human complication beyond the reach of morals. From it there spring, alongside the unreason and slaughter, decent people and good deeds, beautiful cathedrals, mosques, cantatas, poetry. Even the denial of God, he was once amazed and indignant to hear a priest argue, is a spiritual exercise, a form of prayer: it's not easy to escape from the clutches of the believers.*

He is constantly debating his daughter and his father in law about the role of literature and poetry in the real world, particularly the literary supernatural that seems to perpetually occupy the best selling lists. His daughter has given him a "reading list" of novels, but Henry protests: *A man who attempts to ease the miseries of failing minds by repairing brains is bound to respect the material world, its limits, and what it can sustain -- consciousness, no less. It isn't an article of faith with him, he knows it for a quotidian fact, the mind is what the brain, mere matter, performs. If that's worthy of awe, it also deserves curiosity; the actual, not the magical, should be the challenge. This reading list persuaded Perowne that the supernatural was the recourse of an insufficient imagination, a dereliction of duty, a childish evasion of the difficulties and wonders of the real, of the demanding re-enactment of the plausible.*

Then there are times McEwan seems to be influenced by social Darwinism. Here, Perowne is negotiating his car through the left over rubbish from the march, and he sees a street sweeper and their eyes briefly meet: *The whites of the sweeper's eyes are fringed with egg-yellow shading to red along the lids. For a vertiginous moment Henry feels himself bound to the other man, as though on a seesaw with him, pinned to an axis that could tip them into each other's life.....How restful it must once have been, in another age, to be prosperous and believe that an all-knowing supernatural force had allotted people to their stations in life. And not see how the belief served your own prosperity - a form of anosognosia, a useful psychiatric term for a lack of awareness of one's own condition. Now we think we do see, how do things stand? After the ruinous experiments of the lately deceased century, after so much vile behaviour, so many deaths, a queasy agnosticism has settled around these matters of justice and redistributed wealth. No more big ideas. The world must improve, if at all, by tiny steps. People mostly take an existential view - having to sweep the streets for a living looks like simple bad luck. It's not a visionary age. The streets need to be clean. Let the unlucky enlist.*

His eye for the common street sweeper is later turned to the fishmonger and McEwan weaves a philosophical observation into his observation: *The fishmonger is a polite, studious man who treats his customers as members of an exclusive branch of the landed gentry. He wraps each species of fish in several pages of a newspaper. This is the kind of question Henry liked to put to himself when he was a schoolboy: what are the chances of this particular fish, from that shoal, off that continental shelf ending up in the pages, no, on this page of this copy of the Daily Mirror? Something just short of infinity to one. Similarly, the grains of sand on a beach, arranged just so. The random ordering of the world, the unimaginable odds against any particular condition, still please him.*

And then, he turns to humanity in general. Henry is now stuck in traffic, the late aftermath of the march. Does he become irate, frustrated by the traffic? No, he is transported to a breathtaking view from a historical perspective: *Dense traffic is heading into the city for Saturday night pleasures just as the first wave of coaches is bringing the marchers out. During the long crawl towards the lights at Gypsy Corner, he lowers his window to taste the scene in full - the bovine patience of a jam, the abrasive tang of icy fumes, the thunderous idling machinery in six lanes east and west, the yellow street light bleaching colour from the bodywork, the jaunty thud of entertainment systems, and red taillights stretching way ahead into the city, white headlights pouring out of it. He tries to see it, or feel it, in historical terms, this moment in the last decades of the petroleum age, when a nineteenth-century device is brought to final perfection in the early years of the twenty-first; when the unprecedented wealth of masses at serious play in the unforgiving modern city makes for a sight that no previous age can have imagined. Ordinary people! Rivers of light! He wants to make himself see it as Newton might, or his contemporaries, Boyle, Hooke, Wren,*

Willis - *those clever, curious men of the English Enlightenment who for a few years held in their minds nearly all the world's science. Surely, they would be awed. Mentally, he shows it off to them: this is what we've done, this is commonplace in our time. All this teeming illumination would be wondrous if he could only see it through their eyes.*

Back in the operating theatre (now late Saturday night), Henry's awe of science, the brain he is operating on, and what does consciousness mean, all converge: *He's looking down at a portion of Baxter's brain. He can easily convince himself that it's familiar territory, a kind of homeland, with its low hills and enfolded valleys of the sulci, each with a name and imputed function, as known to him as his own house. Just to the left of the midline, running laterally away out of sight under the bone, is the motor strip. Behind it, running parallel, is the sensory strip. So easy to damage, with such terrible, lifelong consequences. How much time he has spent making routes to avoid these areas, like bad neighbourhoods in an American city. And this familiarity numbs him daily to the extent of his ignorance, and of the general ignorance. For all the recent advances, it's still not known how this well-protected one kilogram or so of cells actually encodes information, how it holds experiences, memories, dreams and intentions. He doesn't doubt that in years to come, the coding mechanism will be known, though it might not be in his lifetime. Just like the digital codes of replicating life held within DNA, the brain's fundamental secret will be laid open one day. But even when it has, the wonder will remain, that mere wet stuff can make this bright inward cinema of thought, of sight and sound and touch bound into a vivid illusion of an instantaneous present, with a self, another brightly wrought illusion, hovering like a ghost at its centre. Could it ever be explained, how matter becomes conscious?*

One of my favorite, very poignant passages, probably because it touches me very directly, my mother-in-law, uncle, and now our cousin, suffering from Alzheimer's disease, involves Henry's mother, Lily, who he visits (same Saturday!) at the home she is being cared for -- with advance stages of that dreaded disease. Henry remembers when they had to take her from her home, the very one he grew up in, as she could no longer care for herself and in fact was failing to recognize family members. He enlists the help of his wife and his children: *The family packed up clothes and kitchenware and unwanted ornaments for the charity shops - Henry never realised before how these places lived off the dead. Everything else they stuffed into bin liners and put out for the rubbish collection. They worked in silence, like looters - having the radio on wasn't appropriate. It took a day to dismantle Lily's existence.... She's not dead, Henry kept telling himself. But her life, all lives, seemed tenuous when he saw how quickly, with what ease, all the trappings, all the fine details of a lifetime could be packed and scattered, or junked. Objects became junk as soon as they were separated from their owner and their pasts - without her, her old tea cosy was repellent, with its faded farmhouse motif and pale brown stains on cheap fabric, and stuffing that was pathetically thin. As the shelves and drawers emptied, and the boxes and bags filled, he saw that no one owned anything really. It's all rented, or borrowed. Our possessions will outlast us, we'll desert them in the end.*

I don't think I've given away any significant plot details that will ruin one's reading of this novel of suspense. I mentioned earlier that the novel remains in the shadow of 9/11 and it circles back to the beginning at the end. Henry now thinks what the future might bring, by thinking of what the past was like --as the future might have been seen through the eyes of a physician such as himself, one hundred years ago. It is a powerful message brilliantly expressed, one of foreboding by McEwan.

Inevitably I will think of this novel on some future Saturdays as well, hoping that it is not in the context of a "mass killing," but that specter of terrorism hangs heavily. In his own post 9/11 novel, *The Terrorist,* John Updike struggled to reconcile the fundamentalist Muslim view of American society and what the future might hold. Both novels leave one with the ambiguities of an unknown resolution. Both are novels of peerless writing.

Tuesday, June 4, 2013 **"It Saddens Me to Leave the Field"**

I haven't written lately about baseball, my favorite sport, one I played constantly as a kid, pitching in sort of a combination Little League/Babe Ruth league (very informal and disorganized, more like pick-up games with uniforms) for the Highland Park Terriers, taking the old Jamaica Avenue El to get to the field in Highland Park. I am a lefty and even though I could not crank up an intimidating fast ball, I compensated with breaking balls and placement. I was constantly practicing with neighborhood kids, with dreams of big league ball, but high school and then college teams put those dreams to rest. When I tried out for college baseball I found that most on the team were on an athletic scholarship and although I pitched some batting practice, the first baseman at the time -- forgot his name -- took one of my balls not only over the fence, but to an apartment building way beyond. It was meager compensation to learn, well after I graduated, that he apparently made it to AAA ball.

Although those days are now long gone, there is something about having played the game, knowing its nuances, that still gives rise to fantasies of what might have been, had I been more physically gifted, or worked harder, or had more support from my parents (who pretty much ignored my quest, rarely attending my games). No, mine was a solitary undertaking, getting on the El for practice and then games on Saturday mornings.

To this day I watch baseball with a sense of awe, especially the mental contest between the batter and the pitcher.

So it is no wonder that when the highly praised *The Art of Fielding* by Chad Harbach was published last year, it immediately went on my wish list. One day I was on the phone with one of my best friends, Ron, who, like me, shares a love of the game and he asked whether I had read the book. No, and I explained why. He said, we'll I'm finished with my copy, I'll send it to you! You don't want to keep it, I asked, and he said, no, you enjoy it and only a few days later, Jeff, my postman, handed me the package. So, I put it early in the queue on my bookshelf.

As I started to read it I immediately began to think that if John Irving was a college baseball player instead of a wrestler, this is something he might have written. It has so many Irvingesque features, particularly the quirky nature of the characters, the sexual overtones, not to mention the idiosyncratic names of most characters and places. In fact, one major character, Owen Dunne, had me thinking of Irving's Owen in *A Prayer for Owen Meany*, who as a little-leaguer hits a ball that kills one of his best friend's mothers (Harbach's Owen is hit by a ball and almost dies and like Irving's Owen has a certain presence -- he is known as "Buddha" to his friends).

And that is not the only literary tip of the hat as the novel is set in the fictional Westish, on the shores of Lake Michigan, where in the novel Herman Melville once gave a lecture at Westish College. Guert Affenlight who is now the president of the college had discovered this lecture and wrote his dissertation on it. Hence, there is a Melville statue on the campus, and various references, both direct and implied to Melville's work. Although the college is not exactly the good ship Pequod, it is the place where the lives of the five main characters are transformed through their interaction, Guert and his daughter Pella, and three students (all members of the college baseball team, aptly nicknamed the " Harpooners "), Owen, who is gay and Thoreauesque, and then the larger than life Mike Schwartz who is mentor (sometimes torturer) to the unrealized talents of the baseball prodigy, Henry Skrimshander (yes, you could make the correlation that Mike's project was like a Scrimshaw). But, in the end, Henry takes on some of the characteristics of Bartleby from Melville's short story.

The Art of Fielding begins with the premise and promise of Henry following in the cleats of his idol, the greatest shortstop ever to play baseball, the fictional Aparicio Rodriquez who had written what is more of a philosophical treatise than an instruction book on playing the position, with the fitting title, *The Art of Fielding*. So, in a sense, Harbach's novel is thematically a "play within a play."

One of the nuggets for Henry to ponder from Aparicio's book is *it always saddens me to leave the field. Even fielding the final out to win the World Series, deep in the truest part of me, felt like death*. Harbach writes *There were admittedly, many sentences and statements in The Art that Henry did not yet understand. The opaque parts of The Art though, had always been his favorites...As frustrating as they could be, [they] gave Henry something to aspire to. Someday, he dreamed, he would be enough of a ballplayer to crack them open and suck out their hidden wisdom: Death is the sanction of all that the athlete does.*

As a young ballplayer, Henry was an artist, a lightly hitting but exceptionally gifted fielder who played his position with the grace of a ballerina, capturing the notice of Mike Schwartz when Henry was in high school. (*What [Henry] could do was field. He spent his life studying the way the ball came off the bat, the angles and the spin, so that he knew in advance whether he should break right or left, whether the ball that came to him would be bound up high or skid low to the dirt. He caught the ball cleanly, always, and made, always, a perfect throw.*) Mike recruits him for Westish College on which team Mike is the quintessential catcher, the team captain who plays in pain and on pain killers, a star player whose knees are already giving out.

It is through Mike's quest to build a star out of Henry that some of Harbach's best lapidary baseball prose shines:

The making of a ballplayer: the production of brute efficiency out of natural genius. For Schwartz this formed the paradox at the heart of baseball, or football, or any other sport. You loved it because you considered it an art; an apparently pointless affair, undertaken by people with a special aptitude, which sidestepped attempts to paraphrase its value yet somehow seemed to communicate something true or even crucial about The Human Condition. The Human Condition being, basically, that we're alive and have access to beauty, can even erratically create it, but will someday be dead and will not.

Baseball was an art, but to excel at it you had to become a machine. It didn't matter how beautifully you performed sometimes, what you did on your best day, how many spectacular plays you made. You weren't a painter or a writer—you didn't work in private and discard your mistakes, and it wasn't just your masterpieces that counted. What mattered, as for any machine, was repeatability. Moments of inspiration were nothing compared to elimination of error. The scouts cared little for Henry's superhuman grace; insofar as they cared they were suckered-in aesthetes and shitty scouts. Can you perform on demand, like a car, a furnace, a gun? Can you make that throw one hundred times out of a hundred? If it can't be a hundred, it had better be ninety-nine.

Harbach captures the uniqueness of the game. It's one unlike any other:
Baseball, in its quiet way, was an extravagantly harrowing game. Football, basketball, hockey, lacrosse -- these were melee sports. You could make yourself useful by hustling and scrapping more than the other guy. You could redeem yourself through sheer desire.

And, so, Henry becomes Mike's project. It is a symbiotic relationship. Mike (AKA "artzy") needs to exhort and Henry wants to become the perfect ballplayer.

All he'd ever wanted was for nothing to ever change. Or for things to change only in the right ways, improving little by little, day by day, forever. It sounded crazy when you said it like that, but that was what baseball had promised him, what Westish College had promised him, what 'artzy had promised him. The dream of every day the same. Every day was like the day before but a little better....Hitches, bad habits, useless thoughts - whatever you didn't need slowly fell away. Whatever was simple and useful remained. You improved little by little till the day it all became perfect and stayed that way. Forever.

He knew it sounded crazy when you put it like that. To want to be perfect. To want everything to be perfect. But now it felt like that was all he'd ever craved since he'd been born. Maybe it wasn't even baseball he loved but only this idea of perfection, a perfectly simple life in which every move had meaning, and baseball was just the medium through which he could make that happen. Could have made that happen. It sounded crazy, sure. But what did it mean if your deepest hope, the premise on which you'd based your whole life, sounded crazy as soon as you put it in words? It meant you were crazy.

And so, armed with his glove "Zero" (named so as when his mother asked if he made any errors in a game, he was always able to say "zero!"), Henry becomes a Westish Harpooner, and while Owen, Pella, Mike and Henry are essentially in the same age group and naturally their interactions are the substance of the novel, so is Guert's involvement with his daughter and with Owen. This is a character driven story, one that is hard to put down, particularly if you love the game, and even though the ending seemed to me to be a little contrived ("low and away" in baseball-speak), Harbach's novel is an exceptional first effort.

Monday, July 15, 2013 **We Live Too Shallowly in Too Many Places**

That is an indirect quote from Wallace Stegner's masterpiece, *Angle of Repose*, but more on that later.

I thought of those few words as we headed north on I95 last week, fortified by yet another "book" – actually a 13 hour audio book. Perhaps it was providential that Amazon had a sale on the audio book edition of Jess Walter's most recent novel, *Beautiful Ruins*, right before we departed Florida for Connecticut. While it is very professionally narrated, somehow I think the book might be better read than listened to. I can't really explain why that might be; perhaps having it read to you makes you focus on plot rather than character, or the interruptions while being on the road forces one to stop listening when rest stops dictate.

The story begins with Pasquale Tursi, who, after his father dies in 1962, returns from his partially completed college education to run the family's small hotel in the out of the way Italian coastal town of Porto Vergogna There he has a chance meeting with a minor American actress, Dee Moray (she is in Italy to film *Cleopatra* with Richard Burton and Elizabeth Taylor). The story is a CD page turner (making the drive that much easier), moving back and forth from 1962 to the near present, with the introduction of a number of characters (including Richard Burton). It is like so many good novels, it is the tale of choices and consequences. Walter's characters interact with one another over time, changing the outcome of each others' lives, "beautiful ruins" as is some of the Italian landscape. Their stories devolve into their own "angles of repose." Jess Walter continues his journey as a young ascending American novelist.

The drive up I95 is emblematic of living too shallowly in too many places. As a nation we've become anchorless, a nomadic nation addicted to the so called "pleasures" of travel. Even with gas at $4 plus a gallon the roads were packed, the "rest stops" jammed with those seeking burgers, fries, ice cream, pizza, and sodas.

I have no business wondering the where's or why's of this moving mass of humanity, as I am one of the rootless, but, in our case, trying to "go home" again, to where we spent most of our lives in Connecticut. However, with each passing year, the ties to the past unravel more, and we are more strangers than natives, in spite of our love of the area. One does not put down roots in Florida to offset this loss it seems, as one's neighbors are from someplace else, and they are wanderers as are you. Indeed, we live too shallowly in too many places, bringing me to this great American novel, certainly one of the best of the 20th century, Wallace Stegner's *Angle of Repose*.

The novel was published in 1972. It won the Pulitzer Prize for Literature that year. That fact begs the question of where have I been during those many years since its publication, particularly as I consider myself fairly well read when it comes to contemporary American literature. In my defense, and it's a weak one, perhaps it was a form of cultural snobbism -- not unlike Susan Burling Ward's, the main character in the novel -- that is more East coast focused. When Stegner was writing, I was reading Updike, Cheever, Yates and Roth. Those who wrote about the West, the frontier, did not reach a deep chord in me. But, now, my own sense of place has become diluted. It took this blog to lead me to Stegner's masterpiece. A few months ago I received an unexpected email (this is the truncated version):

Something made me think of you today, so I Googled your name, and Google led me to your blog. I wonder if you'll even remember me. My memories of you are no doubt washed by the passage of time, but how nice that I get to share some of this with you.

In 1969, you hired me as your secretary at Johnson Reprint. I was 20 years old, my typing was pathetic, my shorthand practically non-existent, I had no real secretarial experience, and I had just moved to New York from Meadville, Pennsylvania. Yet for some reason I will never understand you saw potential and offered me the job. It wasn't long after that you left Johnson for greener pastures, and I cut my hair short in protest. Though of course, no one but me cared how long my hair was.

And now, 44 years later, I get to thank you. You were really my first mentor, and you encouraged me to think analytically and take my silly attempts at writing poems to a deeper level. You also taught me a great deal about being a professional--although there was certainly a lot more to learn, you got me over the threshold. And the position itself provided me with skills that served me well throughout my career. A position for which I was completely unqualified. I have always felt that you played a brief but seminal role in my life.

Have you read Wallace Stegner's Angle of Repose? He talks about a Doppler effect (nothing to do with weather) that I couldn't possibly do justice to, so in brief, it is a sort of predestination view but not really. If you are curious and haven't read it, you will just have to do so! Anyhow, I mention it because it has become more and more of an intriguing concept for me over time. When I think back on 1969 as a fragment of my life, I marvel at where my path was to take me. And that at the time, of course, it was unwritten. .... This probably makes no sense whatsoever to you! But it does to me, and it's beginning to feel like I'm writing this more for myself than you. My apologies if it feels that way to you too!

Well, what I started out wanting to say is thank you. For being who you were at a juncture in my life and providing me with a chance, though you didn't know it any more than I did at the time, to build a springboard for myself to carry me into a fascinating and sweet journey. I am truly happy to know that your own life has been, and continues to be, so full of love and friends and success. You earned all that a long time ago just by being your intuitive and generous self.

Naturally, I was moved by this, responded with my thanks and that I haven't read Wallace Stegner's *Angle of Repose*, but have ordered it from Amazon and that it sounds like an ideal summer read. Since then Mary and I have struck up an email relationship, two small characters on the world stage whose lives once intersected and, now, thanks to technology, intersect virtually.

But, there you have it, a bend in time, perhaps the Doppler Effect, leading me to one of the more significant literary works of our time.

Stegner's story is multigenerational; a tale told by Lyman Ward, a 58 year-old former history professor who is now confined to a wheelchair, taken care of by friend and neighbor Ada Hawkes and her daughter Shelly in the home of Ward's grandparents, Susan and Oliver Ward. It was in this California home his grandparents finally settled after living in a number of frontier outposts during the formative years of their marriage. Lyman Ward's father, Ollie, was the oldest of their three children.

Part of Stegner's novel is devoted to present-day Lyman, who is trying to stay independent in spite of his being wheelchair bound, while his only son, Rodman, is trying to place him in an assisted living home. But Lyman is fiercely opposed to the idea. He is now also divorced from his wife, Ellen.

But the majority of the story is the one that Lyman Ward is trying to write about his grandmother, an extraordinary women of letters and an artist as well, who marries a young engineer, reluctantly leaving her best friend Augusta, and the Northeast, to join Oliver (she thinks for only a few years before a planned return to the East) in his quest to pursue a career as a mining engineer in the West.

Actually, the character of Susan Burling Ward is based on the real life of Mary Hallock Foote, and Stegner makes liberal use of Foote's writings in the novel, which led to some controversy although Stegner acknowledges that use saying that he did not hesitate "to warp personalities and events to fictional needs." At times it almost feels like an epistolary novel, although all letters are one sided, from Susan to Augusta. Augusta's life is firmly within the gravitational pull of the eastern intelligentsia, a life that Susan pines for, for herself and for her children.

So, it is Lyman's objective to write this history, to remain independent while doing so, living in the home he used to visit as a child. He thinks of "Angle of Repose" as being an appropriate title, and considers the Doppler Effect as an alternative, "saying" to his grandmother:

If Henry Adams, whom you knew slightly, could make a theory of history by applying the second law of thermodynamics to human affairs, I ought to be entitled to base one on the angle of repose, and may yet. There is another physical law that teases me, too: the Doppler Effect. The sound of anything coming at you - a train, say, or the future - has a higher pitch than the sound of the same thing going away. If you have perfect pitch and a head for mathematics you can compute the speed of the object by the interval between its arriving and departing sounds. I have neither perfect pitch nor a head for mathematics, and anyway who wants to compute the speed of history? Like all falling bodies, it constantly accelerates. But I would like to hear your life as you heard it, coming at you, instead of hearing it as I do, a sober sound of expectations reduced, desires blunted, hopes deferred or abandoned, chances lost, defeats accepted, griefs borne.... You yearned backward a good part of your life, and that produced another sort of Doppler Effect. Even while you paid attention to what you must do today and tomorrow, you heard the receding sound of what you had relinquished.

In recounting the life of his grandparents, Lyman hopes to find something about his own "angle of repose:"

Yet do you remember the letters you used to get from isolated miners and geologists and surveyors who had come across a copy of Century or Atlantic and seen their lives there, and wrote to ask how a lady of obvious refinement knew so much about drifts, stopes, tipples, pumps, ores, assays, mining law, claim jumpers, underground surveying, and other matters? Remember the one who wanted to know where you learned to handle so casually a technical term like "angle of repose"? I suppose you replied, "By living with an engineer." But you were too alert to the figurative possibilities of words not to see the phrase as descriptive of human as well as detrital rest....As you said, it was too good for mere dirt; you tried to apply it to your own wandering and uneasy life. It is the angle I am aiming for myself, and I don't mean the rigid angle which I rest in this chair. I wonder if you ever reached it....

Wheelchair bound, and distraught and cynical about the present (the 1970s), by exploring (and glorifying) her life, Lyman temporarily finds a way out of his: *Fooling around in the papers my grandparents, especially my grandmother, left behind, I get glimpses of lives close to mine, related to mine in ways I recognize but don't completely comprehend. I'd like to live in their clothes a while, if only so I don't have to live in my own.... We have been cut off, the past has been ended and the family has broken up and the present is adrift in its wheelchair. I had a wife who after twenty-five years of marriage took on the coloration of the 1960s. I have a son who, though we are affectionate with each other, is no more my true son than if he breathed through gills. That is no 'gap between the generations, that is a gulf. The elements have changed, there are whole new orders of magnitude and kind. This present of 1970 is no more an extension of my grandparents' world, this West is no more a development of the West they helped build, than the sea over Santorini is an extension of that once-island of rock and olives. ....My grandparents had to live their way out of one world and into another, or into several others, making new out of old the way corals live their reef upward. I am on my grandparents' side. I believe in Time, as they did, and in the life chronological rather than in the life existential. We live in time and through it, we build our huts in its ruins, or used to, and we cannot afford all these abandonings.*

While plot and character development are outstanding strengths of the novel, the sense of place (or displacement) permeates the entire work, the East vs. West, civilization vs. the frontier, and a miscarriage of the American Dream:

I wonder if ever again Americans can have that experience of return-ing to a home place so intimately known, profoundly felt, deeply loved, and absolutely submitted to? It is not quite true that you can't go home again. I have done it, coming back here. But it gets less likely. We have had too many divorces, we have consumed too much transportation, we have lived too shallowly in too many places. I doubt that anyone of Rodman's gen-eration could comprehend the home feelings of someone like Susan Ward. Despite her unwillingness to live separately from her husband, she could probably have stayed on indefinitely in Milton, visited only occasionally by an asteroid husband. Or she could have picked up the old home and remade it in a new place. What she resisted was being the wife of a failure and a woman with no home.

When frontier historians theorize about the uprooted, the lawless, the purseless, and the socially cut-off who settled the West, they are not talking about people like my grandmother. So much that was cherished and loved, women like her had to give up; and the more they gave it up, the more they carried it helplessly with them. It was a process like ionization what was subtracted from one pole was added to the other For that sort of pio-neer, the West was not a new country being created, but an old one being reproduced; in that sense our pioneer women were always more realistic than our pioneer men. The moderns, carrying little baggage of the kind that Shelly called "merely cultural," not even living in traditional air, but breathing into their space helmets a scientific mixture of synthetic gases (and polluted at that) are the true pioneers. Their circuitry seems to include no atavistic domestic sentiment, they have suffered empathectomy, their computers hum no ghostly feedback of Home, Sweet Home. How marvel-ously free they are! How unutterably deprived!

And, indeed, the "place" of frontier and its bearing on his Grandfather's failings, hangs heavily in the novel. Lyman feels empathy for this man who perhaps unwisely trusted others in his pursuit of colossal dreams:

As a practitioner of hindsight I know what Grandfather was trying to do, by personal initiative and with the financial resources of a small and strug-gling corporation, what only the immense power of the federal government ultimately proved able to do. That does not mean he was foolish or mistaken. He was premature. His clock was set on pioneer time. He met trains that had not yet arrived, he waited on platforms that hadn't yet been built, beside tracks that might never be laid. Like many another Western pioneer, he had heard the clock of history strike, and counted the strokes wrong. Hope was always out ahead of fact, possibility obscured the outlines of reality.

The writing is extraordinary. These passages are typical. Susan's letters to Augusta are equally remarkable. There is not one page, not one word in this novel that is superfluous. It's 500 plus pages are filled with energy, beauty, and philosophical contemplation. And I think it so ironic – or is it prophetic – that while this novel was in the process of being published I was hiring Mary who, 44 years later, finds me in the brave new virtual world, and asks me a simple question, "have you read Wallace Stegner's *Angle of Repose*?

Monday, August 12, 2013 **The Orphan Master's Son**

North Korea is an enigma. Only a few months ago the young North Korean leader Kim Jong-un was saber rattling nuclear missiles, threatening not only South Korea, but American bases in the Pacific as well. Bizarrely, at about the same time, basketball celebrity Dennis Rodman visited the country and the new leader (apparently Kim Jong-un likes basketball). Rodman thinks he played peacemaker. How weird to see the heavily tattooed Rodman sitting side by side with the young chubby cheeked dictator.

Did I really want to know more about the circus-like-train-wreck of North Korea? However, the accolades for Adam Johnson's *The Orphan Master's Son* were overwhelming, calling to me. So, I've read it and can understand why it deservedly won the Pulitzer Prize for Literature last year.

This is a compelling novel, such a good story, and so well written. But can life in North Korea really be as Johnson writes? While no one can say whether his depiction is accurate, it is fiction, and it succeeds as an allegory of universal themes.

At times episodic, with shifts in time and voice, mixing the 3rd person narrative of Jun Du AKA Commander Ga, and the 1st person narrative of an interrogator who is dedicated to extracting the "truth" from his interreges by writing their biographies (vs. the brute torture inflicted by the "Pubyok"). Interspersed are propaganda broadcasts which surreally move the story further along. The entire narrative ultimately revolves around the caprice of "The Dear Leader," Kim Jong II, (Kim Jong-il, the father of the present leader) who is the ultimate Orphan Master of an entire nation.

One can only describe the action as an extended nightmare, following the narrative down a rabbit hole into a totalitarian state whose underpinning is brainwashing; its people expecting no more than a life that would seem like Dante's *Inferno* to any westerner. The book makes normalcy of brutality and propaganda, portraying a society where insanity is sanity. In fact, I was constantly thinking of my college psychology professor, Gustave Gilbert, who wrote *The Nuremberg Diary,* and had interviewed all the major Nazi figures who were put on trial there, and came to the conclusion that as they were raised in a culture where deference to authority took precedence over all, their actions would not be considered "insane" in such a society. I also couldn't help but think of another WWII allusion, a work of fiction though, Jerzy Kosiński's *The Painted Bird*, chronicling the horror witnessed by a young boy, who was considered a Jewish stray, during the War.

And similarly, this is a coming-of-age story of Jun Du (or, as some have aptly noted, a "John Doe") who, although the son of a man who ran the "Long Tomorrows" orphanage, is raised as an orphan himself, as his beautiful mother, an opera singer, had been shipped off to Pyongyang for the amusement of the New Class, as is so often the fate of beautiful women in that State. From helping to run the orphanage (his father was frequently drunk), he "graduates" to "tunneler" – working in the dark in tunnels under the DMZ to kidnap South Koreans and then Japanese by boat. He further graduates to study English and becomes a radio surveillance 3rd mate on a North Korean fishing ship, reporting English conversations for reasons unknown. One of those conversations is of two American women rowing across the ocean, one of which figures later in the novel.

Our hero finally metamorphoses into Commander Ga, a hero of the State (and the reader is more than eager to suspend disbelief of this change) as this page turning novel becomes a thriller of the first order. He is united with Commander Ga's wife, Sun Moon who is the State's movie actress, a favorite of "The Dear Leader." From there, all of the main characters in the novel converge, even Sun Moon and the American rower, the propaganda speakers announcing: *Citizens! Observe the hospitality our Dear Leader shows for all peoples of the world, even a subject of the despotic United States. Does the Dear Leader not dispatch our nations' best woman to give solace and support to the wayward American? And does Sun Moon not find the Girl Rower housed in a beautiful room, fresh and white and brightly lit, with a pretty little window affording a view of a lovely North Korean meadow and the dappled horses that frolic there? This is not dingy China or soiled little South Korea, so do not picture some sort of a prison cell with lamp-blacked walls and rust-colored puddles on the floor. Instead, notice the large white tub fitted with golden lion's feet and filled with the steaming restorative water of the Taedong.*

Contrast that Halcyon scene with the reality of our hero's imprisonment: *In Prison 33, little by little, you relinquished everything, starting with your tomorrows and all that might be. Next went your past, and suddenly it was inconceivable that your head had ever touched a pillow, that you'd once used a spoon or a toilet, that your mouth had once known flavors and your eyes had beheld colors beyond gray and brown and the shade of black that blood took on. Before you relinquished yourself – Ga had felt it starting, like the numb of cold limbs – you let go of all the others, each person you'd once known. They became ideas and then notions and then impressions, and then they were as ghostly as projections against a prison infirmary.*

It is a love story as well, and it is the cry for individualism in a totalitarian state. The nameless interrogator's final dreamlike thoughts express it best: *I was on my own voyage. Soon I would be in a rural village, green and peaceful, where people swung their scythes in silence. There would be a widow there, and we would waste no time on courtship. I would approach her and tell her I was her new husband. We would enter the bed from opposite sides at first. For a while, she would have rules. But eventually, our genitals would intercourse in a way that was correct and satisfying. At night, after I had made my emission, we would lie there, listening to the sounds of our children running in the dark, catching summer frogs. My wife would have the use of both her eyes, so she would know when I blew out the candle. In this village, I would have a name, and people would call me by it. When the candle went out, she would speak to me, telling me to sleep very, very deeply...I listened for her voice, calling a name that would soon be mine.*

Adam Johnson has written an epic novel, one that required research and a colossal imagination. Sign me up for his next work!

Tuesday, August 27, 2013 **It's a Wrap**

Hard to believe our summer on the boat is drawing to a close. Next week we'll be on our way to Budapest to begin a river cruise that will take us on the Danube, the Main, and the Rhine, through five countries and many medieval towns and villages.

Our clearing off and packing up signals the end of our boating season here, leaving old friends, the Boat Club we're active in, and neighborhoods that are ingrained in our sub-consciousness. Compounding a sense of sadness was our attendance at two funerals this summer to say farewell to old boating friends, both our age.

I did not read as much as I would have liked during our relatively brief stay here. But in addition to *The Orphan Master* which I described in the previous entry, I recently read and thoroughly enjoyed Tom Wolfe's *The Right Stuff*. It reads like a suspense novel and Wolfe makes you feel as if you are right there. It mostly covers the original Mercury 7 Astronauts' training and launches, but against the background of the Cold War of the late 50s and 1960s, a period I remember so well, but never fully realizing the extent to which it drove the space program. The book begins though with Chuck Yeager's breaking the sound barrier and fittingly ends with Chuck Yeager's

last test flight, the point being that unlike the Mercury 7, Yeager flew a rocket as a pilot. Wolfe's description of Yeager's last test flight is unforgettable, and provides a strong incentive for reading the book. He captures the essence and the meaning of Mercury 7 and defines the intangible, "the right stuff:" ....
Next to Gagarin's orbital flight, Shepard's little mortar lob to Bermuda, with its mere five minutes of weightlessness, was no great accomplishment. But that didn't matter. The flight had unfolded like a drama, the first drama of single combat in American History. Shepard had been the tiny under-dog, sitting on top of an American rocket – and our rockets always blow up – challenging the omnipotent Soviet Integral. The fact that the entire thing had been televised, starting a good two hours before the lift-off, had generated the most feverish suspense. And then he had gone through with it. He let them light the fuse. He hadn't resigned. He hadn't even panicked. He handled himself perfectly. He was as great a daredevil as Lindbergh, and he was purer: he did it all for his country. Here was a man.....with the right stuff. No one spoke the phrase – but every man could feel the rays from that righteous aura and that primal force, the power of physical cour-age and manly honor.

The program and the book culminate with John Glenn's first orbital flight. The adoration of the man knew no bounds and his parade with the other Mercury 7 down Broadway brought even the city of steel and concrete to its knees: ....*And what was it that had moved them all so deeply? It was not a subject you could discuss, but the seven of them knew what it was, and so did most of their wives. Or they knew about part of it. They knew it had to do with presence, the aura, the radia-tion of the right stuff, the same vital force of manhood that had made millions vibrate and resonate thirty five years before to Lindbergh – except that in this case it was heightened by Cold War patriotism, the greatest surge of patriotism since the Second World War....But what the multitudes showed John Glenn and the rest of them on that day was some-thing else. They anointed them with the primordial tears that the right stuff commanded....Somehow, extraordinary as it was, it was...right! The way it should be! The unutterable aura of the right stuff had been brought onto the terrain where things were happening! Perhaps that was what New York existed for, to celebrate those who had it, whatever it was, and there was nothing like the right stuff, for all responded to it, and all wanted to be near it and to feel the sizzle and to blink in the light...Oh, it was a primitive and profound thing! Only pilots truly had it, but the entire world responded, and no one knew its name!*

I also reread Philip Roth's *Goodbye, Columbus* (merely 50 years since the last time). It was a very different experience reading the book now as a septuagenarian. I see Roth as a young colt writing this novella, exploring themes that would develop over the next fifty plus years, with clear signs of the literary thoroughbred he would become. Certainly the work foreshadows my favorite Roth work, *American Pastoral.* Nonetheless, it was somewhat painful reading his youthful work, bringing up issues of my own formative years that were submerged long ago, ones I was hardly conscious of when I first read the book, crazy families' impact on their children, the first real romantic love, and youth's obliviousness that old age would one day arrive. And true to Roth, is a very funny work as well.

The title symbolizes the soon-to-be-lost youth of Brenda's brother, as he is about to be married (like me, at an early age), but still a boy, dreaming of his basketball days at Ohio State, listening to an old radio broadcast of the big game which begins: "The place, the banks of the Oentangy." My friend Bruce and I spent part of the summer at Ohio State University in Columbus as representatives to the National Student Association from our university. It was a different world from New York, indeed, but we, like the youth of Roth's first major work, were ready to be swept along into the stream of life as if it were endless.

The 1984 *Paris Review* carried a remarkable interview with Roth. The interview is a treatise on his process of writing, and I was fascinated by how "fake biography" enters his art, using the analogy of the art of the ventriloquist. As such, Roth himself is omnipresent in his works: ....*Making fake biography, false history, concocting a half-imaginary existence out of the actual drama of my life is my life. There has to be some pleasure in this job, and that's it. To go around in disguise. To act a character. To pass oneself off as what one is not. To pretend. The sly and cunning masquerade. Think of the ventriloquist. He speaks so that his voice appears to proceed from someone at a distance from himself. But if he weren't in your line of vision you'd get no pleasure from his art at all. His art consists of being present and absent; he's most himself by simultaneously being someone else, neither of whom he "is" once the curtain is down. You don't necessarily, as a writer, have to abandon your biography completely to engage in an act of impersonation. It may be more intriguing when you don't. You distort it, caricature it, parody it, you torture and subvert it, you exploit it—all to give the biography that dimension that will excite your verbal life. Millions of people do this all the time, of course, and not with the justification of making literature. They mean it. It's amazing what lies people can sustain behind the mask of their real faces. Think of the art of the adulterer: under tremendous pressure and against enormous odds, ordinary husbands and wives, who would freeze with self-consciousness up on a stage, yet in the theater of the home, alone before the audience of the betrayed spouse, they act out roles of innocence and fidelity with flawless dramatic skill.*

Great, great performances, conceived with genius down to the smallest particulars, impeccably meticulous naturalistic acting, and all done by rank amateurs. People beautifully pretending to be "themselves." Make-believe can take the subtlest forms, you know. Why should a novelist, a pretender by profession, be any less deft or more reliable than a stolid, unimaginative suburban accountant cheating on his wife?

Tuesday, October 15, 2013 "The Master" and" Mistler's Exit"

One of my favorite pastimes on board any vessel is to read some good books. Alas, a river cruise is such an active one, reading time was limited, but between various ports, I managed to read two novels by familiar authors. They were purposely selected for the trip because I admire their fine work and they share Europe as their geographic focal point.

First, I enjoyed *The Master* by Colm Tóibín, and a hat tip to my son, Chris, for sending it to me after he had read it. Chris is a writer of sorts, and this is a writer's book, an interior exploration about how one's life experiences subliminally enter the writing process.

The Master is in fact a highly fictionalized account of Henry James' life during the last decade of the 19th century. Born into a family of wealth and intellect, Henry essentially becomes condemned to a life of inner loneliness, although he was well traveled and had family and friends. Tóibín shows the subtle absorption of those relationships into James' fiction, particularly his sister Alice, his attraction to Minny Temple, his cousin, and later, to a relative of James Fenimore Cooper, Constance Fenimore Woulson (all three of these women die during his lifetime, Constance by suicide). But James' life was one of sexual ambivalence -- as he was equally attracted to three men. There is Hammond (a manservant), Oliver Wendell Homes (after he had returned from the Civil War), and Hendrik Andersen (a sculptor). Tóibín walks the line as many historians do -- that perhaps James was "hopelessly celibate" (as James described himself in one of his own letters).

These relationships, as well as his travels -- to America and throughout Europe, are incorporated into his fiction, and Tóibín imagines how and why in this spellbinding novel, so exacting in its prose. As an example, here is what he writes when Alice dies: *Alice was dead now, Aunt Kate was in her grave, the parents who noticed nothing also lay inert under the ground, and William was miles away in his own world, where he would stay. And there was silence now in Kensington, not a sound in the house, except the sound, like a vague cry in the distance, of his own great solitude, and his memory working like grief, the past coming to him with its arm outstretched looking for comfort.*

In many ways, *The Master* shares some of the characteristics of the next novel I managed to finish during the trip, *Mistler's Exit*. This is also a tale of loneliness, written by one of America's most unique novelists, Louis Begley. I say "unique" as here is a novelist, a very fine writer, who came to his craft decades after being a renowned international attorney, an unusual path for a writer (although ironically Henry James attended Harvard Law School -- as did Begley --, but for only a year as James had no intentions of becoming a lawyer). And I say "loneliness" as the protagonist's sense of solitude is suddenly self-imposed after he receives the diagnosis of inoperable cancer and decides to make a clandestine visit to Venice for a week, keeping the reason for the visit from his wife and only son, in order to take in the city one last time and to think about how to break the news to his family. Instead, he is followed by a young female photojournalist with whom he has intense sex in Venice, although he remains emotionally removed from it. Characters come and go, old acquaintances, including a girl he loved in college, but never slept with at the time. He would like to do so now, but "this time he would not cheat," a double meaning in the word.

Thomas Mistler was born into a privileged family, his father a successful banker, but Mistler charts his own course, breaking from his father's expectations of a successor and instead builds an international advertising business. Begley writes with an eruditeness that is only rivaled by his classmate in Harvard, John Updike, unique in American literature where the norm is great writing often coming from authors not nearly as well educated.

It is a fine introduction to Begley's style, very reminiscent of the "Schmidt" trilogy. In fact, sometimes I thought of Mistler as "Schmidtie."

The epigraph to the novel, taken from Jacques Chardonne's *Demi-Jour*, makes a fitting ending to this entry, a reminder to live every moment as one's last and how meaningless "things" are in one's life.

Too bad about what men will lose; they'll never notice it. Everything ends well because everything ends.

Monday, October 28, 2013 **Nowhere**

Part Franz Kafka, part Woody Allen, and throw in a touch of Mickey Spillane, unlike any book I've read in a long time, *Nowhere* by Thomas Berger is a dystopian view of the "future" which, as it was written in 1985, might as well be now. It's about a second-rate gumshoe (he's no Mike Hammer), who aspires to be a playwright, but never seems to get the second act done, who slides down a rabbit hole into the "Kingdom" of Saint Sebastian, ostensibly on "assignment" by the US Government to find out something about the little Kingdom, its monarch, Prince Sebastian XXIII. It is a little like the country of "Duchy of Grand Fenwick" in *The Mouse That Roared*, one of my favorite films about the Cold War, but far more bizarre.

Things appear to be topsy-turvy in the Kingdom, but are they? Children are formally educated by being forced to watch take-offs of old Hollywood movies, Blonds are second class citizens and in fact are "obliged to have sexual relations with anyone who asks them," and although "condemned to menial work, waiting on tables, pulling rickshaws, they also "practice law (people can be severely punished for rudeness) and certain other professions that are more or less honorific elsewhere" As Russel Wren, our protagonist comments, *and it should be noted that the Blonds are splendid physical specimens, tall and strong and comely, unlike any other oppressed people on record.*

There is a "government" which functions like a parody of *Alice In Wonderland,* where "official scholars" maintain an encyclopedia for the land which no one reads as it is completely idiosyncratic, and hopelessly out of date. Lawmakers are hard to be found or are completely ineffectual. And our Prince is a corpulent over-eater, who encourages sodomy throughout the land, but one who is also considered by the people (that is, the non-Blonds) to be benevolent. No wonder, there is unlimited credit in the country.

Our perplexed gumshoe has an interesting exchange with a clerk concerning credit and economics at the Sebastian cable office (whether and where cables go is unclear):

It would be a profession of lack of faith in one's countrymen. No crime could be more heinous. Every Sebastianer has a God-given right to be owed money by others. Only in this way does he establish the moral pretext for running up his own large debts. Else our economy would collapse.

As it is in part a "mystery" novel, I'll not let on about the final resolution, but, hint, there is a Sebastiani Liberation group -- one of the reasons Wren is thrown into the rabbit hole in the first place. Blond Olga, who Wren first meets as a stewardess on the Sebastiani Royal Airline, is connected to the group, explaining to Wren *Foreigners sometimes do not understand our vays. Ve do not have to screw under every circumstance*, just a little foreshadowing.

Written in 1985, Berger's book is one to be read today and to be pondered, and to be enjoyed for its ironic, satiric sense of humor.

Sunday, November 3, 2013 **Ella Minnow Pea**
Say it quickly as in "LMNOP."

My wife said I should read this book as it's "charming." Charming? I want to read a charming book? But she also added that it has its dark moments. OK, why didn't you say "dark" in the first place, bring it on (I was between reading materials anyhow)!

Well, she was right on both counts. First it appealed to me right out of the gate as it is an epistolary novel, a favorite form of mine, with Helene Hanff's *84, Charing Cross Road* being the best of the lot. I had also read the more recent *The Guernsey Literary and Potato Peel Pie Society* by Mary Ann Shaffer and Annie Barrows which I would definitely put in the "charming" category.

Ella Minnow Pea by Mark Dunn though is in a league of its own. It is first and foremost homage to the English language and a subtle statement about its disintegration -- or even increasing irrelevancy (thanks to our substandard educational system and the onslaught of mass media). It almost reads as a word game.

It's my second straight read about a fabled place (Saint Sebastian being the other one), in this case Nollop, "an autonomous island nation 23 miles southeast of Charleston, SC." In the 19th century it instituted a "monastic devotion to liberal arts education and scholarship, effectively elevating language to a national art form." The nation was renamed Nollop to honor its "native son, Nevin Nollop, the author of the popular pangram sentence *The quick brown fox jumps over the lazy dog*".

Imagine, a peaceful, harmonic small nation which puts language first, and modern technology second. A cenotaph was erected at the center of town, with tiles of that pangram at top to honor Nevin Nollop, who, over the years, became almost a deity. All was well for years. But the "High Council" -- heretofore a compassionate though bureaucratic government of the island -- elevated Nollop to God himself when the masonry holding the letter "Z" crumbled and the letter fell to the ground. The Council chose to interpret this as Nollop's message from beyond the grave that the letter "Z" was to be banned from all speech and written communication, with severe penalties, even death or expulsion from the island by the third offense.

So already, the novel is setting up one of its themes, scientific reasoning vs. religion (the aging of the masonry, the true reason behind the falling tile vs. man's never ending quest to find an explanation for the unknown through religious fanaticism).

As more tiles descend, the consequences for the residents of Nollop become more complicated and severe, having to delete now a continuing barrage of the alphabet when they speak or write, with their correspondence now being confiscated and inspected prior to delivery. The Council becomes more dictatorial, instituting totalitarian government to ensure all citizens worship the dictums of the great Nollop from beyond the grave, even seizing private land to erect a church in his name.

There are some very funny moments in the novel, and some very sad ones. There are themes such as the role of chance in life, and how one neighbor can turn on the other and then eventually seek forgiveness and receive compassion.

And it is all comported in correspondence that becomes increasingly difficult to write as more letters continue to fall to the ground with increasing frequency. There is even some talk of going to a roman numeral form of communication, but, by that time, most of the townspeople have already been banished or worse.

Mark Dunn, who is a playwright by trade, has used all his dramatic skills and his love of language to write this work, such a delight to read as he too obeys the will of the almighty Nollop High Council in writing these epistles that are more and more difficult to discern, but still readable. Sometimes, they reminded me of the ubiquitous ad on the NY Subways systems in the 1960's that read something like this: "if u cn rd ths, u cn lrn spdwrtg."

If you read LMNOP (i.e. *Ella Minnow Pea*), you will not put this down as our young heroine Ella tirelessly works on "Enterprise 32," a pangram that promises to end the whole debacle.

Wednesday, January 1, 2014 **Another New Year. Another Day....**
....Another Hour. Another Minute. Who's counting?

I've been trying to "catch up" with my reading before the New Year and I recently finished two books, both unlikely reads for me, the first recommended by my son, Jonathan, and the second by my friend Emily. These novels, in an odd way, invite comparison, although they are as different as night and day.

Unfortunately, I read *The Fault in Our Stars* on an old version of the Kindle, one that used to be Jonathan's and so he lent me the "book" on that device. It was the first book I have ever read in that manner and it proved to be the frustrating experience I once imagined -- as I was not able to easily make notes for later review (although I understand that this is now a cinch in later versions of the Kindle) and if I accidentally pushed the wrong button, the screen reverted to the beginning and I had to find my place over again (luckily, the book isn't very long).

It's classified as a Young Adult novel so I wondered what business I had reading it, but it had a profound effect on me -- as the protagonist is a cancer victim and has trouble breathing, dragging around one of those oxygen canisters, something she simply accepts. It covers the subject of living one's life and dealing with one's death, not to mention the suffering cancer victims must endure. I'm probably the last person on earth to hear of its author, John Green, but he is one hell of a writer. He reminds me of Jonathan Tropper, but with something more profound to say.

Hazel and Augustus (Gus) are two teenage cancer victims, who meet in a cancer support group and fall in love. It (surprisingly) is not maudlin, and the level of the writing and the philosophical themes examined about the nature of life and death, make this a novel suitable for adult consumption and contemplation. And it is the kind of novel that just breezes along, almost impossible to put down, the reader forming a real emotional attachment to the main characters.

Hazel longs to know more about a novel she has read and is mystified by "An Imperial Affliction" written by an author, Peter van Houten, who lives in Amsterdam and has set his story there. Houten's novel is about a girl dying of cancer and so the implications for Hazel are clear; however the novel has a sudden ending, rather like life itself, without ever revealing what happens to the characters. This naturally leaves Hazel in a bind, but thanks to the equivalent of a "last wish" foundation, Hazel and Gus are cleared to travel to Amsterdam to actually meet Houten himself and try to discover the true outcome. And as often happens in real life, they are disappointed to learn that Houten is a hopeless alcoholic recluse but it is there where Hazel and Gus consummate their love.

The writing is exquisite at times, Gus writing about Hazel in a letter: *She walks lightly upon the earth. Hazel knows the truth: We're as likely to hurt the universe as we are to help it, and we're not likely to do either.*

The ending is, as you might imagine, heart-wrenching, but it is surprising, and to go any further here would be to reveal spoilers. I loved reading this book (which not surprisingly is now being made into a movie).

Contrast that to the novel I just finished, *Emma Who Saved my Life* by Wilton Barnhardt, a coming of age story narrated by the protagonist, Gil Freeman, who leaves his home town in Illinois to become an actor in NYC in the 1970's, moving in with two women who have artistic aspirations themselves. As he says in retrospect, *I can't quite retrieve the young man with all that faith -- where did he get that energy? Didn't he know the odds against being an actor -- or Emma being a poet, or Lisa being a painter? How did he have so much faith in the world? No, it wasn't all stupidity and it wasn't all innocence and youth. I think New York was there too, egging us on.*

Indeed, New York City is the other major "character" in the novel, and Barnhardt covers all of the city, boroughs included, so for me, it was a nostalgic tour, having lived in Manhattan, Queens, and Brooklyn. The novel is as much a love song to NYC as it is a story about the characters, and of the times, each chapter representing a year in the life of the characters, starting with 1974 and ending with 1983. As such it spans the political spectrum from Nixon, to Ford, to Carter, to Reagan, not to mention the changing mores of the times, drugs, sexual liberation, etc. Reading the novel was like reliving the times and it's hard to believe that this was Barnhardt's first novel. I think of influences such as Joseph Heller and J. D. Salinger for some of its humor -- and in parts it is a very funny novel.

But while Hazel and Gus consummate their love, Gil's love for Emma (and it is that love which "saves" his life) essentially goes unrequited (you'll have to read the novel to the very end to understand why I qualify the issue). And while we root for Hazel and Gus, Barnhardt's characters are totally self indulgent and if they ever had to deal with Hazel and Gus' issues, they'd have a hard time.

Although Gil does become an actor and finally makes it to Broadway, he learns that like so many actors he is really mediocre, and he learns it the hard way, first by playing opposite an actress who was once a film star and has come to Broadway, a Rosemary Campbell, to the delight of her adoring fans, Gil knowing that she is a facade of an actress, commenting,

I always wondered if Rosemary knew who the president was, or what year it was, or if World War II was over. Her world had no connection to fact or modern life or normalness or strife and conflict of any kind. One could fantasize about her limo getting hijacked to the South Bronx and her getting turned out somewhere along Southern Boulevard to walk back to the East Side (although with her charmed life she might well have walked back without incident). Scary thing, this kind of insularity that happens with American presidents so they don't even know what's happening and what everyone is thinking, and American pop stars in their own little fantasy worlds-god, the cossetings, the emoluments, the unsparing and unceasing effort not to contradict the SUCCESS, these crazy Howard Hughes worlds of yes men and twenty personal bodyguard-staff -people scurrying about to make sure you never have to soil your hand with opening a door or taking a cap off a pen. I guess you live in that nonsense long enough and you too can be Rosemary Campbell with all the dimension and scope of a touched-up airbrush '30s movie still.

And the real truth about his acting is revealed to Gil with another big role, a leading one, but off Broadway, opposite a Reisa Goldbaum:

But, I'm telling you, it's truly difficult to leave the stage. For so long people ask, friends call up: What are you up to? And you tell them I'm mad this week because I'm Hamlet, or I'm drunk and homosexual this week because I'm Brick in Cat on a Hot Tin Roof, and next month I'll be nobody at all in an evening of Beckett pieces. Then one day you put all those people away, all the masks, all the gestures and reserves of carefully processed emotion, and people ask you what role are you working on this month ... and for once it's your own life, the hardest role of the bunch. You gotta say the lines with a straight face. I was not a great actor. For me acting was pretending I was someone; learn the accent, develop a little shtick, put on the makeup, use every trick I knew and half the time you'd believe I was who I said I was. But you look at a Reisa Goldbaum, someone with a natural gift, and you see that she can reach down into a deep and rich humanity and draw up a true-to-life Williams heroine, a Greek tragic figure, an Ophelia, a Neil Simon one-liner queen. I put on the trappings, she had it in her heart. There was only one role in my heart, only one in my repertoire that could draw upon everything I had, only one I could pull off, in New York or goddam Peoria: myself.

But ultimately, it's the city itself that overpowers Gil:

Emma, you and your poetry, me and my acting-what are we trying to do? We can't top this city. We poor would-be artists can't compete with or improve on the rich density of human experience on any random, average, slow summer night in New York-who are we trying to kid? In the overheard conversation in the elevator, in the five minutes of talk the panhandler gives you before hitting you for the handout, in the brief give-and-take when you are going out and the cleaning lady is coming in-there are the real stories, incredible, heart-breaking and ridiculous, there are the command performances, the Great American Novels but forever unwritten, untoppable, and so beautifully unaware.

Finally, Gil exits from NY with the realization: *Don't get me wrong, there's a lot to be said for the American Dream. But you wake up from Dreams.* Emma goes her way and so does Lisa (who sells out to marriage much earlier in the novel and is yuppiefied).

As a first novel, it is an admirable piece of work, another "can't be put down" page turner, and in the case of this edition, a real hardcover book (not a Kindle -- one of the reasons I can quote extensively from it with ease to demonstrate Barnhardt's writing). Plus, as it was originally published in 1989, there are some nice bookmaking features, the deckled edges, headbands and footbands, the three piece binding, but, best of all, endpapers photographed by Jerry Speier and hand-colored by Doris Borowsky. You can't get these attributes on a Kindle.

Thursday, January 9, 2014 **Russo's Elsewhere**

Richard Russo's *Elsewhere* is a painfully honest memoir. It is lovingly detailed. It appears that we have some shared family history, his novels focusing on many similar issues particularly his relationship with his mother, the theme of *Elsewhere*.

Russo's writings seem to come closest to my own family angst, and *Elsewhere* hits my funny bone as well and reveals the roots of his fictional world. Russo almost had an approach-avoidance issue with his mother who on the one hand he tried to keep at whatever distance he could (without much success), for the sake of his individuality and for the sake of his family, but, on the other, obligingly (and lovingly), took responsibility for, particularly as she aged.

When Russo was a young child, his mother worked for GE in Schenectady, living with Russo's grandparents in Gloversville and commuting (after divorcing her ne'er-do-well husband - the kind portrayed in Russo's *Nobody's Fool* and *The Risk Pool*), asserting her independence by paying her parents rent.

During WW II, when my father was away at the front, my own mother worked for Atlantic Burners (a local heating oil distribution company) in Queens, NY as a secretary/administrative assistant and for years I would hear about how much she missed being a professional woman. We too lived with her parents at the time, with my primary care being passed onto my grandmother and great-grandmother, who lived with us as well.

Russo details the decline of the leather business, it's impact on his home town, Gloversville, and his family, a story eerily close to Philip Roth's family's leather business, and the decline of Newark, as told in his novel *American Pastoral*. These were generations of families in the same business, as mine was in the photography business for more than 100 years, and, that kind of business too changed to such an extent that it eventually just faded away.

I was amused by Russo's statement" *my mother did love mirrors, often practicing in front of them.* My mother too liked to pose and preen in front of mirrors, painstakingly putting on her make-up. In fact, she was very caught up in her appearance and good looks. She knew she attracted men, something that infuriated my father at times.

But from there, Russo's relationship with his mother, and me with mine, diverge greatly, mostly because, unlike Russo's parents, my parents stayed married (when they should have been divorced) and I was not an only child.

Russo reveals a devotion of a saint toward his mother, who had declared, basically that it was he and she against the world, making him promise (as a child) to always look out for one another, almost as if he were her spouse, not her son. Even in later years, after Russo had married (his wife, Barbara, another saint as well) and had daughters of his own, she reminded him of their "pledge" to one another:

One of my mother's most cherished convictions was that back on Helwig Street - she and I had pledged an oath, each to the other. She and I would stand together against whatever configuration the world's opposition took - her parents, my father, Gloversville, monetary setbacks. Now, forty-some years later, I was a grown man with a wife and kids, but this original bond, she believed, was still in force. However fond she was of Barbara, however much she loved her granddaughters, none of that altered our original contract, which to her way of thinking made us indivisible. She'd never really considered us two separate people but rather one entity, oddly cleaved by time and gender, like fraternal twins somehow born twenty-five years apart, destined in some strange way to share a common destiny.

His dissection of her motives, self defense mechanisms, lack of friendships, and dependency on him demonstrates that great writers are great psychologists. Later he learns that his father's offhand foreboding that "she's crazy" had some grounding in that she was OCD.

Still, his mother taught him to persevere (although never understanding why he would want to be a writer with his fine academic credentials that would assuredly lead to a tenured, secure position). He even chose lower paying positions. teaching less, to pursue his writing objectives, not succeeding at first, sort of like when I decided to go into publishing rather than into a more lucrative insurance underwriting position (at the time), as well as choosing not to go into my father's business

Long after she returned to Gloversville from Tucson, I began a decade-long academic nomadship during which I jumped from job to job, trying to teach and be a writer at the same time. For a while, after our daughters came along, we were even poorer than we'd been as graduate students. And I was a bad boy. Caring not a whit about tenure and promotion, thumbed my nose at the advice of department chairs about what I needed to do to succeed in the university. I left jobs for other jobs that paid less but offered more time out of the classroom, In the summer, when many of my colleagues taught extra classes, I wrote stories and spent money we didn't have on postage to submit them to magazines. I wrote manically, obsessively, but also, for a time, not very well. I wrote about crime and cities and women and other things I knew very little about in a language very different from my own natural voice, which explained why the editors weren't much interested.

Later in life Russo finds that voice, and a discipline, and has an epiphany one day as he is looking at the books and periodical articles he had published -- that his writing was the result of an obsessive personality, like his mother's ...

The biggest difference between my mother and me, I now saw clearly, had less to do with either nature or nurture than with blind dumb luck, the third and often lethal rail of human destiny. My next obsession might well have been a woman, or a narcotic, a bottle of tequila. Instead I'd stumbled on storytelling and become infected.

It didn't take long for me to learn that novel writing was a line of work that suited my temperament and played to my strengths, such as they were. Because - and don't let anybody tell you different - novel writing is mostly triage (this now, that later) and obstinacy. Feeling your way around in the dark, trying to anticipate the Law of Unintended Consequences. Living with and welcoming uncertainty. Trying something, and when that doesn't

work, trying something else. Welcoming clutter. Surrendering a good idea
for a better one. Knowing you won't find the finish line for a year or two,
or five, or maybe never, without caring much. Putting one foot in front of
the other. Taking small bites, chewing thoroughly. Grinding it out knowing
that when you've finally settled everything that can be, you'll immediately
seek out more chaos. Rinse and repeat. Somehow, without ever intend-
ing to, I'd discovered how to turn obsession and what my grandmother
used to call sheer cussedness - character traits that had dogged both my
parents, causing them no end of difficulty - to my advantage. The same
qualities that over a lifetime had contracted my mother's world had some-
how expanded mine. How and by what mechanism? Dumb luck? Grace? I
honestly have no idea. Call it whatever you want - except virtue.

It's a writer's astute introspective view of what writing is all about. And
how one's upbringing and genes ebb and flow in his fiction.

His mother passed on a love of reading, and as Russo says, you can't be
a writer without first being a reader. My own childhood was spent bereft of
books and I can't remember my parents reading other than the occasional
potboiler.

Russo was looking at his mother's book collection during one of her
many, many moves, all of which Russo was left the responsibility for engineering, commenting...

Still, illuminating though literary taste can be, the more I thought about
it, neither my mother's library nor my own meant quite what I wanted it to.
If my books were more serious and literary than hers, that was due more to
nurture than nature. If I didn't read much escapist fiction, it was because
I lived a blessed life from which I neither needed nor desired to escape. I
wasn't a superior person, just an educated one, and for that in a large mea-
sure I had my mother to thank. Maybe she'd tried to talk me out of becom-
ing a writer, but she was more responsible than anyone for my being one....
You can't make a writer without first making a reader, and that's what my
mother made me

I can't help but think of Pat Conroy's *My Reading Life* also memoir in which
his mother plays a central role in Conroy's love of reading and then writing.
There are so many similarities, including their mothers' shared love of the same
novel, *Gone With the Wind*.

I had a dream after I had read *Elsewhere*, during the early morning
hours when I can at least remember a snippet of what I dream. I was sitting with Richard Russo's son (he has only daughters), and I mentioned to
him that I would like to meet his father, something I didn't feel daunted
about (as I felt the one time I might have had the opportunity to meet John
Updike). That little boy I was talking to in the dream was obviously me, and
as I talked to him, I gradually woke up with a sense of sadness overcoming

me, for the lost opportunity, wanting to ask my mother one last question: Why, Mom?

But Russo's childhood was far from "ideal" as well (is there such a childhood?), such a burden -- the "pledge" his mother made him take as a child. And yet, he is one of our finest storytellers today. Richard Russo, thank you for sharing your story with us, for your honesty, and for being the writer you've become. *You were a good son.*

Thursday, January 23, 2014 Compare and Contrast

Two recently read novels were as unlike as they were alike, I know a confusing contradiction. If I was an English teacher I would assign them for the classic compare and contrast assignment. Julian Barnes' Booker-winning novella, *The Sense of an Ending* is about the meaning of memory in one's life (or how we prefer to remember things, or how the gaps in our memory are as significant as those moments we remember) whereas Louis Begley's *Shipwreck*, is about an unidentified narrator who is approached by a stranger who over the course of three days confides a story of exacting detail, with the impeccable memory of an observant writer (who is indeed the stranger). In a sense, they both have elements of mystery novels, with endings that leave as many questions as answers.

Each have three major characters, are both first person narratives (although Begley's book is "told" through the unidentified narrator), with the introspective view of character driven novels. They are each concerned with the unexamined life, anxieties of self doubt, Begley's set in a middle age crisis while Barnes' is looking back from the perspective of a retired protagonist. Begley's novel has many erotic elements while the sexuality of Barnes' novel is one of sexual frustration, the young woman who latches onto Begley's protagonist bordering on nymphomania while Barnes protagonist's main love interest is completely repressed. And we all like to see a little bit of ourselves in what we read, with both protagonists expressing parts of my own, such as Tony in Barnes' book, *I had wanted life not to bother me too much.* (Playing it safe in one's personal life and career.) And, like John in Begley's novel, *I'm no good at joining groups and rather proud of my misanthropy.* Both lines resonate.

Barnes' book, as a novella, is a fast and engaging read. An English writer of a number of novels and short stories, Barnes was somewhat of a departure for me. Perhaps it is the "Downton Abbey influence" that has awakened a long dormant interest in English writers. Thomas Hardy and Charles Dickens were among my earlier reading interests. I need to go back to them. Most recently, I've been drawn to Ian McEwan's work but I had heard much about Barnes, so why not start with a Booker Prize winning novel?

The three main characters in the novel are the narrator/protagonist, Tony (who is now divorced and retired), Veronica, perhaps the love of his life (or perhaps not?) when he was in school, and Adrian, a brilliant school-mate who commits suicide later in life. Along with two other friends, we are treated to a description of English school life of the 60s, and Tony's obses-sion with Veronica which culminates in one dry hump and Tony mastur-bating while visiting Veronica at her parents' house. Meanwhile, Veronica finally pairs off with the intellectually gifted Adrian, leaving Tony bereft. Later, we learn that he wrote a letter to Adrian, about Veronica (and more -- don't want to reveal any spoilers), a letter he has completely forgotten until some forty years later, and his complicity in a series of events that may (or may not?) have led to Adrian's suicide, Veronica's unhappiness (although that seems to be her natural state), and an institutionalized (now adult) child (there are interpretations of whose child it might be; I have mine, not to be revealed here). The letter begins, *Dear Adrian -- or rather Adrian and Veronica (hello, Bitch, and welcome to this letter)* so one can imagine its contents.

But all of this is woven in memory, faulty, unreliable memory. After all, what is memory other than certain significant moments in our life, with great gaps in between? And memories are sometimes stories we tell ourselves about our life -- almost a form of cognitive dissonance -- and perhaps I told some myself. There is certainly large chucks of personal information I've written about, but they are my interpretations of the past, not necessarily the same past as one would have witnessed via a video tape. And, perhaps, the most important memories are the ones I've chosen to forget or not to reveal.

That is why Barnes' novel appeals so much to me. Tony Webster's memo-ries may be self serving, or maybe not: *How often do we tell our own life story? How often do we adjust, embellish, make sly cuts? And the longer life goes on, the fewer are those around to challenge our account, to remind us that our life is not our life, merely the story we have told about our life. Told to others, but -- mainly -- to ourselves.* As Veronica accuses Tony, in the beginning and at the end, an accusation he even considers for his epitaph: "Tony Webster — He Never Got It."

Is what we remember called history or is history the accurate recount-ing of memory? When Tony first meets Adrian Finn at school, he seems to be a shy, introspective boy. The school master is discussing the causes of WW I and puts the question to Finn, *"Finn, you've been quiet. You started this ball rolling. You are, as it were, our Serbian gunman....Would you care to give us the benefit of your thoughts?"* One can only imagine the impact the heretofore unknown Finn had on his schoolmates with the remainder of the exchange (and his answer feeds into the heart of the novel, memory and consequences):

"I don't know, sir."

"What don't you know?"

"Well, in one sense, I can't know what it is that I don't know. That's philosophically self-evident." He left one of those slight pauses in which we again wondered if he was engaged in subtle mockery or a high seriousness beyond the rest of us. *"Indeed, isn't the whole business of ascribing responsibility a kind of cop-out? We want to blame an individual so that everyone else is exculpated. Or we blame a historical process as a way of exonerating individuals. Or it's all anarchic chaos, with the same consequence. It seems to me that there is-was-a chain of individual responsibilities, all of which were necessary, but not so long a chain that everybody can simply blame everyone else. But of course, my desire to ascribe responsibility might be more a reflection of my own cast of mind than a fair analysis of what happened. That's one of the central problems of history, isn't it, sir? The question of subjective versus objective interpretation, the fact that we need to know the history of the historian in order to understand the version that is being put in front of us."*

Once Adrian was long gone, Tony, from the perspective of a senior citizen, ruminates about him and in so doing, the inadequacies of his own life: *From the beginning, he had always seen more clearly than the rest of us. While we luxuriated in the doldrums of adolescence, imagining our routine discontent to be an original response to the human condition, Adrian was already looking farther ahead and wider around. He felt life more clearly too-even, perhaps especially, when he came to decide that it wasn't worth the candle. Compared to him, I had always been a muddler, unable to learn much from the few lessons life provided me with. In my terms, I settled for the realities of life, and submitted to its necessities: if this, then that, and so the years passed. In Adrian's terms, I gave up on life, gave up on examining it, took it as it came.*

Tony had imagined a different kind of retirement (as a retired person myself, I can vouch for the veracity of this observation -- it's profound): *Later on in life, you expect a bit of rest, don't you? You think you deserve it. I did, anyway. But then you begin to understand that the reward of merit is not life's business. Also, when you are young, you think you can predict the likely pains and bleaknesses that age might bring. You imagine yourself being lonely, divorced, widowed; children growing away from you, friends dying. You imagine the loss of status, the loss of desire-and desirability. You may go further and consider your own approaching death, which, despite what company you may muster, can only be faced alone.*

But all this is looking ahead. What you fail to do is look ahead, and then imagine yourself looking back from that future point. Learning the new emotions that time brings. Discovering, for example, that as the witnesses to your life diminish, there is less corroboration, and therefore less certainty, as to what you are or have been. Even if you have assiduously kept records-in words, sound, pictures-you may find that you have attended to the wrong kind of record-keeping.

The novel is not all about looking back though and its ending (or the "sense of an ending") is filled with unanswered questions, intentional vagaries, and with the reader having to make his own interpretations. I found myself rereading the end several times to come up with my own conclusions, perhaps the hallmark of a good mystery novel. Barnes book is well worth reading.

What a change of pace was Begley's *Shipwreck* (an ironic title given I was reading this on board a ship).

Like the old joke goes, a man walks into a bar (the L'Entre Deux Mondes -- which could be anywhere), and then.....Well in this case, it's not a joke, unless you consider three days of story-telling to a stranger in a bar, over innumerable drinks, a preposterous tall story. The man who has walked into the "between two worlds" is the famous author, "John North," going up to a stranger to tell the entire content of the book I was about to read. The stranger is never named, and although he is the "narrator" mostly he is conveying, word for word, what he is hearing from North. He is us, the reader, although he does have a few things to say, especially at the strange initial meeting, describing North as *this man so like me in appearance and demeanor, from the crown of his neatly barbered head to the tips of his brogues, well worn but beautifully polished. Listen, he said. Listen, I will tell you a story I have never told before. If you hear me out, you will see why. I would have been a fool to tell it. With you, somehow I feel secure. Call it instinct or impulse or fate -- your choice.*

And so the story begins, involving three major characters, North, his wife Lydia, and North's dalliance with a young French journalist who he met when she interviewed him for the Paris Vogue magazine, Lea Morini. There are several dimensions to this novel, the story itself of choices made, how North cheats on his wife, who he dearly loves, acknowledges the dangers of his extramarital affair, but is so helpless to end because of, to put it mildly, the incredible sex (mostly in Paris), realizing later in the tale how the walls are closing in on him and what limited choices he has for ending the affair. It's a good tale, and the title of the book foreshadows its conclusion, but, like Barnes' book, it is an ending that leaves some questions. But what really interested me is that North is a writer, so why tell the tale verbally to a stranger?

Begley, who comes to the literary world late in life after a career as an attorney, writes with the lapidary precision of his former profession. And I don't mean this in a negative way as he is a pleasure to read, words chosen carefully and gracefully as well. His novels exude erudition and in my opinion he has become one of the best writers today. His Schmidt trilogy alone makes him a novelist of importance. One could say that *Shipwreck* is somewhat a variation of the Schmidt novels, the older man with the younger woman, but it is much more than that. In particular, Schmidt is an attorney, just like Begley WAS, but North is a writer, just like Begley IS. So the many passages about writing, and a description of the literary scene, held my close attention.

North has written an "important" novel, *The Anthill*, which takes place in Paris, one that is being made into a film, and he is currently working on a new novel, *Loss*. Although an accomplished novelist, he is racked by self-doubt (perhaps like Begley?), questioning whether his writing is REALLY that good. His wonderful, faithful wife, Lydia, is his biggest supporter, but nonetheless, his doubts remain. One has to wonder whether this is universal of all good writers. At one point, North goes to the shelves of his library:

There are things you do only when you are alone. I sauntered over to the shelves reserved for the first editions of my novels and their translations and stroked the familiar spines. Then, as though under a compulsion I was unable to resist, I took down first the new book and later all the others and looked at certain passages. I was to remain in my armchair the whole night and the next day, and most of the night that followed, with hardly any pause, although I suspected that I had a fever. I reread my production. At a certain point, entire sentences I had written seemed to disintegrate like figures in a kaleidoscope when you turn the tube, only my words did not regroup and coalesce as new wonders of color and design. They lay on the page like so many vulgar, odious pieces of shattered glass. The conclusion I reached came down to this: none of my books, neither the new novel nor any I had written before, was very good. Certainly, none possessed the literary merit that critical opinion ascribed to them. Not even my second novel, the one that won all the prizes and was said to confirm my standing as an important novelist. No, they all belonged to the same dreary breed of unneeded books. Novels that are not embarrassingly bad but lead you to wonder why the author had bothered. Unless, of course, he had only a small ambition: to earn a modest sum of money and short-lived renown.......And what should one think of a man who writes such books, he continued, where does he belong if not to the race of trimmers, men who live without infamy and without praise, envious of any other fate?

The self-doubt of the nature and quality of his work is again expressed in the context of the movie that was being made of his award-winning The

Anthill. I found this fascinating as Begley's *About Schmidt* was adapted for the screen, and the movie bore little resemblance to the novel. I wonder what Begley thought about it, how much he might have protested. The novel is much better than the movie and I had to erase the memory of the movie from my mind to read the novel. I could never get the lead, though, Jack Nicholson, out of my head and that's the way I see Schmidtie in my mind's eye. Again, North labors with the anxiety that his work is poor: *The proposition was brutally simple and dreadful to consider: if the books are no good, if they are unnecessary books, then my life, of which I had given up so much in order to write them, had been wasted. What set me off was nothing directly concerning Loss; its progress had been slow, but I was moving along and, from time to time, when I reread and corrected the text I was even amused and surprised. I couldn't imagine where I had gotten some of the stuff I had written down, but I was glad to see it was there. The screen adaptation of The Anthill was the immediate cause. I received from the producer a text he described as the almost final version of the screenplay. According to the contract, I had the right to review it and send in my suggestions, revisions, and so on for his and his colleagues' consideration. Nothing more than that. As drama, the screenplay struck me as pretty good. Certainly, it wouldn't put audiences to sleep. I was distressed, though, by the sentimentality of the story and the main characters. That was certainly not what I had intended, what I remembered writing, and that is not, I made quite sure of it, a defect of the novel, which I very conscientiously reread. But was it not possible that the screenwriter- I knew him and knew he was no fool-had seen through some flaw at the core of my book? Something I had not been conscious of that he had brought to the surface? And there was a touch of vulgarity to the screenplay. Had my book invited it? Or, equally sad, was there such a huge and unsuspected gulf that separated me from most of my readers? I asked Lydia her opinion. She reassured me: there was no such flaw and no such gulf. In that case, was she the only reader who understood me?*

The most introspective passage about writing comes from North when he turns back to his new novel, *Loss,* which he had abandoned for awhile. The process of writing and revision he describes, I bet, comes closest to Begley's own painstaking prose: *The manuscript of Loss was waiting for me; finishing it, I decided, was a challenge I had to meet. I reread the hundred eighty or so pages anxiously, and was relieved to find I didn't completely distrust or dislike the story I had written. It would be a rather short novel in an age when it seemed that the proof of serious purpose and rich imagination was to write a work of eight hundred pages without a plot and without a single memorable character. But my method of composition has always been to write down all that I have to say on a given subject and stop. To strain for more is like adding Hamburger Helper.... You must understand that revisions are a task to which I invariably look forward, however long I estimate they may take, because at least the book is palpably there. It's a blessing to be relieved of every writer's recurring nightmare: that he will find himself, perhaps without warning, unable to complete what he has begun.*

So, there it is, the "other" story in *Shipwreck*, about the creative process. But getting back to the plot, one knows that North's liaison with Lea is moving to some sort of conclusion; in fact, it must move in that direction as North loves his wife Lydia, and one can carry on a duplicitous life for just so long without disastrous consequences. And while telling the end of the novel is not my intention, the very last line is not a spoiler -- North says to the stranger who has listened to all of this *...you know more about me now than anyone else alive.* Indeed, and this may refer as much to Begley the writer, as the protagonist North.

Friday, May 16, 2014 **Updike Revealed**

I eagerly bought one of the first copies shipped of Adam Begley's biography, *John Updike.* Unlike most of his contemporaries, he flourished in all venues, poetry, short story, novels, as well as being a brilliant man of letters. As George Gershwin was to American music, Updike was to American Literature.

I wondered whether any biographer would be up to the task of capturing the breadth of his accomplishments. The literary biography bar had already been set very high by the relatively recent biographies of other important late twenty century writers, Carol Sklenicka's *Raymond Carver: A Writer's Life,* Blake Bailey's *Cheever, A Life,* and also by Blake Bailey, *A Tragic Honesty; The Life and Work of Richard Yates.*

In fact, I thought Blake Bailey would emerge as the ideal biographer of John Updike (but he is now working on a biography of Philip Roth). Adam Begley may have had an inside track. His father, Louis Begley, knew Updike. They were at Harvard together as undergraduates, although Begley went in a totally different career direction upon graduation, into the law, until he found himself writing novels towards the end of his career and now into retirement. For me, there is an uncanny connection between Louis Begley and John Updike as social commentators, capturing the times I've lived.

And so back to Adam Begley's biography of John Updike, a writer who I felt I "grew up with" and admired from afar, reading most of his incredible output with such admiration and wonder that one person could write so prodigiously and with such high literary quality. Like Roy Hobbs, Updike was a "natural." He made poetry out of the quotidian.

Begley's biography is superb, treating Updike with both reverence and objectivity. In fact, my rose colored glasses of Updike were somewhat removed by the biography. To my surprise, Updike was less than a perfect human being! And he indeed lived the life he described in the novel so often associated with him, *Couples*. I don't make this observation as a moral criticism, but more as an abandonment of a certain naiveté I've had about Updike. It doesn't change my love of his work or my assessment of his importance to the world of American literature. In fact, I think Begley's biography will go a long way in assuring his place as one of the most important American writers.

Begley well documents Updike's four stages of life, his cloistered childhood in Shillington and Plowville, PA, his Harvard years where he acquired "a monumental erudition," the period of his first marriage to Mary during which time they raised a family of four children in Ipswich, MA and he established himself as a writer of consequence, and his second marriage to Martha during which time he wrote from the perspective of an acknowledged senior statesman of American literature.

Although Updike finally left his home town of Shillington, PA, that town never left him or his fiction, nor did his later residence in Ipswich MA after he graduated from Harvard (and married in his Junior year, just as I did). But before Ipswich, he worked at *The New Yorker* for a while and lived the life of a young NY writer. *The New Yorker* and Updike were inseparable during his entire career. In fact there were generations of Updikes published in that venerable magazine, some of his mother's short stories and stories by his son, David. All three mined autobiography for their fiction and Updike felt a little "crowded" by his mother and then son appearing in the same pages (although their contributions were minimal compared to his).

Having left New York, as well as Shillington, he developed two alter egos to deal with "what might have been." He imagined a life of Harry Angstrom in his *Rabbit* tetrology....a high school basketball star in PA, but then what? And in a number of short stories he imagined a life of Henry Bech, a writer from the "New York school of writing." The Maple short stories, on the other hand, closely chronicled his deteriorating first marriage even detailing his own children. In fact if there was anything that stands out in Begley's biography it is how Updike extracted fiction from his personal experiences; absolutely nothing escaped his omniscient eye.

After his second marriage, Updike and Martha moved more inland, away from Ipswich, to Georgetown, MA (and years later to Haven Hill, a mansion in Beverly Farms MA, and although on the sea, still secluded). He lived a more isolated life during his later years. Begley notes that there he was *settled and safe – out of harm's way – and free from the time – and energy-consuming entanglements of the riotously unmonogamous Ipswich lifestyle. But he worried that he was putting too much distance between himself and the sources of his inspiration.* Updike himself, after nine months into his second marriage said, *One of the problems of being a fiction writer is that of gathering experience. The need for seclusion and respectability that goes with some success, both are very sheltering – they cut you off from painful experience. We all want to avoid painful experience, and yet painful experience is your chief resource as a writer.*

Curiously enough, as Begley points out, as a young writer Updike made his mark without the anger and torment of so many of his contemporary writers. *He wasn't despairing or thwarted or resentful; he wasn't alienated or conflicted or drunk; he quarreled with no one. In short, he cultivated none of the professional deformations that habitually plague American writers. Even his neuroses were tame. Except for his psoriasis, his stutter, and his intermittent religious doubts, he faced no obstacle that hard work and natural talent couldn't overcome.* Perhaps that is because Updike came from a cocoon of love and protection and adulation, his mother recognizing his genius (and he was a bone-fide one), fostering it and in a sense living out her own dream as a writer through her only child. They had a close relationship throughout Updike's life. In fact, his mother was a published author, but her focus was always on her son

And indeed, Updike was a hard worker and devoted himself to writing most days of his life when he was not travelling, playing golf or sometimes poker, or philandering (although, gathering information from all those activities).

I think Begley gets to the heart of "what made Updike run" – especially during his Ipswich years, by putting his finger on what always puzzled me about Updike, his strong religious vein, usually disguised in his novels but prominent in works such as *Roger's Version*. It seemed to be somewhat inconsistent with the life he led. In Ipswich he joined the First Congregational Church (ironically the same religion in which I was brought up, but abandoned as an adult). Religion to Updike was a constant fulcrum in his life, a hinge on which to swing between the fear of death, to his infidelities. Begley hones right in on the issue:

Surrounded by disbelief more or less politely concealed, he refused to play along -- "I decided ... I would believe." Though he disapproved of pragmatic faith, he was well aware of the utility of his own special brand of piety: "Religion enables us to ignore nothingness," he wrote, "and get on with the jobs of life." He explained the tenacity of his faith by pointing to the part played by fear: "The choice seemed to come down to: believe or be frightened and depressed all the time." On a good day, faith in God gave him confirmation that he mattered -- "that one's sense of oneself as being of infinite value is somewhere in the universe answered, that indeed one is of infinite value." Religion eased his existential terror, allowing him to do his work, and to engage in the various kinds of play that best amused him- among them the hazardous sport of falling for his friends' wives. He was caught in a vicious circle: he fell in love, and his adulterous passion made him feel alive, but also sparked a religious crisis that renewed his fear of death -- so he fell in love some more and read some more theology. Not surprisingly, his wife found that she couldn't tell when he exhibited signs of angst, whether he was suffering from religious doubt or romantic torment.

Furthermore, Updike recognized his exceptionalism as a writer and hoarded every document, doodling (he was an expert cartoonist and almost went into the profession of animation), every letter he received. These, he knew, would be a treasure trove for future literary researchers after his death. Even by the time he was in college, Updike had a literary vision of his future, one he described to his mother in a letter: *We need a writer who desires both to be great and to be popular, an author who can see America as clearly as Sinclair Lewis, but, unlike Lewis, is willing to take it to his bosom...[one who could] produce an epic out of the Protestant ethic* A mighty lofty vision for a young man who then carved that future for the rest of his writing life.

Begley's writing itself is superb with the biography reading like a novel, integrating his observations, bolstering them from Updike's own fiction. Consider just this one passage: *...Mary's knack of keeping her husband at a distance, her studiously unruffled passivity – leavened by dry humor, bolstered by tenacious dignity, and sealed with maturing beauty – helped to hold the marriage together. Like many of his damaged fictional couples, they 'hunkered down in embattled, recriminatory renewal of their vows, mixed with spells of humorous weariness.'* Between his own elegant writing, and plentiful quotes, Begley has managed to create a verisimilitude approaching a virtual hologram of Updike's life.

In reading this work, I accumulated six single spaced pages of notes and in reviewing them, realized it would be silly to go into detail on all. I'd end up practically reprinting the essence of Begley's extraordinary biography and as such I've omitted so many other issues that "made Updike run" and many of the controversies. My heartfelt suggestion: read the biography!

In some ways this was a difficult one for me to read. We all have a favorite writer, but I also thought of Updike as a distant friend, a one way relationship of course, but an intimate one. His passing was a loss to me. We had so many commonalities as well, with a number of uncanny things in common (I don't mean to compare myself to him in any way however). We lived through the same eras. What he wrote about I experienced.

Towards the end of his life, he gave a talk at the National Booksellers Association in 2006 entitled "The End of Authorship" – a defense of the printed word in which he felt threatened by Google's attempt to digitize, well, everything. He loved the texture of the book as I do. As Begley recounts,

Updike saw [the universal digitized library] as ruin for writers dependent on royalties. Defending not only the economic model that had sustained him but his fundamental conception of literature, which he understood to be a private, silent communication between two individuals, author and reader, he was arguing for 'accountability and intimacy.'....His identity was forged in solitary communion with an open book.

His was a life of productivity and meaning, and now immortality, a writer who will be read for generations. We would all like to be remembered. It was his intention, even as a young man, to achieve exactly what he achieved (and he did it through assiduously hard work, not to mention having a pure genius for writing). How many of us can say that? My life in publishing was something I loved, but now that is gone, receding in my retirement years to the point I sometimes wonder whether it was a dream and what exactly did I accomplish? Reading Begley's acknowledgments I was heartened that he gave attribution to Jack De Bellis: *Without the herculean efforts of Jack De Bellis, a tireless collector of Updike facts and Updike treasure, all Updike scholars would have to work twice as hard as they do.* I cite this as at the end of my publishing career my company published his *John Updike Encyclopedia.* Before that we published his *John Updike, 1967-1993: A Bibliography of Primary and Secondary Sources.* Updike reviewed the chronology for the former and wrote an introduction for the latter. So the circle closes for me. Books matter, great literature captures life better than any compilation of digital photographs, and Updike's works will be read and studied by generations and generations to follow.

His was indeed a life well led as documented by Adam Begley in this inspired biography.

Saturday, July 12, 2014 *First Novels*

I'm always on the lookout for the emergence of new American literary talent. So behind the times as usual, I just read another worthy first novel, an extraordinarily sensitive work, Dave King's *The Ha-Ha*, published almost ten years ago.

It is everything a good novel should be, <u>intensely</u> readable, one you can hardly put down, while dealing with huge themes in the lives of ordinary people who simply are trying to survive and connect. It is also a coming of age novel, with hints of *Huckleberry Finn*. <u>Spoiler alert</u>, I discuss aspects of the novel below which reveal things you might want to discover for yourself if you should choose to read it.

It is the story of Howard Kapostash, "Howie" and how his life is changed, not once but twice by seismic events, one a war and the other love. The tidal wave of the Vietnam War continues to ripple throughout our lives and especially through its veterans. The "ha-ha" of the novel ("a boundary wall concealed in a ditch so that it does not intrude upon the view") from which the novel derives its ironic title is a metaphor for the barriers Howie faces and a celebration of the individual will as he navigates them.

Dalton Trumbo's *Johnny Got His Gun* floated through my mind while reading the novel, Trumbo's portrayal of the destruction of an individual by war (WW I) being the most extreme rendering ever written (and filmed). In a sense, Howie bears some resemblance to Trumbo's Joe Bonham, a soldier who is a quadruple amputee, trapped in his own body with no way to move or to communicate. Howie, after only 16 days in Vietnam is hurled into the air by a land mine, and emerges brain damaged, but with therapy he is finally able to resume his day to day physical activities (unlike Bonham), able to take care of himself, although permanently unable to speak, read, or write. He returns to his parents' house where he grew up, at first descending into drugs and self pity until finally resurrecting himself, inheriting their home after his parents die and some money and taking in borders to help defray the cost of running it. One of these is a young Asian woman, Laura, who makes soups for a living, using the well-supplied kitchen in Howie's home. Laura becomes his secretary in a sense, taking care of the bills, assisting him to continue to live somewhat independently on his own. She does this in return for a rent-free residence and because she feels admiration, perhaps even love, for Howie.

Howie makes a life as a mute, working at a nearby convent, mowing the lawn, occasionally playing a game with his John Deere tractor, coming precariously close to the ha-ha. He stays in touch with his first and only love, Sylvia. They shared one idyllic, sex-filled weekend before he went to Vietnam but now are only friends. Sylvia has a drug addiction, as well as a 9-1/2 old son, Ryan, who has a nameless, absent black father, so Sylvia and Ryan are two other characters trying to scratch out a life.

The action at this point is fomented by Sylvia's sister who performs an intervention, hauling Sylvia off to a rehab center to kick her drug habit. But what to do with Ryan? Without notice, Howie finds that he will be Ryan's caretaker for an indeterminate amount of time, two damaged people, one a mute and the other a confused angry young boy who will have to live in this non-traditional household while his mother recovers. Howie's covert love for Sylvia makes it impossible for him to refuse.

King beautifully summarizes how Howie has arrived at this point: *It's all the things that I've gone down, everything that didn't happen to me that I always thought would. It's being an exemplar of the admirably rebuilt life, the days spent zigging a holy lawnmower around paradise, the nights with strangers in my home. It's having a child on furlough from another family, from Sylvia's family it's wanting to do the best I can. Pretending I don't still suffer from nightmares that set me bellowing in my sleep, while Laurel and the others pretend they don't hear. It's that maybe I wasn't so much to begin with, but everything that was worth parading has been gone for so long I barely remember it. It's wondering by what queer twist I survived, and why I was given sixteen days and a lifetime of bleak endurance. It's the futility, always, of being understood.*

And so the novel then unfolds, how our mute protagonist who has led a lonely love-starved life for so long, and how the nine and a half-year-old son of a former girlfriend he must suddenly care for change each other. They warily bond through baseball (another metaphor for bringing them into society) and along with Howie's roommates they cobble out a nontraditional family as they wait Sylvia's emergence from rehab.

Howie's feelings for Sylvia, if anything, have deepened while she's in rehab. He even fantasizes a life with her upon her return when he checks on her house, walking though it imagining how things could be, knowing full well, they will never be like this: *All these photos and keepsakes are so familiar that I rarely give them thought when I come in. In my mind I walk through the door and this is my house and I call out, "Honey I'm home!"—a phrase so familiar it's become a joke. Sylvia doesn't answer but I hear her chuckle. She's in the kitchen making sandwiches. There's a knife-tap on the mayonnaise jar and the movement of the shadow on wallpaper. I take a breath. The house smells fresh, it's summer and we keep our windows open. I don't smoke a pipe. I brought our boy back from baseball practice, and I can't wait to tell my wife how he hustled when he hit that double. "You should've seen it," I'll say, and give her a peck. "Beat the throw by a mile!" Then Sylvia will say she'll catch a game soon, and that's enough to look forward to, because really it's father-son time this Saturday morning sports thing and that's how we like it.*

Consequences of actions hang heavily over the novel, how Howie has developed a certain dignity in spite of his travails and then how they unravel as Ryan's mother's impending arrival approaches, finding himself almost in the same condition as when he returned from Vietnam, a victim of a war. He knows any relationship with Sylvia is impossible, but he realizes how achingly he will miss Ryan. Ultimately, it is a tale of how people connect, amend adversity, and are held together by love. One last visit to the ha-ha by Howie in the middle of the night brings everything together:

I wonder if I should say a prayer or if I'm being influenced by the surroundings. I feel a little drunk. Through the silence the echoey whoosh of traffic below the ha ha, a sound like waves. The moon slips behind a cloud, the night is dark again and I decide to pray something that's not a prayer so much as an imagined wish; and I wish the first thing that bubbles into my head. I wish for Ryan to be well loved his entire life. That's the key to happiness I think. I wonder what Sylvia wishes for Ryan; then my mind is pulled from my prayer, and I think that for a few weeks he was well loved by all of us, and we were loved in return. I was loved by Sylvia once –I'll always believe that -- and I was loved more than I deserved by my mother and dad. And I loved them. I wonder what kind of tally this makes for one life but I have my excuses. I'd loved more people if I hadn't been injured. I never knew why I survived, but I was glad I made it. I didn't imagine any other way to feel. There's the period to be proud of, two years of autonomy, sobriety, and endurance. Why does nothing stand out?

Tuesday, July 15, 2014 *A Life Well Lived*

Before leaving for Connecticut I felt inclined to read Julian Barnes' *Nothing to be Frightened Of*, a strange potpourri of philosophy, memoir and literary commentary, along with some ghoulish humor, on death.

Here Barnes turns to essay format to deal with what awaits all of us, something we intellectually accept, but in the gut? Barnes approaches the topic as an agnostic, although he was a declared atheist earlier in life – the difference between the two terms as he expresses his philosophy seems like a thin line. Here's but one example of a fine writer at work on such a topic: *It is not just pit-gazing that is hard work, but life-grazing. It is difficult for us to contemplate, fixedly, the possibility, let alone the certainty, that life is a matter of cosmic hazard, its fundamental purpose mere self-perpetuation, that it unfolds in emptiness, that our planet will one day drift in frozen silence, and that the human species, as it has developed in all its frenzied and over-engineered complexity will completely disappear and not be missed, because there is nobody and nothing out there to miss us. This is what growing up means. And it is a frightening prospect for a race which has for so long relied upon its own invented gods for explanation and consolation."*

I must confess I share the universality of the "fear" of death, not so much of the mystery of a so-called afterlife, but of the process itself. I don't feel like Barnes' often quoted 19th century French writer Jules Renard who once said: "Don't let me die too quickly." It's one of life's experiences, so why miss it? I say, why revel in the experience of it (especially today's medically prolonged version) when you'll not remember it? To me life is about memory.

And the operative word of the last sentence is "me," the persona that remains in others' memory for a while, especially family and close friends, but in another generation or at most two that disappears as well. And against the backdrop of the limited life span of the sun and therefore the earth itself (limited when comparing it to "eternity"), we all make a forgotten appearance. Perhaps that in itself is the most frightening aspect of our "appointment in Samarra."

So the lesson is to live well and cherish the few in our lives to whom we are close and in a sense validate our own existence. As we age, this is an ever diminishing circle.

Tuesday, August 12, 2014 &Sons -- an Ambitious Noteworthy Novel

&Sons, is by another talented "youngish" American writer, David Gilbert. It is encouraging to see a wave of emerging American writers.

Gilbert's &Sons is Dickenesque in its plot and subplots, Irvingesque in the characters eccentricities, and thematically one can sense the shadow of his contemporary, Jonathan Franzen dealing with family issues. I could also throw in a little Tom Wolfe and the influence of the great Canadian short story writer, Alice Munro. This doesn't mean Gilbert isn't original, but all writers have their progenitors. The writing is a hat tip to Salinger as well. The novel within this novel, *Ampersand*, was written by our protagonist, the reclusive writer A.N.Dyer. *Ampersand*'s mystique is similar to *The Catcher in the Rye*.

For me the novel was sometimes emotionally lacking, just the opposite of Zach Braff's recent movie (and script), *Wish I Was Here*, which is also about idiosyncratic sons and their father where I experienced more of an emotional connection to the main characters. (Unfair, I know, to compare a movie to a novel.) Gilbert somewhat misses the boat on that one, but catches a love sonnet to NYC, its Central Park, and some of the "in" places -- many of which didn't exist during my salad days in the City or I was just not "in that crowd."

I found the first third of the novel slow to get going, but once it does, it becomes a fast, compulsive read. Gilbert leans on a slightly science fiction like detail (if you believe A.D. Dyer's tale to his family) to turn the corner in the novel.

These criticisms are not to diminish the quality of Gilbert's writing, which puts him in the running for one of the promising upcoming American authors. It is a complicated novel, but constructed with care and some of the writing is, well, breathtaking.

This passage about friends resonates from my perspective as a septuagenarian. Much of the novel is about the decline during those years. By the 70's one feels the weight, both physically and metaphysically. I continue the journey with, alas, a diminishing number of friends... *Our oldest friends, their faces, never really change as we both travel at the same speed of life. Parents and children are different. They help us measure our existence like the clock on the wall or the watch on our wrist. But all friends carry with them a braided constant, part and hole, all the days in the calendar contained in a glance.*

I like Gilbert's description of the divergence of the roles of mothers and fathers, a common theme in literature and theatre.... *I remember summer beach picnics organized by the Dyer and Topping women, the mothers curating our good cheer; Isabel took the photographs as Eleanor posed the players, the two of them hoping that these happy pictures might stand in for how we looked back, a prefabricated nostalgia. If fathers are unknowable, then mothers are all too visible, a reminder of our earthly attachments.*

Might Gilbert share some of A.D. Dyer's feelings about the writing process? After all, writing is work. Gilbert took six years to write *&Sons: The irony I would like to communicate to you boys is the fact that I never enjoyed writing very much. Oh, maybe I enjoyed the moments before writing, the thinking about writing, when the story starts to form around its cagey heart, a word an image, like with bodysurfing: in a flash I know everything, the themes, the metaphors, five of the characters, the setting, the time frame, the beginning, the middle, the end. It's a strange kind of fission, with a single atom of imagination radiates all this energy, splitting and splitting and splitting, endlessly splitting until you get Bodysurfing or The Bodysurfer which is probably better if perhaps bumping elbows with Cheever.*

Having been a publisher all my life, I can attest to the veracity of Gilbert's description of a publisher's party to introduce a new author. I've been to a few, although my kind of publishing – professional and academic – did not lend itself (thankfully) to a steady diet of these – they were the norm in trade publishing and I suppose they still are... *These were the people who worked in publishing: the editors, the publicists, the marketers, the agents, all of whom arrived on time if almost early, not just because this was a work event but because this promised to be a rare work event that reminded them of when their industry burned bright in the New York sky, a place of true atmosphere instead of greenhouse gases. The excellent catering was also a draw. Dinner tonight came in a dozen bites. These people generally clustered in small groups mainly so they could gorge without embarrassment -- oh my God, the artichoke hearts with veal and ricotta is not of this world -- but also so they could rain down sulfur on the contemptible around them, right out of Trollope or Balzac, they might mutter, gesturing with herbed cheese straws.*

Friday, October 24, 2014 **Three for the Road**

Some ostensibly very different works of fiction are discussed here, Ian McEwan's *Sweet Tooth*, John Updike's *The Maples*, and *The Portable Library of Jack Kerouac*. But they are tied together in some ways, particularly as I read them somewhat concurrently over the last month or two

-- mostly during our trips to Alaska and Seattle -- and each in its own way has struck a chord in me.

After reading McEwan's *Saturday* which I thoroughly enjoyed, everything taking place in one day (Saturday, naturally), I read his *Solar* -- a good story but not in the same league as *Saturday*. I stumbled upon his *Sweet Tooth*, a mystery and a love story, and written from a woman's first person point of view. Much in the novel is about writing itself, a novel within a novel with detailed outlines for some short stories as well, all fitting together like a literary jig saw puzzle.

It takes place during the paranoid cold war 1970s when a young Cambridge graduate, a mathematician by training but a compulsive inveterate reader by avocation, Serena Frome, joins the M15, the British intelligence agency. Ultimately she moves up the ranks and is given a "soft" assignment, nothing too dangerous, of following young British writers, ones that M15 might think would benefit by clandestine financial support, in the hope that their writings might have some use in the macro setting of the cold war. So, the beautiful Frome is assigned to bestow a grant to a young writer, Tom Haley. How was she to know that they would fall in love, his never realizing her association with M15 (thinking she represents a nonprofit group that bestows literary endowments)? Where there is such a secret there are the underpinnings for tension throughout the novel and McEwan capitalizes on every twist and turn. To say any more is to give away an ingenious ending to the novel, where everything finally coalesces.

But how real life enters and is transformed by fiction is at the heart of the novel. As an example, Serena and Tom discuss probability theory (as a reminder, Serena is a trained mathematician). Tom doesn't get it. But ultimately it enters one of the short stories he is writing He gives it to Serena to read. She fails to see how it coalesced in the creative process until she tries to go asleep and in that state finally realizes how Tom did get it: *As I lay in the dark, waiting for sleep, I thought I was beginning to grasp something about invention. As a reader, a speed-reader, I took it for granted, it was a process I never troubled myself with. You pulled a book from the shelf and there was an invented, peopled world, as obvious as the one you lived in.... I thought I had the measure of the artifice, or I almost had it. Almost like cooking, I thought sleepily. Instead of heat transforming the ingredients, there's pure invention, the spark, the hidden element. What resulted was more than the sum of the parts.... At one level it was obvious enough how many separate parts were tipped in and deployed. The mystery was in how they were blended into something cohesive and plausible, how the ingredients were cooked into something so delicious. As my thought scattered and I drifted toward the borders of oblivion, I thought I almost understood how it was done.* Just a wonderful description of the creative process, how life is reflected and filtered by a writer's story.

This is a page turner, somewhat of a classic spy story, besides being a primer on writing itself. Ian McEwan is becoming one of the more interesting writers of the 21st century.

But I return, now, to a different kind of 20th century story (actually stories), having had the pleasure of also reading Updike's *The Maples Stories*. Although these were published during his lifetime, they have been posthumously issued as an "Everyman's Library Pocket Classic" in hardcover, a volume to treasure. I had read most of these before, but to read the eighteen stories that span from 1956's "Snowing in Greenwich Village," to "Grandparenting" published in his favorite venue *The New Yorker* in 1994 is to view the life of the great literary man himself. It took Adam Begley's brilliant literary biography, *Updike,* to see that "the Maples" were in fact Updike and his first wife Mary. The closest Updike had delved into autobiography was his work *Self-Consciousness: Memoirs,* published in 1989 but that is greatly about his growing up in Shillington, PA.

The Maples chronicles the jealousies, infidelities, the love and the hurt, and the intimacies and the breakdown of his marriage. Consider the aching beauty of his writing, so finely crafted in this description of when Richard Maple picks up his wife Joan in his car to finally go to court for their no fault divorce: *She got into the car, bringing with her shoes and the moist smell of dawn. She had always been an early riser, and he a late one. "Thanks for doing this," she said, of the ride, adding, "I guess.""My pleasure,""Richard said. As they drove to court, discussing their cars and their children, he marveled at how light Joan had become; she sat on the side of his vision as light as a feather, her voice tickling his ear, her familiar intonations and emphases thoroughly musical and half unheard, like the patterns of a concerto that sets us to daydreaming. He no longer blamed her: that was the reason for the lightness. All those years, he had blamed her for everything - for the traffic jam in Central Square, for the blasts of noise on the mail boat, for the difference in the levels of their beds. No longer: he had set her adrift from omnipotence. He had set her free, free from fault. She was to him as Gretel to Hansel, a kindred creature moving beside him down a path while birds behind them ate the bread crumbs.*

"Grandparenting" which takes place well after the Maples divorce is an act of atonement for Updike as it brings together the now divorced Maples one last time to participate in the birth of their first grandchild. Indeed, Updike is for the ages.

And what could be more different from Updike than Jack Kerouac's *Portable Library* which I managed to fit in here and there, making it mostly bedtime reading. I read *On the Road* ages ago so that and his other writings in the *Portable Library* edition seemed new to me. Oh, man, this is the beat generation, a step before mine, but I remember it well as it played out in the late 50s and 60s. Kerouac writes with a pulsating persistence, almost stream of consciousness, as if he just cannot fit enough life on a physical page. It throbs with energy as he tries to absorb the "real" underbelly of America in every place imaginable, with the help of drugs, alcohol, sex, and, man, cool beat music. It's almost as if he did not live in the same world as an Updike who crafted his sentences like a sculpture. No, Kerouac was more like a Jackson Pollack, frenzied by getting the colors of life just right (to him), writing in riffs like Charlie Parker (both mentioned by him in his writings).

It was only after reading *The Portable Jack Kerouac* that I realized I have some 'six degrees of separation' with him. Over a period of 12 years he lived within two miles of where I lived as a kid (92-18 107th Street, Queens, NY), first at his parent's house at 133-01 Cross Bay Blvd, Queens, NY and then for five years at 94-21 134th Street, his frequently hanging out at Smokey Oval Park on Atlantic Avenue, where I used to practice with the Richmond Hill HS baseball team. This park was later renamed the Phil Rizutto Park as Rizutto played at Richmond Hill High School, and was a classmate of my father's.

Then, another association from my past: a close friend early in my high school years, Paul Ortloff, apparently began a relationship with Kerouac's daughter, Jan, when he was attending Cooper Union for art. For the first nine years of Jan's life Kerouac had denied being her father but after a blood test he acknowledged the fact. She only met her father two or three times. As one might imagine, Jan was psychologically damaged by this rejection which haunted her for her entire short life (died in her mid 40s) but as a teenager she fell head over heels in love with Paul. I can understand why. He was charismatic, bright, and as Jack Kerouac was to the Beat generation I suppose Paul was to psychedelic and tattoo art. He was a rebel with a James Dean aura. In later life Paul became a psychedelic artist. When I read John Irving's haunting and enigmatic "Until I Find You" I couldn't help but think of Paul.

Paul and I lost contact well before we graduated from high school, his going his way into psychedelic art, ultimately moving to Woodstock, NY, my going the so called straight and narrow. Reading about him in James T. Jones' *Use My Name: Jack Kerouac's Forgotten Families* brought up a lot of memories, but his relationship with Kerouac's daughter was unknown to me at the time. Of course I cannot verify any of this other than Jones' account.

Interesting where reading takes you. All three of these books brought me inward, a self examination at this stage of my life. Simply put, they spoke to me very personally, one about writing, one about the marriage and craft of the short story by a writer I deeply admire (and miss), and the other about a parallel universe, one of which I was aware, but only lived through tangentially.

Sunday, November 2, 2014 **Carver and Birdman**

I don't see many movies in the theater. I'll tape (well, DVR nowadays) an occasional classic on Turner Classic Movies, and see a Woody Allen film, or one of that genre, but I prefer live theatre and reading. However, I made an exception for *Birdman or (The Unexpected Virtue of Ignorance)* as central to its story is Carver's "What We Talk About When We Talk About Love," a short story that resonated so much with me that I decided several years ago to adapt it into play form along with a couple of other short stores, as part of a larger dramatic work, *When We Talk About Carver.*

I had thought the time had come for this little known writer (to the general public) to be acknowledged, celebrated as one of the finest short story writers of our time. What better way to do it than by developing a dramatization of some of his works, centered on his masterpiece, "What We Talk About When We Talk About Love." This was no small feat for me. I love the theatre but adapting a short story to the structure of a drama is not for amateurs. So I loaded up my bookshelves with guides to playwriting and installed some good software, Word.doc templates for dramatic structure and presentation.

Then, when it came to dramatizing the story, there was the conflict of deciding on which version to use, the one Carver originally wrote "The Beginners" and later edited by his editor at Esquire (and later Knopf), Gordon Lish, and then edited again by Lish, under the new title as we now know it. Lish's version distills the story to the bare essentials, including the dialogue. It was the better version to work with as part of the play I envisioned. The Carver estate had granted permission to do this but after a year of trying to place the work, it has languished.

So, given this background, I had to see *Birdman* as soon as it opened nearby. Very little of the short story's dialogue is actually used in the movie, but it anchors the film in many ways. (It was nice to see the set though, a 1970's kitchen, exactly the way I envisioned it.) The Carver short story is about love in all its manifestations, from spiritual love to obsessive, violent love, but is set in its time, alcoholism as the primary social lubricant, and in literary realism. *Birdman* is about love as well, updated for the 21st century, which now includes self-obsessive love strongly influenced by the power and effect of social media along with "magical surrealism" dominating the canvas of the story.

Fascinating for me, the film opens with a quote from Carver, one of the last poems he ever wrote as he was dying of cancer -- his epitaph -- "Late Fragment," published in a collection *A New Path to the Waterfall* with an introduction by his wife, also a poet, Tess Gallagher. One thinks of Carver only as a short story writer, but he wrote poetry as well. As Gallagher put it "...Ray's new poems blurred the boundaries between poem and story, just as his stories had often taken strength from dramatic and poetic strategies."

LATE FRAGMENT

And did you get what / you wanted from this life, even so? / I did / And what did you want? / To call myself beloved, to feel myself / beloved on the earth.

And that is the theme of this movie – wanting to be beloved on earth. All the characters are struggling in their own way to find approbation and love. Aren't we all?

The plot in a nutshell involves a has-been superhero (The Birdman) film actor, Riggan Thomson (played brilliantly by Michael Keaton), who seeks "legitimacy" on the Broadway stage by adapting Carver's short story, and then producing, directing and starring in it. He is haunted by his alter ego, Birdman (this is where the surrealistic element emerges), who declares him as still having superpowers (he is seen levitating in a yoga pose in the first frame). His struggle with his past self and what he envisions as his future artistic self is what propels this frenetic film from its beginning to its end. Also in the cast is his sympathetic former wife, Sylvia (Amy Ryan), their daughter, Sam (Emma Stone) a recovering addict, and the co-stars in the play, one of which he was recently involved with, Laura (Andrea Riseborough) and Lesley (Naomi Watts) a girlfriend of a well-known Broadway method actor, Mike Shiner (Edward Norton). Riggan's only friend and business manager, Jake (Zach Galifianakis) persuades Riggan to hire Mike at the last minute for the other male character part in the play. Mike and Riggan come to blows and yet the show goes on. All the ingredients are here for love relationships in all their variations, good and bad, not unlike the heart of the Carver story. I'm trying to avoid spoilers here.

I mentioned that the Carver quote is the central theme of the movie. There is one exchange between Riggan and his daughter Sam where this resounds loudly. I remember tapping my wife Ann on the shoulder as Sam was in the middle of delivering her monologue. After that climatic moment, Riggan is on track to shred his "unexpected virtue of ignorance":

Riggan: "This is my chance to finally do some work that actually means something."

Sam: "That means something to who? You had a career, Dad, before the third comic book movie, before people started to forget who was inside that bird costume. You are doing a play based on a book that was written 60 years ago for a thousand rich old white people whose only real concern is going to be where they have their cake and coffee when it's over. Nobody gives a shit but you! And let's face it, Dad; you are not doing this for the sake of art. You are doing this because you want to feel relevant again. Well guess what? There is an entire world out there where people fight to be relevant every single day and you act like it doesn't exist. This is happening in a place that you ignore, a place that, by the way, has already forgotten about you. I mean, who the fuck are you? You hate bloggers. You mock Twitter. You don't even have a Facebook page. You're the one who doesn't exist. You're doing this because you're scared to death, like the rest of us, that you don't matter and, you know what, you're right. You don't! It's not important, okay? You're not important! Get used to it."

Where did Riggan get the idea of adapting a Carver short story? It's revealed that when he was a young actor, Carver was in the audience and wrote a note to him on a cocktail napkin to say that he admired the performance. Decades later he still carries the napkin, presents it as his trump card to the *New York Times* critic who says she's going to pan the play as she doesn't admire movie actors who try to cross the line into legitimate theatre.

And so still another theme unfolds in the film. Movie actors are celebrities, have fame but do they have the right stuff? How does live theatre stack up against film? There is no contest as each art form functions on a different plane. Carver's short story could make great theatre, but *Birdman* needs to soar on film, and what a film it is. Ironically, as Riggan is the writer, producer, and director of the Carver play in the film, *Birdman* was co-written, produced, and directed by one person as well, Alejandro González Iñárritu. The only thing he did not do, as did the main character in the film, was to become a character.

The movie has the feeling of being filmed as one long continuous take. It is two hours of breathtaking cinematography perfectly accompanied by music selections, mostly the pulsating drums of Antonio Sánchez who even makes a brief passing appearance in the film. One can imagine those beating in Riggan's head. Nothing is out of bounds for this film and only film could capture the gestalt, the play within the film, the character's intense relationships, Riggan's journey, and the alternative universe of the Birdman which, no pun intended, gives this film breathtaking wings. It is also a love poem to the New York City theatre district.

This film is revolutionary and expect to hear it nominated for a host of Academy Awards, best picture, screenplay, directing, not to mention best actor as Michael Keaton gives a once-in-a-lifetime performance, best supporting actor (Edward Norton was outstanding as a foil to Riggan), best supporting actress, Emma Stone (who can forget her mesmerizing eyes as well), best cinematography, best original soundtrack, and I could go on and on.

Saturday, November 8, 2014 *A Stay at Brookner's 'Hotel Du Lac'*

That's the way I felt reading this deliciously elegant novel by Anita Brookner: I too in the late fall, out of season, was ensconced in the *Hotel Du Lac*, observing the eccentricities of the characters staying there and, in particular, those of our protagonist, Edith Hope. She is a writer of romance novels and she has come to the hotel from her home in England more as banishment than a vacation. But for what reprehensible indiscretion? We have to wait until about midway through the novel to find that out and while it's a surprise, it is totally understandable in context. Meanwhile, Edith who is determined to finish her next novel while staying at the hotel becomes more tangled with the few other people staying there at the end of the season, each with reasons for their own self-exile. In fact if anything stands out in the novel, particularly for Edith, it is a sense of estrangement. But as her own life becomes involved with the lives of the others there on the increasingly frigid misty shores of Lake Geneva, Edith is changed, seeing herself in a different light.

If one had asked Edith before, she would have prided herself on her independence, but, now, she is no longer sure how independent a woman should or can be. After all, one returning visitor there, Mrs. Pusey, and her middle aged daughter, Jennifer, come at that time every year with the singular purpose to shop. *And she was enabled to do this by virtue of the fact that her late husband had prudently deposited certain sums of money in an account in her name in a Swiss bank.*

Edith is a writer, so Mrs. Pusey *presented her with the opportunity to examine and to enjoy, contact with an alien species. For in this charming woman, so entirely estimable in her happy desire to capture hearts, so completely preoccupied with the femininity which had always provided her with life's chief delights, Edith perceived avidity, grossness, ardour.*

As these brief quotes attest, there is a 19th century quality to the writing, even 18th century. Consider what Edith remarks in a letter to her lover, David (married, unlike Edith), back home when imagining the kind of man Mrs. Pusey's daughter, Jennifer, would ever marry:

I wonder if Jennifer is ever to marry. On which outsider will descend the supreme accolade of becoming an insider? How will he be recognized? He will have to present impeccable credentials: wealth equal to theirs, or, if possible, superior, a suitably elevated style of living, an ideally situated residence, and what Mrs. Pusey refers to as "position". All these attributes will come before his physical appearance, for Jennifer might be led astray by that into making a hasty judgment. My feeling is that the chosen one will be agreeably but perhaps not emphatically masculine; he will be courtly and not too young and very patient and totally indulgent. He will have to be all of these things because if he is to be a match for Mrs. Pusey's vigilance he will have to spend a great deal of time with her. With them both....

Isn't this something almost out of Jane Austen? But of course, this is a 20th century novel, and men do figure differently in the equation, particularly for Edith, who has a long term dalliance home in England (is David the reason she has been banished to the Hotel we wonder?) and at the hotel she meets her match (intellectually), Mr. Neville, with whom she spars as the novel progresses. He figures in a double surprise ending, one we sort of suspect and the other we do not. Can't say much more about the characters here or spoilers would be self evident. But I will say one thing, the solitary women there at the hotel, Monica, Mme de Bonneuil, as well as Mrs. Pusey, are there, one way or another, because of men. And so is Edith.

Brookner displays tightly woven prose, almost like a short story, each word carefully chosen and measured. It is elegant and it glitters throughout her work, especially enjoyable when writers write about writing. And Edith Hope is ironically a writer of popular romance novels, one she herself recognizes is not about the real world. She's working on a new novel, *Beneath the Visiting Moon*, one she imagines she'll make great progress on while at the hotel, trying to keep to a daily schedule of writing, *[bending] her head obediently to her daily task of fantasy and obfuscation.*

But she is mired now in the lives of the people at the hotel, and as determined as she is to keep up the daily grind, she has difficulty. She imagines she'll have to read fiction to restart her creative juices:

Fiction, the time-honoured resource of the ill-at-ease, would have to come to her aid, but the choice of a book presented some difficulties, since when she was writing she could only read something she had read before, and in her exhausted state, a febrile agitation, invisible to the naked eye, tended to distance even the very familiar. Words became distorted: 'pear', for instance, would become 'fear'. She dreaded making nonsense of something precious to her, and, regretfully, disqualified Henry James. Nothing too big would do, nothing too small would suffice. In any event, her attention was fragmented.

No small coincidence that Edith mentions Henry James as Brookner writes with a similar style and interest in the complexities of human psychology. *Hotel Du Lac* deservedly won the Booker Prize in 1984, a "hotel" which merits a visit!

Thursday, November 20, 2014 **Perfectly Frank**

Richard Ford is one of the few authors that'll I'll buy any book he writes as soon as it is published in hardcover. I'm particularly fond of the Frank Bascombe novels, Ford's protagonist from *The Sportswriter, Independence*

Day, and *The Lay of the Land*, written in the first person by a "familiar old friend" from New Jersey. I feel I know this person as I knew Updike's Harry "Rabbit" Angstrom. Frank is four years younger than I and Rabbit was ten years older. But the times recounted by these characters are of my era. No wonder I'm so familiar with the landscapes of their lives. And it is interesting that both Updike and Ford had declared the end of their Angstrom and Bascombe novels with the completion of their trilogies, only to come out with one more, as if the character told the writer he had something else to say. I certainly thought the Bascombe works had come to an end when he wrote *Canada*, a fine novel.

Let Me Be Frank With You is Frank's voice, the way he thinks, that connects with me -- plaintive, sardonic, ironic, perplexed, now somewhat resigned, and with a wry wit. It is not a novel but instead four lengthy short stories, loosely held together by Hurricane Sandy and the theme of aging.

The leitmotiv of the Hurricane is actually central to the first story, "I'm Here." At the request of an old real estate client, Arne Urguhart (Frank became a real estate agent after he was a sportswriter and an aspiring novelist), he goes to the Jersey shore to see what's left of the house he sold Arne, actually the house that Frank lived in with his ex-wife Ann.

In the second story, "Everything Could Be Worse," he is visited in his present home in Haddam, the town where Frank began his journey in the *The Sportswriter,* by a Mrs. Pines, who has become displaced by the Hurricane, and injured as well, a cast on her arm, and has an unexpected urge to see the home in which she grew up and in which a terrible crime was committed. Frank invites her to tour the house and her story unfolds.

From there we segue to "The New Normal" where Frank goes to visit his ex-wife who is now a resident of a high-end retirement community, with progressively deteriorating Parkinson's disease, one she even blames on the Hurricane as a *super-real change agent. It was in the air.*

The concluding story says much about the underlying theme of the entire collection, "Death of Others." Here he goes to visit a friend who is literally at death's door, living in a home he's occupied for scores of years, being attended to by hospice. Frank was once his neighbor. The dying man, Eddie Medley, makes a startling confession to Frank. The Hurricane in this story hangs in the background on Eddie's silent TV, a program surveying the damage.

I thought I might be disappointed by this book as it is not another Bascombe novel. *Independence Day*, the second Bascombe novel, which won the Pulitzer Prize, is probably his best. Just the opening sentence of that one expresses his love of the geographic territory: *In Haddam, summer floats over tree-softened streets like a sweet lotion balm from a careless, languorous god, and the world falls in tune with its own mysterious anthems.* In his new short story collection, such a sentence would seem to be impossible. Why? Because Bascombe has aged. He sees life and Haddam differently now.

So, if one concentrates on "the voice" and the themes, perhaps it actually works better as a number of loosely connected short stories. I think that genre feels so natural for what Ford has to say. What Frank says about "love" could be said about his life — *Love isn't a thing, after all, but an endless series of single acts.* And so these stories represent single acts, making up Frank as he enters old age.

When you grow old, as I am, you pretty much live in the accumulations of life anyway. Not that much is happening, except on the medical front. Better to strip things down. And where better to start stripping than the words we choose to express our increasingly rare, increasingly vagrant thoughts.

It's not true that as you get older things slide away like molasses off a table top. What is true is I don't remember some things that well, owing to the fact that I don't care all that much. I now wear a cheap Swatch watch, but I do sometimes lose the handle on the day of the month, especially near the end and the beginning, when I get off-track about "thirty days hath September ... " This, I believe, is normal and doesn't worry me. It's not as if I put my trousers on backwards every morning, tie my shoelaces together, and can't find my way to the mailbox.

And I was also amused by Frank's description of the dangers of falling as a senior citizen. I've been warned as well because one of my so-called "necessary" medications has the side effect of thinning bones. They even wanted to give me other medication to combat those side effects, but that one has its own likely side effects (I refused). Pick your poison I'm told, although as one doctor empathetically told me, "it's not your bones that's gonna get you, it's something else." I could not have said it any better than Frank, though, and reading this book should be required as one enters the final stage of one's life.

Here's Frank's take on it: *... because of something Sally said, I feel a need to more consciously pick my feet up when I walk-"the gramps shuffle" being the unmaskable, final-journey approach signal. It'll also keep me from falling down and busting my ass. What is it about falling? "He died of a fall." "The poor thing never recovered after his fall." "He broke his hip in a fall and was never the same." "Death came relatively quickly after a fall in the back yard." How fucking far do these people fall? Off of buildings? Over spuming cataracts? Down manholes? Is it farther to the ground than it used to be? In years gone by I'd fall on the ice, hop back up, and never think a thought. Now it's a death sentence. What Sally said to me was "Be careful when you go down those front steps, sweetheart. The surface isn't regular,* *so pick your feet up." Why am I now a walking accident waiting to happen? Why am I more worried about that than whether there's an afterlife?*

He somewhat reluctantly, but obligingly, goes once a month to visit his ex-wife (his present wife, Sally, is fine with this) Ann who now lives in cutting edge senior care center, one in which there is progressive health care, right to the grave. At Ann's new home, Carnage Hill (love the name of the place), *being sick to death is like a passage on a cruise ship where you're up on the captain's deck, eating with him and possibly Engelbert Humperdinck, and no one's getting Legionnaires' or being cross about anything. And you never set sail or arrive anywhere, so there're no bad surprises or disappointments about the ports of call being shabby and alienating. There aren't any ports of call. This is it.*

Ann gets under Frank's skin. *And she has a knack of getting me under her magnifying glass for the sun to bake me a while before I can exit back home to second-marriage deniability.*

He handles his visits by displaying his "default self." *The Default Self, my answer to all her true-thing issues, is an expedient that comes along with nothing more than being sixty-eight - the Default Period of life. Being an essentialist, Ann believes we all have selves, characters we can't do anything about (but lie). Old Emerson believed the same. " ... A man should give us a sense of mass ... ," etc. My mass has simply been deemed deficient. But I believe nothing of the sort. Character, to me, is one more lie of history and the dramatic arts. In my view, we have only what we did yesterday, what we do today, and what we might still do. Plus, whatever we think about all of that. But nothing else - nothing hard or kernel-like. I've never seen evidence of anything resembling it. In fact I've seen the opposite: life as teeming and befuddling, followed by the end.*

His move back to Haddam -- where he originally began as a sportswriter aka aspiring novelist – gives him both a sense of place and an opportunity to express his sense of change. Wallace Stegner commented "we have lived too shallowly in too many places." Not Frank Bascombe.

Our move to Haddam, a return to streets, housing stocks and turbid memories I thought I'd forever parted with, was like many decisions people my age make: conservative, reflexive, unadventurous, and comfort-hungry - all posing as their opposite: novel, spirited, enlightened, a stride into the mystery of life, a bold move only a reckless few would ever chance. As if I'd decided to move to Nairobi and open a Gino's. Sadly, we only know well what we've already done.

Indeed, neighborhoods change and new neighbors are remote....

In the eight years since Sally and I arrived back from Sea Clift, we haven't much become acquainted with our neighbors. Very little gabbing over the fence to share a humorous "W" story. Few if any spontaneous invitations in for a Heineken. No Super Bowl parties, potlucks, or house-warmings. Next door might be a Manhattan Project pioneer, Tolstoy's grand-daughter, or John Wayne Gacy. But you'd hardly know it, and no one seems interested. Neighbors are another vestige of a bygone time. All of which I'm fine with.

Code variances have led to such unpredictable changes, especially for Frank's neighborhood which has been recodified as a "mixed use" neighborhood, the end of life as we know it. Though my bet is I'll be in my resting place before that bad day dawns. If there's a spirit of oneness in my b. '45 generation, it's that we all plan to be dead before the big shit train finds the station......How these occurrences foretell changes that'll eventuate in a Vietnamese massage becoming my new neighbor is far from clear. But it happens – like tectonic plates, whose movement you don't feel 'til it's the big one and your QOL goes away in an afternoon. From my own experience, Amen to that.

The last story seems to tie everything together. It carries the ironic title of "Death of Others" as if it can't happen to us. In the mornings as he has his breakfast Frank listens to the local call in radio station, a program called Yeah? What's It To You? Most of the discussion lately has been about the "killer storm." He enjoys listening to his fellow Haddam citizens, their views and personal life evaluations...as nutty as they sometimes are. For a man in retirement, those brief immersions offer a fairly satisfying substitute to what was once plausible, fully lived life.

He also reads the local obits to honor the deceased, but also quietly to take cognizance of how much any life can actually contain (a lot!), while acknowledging that for any of us a point comes when most of life's been lived and there's much less of it than there used to be, and yet what's there is not to be missed or pissed away in a blur.

On that radio program he hears the labored voice of Eddie Medley, ex neighbor, and a Michigan Wolverine alumnus like Frank. An old friend. A dying friend. Eddie also leaves a message on Frank's answering machine. Something in his voice...frail, but revealing of an inward-tenderness that spoke of pathos and solitude, irreverence and unexpected wonder. More the tryer than I'd first thought, but caked over by illness and time. Even in a depleted state, he seemed to radiate what most modern friendships never do, in spite of all the time we waste on them: the chance that something interesting could be imparted, before-the-curtain-sways-shut-and-all-becomes-darkness. Something about living with just your same ole self all these years, and how enough was really enough. I didn't know anyone else who thought that. Only me. And what's more interesting in the world than being agreed with?

Frank really doesn't want to see him, a dying man. He tells him on the phone he's too busy. Eddie replies: *I'm busy too. Busy getting dead. If you want to catch me live, you better get over here. Maybe you don't want to. Maybe you're that kind of chickenshit. Pancreatic cancer's gone to my lungs and belly...It is goddamn efficient. I'll say that. They knew how to make cancer when they made this shit.*

At his advancing age Frank has also been *trying to jettison as many friends as I can, and am frankly surprised more people don't do it as a simple and practical means of achieving well-earned, late-in-the-game clarity. Lived life, especially once you hit adulthood, is always a matter of superfluity leading on to less-ness Only (in my view) it's a less-ness that's as good as anything that happened before – plus it's a lot easier.*

Although Frank does volunteer work, reading for the blind and welcoming veterans back home, he leaves *60 percent of available hours for the unexpected – a galvanizing call to beneficent action, in this case. But what I mostly want to do is nothing I don't want to do.* Nonetheless, as he has the time for the "unexpected," he goes to see his old friend.

He finally gets to Eddie's house and is admitted by the hospice worker to the bedroom. Eddie looks like a skeleton, has trouble even talking, breathing, but he is trying to tell him something. Frank bends down to listen *'That's what I'm here for.' Not literally true. Eddie may mistake me for the angel of death, and this moment his last try at coherence. Death makes of everything in life a dream.* Eddie reveals an old, dark secret, one impacting Frank. No spoilers here.

The take away of this splendid collection of Bascombe stories is if you are planning to grow old, or if you have already joined our group, this is a primer of what is in store. But it's more than the content, it's the unique voice of Frank Bascombe, and hopefully there will be other such works from Ford in the future. And remember, *there's something to be said for the good no-nonsense hurricane, to bully life back into perspective.*

Monday, December 1, 2014 **Trevor's Little People**
I've just begun to plow through William Trevor's massive *The Collected Stories*, a treasure house of some eighty five short stories, all 1,250 pages of them. One can appreciate why he has been called one of the greatest UK short story writers. They are masterful stories and although my preference for American literature had – until now -- overridden my desire to read Trevor, I knew Updike had a high regard for his work (and Trevor reciprocated his admiration for Updike's). It took the mention of a Trevor short story in an Ian McEwen novel, *Sweet Tooth*, to remind me that there is a world of literature out there I haven't yet uncovered and as I'm trying to write some of my own short stories, I picked up this gem from one of Amazon's partners

for less than a buck plus shipping. An incredible bargain, if you have the strength to hold the book, especially when reading in bed, a habit I've developed in the quiet of the night. But this 2 plus lb book requires support on a pillow! Sometimes, as much as I enjoy reading at that particular time, I find myself falling asleep with my glasses on, still holding the book on the pillow, my wife finally turning off the light, removing the book from my sleeping hands, marking the page, and removing my glasses.

It'll be some time before I'm "finished" with these stories (other than for reasons of occasionally falling asleep!). First, they are to be savored and thought about. It's not a fast read, particularly for someone who is trying to better understand the short story craft and is taking notes here and there. Some stories are best appreciated when reread as well. Reading is what is left over to do after a busy day. Therefore, these early comments on what I've read thus far.

How do I possibly categorize these stories? As Updike had his characters -- such as *The Maples* --- mostly modeled after friends and family, highly educated, upper middle class folk with an excessive libido, Trevor has his "little people," people eking out a life in the UK after WW II, some of whom have allowed their fantasy lives to take over, living with illusions frequently to the very end of the story, ones of which they may not even be aware. It leaves the reader with a sense of wonder, about human nature, about the miracle of day to day existence in general. How do we all get by, burdened by the past or by expectations? Trevor once defined the short story as "an art of the glimpse," whose "strength lies in what it leaves out." It's the reader's job to fill in the latter.

Many of the characters begin at one level of a story, exemplary folk in the reader's mind, only to have life take them down a peg or two, then three, to the end of the story. One such story, "The General's Day," concerns a retired General, well known in his town, who leaves his housekeeper during the day to explore the town, usually with fantasies of meeting a younger woman, or seeing friends (who assiduously avoid him), meanwhile suspecting his housekeeper of stealing from him or secretly imbibing his liquor. And yet he goes off, and not everything goes as he's imagined. But there is the past to cling to, as do many of Trevor's characters, along with their hopes. Here's just a piece of Trevor's prose which makes this point:

The General walked on, his thoughts rambling. He thought of the past; of specific days, of moments of shame or pride in his life. The past was his hunting ground; from it came his pleasure and a good deal of everything else. Yet he was not proof against the moment he lived in. The present could snarl at him; could drown his memories so completely that when they surfaced again they were like the burnt tips of matches floating on a puddle, finished and done with. He walked through the summery day, puzzled that all this should be so.

Not wanting to give away spoilers, it's hard to go on with this story gem. Suffice it to say, the General's day ends not as he hoped, but apparently as it always has, and the reader observes human nature stripped threadbare. In fact, if anything characterizes Trevor's stories, it is his unrelenting dissection of lives, bit by bit, getting to core truths, ones not evident at the beginning.

Thus far my favorite story is "In at the Birth" but to try to analyze it or say anything about it is just to spoil another reader's enjoyment of the story. But I will say it is constructed with such care that the outcome, surreal in many respects, is still in keeping with Trevor's love of his "little people." Meanwhile, I still have scores of his stories to read and perhaps I'll revisit Trevor in these "pages" sometime again in the future. Must confess, the sheer bulk of the collection starts to make sense reading on a Kindle, something I have resisted, not because I am a Luddite, but I've been a book person all my life (personally and professionally).

I remember commuting to my first publishing job in 1964 from Brooklyn to Manhattan on the BMT. As any veteran "strap-holder" will know, it took a certain skill to hold on with one hand, and read a paperback book with the other, turning the pages with that one hand. It's a skill that is not applicable to this book! Nonetheless, *The Collected Stories* of William Trevor is highly recommended if you like the genre.

Saturday, December 13, 2014 **Stoner Redux**

I'm astonished that this book was published in 1965 and until now I was unaware of it. A *New Yorker* article by Tim Kreider, "The Greatest American Novel You've Never Heard Of" was a wake-up call to read John Williams' *Stoner.*

The book had been rediscovered abroad, and brought back into print by the New York Review of Books. Ian McEwan had championed the book across the pond when interviewed for an article; "Literature needs more Lazarus miracles like *Stoner*."

It was republished with an insightful essay by John McGahern who, sadly, died at about the time his paperback edition was published (2006). The author of *Stoner*, John Williams, died in 1994, never to see his greatest work become critically acclaimed.

My intention was to put *Stoner* in my reading queue which is building, and building. But when the novel arrived, the *New Yorker* article kept reverberating, and I was fascinated by the cover of the paperback (apparently you CAN tell a good book by its cover!) and I found myself putting it at the top of the queue and, ultimately, interrupting reading the Trevor collection.

One of the points made in the *New Yorker* article is somewhat inexplicable to me: *Despite its pellucid prose, "Stoner" isn't an easy book to read—not because it's dense or abstruse but because it's so painful. I had to stop reading it for a year or two, near the middle of the book....* Yes, it is painful at times, but still compulsively readable. How anyone could put this compelling novel aside is bewildering. The author of *Stoner* articulated the very reasons I "fell in love" with the protagonist. John Williams was once interviewed and said:

I think he's a real hero. A lot of people who have read the novel think that Stoner had such a sad and bad life. I think he had a very good life. He had a better life than most people do, certainly. He was doing what he wanted to do, he had some feeling for what he was doing, he had some sense of the importance of the job he was doing. He was a witness to values that are important ... The important thing in the novel to me is Stoner's sense of a job. Teaching to him is a job-a job in the good and honorable sense of the word. His job gave him a particular kind of identity and made him what he was .... It's the love of the thing that's essential. And if you love something, you're going to understand it. And if you understand it, you're going to learn a lot. The lack of that love defines a bad teacher.... You never know all the results of what you do. I think it all boils down to what I was trying to get at in Stoner. You've got to keep the faith. The important thing is to keep the tradition going, because the tradition is civilization.

The essence of the story is about a man who grew up working with his parents on their farm. The time is before the onset of WW I. He knew nothing else but scratching out life from the fields, his worn hands those of a laborer. It was hard work and there were diminishing returns from the land so when his father heard about the state college having a program to study Agriculture. He sent his only son there, with the hope he would emerge with new techniques which would lessen their burdened lives. But William Stoner would never return to his former life, becoming instead a teacher of English.

Here the exterior story and the inner story run parallel but at odds with one another. His life is besieged by an unhappy marriage, isolation from his wife Edith and daughter Grace, and plagued by an enemy in his English Dept., its Chairman, Lomax (as evil a character towards Stoner as Claggart was to Melville's *Billy Budd*), and by Lomax's favorite student, Walker, who Stoner thinks unworthy of becoming a teacher. He argues this with his one friend, the Dean, Gordon Finch, *it would be a disaster to let him [Walker] in a classroom.....if we do, we become like the world, just as unreal, just as.... the only hope is to keep him out.* But Finch is also now part of the real world and he has become increasingly removed from Stoner. Then finally the real love of his life materializes, Katherine, a student, but ultimately it is to be a love denied. Meanwhile his inner life is blossoming, finding in literature a certain kind of perfect harmony and tranquility.

Both the *New Yorker* article and the Introduction to the NYRB edition quote the same nearly opening lines as I bracketed in pencil in the book. It sets the tone and the themes like a piece of sculpture captures the essence of its subject. It foreshadows the very end at the beginning, unusual for opening lines: *An occasional student who comes across the name may wonder idly who William Stoner was, but he seldom pursues his curiosity beyond a casual question. Stoner's colleagues, who held him in no particular esteem when he was alive, speak of him rarely now; to the older ones, his name is a reminder of the end that awaits them all, and to the younger ones it is merely a sound which evokes no sense of the past and no identity with which they can associate themselves or their careers.*

His discovery of the love of learning and literature comes at the end of his college years and he comes to his profession almost by accident, his mentor, Professor Sloane saying *"but don't you know, Mr. Stoner?...Don't you understand about yourself yet? You're going to be a teacher." Suddenly Sloan seemed very distant, and the walls of the office receded. Stoner felt himself suspended in the wide air, and he heard his voice ask, "Are you sure?" "I'm sure," Sloane said softly. "How can you tell? How can you be sure?" "It's love, Mr. Stoner," Sloane said cheerfully. "You are in love. It's as simple as that."*

The joys of learning, teaching, moving forward in intellectual endeavors, counter balance worldly affairs. The University is a refuge from life itself. And then he finally discovers he is indeed a teacher.

However, his personal life is not what he imagined it would be. Edith, his wife, is reminiscent of F. Scott Fitzgerald's Zelda (and as the *New Yorker* article astutely observes, "you could almost describe [Stoner] as an anti-'Gatsby'"). Edith is unstable, almost child-like, and like Zelda ultimately tries to find some self identity in the arts. They are totally estranged from each other, although living under the same roof. As one would imagine, their daughter, Grace, is impacted by this, ultimately getting pregnant to escape their home, moving to St. Louis, her husband (who she marries after she finds she's pregnant) dying in WW II (in fact, the novel bridges WW I and WW II). She remains more or less in a trance, answering most questions Stoner asks with "it doesn't matter," over and over again, perhaps homage to Melville's Bartelby similarly saying "I prefer not to." She becomes an alcoholic.

The absolutely exquisite, compact writing is what makes this novel great. Ashes to ashes, dust to dust, where we come from and where we go during this brief encounter with life resonates in the pages. Shadows, light, darkness, death, and nature figure prominently in the narrative, particularly the farmers' fields Stoner comes from. Here he is burying his father: *They buried his father in a small plot on the outskirts of Booneville, and William returned to the farm with his mother. That night he could not sleep. He dressed and walked into the field that his father had worked year after year, to the end that he now had found. He tried to remember his father, but the face that he had known in his youth would not come to him. He knelt in the field and took a dry clod of earth in his hand. He broke it and watched the grains, dark in the moonlight, crumble and flow through his fingers. He brushed his hand on his trouser leg and got up and went back to the house. He did not sleep; he lay on the bed and looked out the single window until the dawn came, until there were no shadows upon the land, until it stretched gray and barren and infinite before him.*

After his mother dies, he lays her beside his father, and probably this is where the novel's prose is bleakest, but rings so true. *Their lives had been expended in cheerless labor, their wills broken, their intelligences numbed. Now they were in the earth to which they had given their lives, and slowly, year by year, the earth would take them. Slowly the damp and rot would infest the pine boxes which held their bodies, and slowly it would touch their flesh, and finally it would consume the last vestiges of their substances. And they would become a meaningless part of that stubborn earth to which they had long ago given themselves.*

But counterbalancing the dark aspects of life pushing Stoner along (sometimes the reader wondering whether he is a participant in his choices), is Stoner's euphoric discovery that his choices are one of the mind, not in day to day living: *But choices is what excited him in his work, such as when he was planning his own book, an esoteric study of the English Renaissance. He was in the stage of planning his study, and it was that stage which gave him the most pleasure – the selection among alternative approaches, the rejection of certain strategies, the mysteries and uncertainties that lay in unexplored possibilities, the consequences of choice....The possibilities he could see so exhilarated him that he could not keep still.*

And it is his love of his work, in spite of the slings and arrows dealt by his exterior life, which grows and grows in the novel. He stands up for academic integrity, at a great cost to himself, but on his death bed has his doubts about the meaning of it all: *He had dreamed of a kind of integrity, of a kind of purity that was entire; he found compromise and the assaulting diversion of triviality. He had conceived wisdom, and at the end of the long years he had found ignorance. And what else? he thought. What else?*

It is a remarkable novel, doubly remarkable that it went unnoticed for so long. As the *New Yorker* article points out, so was *Revolutionary Road* by Richard Yates. John Williams' *Stoner* can easily stand beside that work as one of the more important American novels of the 20th century.

Saturday, January 3, 2015 *Crossing to Safety*

I had raved about Stegner's *Angle of Repose*, his Pulitzer Prize winning novel, written earlier in his career. I had hoped to read more by him, but which one of his many works? I was led to this one by Julie Schumacher's article in the *Wall Street Journal* "On Writing about Writers."

It was strange to segue from what I recently read, *Stoner*, to *Crossing to Safety* by Wallace Stegner, the first one a very dark view of academic life and the other an uplifting one although academic politics and anxiety is a minor theme. *Crossing to Safety* is Stegner's last novel, the work of a mature writer, with its philosophical underpinnings and its beautiful effortless flow.

To me, perhaps this should have been his prize-winning novel, but perhaps I am biased as he wrote this when he wasn't much older than I am now, and I closely identify with many of the themes.

The story over four decades unfolds mostly between Madison, Wisconsin and Battell Pond, a small Vermont town *out of a Hudson River School painting, uniting the philosophical-contemplative with the pastoral-picturesque.* Two couples meet at the University in Madison, Sid Lang and his wife Charity, and Larry Morgan and his wife Sally. The two men are instructors hoping to move up the ladder to tenured professorship. Sid and Charity are wealthy and "well-bred" while Larry and Sally are church mice, struggling to stay financially afloat. Sid is a poet and although a competent teacher, Larry is the writer, the one with talent, but one who realizes that teaching might be the only way for he and his wife Sally to survive. Writing would have to be delegated to part time. One would think the two men are being set up by Stegner as competitive gladiators early in the story, but it is quite the opposite. The two couples fall head over heels in Platonic love with each other and each couple "serve a purpose" to the other, Sid and Charity sharing their compound at Battell Pond each summer with them (so Larry can write), and their benefactors having (in return) the close companionship of the author and his wife.

The story, naturally, is told by Larry, covering the gamut of the Zeniths and the Nadirs of their relationship but the latter is rare and it is a friendship unlike most friendships today. The characters are finely drawn by Stegner (aka Larry), and in particular Charity. If I were filming this book decades ago, Katherine Hepburn would have been my choice to play Charity.

But as Julie Schumacher said, this book has writing as one of its central themes. To be a meaningful writer, one must have a philosophical premise, and in the first few pages Stegner reveals his:

In fact, if you could forget mortality, and that used to be easier here than in most places, you could really believe that time is circular and not linear and progressive as our culture is bent on proving. Seen in geological perspective, we are fossils in the making, to be buried and eventually exposed again for the puzzlement of creatures of later eras. Seen in either geological or biological terms, we don't warrant attention as individuals. One of us doesn't differ that much from another, each generation repeats its parents, the works we build to outlast us are not much more enduring than anthills, and much less so than coral reefs. Here everything returns upon itself, repeats and renews itself, and present can hardly be told from past.

In fact there is a heavy dose of Thomas Hardy in Stegner's novel, along with the role of chance and fatalism. Larry even brings up Hardy and then launches into his own interpretation:

Thomas Hardy, whom I had recently been teaching to Wisconsin high school teachers, might have guessed that the President of the Immortals had other sport in mind for us. My own view is less theatrical. Order is indeed the dream of man, but chaos, which is only another word for dumb, blind, witless chance, is still the law of nature. You can plan all you want to. You can lie in your morning bed and fill whole notebooks with schemes and intentions. But within a single afternoon, within hours or minutes, everything you plan and everything you have fought to make yourself can be undone as a slug is undone when salt is poured on him. And right up to the moment when you find yourself dissolving into foam you can still believe you are doing fine.

That last sentence merits reading over and over again. But in the Hardy universe a "slug" can become a writer, by the same fluke of chance:

Talent lies around in us like kindling waiting for a match, but some people, just as gifted as others, are less lucky. Fate never drops a match on them. The times are wrong, or their health is poor, or their energy low, or their obligations too many.

At one point Larry thinks about writing a novel about the two couples (ironically, Stegner, aka Larry, is doing that very thing):

Human lives seldom conform to the conventions of fiction. Chekhov says that it is in the beginnings and endings of stories that we are most tempted to lie. I know what he means, and I agree. But we are sometimes tempted to lie elsewhere, too. I could probably be tempted to lie just here. This is a crucial place for the dropping of hints and the planting of clues, the crucial moment for hiding behind the piano or in the bookcase the revelations that later, to the reader's gratified satisfaction, I will triumphantly discover, if I am after drama. Drama demands the reversal of expectation, but in such a way that the first surprise is followed by an immediate recognition of inevitability. And inevitability takes careful pin-setting. Since this story is about a friendship, drama expects friendship to be overturned. Something, the novelist in me whispers, is going to break up our cozy foursome.

Writing about Sid and Charity not only might have to "break up our cozy foursome" but there is also the problem of the nature of their lives.

Contemporary literature is littered with sex and violence, and the charred remains of unsatisfied lives. So how does Larry take that into account if he "were" to write a novel about this unique relationship?

How do you make a book that anyone will read out of lives as quiet as these? Where are the things that novelists seize upon and readers expect? Where is the high life, the conspicuous waste, the violence, the kinky sex, the death wish? Where are the suburban infidelities, the promiscuities, the convulsive divorces, the alcohol, the drugs, the lost weekends? Where are the hatreds, the political ambitions, the lust for power? Where are speed, noise, ugliness, everything that makes us who we are and makes us recognize ourselves in fiction?

Friendship is the bond of this novel. But what is friendship, especially such a unique one?

It is a relationship that has no formal shape, there are no rules or obligations or bonds as in marriage or the family, it is held together by neither law nor property nor blood, there is no glue in it but mutual liking. It is therefore rare. To Sally and me, focused on each other and on the problems of getting on in a rough world, it happened unexpectedly; and in all our lives it has happened so thoroughly only once.

But friendship is a two way street. If Larry and Sally were "rescued" by their friendship with Sid and Charity, what do the benefactors get out of it? Larry wants to "repay" Sid and Charity, but Charity sees it another way:

As for repaying," she said to me in rebuke, "friends don't have to repay anything. Friendship is the most selfish thing there is. Here are Sid and I just licking our chops. We got everything out of you that we wanted." So they did. They also got, though that they would never have permitted to figure in our relations, our lifelong gratitude. There is a revisionist theory, one of those depth-psychology distortions or half-truths that crop up like toadstools whenever the emotions get infected by the mind, that says we hate worst those who have done the most for us. According to this belittling and demeaning theory, gratitude is a festering sore. Maybe it is, if it's insisted on. But instead of insisting on gratitude, the Langs insisted that their generosity was selfish, so how could we dislike them for it?

Another theme driving the novel is ambition. Sid is a poet (and sometimes chided by Charity for not working harder to write academic treatises instead, the old "publish or perish" route to academic success). But his ambition is not the high test blend that fuels Larry, who comes from nothing and knows that unless he works and works some more, he and Sally would not make it. In some ways it reminds me of my own salad days, having come from parents who survived the depression and doing nothing more than the barely-expected parental things for me as I grew up, with little encouragement, or expectations to pursue any kind of academic life.

I nonetheless left their house for college and never looked back. Luckily I loved my work (publishing) and Ann and I raised our family while I was totally immersed in my work, perhaps too much so, with too much anxiety about the future. But I am who I am, an overachiever, who tried to make do with what talent I did have. As Larry so aptly puts it, *ambition is a path, not a destination...I was your basic overachiever, a workaholic, a pathological beaver of a boy who chewed continually because his teeth kept growing. Nobody could have sustained my schedule for long without a breakdown, and I learned my limitations eventually. Yet when I hear the contemporary disparagement of ambition and the work ethic, I bristle. I can't help it....I suspect that what makes hedonists so angry when they think about over-achievers is that the overachievers, without drugs or orgies, have more fun.*

Indeed, I hope I didn't turn my ambition into a vice, but I did have fun working hard, and it was "without drugs or orgies."

There were several deaths that touched Stegner's life at about the time he wrote the novel, all from cancer. These impacted the novel as well. When he wrote *Crossing,* and are in your 70's one thinks more about "purpose" in life, especially given the inexplicable transitory nature of it all. Our heaven or hell is right here, right now. And how does one die, accepting it, experiencing it? Heavy questions, voiced by Charity:

There's no decent literature on how to die. There ought to be, but there isn't. Only a lot of religious gobbledygook about being gathered in to God, and a lot of biological talk about returning your elements to the earth. The biological talk is all right, I believe it, but it doesn't say anything about what religion is talking about, the essential you, the conscious part of you, and it doesn't teach you anything about how to make the transition from being to not-being. They say there's a moment, when death is certain and close, when we lose our fear of it. I've read that every death, at the end, is peaceful. Even an antelope that's been caught by a lion or cheetah seems not to struggle at the end. I guess there's a big shot of some sedative chemical, the way there's a big shot of adrenaline to help it leap away when it's scared. Well, a shot will do for quick deaths. The problem is to get that same resignation to last through the weeks or months of a slow one, when everything is just as certain but can't be taken care of with some natural hypo. I've talked to my oncologist about it a lot. He has to deal with death every day...But he can't tell me how to do it, or give me any reference in medical literature that will help....So I'm having to find out my own way.

The novel's title, *Crossing to Safety,* comes from a Robert Frost poem, "I Could Give All to Time." Not surprising, as Stegner and Frost were friends, with Frost becoming his mentor to a degree. They had met at a writer's conference in Vermont, not far from the setting of much of this story. Sense of place is strong in both of their writings, as well as love of nature. The final stanza of Robert Frost's poem became Stegner's prologue to the novel: *I could give all to Time except – except / What I myself have held. / But why declare The things forbidden that while the Customs slept / I have crossed to Safety with? For I am There / And what I would not part with I have kept.*

Saturday, January 10, 2015 **Rules of Civility and A Dog's Purpose**

Rules of Civility is the debut novel of Amor Towles who in "real life" is a "principal at an investment firm in Manhattan." In this regard he reminds me of a much younger version of Louis Begley, another professional (although a lawyer), who also stepped across the line into fiction writing. Towles does so successfully as well, managing to capture a time, place, and social strata with a keen eye, one that makes the novel compelling reading. Think of the times of F. Scott Fitzgerald, combined with the insights of Edith Wharton into privileged society, along with some punchy sentences reminiscent of Mickey Spillane. (*E.G.: The driver put the cab in gear and Broadway began slipping by the windows like a string of lights being pulled off a Christmas tree.* Or *They looked like they wouldn't know skinny if it was wrapped in cellophane and sold at the five-and-dime.*)

Unusual, it's a first person female narration. Our likeable protagonist, Katey Kontent, with grit and some fortuitous luck, finds herself navigating from her start in a secretarial pool into the somewhat shark infested waters of New York City's upper class in 1938. The art deco style scene is infested with some very rich people, and she and her friend Eve – actually roommates at the time – both set their sights on Tinker, an ostensibly very rich, attractive man. Eve is the Machiavellian predator while Katey actually loves him. But like much of life, things are not the way they seem. Tinker has a dark secret as he follows his guide, the "110 rules" originally penned by the young George Washington, from which the novel derives its title, *Rules of Civility and Decent Behaviour in Company and Conversation.*

And there is a central theme that ties everything together in the novel when Katey realizes....

It is a bit of a cliché to characterize life as a rambling journey on which we can alter our course at any given time-by the slightest turn of the wheel, the wisdom goes, we influence the chain of events and thus recast our destiny with new cohorts, circumstances, and discoveries. But for most of us, life is nothing like that. Instead, we have a few brief periods when we are offered a handful of discrete options. Do I take this job or that job? In Chicago or New York' Do I join this circle of friends or that one, and with whom do I go home at the end of the night? And does one make time for children now? Or later? Or later still?

In that sense, life is less like a journey than it is a game of honeymoon bridge. In our twenties, when there is still so much time ahead of us, time that seems ample for a hundred indecisions, for a hundred visions and revisions-we draw a card, and we must decide right then and there whether to keep that card and discard the next, or discard the first card and keep the second. And before we know it, the deck has been played out and the decisions we have just made will shape our lives for decades to come.

Rules of Civility is a noteworthy first novel and I am looking forward to Towles' next work.

On to a touching work, very original as it is written from a "first dog's" point of view. Yes, dogs can think and write! We just have to suspend belief and sit back and enjoy. It is sort of a children's book for adults, a simple and moving parable. I think you have to love dogs to read *A Dog's Purpose* by W. Bruce Cameron. Dogs have been a good part of my life, but, alas, not for the last ten years.

A Dog's Purpose's narrator is not only one dog, but one who is reincarnated to truly discover "a dog's purpose." He/she segues from Bailey to Ellie to Buddy in the novel, three separate but related lives, learning in the first life the meaning of love, "the boy" as Bailey refers to Ethan, *this was, I decided, my purpose as a dog, to comfort the boy whenever he needed me.* But dogs (see my own story) do not live long, and eventually Bailey must "leave," being reassured by "the boy" as he departs this life, that *you were a good dog.*

He is reincarnated as a new-born pup, eventually named Ellie, and trains as a search and rescue dog and during her career makes a number of rescues, including the emotional rescue of his masters, first Jakob, and then Maya, *I had a clear purpose – to Find, Show, and save people. I was a good dog. Both Maya and Jakob were focused on work, and that meant neither one of them could ever love me with the utter abandon of Ethan.*

Ellie is then reborn as Buddy, but it is a rocky start for him (first named Bear-Bear by uncaring owners). He is abandoned in the woods by them, and by the time he finds himself back to civilization – eating garbage along the way, he is distraught. *I was a dog who had learned to live among and serve humans as my sole purpose in life. Now, cut off from them, I was adrift. I had no purpose, no destiny, no hope.* However, he finally finds a new owner, is renamed "Buddy," and to go into much more detail is to get into spoilers although I sort of guessed where it was going.

This novel would devour a full tissue box if Ann had read it. It was touching and one must credit the author, W. Bruce Cameron, for his imaginative tale. It is a gentle reminder that we all need to find our purpose in life and then find a way to fulfill it. Buddy nee Ellie nee Bailey certainly did.

As Bailey exclaims: *dogs have important jobs, like barking when the doorbell rings, but cats have no function in a house whatsoever.*

Thursday, February 12, 2015 Conroy's Final Memoir?

This is the third "non- fiction" book I've read by Pat Conroy. I put that in quotation marks as the line separating his novels and his memoirs of his youth at the Citadel (*My Losing Season*), the influence of his mother and teachers on his maturation as a writer (*My Reading Life*), and now, finally, this tortured history of his entire family (*The Death of Santini*) completes the trilogy of his autobiographical works. His memoirs are the building blocks of his fiction. And that is not a criticism, but a fact. For some writers it may be more subliminal, but where else does a writer derive his/her deepest experiences other than those lived? That is what makes moving, meaningful literature, theatre, paintings, you name the art.

I have a profound respect for Conroy's writing ability. It flows, whether it's memoir or fiction. This particular work, I would think, puts his life story to bed, or one hopes so. As he movingly puts it at the onset ...*in the myth I'm sharing I know that I was born to be the recording angel of my parents' dangerous love. Their damaged children are past middle age now, but the residues of their fury still torture each of us...Our parents lit us up like brandy in a skillet. They tormented us in their own flawed, wanton love of each other. This is the telling of my parents' love story – I shall try to write the truth of it as best I can. I'd like to be rid of it forever, because it's hunted me down like some foul-breathed hyena since childhood.*

Throughout this angst-ridden work I hear the refrains of John Bradshaw. I've met Bradshaw. I wish Conroy had, although he himself has gone through years and years of therapy. Bradshaw puts his case very clearly in his seminal work *The Family* – the family is a system which shapes our lives and survival in a dysfunctional family involves creating a false self, playing a role – getting typecast so to speak – and it is multigenerational.

It was not until Conroy wrote *The Great Santini* at the age of 30 that he first heard the phrase "dysfunctional family:" *Because I had studied the biography of Thomas Wolfe with such meticulous attention, I thought I knew all the pitfalls of and fly traps into which I could fall by writing on such an incendiary subject as my own family. When I began to write the book, I had never heard the phrase "dysfunctional family." Since the book came out, that phrase has traveled with me as though a wood tick has attached itself to my armpit forever...My portrait of my father was so venomous and unforgiving that I had to pull back from the outraged narrative voice and eventually decide to put the book into third person. But even then, the words flowed like molten steel instead of language.*

As the oldest in the family of many siblings, Conroy bears the brunt and he is trying to excise those demons in his memoirs and fiction.

It was not until after he had a physical confrontation with his father that the impact of multigenerational family sickness dawned on him. His father had left Conroy's house drunk after being plummeted by his son. It suddenly dawned on Conroy that his father had no business driving a car in that condition and ran down the street to find the car – which he did with his father passed out in the driver's seat. He studied his father's face. *I realized I would always be serving a life sentence without parole because of the unpardonable cruelty of this one man. Now on this night, my father had proffered his final gift to me – because I had kicked him across the lawn and beat him with my fists, I sat studying him at my leisure, deep in thought on the first night I ever thought of myself earning my natural birthright as a violent man. I was devastated. All during my childhood, I had sworn that I would never be like him, and here before me, drunken and beaten, was living proof that I was the spitting image of Don Conroy.*

As Tolstoy posited "happy families are all alike; every unhappy family is unhappy in its own way." I've heard of such families (the happy ones), although I've rarely met one without some secret lurking. I think a more benign way of putting it is that some families get along better than others, but all families have their crucibles to bear. I like Conroy's way of putting it: *I don't believe in happy families. A family is too frail a vessel to contain the risks of all the warring impulses expressed when such a group meets on common ground. If a family gathers in harmony for a reunion, everyone in attendance will know the entryways and exits have been mined with improvised explosive devices. The crimes of a father or the carelessness of a mother can defile the taste of oyster dressing and giblet gravy on the brightest Thanksgiving Day....The pretense of being festive at these events is both crushing and debilitating to me...My parents taught me many things, but they never taught me a thing about faking joy...The happy family is one of the treasured romances of the American epic, something akin to the opening of the West.* Holidays brought out the worst in my own family, hopes ridding high, with no way of scaling those walls of expectations.

Much of the book is devoted to the ironic reconciliation with his father. I say "ironic" as it was through the publication (and ultimately the making of the movie) of *The Great Santini*, the main character, "Bull" Meecham being based on his father, that a reconciliation becomes possible. It was not an attractive portrait, so much based on Don Conroy's incendiary persona. Upon publication -- as in the case of Conroy's literary hero Thomas Wolfe when his autobiographical *Look Homeward Angel* was published -- there was an upheaval in the family. But eventually Don Conroy became proud to be known as the "Great Santini," talking down the unflattering parts as being due to his son's "over imagination" and playing up the heroic parts. To Pat Conroy's credit he accepted this part of the reconciliatory bargain and even allowed his father to participate in book signings, his father becoming sort of a "wingman" to Pat for the rest of his life on those occasions.

The deaths of his mother (who had divorced his father years earlier) and then the Great Santini himself are movingly described by Conroy. The affect the family dynamics had on the siblings and particularly his estrangement from his sister Carol Ann (*her talismanic powers over me extended into the deepest realms of self*) and the suicide of his youngest brother (*Tom was born to hurt*) are detailed. His beautiful eulogy to his father is appended at the end of the book.

Towards the end of his father's life, *we began a year of submitting to Dad's whims as he made a final tour of the most significant places in his life. He planned visits to every person he'd ever considered a friend, paying special attention to my daughters, who had worshiped him ever since they had learned to talk... He connected himself to Chicago, to Atlanta, and the surprising realm of Beaufort, where his children had planted their own flags of belonging and home.*

Finally the end of this cathartic work, Conroy saying *I will not write about you again* to his now dead parents, He also has found peace in his marriage to Cassandra King, a novelist as well. And they have settled in the low country of Beaufort, a place he loves, a place Conroy can call home in spite of being an army brat and having moved all over God's creation. I hope for no more non-fiction from Conroy as he promises. Yes, any future novel he may write may be steeped in the roots of his own life, but that is how it should be. The book's dedication is lovingly made to his all his brothers and sisters, a sure sign of healing.

It's all out there now, other than the parts which, for whatever reasons, he has chosen to keep private. Thomas Wolfe is Conroy's spiritual literary mentor, both southerners, poetic writers, embracing family history as fiction.

Saturday, March 7, 2015 *Tyler Shows Her Age in A Spool of Blue Thread*

Anne Tyler has joined my growing group of septuagenarian authors and her latest novel *A Spool of Blue Thread* seems to profoundly reflect her initiation. We now deal with the travails of aging in its broadest sense, the decline of our own physicality, our illnesses, deaths of friends and loved ones, and anxiety about the passage of time as we near the end of the hour glass. For many of us, there are our adult children, and our grandchildren to worry about, in a changing world that bears no resemblance to the one we grew up in. Essentially, this is what Anne Tyler speaks to in *A Spool of Blue Thread*, a metaphor that ties together four generations of the Whitshank family, which Tyler describes as being such a *recent* family that they were *short on family history. They didn't have that many stories to choose from. They had to make the most of what they could get.*

I loved this novel, for personal reasons as well as admiring Tyler's writing skills. She is one of America's best living writers.

This is a family history told in typical "Tyleresque," and set mostly in the "Tylertown" of Baltimore. The women are mostly stalwartly idiosyncratic homebodies. The men are mostly craftsmen, homebuilders. At the top of the Whitshank family tree there is the grandfather, Junior, and his wife, Linnie Mae. We learn that she had basically forced herself upon him, first as a 13 year old and five years later, after Junior moved to a boarding house in Baltimore (and completely forgot Linnie Mae, his own family, the feeling mutual, hence being short on family history) Linnie Mae just turned up, suitcase in hand, to move in with him, although they had no contact during those five years: *She was the bane of his existence. She was a millstone around his neck. That night back in '31 when he went to collect her from the train station and found her waiting out front – her unevenly hemmed gray coat too skimpy for the Baltimore winters, her floppy wide-brimmed felt hat so outdated that even Junior could tell – he'd had the incongruous thought that she was like mold on lumber. You think you've scrubbed it off but one day you see it's crept back again.* So, indeed, she did creep back into his life but he finally acknowledges that his ultimate success in the building business was in part due to her people skills. (Junior is a craftsman, a perfectionist, but not very good with the customers.) He builds a home for a Mr. and Mrs. Brill, but: *This was the house of his life, after all (the way a different type of man would have a love of his life), and against any sort of logic he clung to the conviction that he would someday be living here.*

And indeed in due course they did, bringing up their two children, daughter Merrick and son Redcliffe, in that home. "Red" follows in his father's footsteps with the business, marrying Abby (the main character in the novel) and they have four children, Amanda (*who had a bossy streak*), Jeannie (tomboyish when young), Denny (whose story becomes the beginning and end of the novel) and Stem (who was adopted when Denny was four). Stem is called "Douglas" by his wife, Nora, later on in the novel. Both Amanda and Jeannie ultimately marry men with the same name, Hugh, *so...*

their husbands were referred to as 'Amanda's Hugh' and 'Jeannie's Hugh', just another "family quirk." Naturally, Red and Abby ultimately move into the house Junior built, the bedrock for the Whitshank chronicles.

The opening chapter reads almost like a self-contained short story – about the black sheep of the family, Denny. Personality is established at an early age, and this incident takes place when he was 9 or 10: *One time in the grocery store, when Denny was in a funk for some reason, "Good Vibrations" started playing over the loud- speaker. It was Abby's theme song, the one she always said she wanted for her funeral procession, and she began dancing to it. She dipped and sashayed and dum-da-da-dummed around Denny as if he were a maypole, but he just stalked on down the soup aisle with his eyes fixed straight ahead and his fists jammed into his jacket pockets. Made her look like a fool, she told Red when she got home. (She was trying to laugh it off.) He never even glanced at her! She might have been some crazy lady! And this was when he was nine or ten, nowhere near that age yet when boys find their mothers embarrassing. But he had found Abby embarrassing from earliest childhood, evidently. He acted as if he'd been assigned the wrong mother, she said, and she just didn't measure up.*

As a young adult, Denny comes and goes, disappears for large amounts of time and then suddenly shows up. *And whenever he did come home, he was a stranger.* Naturally, parents try to "figure out" their troubled offspring.

Denny is shipped off to a small private college, but that didn't change his nature. *He was still the Whitshank's mystery child.* He bounced around from here to there, occasionally keeping in touch by phone, Tyler describing it with her typical humorous slant: *He had this way of talking on the phone that was so intense and animated; his parents could start to believe that he felt some urgent need for connection. For weeks at a time he might call every Sunday until they grew to expect it, almost depend on it, but then he'd fall silent for months and they had no means of reaching him. It seemed perverse that someone so mobile did not own a mobile phone. By now Abby had signed them up for caller ID, but what use was that? Denny was OUT OF AREA. He was UNKNOWN CALLER. There should have been a special display for him: CATCH ME IF YOU CAN.*

Denny suddenly marries. The Whitshank family is invited to the wedding in NYC. *The preacher was a bike messenger with a license from the Universal Life Church.* Denny and his wife Carla have a baby, Susan, with whom at one stretch Denny regularly takes (without Carla) to visit his parents. Suddenly, no word again, and it goes on for three years and after 9/11 Abby can take it no longer, afraid for her son and their granddaughter and they finally trace him. After several failed attempts to contact him, they ask his older sister Amanda to call. Abby and Red stand by the phone as the call is placed. Denny answers. Although the Whitshank's couldn't hear what Denny said after Amanda identified herself, they could imagine by what Amanda continued to say: *Someday you're going to be a middle-aged man thinking back on your life, and you'll start wondering what your family's been up to. So you'll hop on a train and come down, and when you get to Baltimore it will be this peaceful summer afternoon and these dusty rays of sunshine will be slanting through the skylight in Penn Station. You'll walk on through and out to the street, where nobody is waiting for you, but that's okay; they didn't know you were coming. Still, it feels kind of odd standing there all alone, with the other passengers hugging people and climbing into cars and driving away. You go to the taxi lane and you give the address to a cabbie. You ride through the city looking at all the familiar sights-the row houses, the Bradford pear trees, the women sitting out on their stoops watching their children play. Then the taxi turns onto Bouton Road and right away you get a strange feeling. There are little signs of neglect at our house that Dad would never put up with: blistered paint and gap-toothed shutters. Mismatched mortar patching the walk, rubber treads nailed to the porch steps-all these Harry Homeowner fixes Dad has always railed against. You take hold of the front-door handle and you give it that special pull toward you that it needs before you can push down the thumb latch, but it's locked. You ring the doorbell, but it's broken. You call, 'Mom? Dad?' No one answers. You call, 'Hello?' No one comes running; no one flings open the door and says, 'It's you! It's so good to see you! Why didn't you let us know? We'd have met you at the station! Are you tired? Are you hungry? Come in!' You stand there a while, but you can't think what to do next. You turn and look back toward the street, and you wonder about the rest of the family. 'Maybe Jeannie,' you say. 'Or Amanda.' But you know something, Denny? Don't count on me to take you in, because I'm angry. I'm angry at you for leading us on such a song and dance all these years, not just these last few years but all the years, skipping all those holidays and staying away from the beach trips and missing Mom and Dad's thirtieth anniversary and their thirty-fifth and Jeannie's baby and not attending my wedding that time or even sending a card or calling to wish me well. But most of all, Denny, most of all: I will never forgive you for consuming every last drop of our parents' attention and leaving nothing for the rest of us.*

This is a poignant piece of writing, a cautionary note about the passage of time and the dangers of ignoring family and the ordinary details of our lives. Abby wonders how they settled for so little when it came to their prodigal son. And this is just the first chapter, and it sets the stage for everything that follows.

Tyler though does not construct the novel chronologically, instead moving back and forth in time. Regarding the grandfather, Junior, in her usual good humor Tyler explains; *If it seems odd to call a patriarch 'Junior,' there* was a logical explanation. *Junior's true name was Jurvis Roy, shortened at some point to J.R. and then re-expanded, accordion-like, to Junior.* As noted, Junior builds the house of his dreams for Mr. Brill, knowing full well in his heart that eventually he would be able to buy it, which he did. He fidgets with it for the rest of his life as a builder, head of Whitshank Construction, then carried on by his son Red who moves his family into the house. The house stands as a bulwark in juxtaposition to the fragility of the family.

Then another time leap to Abby who comes from another section of Baltimore and marries Red. Skipping to the very present, we learn that Abby has a form of dementia. This begins a progression of events and the eventual rallying of the family, even Denny. On one lovely day, with the family on the porch Denny was recollecting to Stem (who is now running the business for aged Red) about his earliest recollection of his grandfather ripping out the walkway and resetting the stones, Abby comments *'Oh, you men, stop talking shop!....Weather like this always takes me back to the day I fell in love with Red'...The others smiled. They knew the story well....'It was a beautiful, breezy, yellow-and-green afternoon' Abby began. Which was the way she always began, exactly the same words, every single time. On the porch, everybody relaxed. Their faces grew smooth, and their hands loosened in their laps. It was so restful to be sitting here with family, with the birds talking in the trees and the crosscut-sawing of the crickets and the dog snoring at their feet and the children calling, 'Safe! I'm safe!'*

That's as good as it gets for any writer, to be able to conjure up such images. I read and reread the passage again and again. Even in my own twisted childhood there were times I felt "I'm safe."

For some time the adult children, along with spouses and Abby and Red's grandchildren come and go to help their aging parents. There we learn much about the internal sibling rivalry, the hurts, the jealousies, and how these emotions relate to their upbringing. In particular, Stem (Douglas) and Denny come to blows, literally.

Abby, even in her condition, comes upon certain truths about life such as, *you wake in the morning, you're feeling fine, but all at once you think, 'Something's not right. Something's off somewhere; what is it?' And then you remember that it's your child – whichever one is unhappy.*

She is seeing a doctor about her condition but she wants to discuss philosophical issues: *'And time,' she would tell Dr. Wiss. 'Well, you know about time. How slow it is when you're little and how it speeds up faster and faster once you're grown. Well, now it's just a blur. I can't keep track of it anymore! But it's like time is sort of ... balanced. We're young for such a small fraction of our lives, and yet our youth seems to stretch on forever. Then we're old for years and years, but time flies by fastest then. So it all* comes out equal in the end, don't you see.' I'm sure even Einstein would agree. It's all relative!

To go on with more about Abby's fate is to reveal too much. The house of the Brills, then Junior's, and then Red's stands steadfast front and center, almost like another character in the novel, but even that eventually devolves. Everything changes over the course of time, but the spool of blue thread runs from generation to generation to generation. Tyler captures this in perhaps her most ambitious novel ever, showing her abiding sympathy for her characters, and there are many in this novel.

It fittingly ends as it begins, focused on peripatetic Denny, who is searching for his own sense of belonging and place, as he boards a train for New Jersey on the eve of hurricane Sandy, an interesting image to leave the reader with towards the conclusion of this wonderful, evocative, but essentially melancholy, novel. Tyler may be showing her age, but clearly with no diminution of her writing skills.

Wednesday, June 17, 2015 **Trevor Revisited**

My first entry on William Trevor was last December when I began to savor his huge *The Collected Stories* (1992), but that was a thousand pages ago.I'm still reading the book! His stories require close reading, even a second reading, as there is the story itself and then the meaning along with all the underlying emotions. There are also the settings and cultural references, typically UK and Irish or along the Amalfi coast or Tuscany, that often requires some additional research by me. The further he strays from London and its environs which I'm familiar with to a degree, the more demanding the task becomes. What did we do before Google?

However in the end, it's almost unnecessary to understand all those references as Trevor primarily deals with universal truths mostly borne by the experiences of everyday people. As John Updike noted in his 1981 review of one of Trevor's collections, "Mr. Trevor knows, and dramatizes, two principal truths about low life: it never utterly lies down, but persists in asserting claims and values of its own derivation; and it cannot be fenced off and disowned by the fortunate."

Trevor himself refers to fiction writers as "outsiders," ones who have no place in society because society is what we're watching" and that he "hang[s] about the shadows of the world, that he "likes to dwell upon it rather than in it," can be seen in each and every one of his short stories.

Here are widows and widowers, miscreants and innocents, the travails of the elderly juxtaposed to the innocence of youth, the dilemmas of the middle aged and the divorced, so often lonely people trying to connect with someone who is inappropriate, and people from all economic stations of life.

His characters are victims of their own actions, sometimes "imagining" (the number of times Trevor says, "he [or] she imagined" is countless) different outcomes and different realities. There is a Pinteresque quality to many of the stories, showing humanity, some humor, and a hint of the absurd.

We identify with his characters, perhaps their taking the wrong fork in the road as we might be prone to do, and the consequences of their actions. He spotlights that inherent loneliness we sometimes feel at social gatherings, or in our everyday relationships. The mistakes of our lives add up but so do our little victories, our justifications of our actions making things seem alright.

Sometimes I sense the shadow of Thomas Hardy reading Trevor, Hardy's sense of realism, even suffering. And a few stories slightly reminded me of Edgar Allan Poe, not that Trevor delves into horror, but there is a mysterious quality to many of his stories and tension. I also suspect he is a "fan" of A.J. Cronin, a popular English storyteller of the 1930's and 40's, who wrote in a similar style. He mentions A.J. Cronin in a couple of stories and even one of his characters is named "Cronin." I read Cronin's *The Citadel* in high school, a book I read for pleasure, and remarkably it held my attention (at the time I read mostly science fiction for my pleasure reading). Perhaps Cronin merits a revisit.

Trevor's stories take place in boarding schools, social gatherings, the office, small towns, dance ballrooms, and hotels and pensiones making them central scenes for these mostly melancholy, moving tales to play out. Here he can observe his characters while he moves them about like pieces on a chessboard, his detailed descriptions always precise. Humiliation seems to run through his stories as a leitmotif.

Interestingly he seems to find women, not the men, the most interesting subjects simply because, as he's said, "I write out of curiosity more than anything else. That's why I write about women, because I'm not a woman and I don't know what it's like. The excitement of it is to know more about something that I'm not and can't be."

In spite of the foibles of his characters, Trevor mostly manages to demand our empathy for them. We've all known people such as Trevor describes or recognize ourselves, sharing similar emotions. On the other hand, there are also hints of misanthropy, a sense that to be human is to be imperfect, even a species to be deplored. Always, his stories are memorable and haunting, people who are as real as your best friend. They are unforgettable.

I'm tempted to write about some of the specific stories in this collection, as I began to do in my last entry on Trevor, but to do so, without revealing key turns in character and plot is next to impossible. A short story is not like a novel; it's about (as Trevor said), a "glimpse" and to describe the glimpse is to, well, ruin another reader's enjoyment of the story.

Here is a writer you can read again and again. His stories provoke introspection and reflection. He is certainly in the class (or the head of it) of the
other great contemporary short story writers, Cheever, Updike, Carver, and
Munro. It is rare to be so profoundly moved and amazed by one short story
collection, *The Collected Works*, by William Trevor (Penguin Books, 1992).

Thursday, July 23, 2015 *Hitchens' Final Thoughts on Religion*

It's a masterpiece of logic and freethought: Christopher Hitchens' *God is
Not Great; How Religion Poisons Everything*. In the small world department, it's dedicated to his close friend and now one of my favorite contemporary English novelists, Ian McEwan, with whom he no doubt extensively
discussed the book's contents as it was being written.

I've never forgotten Cal Thomas' reprehensible "Christmas message"
extolling the death of the atheist Hitchens who died of esophageal cancer
more than three years ago. As a secularist, I'm predisposed to Hitchens'
arguments, but as I've only read some of his essays in the past; it was time
to read the book which Thomas castigates. While Hitchens carefully builds
his arguments free from external dogma, Thomas uses the bible as his reference source. Hitchens would have annihilated him in a public debate.

Hitchens' book begins with two brilliant introductory chapters. The
first, "Putting it Mildly," sets out his fundamental arguments: *How much
vanity must be concealed – not too effectively at that – in order to pretend that one is the personal object of a divine plan? How much self-
respect must be sacrificed in order that one may squirm continually in
an awareness of one's own sin? How much needless assumptions must
be made, and how much contortion is required, to receive every new
insight of science and manipulate it so as to 'fit' with the revealed words
of ancient man-made deities? How many saints and miracles and coun-
cils of conclaves are required in order to first be able to establish a dogma
and then – after infinite pain and loss and absurdity and cruelty –
to be forced to rescind one of those dogmas? God did not create man in
his own image. Evidently, it was the other way about, which is the painless explanation for the profusion of gods and religions, and the fratricide
both between and among faiths, that we see all about us and that has so
retarded the development of civilization.*

What are the alternatives to organized religion? *Literature, not scripture, sustains the mind and – since there is no other metaphor – also the
soul. We do not believe in heaven or hell, yet no statistic will ever find that
without these blandishments and threats we commit more crimes of greed
or violence than the faithful....We are reconciled to living only once, except
through our children, for whom we are perfectly happy to notice that we*

must make way, and room. We speculate that it is at least possible that, once people accepted the fact of their short and struggling lives, they might behave better toward each other and not worse. We believe with certainty that an ethical life can be lived without religion. [Emphasis is mine-- Ann and I were married at NYC's Ethical Cultural Society which practices the "religion" of humanism – valuing the importance of each individual, celebrating diversity, and believing that our collective deeds create our own heaven or hell right here.] *And we know for a fact that the corollary holds true – that religion has caused innumerable people not just to conduct themselves no better than others....*

No wonder Thomas went off the deep end reading this book. The title of the second chapter is "Religion Kills" and is self explanatory. How many people have died because of, or in the name of, religion? How many wars were fought with both sides praying to "their" God to annihilate the other?

Much of the rest of the book examines religion by religion, showing the contradictions and logical fallacies of their scriptures, their inherent harshness, and their indoctrination procedures. Get them while they're young. In fact one chapter questions whether religion could be considered child abuse. I felt that way during my "religious training." *How can we ever know how many children had their psychological and physical lives irreparably maimed by the compulsory inculcation of faith....[We] can be sure that religion has always hoped to practice upon the unformed and undefended minds of the young, and has gone to great lengths to make sure of this privilege by making alliances with secular powers in the material world.*

As I said, I speak from experience. I was baptized in a Presbyterian Church (as it was nearby the apartment my parents then lived in), and although my grandparents went to a Baptist Church (I think occasionally, not regularly), for some reason I wound up in the Congregational Church across the street. My parents rarely went, but I was sent there for "religious training," something to make me a better person. This included training during "release time" while I was in grammar school. Kids had Wednesday afternoons off to go to their churches for even more religious instruction. So public schools were in this indoctrination scheme as well. I was "confirmed" into the church as a 13 year old, but continued to go to Sunday school.

I'm not sure whether it was unique with my particular Congregational church or it is a basic tenet of the sect, but Calvinism ran deeply in its teaching. Hard work and good deeds will get you into heaven. That part of the equation was OK by me at the time, but the corollary, the burning in hell part for eternity did not – even for the slightest of "sins." As a young child I had nightmares about the devil and hell.

The last time I went to church was when the minister urged the congregation to vote for Nixon as he warned that voting for Kennedy would mean control by the Vatican, just another missile thrown in the war of Protestants and Catholics. (The Irish short story writer, William Trevor, deals with this issue in many of his writings, in particular "Lost Ground" where a Catholic saint appears to a Protestant boy and the outrage it creates in the town – *Why should a saint of [the Catholic] Church appear to a Protestant boy in a neighbourhood that was overwhelmingly Catholic, when there were so many Catholics to choose from?*). Other than attending weddings and funerals, organized religion lost its hold on me then and there.

Hitchens is an equal opportunity exposer of religions, analyzing the hocus pocus of each. He is most familiar with Christianity, but is well schooled in other religious texts, particularly the other Abrahamic religions, Judaism (he found out later in life that his mother was Jewish) and Islam. Fascinating – his analysis of the schism within Islam -- and I'm wondering what he would say about ISIS, the latest incarnation claiming to be the caliphate.

Unlike other religions, the Islamic tenet is that the Koran can never be translated and therefore be open to free inquiry by "non-believers." *This is why all Muslims, whatever their mother tongue, always recite the Koran in its original Arabic....Even if god is or was an Arab (an unsafe assumption), how could he expect to 'reveal' himself by way of an illiterate person who in turn could not possibly hope to pass on the unaltered (let alone unalterable) words?*

I understand why a very religious person may dismiss this as a polemic, but anyone with an open mind will perhaps agree that organized religion just seems to complicate everything, and extreme interpretations of the scriptures, whether Christian, Muslim, etc. add violence to the equation. I've always wondered how any religion can claim to be the "true" one when there are so many other ones including splinter sects claiming the same. Surely, at least the majority is wrong if not all. Of course, these are individual decisions and I try to respect all religions provided they are non-violent and do not proselytize. In fact, there is something to envy about someone who is so confident that there will be a happy afterlife instead of the nothingness from which we came.

Friday, August 14, 2015 *Fortune's Rocks*

One of the books that I squirreled away on the boat some time ago for "summer reading" was Anita Shreve's *Fortune's Rocks*. I keep a number of "emergency books" on our bookshelf in our dinette in case I "tire" from other summer reading I bring up from Florida. I've been reading William Trevor's short story collection, *Selected Stories*, interspersing Thomas McGuane's new short story collection, *Crow Fair*, focusing on short stories with the hope I will learn more about the art of the short story so I can successfully carry forward my own stories (thus far, the osmotic learning method has failed as it's difficult on the boat to concentrate on writing – it's just much easier to read). The Trevor collection has become increasingly maudlin and focused on rural Ireland, not that I mind either, but I felt I just needed a break. Although McGuane's collection provides a stark contrast to Trevor's, his writing reminding me more of a cross between Raymond Carver's short stories and Sam Shepard's plays, I needed a novel to break up the routine. Anita Shreve to the rescue!

I've always admired Shreve who loves to write period pieces or contemporary ones set on the New England coast, but at the core of her works are affairs of the human heart -- I'm thinking of *The Weight of Water*, *Body Surfing*, and *Sea Glass* in particular. *Fortune's Rocks* is in that ensemble, a novel rich in 19th century language with Shreve's unique eye to detail. As she's successfully done before, she writes this novel in the present tense, rendering the reader a sort of eavesdropper onto unfolding events. She also juxtaposes the present tense narrative to the omniscient author's eye, commenting on various social issues.

It is a page turner or perhaps I should say a page burner as it is reminiscent of a high brow Harlequin Romance. It is the "steamiest" novel I've ever read by Shreve, particularly unusual given the late 19th century setting. It is even shocking in some respects, not because of the language but because of the story in the context of the times.

Precocious fifteen year old Olympia Biddeford is the daughter of a prominent and wealthy Boston family who own a vacation cottage, formerly a commodious Convent, on the New Hampshire coast. This well connected summer community at Fortune's Rocks borders Ely Falls, a mill town where immigrant Franco—Americans toil away in noxious factories. She and her parents arrive for their summer on the eve of her 16th birthday. Olympia's perspicacity has not escaped notice of her father, who has removed her from school and taken upon himself the extensive education of his daughter at home. They are very close.

Shreve's superlative prose sets the tone: *It is the late morning of the day of the summer solstice, and through an open window Olympia is trying to capture on her sketch pad the look of a wooden boat, unpainted, its sails old, a dirty ivory. But she is not, she knows, terribly gifted as an artist and her attempts of rendering this boat are more impressionistic than accurate, the main purpose of her sketching being not so much to improve her drawing skills as to provide herself with an opportunity for idle thought. For at this time in her life, Olympia is much occupied with the process of thinking: not constructive thinking necessarily, and nothing that will produce brilliant solutions to problems, but rather drift thinking, like dreaming, the thoughts moving randomly from one place to another, picking something up, looking at it, putting it down again, the way people move through shops.*

But it is not only the maturation of her mind this summer, but the emergence of a woman from the body of a child. In this regard, she meets one of her father's married friends, John Haskell, a physician who is opening a clinic in Ely Falls, a progressive-minded man. He is building a cottage in Fortune's Rocks which he will soon occupy with his wife and children.

Without going into spoiler details, suffice it to say, one of the novels Olympia is reading that summer is Hawthorne's *The Scarlet Letter.* Olympia and Haskell are enveloped in a relationship that has disastrous consequences, Olympia becoming utterly ostracized in an era that is intolerant of straying from social norms.

The novel reads like a mystery in many respects. It also reminded me a little of Dickens' social commentary on the ills of 19th century mill life working conditions. In fact, as much as the novel is about the coming of age of Olympia, it is about her growing awareness of the schism between the wealthy and working classes.

Ultimately, the novel brings these two worlds in direct conflict: the Franco-Americans working in the mills of Ely Falls and Olympia's, a clash of class and culture.

It is a testimony to Shreve's ability to create a compelling architecture for her novel — not merely a passionate love story, but one told on a broader canvas of issues.

Wednesday, August 19, 2015 *Time and Again – and Again*

Time and Again by Jack Finney is a 1970's novel that was languishing on my "bullpen bookshelf."

Compared to *Fortune's Rocks,* the novel I wrote about in a prior entry, this is lightweight as far as literature is concerned but a compelling read nevertheless. It harkens back to the nascent roots of my reading life. My parents were not readers, so I had to fend for myself. As a teenager I discovered science fiction, particularly H.G. Wells and his classic, *Time Machine.* His novels ultimately led to other SF writers such as Jules Verne, Ray Bradbury and Isaac Asimov (with whom I briefly worked early in my career on a series of SF reprints). Finney's novel is science fiction, but it is also a mystery and romance novel as well, and most prominently, an historical portrayal of NYC in the early 1880's.

The novel's protagonist, Si Morley, is an illustrator for a magazine in 1970 (when the novel was written) and he is selected for a secret government project involving time travel. No complicated machinery involved, but instead a clever conceit involving hypnosis and self-hypnosis, so the reader needs to merely suspend belief.

Needless to say, there are the obvious themes such as the danger of disturbing the past so as not to affect the present, and that is a fine line Si has to walk. He makes multiple visits and has follow up debriefings from his government overseers. His last visit becomes a more involved and revelatory one, his becoming more a person of the late 19th century and getting to know the people of the time, not as images of the long deceased, but real, living people. When Finney deals with that, it gave me the chills. These are the New Yorkers who passed through Ellis Island.

Si catches a Third Avenue horse drawn bus, on a cold winter's night in 1882: *Here in the Third Avenue car, my feet ankle-deep in dirty straw but still cold, toes a little numb, I caught a glimpse – through the window of the closed door ahead – of the driver as he drew back on the reins to bring the car to stop. A middle-aged woman, her face as Irish as an anti-Irish cartoon on a back page of most any "Harper's Weekly," climbed aboard. She wore a heavy knitted shawl over her gray hair that covered her shoulders too; she had no other coat; she carried a basket on one arm. As she opened the door, the cold air rolling in and stirring the straw in the aisle, I heard the horse's hoofs slipping and clattering for a purchase, heard the crack of the driver's whip, and just as the door closed I saw the driver's body move as he stamped his feet, hearing the muffled sound of it, and he suddenly turned real for me as I understood how cold he must be out there on that open platform.*

And then the city, too, turned real, this car no longer a quaint museum piece of the future, but of the here and now: solid, scarred, uncomfortable, dirty because the straw on the floor was stained with tobacco spit driven by a harassed overworked man and pulled by a badly treated animal. It was cold out on that platform, I knew that, but I got up, walked up front, slid open the door, and stepped out pulling the door closed behind me. I had to talk to this man.

And indeed Si does, nearly freezing in the process, learning of the man's struggle to make a living at $1.90 a day to support his wife and two children, working 14 hours a day. The heart of the issue, which is also examined in Anita Shreve's novel *Fortune's Rocks*, is the extreme differences in social strata, still rife in our modern times. Our families economic and class status still governs much of our future working lives, hard work being secondary. As the driver relates to Si: *Nine tenths of the people in New York find scarcely a moment in their lives which they can call their own, and see mightily little*

*but misery from one year's end to the other. How is it possible for me to
thank God in my heart for the food he gives me for life, while every morsel
I eat I earn with my toil and even suffering? There may be Providence for
the rich man, but every poor man must be his own Providence. As for the
value of life, we poor folks don't live for ourselves at all; we live for other
people. I often wonder if the rich man who owns great block of stock in the
road and reckons his wealth in the millions does not sometimes think, as
he sits at his well-filled table and looks at the happy faces of his children, of
the poor car driver who toil for his benefit for a dollar and ninety cents a
day, and is lucky if he tastes meat twice a week and can give the little ones
a home, warm clothes and blankets for the winter.* Could Dickens have said
it better?

The guiding rule for Si during his time travel is "observe, don't inter-
fere." To do the latter is to possibly change the present, perhaps substan-
tially. Can the empathetic Si actually abide by the rule? That is one of the
mystery themes running through the novel. I'll leave the ultimate answer
to the reader, but suffice it to say, *Time After Time* is a compulsive read,
especially for an old Sci-fi veteran like myself. I found it particularly
amusing, though, when Si finally returns to 1970 from his last round trip,
the world he describes, one from 45 years ago, seems as foreign to me
now as the 1880's did to Si. Change, one of the few things one can count
on in life, in our hyper-cyber world seems to have taken on a geometric
construct.

Tuesday, September 1, 2015 **When She Was Good – and Roth is Great**

The time had come to leave our boat and return to Florida. Right before
leaving I picked up a novel I had brought, Philip Roth's *When She Was
Good*. Although I've read a lot of Roth, this one is not often discussed. To
my knowledge its Roth's only novel with a woman (Lucy Nelson / Bassart)
as the protagonist. How does this square with the accusations over the years
of Roth being a misogynist?

What held me is Roth's lapidary characterization of Lucy. This is a character, like the one in Dreiser's *Sister Carrie*, who you are unlikely to forget
and it is Roth's characterizations and dialogue which sets this novel apart. It
reminded me of my own mother's struggles in a man's world. There are two
edges to this sword, though, Lucy as standing for and rationalizing what she
considers "the truth" and then where her expectations stemming from" the
truth" almost borders on mental illness. Although she is described as a "ball
buster" at one point, I think Roth is clearly rooting for Lucy in a world that
does not reward her stalwart individualism. Like Anita Shreve's Olympia
in *Fortune's Rocks*, Lucy is a woman before her time. And like Anne Tyler's

A Spool of Blue Thread, this is a multigenerational novel, but with a darker view.

Willard Carroll is from a dysfunctional family but as a young man he finds the American Dream waiting for him in "Liberty Center:"

So at the sight of Liberty Center, its quiet beauty, its serene order, its gentle summery calm, all that had been held in check in him, all that tenderness of heart that had been for eighteen years his secret burden, even at times his shame, came streaming forth. If ever there was a place where life could be less bleak and harsh and cruel than the life he had known as a boy, if ever there was a place where a man did not have to live like a brute, where he did not have to be reminded at every turn that something in the world either did not like mankind, or did not even know of its existence, it was here. Liberty Center! Oh, sweet name! At least for him, for he was indeed free at last of that terrible tyranny of cruel men and cruel nature.

He found a room; then he found a job-he took an examination and scored high enough to become postal clerk; then he found a wife, a strong-minded and respectable girl from a proper family; and then he had a child; and then one day-the fulfillment, he discovered, of a very deep desire-he bought a house of his own, with a front porch and a backyard: downstairs a parlor, a dining room, a kitchen and a bedroom; upstairs two bedrooms more and the bath. A back bathroom was built downstairs in 1915, six years after the birth of his daughter, and following his promotion to assistant postmaster of the town.

That daughter, Myra, becomes the mother to Lucy, Willard's grandchild. But Myra married a man with a drinking problem and as a young girl Lucy calls the police as her mother was hit by her drunken husband, Whitey, blackening her eye. The shame of having the police involved, and their name the subject of gossip, seems worse to Lucy's grandparents, and even her mother, than the act itself. It is from this action that the novel finds its themes and its energy, Lucy condemning her father, totally ostracizing him, and men in general, unless they tell the "truth" and abide by her expectations of how a man should behave, taking responsibility, doing the right thing.

These threads of shame and anger and expectations culminate in her savage condemnation of her malleable husband, Roy, with whom they now have a child, the fourth generation in the novel. These very words could have been spoken by my own mother during the height of her own unhappy marriage to my father:

"You worm! Don't you have any guts at all? Can't you stand on your own two feet, ever? You sponge! You leech! You weak, hopeless, spineless, coward! You'll never change- you don't even want to change! You don't even know what I mean by change! You stand there with your dumb

mouth open! Because you have no backbone! None!" She grabbed the other cushion from behind her and heaved it toward his head. "Since the day we met!" ....

    She charged off the sofa. "And no courage!" she cried. "And no determination! And no will of your own! If I didn't tell you what to do, if I were to turn my back-if I didn't every single rotten day of this rotten life ... Oh, you're not a man, and you never will be, and you don't even care!" She was trying to hammer at his chest; first he pushed her hands down, then he protected himself with his forearms and elbows; then he just moved back, a step at a time.

    This tirade is in front of family and in front of their child. It is a novel that resonates with me for personal reasons. I'll leave it to the reader as to whether Lucy is a "ball buster" or just a person living in a world that has turned on her because "of that terrible tyranny of cruel men and cruel nature" -- as experienced by her own grandfather before he fled to "Liberty Center."

    I'll miss Roth (who has vowed to write no more) as I've missed Updike. To hear from them no longer is like losing close friends.

Saturday, November 14, 2015 *Light Years*

Can it be? Eight years in my elementary school seem to be light years in the distant past, but at the time they were an eternity. And four years in high school were equally drawn out, anticipating adulthood, the point at which I could leave the turmoil of my parent's home. Time accelerated in college, came on full speed during my career and raising a family, and now it's a year in a blink.

    This is a natural segue into a book I recently read, *Light Years* by James Salter. We're talking about elegant masterpiece writing here -- an author I should have read long ago, known as a "writer's writer" by many, a prose stylist. Perhaps I failed to come to his writing as his earlier work was based on his years as a fighter pilot in the Korean War. His novel *The Hunters* was made into a movie starring one of my favorite film noir actors, Robert Mitchum. Little did I know when I saw the film, it was based on James Salter's novel of the same title. It is so incongruous that the same person wrote both novels.

    Salter died only recently, having just turned 90, in Sag Harbor, where I spent part of the summers of my childhood.

    So I am very late to discovering Salter, although his *Light Years* is closely related to other authors I have admired, ones who have written about marital implosion (the subject of Salter's great work), Updike, Cheever, Yates, Ford, to name but a few.

    Ethereal, poetic prose fills the pages of *Light Years*. The plot almost exists out of time and place – although it's set in the 70s, mostly in the northern suburbs of New York. The dissolution of a marriage is presented as a case of everyday entropy, but in stunning language and descriptions. Think Hemingway's short, rhythmic sentences and F. Scott Fitzgerald's lyricism. It's unlike anything else I've read.

It is the story of Viri Berland, a moderately successful architect, and Nedra his beautiful free-spirited wife. Mind you, this was written in the nascent days of feminism. Much of the novel is viewed from Nedra's viewpoint. They live in the Hudson Valley, with their children. Days pass, light into darkness, darkness becomes new days, years. Light years. (The light imagery is omnipresent.) They have a social life, parties, each have dalliances, quiet ones, not the kind which lead to nasty marital confrontations. Time passes until they find they are empty nesters and now what?

Nedra is the one who makes the break but it is Viri, confounded by the change in his life who moves on to another marriage, one he regrets. To indulge in more detail about the plot, though, is senseless as it is the feeling that one derives from reading *Light Years* which is the point. We're all just brief flickers of light in the annals of time, eternity of nothingness before we are born and a similar eternity when we are gone. We believe in endless tomorrows while living out our younger years, the sum of countless moments, most not remembered later, but near the end, the hour-glass so one sided, we look back and wonder where it all went.

Salter tells his story in lush language. Of those parties in their early years of marriage: *Country dinners, the table dense with glasses, flowers, all the food one can eat, dinners ending in tobacco smoke, a feeling of ease. Leisurely dinners. The conversation never lapses. Their life is special, devout, they prefer to spend time with their children, they have only a few friends.*

Or, when Nedra goes to the city to shop: *Life is weather, Life is meals. Lunches on a blue checked cloth on which salt has spilled. The smell of tobacco. Brie, yellow apples, wood-handled knives. It is trips to the city, daily trips. She is like a farm woman who goes to the market. She drove to the city for everything, its streets excited her, winter streets leaking smoke. She drove along Broadway. The sidewalks were white with stains. There were only certain places where she bought food; she was loyal to them, demanding. She parked her car wherever it was convenient, in bus stops, prohibited zones; the urgency of her errands protected her.*

In his prime, Viri thinks about his career as an architect: *I must make one building, even if it's small, that everyone will notice. Then a bigger one. I must ascend by steps....He wanted one thing, the possibility of one thing: to be famous. He wanted to be central to the human family, what else is there to long for, to hope? Already he walked modestly along the streets, as if certain of what was coming. He had nothing. He had only the carefully laid out luggage of bourgeois life, his scalp beginning to show beneath the hair, his immaculate hands. And the knowledge; yes, he had knowledge.... But knowledge does not protect one. Life is contemptuous of knowledge; it forces it to sit in the anterooms, to wait outside. Passion, energy, likes: these are what life admires. Still, anything can be endured if all humanity is watching. The martyrs prove it. We live in the attention of others. We turn to it as flower to the sun....There is no complete life. There are only fragments. We are born to have nothing, to have it pour through our hands. And yet, this pouring, this flood of encounters, struggles, dreams ...one must be unthinking, like a tortoise. One must be resolute, blind. For whatever we do, even whatever we do not do prevents us from doing the opposite. Acts demolish their alternatives, that is the paradox. So that life is a matter of choices, each on final and of little consequence, like dropping stones into the sea.*

Viri's and Nedra's time with their children is precious: *Children are our crop, our fields, our earth. They are the birds let loose into darkness. They are errors renewed. Still, they are the only source from which may be drawn a life more successful, more knowing than our own. Somehow they will do one thing, take one step further, they will see the summit. We believe in it, the radiance that streams from the future, from days we will not see. Children must live, must triumph. Children must die; that is an idea we cannot accept....There is no happiness like this happiness: quiet mornings, light from the river, the weekend ahead. They lived a Russian life, a rich life, interwoven, in which the misfortune of one, a failure, illness, would stagger them all. It was like a garment, this life. Its beauty was outside, its warmth within.*

When Nedra begins to hint at leaving, Viri is stunned, especially now that he was approaching late middle age.And when she is gone, he is left in the house: *Dead flies on the sills of sunny windows, weeds along the pathway, the kitchen empty. The house was melancholy, deceiving; it was like a cathedral where, amid the serenity, something is false, the saints are made of florist's wax, the organ has been gutted. Viri did not have the spirit to do anything about it. He lived in it helplessly as we live in our bodies when we are older....alone in this city, alone on this sea. The days were strewn about him, he was a drunkard of days. He had achieved nothing. He had his life--it was not worth much--not like a life that, though ended, had truly been something. If I had had courage, he thought, if I had had faith. We preserve ourselves as if that were important, and always at the expense of others. We hoard ourselves. We succeed if they fail, we are wise if they are foolish, and we go onward, clutching, until there is no one--we are left with no companion save God. In whom we do not believe. Who we know does not exist.*

As one might imagine from the last quote alone, the novel comes to a profoundly sad ending, disturbing in so many ways.

Saturday, December 12, 2015 *All That Is*

Having read James Salter's *Light Years* I was eager to read his last work, one that was written and published only two years before his death at the age of 90. Why does a person nearing the end of his life take one last plunge into writing a novel after such a long absence (the previous one was written more than 30 years earlier)?

That is immediately answered in the epigraph preceding the half title page: "There comes a time when you / realize that everything is a dream, / and only those things preserved in writing / have any possibility of being real." Salter has important things to say about that "dream," and thus this novel.

Light Years is poetic whereas *All That Is* is more episodic, covering the events of the entire adult life of Philip Bowman, a naval officer in WW II, Harvard educated. He takes a circuitous route to becoming one of the leading editors in a well-known New York City literary publishing house, one that could be a veiled version of Farrar, Straus and Giroux. The novel contains a number of publishing references that are familiar to me, particularly the London and Frankfurt Bookfairs and ABA in Chicago. So reminiscence was an added layer of meaning while reading this tale.

The novel opens during WWII. Bowman is a navigator aboard a destroyer in the Pacific. The man he most admires is his bunkmate, Kimmel, who is known for his sexual exploits. Bowman is completely inexperienced with women. During a ferocious kamikaze battle, Kimmel jumped into the water during the attack, abandoning ship as he was convinced the ship's magazine would blow, only to be picked up by another destroyer that was then almost immediately sunk. *Kimmel ended up in a naval hospital. He became a kind of legend. He'd jump off his ship by mistake and in one day had seen more action than the rest of them would see in the entire war. Afterwards, Bowman lost track of him.*

I make a point of this as the life Bowman imagined of Kimmel, he eventually tries to create for himself, seeking sexual experience (first through a totally inappropriate marriage to an affluent and inexperienced young women from a wealthy Virginia family, a marriage which rapidly ends in divorce) and then through what constitutes a slowly revolving door of sexual partners. These women were all well educated, some married, attracted to Bowman no doubt as he matured into a New York City sophisticate, well connected to artists and writers in particular, the names of which are dropped freely throughout the novel.

Yet, there is the strong theme of Bowman leading essentially a solitary life populated by the activities of his profession and his dalliances. A couple of these relationships become quite serious, even leading to the thought of a second marriage. One in particular seems to be heading right there until it explodes into deception and even more startling in the context of this tale, revenge. It is the only moment in the novel that truly takes the reader by surprise.

It reminds me in many ways of *Stoner* by John Williams, although that is a much darker tale. There is a sense of "aloneness" in each novel. These men have their work, work they love, but relationships break down or are fleeting. Each protagonist marries only once.

Bowman and Stoner move in different circles, Bowman's world being the well-traveled, the affluent and sophisticated. Salter's characters move in and out of the novel not unlike life itself where acquaintances reappear in the most unlikely places or at the most unlikely times.

Two such characters (and there are scores of such minor players) in the novel are Neil Eddins, "the other editor,…a southerner, smooth faced and mannerly, who wore striped shirts and made friends easily," and Charles Delovet a literary agent. Salter describes a meeting between Eddins and Delovet, and the description is typical of Salter's prose and the kind of people he writes about: *In the city one day Eddins had lunch at the Century Club, in the distinguished surroundings of portraits and books, with a successful literary agent named Charles Delovet, who was well-dressed and walked with a slight limp said to be from a ski accident. One of his shoes had a thick heel though it was not obvious. Delovet was a man of style and attractive to women. He had some major clients, Noel Coward, it was rumored, and also a yacht in Westport on which he gave parties in the summer. In his office he had a ceramic ashtray from the Folies Bergere with a dancer's long legs in relief and, imprinted around the rim: Pour plaisir aux femmes, ca coute cher-women are expensive. He'd been an editor at one time and he liked writers, loved them, in fact. He rarely met a writer he didn't like or who didn't have some quality he liked. But there were a few. He hated plagiarists.*

Salter's prose can be lyrical, evocative, and nostalgic, such as this description of Bowman going to see his ailing mother, leaving New York City by train: *Bowman came by train, looking out at the haze of the Jersey meadows, marshes really. He had a deep memory of these meadows, they seemed a part of his blood like the lone gray silhouette of the Empire State Building on the horizon, floating as in a dream. He knew the route, beginning with the desolate rivers and inlets dark with the years. Like some ancient industrial skeleton, the Pulaski Skyway rose in the distance and looped across the waters. Nearer, in a rush, blank factories of brick with broken windows went past.* Then there was Newark, the grim, lost city of *Philip Roth, and churches with trees growing from the base of neglected spires. Endless quiet streets of houses, asylums, schools, all of an emptiness it seemed, intermixed with bland suburban happiness and wholesome names, Maplewood, Brick Church. The great, smooth golf courses with immaculate greens. He was of it, from it, and as he rode, unconnected to it.* I know those sites too, but it takes a special writer to connect the reader to those feelings.

Salter takes the opportunity to opine on literature's place in contemporary culture (or lack of place to be more precise) and the decline of publishing (something I felt very acutely at the end my own career): *The power of the novel in the nation's culture had weakened. It had happened gradually. It was something everyone recognized and ignored. All went on exactly as before, that was the beauty of it. The glory had faded but fresh faces kept appearing, wanting to be part of it, to be in publishing which had retained a suggestion of elegance like a pair of beautiful, bone-shined shoes owned by a bankrupt man. Those who had been in it for some years....were like nails driven long ago into a tree that then grew around them. They were part of it by now, embedded.*

The novel's dialogue is as first-rate as the narrative (he has a good eye and ear for detail), so natural, and sometimes going on for pages. As I suspected, Kimmel comes back into the novel, almost like a coda and that dialogue between he and Bowman is as good as it gets. Real people. And at times the novel reaches the level of eroticism, unusual for a man of his age, but remembering the "beauty of fire from the beauty of embers" (John Masefield).

At the conclusion all things come together, the sea, a woman, a future, even an amusing expression of vanity, shocked by his own aging appearance: *He had been weeding in the garden that afternoon and looked down to see, beneath his tennis shorts, a pair of legs that seemed to belong to an older man. He mustn't he realized, be going around the house in shorts like that....he had to be careful about such things.*

And finally thoughts about death, not too far removed from those anyone his age (or mine) might have: *He had always seen it as the dark river and the long lines of those waiting for the boatman, waiting in resignation and the patience that eternity required, stripped of all but a single, last possession, a ring, a photograph, or letter that represented everything dearest and forever left behind that they somehow hoped, it being so small, they would be able to take with them. What if there should be no river but only the endless lines of unknown people, people absolutely without hope, as there had been in the war? He would be made to join them, to wait forever. He wondered then, as he often did, how much of life remained for him. He was certain of only one thing, whatever was to come was the same for everyone who had ever lived. He would be going where they all had gone and-it was difficult to believe-all he had known would go with him, the war, the butler pouring coffee...names, houses, the sea, all he had known and things he had never known but were there nevertheless, things of his time, all the years, the great liners with their invincible glamour readying to sail, the band playing as they were backed away, the green water widening... and the small boats streaming, following behind. The first voice he ever knew, his mother's, was beyond memory, but he could recall the bliss of being close to her as a child. He could remember his first schoolmates, the names of everyone, the classrooms, the teachers, the details of his own room at home-the life beyond reckoning, the life that had been opened to him and that he had owned.*

Essentially this is a work of closure, a statement that life passes quickly and before one knows it there is little to the future and the past cannot be undone. Yet in his inherent aloneness, Bowman's life is one of content.

Monday, February 15, 2016 **American Rust – A Modern American Tragedy**

Philipp Meyer's first published novel, *American Rust* is a work of merit by a writer of promise, almost a dystopian piece of fiction, the inverse of the American Dream, depicting the demise of the middle class and the seismic changes to the American landscape. It is also a Bildungsroman, the protagonist, Isaac English, having to embark on an odyssey to escape the "American rust" of the Pittsburgh valley and its failed steel industry and his father as well, having to endure beatings, starvation and exhaustion during his journey, but ultimately returning home to save his friend Poe, and to find salvation.

This is a well-crafted character driven novel with each carrying a piece of the story, frequently that piece unknown to the others, at least in its entirety, and leaving the reader the omniscient observer. Meyer skillfully maintains the suspense, making the book a page turner, to me one of the marks of a good writer.

The other characters are intertwined with the 19 year old Isaac English who was expected to go to any top college of his choice as he excelled in high school, as did his older sister, Lee, who went on to Yale on scholarship, and married wealthy right out of school. Isaac stayed behind in the prison of his environment, to care for his father Henry who is in a wheelchair and also to be with his only friend, Billy Poe, two years older than Isaac, a star football player in high school who was expected to get an athletic scholarship to college, but ended up hanging around the dilapidated mill town mainly out of loyalty to his mother who is divorced, and living in a trailer. There is the chief of police, Bud Harris, who loves Billy's mother and has moved mountains to keep Billy on the straight and narrow. And to further add complexity to the plot, there is the residual love affair between Billy and Isaac's sister, the now married Lee, who returns to check on her father and finds her brother leaving.

There are acts of sacrifice and love that ultimately set Isaac and Billy free bringing these threads together. Lurking in the background at all times though, are the remnants of the steel towns, the low-paying jobs left behind for those who have stayed and can find them, a future without a real future and violence. The same feelings were invoked when I read about the empty mill towns of Richard Russo and the trailer parks of Russell Banks. But Meyer's writing is his own, and clever as he builds his novel chapter by chapter, from those different viewpoints, converging at the end. There is a little bit of modern day Kerouac here and even Salinger (such as the way Isaac in stream of consciousness refers to himself in the third person as "the kid").

What came to mind over and over again is this election year. Here we have two revolutionary yet entirely polarized players, the "democratic-social-ist," Bernie Sanders, and the "alpha male, say-anything-you-want" Donald Trump. Each in their own way has forged a strong connection with the disen-franchised white middle class, or the young. What used to be a mainstream American Dream now exists mostly for the deliriously wealthy. The phenom-ena of today's Republican and Democratic primaries is the "do-you-hear-the-people-sing" voice of those who have been left holding the bag as we've morphed from a manufacturing economy to a techno-service based one.

In this regard, Philipp Meyer's *American Rust* speaks like John Dos Passos' *USA Trilogy*, or John Steinbeck's *The Grapes of Wrath*. The topogra-phy of the problem is laid down in similar social commentary. Lee is driving her father for a medical appointment and Meyer observes: *Farther along she couldn't help noticing the old coal chute stretching the length of the hillside, passing high over the road on its steel supports, the sky visible through its rusted floor; the iron suspension bridge crossing the river. It was sealed at both ends, its entire structure similarly penetrated and pocked by rust. Then it seemed there was a rash of abandoned structures, an enormous steel-sided factory painted powder blue, its smokestacks stained with the ubiquitous red-brown streaks, its gate chained shut for how many years, it had never been open in her lifetime. In the end it was rust. That was what defined this place.*

Isaac in his travels on foot is approaching a western PA town: *From a distance it looked peaceful. Up close it looked abandoned-most of the build-ings in complete disrepair, vandalism and neglect. He passed through the downtown, there were a few cars parked, but mostly it was empty buildings, old signs on old storefronts, ancient For Lease signs in most of the windows. The only hints of life came from the coke plant by the river, long corrugated buildings, a tall ventstack burning off wastegas, occasional billows of steam from the coke quenching. A scooploader big enough to pick up a semitrailer was taking coal from a barge and dumping it onto a conveyor toward the main plant. The train tracks were jammed with open railcars full of dusty black coke but other than Isaac, there was not another actual person in sight.*

The consequences are destroyed lives. Harris describes it as "The Great Migration" as Steinbeck might have defined it himself: *Passing through the town, past the old police station and the new one, he'd seen the Fall, the shuttering of the mills, and the Great Migration that followed. Migration to nowhere-thousands of people moved to Texas, tens of thousands, probably, hoping for jobs on oil rigs, but there weren't many of those jobs to be had. So those people had ended up worse off than they started, broke and jobless in a place they didn't know anyone. The rest had just disappeared. And you would never know it. He'd watched guys go from making thirty dollars an hour to four-fifteen, a big steelworker bagging his groceries, stone-faced, there was no easy way for anyone to deal with it.*

Migration jobs like the ones offered to Billy Poe involve constant traveling to dispose of the flotsam of shutting down our manufacturing facilities and its environmental impact: *There was an opening at a company that did the plastic seals for landfills. Traveling all over the country. At new landfills they would lay down the plastic liners in preparation for garbage to be dumped there, to prevent leakage into nearby streams and such. At the old landfills they would seal them up, it was like a giant ziplock, a heavy layer of plastic overtop the garbage and then they blew them up with air to test them, just before they dumped the soil on top you could run across the acres of plastic, bouncing, it was like running on the moon...it was fourteen dollars an hour to start. But it was not really running on the moon. It was working with other people's trash....The work was all in the Midwest now, taking down the auto plants in Michigan and Indiana. And one day even that work would end, and there would be no record, nothing left standing, to show that any-thing had ever been built in America. It was going to cause big problems, he didn't know how but he felt it. You could not have a country, not this big, that didn't make things for itself. There would be ramifications eventually.*

Lee's teacher in high school had come to the town decades before when the steel mills were thriving. He *moved to the Valley to bring socialism to the mills, he'd been a steelworker for ten years, lost his job and become a teacher. Graduated from Cornell and became a steelworker....It was obvious there were people responsible, there were living breathing men who'd made those decisions to put the entire Valley out of work, they had vacation homes in Aspen, they sent their kids to Yale, their portfolios went up when the mills shut down. But, aside from a few ministers who'd famously snuck into a white-glove church and thrown skunk oil on the wealthy pastor, no one lifted a hand in protest. There was something particularly American about it-blaming yourself for bad luck-that resistance to seeing your life as affected by social forces, a tendency to attribute larger problems to individual behavior. The ugly reverse of the American Dream. In France, she thought, they would have shut down the country. They would have stopped the mills from closing. But of course you couldn't say that in public.*

Philipp Meyer, a writer of great promise. I can now turn to his highly praised, *The Son.*

Tuesday, April 5, 2016 **The Son – There IS Blood**

As in the case of *American Rust*, Philipp Meyer's *The Son* is a story told by different characters, but this is a multigenerational novel, skipping back and forth in time, and on a much, much larger scale. If *American Rust* is a microcosm of the contemporary economy, this is a macrocosm of the dark side of the American soul, with overtones of Theodore Dreiser, John Dos Passos and Herman Melville. It is also historical fiction, well researched, particularly in the ways of the Comanche.

Expansive in scale, it takes place mostly in Texas over more than a century. I kept thinking of the movie *Giant* which I remember seeing as a kid, a sprawling film about a Texas family and oil, James Dean's last film. At some point in the novel the movie is actually mentioned so Meyer too was acutely aware of the same in envisioning location. One could also think of the recent movie *There Will Be Blood,* based on Upton Sinclair's novel *Oil.*

At the heart of *The Son* are violence and racism, man's plundering nature, and the Darwinian reality of the weak being devoured by the strong and them, in turn, becoming victims themselves, if not with their very lives, their souls.

The "story" is begun by the patriarch of the McCullough family, Eli, who as a thirteen year old is abducted by the Comanche, having to witness the brutal murder of his mother and sister. This is only the beginning of scores of brutalities in the novel; one needs a thick skin to wade into the evil of man portrayed in these pages. Be prepared to metaphorically drink turtle and buffalo blood.

Eli tells his story in chapters spread throughout the novel, in the first person, sometimes in retrospect, sometimes in real time. He and his brother are taken by the Comanche as slaves and Eli is given the name "Tiehteti" which he explains "meant pathetic little white man." This is the one thing he vows not to be as he grows up in the tribe, finally rising through his own barbarism to a position of respect, at which point he is "traded" back to white society as there was a premium paid for the return for white captives. Eli becomes a mercenary with the Texas Rangers and ultimately sets out on his own to build an empire, first in cattle and horses and finally in oil. Along the way, the skills and savagery learned as a Comanche serve "Colonel McCullough" (as he is known from his Texas Ranger days) well as an empire builder.

The conscience in the novel is his son, Peter, who is overwhelmed by the Texans' treatment of the Mexican natives of Texas, Mexicans who pre-dated the whites before the Civil War. Once the Civil War ended, there was a steady influx of whites and finally when oil was discovered there, their arrival was as fast as they could dispatch Indians and Mexicans to their graves. Peter is horrified and seeks redemption by falling in love with the sole survivor of a Mexican family destroyed by his father and his henchmen. Peter's story is detailed from the pages of his diary which has survived due to a development that only a spoiler could explain, so enough said.

The other main character is Jeanne Anne, Peter's grandchild and Eli's great-grandchild, into whose veins all this bloodletting and empire building ultimately flows. She must make her way in the world of men, ruthless ones at times. J. A. McCullough's chapters are also intermingled, out of chrono-logical order, Meyer writing her tale in the third person.

She grows into this world of men who perhaps thought that *she was a slut or a dyke or a whore. A man trapped in a woman's body; look up her skirt and you'll see a cock. A liar, a schemer, a cold heart with a cunt to match, ridden hard and put up wet. Though she shouldn't take it per-sonally. No one meant anything by it. To be a man meant not living by any rules at all. You could say one thing in church and another at the bar and somehow both were true. You could be a good husband and father and Christian and bed every secretary, waitress, and prostitute that caught your eye. They all had their winks and nods, code for "I fucked that cheer-leader or nanny or Pan Am stewardess, that maid or riding instructor." Meanwhile, the slightest hint she was anything but a virgin (excepting [her] three children), would get her banned for life, a scarlet letter.*

She's the one who has to manage the empire during the time of burgeon-ing oil prices and shady land grabs. Behind every great wealth is a great sin and behind it all is the sense of a Godless universe of natural selection.

Peter watches his father burn down the hacienda of his long-time Mexican neighbors, an old established family, the Garcia's: *...he is not of our time; he is like some fossil come out of a stream bank or a trench in the ocean, from a point in history when you took what you wanted and did not see any reason to justify. I realize he is not any worse than our neigh-bors: they are simply more modern in their thinking. They require some* racial explanation to justify their theft and murder. *My brother Phineas is truly the most advanced among them, has nothing against the Mexican or any other race, he sees it simply as a matter of economics. Science rather than emotion. The strong must be encouraged, the weak allowed to perish.* Though what none of them see, or want to see, is that we have a choice.

Jeanne has her own view on the topic: *Even if God existed, to say he loved the human race was preposterous. It was just as likely the opposite; it was just as likely he was systematically deceiving us. To think that an all-powerful being would make a world for anyone but himself, that he might spend all his time looking out for the interests of lesser creatures, it went against all common sense. The strong took from the weak, only the weak believed otherwise, and if God was out there, he was just as the Greeks and Romans had suspected; a trickster, an older brother who spent all his time inventing ways to punish you.*

The Meyer's overarching philosophical view is expressed by Jeanne as well (helpful to be doing Google lookups to get the full scope of Meyer's research): *As for JFK, it had not surprised her. The year he died, there were still living Texans who had seen their parents scalped by Indians. The land was thirsty. Something primitive still in it. On the ranch they had found points from both the Clovis and the Folsom, and while Jesus was walking to Calvary the Mogollon people were bashing each other with stone axes. When the Spanish came there were the Suma, Jumano, Manso, La Junta, Concho and Chisos and Toboso, Ocana and Cacaxtle, the Coahuiltecans, Comecrudos ... but whether they had wiped out the Mogollons or were descended from them, no one knew. They were all wiped out by the Apaches. Who were in turn wiped out, in Texas anyway, by the Comanches. Who were finally wiped out by the Americans.*

A man, a life - it was barely worth mentioning. The Visigoths had destroyed the Romans, and had themselves been destroyed by the Muslims. Who were destroyed by the Spanish and Portuguese. You did not need Hitler to see that it was not a pleasant story. And yet here she was. Breathing, having these thoughts. The blood that ran through history would fill every river and ocean, but despite all the butchery, here you were.

The writing is prodigiously powerful, the research exhaustive. One could say this is a Western novel, but it is so much more: it is the promise of great things to come from Philipp Meyer.

Wednesday, July 13, 2016 *Jim Harrison, a Singular Writer*

Jim Harrison produced an extensive number of novels, novellas, poetry, and screenplays, yet I had never read his work (other than seeing his screenplay version of *Legends of the Fall*, perhaps his most famous novella). When I saw his obituary earlier this year I made a mental note to remedy this.

I chose to read one of his more recent works, *The River Swimmer*, which is the title of one of the two novellas therein, the other being *The Land of Unlikeness*. I forgot what a joy it is to read a novella, which can be read in one sitting (but in my case taking my time, savoring the language, the perfect literature to read at bedtime, being able to expunge the real world and take in the rural north of Harrison's world). These two works are about two men, one young, one old, each on a journey to find his true self.

The Land of Unlikeness especially resonates as it is about a man much closer to my age who is going through a late life identity crisis. Clive was an artist who became a renowned art appraiser and as such traveled throughout Europe on behalf of his clients, leaving far, far behind the farm on which he was raised in Michigan. There, his mother lives with his sister. Suddenly he finds himself obligated to return home for a summer, when his sister wants to see Europe for the first time and expects her brother to step into a caretaking role for the mother. He does so reluctantly, finding himself back in his boyhood room. And then things change.

His first love, Laurette, now owns the old stone farmhouse of her parents, visits there on weekends, her "housesitter" or "whatever" Lydia living there as well. It brings back memories of Clive's nearly consummated sexual encounter with her as a teenager. But it also brought to surface the truth about his life: *He was suddenly quite tired of the mythology he had constructed for his life. The idea of having quit painting was far too neat. He had lost heart, run out his string, or the homely idea he had painted himself into a small dark corner.*

Meanwhile, he had his mother to care for and all she wants to do is to be taken out for bird-watching expeditions early in the morning. *The dawn was loud with the admittedly pleasant chatter of birds.* These expeditions, although obligatory, become pleasurable. More things change. Laurette and Lydia come to visit the mother as they have been neighbors for a long time. Clive awakens from a nap and observes the women on the patio and goes downstairs to join them and have a martini. *Even more prepossessing was a casserole of lasagna she had brought over which was on a table beside an empty wine bottle. The smell of garlic and tomato sauce, Lydia's thighs, and the sunlight dappling through the willow tree overwhelmed him and he drank deeply.*

He and Laurette wander to the back of the garage nearby. *He found himself pressing her against the hood of his mother's car, trying to kiss her but she averted her face. His hands kneaded her buttocks and he was becoming hard at an amazing speed. "Jesus Christ, I have to think about this. I can't fuck you in a garage with people outside." She slipped away laughing. "Why" he said glumly. He stood there waiting for his penis to slump. It seemed comic at best that this woman could still bowl him over after forty years. How wonderful it would be to find a '47 Plymouth and paint her slouched in the corner with her pleated skirt up.*

Just superb erotic imagery as Clive works towards that wishful goal of finally consummating their teenage relationship while still caring for his mother. Then he finds himself painting once again. In fact, *on a warm-hearted whim he did a small portrait of a bluebird for his mother and then was embarrassed when she was overwhelmed.* It is at this point that I totally identified with Clive, his love of painting is akin to my love of writing, but to say I'm a writer, or that I'm a pianist, my other great interest, is to endow an obligation and subjects the passion to categorization: *Now he was speculating whether or not Laurette would pose half-nude on the car seat. The whole idea was preposterously silly but why not? It was not more cheeky than the idea of his resuming painting. Part of the grace of losing self-importance was the simple question "Who cares?" More importantly, he didn't want to be a painter, he only wanted to paint, two utterly different impulses. He had known many writers and painters who apparently disliked writing and painting but just wanted to be writers and painters. They were what Buckminster Fuller might have called 'low-energy constructs.' Clive didn't want to be anything any longer that called for a title. He knew he wanted to paint so why not paint. Everybody had to do something while awake.* A priceless paragraph of writing and wisdom.

A subplot in the novella is his being estranged from his daughter Sabrina and their eventual reconciliation, all part of his becoming himself, they sharing a camping trip to Marquette on Lake Superior. But it was stormy and that first night they had to take a hotel room on the lake. Finally, they were able to camp. *Behind Sabrina there was a shade of green on a moss-colored log he had never seen before. And on that first afternoon in Marquette there had been a splotch of sunlight far out on the dark stormy lake, golden light and furling white wave crests.* In nature Harrison finds his halcyon home and his most beautiful writing is centered there.

Nature figures even more prominently in *The River Swimmer*, the second story in the book. Here Harrison moves into the realm of magical realism. Thad is a young man who wants to swim all the rivers of the world. Cheever's *The Swimmer* merely swims the suburban sins of Westchester. Thad wants to take in all of nature and in fact has a mystical relationship with "water babies" which his American Indian mentor, Tooth, called them. She was born on the same land as Thad and was allowed to stay there when Thad's father bought the land. Tooth says they may be the souls of lost children who became aquatic infants. These apparitions frequently accompany Thad on his journeys but the demands of two young women conflict him, Laurie and Emily: *Thad felt a slight wave of nausea over money and power, including Laurie and Emily. Nothing ever seemed to be denied to rich girls....What kind of preparation for life can wealth be except to make it easy? Thad preferred Tooth's niece, Dove, in many ways....They had such a good time his heart broke apart when they split up and she said, "You like those rich pretty cunts not a big-nosed Chip girl."*

As in any piece of magical realism, one has to suspend belief to get the most out of the tale. Thad endures criticism, even violence, in his pursuit of his aquatic life. *In periods of extreme loneliness we don't know a thing about life and death and the reality of water consoles us. In school he had long thought that history, the study of it, was an instrument of terror. Reading about either the American Indians or slaves can make you physically ill. He wanted a life as free as possible from other people, thus simply staying on the island was tempting. The possibility of stopping people from doing what they do to other people seemed out of the question.*

He makes compromises towards the end, but one in keeping with *the idea that he was a whore for swimming, the only activity that gave him total pleasure and a sense of absolutely belonging on Earth, especially swimming in rivers with the current carrying your water-enveloped body along at its own speed. It was bliss to him so why shouldn't he be obsessed?*

As painting was an obsession to his older version, Clive. They both found solace in nature, doing what they were born to do. Jim Harrison, a unique writer, who died while writing long handed at his desk.

Tuesday, August 16, 2016 **Crow Fair and Desperate Characters**

Thomas McGuane's short story collection, *Crow Fair* impressed me, reading one short story each evening to completion. He is a gifted writer and although Montana is his focus and thus the western experience of writers such as Wallace Stegner and Raymond Carver encroach, there are also palettes of Updike and Cheever. His characters are universal, flawed, sometimes funny, but fundamentally ones you identify or sympathize with, real people in stories that are so natural the denouement suddenly seizes you. Above all, survival, emotionally as well as physically, is a leitmotif threaded in these stories. Now I fully understand his close friendship with Jim Harrison.

His story "Hubcaps" has an exposition that is reminiscent of a Cheever story....*By late afternoon, Owen's parents were usually having their first cocktails. His mother gave hers some thought, looking upon it as a special treat, while his father served himself a 'stiff one' in a more matter-of-fact way, his every movement expressing a conviction that he had a right to this stuff, no matter how disagreeable or lugubrious or romantic it might soon make him....Owen's mother held her drink between the tips of her fingers; his father held it in his fist. Owen could see solemnity descend on his father's brow with the first sip, while his mother often looked apprehensive about the possible hysteria to come.*

"On a Dirt Road" is particularly Carver-like. Ann and the protagonist "need new friends." A couple moves in a home on their shared dirt road where two cars can hardly pass, and they only see their new neighbors on the road neither acknowledging the other. Ann wants to have dinner with the Clearys, old friends, of whom our protagonist has tired. Ann says she'll go alone with Clearys to a local pizza joint. Off she goes and our protagonist decides to go meet the new neighbors who turn out to have "issues." Nonetheless on the spur of the moment he invites them to go to the pizza place to surprise his wife, but the surprise is on him.

In "A Long View to the West" a man is caring for his dying father who is in the habit of telling or I should say retelling the same stories. Clay asks his father how he feels about dying, the reply being *How should I know? I've never done it before.* This is when he realizes that he is more frightened than his Dad, also realizing that he needs those stories.

"Motherlode" is about a "cattle geneticist" who gets caught up in a dangerous scam, way beyond his level of expertise, and he pays the consequences. The suspense is so carefully built by McGuane that the reader is caught unawares at the end of the story.

In "Prairie Girl" a woman rises from "Butt Hut," a brothel to bank president, by marrying a gay man from the banking family, having a child by him, and raising the boy as the true love of her life. Peter always wonders about his Mom, never realizing the truth.

"River Camp" incorporates all the writer's themes, the role of nature in our insignificant lives, dysfunctional relationships, and the danger that lurks just below the surface because of something which is greater than ourselves. Two old friends, sometimes adversaries, book a strange guide to lead them on a camping trip in the wilderness, learning more about each, their wives, and then the brutal truth about the guide and what nature has in store for them.

The title story "Crow Fair" concerns two brothers who learn that their dying mother, suffering from dementia, had a long affair with a Crow Chief who they set out to find. In so doing, the brothers go their separate ways.

Idiosyncratic, funny and sad at the same time, and beautifully written, McGuane tugs at the reader's heart with simple truths about life. I've mentioned only a few of the stories. These stories, like Cheever's and Carver's deserve to be reread.

Now on to an outstanding novel. Thanks to Jonathan Franzen's unremitting praise of a "forgotten novel," I picked up Paula Fox's *Desperate*

Characters. Here is yet another American classic I could put in the same class as John Williams' *Stoner* which was written only five years earlier (*Stoner* 1965; *Desperate Characters* 1970). Those were turbulent years and each novel deals with the turmoil in subtle ways, but mostly through relationships. Each is written in absolutely exquisite, compact prose.

Fox's novel has a special familiarity to me as it is set near Brooklyn Heights in the late 1960s, my last Brooklyn years in the exact same place and time. Her descriptions of the decadence of New York City of the time are real as I remember. This is juxtaposed to the decay of the inner lives of the two main characters, Sophie and Otto Bentwood. They are a childless couple, in their early 40s, living in the slowly gentrified neighborhood bordering Brooklyn Heights. They also have a Mercedes and a house on Long Island with a barn. They should be happy, right?

Early in the novel, to Otto's displeasure, Sophie feeds a feral cat who suddenly lashes out at Sophie, sinking its teeth in her hand. The incident is the undercurrent of the entire novel as the reader is left wondering whether her decision to not immediately seek medical attention will have serious consequences. In this regard it is a novel of suspense. Otto advises that she do so, although, interestingly, he is not absolutely insistent.

Otto is breaking up with his law partner, Charlie Russell, who has his own marriage difficulties. However these partners, friends from college have gone their separate ways professionally. But the plot is secondary to the crafted writing, sentences, paragraphs you just find yourself dwelling over.

When the cat first appears, ramming its head against the glass door, Otto explains *'Ugly Bastard!' The cat looked at him, then its eyes flicked away. The house felt powerfully solid to him; the sense of that solidity was like a hand placed firmly in the small of his back. Across the yard, past the cat's agitated movements, he saw the rear windows of the houses on the slum street. Some windows had rags tacked across them, other, sheets of transparent plastic. From the sill of one, a blue blanket dangled.*

When Otto is out of sight, Sophie defies him by feeding the cat, even petting the cat as she serves up some milk. *The cat's back rose convulsively to press against her hand. She smiled, wondering how often, if ever before, the cat had felt a friendly human touch, and she was still smiling as the cat reared up on its hind legs, even as it struck at her with extended claws, smiling right up to that second when it sank its teeth into the back of her left hand and hung from her flesh so that she nearly fell forward, stunned and horrified, yet conscious enough of Otto's presence to smother the cry that arose in her throat as she jerked her hand back from that circle of barbed wire.*

What struck me was that "friendly human touch" is absent from her marriage and that she suppressed her cry because of Otto being nearby. This is a marriage in crisis.

Fox is one of these rare writers who can capture the essence of a person in few words, such as her description of one of their friends, a psychiatrist, Myron Holstein who caters to writers and painters: *He didn't know a thing about her, not even after ten years, but she loved the air of knowingness; the flattery that didn't obligate her. And she liked his somewhat battered face, the close-fitting English suits he bought from a London salesman who stopped at a mid-town hotel each year to take orders, the Italian shoes he said were part of his seducer's costume. He wasn't a seducer. He was remote. He was like a man preceded into a room by acrobats.*

That last sentence reminds me of Sondheim's *Send in the Clowns* or George Barker's poem *To My Mother:* "She is a procession no one can follow after / But be like a little dog following a brass band."

It's a stalemate relationship between Otto and Sophie. He refuses to answer the telephone. She asks, why? *"Because I never hear anything on it that I want to hear any more." They were both standing rigidly, each half-consciously amassing evidence against the other, charges that would counterbalance the exasperation that neither could fathom. Then he asked her directly why she was angry. She said she wasn't angry at all; it was just so tiresome of him to indulge himself about the telephone, to stand there so stupidly while it rang, to force her to do it.* How many of us have played the same tug of war with our spouses?

As a woman in her early 40's, Sophie's body is changing. It comes somewhat as a shock to her: *Her body was not her own any more, but had taken off in some direction of its own. In this last year she had discovered that its discomforts once interpreted, always meant the curtailment, or end, of some pleasure. She could not eat and drink the way she once had. Inexorably, she was being invaded by elements that were both gross and risible. She had only realized that one was old for a long time.* Old for a long time, how familiar! Brilliant writing!

Yet the heart of the novel is a philosophical question as "desperate characters" seek meaning in a hostile universe, a snapshot of New York City when it reached its nadir in the late 1960s. As Franzen asks in his introduction: "What is the point of meaning – especially literary meaning – in a rabid modern world? Why bother creating and preserving order if civilization is every bit as killing as the anarchy to which it's opposed?" Striving for the answer, Franzen has read and taught the novel many times.

John Williams' Stoner has been called "the greatest American novel you've never heard of." Paula Fox's *Desperate Characters* is in the same league.

Wednesday, September 28, 2016 **Home at Last!**
Much of this entry was about spending a week in London, going to theatre (see Chapter II), and then we went to Southampton to catch our ship and begin a trip of some 5,700 statute miles to Rotterdam in the Netherlands, Bergen and Flam in Norway, a scheduled stop in the Shetland Islands, Lerwick (which we were unable to visit because of rough seas, a great disappointment), and then three stops in Iceland (one of our favorite destinations), Akureyri, Isafjordur, and finally Reykjavik. The leg from Akureyri to Isafjordur was rough, a head sea of up to 27 feet, with a 40 MPH head wind. The ship's bow would come off of one of the crests and plunge into the trough. It was so rough forward (we were more aft) that staterooms were in disarray from flying drawers and loose objects and some passengers even put on their life jackets and tried to sleep in lounges near muster stations. Also, in the bad weather department during the cruise, we were pinned to the dock in Reykjavic by high winds for 18 hours beyond our departure time and therefore the ship had to make up time for the next 2,301 nautical mile leg to Boston. The seas to Boston were benign. I could have crossed it in my own boat (had there been enough fuel!).

That crossing took five days and we settled into a routine, my attending daily enrichment lectures in the morning, one on astronomy and the other on writing historical fiction. Ann meanwhile had organized morning AND afternoon Mah Jongg games, we meeting for lunch. This left me free in the afternoon to first go to the gym and walk off some of the calories and then to settle down to catch up on my reading.

Luckily I had two books on my Kindle app (yes, I broke down and got an iPad, not that I was abandoning print forever, but there are times when this is a great convenience) and I thought I'd go to the ship's library in case they didn't last. I found the library threadbare, empty shelves, the few books disheveled and uninteresting.

Thinking that two books would not last, I panicked and went to a store on board where they had a rack of paperbacks for sale. Mostly potboilers and romance novels, nothing that would appeal to me, but luckily they had one copy of a book recently made into a film (which I haven't seen), by an author who I admire, Dave Eggers: *A Hologram for a King*. I snapped it up and was confident I was set.

My first read (and my very first iPad electronic book that I've read as I'm from the "old school" and love the printed page – after all, that was my business) was *White Noise* by Don DeLillo, a dystopian work of post modern fiction., the underlying theme of which I can summarize from a quote in the novel: *"That's what it all comes down to in the end," he said. "A person spends his life saying good-bye to other people. How does he say good-bye to himself?" "What if death is nothing but sound?" "Electrical noise." "You hear it forever. Sound all around. How awful." "Uniform, white."*

It's dark, a chemical cloud consuming the main characters. Yet there are some funny, laugh out loud passages, such as this quote from the aging father saying goodbye to his daughter, probably for the last time, as he drives off: *"Don't worry about me," he said. "The little limp means nothing. People my age limp. A limp is a natural thing at a certain age. Forget the cough. It's healthy to cough. You move the stuff around. The stuff can't harm you as long as it doesn't settle in one spot and stay there for years. So the cough's all right. So is the insomnia. The insomnia's all right. What do I gain by sleeping? You reach an age when every minute of sleep is one less minute to do useful things. To cough or limp. Never mind the women. The women are all right. We rent a cassette and have some sex. It pumps blood to the heart. Forget the cigarettes. I like to tell myself I'm getting away with something. Let the Mormons quit smoking. They'll die of something just as bad. The money's no problem. I'm all set incomewise. Zero pensions, zero savings, zero stocks and bonds. So you don't have to worry about that. That's all taken care of. Never mind the teeth. The teeth are all right. The looser they are, the more you can wobble them with your tongue. It gives the tongue something to do. Don't worry about the shakes. Everybody gets the shakes now and then. It's only the left hand anyway. The way to enjoy the shakes is pretend its somebody else's hand. Never mind the sudden and unexplained weight loss. There's no point eating what you can't see. Don't worry about the eyes. The eyes can't get any worse than they are now. Forget the mind completely. The mind goes before the body. That's the way it's supposed to be. So don't worry about the mind. The mind is all right."*
Just a little guilt trip!

It was a striking change to then turn to Richard Russo's *Everybody's Fool*, his long anticipated sequel to *Nobody's Fool* which I read in the early 90s and later saw the movie version with Paul Newman playing the iconic Sully. It is a rollicking multiple plot tragic comedy. It too is dark in some ways and Russo falls a little short of the natural humor of another earlier work of his, *Straight Man*. To me, it was sad to witness Sully and friends in their twilight years. But this is a writer who loves his characters and imparts that love to the reader. Everyone in the novel is a fool one way or another. I couldn't help but see Paul Newman in my mind's eye as I read this sequel. He lived in my former home town, Westport, CT, and I used to see him around from time to time. But Sully's story is only one in the novel and Russo uses his story to tie together others, particularly that of Douglas Raymer, the chief of police who was only a minor character in the prior novel, but a major one here. At one point he wonders: *Where were fools supposed to go? Was there someplace known for welcoming them, where he might blend in with others of his ilk? A place inhabited by middle-aged men who found it impossible to put their deceased wives' infidelities behind them? Who fell in love again in the manner of teenage boys, too self-conscious and clueless to figure out whether their affections were returned? Was there such a place anywhere in the world?*

A Hologram for a King by Dave Eggers in some respects reminded me of Camus' *The Stranger* written in a Hemingway style about the modern dilemma and the existential threat of globalism and its effect on jobs. Like *The Stranger* it has a strong absurdist quality to it as well as being set in the Middle East (in Saudi Arabia vs French Algiers). It is very carefully constructed with simple prose, but with profound meanings running beneath.

Alan Clay is a 54 year old "consultant," hired by a major telecommunications company to sell an IT system to King Abdullah who is creating a city in the white sands outside Jeddah, the King Abdullah Economic City. Will it ever happen though? Will the King ever show up so Alan and his team of three young techies can demonstrate the power of their system, the only one that can create a Hologram of a person speaking from another part of the world?

Alan was a seasoned executive with Schwinn Bicycles before the company slowly imploded from a combination of poor business decisions and globalism. He's in debt and is obsessed with trying to explain to his daughter, Kit, why he might not be able to afford her next semester's college tuition unless this sale goes through. But every attempt to set up a firm appointment with the King seems impossible. Days turn into weeks as Alan becomes unglued.

He wonders where meaningful work has gone. He once built a stone wall at his home, remembering the satisfaction of working with his hands. Sure, it was crooked, not very attractive, but he did this. With his own hands. Nonetheless his town made him remove it as he did not have a permit and it did not meet code. But where was work satisfaction today? -- that was the more important question.

Alan's team is ensconced in a tent. It's hot. The Wifi doesn't work. He supposedly has a contact, a Mr. al-Ahrnad who is to meet him at the main building, the "Black Box," but his repeated attempt to contact him there is rebuffed by the receptionist, Maha. And there is no getting to the King without settling issues first with Mr. al-Ahrnad. Eggers dialogue does not employ quotation marks, but it is clear as to what is description and what is dialogue. This is just a sample of the absurdist loop that Alan finds draining and bewildering, a man from the old school thrust into the modern dilemma:

Alan left the tent and walked up to the Black Box. He was soaked when he arrived, and again he was greeted by Maha. -Hello Mr. Clay.-Hello Maha. Any chance of seeing Mr. al-Ahrnad today?

-I wish I could say yes. But he is in Riyadh today.-Yesterday you said he'd be here all day.-I know. But his plans changed last night. I'm so sorry. -Let me ask you something, Maha. Are you absolutely sure that we shouldn't be meeting with anyone else here? -Anyone else?-Anyone else who might be able to help us with the wi-fi, and might be able to give us some prognosis about what will happen in terms of the King, our presentation?-I'm afraid not, Mr. Clay. Mr. al-Ahrnad really is your primary contact. I'm sure he's very anxious to meet you, but has been unavoidably delayed. He will be back tomorrow. He has guaranteed it.

Of course he doesn't show again.

Meanwhile, Alan has befriended Yousef, a young man who is his driver at times, and who introduces him to a different world, the one below the façade of a city which may never be built. In so doing, Alan comes to terms with his human frailties, and even love and patience in a world over which he is but a meaningless cog. Highly recommended and I guess I'll have to see the film.

A footnote to the foregoing. I've never had an author, and I've worked with thousands as a publisher, take the time in the acknowledgements to thank by name the entire staff of the printer of the book as Eggers does here (Thomson-Shore in Dexter, Michigan -- printers of the hardcover edition). I met with Ned Thomson and Harry Shore when they founded the company in 1972 in Michigan and my company was among their first customers, if not their first. It's just a serendipitous tangential connection between this novel and my distant past.

Saturday, November 26, 2016 *A Sport and a Pastime; Another James Salter Masterpiece*

Salter chisels precise sentences, ones Hemingway himself would envy. And there are flashes of Fitzgerald as well, colorful and lyrical. It's long been said that Salter is a writer's writer and in *A Sport and a Pastime* ("Remember that the life of this world is but a sport and a pastime..." from *The Koran*) he spins the tale of three people, one the narrator, and then the story of the 24 year old Philip Dean and his young lover, an 18 year old French shop girl, Anne-Marie. We follow their pleasures of eating, sex, motoring about the French countryside, from hotel to hotel and restaurant to restaurant, all related through the imagination and recollection of our voyeur narrator. Sexually, every major position from the *Kama Sutra* is explicitly explored and yet the novel is not pornographic, Salter weaving eroticism into his panoply of French provincial images and the strange relationship of the narrator to the two main characters.

The narrator warns the reader that his tale is as much fabricated as it is real. What is real and imagined is left to the reader. We know little about the unnamed narrator who is staying at his friends' country home in Autun, France (the Wheatlands, who live in Paris) as he has done many times before. It is here that he befriends Dean. He is fond of the French countryside and he imagines a love interest in a woman there, Claude, who he only glimpses from afar. He fantasizes about her and here is the genius of Salter who skillfully foreshadows the narrator's interest in Dean and Anne-Marie. Salter's writing is exquisite:

I have discarded my identity. I am still at large, free of my old self until the first encounters, and now I imagine, very clearly, meeting Claude Picquet. For a moment I have the sure premonition I am about to, that I am really going to see her at the next corner and, made confident by the cognacs, begin quite naturally to talk. We walk along together. I watch her closely as she speaks. I can tell she is interested in me, I am circling her like a shark. Suddenly I realize: it will be her. Yes, I'm sure of it. I'm going to meet her. Of course, I'm a little drunk, a little reckless, and in an amiable condition that lets me see myself destined as her lover, cutting into her life with perfect ease. I've noticed you passing in the street many times, I tell her. Yes? She pretends that surprises her. Do you know the Wheatlands, I ask. The Wheatlands? Monsieur and Madame Wheatland, I say. Ah, oui. Well, I tell her, I'm staying in their house. What comes next? I don't know-it will be easy once I am actually talking to her. I want her to come and see it, of course. I want to hear the door close behind her. She stands over by the window. She's not afraid to turn her back to me, to let me move close. I am going to just touch her lightly on the arm ... Claude ... She looks at me and smiles.

Ultimately, his inner life becomes consumed by his thoughts and observations of Dean and Anne-Marie, Salter making the point that memory is not a photograph but a construct:

Certain things I remember exactly as they were. They are merely discolored a bit by time, like coins in the pocket of a forgotten suit. Most of the details, though, have long since been transformed or rearranged to bring others of them forward. Some, in fact, are obviously counterfeit; they are no less important. One alters the past to form the future. But there is a real significance to the pattern which finally appears, which resists all further change. In fact, there is the danger that if I continue to try, the whole concert of events will begin to fall apart in my hands like old newspaper, I can't bear to think of that. The myriad past, it enters us and disappears. Except that within it, somewhere, like diamonds, exist the fragments that refuse to be consumed. Sifting through, if one dares, and collecting them, one discovers the true design.

The narrator is awed by Dean, knowing he can never experience his ease in matters of love and profligacy:

I am only the servant of life. He is an inhabitant. And above all, I cannot confront him. I cannot even imagine such a thing. The reason is simple:

I am afraid of him, of all men who are successful in love. That is the source of his power.

This is eerily similar in its conceit to Salter's last novel, *All that Is*. Its main character, Bowman, tries to imagine the sexual life of a person he once admired, Kimmel, and goes on to try to recreate that life for himself.

Dean subsists on money from his father. He is a Yale drop out. He knows that it will end but meanwhile this intense relationship with Ann-Marie blocks out all light about choices and planning for the future. Dean is a blind man to it all.

We all know how this must end, much like Dean's rare sports car, a Delage, one he abandons, which immediately atrophies with Dean's departure. I think of Dean as a Gatsby and the narrator as his Nick Carraway. Perhaps this is intended all along by Salter, his hat tip to Fitzgerald...

We are all at his mercy. We are subject to his friendship, his love. It is the principles of his world to which we respond, which we seek to find in ourselves. It is his power which I cannot even identify, which is flickering, sometimes present and sometimes not – without it he is empty, a body without breath, as ordinary as my own reflection in the mirror – it is this power which guarantees his existence, even afterwards, even when he is gone.

Although Salter wrote six novels as well as a number of screenplays, *A Sport and a Pastime, Light Years*, and *All that Is* are probably his finest. His first novel, which I have on my shelf to read is considered a masterpiece of wartime aviation fiction, *The Hunters* published in 1956 (Salter was a West Point graduate and a jet pilot during the Korean conflict, a remarkable background for a writer of his stature). That is a span of 57 years during which he wrote his few novels. His output was not great, but his writing is.

Friday, December 9, 2016 *American Ingenuity and Pragmatism – The Wright Brothers*

For a change of pace from the constant drum beat of politics by Twitter and the soul-searching fiction I usually read, I needed a non-fiction reminder of what made this country so unique and special. Toward that end, I turned to David McCullough and his biography, *The Wright Brothers*. McCullough has the ability to present history as a living entity, a time machine into the past. Once you read something by him, you feel connected to that era. I read his award-winning *1776* and *John Adams* before I started writing this blog and later returned to his *The Great Bridge* which he wrote early in his career. It is the story of the building of the Brooklyn Bridge and particularly relevant as Brooklyn is near and dear to my heart.

He is a natural born writer and honed his craft as an English major at Yale University. He is not an historian by education, but historical literature

is nothing more than great story telling using facts where possible and filling in the blanks.

In *The Wright Brothers* he captures the persona of two distinctly
American men, Wilbur and Orville Wright, problem solvers and entrepre-
neurs who after establishing a successful bicycle manufacturing business
in Dayton, Ohio around the turn of the century became fascinated by flight,
studying birds for their beginning education in aerodynamics. Against the
then current belief that human flight (other than by balloon) is impossible,
and without funding, they methodically and pragmatically tinkered with
glider design, picking the Outer Banks -- Kitty Hawk, NC -- as their testing
site because of the unrelenting winds there -- not exactly around the corner
from Toledo, Ohio. It was completely desolated during those times and at first
they lived in tents, graduating to a little shop they set up. Not many people
followed them, thinking they were just eccentric.

Having access to the extensive Wright Family papers allowed
McCullough to tap into primary source documentation, quoting sometimes
from these to tell the story. Imagine Wilbur setting up camp, awaiting the
arrival of Orville, writing a letter to his father which so clearly sets out the
methodical thinking behind their experiments with flight:

*I have my machine nearly finished. It is not to have a motor and is
not expected to fly in any true sense of the word. My idea is merely to
experiment and practice with a view to solving the problem of equilibrium. I have plans which I hope to find much in advance of the methods
tried by previous experimenters. When once a machine is under proper
control under all conditions, the motor problem will be quickly solved. A
failure of a motor will then mean simply a slow descent and safe landing
instead of a disastrous fall.*

This was the genius behind the Wright Brothers experiments, start
with the obvious, recognizing that like a bicycle, lack of control will defeat
this mode of transportation. Well funded experiments such as those conducted by Samuel Langley, with a machine called "The Great Aerodrome"
which had the backing of $50,000 in public money from the U.S. War
Department and another $20,000 in private backing, including an invest-
ment by Alexander Graham Bell, was doomed to crash. Contrast that to the
total of $1,000 the Wright Brothers invested in their successful experiment
and you have yet another example of private pragmatism triumphing over
public profligacy.

Much of their work was done almost secretly, which is the way Wilbur
and Orville wanted it, eschewing publicity and crowds until, well, their
experiments resulted in a real flying machine. In fact they had to take it to
Europe to make their mark publicly. That is an interesting story onto itself,
particularly given the fact that the European phase of their lives involved

not only them, but their sister Katherine as well. She became increasingly involved with their work after Orville was seriously hurt (but fully recuperated with her help) after their one serious accident. They knew the work was dangerous and for that reason they had a cardinal rule never to fly together (their next generation of the "Wright Flyer" was outfitted for two people), a practice they dutifully followed until later in Wilbur's life when flying was more commonplace.

While inspiration and perspiration were in large part the necessary ingredients in their ultimate success, so was fortuity. The unsung hero which McCullough cites in his story is Charlie Parker, an itinerant mechanic who the brothers occasionally used for making parts for their bicycles, who was finally hired full time. As he later recalled: *They offered me $18 a week.....that was pretty good money...Besides, I liked the Wrights....So far as I can figure out, Will and Orv hired me to worry about the bicycle business so they could concentrate on their flying studies and experiments... And I must have satisfied them for they didn't hire anyone else for eight years.*

Indeed, Parker ran the business while the brothers were working on their experiments, but that was just a small part of Parker's contribution to solving the riddle of powered flights. When the brothers finally felt they licked the problem of controlled glider flight, they were ready to add an engine for powered flight. Accordingly, they asked various automobile manufactures to submit specifications for a light engine with sufficient power but received only one reply and that engine was too heavy. They themselves had insufficient knowledge to build such an engine but happenstance there was Charlie Parker, a brilliant mechanic. As he later recalled and recounted by McCullough: *While the boys were handy with tools, they had never done much machine-work and anyway they were busy on the air frame. It was up to me....We didn't make any drawings. One of us would sketch out the part we were talking about on a piece of scratch paper and I'd spike the sketch over my bench.*

Does it get any more seat of the pants than that?

The brothers led a monastic life, totally dedicated to their work. They were bachelors and except for strict observance of the Sunday Sabbath, it was work 24 x 7. All that sacrifice and McCullough movingly recounts the moment in time when they alternatively flew the first four successful times, the last by Wilbur, 852 feet in 59 seconds.

After that their life changed, becoming celebrities of sorts, but still focusing on their work for the next several years, better known in Europe than here in many ways as they went to France to demonstrate their work to the government who had more interest at the time than their own. Wilbur was the first to go abroad. His time there was unlike any he'd known back in Dayton, beginning with his first transatlantic voyage on the Cunard Line's *Campania* which was advertised as "a flying palace of the ocean," a phrase which of course appealed to Wilbur. *We made 466 miles the first day* he wrote back home and he took a tour of the engine room, amazed at those engines delivering 28,000 horsepower vs. the 25 of the new engine for the Flyer III he was about to demonstrate across Europe. He took copious notes during the crossing and walked its decks up to 5 to 10 miles a day. Wilbur was a person of contemplation and action.

One would think this methodical, technical man might not appreciate all that Paris could offer but he became a regular visitor to the Louvre and spent countless hours among its masterpieces. Ultimately Orville and Katherine joined him and they became the toast of France, Wilbur at first. *As said by the Paris correspondent for the Washington Post, it was not just his feats in the air that aroused such interest but his strong 'individuality.' He was seen as a personification of 'the Plymouth Rock spirit,' to which French students of the United States, from the time of Alexis de Tocqueville, had attributed 'the grit and indomitable perseverance that characterize American efforts in every department of activity.'*

I think that observation is the essence of McCullough's biography about the two brothers, their pragmatic approach to problem solving and faith in doing what no one thought possible. They were finally recognized back home at the White House, President Taft himself presenting medals and acknowledging the tardiness of their recognition at home and the accomplishment which given their lack of support is uniquely American, diligence prevailing above all:

I esteem it a great honor and an opportunity to present these medals to you as an evidence of what you have done. I am so glad-perhaps at a delayed hour-to show that in America it is not true that 'a prophet is not without honor save in his own country.' It is especially gratifying thus to note a great step in human discovery by paying honor to men who bear it so modestly. You made this discovery by a course that we of America like to feel is distinctly American-by keeping your noses right at the job until you had accomplished what you had determined to do.

This recognition was finally followed by the largest celebration ever staged in their home town of Dayton, Ohio. It is mind boggling to think that the invention of flight was only little more than 100 years ago. It demonstrates the rapidity of change today.

Reading this masterful biography was the perfect antidote to a disheartening election and now post election season, with its invective rhetoric, a display of American unexceptionalism and gullibility. One can only hope this too shall pass and we will revert to the mean that made this nation so special, as typified by the Wright Brothers and so brilliantly portrayed by David McCullough.

Tuesday, January 10, 2017 *The Hunters*

How many men start out as an F-86 pilot during the Korean War and then become a writer over the next 50 years? Having read virtually all of James Salter's novels, it was inevitable that I needed to read his first I'm generally not "into" war novels (although will never forget reading Herman Wouk's *The Winds of War* and *War and Remembrance*, tears streaming down my face reading the concentration camp chapters), so to this point I had avoided Salter's *The Hunters*. Perhaps this is also because I had seen the movie version on Turner Classic Movies, staring my favorite film noir actor, Robert Mitchum (also with Robert Wagner and May Britt). The novel is very different than the film, hardly bearing any resemblance, other than a story of F-86 fighter pilots during the Korean War. Salter's novel is so superior, but of course it's literature, not Hollywood. Salter must have agonized over the changes that were made to his novel for the screen version.

Cleve Connell arrives at Kimpo air base at the height of the Korean War. There, the F-86 pilots do a dance of death with their MIG-15 enemies. Connell learns this dance means to hunt or be hunted, kill or be killed, a path to fame or ignominy.

The wonder of flying, only decades after flight itself was pioneered by the Wright Brothers, is encapsulated by Salter, an experienced F-86 pilot. This novel could not have been written without that credential or by a person indifferent to the joys of flying. Cleve is ready for one of his early missions, congregating with the other pilots while waiting to go out to his "ship" as they referred to their F-86's: *He was not fully at ease. It was still like being a guest at a family reunion, with all the unfamiliar references. He felt relieved when finally they rode out to their ships. Then it was intoxicating. The smooth takeoff, and the free feeling of having the world drop away. Soon after leaving the ground, they were crossing patches of stratus that lay in the valleys as heavy and white as glaciers. North for the fifth time. It was still all adventure, as exciting as love, as frightening. Cleve rejoiced in it.*

Cleve fantasizes about turning his flying skills into a sport, becoming an ace (5 kills). He romanticizes to his wingman, while being aware that it's not necessarily the best prepared pilots who become aces: *Odd. Everything about this ought to be perfect for you and me. Here we are, by sheer accident, in the most natural of worlds, and of course that means the most artificial, because we're very civilized. We're in a child's dream and a man's heaven, living a medieval life under sanitary conditions, flying the last shreds of something irreplaceable, I don't know what, in a sport too kingly even for kings. Nothing is missing, and yet it's the men who don't understand it at all that become its heroes.*

By then, though, he is already transitioning into some self doubt, even after a brief burst of confidence after his first kill. Soon he sinks into an even larger sinkhole of remorse, and finally finding an acceptance of his self worth in the end. He is tormented, directly or indirectly by his arch rival, Pell, a man he learns would claim unsubstantiated kills or even put his wing-man in harm's way to get a kill....*he hated Pell. He hated him in a way that allowed no other emotion. It seemed he was born to, and that he had done it from the earliest days of his life, before he ever knew him, before he even existed. Of all the absolutes, Pell was the archetype, confronting him with the unreality and diabolical force of a medieval play, the deathlike, grinning angel risen to claim the very souls of men. When he dwelt upon that, Cleve felt the cool touch of fear. There was no way out. He knew that if Pell were to win, he himself could not survive.*

But these opportunities for wins frequently were the consequence of just sheer luck. The squadron flew three or four missions a day and pilots are not assigned to all. Some came back their noses blackened, the fuel tanks dropped, indicating a dog fight while others do not see MIGs during the entire mission. Cleve's pick of the litter tended to be in the latter category while Pell's were in the former, so no wonder.

The Hunters is a well developed novel, gathering momentum to the end, becoming so compelling one can't put the book down the deeper you get into it. Although a war novel, it is written by a then young writer whose prose, you can tell, would lead him to greatness, not in the air, but on the page.

Thursday, May 11, 2017 **Peanut Island, Trevor, and Politics**

Tuesday dawned a beautiful day, a day to be on the water, to escape the constant political drumbeat, and to enjoy what led us to Florida in the first place. Ann was busy, so that meant going out on my own so off to Peanut Island, a publically owned and maintained place of solace during the weekdays. I went. The island was indeed mostly deserted, just what I sought, some peace and quiet. Brought a sandwich and some Perrier, tied the boat up at the floating docks in the Peanut Island Boat basin, and then walked the quarter mile or so to "my" beach, with a beach chair and reading material, the second collection of short stories by William Trevor who I haven't returned to ever since the election and getting sucked into the abyss of political news.

Time to turn to an old friend to accompany me on "my" island and forget about everything else.

His second short story anthology *Selected Stories* consists of ones he wrote later in life, many when he was my age, so I particularly relate to them. As an "Anglo-Irish" writer his shift seems to be more towards where he grew up, Ireland, and not where he lived most of his adult life, England. He is indeed an Irish story teller.

After a swim (or more like floating) in the clear Bahamian-like waters of Peanut Island, I had my lunch and settled down with my companion. I read and pretty much reread his story *Widows*, classic Trevor, a story about a slice of life of persons of no particular interest, attribute, or fame, everyman in his naked self. The story starts off with such a memorable line, immediately bringing you into the story: *Waking on a warm, bright morning in early October, Catherine found herself a widow.* Her husband, Mathew, died in his sleep right next to her. Then in one sentence you get a good idea of both of them: *Quiet, gently spoken, given to thought before offering an opinion, her husband had been regarded by Catherine as cleverer and wiser than she was herself, and more charitable in his view of other people.*

He was well thought of, organized and professional as a seller of agricultural equipment. He even anticipated the inevitable day when they would be separated by death: *Matthew had said more than once, attempting to anticipate the melancholy of their separation: they had known that it was soon to be. He would have held the memories to him if he'd been the one remaining. 'Whichever is left,' he reminded Catherine as they grew old, 'it's only for the time being.'...Matthew had never minded talking about their separation, and had taught her not to mind either.*

It is not until the funeral that we are introduced to another key character, the other widow (after all the title of the short story is *Widows*) and that person is Catherine's sister, Alicia. She had been living in the house with Catherine and Matthew since her own philandering husband had died nine years earlier. So there is now the contrast of a happy marriage and Alicia's unhappy one. The sisters are now alone in the house. Alicia is the older, and their relationship seems to be reverting into one before their marriages, the older helping, guiding the younger.

Until the other major character emerges, a painter, Mr. Leary, who brought *no special skill* to his work and was *often accused of poor workmanship, which in turn led to disputes about payment.* Weeks after the funeral he comes by the house to discuss *an outstanding bill,* an *embarrassment* because of the death. He explains that work he had done for Matthew on the house, for cash, £226 to be exact, had not been paid. Catherine clearly remembers withdrawing the money in that exact amount for Matthew to give to him, and even has the bank records to that effect, but Mr. Leary asks whether she had a receipt. Mrs. Leary always issued a receipt and there was none in her receipt book. Are you sure the money was delivered to Mrs. Leary? The reader is left with the insinuation that perhaps Matthew used the money for something tawdry or at least was careless. Catherine and her sister think that this is just a clever scheme by the Leary's to be double paid. She ignores it for awhile but still ponders the possible reasons and then a statement is delivered by mail that the amount is past due. And that's part of the genius and wonderment of the story: we never really know whether it was paid or not and if not why (although one is left with the feeling it was).

Catherine is tortured by this knowing a statement will come month after month and finally declares to her sister her intention to pay the bill (probably again). *Catherine was paying money in case, somehow, the memory of her husband should be accidentally tarnished. And knowing her sister well, Alicia knew that this resolve would become more stubborn as more time passed. It would mark and influence her sister; it would breed new eccentricities in her. If Leary had not come that day there would have been something else.*

So, in a sharp turn in the story, the spotlight now shines on the relationship between the sisters. This is another Trevor technique of shifting the story suddenly to the real one: an old power struggle to a degree, Alicia being the older and when they were younger considered the more beautiful. Why shouldn't things return to the way they were? The disagreement between the sisters, to pay or not, reaches a climax one night. *They did not speak again, not even to say goodnight. Alicia closed her bedroom door, telling herself crossly that her expectation had not been a greedy one. She had been unhappy in her foolish marriage, and after it she had been beholden in this house. Although it ran against her nature to do so, she had borne her lot without complaint; why should she not fairly have hoped that in widowhood they would again be sisters first of all?....By chance, dishonesty had made death a potency for her sister, as it had not been when she was widowed herself. Alicia had cheated it of its due; it took from her now, as it had not then.* Talk about great writing. That last sentence is a gem. And that is what Trevor's writing is all about, the commonplace, but those profound moments in each "everyman's" life.

So, my day at Peanut passed with natural beauty and my renewed "friendship" with William Trevor, to be revisited as time permits. I packed up, walked back to the boat, the late afternoon sun now beating heavily, boarded the boat and went north on Lake Worth back to my dock to clean up the boat and get ready for dinner with friends. It was a day away from Twitter and current news so it was not until later that I learned that FBI Director James Comey was abruptly fired by Trump, the details of which as we get deeper and deeper into it are as bizarre as any fiction I've ever read.

Wednesday, June 28, 2017 **News of the World**

Funny how what we sometimes read is based on serendipity rather than carefully thought out choices. After all, reading time is precious, especially with multifaceted activities whirling around in the modern world, all calling for our attention or participation. It's one of the reasons I welcome the summer and returning to our boat in Connecticut for a long stay. No pressing commitments, no piano, and although there is work to be done on the boat, incomparable to "running" the house. I welcome the change.

So I've been happily arranging my reading, lining up all the novels I hope to finish, no sense listing them here. In fact, I had already started one, when our good friend, Nina, sent us an email with the subject "beautiful writing," starting out her message "…. *It was March 5 and cold, his breath fumed and his old muffler was dank with the steam. Above and behind them the Dipper turned on its great handle as if to pour night itself out onto the dreaming continent and each of its seven stars gleamed from between the fitful passing clouds….." This is a passage from the book I'm reading and loving): News of the World by Paulette Jiles. It's a story of a printer turned newsreader in the 1870's and what happens to him.*

So I sagely replied, Yes, Beautiful. Lend me your copy!

Jiles' novel reminded me a little of Philipp Meyer's, *The Son*, (although Meyer's is written on a much grander scale). Yet each makes its points about man's inhumanity to man and survival being a paramount issue. However *The Son* is a sledgehammer of a novel while *News of the World* is delicate and uplifting.

Here's another comparative observation to other novels I've reviewed, and this might seem to be strange, yet there is an interesting connection. Jiles dispenses with the use of quotation marks as does Dave Eggers' *Hologram for a King* and Louis Begley's *About Schmidt*. This technique, while off putting at first, works very well as you get used to it and I find that it makes great story telling even more energizing; it's almost reading like screenplays, easily adaptable to that medium. The novels I mentioned were made into films. *News of the World* would be a perfect film as well I thought. Therefore I Googled the title and "film" and found that Tom Hanks had just signed up for a movie version!

Perfect casting as "The Captain" and ideally suited to Hanks' sensibilities and temperament. He's a little young for the part, the main character being closer to my age (nearing mid-70s than Hanks at 60), but just perfect otherwise. Ironically he starred in the movie version of *Hologram for a King* so maybe he has a penchant for story narratives and dialogue without quotation marks as well!

The Son also made its way to film, a recent 10 part TV miniseries. Great stories about the West and the real back story of the unimaginable cruelties and hardships have power.

I found *News of the World* a metaphor for today's developing dystopian world. There was extreme political dissention in Texas during post Civil War years. Edmund Davis, considered a radical, was elected governor against Andrew Jackson Hamilton, a Unionist Democrat. Davis supported the rights of freed slaves and wanted Texas to be divided into a number of Republican-controlled states. This leitmotif works in the background of the novel and the political polarity resembles today. You were either pro Davis or anti-Davis.

It was also a time of great fear, Mexicans being hunted and murdered, Indian wars continuing, and marauding bands of outlaws, lawlessness and violence, not exactly an excellent time for a 70 plus year old man to take a newly freed Indian captive on a 400 mile journey south through Texas.

Captain Jefferson Kyle Kidd is no ordinary man of the times, though. He's been through two wars, including the war of 1812 but that experience is secondary to his nature. He's a good man, trustworthy, honorable, and as an ex-printer he is interested in and makes his living from "the news of the world." These attributes put him in a situation where he is inveigled to return a captive of the Kiowa tribe, a 10 year old white girl, captured when she was six, to her aunt and uncle some four hundred grueling and dangerous miles from Wichita Falls northwest of Dallas to Castroville, southwest of San Antonio.

He's also not ordinary as he embraces information (a modern man!), believing that *"If people had true knowledge of the world perhaps they would not take up arms and so perhaps he could be an aggregator of information from distant places and the world would be a more peaceful place."*

So the story begins when Britt Johnson, a free black man, asks Captain Kidd to deliver the child, who was left to him by a government agent, back to her family. After all she's a white girl and if Johnson attempts the three plus week journey, there could be consequences. *You take her and the fifty dollar gold piece I was given to deliver her. Hard to find somebody to trust with this.* Thus the Captain was given the responsibility of delivering Johanna Leonberger under contract with a government agent (Johnson gives him papers to that effect) and as Kidd himself says: *I am a man of my word.*

He was a runner during the war of 1812. *He had good lungs and knew the country...covering ground at a long trot was meat and drink to him.... Nothing pleased him more than to travel free and unencumbered, along, with a message in his hand, carrying information from one unit to another, unconcerned with its content, independent of what was written or ordered therein...A lifting, running joy. He felt like a thin banner streaming, printed with some real insignia with messages of great import entrusted to his care...He always recalled those two years with a kind of wonder. As when one is granted the life and the task for which one was meant. No matter how odd, no matter how out of the ordinary. When it came to an end he was not surprised. It was too good, too perfect to last.*

And since the Civil War he has been an itinerant news provider, going from town to town reading news articles at assemblages of people in the town for 10 cents apiece. But now he had to combine his living with the solemn oath of delivering the child safely, *in his mild and mindless way still roaming, still reading out the news of the world in the hope that it would do some good, but in the end he must carry a weapon in his belt and he had a child to protect and no printed story or tale would alter that.*

When he first sees Johanna he says *The child seems artificial as well as malign.*

She says (inaudible to them): *My name is Cicada. My father's name is Turning Water. My mother's name is Three Spotted. I want to go home. She doesn't speak these words though as the Kiowa words in all their tonal music lived in her head like bees.*

Thus, the journey begins and here in the best interest of spoiler alerts, I'm deserting plot and delving into some of Jiles' sparse writing and some of the themes that emerge.

The Captain is not only a man of honor, but a person of great sensitivity. In spite of the travails of trying to transport her, and the frustrations of trying to teach her some of the ways of the white world which she had entirely forgotten, his inherent humanity prevails: *He was suddenly almost overwhelmed with pity for her. Torn from her parents, adopted by a strange culture, given new parents, then sold for a few blankets and some old silverware, now sent to stranger after stranger, crushed into peculiar clothing, surrounded by people of an unknown language and unknown culture, only ten years old, and now she could not even eat her food without having to use outlandish instruments....Her sufferings were beyond description.He worried all up and down every street and with every tack he drove in. Worried about the very long journey ahead, about his ability to keep the girl from harm. He thought, resentfully, I raised my girls, I already did that. At the age he had attained with his life span short before him he had begun to look upon the human world with the indifference of a condemned man.* Oh do I identify with the last sentence!

He is a man who lives in the real world and his flight with Johanna brings these thoughts to the surface, *more than ever knowing in his fragile bones that it was the duty of men who aspired to the condition of humanity to protect children and kill for them....Human aggression and depravity still managed to astonish him....Some people were born unsupplied with a human conscience and those people needed killing.*

Yet, as he turns 72 on the road, and is fending off threats to follow through on his promise and in the process gradually bonding with Johanna, he is "beyond belief "at his age, still traveling, alive, and thus "unaccountably happy."

Maybe life is just carrying news. Surviving to carry the news. Maybe we have just one message, and it is delivered to us when we are born and we are never sure what it says; it may have nothing to do with us personally but it must be carried by hand through a life, all the way, and at the end handed over, sealed.

This is a beautiful novel and I was glad to put down my other reading to enjoy *News of the World*. I'll look forward to Tom Hanks' interpretation of it, an actor I admire. He will make a great Captain Kidd.

Thursday, August 24, 2017 Rabbit at Rest -- Art as Life Itself

For years I've had a copy of John Updike's *Rabbit at Rest* sitting on the small bookshelf of our boat, where we have spent a part of the summer for each of the last eighteen years. Each stay grows a little shorter as we age. Perhaps that is because the boat seems to get smaller but the truth is it's just more difficult. Boating demands strength and agility and a touch of fearlessness, all of which we had in abundance when we first started to boat on the Long Island Sound almost forty years ago, visiting most ports from Norwalk, CT to Nantucket, with yearly stopovers at Block Island. Our stays now are mostly at the home port dock, but fortunately we are far out into the Norwalk River so it's almost like being at a quiet mooring, with just more creature comforts when needed, like air conditioning. But occasionally we go out to the Norwalk Islands where we still have a mooring, especially on a fine day like this, leaving our home port.

I'm not sure why I kept this duplicate copy of what I consider to be Updike's finest novel, *Rabbit at Rest*, on the boat, but now I know, having picked it up again. I'm steeped in nostalgia. When I first read it I felt I was looking into my future. Now I'm looking into my past. No one is a better social historian than Updike, the novelist. I miss him so much.

Simply put, Updike peers into the abyss of death in this novel. It hangs heavily in some way on every page and having gone through some of the same experiences with angioplasties and more, I closely identify. He's now a snowbird in this novel, 6 months in Florida and 6 months in his familiar Pennsylvania environs. Rabbit (Harry Angstrom) has let himself go, however. His little exercise is golfing but even that goes by the wayside. On the other hand he is addicted to fast food, salt, you name the poison. *Harry remorsefully feels the bulk, 230 pounds the kindest scales say, that has enwrapped him at the age of 55 like a set of blankets the decades have brought one by one. His doctor down here keeps telling him to cut out the beer and munchies and each night...he vows to but in the sunshine of the next day he's hungry again, for anything salty and easy to chew. What did his old basketball couch...tell him toward the end of his life, about how when you get old you eat and eat and it's never the right food? Sometimes Rabbit's spirit feels as if it might faint from lugging all this body around.*

This last sentence really gets to the heart of the novel. It makes me wonder whether Updike was unconsciously elaborating on the great Delmore Schwartz poem, *The Heavy Bear Who Goes With Me*

With that as the essential theme, nothing escapes the granular examination of Updike the social historian, the sterility of Florida life, the inherent difficulty of the father – son relationship (poor Nelson becomes hooked on drugs, always having to live in the larger than life shadow of his father, and leads the family into financial crisis), the political back drop of the time – Ronald Reagan and George Bush, the cupidity of corporate America, driving real industry overseas and becoming a nation of financial engineering. In fact, so much of the novel stands up to today's world that one can see the foreshadowing of the Age of Trump. There is even a swipe at Trump on the front page of Rabbit's local Florida paper of the late 80s, a picture of Trump with the headline (*Male call: the year's hottest*). One would have to wonder what Updike would have written with the last few years as political fodder.

Rabbit maintains a little garden at his house in Pennsylvania, but he's also planted the seeds of what his family has become, his wife Janice yearning for a life of her own as a real estate broker, his son Nelson running their car dealership into the ground with debts to finance his cocaine habit, his daughter in law, Pru, hanging onto a loveless marriage, his two grandchildren looking to their grandpa for love and guidance, and Rabbit like a deer caught in the headlights. *Family life with children, is something out of his past, that he has not been sorry to leave behind; it was for him like a bush in some neglected corner of the back yard that gets overgrown, a lilac bush or privet some bindweed has invaded from underneath with leaves so similar and tendrils so tightly entwining it gives the gardener a headache in the sun to try to separate bad growth from good. Anyway he basically had but the one child, Nelson, one lousy child.*

But that is not the only thing that is entwined, being strangled; it's his heart and the American soul. *As the candy settles in his stomach a sense of doom regrows its claws around his heart... With [his golf partners], he's a big Swede, they call him Angstrom, a comical pet gentile, a big pale uncircumcised hunk of the American dream.* And when he finally has a heart attack on a Gulf of Mexico beach, *he lay helpless and jellyfishlike under a sky of red, of being in the hands of others, of being the blind, pained, focal point of a world of concern and expertise, at some depth was a coming back home, after a life of ill-advised journeying. Sinking, he perceived the world around him as gaseous and rising, the grave and affectionate faces of paramedics and doctors and nurses released by his emergency like a cloud of holiday balloons.*

He has an angioplasty when he should have had a bypass, but he doesn't want anything done in Florida instead returning to his home soil of Pennsylvania. *Harry always forgets, what is so hard to picture in flat Florida, the speckled busyness, the antic jammed architecture, the distant blue hilliness forcing in the foreground the gabled houses to climb and cling on the high sides of streets, the spiky retaining walls and sharp slopes....* But once back home there are problems, family problems, money problems, leading to marital discord, and Rabbit on the run again, but to where, back to Florida, bringing his compromised heart, and his focus more and more on death. *It has always...interested him, that sinister mulch of facts our little lives grow out of before joining the mulch themselves...*

And yet, on the lonely drive down I95, one that I've done scores of times myself, Updike's penchant for social commentary and his ear for dialogue dominates. Nearing the Florida border Rabbit turns to a man one empty stool away from the counter of a rest stop restaurant, asking:

"About how many more hours is it to the Florida line?" He lets his Pennsylvania accent drag a little extra, hoping to pass. "Four" the man answers with a smile. "I just came from there. Where you headin' for in Florida?" "Way the other end. Deleon. My wife and I have a condo there, I'm driving down alone, she'll be following later." The man keeps smiling, smiling and chewing. "I know Deleon. Nice old town." Rabbit has never noticed much that is old about it. "From our balcony we used to have a look at the sea but they built it up." "Lot of building on the Gulf side now, the Atlantic side pretty well full. Began my day in Sarasota." "Really? That's a long way to come." "That's why I'm makin' such a pig of myself. Hadn't eaten more than a candy bar since five o'clock this morning. After a while you got to stop, you begin to see things." "What sort of things?" "The stretch I just came over, lot of patchy ground fog, it gets to you. Just coffee gets to your stomach." This man has a truly nice way of smiling and chewing and talking all at once. His mouth is wide but lipless, like a Muppet's He has set his truck driver's cap, with a bill and a mesh panel in the back, beside his plate; his good head of gray hair, slightly wavy like a rich man's is permanently dented by the edge of the cap. "You driving one of those big trucks? I don't know how you guys do it. How far you goin'?" All the salad on the plate has vanished and the smile has broadened, "Boston." "Boston! All the

way?" Rabbit has never been to Boston, to him it is the end of the world, tucked up in under Maine. People living that far north are as fantastic to him as Eskimos.

There is more to the dialogue than that but it exhibits Updike's keen ear for ordinary talk. I could have had the same conversation as that (although Boston is not fantastic to me in the same way).

Arriving in Florida, without his wife, who is really not following him, he is alone, with his failing heart and his dimming dreams, the heavy bear that goes with him, dragging him down, down. *Rabbit at Rest*. Brilliant, one of the best novels of the late 20th century along with Roth's *American Pastoral*.

Not having Updike's decade by decade commentary of the Rabbit series feels like the same galactic void from his sentence: *The stark plummy stars press down and the depth of the galactic void for an instant makes you feel suspended upside down....We are each of us like our little blue planet, hung in black space, upheld by nothing but our mutual reassurances, our loving ties.*

Saturday, November 4, 2017 *Two Unlikely Companion Pieces*

I just read my first illustrated book, an idiosyncratic history of New York City, *Tenements, Towers & Trash: An Unconventional Illustrated History of New York* by Julia Wertz. The genre is "comics," but the *New York Times* gave it such a glowing review, and since my love of NYC – where I grew up and lived as a young adult --- is so deep, I couldn't resist owning this fetching coffee table book. It's easy to read and a candy feast for the eyes for an old New Yorker, although as a kid I grew up in Queens, but that still counts!

Obviously, it can't be a comprehensive history. Wertz takes bits and pieces of the city's history – the ones that particularly appeal to her -- and weaves them together in a graphic time machine of sorts, frequently juxtaposing the "then" and "now" scenes. Just a glance at the "Table of Contents" underscores the eclectic nature of the history.

She tends to focus on those aspects that are not touristy. It reaches across generations. She's young enough to be my daughter or perhaps even granddaughter. As she is not a New Yorker by birth, and no longer lives there, she sees the city in a way a native New Yorker might not, in the way that I do. I took all those sites for granted and it makes more of an impression in retrospect than it did then.

I enjoyed her journey through parts of NYC I've known and other parts I did not. Also I appreciated her quirky selection of topics such as the origins and "formula" for the "egg cream" which took me back to my childhood at a local luncheonette in Richmond Hill, Queens, 107th Street and Jamaica Avenue, called Freers.

In fact, if there is one disappointment in the book, it is that she tends to give short shrift to Queens, as opposed to Brooklyn where she lived in

Greenpoint during her NY years. Missing are iconic scenes of my youth and I think of the confluence of Myrtle, Hillside, and Jamaica Avenues as ground zero where Jahn's, the RKO Keiths, and the Triangle Hofbrau still live large in my memory!. All gone now.

Those figured prominently in my teenage years whereas during grammar school days other beloved places were in South Richmond Hill, 107th St near Atlantic Avenue. One of the first Carvel's was there or some days we'd bike over to Jamaica, Queens where there was a Wonder Bread factory where workers would give us hot bread from their oven. There was also a slaughter house not too far away and we'd peer through knotholes to see chickens dancing around without their heads before we were chased away. Also on Atlantic was a park on 106th St. where we played stickball, punch ball, handball, any kind of game you could play with a Spaldeen.

Along Jamaica Avenue I remember the Gebhardts bakery off of 111th street whose crumb cake was divine. Also there was a fish store around 112th where they also cooked greasy French fries and served them wrapped in newspaper. We got our school supplies from Lipchitz or Woolworths. Right near Lipchitz was the Richmond Hill Savings bank where my mother encouraged me to open an account to save my pennies, and I always felt I was entering a church when I went there with my junior savings account.

Overhead was the Jamaica Avenue El which on rare occasions was our escape into NYC, a great adventure as a kid, but I usually took it early Saturday morning to go to the Van Wyck Lanes where I could bowl a few games for 15 cents each if I got there before 9.00 am with my own ball.

We'd play ball until dark, a round sewer top for home plate, or stoop ball, eat dinner and then wait for the ring of the Bungalow Bar Man, begging our parents for a 10 cent chocolate pop. The games we played. Anything to stay out of the house. Steal the bacon, Ringolevio, yo-yo duels, card games like war, flipping baseball cards, dodge ball and the list goes on.

Forest Park was a draw, with a carousel and later in my teenage years, a walk along the railroad tracks with friends, putting pennies on the rail and then running back to see them after a freight train had passed. The Park was also a great place to build a secret fort. Or for sledding. And for playing baseball at Victory Field.

On Halloween we would get apples, popcorn or crackerjacks, just take a handful, no need to worry back then that there would be a razor blade in the apple or the popcorn poisoned. And on Thanksgiving our parents would blacken our faces with burnt cork, dressing us as bums, and we would go around the neighborhood asking "anything for Thanksgiving?" I think we normally received a few pennies. Into the bank account! Little did I know then how non PC such an activity was.

We got around on our Schwinn bikes, clothes-pinning playing cards to the wheel frames so the spokes would make a racket. As teenagers we sought out older kids to cruise Queens Blvd or hitch a ride to Rockaway Beach where we would work hard to get a tan, but usually left with a blistering sunburn (my Dermatologist now thanks me for my stupidity). Also part of our teenage years was spent at the Hillside Rollerdrome Skating Rink on Metropolitan Avenue.

I could go on and on. But I see I am digressing into reveries, none of which I could criticize our author, Julia Wertz, for not including in her "unconventional history." It would have been nice though to include the institution that was Jahn's Ice Cream Parlor! I'm also sorry she failed to include the Brooklyn Paramount in her illustrations of iconic NY theaters,

Her writing this history has naturally given rise to these memories and her work is a "must have" for an incurable (albeit former) New Yorker. Plus there are a number of scenes which struck home in the book, but I'll mention only a few. The first is her illustration of Max's Kansas City, a joint, restaurant, theatre which I used to go to with other colleagues on special occasions from the publishing company I worked for in the mid 1960s. We always had to have one of their iconic Bloody Mary's. Sometimes they would have an experimental theater production on the second floor, the kind you'd see at Café La MaMa in the East Village.

But the illustration that really hit home is coincidentally both on the cover and at the end of the book, a stroll down the Bowery. I kept looking at it and said I know this illustration for some reason. Well, when researching the history of my family photography business, Hagelstein Brothers, I found the building my great grandfather and great uncle bought in 1866 to begin a business which would survive 120 years in NYC. That building was 142 Bowery and there it was in Wertz's book as well as her selection for the cover. So, I found that sort of thrilling.

She's also irreverent, and I don't mean that in a nasty way, but very respectfully. She's downright funny such as her quip about "micro-living" this, as she points out, is a trumped up idea of justifying astronomical rental fees for small spaces

She can also be very philosophical as one illustration has her on one of her "long city walks" saying to a friend, *I'm perpetually fantasizing about a time I never experienced, and imagining a life I'll never live.* I might know a little more about the former but we're in the same boat regarding the latter.

Most of all, I am regretful that I didn't take more careful notice of everything when I was roaming NYC, having lived in Queens, Brooklyn (Park Slope and Downtown), the East Village (only briefly with a friend), and then the upper West Side. And, not only regretful because of that, but my encroaching old age makes only an occasional return to the city possible now, never to live there again.

While I was reading and enjoying Wertz's "comic" table top book, I was also engrossed in another work by a New Yorker, the great writer, particularly known for his professional writing on baseball, Roger Angell. But he is so much more than a baseball writer, and I'm closer in age to him (he's turning 98 and still writing!) than I am to Julia Wertz. They actually have *The New Yorker* magazine in common, Wertz contributing cartoons and Angell a long, long established writer for them.

This Old Man: All in Pieces is a potpourri of memories, the consequences of what it means to be the last man standing, the losses, and homage to NYC. I feel that I'm right behind him on the journey, the realization that my much operated on body is moving into the category of "this old man" as well.

The title of the collection is derived from his essay which appeared in *The New Yorker* in 2013, a display of his writing talents, so effortless and natural. It includes "farewells, letters, and tributes" to those he has known, *our dead are almost beyond counting and we want to herd them along, pen them up somewhere in order to keep them straight. I would like to think of mine as fellow voyagers...Here in my tenth decade, I can testify that the downside of great age is the room it provides for rotten news.*

His tribute, "Over the Wall " to his late wife, Carol, written only months after her death starts with *Carol doesn't know that President Obama won reelection last Tuesday, carrying Ohio and Pennsylvania and Colorado, and compiling more than three hundred electoral votes. She doesn't know anything about Hurricane Sandy. She doesn't know that the San Francisco Giants won the World Series, in a sweep over the Tigers. More important, perhaps, she doesn't know that her granddaughter Clara is really enjoying her first weeks of nursery school and is beginning to make progress with her slight speech impediment. Carol died early last April....*

What the dead don't know piles up, though we don't notice it at first. They don't know how we're getting along without them, of course, dealing with the hours and days that now accrue so quickly, and, unless they divined this somehow in advance, they don't know that we don't want this inexorable onslaught of breakfasts and phone calls and going to the bank, all this stepping along, because we don't want anything extraneous to get in the way of what we feel about them or the ways we want to hold them in mind. But they're in a hurry, too, or so it seems. Because nothing is happening with them, they are flying away, over that wall, while we are still chained and handcuffed to the weather and the iPhone, to the hurricane and the election.....

There are scores of writers he worked with and befriended, one in particular, John Updike, who comes up again and again in these essays, bringing the writer to life with personal quips. He also recognizes the genius of Updike's writing: *Updike's writing is light and springy, the tone unforced; often happiness is almost in view, despite age or disappointments. He is not mawkish or insistently gloomy. Death is frequently mentioned but for the time being is postponed. Time itself is bendable in these stories; the characters are aware of themselves at many stages. This is Updike country: intelligent and Eastern, mostly Protestant, more or less moneyed.*

Angell relates an anecdote regarding how Updike accidentally got to see and write about Ted Williams' final at bat of his career at Fenway Park, hitting a home run. Updike was in the area to meet a woman at her place on Beacon Hill and stood him up! So he made his way to Fenway and was there to witness the consecrated moment and famously wrote about it in a piece for *The New Yorker*, "Hub Fans Bid Kid Adieu." Here is the confluence of literature and baseball, a legend elevated into a literary masterpiece:

Fisher threw [a] third time, Williams swung again, and there it was. The ball climbed on a diagonal line into the vast volume of air over center field. From my angle, behind third base, the ball seemed less an object in flight than the tip of a towering, motionless construct, like the Eiffel Tower or the Tappan Zee Bridge. It was in the books while it was still in the sky. [Center fielder Jackie} Brandt ran back to the deepest corner of the outfield grass; the ball descended beyond his reach and struck in the crotch where the bullpen met the wall, bounced chunkily, and vanished. Like a feather caught in a vortex, Williams ran around the square of bases at the center of our beseeching screaming. He ran as he always ran out home runs-hurriedly, unsmiling, head down, as if our praise were a storm of rain to get out of. He didn't tip his cap. Though we thumped, wept, and chanted "We want Ted" for minutes after he hid in the dugout, he did not come back. Our noise for some seconds passed beyond excitement into a kind of immense open anguish, a wailing, a cry to be saved. But immortality is nontransferable. The papers said that the other players, and even the umpires on the field, begged him to come out and acknowledge us in some way, but he never had and did not now. Gods do not answer letters.

In accepting the J.G, Taylor Spink Award at the American Baseball Museum and Hall of Fame at Cooperstown, N.Y. Angell acknowledged his debt to baseball:

My gratitude always goes back to baseball itself, which turned out to be so familiar and so startling, so spacious and exacting, so easy-looking and so heart-breakingly difficult that it filled up my notebooks and seasons in a rush. A pastime indeed. Fans know about this too. Nowadays we have

all sports available, every sport all day long, but we're hanging on to this
game of outs, knowing how lucky we are.

Roger, I know what you mean! In this crazy world baseball remains essentially unchanged except for the amusement park nature of many of today's fields. I liked it more in the days of no mascots, flashing scoreboards, fireworks, enclosed stadiums, constant "music." Let 'em play ball!

Tying these two books together may be a stretch, but there is also Roger Angell the inveterate New Yorker. In a letter to Tom Beller who was researching a book about J.D. Salinger, Angell imagines what Madison Avenue was like when he probably passed "Jerry" as he refers to J.D., both unaware of the other....

I'm pretty sure that Jerry Salinger would have walked toward
Madison, not Lex, in search of that pack of cigarettes. He could have tried
at the little Schmidt's Drugstore, two doors north of 91st Street on the NE
corner of Park, but probably that was still a pure drugstore. It had one of
the pharmacist's vases of mauve water hanging in the window.... Madison
then was nothing like Madison now. The gentrification began in the 1980s,
I believe. It was a businesslike avenue before that, and in Jerry's time,
with two- way trolley tracks in the middle. All traffic was two-way. It
had newsstands, a Gristede's (on the NE corner of 92nd); a liquor store or
two; a plumber's store, with a bathtub in the window (mid 91st-92nd, on
the east side of the avenue); a florist's (J. D. Flessas, on the SW corner of
91st); numerous drugstores (including Cantor's on NE or SE corner of Mad
and 93rd, depending on which year we're talking about, and, maybe a bit
earlier, a nearby Liggett's); plus shoeshine and shoe repair shops, hard-
ware stores (probably Feldman's, even then), etc., etc. The Hotel Wales was
already there, east side of the avenue between 92nd and 93rd, but much
seedier then....Salinger and the younger me probably passed each other
more than once on the street back then, all unknowing. We each knew that
the wind was from the east on gray mornings when we woke up with the
smell of hops in the air, blown from the huge Ruppert's Brewery, which lay
east of Third and north from 90th Street.

Two entirely different generations, but dealing with life in the Big Apple, then and now.

Sunday, January 14, 2018 **The Solitary Journey**

Last week my long-time college friend, Bruce, wrote "My brother died this morning. I tell you because you are my oldest friend, and also, because I sat down just now in front of our fireplace with the logs burning and read 'On Growing Old' and remembered that we memorized that poem together."

My first thought reading his note was of Camus's novel *L'Étranger* which I read in French in school (alas, no longer have any ability in that beautiful language). But those haunting first words sprang to mind: "Aujourd'hui, maman est morte." There is finality about it. This is part of life.

I also remember memorizing John Masefield's great poem 'On Growing Old' with Bruce. We were romantics back then and Masefield wrote so poignantly about what we thought was the unthinkable in our youth.

I bring this up because last Saturday night I had to go to the local hospital ER. I had been on antibiotics and Prednisone for a bronchial infection and late Sat. night I could hardly breathe, persistent uncontrollable cough in the chest in spite of all my medications. Pulmonary Embolism? Congestive Heart Failure? That was the motivation to go.

My wonderful wife, Ann, was with me every step of the way but eventually, when they get you in that ER bed, everything is out of your control and even trying to explain my complicated health history seems of little interest except for recent medications.

She was exhausted by midnight and as our home is five minutes from the hospital, I asked her to go. And so, alone. Then I was sent off for tests, x-rays, CAT scan, blood tests, finally being admitted to a room at 3.00 AM. Indeed, a solitary journey.

Hospital life: constant interruptions, no rest with nurses and Doctors (most of whom I don't know) popping in unexpectedly at all times. Nighttime is the worst. TV is useless of course so I brought one book in particular that turned out to "save" me. It calmly and poetically put living (and dying) in perspective. It is a recent book by one of my favorite writers, Richard Ford and in particular his earlier Frank Bascombe novels.

His latest work is essentially a memoir *Between Them; Remembering My Parents*. It was particularly affecting reading it in my hospital stupor and I felt that Ford drew me away from the illness into the very private lives of two ordinary people, who did the best they could, swept along by the rivers of time and chance. Edna and Parker married early in life, both from the deep south, building their lives as a partnership, accustomed to living on the road together as he was a salesman, even successfully surviving the depression. It was just the two of them until later in life (in their 30s) along came their only child, Richard Ford. The title of the book is particularly revealing. It was in effect a life separately lived by the parents, and then Richard coming between them. It changed the formula and as life dishes out the unexpected, so we make our adjustments.

For Richard, this meant having a part-time Dad, who, even when he was in Richard's life, wasn't particularly interactive with him. Neither was my father, who I loved dearly, and although he returned from work each night, he lived in a marriage which was essentially unhappy.

What stunned me about Richard Ford's sparse lapidary memoir is he poses as many questions about the multitude of blanks, things he could not even conjecture at, regarding his parents' relationship. Here he shines as a creative writer. Ford engages the reader to think about those blanks as well, whereas I've tried to define some, probably woefully incorrectly. Memory is so faulty, so fungible.

My own mother carried most of the fury of my parents' marriage. My father was the "beaten" one emotionally. One neatly fed into the other. But Ford's memoir, reading it while I lay vulnerable in my hospital bed, reminded me there was another side to her. The loving one. Memories swelled, one's I've forgotten.

Silly ones, like the time we were driving back from my cousin's house in New Hyde Park to our home in Queens one late Sunday night and my mother and I asked my father to stop at a drug store as we both were dying of thirst. We jumped out of the car and in the paperback rack I saw one of the then best-selling books, *Don't Go Near the Water*, a 1956 novel by William Brinkley. I showed my mother the cover as we were asking for water and we began to laugh so uncontrollably that those in the drug store probably thought we were wacky. Strange how a memory like that, unlocked for years, could be unleashed in a hospital bed in the middle of the night while reading about someone else's parents.

In Ford's skillful hands, the very ordinariness of these two forgotten people, his parents, is elevated to a kind of tribute to the human condition: the solitary journey we're all on.

Some other writer's memoirs emphasize how they developed as writers, influenced by parents, particularly mothers. Ironically, I read the late Pat Conroy's *My Reading Life* after emerging from open heart surgery now seven years ago. His mother used to read him *Gone With The Wind,* instilling a love of reading.

I had no such mentoring and apparently neither did Richard Ford, although Ford supplies a teaser on that subject. One day the young Richard and his mother were shopping at the "Jitney Jungle grocery," and his mother asked him to look at a woman in the store. Richard looked and saw *someone I didn't know – tall and smiling, chatting with people, laughing.* His mother said, *"That's Eudora Welty. She's a writer," which was information that meant nothing to me, except that it meant something to my mother, who sometimes read bestsellers in bed at night. I don't know if she had ever read something Eudora Welty wrote. I don't know if the woman was Eudora Welty, or was someone else. My mother may have wanted it to be Eudora Welty for reasons of her own. Possibly this event could seem significant now, in view of my life to come. But it didn't, then. I was only eight or nine. To me, it was just another piece in a life of pieces.*

In Ford's Acknowledgements at the end of the book he gives thanks (among others) *to the incomparable Eudora Welty, who in writing so affectingly about parents, have provided models for me and made writing seem both feasible and possibly useful.* So there is an arc there, from that vague memory of being with his mother to becoming a writer. Although in the Afterward he says something that Updike might have said as well about writing: *Mine has been a life of noticing and being a witness. Most writers' lives are.*

Unfortunately for me, I did not come from a reading family. My father read Reader's Digest Condensed books. I can't remember my mother reading anything but magazines. But Ford and I share the fact we were poor students in high school. He refers to a disability. I had several, one an emotional one coming from a troubled family, feeling shame, and I was a small kid, trying to make up for it by excelling in baseball, and even basketball to a degree, anything to fit in. But I also think I had a form of dyslexia. My mother interpreted my disability as the need for speech therapy, which was also embarrassing as the speech therapist worked at the high school and I was still in elementary school, and had to walk through the halls with the high school kids, standing out as any young kid would. I hated it.

And that of course was not the only problem. My spelling was atrocious. And as I said although my parents generally did not read to me as a kid, I do remember one that was read. I loved to look at the pictures. It was probably their sense of well-intended therapy: *Boo Who Used to be Scared of the Dark.* I had reason.

In school I read only what was assigned and it wasn't until I came under the influence of two great teachers in my life while a senior in high school that I discovered the joys of reading. After publishing thousands of books in my publishing career, I guess I learned to compensate, word processing being a good crutch for poor spelling.

Ford does not deal with the leap from his hardship in high school to his days at Michigan State to writer. Not appropriate in this work as it is about THEM and less about HIM. And there is yet another ironic thing we had in common. He first thought of going into Hotel Management. It is no wonder; his parents frequently took him on his father's road trips, living in hotels all over the Deep South. No such explanation for me other than Kent State had such a program and I vaguely thought of that as an escape route from my family (this plan did not work out thankfully). I was flotsam in the tide of life.

Between Them is really two separate works, one about his mother which he wrote soon after she died, and the other about his father, which he recently wrote. But you wouldn't know it, as it flows with such continuity. His prose is breathtaking. Here is one paragraph that was particularly affecting (to me), about his father:

But hardly an hour goes by on any day that I do not think something about my father. Much of these things I've written here. Some men have their fathers all their lives, grow up and become men within their fathers' orbit and sight. My father did not experience this. And I can imagine such a life, but only imagine it. The novelist Michael Ondaatje wrote about his father that '... my loss was that I never spoke to him as an adult.' Mine is the same - and also different - inasmuch as had my father lived beyond his appointed time, I would likely never have written anything, so extensive would his influence over me have soon become. And while not to have written anything would be a bearable loss - we must all make the most of the lives we find - there would, however, not now be this slender record of my father, of his otherwise invisible joys and travails and of his virtue - qualities that merit notice in us all. For his son, not to have left this record would be a sad loss indeed.

Yes, a sad loss, especially from such an exceptional writer, Richard Ford. The book was a gift from my wife for my birthday and the coincidence of it landing in my hands while in the hospital, helped deal with the travails of my setback. I got to know two perfect strangers, now memorialized, and appreciate Ford's writing even more.

Wednesday, May 23, 2018 *Goodbye, Philip Roth*

I feel as if I have lost a good friend, similar to the way I felt when John Updike died now more than nine years ago. I grieved then and I grieve now. These are <u>the </u>two towering writers of my lifetime and no one, for me at least, will even begin to approach them. They were not only the most prolific writers of our era, but were the most perceptive observers of our cultural scene, now turning into a cultural wasteland. And they spoke personally to me in ways other writers often have as well, but never with such fecundity.

Roth was ten years older than I am (and Updike was about the same number of years older than I was when he died), a coincidence which does not fail to strike a looming chord in me.

A few years after Roth decided to stop writing fiction he gave an interview, one of his few in his later years, where he commented on that decision: *It is now truly a great relief, something close to a sublime experience, to have nothing more to worry about than death.*

Indeed, the few slender novels he produced towards the end of his writing life are ruminations about death. They are hard to read and yet mesmerizing, a phase of life for which we are all preparing. Now a great voice has been silenced, but what he had to say will live into the future of American fiction and thought.

There is a coincidence to his death yesterday. The day before my wife, Ann, met someone who revealed he was a childhood friend of Philip Roth.

How the conversation turned to Philip Roth was preternatural. Ann told him how much I (and she) admire Roth. He suggested we talk and provided his email contact. I wrote him a long, chatty email suggesting we meet, maybe over lunch, as I'd love to hear about him as he was then. That was yesterday, the day Roth died. I grieve for his childhood friend and for us all. There will never be another like him.

Fortunately Blake Bailey who wrote two superb literary biographies, one on John Cheever and the other on Richard Yates, has been working with Philip Roth on his life's story, with unfettered access to Roth's papers, friends, and relatives. This authorized biography will be the final chapter of a remarkable literary life.

An absolutely fascinating, revealing, brilliant interview was given by Philip Roth to a Swedish journalist, Svenska Dagbladet, for publication there on the occasion of his novel, *Sabbath's Theater* being translated into Swedish.

Asked about his generation of writers and the state of contemporary American fiction, he morphs from fiction to his feelings about the world we now inhabit. His observations on today's world are particularly profound: *Very little truthfulness anywhere, antagonism everywhere, so much calculated to disgust, the gigantic hypocrisies, no holding fierce passions at bay, the ordinary viciousness you can see just by pressing the remote, explosive weapons in the hands of creeps, the gloomy tabulation of unspeakable violent events, the unceasing despoliation of the biosphere for profit, surveillance overkill that will come back to haunt us, great concentrations of wealth financing the most undemocratic malevolents around, science illiterates still fighting the Scopes trial 89 years on, economic inequities the size of the Ritz, indebtedness on everyone's tail, families not knowing how bad things can get, money being squeezed out of every last thing — that frenzy — and (by no means new) government hardly by the people through representative democracy but rather by the great financial interests, the old American plutocracy worse than ever....You have 300 million people on a continent 3,000 miles wide doing the best they can with their inexhaustible troubles. We are witnessing a new and benign admixture of races on a scale unknown since the malignancy of slavery. I could go on and on. It's hard not to feel close to existence here. This is not some quiet little corner of the world.*

His comments on American popular culture are priceless and prescient: *The power in any society is with those who get to impose the fantasy.... Now the fantasy that prevails is the all-consuming, voraciously consumed popular culture, seemingly spawned by, of all things, freedom. The young especially live according to beliefs that are thought up for them by the society's most unthinking people and by the businesses least impeded by innocent ends. Ingeniously as their parents and teachers may attempt to protect the young from being drawn, to their detriment, into the moronic amusement park that is now universal, the preponderance of the power is not with them.*

Among the tributes published in the *New York Times* on Roth was one which quoted a paragraph from *American Pastoral*. I remember reading this exact paragraph out loud to my wife when I first read it. Great literature captures universality. My father was not Jewish but this could mostly apply to him, as it could to almost anyone "for whom there is a right way and a wrong way and nothing in between" and whose "most serious thing in life is to keep going despite everything." Here's what Roth wrote:

Mr. Levov was one of those slum-reared Jewish fathers whose rough-hewn, undereducated perspective goaded a whole generation of striving, college-educated Jewish sons: a father for whom everything is an unshakable duty, for whom there is a right way and a wrong way and nothing in between, a father whose compound of ambitions, biases and beliefs is so unruffled by careful thinking that he isn't as easy to escape from as he seems. Limited men with limitless energy; men quick to be friendly and quick to be fed up; men for whom the most serious thing in life is to keep going despite everything. And we were their sons. It was our job to love them.

And as readers it is our job to love Philip Roth and remember him always.

Friday, October 12, 2018 *Clock Dance by Anne Tyler Marks our Time(s)*

"Time, time, time see what's become of me" (Paul Simon, "A Hazy Shade of Winter"). That pretty much describes the action of most of Anne Tyler's *Clock Dance*. "Tylerville" (my moniker for Baltimore, if you want to put it in a real world context) is where everyday people live, made memorable by Tyler's gift for characterization.

We follow the main character in the novel, Willa Drake, kaleidoscopically, chapters devoted to 1967, 1977, 1997, 2017 from the vicinity of Harrisburg, Pennsylvania, to Coronado, California, to Tucson, Arizona, and finally and fittingly, Baltimore. In her last novel, *A Spool of Blue Thread*, it was the protagonist's son who ends up searching for his own sense of belonging and place. In this novel, it is Willa.

In her "Tyleresque," prose we learn of the deaths of her parents, about her two sons, Ian (now living in Colorado, and mostly out of cell phone range) and Sean (in Baltimore, explaining Willa's connection there in part), the death of her first husband, her estrangement from her sister, Elaine, and her wifely obligations to her second husband, Peter, a semi retired lawyer who calls her, affectionately (but personality appropriate) "little one." As years wear on, she also becomes somewhat estranged from her two sons and finds herself living without purpose. Until the call from Baltimore, but to tell more about the nature of that call is a spoiler.

In Baltimore we are introduced to a number of quirky characters, so typical in Tyler's works. She has the ability to create memorable people, all the pieces needed for a character driven novel. Be prepared to share Willa's journey with her collection of friends in Tylerville, Denise and her daughter Cheryl, Mrs. Minton, Callie, Ben Gold, Erland, Sir Joe, Hal, Richard, Barry, and let's not forget Robert, the cat and Airplane, the dog. All have their lives changed or touched in some way by Willa and in turn so is Willa's.

At first I found the novel slow, even maudlin. Did I care about Willa or just feel sorry for her? Just at the point of fish or cut bait, I'm hooked by Tyler as the plot gathers momentum and Willa makes the transition from an after-thought in a male dominated world to something she desperately needs: to be needed. At 61 she laments not having a grandchild, not having a daughter and through a slow osmotic process SHE adopts not only a family, but a place to live that finally feels like home.

Time and aging hang heavily on every page. Willa's father explains how he finally dealt with his days alone after the death of her mother (after Willa lost her first husband): "I broke my days into separate moments," he said. "See, it's true I didn't have any more to look forward to. But, on the other hand, there were these individual moments that I could still appreciate. Like drinking that first cup of coffee in the morning. Working on something fine in my workshop. Watching a baseball game on TV." She thought that over. "But..."she said. He waited. "But...is that ENOUGH?" she asked him. "Well, yes it turns out that it is,"he said.

Three pre-teen girls play a game, each standing behind the other, their arms extended, all six moving in stiff, stop-and-start arcs in time to the clicking sounds that Willa could hear now punctuating the music. "It's a clock dance!" Cheryl shouted, briefly peeking out from the tail end. "Can't you tell?" Of course: those clicks were tick-tocks. Those arms were clock hands, jerking in time to the tick-tocks like the hands of those stutter clocks on the walls of grade-school classrooms.

But when Willa thinks of her own version of a clock dance many pages later, it is a powerful reminder of our mortality: If Willa were to invent a clock dance, it wouldn't look like the one the three little girls had shown her. No, hers would feature a woman racing across the stage from left to right, all the while madly whirling so that the audience saw only a spinning blur of color before she vanished into the wings, POOF! Just like that. Gone.

The theme of the novel and the last chances presented to Willa couldn't be any clearer than that. Change or poof, gone.

Reviewing her last novel, *A Spool of Blue Thread*, I said Tyler was showing her age. Even more so here, now three years later. Although Willa is "only" a 61 year old, I look to another character, Mrs. Minton as the future one Anne Tyler fears, a widow (like Tyler who lost her husband in 1997, the same year Willa loses her husband) who now uses a walker ("just for balance"), and when Willa first sees her "out of her housecoat" notes: *Her skirt was unbecomingly short, barely knee-length, so that her blue-white mottle shins showed, and her sleeveless blouse exposed her stringy arms.* Aging is not a pretty process in Tyler's eyes, but what is the alternative?

Her detailed descriptions, noting all things relating to her characters, make her our very own Jane Austen, although sweeping love affairs are not her province. Tyler is one of our finest living novelists, still going strong. I only buy her books in hardcover, to enjoy them as permanent additions to our bookshelves, and as evidence that we still know how to make a real book. As I concluded in my last review, "Tyler may be showing her age, but clearly with no diminution of her writing skills."

Friday, August 9, 2019 *A Fan's Notes by Frederick Exley is an American 20th Century Classic*

My good friend, a fellow boater and a terrific actor, James Andreassi, turned me on to this book, *A Fan's Notes* by Frederick Exley. Jim knows my love of American literature and as we are both NY Yankee fans, we also naturally share an interest in the NY Giant football team. Back in my college days I used to go to Yankee Stadium to see YA Tittle and Frank Gifford star in the NFL in the early 1960s.

I think Jim was surprised that I wasn't familiar with this book but now I understand why: you won't find it on those lists of important American novels of the 20th century. It ought to be. It's an under-the-radar American classic. I felt the same way when I read *Stoner* by John Williams and Paula Fox's *Desperate Characters*.

Not that Exley's work shares a similar writing style but its importance to the canon of American literature cannot be underestimated. It certainly does not deserve its general anonymity. Its acclaim now depends on keepers of the flame (of which I am now one).

Exley describes his work as a "fictional memoir" and I sometimes wonder whether, when it comes down to it, other great pieces of writing should be similarly described. But Exley puts it right out there with self-deprecation and hilarity equally balancing the forces of life that tear away at him. No doubt he had ridden life hard and in turn was ridden, roaming between cities, women, bars and mental institutions. These experiences permeate the novel, making it almost a documentary of the beat 50s and the turbulent 60s, and an astute commentary on the chimerical American dream.

Because of his bouts with alcoholism and mental illness, the novel similarly drifts in and out of consciousness, but even at its less lucid moments captures one's attention. His writing process is best described by himself in the novel. He goes back and forth to "Avalon Valley" a mental institution where he finally begins to put pen to paper: ... *what I was doing at Avalon Valley has begun to haunt me, and taking a deep breath, I started fearfully into the past in search of answers. In many ways that book was this book, which I wasn't then ready to write. Without a thought of organization I wrote vignettes and 30 page paragraphs about anything and everything I could remember. There are times now when, in nostalgia, I tell myself I'll never again put down the things I did then, but I know I'm only confusing quantity with quality. If nothing else, I wrote a great deal during those months, writing rapidly, furiously, exultantly, heart-sinkingly, and a manuscript of whatever merit began, page upon page, filling up the suitcase at the foot of my iron cot.*

Indeed, there are resemblances between that "book" and this one, particularly the observation about vignettes, as he goes from one subject, a bar, a person, a city, to another. His character descriptions in particular are superlative, alive in every way. Sometimes in tone, I think of Frederick as a mature Holden Caulfield gone berserk. In fact there are several references to Caulfield in the book and the two characters certainly share a cynical view of the world. There are hints of Amory Blaine from Fitzgerald's first novel *The Far Side of Paradise* (in Exley's more lyrical, optimistic moments) but also a reminder of the admonition from Fitzgerald's *Crack Up*: "Of course all life is a process of breaking down ...."

One would think by the title that this is a sports book and it is as far as it serves as a metaphor. In this regard it reminds me of the English novelist David Storey's early 1960 novel, *This Sporting Life*, made into a movie starring Richard Harris, his first major screen role. I reviewed that for my college newspaper at the time, saying "The challenge of the rugby game is juxtaposed to the challenge of life. Frank accepts both and deals with them in the only manner he knows how: using brute force. Although a vigorous, powerful, and relentless symbol of strength throughout the film, he is unable to dominate life entirely."

That juxtaposition of sport to life is evident here as well, but unlike the main character of *This Sporting Life*, Fred's sporting life is that of a fan, in particular, of Frank Gifford of the New York Giants. He first comes across Frank when he's in college at USC and naturally, Frank is playing for his college team and he is the Big Man on Campus, and is spoken of in reverential tones. Unknown to Fred, it is Frank's girl he spots on campus, his knees buckling at her beauty, never to be his though as he is "not in the game." It is just the beginning of his realizing that his life, no matter how far he stretches for the golden ring, will never attain the heights enjoyed by our sports heroes such as Frank Gifford. Exley's description of Frank's girl when he first sees her on campus as well as his first roommate at college is testimony to Exley's descriptive powers: *I saw her first on one stunning spring day when the smog had momentarily lifted, and all the world seemed hard bright blue and green. She came across the campus straight at me, and though I had her in the range of my vision for perhaps a hundred feet, I was only able, for the fury of my heart, to give her five or six frantic glances. She had the kind of comeliness -- soft, shoulder-length chestnut hair; a sharp beauty mark right at her sensual mouth; and a figure that was like a swift, unexpected blow to the diaphragm-that to linger on makes the beholder feel obscene. I wanted to look. I couldn't look. I had to look. I could give her only the most gaspingly quick glances. Then she was by me. Waiting as long as I dared, I turned and she was gone.*

Fred's father, Earl, was a football star in school and between his expectations and those fostered on him by society he seemed condemned to live a life of failure, especially trying to attain vestiges of the American Dream such as finding the girl next door. He thinks he's found her, when he meets Bunny Sue, who *had honey-blonde, bobbed hair and candid, near-insolent green eyes. She had a snub, delightful nose, a cool, regal, and tapering neck, a fine intelligent mouth, that covered teeth so startling they might have been cleansed by sun gods....she was so very American. She was the Big Ten coed whose completeness is such that a bead of perspiration at the temple is enough to break the heart.*

She is so, so perfect, though; he is totally impotent trying to make love to her. She lives a placid life in the suburbs where her father boasts the tallest TV antenna in the area to bring in far away stations. Is this to be his life too? No, he was to be condemned again, and again, becoming a vicious alcoholic, coming home to his mother and step father when he could no longer function, and then, ultimately being sent back to Avalon for treatment. He was a "repeater," the underbelly of the American dream:

These repeaters were the ugly, the broken, the carrion. They had crossed eyes and bug eyes and cavernous eyes. They had club feet or twisted limbs — sometimes no limbs. These people were grotesques. On noticing this, I thought I understood: there was in mid century America no place for them. America was drunk on physical comeliness. America was on a diet. America did its exercises. America, indeed brought a spirituality to its dedication to pink-cheeked straight-legged, clear-eyed health-exuding attractiveness -- a fierce strident dedication....To what, I asked myself, was America coming? To no more it seemed to me, than the carmine-hued, ever-sober 'young marrieds' in the Schlitz beer sign.

The process of his returning to a modicum of sanity brings the novel back to the sports metaphor. Constantly in bar rooms or street fights, he emerges from one such fight with bruises as well as an epiphany, one perhaps delayed too long in the novel, and in his life, but climatic nonetheless:

In a moment I would fall asleep. But before I did, all the dread and the dismay and the foreboding I had been experiencing disappeared, were abruptly gone, and I feel quiet. They disappeared because, as I say, I understood the last and most important reason why I fought. The knowledge causes me to weep very quietly calmly, numbly, caused me to weep because in my heart I knew I had always understood this last and most distressing reason, which rendered the grief I had caused myself and others all for naught. I fought because I understood, and I could not bear to understand, that it was my destiny – unlike that of my father, whose fate it was to hear the roar of the crowd — to sit in the stands with most men and acclaim others. It was my fate, my destiny, my end, to be a fan.

He becomes an English teacher and is able to express empathy: *...having attempted merely to dazzle the kids with the Bard's poetry, with ever so much scholarly caution and hemming and hawing, I was one day starting back through the text elaborating this theory when a point eluded me, I looked up and off into the class, and my eyes came to rest on a girl who was smiling and weeping simultaneously. A stunningly salubrious and tall maiden with glittering teeth, brilliant blue eyes, and a wondrous complexion, the smile was with her a perennial characteristic – though it was not in the least insinuative or licentious. If a teacher is in the least a man, he soon comes to imagine that his female trusts spend half their nocturnal hours masturbating to his summarily called up and glamorized image; her smile had never seem to have that kind. An abstract of guileless amiability, as though her heart were large and airy and glad, hers, rather, had always seem the smile of an innocent as yet unprepared to determine what should penetrate that heart. A poor student, her countenance exuded remarkable intelligence; both her modish dress and fine carriage intimated 'background'; when she finally surmised what I demanded by way of examination answers, I had thought her grades would improve. Above the smile on this day, above the lovely Grecian nose and vigorous colored cheeks were two great lipid pools of astonishingly blue tears. My first impression was that it was her time of the month, my first impulse to hurry her discreetly to the girls' room. With an alarming suddenness, though, and accompanied immediately by an almost feverish remorse, the blood rushed to my face, I turned away from her, and my eyes fled back to the text: she was frightened to death of me.*

Yes, Exley was hung up on masculinity and is even misogynistic at times, with clearly suicidal tendencies in his compulsion to drink. Yes, he will never measure up to his father or Frank Gifford in sports. But merely recognizing that his student "was frightened to death of me," is a far cry from where he began. Every step of the way, his writing, although sometimes disjointed, is lyrical, even magical at times, clearly a novel to be included in the canon of important literature of a unique American era. And ironically, over time, this one work will endure while his father's sports accomplishments have been forgotten and Gifford's will merely be impressive statistics one can Google. Sadly, Exley produced very little after this titanic novel but it is enough for one to take serious note of *A Fan's Notes*.

Wednesday, December 4, 2019 **'Quichotte' by Salman Rushdie - Making sense of Y2K's Second Decade**

While we were at the Malaprop's Bookstore/Café in Asheville I spied a signed edition of Salman Rushdie's recently published novel, *Quichotte* (pronounced "key-shot"). I vaguely remembered reviews that recommended the work. I looked it over and the jacket copy hooked me: "Just as Cervantes wrote Don Quixote to satirize the culture of his time, Rushdie takes the reader on a wild ride through a country on the verge of moral and spiritual collapse." Having never read Rushdie, I snapped up that next to last copy, although reading a signed edition has its downsides: no marginal note taking allowed, no turned down corners of pages to mark important passages. Plus, I knew I wouldn't get to it for a while.

"A while" stretched well into the fall and, finally, I began it, clearly a modern day take off on Don Quixote (from which our main character derives his name), but the character Quichotte is a creation of another character, a crime fiction writer, "Brother" with a pen name of Sam Duchamp. If you are looking for a logically organized, cohesive novel, this is not the one, but if you value a writer's ability to capture the soul of society in a "moment" in time, then you simply must admire Rushdie's work.

There are so many characters contributing to the overall sense of a world gone terrifyingly out of control, a sprawling novel in its allusions and conceits, a brilliant work of postmodern fiction, with metafictitious elements so you are constantly caught off guard. There are stories within stories oftentimes with the identity of the author unclear. There are pastiches of popular culture the sum of which point the way to the vapid disintegration of values and truth, making it a hallmark work of dystopian literature.

Perhaps it is Rushdie's age. He, as with Quichotte (and Brother), as well as myself, are only too aware that time is running out. Is there enough left to put our personal lives in "order" while the societies we inhabit (in this novel, America, England, and India) are teetering on the precipice of chaos? There are constant veiled allusions to absurdists such as Ionesco and Beckett. The elderly Quichotte has by pure will conjured up a son, "Sancho" to accompany him on his "quest" to find his true love, Salma R., a reality TV star (magical realism and phantasmagoria abound throughout the entire novel). "Father and son" had been sleeping under the stars but they've had a quarrel. Quichotte has gone back to sleep, but Sancho, half ghost at this point, half real person, has climbed to the roof of their Chevy, *listening to the crickets and looking up at the humbling wheel of the galaxy. There was a sign if you wanted one, he thought, a gigantic starlight finger flipping the bird at the Earth, pointing out that all human aspiration was meaningless and all human achievement absurd when measured against the everything of everything. Up there was the immensity of the immensity, the endless distance of the distance, the impossible scale, the thunderous silence of all that light, the million million million blazing suns out there where nobody could hear you scream. And down here the human race, dirty ants crawling across a small rock circling a minor star in the outlying provinces of a lesser galaxy in the inconsequential boondocks of the universe, narcissistic ants mad with egotism, insisting in the fact of the fiery night-sky evidence to the contrary that their puny anthills stood at the heart of it all.* (Do I hear the echo of Samuel Beckett's *Happy Days?*)

As a picaresque novel it savagely satires the entire America of now, a society gone wild with the self indulgent consumption of popular culture, conspiracy theories, xenophobia, opioid addition, and political polarization. Rushdie skillfully moves his characters from one story to another, sometimes intersecting, part of his metafictional technique, with such alacrity that the novel is best read not in little sips before bedtime as I did, but in a few large gulps. Still, you'll wonder about it all. It is not easy to follow, but it is compelling to follow. I found that I had to read the prior few pages before I picked it up again.

In addition to Quichotte, who used to be a pharmaceutical salesman for his relative, "Dr. Smile," there is the good doctor's wife, "Happy" who pushes her husband to become successful which leads to Smile's highly addictive sub-lingual Fentanyl spray called "InSmile." This ultimately connects Quichotte to Salma R., the reality TV star (and InSmile addict) whose mother and grandmother were also TV stars in her place of birth, India, which not coincidently is where Quichotte was born (and, of course, Rushdie as well).

Quichotte has problems with his sister, as does "Brother" in a parallel story and as the novel progresses; these tend to run less side by side but converge. As I said, it's an unreal novel, hard to follow, but necessary to read. Why necessary?

Well, for me, it so eloquently suggests answers to some questions I raised in *Waiting for Someone to Explain It; The Rise of Contempt and Decline of Sense.*

When I complied that book from my political musings in my blog, its tongue in cheek title expressed the increasing questions that seem to rise as I age and with these times seemingly spinning apart. I think Rushdie is similarly expressing a feeling of hopelessness for the human race, and in particular, our nation. I realize that this belief is nihilistic and cynical, but in fiction he presents abounding evidence.

Dues ex machina! In the end Quichotte and Salma R. take an "impossible journey" across an America that has devolved into a dystopian landscape to get to California to find one of Salma R's TV guests, the Elon Muskian (mad? evil?) scientist "Evel Sent", who claims he has invented a portal to an alternative Earth. Seriously, he's sent a dog though there and brought him back, although, as the dog can't speak, we really can't quite be sure (yes, the novel is also very funny at times). If only Quichotte and Salma R can get to the portal, and they do! But what happens then? Not wanting to float a spoiler, I'll end this paragraph here.

Quichotte in answering a question posed by his "son" Sancho, sums up the importance of what our novelists contribute to the enigma of our times: *"I think it's legitimate for a work of art made in the present time to say, we are being crippled by the culture we have made, by its most popular elements above all...and by stupidity and ignorance and bigotry."*

And then there is the ultimate absurdist question, <u>does it matter at all</u>? This is where the process of aging and the very nature of existence converge: *What vanishes when everything vanishes: not only everything, but the memory of everything. Not only can everything no longer remember itself, no longer remember how it was when it still was everything, before it became nothing, but there is nobody else to remember either, and so everything not only ceases to exist but becomes a thing that never was; it is as if everything that was, was not, and moreover there is nobody left to tell the story, not the whole grand story of everything, not even the last sad story of how everything became nothing, because there is no storyteller, no hand to write or eye to read, so that the book of how everything became nothing cannot be written, just as we cannot write the stories of our own deaths, which is our tragedy, to be stories whose endings can never be known, not even to ourselves, because we are no longer there to know them.*

And, so, the second decade of the 21st century draws to its end.

CHAPTER II

PALM BEACH DRAMAWORKS

To date a fair amount of my writing has been reviews of plays performed at regional theatres and in particular, one of the best regional theatres in the country, Palm Beach Dramaworks. This company is the brainchild of William Hayes, now Producing Artistic Director, and his wife, Sue Ellen Beryl, Managing Director. Hayes has a gift for putting together, season after season, well-balanced fare. He is equally gifted in casting and, remarkably, also serves as the director for many of the shows.

My connection to Dramaworks as a reviewer over the last 10 years has deepened my love of professional theatre. Its principal mission -- "to engage and entertain audiences with provocative and timeless productions that personally impact each individual" -- is one that the company accomplishes performance after performance. The key words, "personally impact" are exactly what I have tried to convey in my reviews, although of course the themes are universal.

My only regret is that I was not reviewing their productions during the entire span of their history. They celebrate their 20th anniversary next season.

Of course we attended many plays and musicals during my publishing years, but I missed many contemporary and classic plays because of the demands of my workplace. Dramaworks has helped me fill the gaps of those years. More than that, it has served like a post graduate education, under the tutelage of some of our greatest playwrights: David Mamet, Edward Albee, Martin McDonagh, Arthur Miller, Athol Fugard, Lorraine Hansberry, Eugene Ionesco, Harold Pinter, Horton Foot, Thornton Wilder, Sam Shepard, William Inge, Alan Bennett, Eugene O'Neill, John Patrick Shanley, Tennessee Williams, Donald Margulies, Tom Stoppard, Lillian Hellman, David Hare and August Wilson, to name just a few. That is but a partial playwright list of the fifty Dramaworks plays reviewed here.

227

Indeed, by sticking with classics of contemporary theatre, the essence of Dramaworks' oeuvre is relevancy, to our times, and to the experience of its audiences. They tap into the Zeitgeist like no other theatre company we have known.

And yet in recent years Dramaworks has recognized that as a regional theatre it has the obligation to go beyond their original manifesto. If regional theatres do not give voice to new playwrights and plays, who will? A theatre cannot survive without fresh new ideas, and it cannot flourish without engaging broader, younger, and more diverse audiences. Thus, their Dramaworkshop was born, dedicated to developing new plays, through a selection process and readings, with audience feedback, the objective of which is to enable significant new works to join the classics on their main stage. Several have already found their place there and are reviewed here.

Palm Beach Dramaworks, now entering its 20th year, will undoubtedly continue to impress us with its outstanding achievements.

Thursday, February 18, 2010 'American Buffalo' Soars

Dramaworks dares to produce mostly classics such as the recent Ibsen's *A Doll's House*, Frayn's *Copenhagen*, O'Neill's *A Moon for the Misbegotten*, and one of my favorites, Ionesco's *The Chairs*, simply serving up the very best in theatre, in a highly professional manner.

Their production of *American Buffalo* fits their mission to engage the audience with meaningful, classic drama. This is a provocative work, its nearly two hour run time going by with such pacing and great acting that the evening seemed to be compressed into mere minutes. David Mamet's play is presented as he probably intended, with a perfect set design of a 70's junk shop, the microcosmic universe where three small-time crooks, inherent losers, but ones with the needs of *everyman* for respect, friendship, even love, bungle their way through a botched job of stealing a coin collection from a "mark." It is darkly humorous throughout.

Mamet's staccato dialogue, although stark and profane, is pure poetry. It has a cadence that carries along the characters' interaction and the plot. This is how people talk, and Donny (Dennis Creaghan), Teach (John Leonard Thompson), and Bobby (Matthew Mueller) become vividly real. An amusing sidebar is the fourth character in the play, Fletch, who we, the audience never see, but we join the characters in the play, questioning what kind of guy he might be, first thinking he's the "brains" and then thinking he is nothing but a card shark and cheat, but then learning he was assaulted and is in a hospital with a broken jaw (ironic as he can't speak in the play anyhow). It's an interesting conceit that Mamet employs to bring us, the audience, further into the heart of the play.

And on a smaller scale the play is emblematic of today's Madoffian barbaric business world, and the collapse of moral values. Director William Hayes keeps these characters in a state of unease, the only certainty being the refrain of the play "hey, we're talk'n business here."

Thursday, April 22, 2010 'Three Tall Women' Stands Tall

Although Dramaworks bills itself as "Theater to Think About," with this production of Edward Albee's *Three Tall Women*, it's more like theatre that thinks about me. Maybe it is their knack for choosing pieces, or it's the fact that anyone from a dysfunctional family (the "me" in this case), by definition, comes from a "story" of what makes interesting theatre. What point is the writing about characters not in conflict, those who do not feel wounded, and who are not constantly striving for redemption?

With *Three Tall Women*, a 1994 Pulitzer prize-winning play, Albee comes to grips with his adoptive mother, and the process and mystery of ageing, so it is both a very personal work for the playwright and a philosophical tour de force about the universality of life's inexorable path. The three female characters, "A," "B" and "C" in the first act are three distinctive characters, an elderly woman, her caretaker, and her attorney's representative, aged 92 (or 91), 52, and 26. In the second act they become the three faces of the same person (A) at different stages of her life, speaking to one another about her (their) life, recounting many of the regrets and some of the happiness. It is a platform for recriminations, at one emotional high point in the play, A, B, and C "denying" each other as well as A's son who makes a speechless appearance at his mother's deathbed. It is the perfect conceit for Albee to come to an emotional reconciliation about his own life.

It is also the perfect vehicle for Albee's thoughts on the vicissitudes of aging, the loss of friends, either through death or simply change. The twenty six year old version (C) is particularly horrified to learn what awaits her in the future, wondering "why aren't we told?" (about ageing, illness and dying) to which B's response is *if we were taught that in school, the streets would be littered with adolescent corpses.*

Dramaworks captures this work beautifully, passionately, powerfully, the three actors Beth Dixon (A), Angie Radosh (B), and Gen Rae (C) at the top of their game. Beth Dixon has the most difficult role, having to carry most of the dialogue in the first act. Radosh's and Rae's performances are memorable and distinctive as well. Chris Marks makes a moving appearance as "The Boy," the speechless recipient of his mother's derision. This performance had great pacing, not one self-conscious moment on stage, a tribute to the directing of J. Barry Lewis. It is the kind of play that could be effective even as a reading, but Dramaworks has gone all out with wonderful scenic and costume designs.

Thursday, December 16, 2010 **My Second Session with Freud**

In the blink of an eye almost a half year has gone by since we saw the NYC premiere of *Freud's Last Session* by Mark St. Germain, wondering how it will translate to the venue of Dramaworks in West Palm Beach. Last night we attended the preview of the production which was directed by Bill Hayes. He had promised something "different" than the NYC production, and he delivered.

The play is about a fictitious meeting between two great thinkers, C.S. Lewis, the Christian apologist, and Sigmund Freud, the father of psychoanalysis and a staunch atheist, towards the end of Freud's life and at the onset of WW II and is set in Freud's study in London. In a sense, the outbreak of war is another "character" in the play, one which helps develop the dramatic tension. It is a perfect conceit to spin a play about great ideas confronting the inexplicable transience of life and the gathering storm of man's inhumanity to man. Still there is a playful humor between these two great philosophers and this helps to relieve some of the tension of the intellectual dialogue. They both seem to agree on one thing: "humor tips the scales."

The *New York Times* review of the NYC production, while overall praising the work, was critical of there being a "lack of tension" or lack of "suspense." Dramaworks has addressed that, getting to more of the core emotions of the two, sometimes finding they share more as human beings in spite of their philosophical differences. Of course it helps to have two fine actors to direct, Dennis Creaghan who I will always remember for his role as Don, the owner of the junk shop in David Mamet's *American Buffalo* which played last year. It shows the range of his acting abilities to go from the staccato street dialogue of Mamet to the thoughtful, brooding pronouncements of a Freud. Chris Oden, playing Freud's foil, C.S. Lewis, always seems to have the perfect theist rejoinder to Freud's scientific view, and Oden plays the role convincingly with passion.

I had said in my review of the NYC production (in Chapter III of this book) that we felt as if we were in Freud's study, but that sensation has been used to even greater advantage by Hayes, and his set designer Michael Amico, in the intimate setting of Dramaworks' theatre, where the audience sits, literally, on the very edge of the stage in a stadium seating configuration -- rather than having to look up at the action as it was presented in NY. Dramaworks has perfectly replicated a typical London mews apartment and faithfully captured Freud's study with his ancient artifacts, even down to copying the chair he sat in!

Thursday, February 24, 2011 'Dinner With Friends' Served up at Dramaworks

As my literary maturation was greatly impacted by the likes of Updike, Yates, Cheever, and Carver (each of whom wrote numerous stories about couples), not to mention having lived most of my life in Connecticut (where *Dinner with Friends* is set), Donald Margulies' play strikes a familiar funny bone. I know these people.

I can only wonder how the incredibly intimate stage of Dramaworks' quarters on Banyan Boulevard will translate into their more substantial Clematis Street home next November.

On its present postage stamp sized stage, Dramaworks effectively deals with the seven scene changes required by the play in its two acts, the action shifting from the present in act one to the past at the opening of act two and then back again to the present. The scene changes are effortless as the staging is simple, using mostly three props that can be shifted from being used as table and chairs and, when put together, can be turned into a bed. The changes, rather than being an impediment, seem to move the action along in an engaging way and on Dramaworks' present stage, all of this is happening right before you, bringing the audience into the performance.

The play strikes blunt truths in the finest tradition of tragicomedy, Margulies offering up both the humorous aspects of male female relationships and the wearing of time which can lead to destructive outcomes. Margulies said in a PBS interview concerning his plays: *The ways that people deal with the effect of time, which invariably entails loss, is probably what unites all these works.*

And loss pervades *Dinner With Friends*, newlywed Gabe (Jim Ballard) and his wife Karen (Erin Joy Schmidt) introducing mutual friends Tom (Eric Martin Brown) and Beth (Sarah Grace Wilson), the two couples becoming best, inseparable friends. But a dozen years later Tom and Beth are breaking up, leaving Gabe and Karen pitching and rocking in their wake, questioning their own relationship and facing the sudden realization of friendships ending combined with the inevitable regrets of middle age.

Scene 1 is a manic dinner conversation between Gabe and Karen about their recent gourmet vacation in Italy, Beth listening passively, finally revealing the real reason why Tom was not there, their marriage ending. She says that Tom said *this is not the life he had in mind for himself.* That becomes a question mark that looms over all the characters for the rest of the play. The shock and betrayal is best expressed by Gabe: *All the vacations we spent together at the Vineyard. How could he walk away?*

The same night, Scene 2, Tom returns to Beth's bedroom and is furious that she has told their friends the news without him. *You've got the advantage, now....They heard your side, so they are with you....You prejudiced my case!* There is some physical violence, culminating in sex. As Tom later explains to Gabe about the incident, *rage can be an amazing aphrodisiac!*

Scene 3 finds Gabe and Karen parsing blame, Karen wondering about Tom, *the person you completely entrusted your fate to is an imposter.... Maybe he never existed before...your friend.* Gabe: *You think you're safe on solid ground and it cracks open."*

The opening of Act II shows the couples on Martha's Vineyard twelve years earlier, when Gabe and Karen brought Tom and Beth together. In their youthful bantering, Tom says of Gabe and Karen, after a show of how happy the newlyweds are: *Their job is to make the rest of the world feel incompetent* and in that statement lies the unspoken friction between the couples in ensuing years.

Scenes II and III analyze the unraveling relationship between Beth and Karen, and then subsequently Tom and Gabe. In fact, there are a number of dynamics throughout the play, between the two couples, the two spouses, and then the two male and female friends. Each of these relationships are challenged and changed. That is the genius of the play, what is unspoken is really as important in these two scenes, as in spite of the friends' surface reassurances about staying in one another's lives (Tom and Beth now with different significant others), one knows that this friendship is irreconcilably over. Gabe sadly says to Tom, *We were supposed to grow old and fat together,* Tom responding, *Isn't that just another way to say misery loves company?*

The last scene finds Gabe and Karen ritualistically making up their bed in Martha's Vineyard, Karen asking *What were all those years about?* The same question we all ask ourselves at times.

Most of us have experienced that unsettling moment when best friends announce they are separating, realizing at the same time one's own life cannot go on as before. The play rings with an inescapable universal truth, further brought home by the fine directing of J. Barry Lewis, who has orchestrated this piece to fully express his vision: *we create family out of our friends and acquaintances....we recognize a bit of ourselves, as we attempt to engage one another in meaningful relationships to fill the powerful need for family.*

The actors are all newcomers to Dramaworks, all pros with extensive credentials. Perhaps the most difficult role to play is Gabe's as he is uptight with a mess of internal contradictions, instinctively empathizing with Tom on the one hand and condemning him on the other. Jim Ballard handles the role convincingly. Ballard is multi talented in that he also has a Broadway quality singing voice having seen him play the Wolf in Sondheim's *Into the Woods* at the Caldwell Theatre in Boca Raton last year.

We saw Erin Joy Schmidt perform the lead a couple of months ago in Florida Stage's *Goldie, Max and Milk*. She was an ideal Karen, absorbing the shock of Beth's accusation of *You love it when I'm a mess...You need me to be a mess...I was comic relief,* Ms. Schmidt dramatically delivering Karen's remorseful reply: *You're my family.*

Eric Martin Brown was a convincing Tom, who feels liberated from what he feels was a loveless marriage: *I always felt inauthentic having this life...most of the time I was just being a good sport* to which Gabe replies, *I thought we were just living our lives.*

Sarah Grace Wilson is wonderful as Beth, the sorrowful little "artist" who awakens to the reality that her passion for art was just a substitute for living. And, we find out to our surprise, had a lover earlier in the marriage.

Having, myself, adapted two of Raymond Carver's short stories to one-act plays (presently waiting for permission rights from the Carver estate), each about couples, I have a new appreciation of how difficult it is for a play-wright to incorporate all the elements of a great play, the humor, the tragedy, doing it all with dialog, no descriptive narrative, making the characters real, having a story the audience will hang onto until the end. Margulies' play is a master class in playwriting, receiving the 2000 Pulitzer Prize in Drama.

And I can more clearly see the incredible confluence that must happen to create great theater, the writing, the directing, the staging, the acting. It is a creative act of teamwork. Arts such as painting and literature are solitary journeys into the soul.

Thursday, May 5, 2011 'The Beauty Queen of Leenane' – A Gritty Play

The small town in Connemara, County Galway, Ireland, called Leenane, is not a place where people really live. They merely exist, watching their lives dissipate. Nothing happens there, except boredom and waiting for the evening news on the "telly." The "beauty queen" of the town is the angry, delusional spinster daughter, Maureen, of a savagely controlling mother, Mag, who are locked together in battle throughout the play. It is an interesting choice of properties by Dramaworks not only to conclude its most successful season ever, it also marks the end of its presence at the diminutive theatre on Banyan Blvd. before moving next season to a larger theatre and stage on Clematis Street.

The Beauty Queen of Leenane by Martin McDonagh works best in the intimate setting of its present location, where the audience is closely caught up in the grimy, gritty substance of the play. Poor Maureen has been abandoned by her two sisters who long ago fled the town, escaping by marriage, leaving their younger sister, now 40, with caretaking responsibility for their 70- year old cantankerous, hypochondriac mother. The play opens ominously, a thunderstorm underway, Mag's face illuminated by the lightening, foreshadowing events to come. Mother and daughter confront each other, Mag with her complaints about the complan (meal supplement) and her porridge, Maureen angry that her mother continues to pour her urine from the bed pan down the kitchen sink. The "u-rey-ene" infection issue is brought up like a leitmotif throughout, part of the dark humor that shrouds the entire play. Maureen admits her fantasy of inviting an imaginary beau to their home, only if he likes to murder old women. Maureen's frustration and fury throughout is for the most part kept tightly under control but omnipresent.

Into every stalemated symbiotic relationship must come a game changer, and it is Pato Dooley, who had fled his hometown for London, but while visiting Leenane invites Maureen to a party where an unexpected flame is ignited between them. It is he who gives Maureen the ironic crowning of "the beauty queen of Leenane." When Maureen feels there is a chance to escape the prison of her surroundings and most particularly, her mother, the tension grows in the play as Mag stands in the way of her daughter's last chance at happiness.

Pato's brother Ray plays a go-between the two would be lovers, but he too is a victim of the town, a bored, restless young man, who can see his own bleak future there, and he impatiently fails to deliver the letter to Maureen that would have changed her life. As it is, that failure leads to other bleak consequences. The letter itself is delivered to the audience as an unforgettable monologue by Pato in the opening scene of Act II. Pato's words could be felt in one's very gut.

Appropriately, this last play in Dramaworks' Banyon theatre is directed by Bill Hayes, the theater's cofounder. The play flows, never a dull moment, but always unsettling. It starts darkly and moves inexorably into tragedy. One is hardly aware of the skilled direction needed to bring this off, and hold the audience mesmerized in spite of the raw elements being presented.

Dramaworks also knows how to pick the most talented actors for its productions. Barbara Bradshaw who was brilliant in Dramaworks' production of *The Chairs* is the perfect Mag Folan. I watched her eyes as Maureen spoke at times, Mag following every hurtful word, but at the same time, using those words as fodder to feed her own controlling revengefulness.

How Kati Brazda, who plays Maureen, could hold onto that anger in such a controlled way for two hours, but with flashes of brief happiness in the presence of Pato, is remarkable. I've known people like her in my own life, damaged people, trying to survive with their anger, but poorly. She was so real and utterly believable.

I already remarked that Pato's monologue letter to Maureen is one of the high points of the production, so impassionedly delivered by Blake

DeLong who almost succeeded in rescuing poor Maureen. His sometimes bumbling, but always frustrated brother, Ray, is competently played by Kevin Kelly who articulates the simple but profound: *This bastard town will kill you.*

My wife Ann saw the original play on Broadway and her only complaint was the difficulty in understanding the thick Irish accents. Every word in this play must be heard and understood to make it successful theatre. To the credit of Dramaworks, they enlisted Lisa Morgan as a dialect and vocal coach for the play, the perfect Irish accent but with a clarity understandable to an American audience. Ann consequently thought it was a more enjoyable production than even the Broadway version.

Original music was written for the brief interludes in this production, Irish music of course, which just added to the enjoyment.

This is not a play for everyone, but it seems to be so fitting for Dramaworks' last at its present intimate location -- an exclamation point added to their artistic mission of "theatre to think about."

Sunday, November 13, 2011 'All My Sons' at Dramaworks' New Home

Life imitating art, the American Dream laid threadbare, the relationship of fathers and sons, themes of individual responsibility to society, all resonate at the new home of Dramaworks, a complete remake of the old Cuillo Theatre on Clematis Street in West Palm Beach, renamed the Don & Ann Brown Theatre. All the credit for maintaining the high quality of Dramaworks' offerings goes to the founders, the Producing Artistic Director, William Hayes, the Managing Director, Sue Ellen Beryl and the Company Manager, Nanique Gheridian. Their vision, dedication, and no doubt huge sacrifices during the formative years of Dramaworks is what gave birth to what is, today, one of the leading regional theatres in the country. Their winning formula, while extremely difficult to execute so professionally, is to focus on classic, award-winning plays, and produce them on a level on par with Broadway or the West End.

We were fortunate enough to attend opening night, the first production in the beautifully renovated theatre, now seating 218 vs. the 84 in Dramaworks' theatre on Banyan Street. It was a special moment to be there for the opening, and attend the celebratory reception afterwards with crew and cast. It was reminiscent of the time we attended the Academy Awards and were guests of the Academy when I published *The Annual Motion Picture Credits Database.*

In designing the new theatre, a special effort was made by Dramaworks to retain the intimacy of the old theatre, still bringing the audience into the production in a visceral way.

In the case of their first play, Arthur Miller's *All My Sons*, Dramaworks could not have chosen a more appropriate offering, for our times and for their new theatre. The production demands of this play, in particular with its larger cast and two story set, would have been impossible in Dramaworks' former home, both technically and financially.

Furthermore, one cannot help but think of the numerous parallels to real life situations such as the Madoff scandal leaving the family with the shame brought on by the father, or the ignored cries of the helpless Kitty Genovese who was murdered in the neighborhood where I grew up, or the most recent failure of assuming individual responsibility in the Penn State debacle. These themes are played out in life and in art.

No doubt Madoff, in the process of destroying countless individuals, thought, as Joe Keller, that he was doing something "for family and for his sons," thus justifying his actions. And how do ordinary citizens become bystanders while their neighbor is being murdered or a child sexually assaulted? Miller deals with similar issues in a play written decades before.

Miller once said "The American Dream is the largely unacknowledged screen in front of which all American writing plays itself out," and what is more American than dreaming of riches and the so called "good life." Some men kill for that, some do it with Ponzi schemes and others with defective parts sold to the government at huge profits which cost American servicemen their lives. Or to paraphrase Balzac, behind every great fortune lies a great crime.

And part of the "Dream" is living with illusions that try to make life more bearable. The mother, Kate, voices this facet of the play believing that her son, Larry, is still alive and will miraculously return home three and a half years after the war has ended. When Ann Deever, the daughter of Joe Keller's former partner who is now in prison, paying for a crime Joe is also guilty of, questions why Kate still believes that Larry is alive, she answers: *Because certain things have to be, and certain things can never be. Like the sun has to rise, it has to be. That's why there's God. Otherwise anything could happen. But there's God, so certain things can never happen.* The drama heightens to the inevitable converging lines of fantasy and reality, when Kate admonishes her other son, Chris: *Your brother's alive, darling, because if he's dead, your father killed him. Do you understand me now? As long as you live, that boy is alive. God does not let a son be killed by his father.*

Dramaworks' production powerfully captures Miller's modern telling of the elements of a Greek tragedy, characters making choices that lead to their own downfall, leaving the audience feeling pity on the one hand and fearing this could be any person, including themselves or their own neighbor.

My wife, Ann, and I felt as if we had a blow to our solar plexus. The acting, directing, every element was close to perfection.

All My Sons has the largest cast we've ever seen in a Dramaworks production, ten highly capable actors, some of whom are Dramaworks veterans. All were excellent, but the especially heavy lifting was done by Kenneth Tigar (Joe Keller), Jim Ballard (Chris Keller), Elizabeth Dimon (Kate Keller), and Kersti Bryan (Ann Deever). Their performances were amazing, physical and emotional, resonating with the full force of Miller's words. One wonders how these actors can sustain such emotional levels and then do it again the next day!

The remainder of the cast supported the leads with fine performances: Cliff Burgess (George Deever), Nanique Gheridian (Sue Bayliss), Dave Hyland (Frank Lubey), Kenneth Kay (Dr. Jim Bayliss), Margery Lowe (Lydia Lubey), and Kaden Cohen alternating with Leandre Thivierge (Bert).

The production was directed by another Dramaworks veteran, J. Barry Lewis. Lewis used the larger stage, as well as the lighting and the set, to bring out the best in his actors. I would imagine it is precisely what Arthur Miller himself envisioned.

The meticulous stage settings which have characterized Dramaworks' past productions, endures now on a larger scale -- a much larger scale in fact, a two story house on stage and its backyard -- thanks to the scenic design of Michael Amico. We felt as if we were sitting in the backyard of Anywhere, Midwest, USA. When the play opens the audience is drawn to a fallen tree, one that was planted in memory of the Keller's son, Larry, which now lies toppled by a storm in the night, a symbol of another encroaching storm that culminates in the powerful dramatic resolution. The scenic architecture perfectly connects the audience to the play, the same kind of intimacy that characterized Dramaworks' productions in their former venue.

Congratulations Dramaworks, the crew and cast, and best wishes to you all in your new home!

Thursday, January 5, 2012 **'Man-in-the-Moon Marigolds' Bloom at Dramaworks**

There seems to be a pattern in Dramaworks' choice of productions or perhaps it is just a theme that permeates fine playwriting, mothers (or fathers) that are controlling in some way, by playing on sympathies, living within illusions, or by downright emotional abuse. According to Bill Hayes, the Producing Artistic Director of Dramaworks and the Director of its new production, *The Effect of Gamma Rays on Man-in-the-Moon Marigolds* by Paul Zindel, "Zindel wrote a brutally honest piece about a family much like his own; the father is gone, and the mother is impoverished – not just financially, but emotionally." And for Hayes, the play "resonates so deeply for me....[as it], in the end, celebrates teachers."

It is an interesting choice of plays, all female actors, although there is the off stage character of Mr. Goodman, a teacher, who nonetheless figures prominently in the plot. The play was chosen, not only because of its relevancy (perhaps more relevant today than when it was written in 1964), but it also balances the more male dominated play that preceded it at Dramaworks, *All My Sons*, and the one that will follow this season, *The Pitmen Painters*.

Indeed, the themes of *The Effect of Gamma Rays on Man-in-the-Moon Marigolds* pack relevancy in today's world, the single working mother, bully victimization of a child by her peers, alcoholism, parent abuse, and the role of the teacher beyond the classroom. We've all had a teacher that has changed our lives in some way.

The three girls in the play, Arielle Hoffman. Skye Coyne, and Gracie Connell are all 17 in real life, just beginning their journeys into the artistic world, and one can tell they bonded as they prepared for this production.

Laura Turnbull, a veteran actor who plays the lead, acts opposite her own daughter, Arielle Hoffman. Her daughter is going off to college next year and this was Laura's opportunity to work with her professionally.

Interestingly, many of Dramaworks past productions have touched upon similar themes. The most recent one, *All My Sons,* where the parents live a life of illusions and lies. And then there was last year's masterful production, *The Beauty Queen of Leenane,* with some parallels to Marigolds, where daughter Maureen is left with caretaking responsibility for her 70- year old cantankerous, controlling mother. Also from the prior year, is their production of Edward Albee's *Three Tall Women,* yet another Dramaworks choice I take very personally: dysfunctional families are the stuff of great modern theatre.

So Dramaworks is walking on familiar ground with its new production about a single mother, Beatrice Hunsdorfer, who has had some bad breaks in life and now is left with two daughters and herself to support and ends up turning all her disappointment and anger towards them. She is a misanthrope with the mission of destroying happiness where she sees it, a formidable antagonist for her introverted younger daughter, Tillie, who is also bullied by her classmates. A life buoy is thrown to Tillie by her science teacher, Mr. Goodman, in the form of a science project, to study the effects radiation has on marigolds. Her teacher also gives her a pet rabbit, which becomes just another object of Beatrice's hatred, and something Tillie's older sister, Ruth, jealously yearns to possess. Ruth is fighting for her life too, but more under the spell of her mother, more like her mother, unlikely to break free.

One of the difficulties playing Beatrice is to try to preserve some sympathetic reaction by the audience as Beatrice's path to self-destruction has to an extent been paved by circumstance. Laura Turnbull gave a bravura performance, one of the most memorable ones we've seen in a long time. I was particularly drawn to it as there are parallels to my own life and mother, who never really understood her self-imposed prison of a miserable marriage. She was racked with guilt and rage, sometimes turning to alcohol for consolation. I have seen my mother in the same drunken stupor as Beatrice, although Beatrice mostly lives in that stupor on a daily basis. Beatrice is a "crazy-maker," leaving emotional destruction to most in her wake.

Laura Turnbull's performance is full of passion, physically demanding, and if one had only a single reason to see this play, her extraordinary accomplishment inhabiting this role would be it. You have only to hear her deliver the line that ties the play's title to her sad life: *Half-life! If you want to know what a half-life is, just ask me. You're looking at the original half-life!'*

Arielle Hoffman gives a carefully measured performance as the shy, abused, vulnerable daughter, Tillie, a perfect balance in the play, the voice of hope for the future -- that a *good mutation* will come out of the muck and the mire of her upbringing. She strives to escape the gravitational pull of her mother, simply stating *my experiments make me feel important.* Arielle Hoffman has the audience carefully listening to her every word.

Her sister in the play, Ruth, is played by Skye Coyne, who, like Laura Turnbull's role, requires a dialed-up emotional level. Ruth is also abused by her mother, but protects herself by simply taking it, or by giving it back. There are some dark undertones in her character, the intimation that she was treated for mental illness (no wonder) and that she suffers from epilepsy. If Beatrice's life was ruined by circumstances, Ruth seems to be heading towards the same end. And while Ruth can be cruel towards her younger sister, Coyne walks a fine line as well, tugging at the audience's empathy. Her performance is equally memorable.

A minor role goes to Gracie Connell as Janice Vickery, Tillie's science fair adversary. She gives almost a tongue in cheek recitation of how she boiled the skin off a dead cat to use its skeleton so one can imagine what kind of person she is and how she treats Tillie.

The other minor role, that of Beatrice's boarder, Nanny, involves no dialogue but is actually a substantive role in the play and is wonderfully performed by Harriet Oser, a veteran of many Florida theatre productions. Although Nanny ostensibly serves little function in the plot, Nanny's role is highly symbolic. She is there to share in the abuse that Beatrice spares for no person or rabbit, and she is there as a harbinger of Beatrice's future (assuming she doesn't kill herself or die early of alcoholism). We also learn that Beatrice has had other boarders before, ones who have died, or have gone away, not surprising given they were all exposed to Beatrice's toxicity. I particularly noted the brilliant contrivance that was used on stage by

Nanny, her medical walker for getting about, the slow cadence of which is like a leitmotif of time's passing, running out for all on stage but Tillie who carries the hope of the future.

The Effect of Gamma Rays on Man-in-the-Moon Marigolds is Paul Zindel's best known work, winning the 1971 Pulitzer Prize, and one can see the influences of Tennessee Williams and Edward Albee. In fact, Albee was Zindel's mentor and creative writing teacher in the late 1950's. In many ways, it is a play to simply be experienced rather than to be analyzed. It is an actor's play and its measure of success will hinge on their performances, and Dramaworks has pros at work in this production, some experienced and some upcoming.

Bill Hayes is the Director, but he is more than that, having the opportunity to mentor three young actors, his giving that special gift as he received it from his mentor, Steve Mouton, decades before. And Hayes has some masterful help in the production, a fabulous set by Michael Amico, taking advantage of every square inch of Dramaworks' new, expanded theatre, the careful detail of James Danford, the Production Stage manager, Lighting (subliminally communicating gamma rays) by Sean Dolan, and Sound by Steve Shapiro.

Thursday, February 16, 2012 **'Pitmen Painters' Portrayed by Dramaworks**

The life of a miner is like no other. Miners are born into a mining family. Their fathers did it before them and their fathers before. It was the lucky son who broke away, but most miners did not leave, could not leave, and they slogged through their days, and those who did not die because of mining accidents, could be expected to die at an early age because of black lung disease from coal dust, or live with emphysema or chronic bronchitis. As hostile as the environment was to the body, it also wrecked the soul.

The Pitmen Painters is a true story about English miners who in 1934, with the assistance of the "Workers Educational Association," engaged an academic art teacher, Robert Lyon, for an "art appreciation" class, but as these workers had never even seen a painting, and didn't have the vocabulary to discuss painting, Lyon turned it into a class of "doing" painting instead of teaching. Their first assignment was to paint something that relates to their work, which of course is the only thing they ever had known. From that point they went on the most unlikely artistic journey as a group, which is what the play is all about, unleashing their individual creative spirits. Although the painting miners embrace their new passion, they still go back to the mines to work each and every day.

The play is by Lee Hall, creator of the film and musical Billy Elliot. Hall grew up in Northumberland in northeast England, the home of the great mines that fueled the industrial revolution. By chance he came across a copy of *The Pitmen Painters* by William Feaver in the bin of a bookshop on the Strand near Covent Garden, a familiar a scene to me as our UK publishing distributor was at 3 Henrietta Street and I can imagine his thrill discovering the work nearby. The play was inspired by Feaver's history.

The basic staging is a simple barren brick meeting hall of the Ashington miners which serves perfectly for the many scene changes in conjunction with the overhead visual projections which illuminate the various paintings that scroll by during the evening.

And the play is brought to life by its director J. Barry Lewis, taking full advantage of Dramaworks' new audio visual technical muscle as the play progresses through a fluid chorography of audio visual montages. In other words, the scenic design is an ever changing one, the timing of the changes critical to the movement of the play and the role of the actors. J. Barry Lewis noted that "the design of the play is a work of art itself." Indeed it has an intricate interactive nature.

There are many themes that Hall deals with, class immobility, socialism, the drudgery of the mines juxtaposed to the ethereal nature of art, but the tension of the play comes from the rights or expectations of the individual vs. the group and Hall combines this with a shrewd sense of humor and timing. In fact most of the play's miners frequently have comic roles in contrast to the one who succeeds most as an artist, Oliver Kilbourn. I loved the exchange between Oliver, the "student" and Robert the "teacher" who, when sketching Oliver, is criticized by Oliver for not capturing his essence as a human being. The student becomes the teacher. Societal class becomes topsy-turvy.

As the art establishment eventually "finds" the Pitmen Painters -- and they had a number of exhibits which encompass much of the play -- their fame gives Oliver an opportunity to leave the group to become a professional artist when he is offered a stipend, more than he is paid in the mines, by a wealthy art benefactor, Helen Sutherland. This becomes the core dramatic element of the play, as Oliver agonizes about leaving the group and everything he knows -- after all, mining is his "family" -- and the group itself debates on whether that is proper and who "owns" the paintings, the individuals, or, as is argued by George Brown, who represents the Workers Educational Association, the Association itself. Ironically, Oliver meets a professional painter he has admired, Ben Nicholson, a member of the British educated class, and who is also the recipient of a stipend from Helen. But it is Nicolson who professes *his* admiration of Oliver as he is "free," unbounded by the shackles of being attached to a patron. So Oliver does not become dependent on Helen and remains the "miner-painter."

After WW II the group eagerly looks forward to the benefits of socialism, the National Health Service, and the continuing support of the Workers

Educational Association. But change is underfoot and by 1984 the group is disbanded, but not without their realization of what art has meant to their lives, as a group and as individuals. In our own economic times, when government is so eager to undermine the support of the arts under the guise of economic prudence, there is much gleaned from this play.

When towards the end Oliver again meets Helen at one of the exhibits of the Ashington miners, she is more critical of the group's work, saying it lacks a certain "sexuality" or passion. The play itself leaves something wanting in that area. It is a wonderful dramatized story, well worth the 2-1/2 hour running time, including intermission -- and never a dull moment -- but *Pitmen Painters* is not great drama per se. Nonetheless, Dramaworks makes it great theatre.

Professionalism characterizes the production and this is no more evident than the choice of actors, in this case all members of Actors' Equity, and many veterans of previous Dramaworks productions or other South Florida stages. Foremost, is Declan Mooney's heartrending portrayal of Oliver Kilbourne's journey from naiveté to knowledgeable artist. He is the dramatic center of the action. Two other Dramaworks veterans, Dennis Creaghan (George Brown) and Colin McPhillamy (Jimmy Floyd) demonstrate outstanding comic timing which is so important to the play, the perfect offset to the weighty themes of the production. John Leonard Thompson (Robert Lyon) plays his role as the London art instructor with intensity and sensitivity toward his unlikely students, a stark contrast to his role as "Teach" in *American Buffalo*, showing his range. Newcomer to Dramaworks (but highly experienced actor who acted once with my heartthrob, (Ann-Margret) Rob Donohoe (Harry Wilson) is perfect as the impassioned Socialist who remains a member of the group even though he can no longer mine as he was gassed in WW I and has a breathing disorder, becoming, instead, the group's "dentist" providing still other comic opportunities. Joby Earle competently plays two roles, "the Young Lad" and Ben Nicholson, and last but not least, the two women in the play, Kim Cozort (Helen Sutherland) and Betsy Graver (Susan Parks), were professional in every way and incandescent against the stark stage in their costume designs by Erin Amico.

And kudos to the Dialect Coach, Ben Furey, who helped to make the Ashington accent believable but intelligible to the South Florida audience, and the actors who assimilated that difficult accent.

Thursday, April 5, 2012 **'Master Harold...and the Boys' Triumphs**

This riveting story needs to be performed again and again while we, as a society, still suffer prejudice and intolerance. This new production solidifies

Dramaworks place as a premier serious theater in Southeast Florida. I call it Broadway South.

So much is packed into this production of *"Master Harold"...and the boys* by Athol Fugard that the simplicity of the plot belies its profound intensity, the action slowly building and escalating on two phone calls. Sam (W. Paul Bodie) and Willie (Summer Hill Seven) are servants in the early years of South Africa's apartheid system, 1950, in a St. Georges Park Tea Room where all the action takes place on a windswept rainy Port Elizabeth afternoon. Sam, while not having the benefit of a formal education is nevertheless possessed of a strong native intelligence and kindly disposition, while Willie is somewhat slow, more sensitive and dependent on Sam's guidance. They are casually cleaning the room, but mostly they are playfully teasing each other about an upcoming ballroom dance competition. Enter the son of the couple who owns the tea room, a 17 year old student, Harold, known to Willie and Sam as "Hally" (Jared McGuire). The off stage parents loom significantly in the plot, particularly the father who is both crippled and an alcoholic, an embarrassment to Hally.

The three on-stage characters have a close relationship, even a loving one. In a twist of societal relationships, Sam has become sort of an ersatz father to Hally, recognizing the boy's conflicted feelings towards his father. Sam tells Hally about his mother's phone call. His father is coming home from the hospital. This is strongly denied as a possibility by Hally until he receives the first of two phone calls from his mother. He implores his mother to keep the father there (not wanting him home).

Hally's demeanor changes after the phone call. He becomes obsessed with his homework assignment which is to write about a significant cultural event and Sam suggests the upcoming dance competition as being a worthy subject. Hally is instantly caught up in the possibilities; with the dance competition becoming a metaphor for a perfect world, where people glide in unison, without colliding with others, where there is no hurt or abuse. This good time is interrupted by a second phone call in which Hally's mother tells him that his father insisted on leaving the hospital and now he is expected home immediately after locking up the Tea Room. It is at this turning point that the play goes from benign to dark. Hally is consumed with anger, knowing the consequences and the humiliation of his father's return, and the multigenerational nature of racism rears its head as Sam suddenly becomes the target of "Master Harold." Sam at first feels betrayed. Although this confrontation becomes volatile, the essential goodness of Sam prevails at the end while Hally departs into the symbolically stormy night. Life goes on. Willie and Sam rehearse dance steps to the strains of Sarah Vaughn on the juke box, Willie wanting to believe that nothing has really happened. They have their dignity at the end.

This drama works on so many levels, one hardly knows where to begin. The consequences of family abuse and shame, apartheid, racism in general and how that reverberates throughout society, witness the recent Trayvon Martin tragedy or the virulent anti-Obamanism that seem to be part of today's political landscape, and the multigenerational nature of racism and family abuse. The abusive, alcoholic father in literature and theater is pervasive. The impact on their families is always disastrous and a son's need to find substitute fathers is profound. And what happens when the substitute father is perceived as your inferior? Ironically, who is really in bondage, Hally or Sam?

The innocence and even nobility of Sam is sorely tested by Hally's demeaning and malevolent invectives, but Hally is caught in the irresolvable conundrum of having to become a man at the expense of treating noble Sam as society (and Hally's father) expects a white man to treat a servant in the system of apartheid. And how different is that from even post Civil War America where Afro American's were merely stereotypes and those of us who grew up in the south, such as my wife, were accustomed to segregated schools, buses, bathrooms, lunch counters, everyplace one went, well into the 20th century.

Not surprisingly, Sam mentions Abraham Lincoln as one of history's most significant figures, Fugard's veiled reference to America's race problem. But Sam also mentions Jesus Christ as such a figure and in Sam's goodness and forgiveness and careful nurturing of Hally he too is saying "forgive them for they know not what they do." This is a very autobiographical play. Fugard was 17 in 1950 as well, and this work is his exculpation of the guilt he felt being raised in the system of apartheid.

It is a delicate play to stage successfully. So much depends on the nuances of the set and the acting, the lighting, the ambiance. One thing out of place would be easily noticed and distracting. Here Dramaworks excels, selecting the ideal actors and relying on the behind the scenes talents of the people supporting them.

Under Director Bill Hayes' careful direction, the three actors shine. The pacing of the play makes one completely unaware of time passing, the audience caught in each moment, everything seeming to happen at precisely the right time and place on stage. The metaphor of the dance (of life) is leitmotif that weaves throughout the play, Hayes highlighting those at appropriate moments.

Jared McGuire who plays Hally has played the part before. He knows Hally well and although Mr. McGuire is older than 17 (no seventeen year old actor is going to have the experience to play this pivotal role so well), he passes as such, his boyishness coming through in his relationship with Sam as well as the raging testosterone that gives rise to his misguided attempt at "being a man" -- his trying to become one in a corrupt society and a dysfunctional family. This is a difficult role to play and McGuire nailed it.

W. Paul Brodie turned in a bravura performance as the compassionate Sam, a person who is sorely tested but emerges noble at the end. He is on stage 99% of the time and while there he is a force, either of drama, sadness, or, even laughter in his kidding of Willie and sometimes Hally.

Summer Hill Seven's portrayal of dim-witted Willie is perfect, even his glances at Sam and Hally during their confrontations. But Willie lives in the dream world, looking forward to the dance competition, reconciliation with his girl friend who he has abused (all of society is caught up in being abused and passing it on), and Seven effectively plays this role.

The scenic design by Michael Amico is exacting, recreating what a 1950 Tea Room in South Africa must have looked like, using the full stage of the new Don & Ann Brown Theatre to its greatest advantage. Even the detail of making a real on stage cream soda is portrayed, everything so authentic. Outside, upstage, the pane glass windows of the Tea Room reflect the falling rain, the dreary reality that the Tea Room symbolizes, and, if I'm not mistaken, the rain becoming more intense as the denouement of the play approaches and Hally goes out into the storm.

A wonderful play by a master playwright, performed by one of America's most professional regional theater companies results in dazzling drama.

Thursday, May 24, 2012 'Proof' + Dramaworks = Unforgettable Theatre

Dramaworks concludes an enormously successful 1st season in its new home, with the production of David Auburn's Pulitzer Prize and Tony winning *Proof.*

We've seen *Proof* before, most recently at the Westport Country Playhouse. Its South Florida premiere was at the Coconut Grove Playhouse was some ten years ago. And the play, which was later made into a movie, gets conflated with two other movies in my mind, *Good Will Hunting,* about a young man who is a mathematical genius but instead becomes a janitor at MIT and needs the help of a psychiatrist to straighten out his life, and *A Beautiful Mind,* a story based on the life of John Nash, a real-life mathematical genius who, what else, happens to be delusional and paranoid, although he goes on to receive a Nobel Laureate in Economics. A theme of these films and *Proof* is the close association of mathematical genius and some form of mental illness.

Proof is about such a mathematical genius, the recently deceased Robert, who appears in the play in flashbacks, and in an opening scene fantasy conversation with his daughter Catherine who cared for him during his declining years. She seems to be following in her father's footsteps, having mathematical abilities, and suffering from depression. The play looks at that fine line between genius and mental illness, Catherine's fear of inheriting both, while exploring the subjects of love and trust, the latter themes being the real "proof" of the play.

So, what does Dramaworks bring to the table that the other well-worn productions of *Proof* might have overlooked? Above all, Dramaworks focuses on the play's deep emotional core, with the characters interacting as finely as a string quartet, the story simply unfolding their fears and suspicions, their hopes and their love.

In addition to Catherine and her father Robert, there is Catherine's sister, Claire, the one person who represents the real world vs. the exalted world of theoretical mathematics. Then there is Hal, a PhD who studied under his mentor, Robert, who thinks he finds a mathematical breakthrough in what he assumes is Robert's papers, but Catherine claims its authorship. She also studied math (and perhaps inherited genius) and the question of authorship is the fulcrum of the dramatic tension between Catherine and Hal, and Catherine and her sister. Hal and Catherine have also become lovers, complicating this issue further.

Between the four characters Director Bill Hayes wrings out every drop of meaning intended by Auburn's play, letting the four fine actors find their unique voices in this production. Hayes also exacts the comedic elements from the play and there are some very funny moments, well pared to some of its darker facets.

Kenneth Kay's Robert is measured in his "madness" (but not in his love for his daughters), until he volcanically explodes not accepting, or understanding, his final decline in the cold outside his home on the back porch of an old Chicago neighborhood where he and Catherine live. He has been laboring over equations relating to temperatures and seasons, all gibberish, which Catherine is shocked to discover after his short remission during which she left home to study at Northwestern University. She leads him back into the house and back into her role of caretaker to his death. Kay plays his part perfectly, and you can't help but see in him the decline we all fear or have witnessed in our own families.

The most demanding role is Catherine's played by Katherine Michelle Tanner. She alternates between being strong, as in her contention that the authorship of "proof" is her own, cynical in some aspects of her relationship to her sister, Claire, and fragile and vulnerable as she reacts to Hal and her father. She looks disheveled in most of the play, wearing her inner demeanor on her sleeve. Tanner's performance is compelling and as she is almost nearly always on stage one's eyes are drawn to her and her conflicts.

If Catherine has a demanding role, perhaps Claire's is most difficult, played by Sarah Grace Wilson a PBD veteran. Claire has flown back from New York City to her old childhood home for her father's funeral in which she thinks to rescue her sister and walks into a drama she never expected. (*People like me have to clear up catastrophes* she proclaims at one point.) Hers is the voice of reason, a woman who really loves her sister and father, trying to do "the right thing" but she always seems to become the heavy, in spite of one comic moment joining in a late night party after her father's funeral with geeks from the University, getting drunk and waking with a hangover the next morning, complaining, *those fucking physicists!* You find yourself feeling for her, imagining if you were in a similar position, but she just doesn't understand the weightiness of theoretical mathematics, the implications of a "new proof" or the emotional ramifications of doubting her sister's authorship.

Cliff Burgess is becoming a fixture at Dramaworks, this time playing the nerdish Hal, protégé and admirer of Robert, and who becomes the lover and ultimately the advocate of Catherine. Burgess exacts laughs at times to lessen the tension of the drama. Towards the end he expresses the essence of the play, his support and trust of Catherine

Michael Amico's scenic design is world class. We felt like we were in the backyard of a Chicago home in an old neighborhood, a home that is obviously in some state of decline as is Robert. It is Catherine and Claire's childhood home as well. How often have we visited our own childhood homes to be buffeted by the ensuing emotions of such a visit? That is the feeling one gets from the set design, the lighting, even the music interludes between scenes.

Unlike some other regional theaters that have gone by the wayside in this hostile economic environment for the arts, Dramaworks has been building, step by step, never overreaching itself, into one of the leading regional theaters in the US. We're just lucky enough to live nearby.

Thursday, October 11, 2012 '*Talley's Folly' Successfully Opens Dramaworks' 2012/13 Season*

In a sense, the set of this play is its 3rd "character." It is always being referred to in the script, as a place in time, a place in family history, and a symbol of the emotional disarray of the play's two unlikely lovers.

The Victorian boat house in which the action takes place, the folly of the play's title, where Sally Talley first met Matt Friedman a year earlier, has been worn down by time, neglected, almost an outcast like the characters themselves. Here Dramaworks take full advantage of its new expansive stage, and the experienced Michael Amico, with the help of a book which had actual plans for building a boathouse in 1870, strives to capture play-wright Lanford Wilson's intent.

Wilson's description states said that the boat house set should not look "bombed out" but, instead, should look "run down." Bombed out would imply little hope, but hope gathers momentum as the play progresses. And so as we first see it, the boat house has an almost ghoulish presence but becomes an enchanted place as the play unfolds.

It is July 4th in 1944, at Sally's home near Lebanon, Missouri (inciden-tally, where the playwright was born) and the play begins with an extraor-dinary monologue, Matt breaking the fourth wall, directly addressing the audience, in fact, in this production, even strolling in the first row before the stage, humorously and engagingly setting the time, place, and cir-cumstances of the play. He says the play *is a waltz - a no-holds-barred romantic story that could be done here with a couple of folding chairs, which, hopefully, will end in love, and that it will be performed without an intermission.*

When Sally, the object of Matt's love, enters the dialog abruptly shifts in a 90 minute plus performance, Matt now in full character. It is an inter-esting dramatic device, demanding your attention, and I thought one that endears the audience to Matt's quest.

This is a prequel to Wilson's first play in the Talley series of three, *Fifth of July*, which takes place in 1977. In this, really the first play chronologi-cally, Wilson establishes how Sally and Matt meet only a month after D Day, the implications of the war hanging heavily.

They first had a romance a year before, in this same boat house which has been in Sally's family since her "Uncle Whistler" built it. Everett Talley (known as the "whistler" as he always whistled; everyone in the town think-ing him crazy) wanted to build a gazebo, but it became more of a boat house. It has always been Sally's favorite place and she thinks of her Uncle as one of the healthiest family members in spite of his eccentricities.

Her family is one of the two wealthiest families in town. They are also Protestant and along with that distinction comes some southern bigotry and Matt being a Jewish immigrant and much older, is rendered unwel-come by them. (While Sally says she's a mid-westerner, Matt contends that "anyplace outside of New York City and some suburbs of Boston, is the south!") Her family even threatens to shoot him, calling Matt the *commu-nist traitor infidel.*

Thus the clandestine meeting of Sally and Matt on this July night in the boat house. Even though she at first rejects Matt's advances, in fact tell-ing him to go back to St. Louis, her very presence, and in a new dress no less, sort of belies her protestations. (Matt, by the way, is wearing a new tie instead of the same one he has worn for years in his office.) Matt has sent

Sally letters for the past year, all unanswered (she complains that they were mostly details about his work as an accountant).

So during that night they exchange stories about their past. In spite of being from a well-established family, Sally feels she is an outsider, carrying a secret with her which she finally reveals to Matt (no spoiler here, see the play!). Once she unburdens herself of that, the walls of Matt's unrequited love are torn down.

Sally questions Matt about his origins and Matt too has his tale to tell, piecing together his Eastern European / German heritage, and revealing a tragic family history of escaping persecution and the pain of his family being killed by the Nazis.

It is a beautiful play of how two emotionally wounded people, ones who feel out of step with the times and society, find a path to happiness. *You and me are so alike, although we are so different* Sally finally says. (And a political awakening has already stirred in Sally, her being fired for teaching Thorstein Veblen's *Theory of the Leisure Class*, in nursery school!)

So much of the play depends on the staging and the acting. As a "two handed" play it is such a delicate balance to keep the action moving forward. At any time one fears their relationship might spin out of control and end badly. And in this respect, Director J. Barry Lewis perfectly choreographs the actors on the multi-tiered stage in harmony with the overall feeling of the play as a waltz, the dialogue shifting back and forth between confrontation and tenderness in 3/4 time. He also finds the right symmetry between the play's humorous and soulful moments.

But when it comes right down to it, the acting makes or breaks *Talley's Folly* and here Dramaworks' casting excels. My wife, Ann, saw Judd Hirsch's performance as Matt in the 1980 award-winning Broadway production, but thought Brian Wallace's performance last night was every bit as credible. Brian has to carry some heavy lifting particularly with the opening monologue. Mr. Wallace, making his first Dramaworks appearance (although an experienced actor in NY and in repertory productions), had the audience rooting for him right from the beginning. His ease in handling the diverse emotions of humor, anger, and disappointment, while practically pleading for Sally's hand, were moving.

Erin Joy Schmidt who plays Sally has appeared in two other productions we've seen, *Goldie, Max and Milk* at the Florida Stage and *Dinner With Friends* at Dramaworks. She can turn an emotion on a dime, her eyes often welling up with tears while Matt is speaking and even though she might be on another part of the stage, the audience knew precisely when to follow her reaction. How does one play the part of a spinster, one who by her own admission regarding her family *are as anxious to get rid of me as I am to leave*, but finds her opportunity with a Jewish accountant of foreign ancestry, and an older man of whom her family disapproves? She's afraid of intimacy and commitment on the one hand and abandonment on the other, and Ms. Schmidt's performance covers the whole range.

A special note about the lighting, designed by Ron Burns as at one point Matt remarks that *there is no color in the moonlight.* It drew my attention to the dappled lighting as if streaking through the trees across the actor's faces, just the perfect ambiance for the play and the setting. Costume design is by Brian O'Keefe, with unerring detail right down to Sally's seamed stockings and her stunningly coifed period hairstyle.

This is indeed a "fitting" production for the first of Dramaworks' new season.

Thursday, December 6, 2012 'A Delicate Balance' -- Vanishing the Impossible

By now we have all been exposed to the famous first line of Leo Tolstoy's *Anna Karenina,* "Happy families are all alike; every unhappy family is unhappy in its own way." If that is the case, great American drama is built on the unhappy family with Eugene O'Neill perhaps being the master and following in his footsteps Tennessee Williams, Arthur Miller, Edward Albee, and others. And when one looks over the offerings of Dramaworks over the years, some of their finest productions are such family dramas, most recently *All My Sons, The Effect of GammaRays on Man-in-the-Moon Marigolds,* and the forthcoming, *A Raisin in the Sun.* I suppose writing a drama about a happy family, would be drama-less, so what's the sense?

This might be Albee's most enigmatic work, with long sometimes disjointed monologues, perhaps less explosive than *Who's Afraid of Virginia Woolf,* but with a deep, deep undertow of modern-day family angst. Tobias and Agnes, living their upper class existence in 1960's suburban Connecticut, along with Agnes' alcoholic sister, Claire, suddenly have visitors, their old and close friends, Harry and Edna. Their friends are in an existential plight, fleeing some unexpected terror in their own home. They have come to move in -- permanently. And into the pot let's stir the arrival of Julia, Tobias' and Agnes' thirty six year old infantile daughter who is returning home after her fourth divorce. (They had a son who died in childhood, just another element in the family's dark past.) It is the perfect mix for the kind of edgy drama that distinguishes the work of one of our greatest playwrights. And it is from these damaged characters that the drama springs.

Albee, even at the age of 84, has not relinquished much control over his plays. He has final say over the selection of actors, the design of the set, and the venue of course, wanting the most professional environment possible. He once said "When you're writing a play, you're attempting the impossible.

When you're directing it, you must do only what is possible, and the impossible must vanish."

So, did Dramaworks vanish the impossible? It is a "delicate balance" between the playwright and the performing team to make a theatrical masterpiece, and Albee and Dramaworks have all the right stuff. Albee's dark view of the human condition emerges with absurdist clarity.

And a word about the set by Michael Amico, an aesthetically perfectly proportioned living room/library in a staid Connecticut home, the bar being a focal point, downstage right. It is of course the first thing the audience takes in as it is being seated, setting a mental marker for what unfolds.

Albee throws down the gauntlet with Agnes saying *I find most astonishing the belief that I may, very easily, as they say, lose my mind one day.* Tobias replies while mixing a drink (there are countless drinks mixed and consumed during the production): *We will all go mad before you.*

One gets the sense as the first act unfolds that the entire family is mad at the starting gate. In fact, the play ends the following morning with Agnes making reference to those opening lines, noting that it is a new day. It might be on the calendar, but their lives go on as before.

There are so many themes in the play, particularly the nature of love and friendship. Is friendship love? Does one have to love one's own blood? What are the obligations of love? At one point, Claire says to Agnes, *Tobias loves you, you love Julia, Julia loves me, and I love Tobias.* Maybe a Venn diagram would reveal that there is some kind of "love" between the two sisters, Claire and Agnes, but Claire has already said she would like to see Agnes dead. But perhaps that emotion can be construed as a loving gesture in the context of this play. One only has to listen to Tobias' disturbing monologue about a cat that fell out of love with him and he had put to sleep.

The Broadway veteran Maureen Anderman plays the highly controlled, haughty, Agnes, delivering her acerbic wit with great ease. Her relationship with her sister, Claire, vacillates from an uneasy truce on the one hand to her attacks on her alcoholism: *If you want to die, don't take your whole life doing it.*

Claire is brilliantly played by the Dramaworks veteran, Angie Radosh, who in spite of her serious drinking is probably the sanest person in the play, somewhat inhabiting the role of a Greek Chorus.

Another Dramaworks old hand, Dennis Creaghan, plays Tobias, capturing a man in the middle of this family/friend crisis, bewildered by it all, expected, as the man of the house to resolve the issue, culminating in one of the most contradictory and demanding monologues in American theatre when confronting his friend, Harry.

Rounding out the cast are Anne Bates as the daughter, Julia, who always seems to prefer the "comfort" of her dysfunctional family to any of her spouses, and two other Dramaworks pros, Laura Turnbull as Edna and Rob Donohoe as Harry play their roles of lost, bewildered, anxiety infested (no, "plague contaminated" as accused by Agnes) "friends" to a tee, friends who insist they have "rights."

Searing and disturbing, but with rich, nonlinear language that really warrants reading the script to more fully understand it, this might not be a play for everyone, but in the annals of American theatre it doesn't get much better than a work by Edward Albee and a production of it by Dramaworks. You will never meet more disconnected characters on one stage, but the Director, Bill Hayes, pull them together in this haunting production. Perplexing at all times, *A Delicate Balance* taps the angst in us all.

Thursday, January 31, 2013 **Dramaworks' 'A Raisin in the Sun' -- a Special Relevancy**

A Raisin in the Sun is based on fact and portrays a time which is indelibly etched in my own memory. Lorraine Hansberry's father bought a house in the Washington Park section on the South Side of Chicago and the Hansberry family became a victim of racially restrictive neighborhood covenants preventing Afro-Americans from renting or buying there. The case ultimately went to the Supreme Court. Meanwhile the young author later remembered the long fight that "required our family to occupy disputed property in a hellishly hostile 'white neighborhood' in which literally howling mobs surrounded our house." The emotional toll this took resulted in the first play by an Afro-American woman to open on Broadway -- a smash hit for two years, with a predominantly black cast, evidence in itself that change was already underway and gathering momentum.

It also has a special relevancy to me as I grew up in a neighborhood not unlike Clybourne Park, the lily-white middle class neighborhood the Younger family in the play plans to move into. Karl Linder (the one white character in the play) portrays Clybourne's residents, as a community of people *who've worked hard as the dickens,....not rich or fancy people,...just hard-working, honest people who don't really have much but those little homes....[And] at the moment, the overwhelming majority of people out there feel that people get along better take more of a common interest in the life of the community when they share a common background.* Where I grew up, Richmond Hill, Queens, a suburb of NYC, could similarly be defined.

Linder's description of course is code for racism and I witnessed it first-hand when I was very young. Of course in the 50s I didn't understand any of this at the time but remember discussions, and "fear" expressed about the "Negroes" who were moving in. It was so endemic in our middle class, mostly German, neighborhood (ironically, Karl Linder's probable ethnic background); it was simply the way things were. You accepted it. It took the Little Rock desegregation crisis to bring another take on "reality" for me, then the three freedom riders that were beaten and murdered by the Ku Klux Klan, and finally seeing Malcolm X in college to raise my consciousness. Amazing to think *A Raison in the Sun* debuted on Broadway in 1959!

But a great play does not merely recount historical facts, it is steeped in profound passion, character development, and universal themes which give meaning to what it is to be human and vulnerable.

In "preparing" to see this production we had secured tickets last summer to see the Pulitzer and Tony award winning *Clybourne Park* by Bruce Norris in New York (reviewed in Chapter III), which is both sort of a prequel and sequel to Hansberry's groundbreaking work. Norris' work is an exercise in cynical acerbity on the topic of racism. Perhaps progress has been too glacial for Norris but I see it differently, and while *Clybourne Park* had its philosophical merits and some clever, even comic dialogue, it lacked the raw emotion of *Raisin*.

Hansberry writes about the Younger family, holed up in a small apartment in Chicago's Southside, but the matriarch of the family has inherited $10,000 from an insurance policy upon the death of her husband and she is intent on using the money for the betterment of her family, all of whom live with her in the apartment, her son, Walter Lee and his wife, Ruth, along with their child, Travis, and Walter's sister, Beneatha.

The title of the play comes from Langston Hughes' poem *A Dream Deferred*. But it is not only that line from the poem that enters the play, it is about "what happens to a dream deferred." Does it "fester," "stink," "become crusty and sugary," "sag," "or does it just explode?" The play is all of these, gathering energy that leads to an explosive climax.

The classic American dream theme that is part of the collective consciousness of the American theatre, and literature as well, the illusion that wealth in itself is the dream, is evident here too, with Walter scheming to use some of his mother's insurance money to buy into a liquor store.

But all the characters are dealing with their own dreams. Mama wants a house and a garden, a better life for her children, and her son to measure up to her dead husband who was honorable and worked all the days of his life : *I seen...him...night after night...come in ...and look at that rug...and then look at me...the red showing in his eyes...the veins moving in his head...I seen him grow thin and old before he was forty...working and working and working like somebody's old horse...killing himself...and you—you give it all away in a day.*

Mama's dream of a better place to live is shared by Walter's wife, Ruth, for themselves, and their child, Travis. And she shares in the hope that Walter will do the right thing, quit drinking, but Walter disappoints more often than not: *Oh let him go on out and drink himself to death! He makes me sick to my stomach!*

And Walter's sister, Beneatha, has dreams about becoming a Doctor. Some of Mama's insurance money is earmarked for medical school. She is also seeking out her identity as an Afro-American through her Nigerian friend, Asagai.

Even Karl Lindner, the spokesperson for the Clybourne Park Association lives in his own dream world, thinking his is a "rational argument" for the Youngers not to move into the community, that *Negro families are happier when they live in their own communities.* And he personifies so much of the problem of racism, believing his own delusions, even thinking he is doing a kindly favor for them.

Hansberry weaves these counterpoint dreams together in an intense drama which Dramaworks brings to life. It is a beautifully written play, gut retching at times.

Director Seret Scott developed a special cohesiveness of the actors. The voices she needed to present the many tiered themes in the play had become bonded to the extent that we felt like we were witnessing a real family on stage. Their joy of working together clearly came through.

Casting is one of Dramaworks' strong points. This is a large cast, all terrific, but it is the four leading roles whose performances were extraordinary.

Ethan Henry who plays Walter Lee Younger carries much of the heavy emotional weight of the play. Walter lives in the shadow of his father but he is a father himself as well as an Afro-American man who, working as a chauffeur, has been exposed to the privileged white man's world, and the consequent humiliation he feels returning each night to his mother's apartment, and to his wife, son and sister. He wants to be a man, the man and his scheme to make a fast bundle with part of his father's insurance money turns bad and just reinforces the humiliation he has carried all his life.

Ethan Henry plays this role with such force and physical presence, it seemed to suck all the air out of the theatre and silence a normally fidgeting audience. I don't like to make comparisons, but he reminded me so much of one of my favorite actors, Denzel Washington. It is no easy feat to pull off this role to such an extent that one does not need to compare his performance to Sidney Poitier's. Ethan Henry establishes his own vision of Walter Lee Younger.

And while Claudia McNeil might be considered the gold standard for playing the role of Lena Younger, the matriarch of the family, Dramaworks' Pat Bowie plays it with such quiet, sometimes agonizing dignity; her performance will be the one I remember going forward.

Her love of her family, her final forgiveness of her son which paves the way for his redemption, is the rock on which the family ultimately builds its future. When she says *child, when do you think is the time to love somebody the most? When he's done good and made things easy for everybody? That ain't the time at all. It's when he's at his lowest......and he can't believe in himself because the world's whipped him so!* I held my hand to my chest, as that line electrically connected to the audience and characterized her performance.

Lena is convinced that by buying a house for her family, it will restore their disintegrating lives to a level of dignity -- especially her son who she no longer understands: *It's just a plain little old house—but it's made good and solid—and it will be ours. Walter Lee—it makes a difference in a man when he can walk on floors that belong to him....* Indeed.

Walter's wife, Ruth, is played by an experienced Shakespearian actor, Shirine Babb. She shares in the horror of witnessing the downfall of Walter, and she fears for her family, her son Travis, as well as her unborn child. Ms. Babb suppresses that horror to a level of stoicism at times which quickly rises to exuberant expectations in anticipation of moving and what that will mean for her family. She sheds tears at one moment, sometimes on the other side of the stage seeing Walter's rage (mostly directed at himself), and then joy as Lena talks about the future and what the house will mean. Ms. Babb was a delight to watch walk that difficult line on stage.

Beneatha is played by Joniece Abbott Pratt who carries the role of the emerging educated generation -- seeking to become a Doctor on the one hand and on the other trying to understand her African roots. She is conflicted as her boyfriend George (played admirably by the New York based actor Jordan Tisdale) is an educated, even wealthy black, but one who is trying to distance himself from his heritage.

On the other hand, she has another suitor, Joseph Asagai (sensitively played by Marckenson Charles) who is a student from Nigeria, wanting to go back to his country and take Beneatha, introducing her to African culture, bringing her recordings of native African drums (to which Beneatha dances in her African dress also given to her by Asagai). He even convinces Beneatha to change her hair to Afro-natural, which shocks George, but Beneatha finally wears with pride.

He is the one who speaks the truth to Beneatha when she is at her nadir after Walter has squandered the money, giving her another perspective, *There's something wrong when all the dreams in this house......depended on something that might never have happened......if a man had not died. We used to say back home......'Accident was at the first and will be at the last......but a poor tree from which the fruits of life may bloom.'....I see only that you, with all of your keen mind......cannot understand the greatness of what your mother tried to do. You're not too young to understand. For all of her backwardness......she still acts, she still believes that she can change things. So she is more of the future than you are.*

So Ms. Pratt has to walk a thin line as part of the family and as a symbol of striving and of the future which she does with aplomb.

David A. Hyland plays the mild mannered Karl Lindner, the representative from the Clybourne Park Association, who has the task of buying off the Youngers so they don't move into his frightened community. It's a difficult role to play as he is not a mean racist, but merely a product of his times, and Hyland makes it look easy.

And finally, not a character, but a symbol, is Lena's plant, a fragile thing that she has nurtured in the mostly sunless apartment, but she is determined to carry with her to her new home. Beneatha asks her what she's doing with that old withering plant and Mama says *Fixing my plant so it won't get hurt none on the way....* Incredulously Beneatha says: *Mama, you going to take that to the new house?...That raggedy-looking old thing?* To which Mama replies, *It expresses ME!*

Originally a three act play, Dramaworks has opted to change it to two acts, the first running about 1 hour 20 minutes, but that time passed quickly. The explosive second act's denouement is one of redemption, not tragedy, and one gets the sense that the future will be better, that progress is being made.

If Lorraine Hansberry had not died so young, in her mid thirties, who knows what other masterpieces she would have written. Let us be thankful for this one great work and for a local theatre company up to producing it at such a high standard. Prediction: a standing ovation after each performance as there was last night.

Thursday, March 28, 2013 **Letting Go -- Dramaworks' 'Exit the King'**

It is the rare regional theatre that would commit to the infrequently performed *Exit the King* by Eugene Ionesco. It is so much easier to win over an audience, particularly here in South Florida, with a traditional play grounded in realism. But Dramaworks is open to almost any theatrical challenge and it has earned the right to take on the occasional unconventional and controversial piece. However, will its loyal devotees follow them into the veritable shadow of the valley of death? I think they will provided they check their usual theatrical expectations at the door, and give themselves over to a leading playwright of the Theatre of the Absurd, a skillful director, an incredibly talented cast, and supporting technicians.

While we are all reconciled to the inevitability of our own deaths, at least philosophically, how about being told you have an hour and a half to live, as does our "everyman" 400 year-old King Berenger in Ionesco's *Exit the King*? Here's a fable on the art of dying, staged with the only sword we can thrust at the thought: humor. The corollary is to learn the art of living.

I was more than curious how Dramaworks would stylize Ionesco's play, recently reading the play to familiarize myself with the possibilities. (The Dramaworks' production is based on the more recent, contemporized translation by Neil Armfield, the director of the 2009 Broadway production, and its star, Geoffrey Rush.) Without the strong hand of a director and superlative performances on the part of the actors, it could be a very maudlin evening -- as some earlier versions were purported to have been when the play was first staged in the 1960's. Fear not, get ready for many hilarious moments with this production.

The "Theatre of the Absurd" finds its philosophical roots in Albert Camus' 1942 essay, "The Myth of Sisyphus" which presents the ultimate philosophical conundrum:....."much of our life is built on the hope for tomorrow yet tomorrow brings us closer to death and is the ultimate enemy; people live as if they didn't know about the certainty of death; once stripped of its common romanticisms, the world is a foreign, strange and inhuman place; true knowledge is impossible and rationality and science cannot explain the world: their stories ultimately end in meaningless abstractions, in metaphors. From the moment absurdity is recognized, it becomes a passion, the most harrowing of all."

Playwrights like Ionesco, Genet, Samuel Beckett and Edward Albee, brought this philosophical view to drama. It was critic Martin Esslin who defined this genre in a 1960's study, stating "the shedding of easy solutions, of comforting illusions, may be painful, but it leaves behind it a sense of freedom and relief. And that is why, in the last resort, the Theatre of the Absurd does not provoke tears of despair but the laughter of liberation."

At the time Esslin considered Samuel Beckett to be the leading playwright of the genre, and having seen his *Happy Days* a couple of years ago at the Westport Country Playhouse (see Chapter III), I understand. That play taught me the lesson of reading the script of an Absurdist drama before seeing it.

But Ionesco is an equal master and Dramaworks' production of his *Exit the King* indeed releases "laughter of liberation" displacing any "tears of despair," watching clown-like King Berenger's kingdom go to rack and ruin as his control over it and as his own life slip away. Although he is given credit for virtually every invention of mankind, he also shoulders the blame for letting his kingdom devolve. He has been oblivious to the passing of time, and has narcissistically whiled away his days. Like the rest of us in our own little kingdoms, we exercise the illusion of control in a world that will forget us in a nanosecond when we are gone.

The play more or less follows the progression of the stages of dying as set forth by Kubler-Ross in *The Art of Dying*: denial, anger, bargaining, depression, and acceptance (not necessarily in that order, and sometimes going back and forth) with all of these stages facilitated by interaction with the five other characters in the play, mostly with the timing of a slapstick comedy. (Ionesco's own stage directions for one scene reads "This scene should be played like a tragic Punch and Judy show").

The skillful hand of director William Hayes applies Ionesco's instruction to much of the production, balancing the weighty philosophical content with some belly laughs. One can clearly see where Hayes is going with the orchestration, having selected the ideal actor for each role, choreographing their intricate movement on (and off) stage, and introducing sound effects of the opening and closing of doors, a cacophony of mostly circus sideshow music, bells, whistles, kettle drums and let's not forget the sound of the cuckoo clock, as well as a strobe light enhanced Keystone Kops chase scene.

Our 400 year old King Berenger is told he is dying and has 1 hour and 30 minutes before the play ends to do it. His kingdom is dying as well. He at first protests: *I'll die when I want to.* He asks the fundamental philosophical question: *Why was I born if it wasn't forever?*

Colin McPhillamy gives a tour de force performance as King Berenger. Even before the actual performance begins he mingles with the audience, in good humor, just a regular guy like the rest of us. His transformation through the various stages of his impending death on the stage requires great poise and physicality, constantly shifting between vaudevillian comedy to great pathos such as this monologue which settles down the hilarity, solemnly delivered with the cadence of a Gregorian chant: *Help me, you countless thousands who died before me! Tell me how you managed to accept death and die. Then teach me! Let your example be a consolation to me, let me lean on you like crutches, like a brother's arms. Help me to cross the threshold you have crossed! Come back from the other side a while and help me! Assist me, you who were frightened and did not want to go! What was it like? Who held you up? Who dragged you there, who pushed you? Were you afraid to the very end? And you who were strong and courageous, who accepted death with indifference and serenity, teach me your indifference and serenity, teach me resignation!*

It is Queen Marguerite, his first wife, played by Angie Radosh, a seasoned Dramaworks actress, (one of our favorites) who provides the constant voice of reason, telling the King over and over again to prepare for the inevitable: *It's your fault if you've been taken unawares, you ought to have been prepared. You never had the time. You'd been condemned, and you should have thought about that the very first day, and then day after day, five minutes every day. It wasn't much to give up. Five minutes every day. Then ten minutes, a quarter, half an hour. That's the way to train yourself.*

Radosh's role is often as challenging as McPhillamy's. Unlike the other characters she does not share in the slapstick frivolity, never appearing like a marionette figure. She is the consummate actress and it is Queen Marguerite who carries the heavy lifting of the final scene in the play, as the King does indeed "exit" (after the other characters have left him alone to do so). Radosh delivers a moving performance in that scene, compassionately assisting the King to the final acceptance of the end of his life.

Countervailing the "old" Queen, is the young and beautiful trophy wife Queen Marie, who entreats the King to live, to fight death by exhorting him to *Cling to me, don't let go! It's I who keep you alive. I keep you alive, you keep me alive. D'you see, d'you understand? If you forget me, if you abandon me, I no longer exist, I am nothing.* Claire Brownell, a newcomer to Dramaworks plays Queen Marie with the right balance of passion, and humor, reminding us at times of a vulnerable Sugar Plum Fairy.

Rob Donohoe another seasoned Dramaworks actor performs the role of the Doctor, also Surgeon, Executioner, Bacteriologist & Astrologist! His riotous first appearance on stage with his wild hair, hack saw in hand and bloody stains on his apron is a harbinger of more humor to come. He sides with Queen Marguerite. The king is dying. Prepare. Although he is mostly playing a caricature, he delivers one of the more profound Ionesco lines concerning the relative insignificance of a single life, even though it is that of the King's: *He will be a page in a book of ten thousand pages in one of a million libraries which has a million books.* (Although, added to this is a line, presumably from the recent translation, *Or they can Google him.*)

Juliette, "the domestic help and registered nurse," is persuasively and amusingly played by Elizabeth Dimon, wearing a sort of worn Raggedy Ann doll attire. The King has always taken her for granted, but she becomes a real person to him while dying, his being accused by the Doctor and Marguerite of trying to "gain time" in taking such interest.

The Guard, performed by a helmeted and heavily armor breasted Jim Ballard, is the comic Greek chorus providing some of the heartiest laughs of the evening. These come from his deadpan announcements of what appears to be happening on the stage such as :*The King is walking! Long live the King!...The King is down! The King is dying!...The King is up! Long live the King!*

Suddenly the Guard has a heart to heart talk with the audience, reminiscing about his great days (centuries) with his King and the King's accomplishments which naturally range from inventing gunpowder, steel, zeppelins, airplanes (*At the start it wasn't a success. The first test pilots, Icarus and the rest, all fell into the sea.*), tractors, the building of Rome, New York, Moscow, Paris. Etc. *He wrote tragedies under [the secret] name of Shakespeare.*

When presenting a play that is not a period piece, but a more abstract philosophical concept, the nuances provided by the set design conceived by Michael Amico go a long way to tie the production together. The set has sort of a three dimensional children's pop out book feel to it. The costume designs by Leslye Menshouse are spot on, mostly emphasizing caricature, but with regal aspects particularly for Queen Marguerite. Lighting design by John Hall and sound design by Matt Corey are equally important to the overall artistic shape of a production such as this.

When the end finally comes, to our poor King, to his kingdom, to the play itself, we are left with an exhausted emptiness. We've laughed in the presence of the human predicament, sadly knowing what will happen sooner or later to each and every one of us.. But we have more time, don't we? It is not a play that will appeal to everyone. The man next to my wife was very uncomfortable during the performance, while the one next to me just laughed the whole night long. We exited to the melody of "Always Look on the Bright Side of Life" from Monty Python.....*Just remember that the last laugh is on you!*

Thursday, May 23, 2013 'Dancing at Lughnasa' -- and at Dramaworks

The personable Resident Director of PB Dramaworks, J. Barry Lewis, said they wanted to end their season with an explanation point -- Brian Friel's best known play (he's written 36!) *Dancing at Lughnasa*. The season began with *Talley's Folly*, a sensitive, delicate two person play about injured lives and it concludes with this eight person production, with much of the focus on five unmarried sisters, but still about injured lives, an ensemble production narrated by Michael, the adult child of two of the play's characters, Chris and Gerry (although we never see Michael as a child on the stage). As a "memory play" we spend time in the past to understand the present. And as an ensemble, there is no real central character, but that of the family unit and how these people come together and relate to each other in their own special ways.

The overriding themes are dreams foregone, and the old world coming into conflict with new world values, such as the Catholic church losing its grip in the face of rising secular activities, like music and dancing. The production is a veritable time machine trip, all layers of the play bringing you to the village of Ballybeg, Country Donegal, Ireland in 1936.

The play also carries forth a recurring theme in Irish theater, suffering, tragic women, and men who are free to drift in and out of their lives.

I think of Martin McDonagh's *The Beauty Queen of Leenane* (performed by Dramaworks last season) and some of the works of Sean O'Casey which explored similar themes.

Gerry, Michael's father, visits once a year, with dreams of being a great gramophone salesman, or an adventurer in the Spanish Civil war. The Uncle, Father Jack, has returned from Uganda where he was a missionary but has returned ill, and has been transformed into a pagan worshiper, very much in conflict with the values of his sister, Kate, who, of the five sisters, still staunchly upholds Catholic traditions. The women are the ones who keep the family going, do the work and have to carry on in the face of adversity, the changing times of the industrial revolution that threaten their meager income (Kate is a school teacher whose income is supplemented by two of her sister's -- Rose and Agnes -- work as piecemeal knitters).

Theirs are dreams constantly deferred but Friel introduces the interesting conceit of an unpredictable wireless radio, one that will occasionally work, and it is then the women can burst into dance, from which the play derives its title after an Irish pagan dance festival. They dance fast and furiously and passionately, with one another and singularly, a sudden, powerful geyser of normally suppressed sexuality and freedom, with animal like cries of joy, but as strangely as this music comes into their lives it fades away and it is back to their mundane lives. The "magic" of the radio -- clearly remembered by Michael with the nickname of Marconi -- opened the outside world to this family for the first time.

Friel uses the stage as a canvas to paint an abstract of family dynamics of the times, ones that mirrored his own life and clearly this is why the play works. Michael is the playwright's voice: "atmosphere is more real than incident." And in order for it to work, the setting must also be perfect and the scenic design by Jeff Modereger has created a startlingly stark depiction of the family's threadbare home and its outside yard, using the full expanse of the stage and compensating for the stage's lack of depth. It is a stage the actors can move freely about without opening and closing doors.

The challenge to the actors who play the sisters is to capture the specific individuality of the different sister relationships. As an ensemble production, the audience needs to get to know each character on his/her own merits, and follow that person's own solitary story.

Kate is the default mother of the family, a schoolteacher and as such the main provider. She is also the upholder of tradition and the values of the Catholic Church (although she, too succumbs to some dancing, but not with wild abandonment). Julie Rowe, who is new to Dramaworks, but not South Florida, plays the role with stoic determination.

She, as are all of the sisters, is protective of Rose, played by Erin Joy Schmidt. Rose is a little slow witted, innocent, and is the first to get caught up in the excitement and dreams of attending the upcoming harvest dance (which they don't). Ms. Schmidt -- who co starred in *Talley's Folly* at the beginning of the season, carries the role with a kind of gullibility and she, of all the sisters, is most transparent to the damage they all feel.

A veteran Dramaworks actor, Margery Lowe, plays Agnes, who takes a special interest in protecting Rose. The two of them knit to supplement Kate's income and they are the ones who become most vulnerable when a factory opens nearby. This is a difficult role, well acted by Ms. Lowe, as Agnes in many ways is the most repressed of the sisters, secretly in love with Chris' Gerry, but never able to reveal anything.

Chris is played by Gretchen Porro, a Dramaworks newcomer who, when with Gerry, becomes almost manic, a schoolgirl in love, and without him, depressive, a "bad woman" as she has an illegitimate child (but, nonetheless, a love child as the pagan convert Father Jack refers to him). It is another difficult role to play (there are really no easy ones).

Meghan Moroney plays Maggie, the homemaker and in many ways comes closest to a central figure as a fun loving family go between, played with indomitable optimism and energy by Ms. Moroney. But her good nature is belied by regret too, occasionally singing with a beautiful voice or humming the then popular song, *Isle of Capri*. She is a powerful figure on stage and as Irish as a shamrock!

And Michael's father, Gerry (played by Dramaworks veteran Cliff Burgess), who occasionally visits to see his son, re-romance his would-be-wife, Chris, with a wink at Chris' sister, Agnes, is not immune to the power of the music, cutting a Fred Astaire with both Chris and Agnes at times to the refrains of "Dancing in the Dark." Burgess walks a line in this role, always erring on the side of likeability. You never feel he is a heel in spite of his dreams of adventure, and his kaleidoscopic, self-servicing visits. He embodies the freedom the women envy, living in the moment.

Our matriarchal Kate worries when her brother, Father Jack, played by Dramaworks veteran John Leonard Thompson, returns from his missionary work in Uganda, as he not only comes back sickly, with memory loss from malaria, but as an admirer of pagan practices of the African people, threatening the Mundy family's reputation -- and putting her Catholic values in direct conflict. Thompson glides around the stage like a gray ghost, dazed most of the time, but slowly getting it together, near the end trading his symbolic British colonial hat for Gerry's straw hat, before, Gerry, himself, sets out to find adventure in the Spanish-American war.

The play opens and closes with two powerful, wonderfully written monologues delivered by the adult son, Michael, who is sifting through his memory to describe his childhood recollections. They are beautiful, delivered with the devotion of a loving son of this decimated family, by

Declan Mooney, another Dramaworks veteran. To quote those is to reveal just too much of the outcomes of these damaged characters.

In fact, there is a pervading sadness emitted by the play. We too briefly get caught up in the spontaneous dancing as a relief from the ennui of despair. And the play seems long, although Dramaworks' pacing felt right; nonetheless there is just so, so much material to cover. J Barry Lewis' direction was flawless, but, a two hour and thirty plus minute play (with a 15 minute intermission) is a challenge to keep the audience engaged when the plot is partially made up of vignettes of despondency.

A few words about the sound (Steve Shapiro), lighting (Ron Burns), and costumes (Brian O'Keefe) -- all flawlessly in synch with the period and the mood of the play. Again, "atmosphere is more real than incident." It is here that the behind the scene technicians shine. Kudos as well to Lynette Barkley, the choreographer, and Gillian Lane-Plescia who was the dialect coach and helped to make the production authentic on the one hand and intelligible to an American audience as well.

Thursday, October 10, 2013 'Of Mice and Men' -- A Bold Production

Robert Burns: "The best laid schemes of mice and men / Go often awry."

I say "bold" in the subject heading but I could have easily said "daring." It's not the type of drama some people seek out. It is delivered with such intensity that some moments land on the audience like a sledgehammer. But if any play suits Dramaworks to a tee, it's *Of Mice and Men*, a play about simple dreams dashed by chance and circumstances, the inherent vulnerability of characters who are striving for the basic things in life, a place to live and some security. Dramaworks knows how to pick great dramas of this nature and breathe life into them.

Of Mice and Men is among one of John Steinbeck's greatest works, not as famous as *Grapes of Wrath* or *East of Eden* of course, but it's a novella consisting almost entirely of dialogue. It reads like a play and it sweeps the reader along into its inevitable, tragic conclusions. Steinbeck designed it as such --- to convert it to a play. Reading stories such as *Of Mice and Men*, where the characters are "acting out" the themes of the work through dialog and their actions, gives it that unique momentum, unlike more descriptive literary works. Seeing it live on stage pushes you to deeply empathize with real people, as if you are transported to their time, place, and circumstance.

There are not many plays more painful to watch in my opinion, because nearly every character is so seriously flawed, and on his / her road to ruin. Alas, "the best laid schemes....often go awry." On a macro level, the setting of the dust bowl migration leaves them even more at risk. These are migratory workers in the field, set in a ranch in California not far from Steinbeck's home town. Here is society's most vulnerable stratum, and it is their inherent loneliness as migrant workers and their unreachable dreams that are laid threadbare in this production.

It takes a certain ear to capture real dialogue, and as Steinbeck himself grew up in Salinas, California during those times, and spent some time on ranches with migrant workers, he is a master, and if you see this play and/or read the novella, this is something to be appreciated, savored, as it is a language that almost manifests the hardship, the loneliness, and the ill-fated destiny of the characters. Ironically, the language itself catapulted the book onto censorship lists, especially when first published, but probably in some sections of the country, it is still not taught.

It is also a work about friendship and trust, a unique, almost symbiotic relationship between two men. They rely on one another, George the orchestrator of their lives (or whatever modicum of control he has) and Lennie, a quiet innocent giant of limited mental capacity dependent on what George says and the dreams that George spins to keep them both going.

In trying to explain their relationship to Slim, the mule driver, perhaps the most "normal" person on the ranch, George says the following, indicating to Lennie with this thumb: *He ain't bright. Hell of a good worker, though. Hell of a nice fella, but he ain't bright. I've knew him for a long time.*

To which Slim replies, *Ain't many guys travel around together. I don't know why. Maybe ever'body in the whole damn world is scared of each other.*

George and Lennie's dreams are just that simple: *Jus livin offa the fatta the lan* with Lennie tending to the rabbits. It is the American Dream at its most basic. A place to live, a little happiness? This a leitmotif in the play.

Crooks, the black stable hand, knows a thing or two about being lonely and ostracized, and recognizes in Lennie a somewhat kindred spirit. More foreshadowing as he says to Lennie: *I seen hunderds of men come by on the road an' on the ranches, with their bindles on their back an' that same damn thing in their heads. Hunderds of them. They come, an' they quit an' go on; an' every damn one of 'em's got a little piece of land in his head. An' never a God damn one of 'em ever gets it. Just like heaven. Ever'body wants a little piece of lan'. I read plenty of books out here. Nobody never gets to heaven, and nobody gets no land. It's just in their head. They're all the time talkin' about it, but it's jus' in their head.*

One of the catalysts in bringing the play towards its dark conclusion is the one truly unlikeable character, Curley, the "The Bossman's" son, constantly needing to prove himself, incredibly possessive of but inattentive to his new wife (unnamed in the play, an interesting subliminal message about Steinbeck's attitude towards women - or at least their place in the play). Candy, the aging worker who is now confined to the most menial tasks around the ranch warns George and Lennie: *Curley's like alot of little guys. He hates big guys. He's alla time picking scraps with big guys. Kind of like he's mad at 'em because he ain't a big guy. You seen little guys like that, ain't you? Always scrappy?*

There are no chances for Lennie and George's simple dream to become a reality (and for Candy as well, who wants to be included). The final catalyst is Curley's wife, who is generally regarded as a slut by the ranch hands, but nevertheless dreams of becoming a movie star, and is the ideal magnet to draw Lennie (and herself) into the play's inevitable conclusion. In the second act Curly's wife and Lennie "talk" to each other, expressing their hopeless dreams, but neither are capable of listening to the other. It is a conversation entirely in counterpoint.

This was an absolutely perfect script for J. Barry Lewis, the veteran, knowledgeable, Resident Director of Dramaworks, to bring out the themes of this play by maximizing the superb talents of his actors and utilizing the 'state of the art' stage now available in their new space. It is truly the ideal designed theatre for both sides of the fourth wall, bringing the audience into the performance.

Many of these artists are veteran Dramaworks' actors or technical people. First and foremost John Leonard Thompson carries a heavy load in the play, being on stage most of the time, playing George with a focused intensity, trying to manage Lennie and keep him out of trouble, keep the dream intact and attempt to fit into the ranch and keep their jobs and at the same time keep their plans secret (unsuccessfully as Candy becomes part of the hopeless scheme and even Crooks tries to join in). And of course trying to avoid the inevitable conclusion of the play, so shocking, even though most in the audience (I hope at least) knew how it would end. It is a part demanding such energy (and ability to memorize massive regional dialogue) so hats off to him.

Brendan Titley is one of the newcomers to Dramaworks, a young but experienced actor who does a heartfelt job portraying Lennie -- a difficult part to play but he always manages to secure the empathy of the audience.

An award-winning supporting performance is given by Dennis Creaghan, an absolutely perfect depiction of the old rancher, Candy, whose beloved old dog has just been shot to put him out of his misery. He fears that he too has become too old and useless and knows that his time at the ranch will be at an end sooner than later. He is irresistibly drawn to the scheme of sharing in George and Lennie's dream of owning a small ranch which he can help them realize (he was given a small amount of money as compensation from an accident that severed his hand).

Cliff Burgess's characterization of Slim, the one person who seems to have reconciled himself to his job on the ranch, goes about his business in an upbeat way -- a fair-minded person. His presence on the stage and the way Burgess comports himself in the part was always a relief, lessening the heavy tension on stage for a moment or two.

W. Paul Bodie is ideal as Crooks, the stable hand, who actually has his own room -- he's not allowed to play cards with the other boys or even enter the bunk house because he is black. He's resentful about that, but ironically, he has something none of the other workers have, his own place. Crooks accepts his lot in life on the one hand and is angry on the other, Bodie expressing that contradiction perfectly.

Curley's wife is admirably played by Betsy Graver and while she is not on stage that often, she creates a contrast to the bland monolithic "colors" of the workers. Simply, she lights up the stage with her seductive looks and dress, a femme fatale in every sense of the term.

The remaining cast members give professional performances in every way, but one last comment on the acting, and that is the brief, but powerful role of "The Boss" by one of the stage's (and movie and TV) most experienced actors, Frank Converse. He is larger than life while on stage. Coincidentally we have a geographic connection as he lives in Weston, CT (where we lived for some 25 years) and were fortunate to see him in some productions at the Westport Country Playhouse over the years.

Michael Amico uses representative design, with one major set -- sort of a Tabula rasa with added extras to effectively portray a sandy bank on the Salinas River, the ranch bunkhouse, the barn, and the stable hand's room. There is actually a hatch that opens on the stage floor filled with water to represent a river and along with the sound effects and lighting, the audience is drawn into the image and supplies the "rest" allowing the characters to do the storytelling. His designs always seem to be exactly the right one for the play, difficult to construct after being properly imagined.

Leslye Menshouse's costumes were designed right out of the Sears, Roebuck catalogues for the times -- probably where the characters would have bought their clothing, and then underwent serious "distressing" to reflect the years of hard labor and the few clothing changes men of the fields wore. They had the look of the WPA photographs from the dust bowl migration.

Lighting shifts are numerous and dramatically effective, using the stage design to its greatest advantage and well coordinated with myriad sound effects, of wildlife, dogs howling in the distance, of men outside the barn, horseshoes thudding and making ringers.

This is a major production, and in the intimate Dramaworks' surround-ings, the audience becomes part of the tragic events that unfold, but also -- hopefully -- with the sense that we all share, as human beings -- the same feelings, wanting to be connected (and I don't mean Facebook) with others. Nonetheless, some will see this production as dark, very dark, and in many ways it is that too, but Steinbeck (and Dramaworks) are striving for a more empathetic appreciation of universal human needs.

Thursday, December 5, 2013 'The Lion in Winter' a "Holiday Show"

While most South Florida stages are basking in the glow of holiday cheer productions, Dramaworks has chosen to present its antithesis, a play set in the Christmas past of 1183, James Goldman's vision of the Plantagenet family reunion (which actually never happened) in Chinon, France, at the castle of King Henry II, along with his wife, Eleanor of Aquitaine who he has briefly released from a prison exile in England, their sons, Richard (the Lionheart), Geoffrey, and John, as well as France's King Philip II, and his half-sister, Princess Alais Capet.

Most of the play circles around alliances made and then broken, focused on which son of Henry's will inherit the throne, who gets what territory, which Prince will marry Princess Alais, or, for that matter whether Henry himself will marry the Princess who is half his age if he can get his marriage to Eleanor annulled by the Pope (who owes him one), whether King Philip can recover territory Henry promised to return when Philip's father was alive, and last but not least, whether Eleanor will be able to secure her freedom from the soul crushing 10 year imprisonment she has endured. As the foregoing suggests, there are endless combinations for alliances between the characters who desperately want to achieve their objectives with the least important factor being family love and loyalty. It is the perfect stuff of tragedy, but this is equally balanced with comedic elements -- sublimely and acerbically written by James Goldman.

What a delicious reprieve from the typical Christmas show as behind the facade of the holiday is probably more family strife than anyone cares to admit. The play has the tone of the cynical Stephen Sondheim song from *Follies*, "Could I Leave You?" and it is no surprise that Goldman and Sondheim were friends and in fact collaborated on *Follies*, for which Goldman wrote the book.

Goldman portrays the dysfunctional Plantagenet family using many factual elements but much of it is totally imagined. They scheme and counter-scheme to the point of exhaustion, mostly out of sheer boredom with their lives, where after a tortuous scene Eleanor hilariously asks, *What family doesn't have its ups and downs?*

The themes are as relevant today as they were in 1183. Just think of the mass killings, lack of gun control, family shootings and the kaleidoscopic wars in which our species seems to indulge. At one point Richard threatens John with a knife, John saying *A knife -- he's got a knife.* Eleanor's reply to her sons covers war and its microcosm, families: *Of course he has a knife.*

He always has a knife. We all have knives. It is eleven eighty-three, and we're barbarians. How clear we make it. Oh my piglets. we're the origins of war. Not history's forces nor the times nor justice nor the lack of it nor causes nor religions nor ideas nor kinds of government nor any other thing. We are the killers; we breed war. We carry it, like syphilis, inside. Dead bodies rot in field and stream because the living ones are rotten. For the love of God, can't we love one another just a little? That's how peace begins. We have so much to love each other for. We have such possibilities, my children; we could change the world.

The language is so rich and witty, and if there is love, it is of the contest itself, a wonderfully choreographed Tarantella of never-ending verbal slings and arrows. Dramaworks takes this splendidly written work and uses all its expertise to bring the play to the level of a Broadway production, one which may not please everyone as it is a complicated, and sometimes disturbing play. Black humor, perhaps, but there is a certain honesty that prevails.

Professionalism shines through in the production, first with the most ambitious set ever undertaken by the company (scenic design is by the highly experienced and gifted Michael Amico), a revolving part of the stage where as one scene is being presented to the audience, the other is being set up behind stage. Goldman's play demands many different scene changes and had Dramaworks not built its mechanized set, the play would have had those dreaded darkened moments while stage hands moved furniture, and this play needs to move along without such interruption. Amico's set allowed Dramaworks to have a perfect scene ready quickly and appropriately decorated with tapestries and furniture, including one with a Christmas tree.

The costume designs by Brian O'Keefe deserve a special mention as they are so integral to the play and to the characters. O'Keefe not only did his extensive period research, but made a careful study of the characters themselves, designing each costume for that character's persona, and then constructed each piece by hand. Only the belts and boots were purchased. As a result, both the King and Queen look entirely regal. Their sons can be easily distinguished by their dress -- Richard the Lionheart in his warlike appearance, Geoffrey the middle son having a tight snake-like fitting attire, and the younger, John, who borders on being a buffoon, dressed in almost a potato sack, all these costumes so suitable to their personalities. The young Princess Alais is attired in simple gowns while King Philip's attire reflects his youth, although a King in his own right.

King Henry and Eleanor of Aquitaine are played by two experienced Shakespearean actors, C. David Johnson and Tod Randolph, respectively, and their classical expertise makes their presence truly stately on stage. Theirs is a battle of wits and wills and Johnson and Randolph make excellent foils, yet easily fall into each other's arms, recalling their shared past. Richard is played by Chris Crawford, with the authority expected of an experienced warrior, and with requisite relentless ambition to succeed Henry.

The Dramaworks veteran, Cliff Burgess, plays the sly Geoffrey with chameleon-like precision, while Justin Baldwin portrays the clueless, infantile John. Katherine Amadeo inhabits Alais with a calculating innocence, entirely in love with and dedicated to Henry, the man, but, still, as a Princess, knows her own mind, holding herself up well to the dominating intellect of both Henry and Eleanor. Pierre Tannous makes his Dramaworks debut as an actor, having been active in the theatre company behind the scenes until now -- playing King Philip, balancing his need to appear regal in spite of his young age.

The production is Directed by William Hayes who orchestrates the play so it evolves naturally, almost as if it has a life of its own. Lighting design is by Ron Burns, and sound design by Matt Corey.

<u>Eleanor:</u> *How, from where we started, did we ever reach this Christmas?*
<u>Henry:</u> *Step by step.*

It's Christmas, 1183 at Dramaworks!

Thursday, January 30, 2014 **Pinter's 'Old Times' -- Dramaworks' Inspired Rendering**

If you try to "figure out" *Old Times* by Harold Pinter you might miss the performance. It is meant to wash over you like a piece of music, performed by the three major "instruments," Deeley (a successful film-maker), Kate (his wife) and Anna, a friend of 20 years ago who is visiting the couple in their gentrified farmhouse near the English coast.

It is about the unreliable, fungible nature of memory and its affect on relationships, told in "Pinteresque," a variation on the theatre of the absurd. The opening of the play introduces us first to the married couple as they are waiting for the arrival of Anna (although she is already on the stage with her back turned to the audience). Parts of their dialogue are like an overture to what will follow -- the ambiguous later recounting of the past in the play. In just the first few minutes, phrases like "I think," "I think so," "what does that mean," "when you look back...all that time," "can't you remember," "it's a very long time," "she remembers you," "do you think," "I didn't know," "I don't know," "I don't think so," and "I hardly remember her" are tossed around, foreshadowing the action (and the pauses) that will follow.

At one point Anna says (reinforcing the dreamlike feeling of the play), *Can you see that tiny ribbon of light? Is that the sea? Is that the horizon?* That sort of sums up how I felt looking for clarity (not Pinter's intention).

Instead, look for transparency in Pinter's pauses, as much of the story is told in those silent moments.

The plot is simple, but beneath the words are questions. An old friend visiting a married couple, Anna now living in Sicily married to a wealthy Italian (an object of some jealousy on Deeley's part? Deeley has been to Sicily. Did he see Anna there?). Anna and Kate were good friends (perhaps lovers?) before Kate met Deeley (or was it before or during the time Deeley knew Anna?). It is a dance of divergent memories and even roles (are they all really one person, or is Anna dead and Kate and Deeley are discussing her?). As Anna says at one point: *There are some things one remembers even though they may never have happened. There are things I remember which may never have happened but as I recall them so they take place.* That sort of sums up the entire play.

There is one particular conflicting memory and that is Deeley's description of his meeting Kate for the first time at a showing of the film, "Odd Man Out" (the title could describe Deeley's relationship with Kate and Anna). Perhaps Kate had gone to the film WITH Anna, as later Anna asks Kate whether she remembers those days when they explored London, they had gone to *some totally unfamiliar district, and almost alone, saw a wonderful film called "Odd Man Out."* (Emphasis, mine.) The opening title of this 1947 British film noir reads in part, *This story...[is] concerned...only with the conflict in the hearts of the people when they become unexpectedly involved.* Indeed, the characters in *Old Times* are "unexpectedly" but, more so, inscrutably involved.

Also, Deeley and Anna might have met (before Deeley met Kate) at the "Wayfarers Tavern," although Anna does not think so, but Deeley claims to remember her vividly, describing exactly what she wore. Later, Anna acknowledges *It was me. I remember your look...very well. I remember you well.* Kate turns to Anna and then says: *But I remember you. I remember you dead."*

Given the ambiguity of this play, its success is even more dependent on the performances of the three characters, their direction and the staging. The actors, as well as the scenic and lighting designers are newcomers to Dramaworks, but all highly experienced professionals.

As the play's Director, J. Barry Lewis has made the most of Pinter's script, making sure the pauses are as significant as what is said. It is part of the rhythm of the play, like gaps in memory the action on stage have their moments of rest so the audience can watch the characters, their bodily reactions having as much (or more) meaning than the words. Nonetheless, Lewis moves the action along and this two act play, without an intermission, and it glides by like a passing dream.

The set is particularly important, as it is real, tangible, denoting something, the action on the stage being so ethereal. Stage designer Victor Becker has created an expansive set for the first act. The play needed something grounded; hence, the beams, reminiscent of the frame of a barn, with the modern windows indicating that the home had been renovated. The second act is in the bedroom, the top part of the set lowered, "raising" the audience to the second floor, with two divans and an armchair replacing the furniture of the living room. It is a more intimate set now and this is where the play's tension rises.

Inevitably, the success of this play depends greatly on the three actors making their company debuts, Shannon Koob (Kate), Pilar Witherspoon (Anna), and Craig Wroe (Deeley). They are more than up to the task, totally consumed with their interpretations of the characters.

Wroe walks a fine line between the loving husband, the jealous lover, the angry "man out" and manages to carry much of the humor in the play (yes, there are some subtle amusing moments, some of which are delivered with a twist of sarcasm).

Koob has a difficult role as Kate as some of her work is done in silence, the bodily reactions to her husband and Anna, her facial expressions of hurt and anger -- actually seething anger at times and one wonders how Koob decompresses after each performance.

Witherspoon plays a more animated character, a catalyst in the lives of Deeley and Kate, almost like a breath of fresh air entering a stale, worn relationship. The actors are simply superb.

Paul Black 's lighting design endeavors to make emotional connections, with the lighting fluid, moving imperceptibly between colors and intensity.

All elements are in sync to make *Old Times* another Dramaworks unforgettable performance. I particularly liked the numerous threads of lyrics briefly sung by Deeley and Anna to Kate, almost as if they were trying to "top" each other, songs written by the likes of Jerome Kern, George Gershwin, Cole Porter, Rodgers and Hart, among others, songs representative of the past, evocative and in keeping with "old times." As Deeley remarks *they don't make them like that anymore.* Similarly, there are few professional theatres that can put together such a seamless, memorable production of *Old Times.*

Thursday, March 27, 2014 'Dividing the Estate,' a Timeless Tale

Dividing the Estate is perhaps as relevant for today's self-centered, materially obsessed culture as it was when it was written in the 1980s. It is a timeless tale of a vanishing way of life, old money being consumed by the expenses of maintaining an estate whose inhabitants do no work and where once bustling towns have become ghost towns because of urban sprawl and a severe economic recession. The real estate bust of the late 1980's was particularly hard on Texas and this play takes place in Horton Foot's mythical town of Harrison, Texas (where many of his plays are set). But the play is also about loyalty and devotion, the playwright empathetically portraying his characters in spite of their weaknesses. And it is a play that puts a smile on one's face with its humor, even with abundant heartrending overtones.

In fact, the play's Director -- also the Producing Artistic Director of Dramaworks -- Bill Hayes, purposely chose this work for its timeliness.

The Texas Gordon clan is divided, torn by feelings of entitlement, jealousy, rapaciousness and the hint that behind every fortune is a great crime. This is family, sometimes at its worst, and sometimes at its best. The family gyroscope is its matriarch, Stella, all the characters spinning around her in one way or another and her control is absolute, sometimes exercised as a benign dictator to her children and sometimes lovingly, particularly to her 92 year old black servant, Doug, who has been with the family since he was five. In fact Stella and Doug basically grew up together, so it is no wonder that Stella seems so devoted. He is indeed a surrogate family member. The other servants, Mildred and Cathleen also interact with the family, and these "downstairs" characters have their own dynamic interplay.

Shades of Chekov's *The Cherry Orchard* reverberate in the play, family coming together over an estate, a subtle drama with the sorrows and desires of ordinary people inextricably culminating in a denouement the audience can feel coming, and yet the characters are left dazed, staring blankly at the audience as the lights fade.

The exception is the one realist in the group, interestingly known as "Son," actually Stella's grandson, the only person in the family with some college education, who manages the estate, doles out "advances" to his alcoholic and philandering Uncle Lewis and the demanding and avaricious Aunt Mary Jo on their shares of the estate. Son's own mother, Lucille, is Stella's "good" child, the perfect foil for the others. Son fully knows what financial shambles the estate is in. Although the signs of decay in their Texas town are omnipresent as well, to varyingly degrees the characters delusionally pin their hopes on a financial reversal from leasing their land for oil exploration.

There are hints that the sins of Stella's long dead husband and her progenitors shadow the family. Stella says to Lucille. *Your father was a sinner -- he fathered children all up and down this county, black and white. I warned him he'd be struck down right in his bed of iniquity, but he never was. He died just as peaceful...,*Lucille interrupting, saying *He didn't die peaceful, Mama. He was in great pain when he died.* Stella replies, *Well he was in his own bed being cared for by his family. I despised him, you know.*

Another telling exchange is between Son, and the family, regarding how the estate came into being, Stella in denial. Son remembers when he was a student a classmate accused him of having *a blue belly just like your Yankee great-grandfather* -- a carpetbagger. They go back and forth recounting the story, Son always referring to his great grandfather, Stella always correcting him saying great-great-grandfather, Son saying that *he stole land right and left by destroying legal records in the courthouse* and Stella protesting *he didn't steal the land. He didn't steal anything.... And my daddy told me that his daddy told him that you could buy land here for a dollar-fifty an acre, and people were abandoning their plantations because they couldn't make a living on them without their slaves, and he saved his money and bought as much land as he could, and that makes up our estate.* One never knows the complete story, but this exchange, which is as humorous as it is revealing, leads to the inevitability of the unfolding drama.

And so this bewildered and torn southern family tries to come to grips with its predicament. They've been accustomed to a life on the dole and now the light of reality is at the end of their fictive tunnel. The 5,000 acre estate is no longer productive, but a burden, taxes and expenses rising while revenue diminishes.

This is a production well worth seeing, a play by one of our most prolific playwrights having written more than fifty, *Dividing the Estate* being his last one before he died at the age of 92. Horton Foote also adapted *To Kill a Mockingbird* for the screen for which he won an Academy Award. A truly remarkable playwright.

And while it is so often referred to as a "comedy" these generally are not belly laughs, but rather, a chortle here and a titter there as we recognize ourselves and members of our own families in Foote's characters. The cast coalesces and you feel that this is family and although set in 1987, as relevant today.

Foote's regional Texas dialogue is lively, lots of give and take between the actors, so the play moves at a good pace, and director Hayes takes full advantage of the script, and the actors -- the largest cast assembled to date at any Dramaworks production -- shine in their roles.

These are all pros and it is hard to single out any one performance. The interplay between Stella (Mary Stout) and her very different (but dependent) children, Lewis (Rob Donohoe), Mary Jo (Kim Cozort), and Lucille (Elizabeth Dimon), reveal well worn hurts, and expectations. The "help," Doug (John Archie), Mildred (Avery Sommers), and Cathleen (Deltoiya Goodman) have their own conflicts, and interaction with the family, many amusing, always touching. Bob (Kenneth Kay), Mary Jo's distraught husband, is now bankrupt, visiting from Houston with their two spoiled generation X children, Emily (Gretchen Porro) and Sissie (Leah Sessa). Son (Gregg Weiner) is now engaged to Pauline (Margery Lowe), a schoolteacher, who tries to introduce news of the world into the family, with no success. And finally, there is the teenager Irene (Natalia Coego), a waitress at the local "Whataburger" who, with great hilarity is introduced by Lewis towards the end of the play, as his beau. The family jokes that soon they'll all be working at Whataburger until Pauline chimes in, *That's what they say America is becoming, you know, a service economy*. Dramaworks lovingly transforms Foote's work into memorable, fun theatre.

Saturday, May 17, 2014 'Tryst' – Trust and Betrayal

The always knowledgeable and charismatic director, J. Barry Lewis, points out that *Tryst* by British playwright Karoline Leach is somewhat of a departure for Dramaworks. It's not a well-known classic play. But judging by the opening night, it was produced with Dramaworks' usual careful detail to scenic design, costumes and lighting, bringing out the best the play has to offer.

And it's an unusual play because of the characters' interaction with the audience, breaching the fourth wall frequently, perhaps more in touch with the audience than with each other, pleading their cases. The overarching themes of reality perceived vs. reality, the struggle between the masculine and feminine, and trusting one's heart, resonate continually. The play is set on the eve of the women's suffrage movement in England further highlighting these issues.

Actors Jim Ballard and Claire Brownell perform in this "two-handed play," both on stage for two hours without relief.

The multiple scenes in the play require the audience's involvement, the actors creating the beginning of the illusion, along with sound effects, lighting, and the swift changing of props, and the audience having to fill in the rest. Don Thomas, who did the lighting design, chose to see the story through the eyes of the cad, George Love, played by Ballard. Side and overhead lighting is extensively used to create shadows (portraying the dark side of the play). The first act alone has some seventy lighting changes.

And indeed the production holds the audience spellbound in its melodramatic grip, set in the period Ann and I enjoy so much, early 20th century England during the times of PBS' *Mr. Selfridge* and *Downton Abbey*. The costumes and the set perfectly capture Edwardian England. Its premise is universal; a con is a con is a con, for monetary gain or in capturing a trusting heart, there is a "Mr. Love" predatorily waiting to take advantage of the weak. Sometimes, and delightfully for the audience, the predator is exposed.

The two hour production, with an intermission, flies by thanks to the skillful direction provided by Mr. Lewis and the compelling performances of Dramaworks' veteran actor Jim Ballard as George Love and Claire Brownell as Adelaide Pinchin in her second appearance at the theatre. In particular, Ms. Brownell inhabits the role of the demure Adelaide, who, during the course of the play, with prodding by George (although that is not his altruistic intention), begins to find her own inner strength while George's perceived charismatic force and ulterior motives are revealed. Indeed, they discover a commonality of abuse they both suffered from their fathers which has crippled both of them in profound ways.

Playwright Karoline Leach uses a number of contrivances to bring the play this far. It would be a spoiler to list them, but the conclusion, in my opinion, which some found disturbing, fits the essence of what was revealed on stage, and how the characters were changed by one another. Is *Tryst* great theatre? Perhaps not, but between the acting and the production elements, Dramaworks' version is well worth seeing.

The production features scenic design by Jeff Modereger, costume design by Brian O'Keefe (whose costumes were designed not only for the period, but for the fast changes that take place on stage), lighting design by Don Thomas, and sound design by Rich Szczublewski. A special mention should be made of the work of the dialect coach, the renowned Gillian Lane-Plescia who indeed helped make the characters sound like they are from their appropriate Edwardian English class (although George is feigning his), enhancing the production's verisimilitude.

Thursday, October 9, 2014 "This Is the Way We Were" – 'Our Town'

Thornton Wilder's *Our Town* is probably the most widely performed play in American theatre. Who hasn't seen it, even at the high school level (my son played George Gibbs in his high school production)? As many times as we've seen the play our one regret was not being able to attend the Westport Country Playhouse's production with Paul Newman as the stage manager in June 2002. Its brief run there ended before we returned to Connecticut from Florida for the summer.

So now we finally had the opportunity to see what a professional theatre company would do with the play. In celebration of Dramaworks' 15th season, it has staged a beautiful, memorable rendering, with the largest cast in its history, many veterans of other Dramaworks shows. As J. Barry Lewis, the play's Director and Dramaworks' Resident Director, said this company had grown so much artistically over the years that it wanted to put their own imprimatur on one of the most revered plays in American theatre history.

Most of the twenty one actors in the play have appeared in other Dramaworks productions, so it was a reunion of sorts, a celebration of their theatre community -- and community in general -- with its choice of another Pulitzer Prize winning play (the company has performed at least one in each of its 15 years).

Dramaworks also put its own spin on the set. Although it is the traditional minimalist set, with no props other than the chairs and tables (actors miming their use of everyday implements such as kitchenware), the back-drop could be anyplace backstage circa 1938 when the play was written (although the play covers the years 1903-1913, set in the mythical Grover's Corners of New Hampshire). It is evocative of New England. It speaks of earlier times, a simpler way of life, but life, nonetheless, as we all still live it in all its cycles. The minimalist set asks us, the audience, to use our own imagination, enter the play, and to fill in the blanks.

So why does this play never tire? It is a play about everyman – us – and it is a celebration of what it means to be part of a community. It's about the transience of life, something we become increasingly aware of as we age, putting our brief humdrum existence in context (*The cottage, the go cart, the Sunday-afternoon drives in the Ford, the first rheumatism, the grandchildren, the second rheumatism, the deathbed, the reading of the will. Once in a thousand times it's interesting.*). It is a call to find beauty and meaning in the ordinary.

The play is like a fine piece of music, where Act I: Daily Life is the exposition, meeting the characters and witnessing their routines, ones they go about sort of unconsciously as they comment about the weather and the ordinary details of their day. Act II: Love and Marriage is the development section, where the characters and the themes are now more in focus; something of consequence is happening, a wedding, perhaps the most significant event in our lifetimes (*People are meant to go through life two by two, 'Tain't natural to be lonesome.*) Act III: Death and Dying is the recapitulation, but, now with an entirely different and solemn look at the characters when they realize their daily life must be lived, and every day, every action, cherished (*Do any human beings ever realize life while they live it?-every, every minute?*). The omniscient Stage Manager then sums up, continuing to pass through the fourth wall, directly wishing the audience a good night.

We never tire of hearing the great masters of classical music, and similarly that is why seeing *Our Town* again (and again) is welcome. We listen for the variations, the spin on the performance a conductor might put on a piece of music and the virtuosity of the musicians, and in this case what a director will do with the tabula rasa of the stage and bringing out the talent of the actors.

How fitting that the Stage Manger role should go to Colin McPhillamy whose previous performances in Palm Beach Dramaworks' *Exit the King, Copenhagen* and *The Pitmen Painters* were outstanding. He is the consummate actor, giving a tour de force performance in the role of the authoritative, omniscient guide for the audience, easily transitioning to briefly becoming a character in the play and then back again as the "stage manager." It must be a difficult role to play. McPhillamy perfectly describes it in his blog: "A man both of the town and beyond it, able to move in several directions in time and with the prescient knowledge of things to come and things past. His voice joins with the author's in the play's great invitation: to notice."

Arguably the other leading characters in the play are Emily Webb and George Gibbs, with their marriage the center of the play's loose plot line which gives rise to the play's major themes on what it means to exist.

Emiley Kiser, a Dramaworks newcomer, plays Emily Webb. She's direct and likable, to George who marries her, and to us, the audience. Yet she dies a young woman, only 26 years old giving birth to their second child. Emiley Kiser is the kind of actress who just radiates her youth, making the transition from teenager to young adult on stage, the perfect choice for the fabled girl next door in the mythical town of Grover's Corner.

George Gibbs is played by another newcomer, Joe Ferrarelli, an all-American boy, baseball is his sport, who hopes to go to college but settles down with Emily instead. He takes the path of most of Grover's Corner's youngsters, 90% of them staying in the same town as they were born. Ferrarelli plays his role with the breathless expectation of the future, a life with his childhood (albeit secret) sweetheart, one that he takes for granted will last, well, forever.

The other major roles are all played by Dramaworks' veterans and their experience and love of working together shines in their professionalism. These include Kenneth Kay (Dr. Gibbs), Elizabeth Dimon (Mrs. Gibbs), Patti Gardner (Mrs. Webb), Dan Leonard (Mr. Webb), and Margery Lowe (Mrs. Soames). Other members of the cast are Michael Collins, John Felix, Cliff Goulet, Dave Hyland, Hal Johnstone, Char Plotsky, Allie Beltran, Sawyer Hyatt, Joshua Stoughton, Justin Strikowski, Patrick A. Wilkinson, Nick Arenstein, and Ashley Horowitz.

In addition to the first-rate acting, it's the "other things" that distinguish a fine professional production from a very good amateur one, specifically the set, lighting, sound, and costumes. Of course professional companies usually have the facilities and the budget to excel in these areas, but one also needs the inspiration and the creativity for them to soar.

I already mentioned the scenic design, but a special mention should be made about the lighting, designed by the same person who handled the scenic design, Paul Black. With lighting, he captured the characters bathed in moonlight, drew the audience focus to certain characters while keeping others in dappled shadows, and making the characters in the cemetery seem, well, other-worldly.

Costumes of the period were spot on, thanks to Robin L. McGee's efforts and when you needed to hear that railroad in the distance, sound designer, Matt Corey was right on cue. Indeed, it's these little things that help make a brilliant professional production.

Finally, it takes a special director to bring all of these elements together into a seamless, fulfilling creation. J. Barry Lewis had never directed *Our Town* during his long career and it took a confluence of events to bring him to Grover's Corner at this time, with a theatre company reaching maturity, with actors uniquely qualified for the roles, and professional designers and a stage well equipped to bring out all Thornton Wilder intended. A deft director's hand is critical to avoid the sense of sentimentality and to focus on the weighty universal truths behind the cycle of life of the play's characters. He is careful to capture the humor Wilder interjects here and there as well as to counterbalance the tragic elements.

So once again Dramaworks kicks off its season with a classic American play, one about a town in the early 20th century, about us. At one point the stage manager speculates about what the townspeople should put in a time capsule they are planning. He thinks this play itself should be among the artifacts, *So - people a thousand years from now - this is the way we were in the provinces north of New York at the beginning of the twentieth century. - This is the way we were: in our growing up and in our marrying and in our living and in our dying."*

Friday, December 5, 2014 **Family Scars Emerge in 'My Old Lady'**

I had thought that the Plantagenet family from last year's Dramaworks' production of *Lion in Winter* took the prize as the quintessential dysfunctional family. Move over, *My Old Lady* by Israel Horovitz has come to town with two adult children tormented by the past and Mommy (the Old Lady) and Daddy (the recently deceased Max) are to blame. As the saying goes, you are only as sick as your secrets and it would take a Jacques Cousteau diving bell to plumb the depths of the ones in this play. But this production comes with a bonus: it features the reigning royalty of theatre with six decades of experience on the stage, Estelle Parsons.

My Old Lady is a very dark comedy, a slice of life that borders on Ibsenesque realism with some Woody Allen thrown in. It certainly has all the elements of dramatic tension, but they are not slam dunk moments, and with much of the action (the secrets) having already taken place in the past it requires the actors to give their all to bring the play to life. The entire first act consists of expository vignettes to set the stage for the more dramatic-packed second act.

Perhaps if all playwrights had an opportunity to constantly revisit their plays, they too would change elements as Israel Horovitz has done with the new Dramaworks production. He's close to the play having recently directed a film version which has led him to readdress aspects of the stage version as well (he perceives the Dramaworks' version as being "slimmer and sleeker"). Having never seen the play, neither when it opened in 2002, nor any subsequent productions, and having purposely stayed away from the film before seeing the Dramaworks production, it was tabula rasa for me.

However, we attended Dramaworks' version of lunch and learn where everyone was in attendance, the actors Estelle Parsons, Angelica Page and Tim Altmeyer, the director William Hayes, and the playwright himself, Israel Horovitz. The actors and the playwright have been involved with the Actors Studio for years, so there was a playful give and take in the lively discussion, with many anecdotes about them working together in the past. Ms. Parsons said she wanted to do the play because it was set in another culture and that she was particularly drawn to the subject matter – "the terrible affect of duplicity and deception in marriage having an impact on the children" as she put it.

Horovitz is the most produced American playwright in France and he said that is a partial reason why he wanted to write a play set there-- as homage to the French for widely accepting his works.

Estelle Parsons and Angelica Page have worked together three times before – each time Ms. Page playing her daughter (most recently in the touring production of *August: Osage County*) and Tim Altmeyer previously worked with Ms. Parsons in a Horton Foote play.

The play's anti-hero Mathias Gold finds himself with a strange inheritance – his remote, unloving father, Max, has left most of his fortune to charity and, mysteriously (but perhaps for a good reason as we find out later) bequeathed to his only surviving son an apartment in Paris, one that is subject to the unique French "viager "contract, a detail of which Mathias is at first unaware.

Mathias believes the apartment will be the ticket to bail him out of a life of divorces and unpublished novels (three each!) and debt. He plans to sell it at once but after making the trip to France spending his last remaining funds on his airline ticket and with only a knapsack of his worldly belongings, he finds out there are those strings attached: the previous owner, Mathilde Girard, who sold the apartment to Mathias' father, has a life-long lease to occupy the apartment and, to make matters worse for Mathias, not only is he now penniless, with not even airfare back home, but he is responsible for the expenses of the apartment, and can't sell it until Mathilde dies. Although 92 years old, she's feisty enough to live another decade.

Complicating the plot is Mathilde's daughter Chloe, an unmarried and unhappy schoolteacher, who vehemently disagrees with her mother's decision to allow Mathias to live in the apartment. (Mathilde has accepted Mathias' gold watch, the only other bequest of his father except for a few French books as payment for his obligatory 2,400 Euro monthly obligation.)

Now, they're all roommates! And you have all the elements to turn this play into a character study the cast and director can sink their teeth into.

Mathias is an existential mess, a man who has created his own life defining predicament, constantly railing at his father for crippling him. He is certainly not "a force of nature" as Mathilde described his father. And now he is mired in the lives of these two women, one an old bohemian and the other just another dependent still living with her mother. Where are the adult people in this drama other than Mathilde? Are they going to blame their parents (his father and her mother) for their misfortunes into perpetuity (or at least throughout the play)? In that respect they have a lot in common and it makes the feisty old lady the real hero in the play, one who has lived life on her own terms, not her parents' or society's.

While the play is riveting at times, it can be tedious hearing the retrospective ranting of "the children." Furthermore, to pull off some kind of satisfactory denouement is difficult. I know how the first draft of this play ended (very differently which would have left the audience in a black hole). I have no idea about the other versions, but clearly Horovitz was reaching for a more positive conclusion, although to me it felt somewhat contrived.

So perhaps in an imperfect play the acting becomes particularly important, with Estelle Parsons anchoring it steadfastly. Her voice alone stands out, all knowing, and in spite of her 92 years (Ms. Parsons is actually in her late 80's), she is sharp, intelligent, and will not allow "the children" to run fully amuck when she's on stage. She ambles with a cane from time to time back and forth on stage, but mostly settles in a chair, stage center, and she is indeed the center of the play, the "kids" whirling around her, satellites in her orbit.

Perhaps the most difficult role is Mathias'. He is on stage most of the time. How do you warm up to a loose cannon, a down on his luck, self pitying, sometimes pathetic, immature and self absorbed character with a penchant for the ultimate truth serum, booze. He's drunk at least half the time on stage. Even though he does indeed wear the scars of his childhood, some very horrific ones, there are times you want to reach out and smack him and say, get over yourself!

Thankfully, we have an actor with the ability to deliver such a performance without totally alienating his audience, Tim Altmeyer. He has to carry the load of discontent in the play, his body language expressing much of his unhappiness, flaying his arms, delivering such lines as *If you don't laugh you cry – it's a Jewish thing.* And that is what makes Altmeyer's fine performance; you either laugh with him or cry for him. He is a loveable loser but as Mathilde so pointedly puts it in the first act, *how did you get to be 53 and have nothing to show for it?*

The equally difficult role of Chloe falls to Angelica Page. Although on stage less than the other two actors, she has to express her more subliminal anger and this comes through her rigid demeanor and facial expressions. Mathias and Chloe are birds of a feather but during the second act they find the enmity they originally felt towards one another was misplaced. Let's both blame the parents!

Page carries her repressed anger to the point of sometimes delivering her lines in a way that the audience has difficulty hearing all the words. In particular there is one brief monologue she utters mostly with her back to the audience upstage looking at the garden outside the apartment's window. "What did she say?" the audience was left wondering.

The set design by K. April Soroko, who is making her debut at the theatre company, creates the illusion that it goes beyond the room, a very substantive Parisian apartment, with the romantic feeling of the park in the background thanks to the lighting design by Ron Burns. The sound design by Rick Szczublewski is an important element, providing a kind of French cafe music during interludes, adding to the flavor of the production. Director Bill Hayes moves things along at a lively pace.

Not wanting to introduce any spoilers about the ending, I'll instead paraphrase one of the concluding lines: *Life is just less terrible* (than the alternative). And I found myself thinking of the great Sondheim song from *Into the Woods*, "Children Will Listen," certainly the other message dominating the work.

Thursday, January 29, 2015 **'Les Liaisons Dangereuses' – Duplicity and Hedonism Abound**

I remember seeing some of Molière's light and relatively harmless farces. Perhaps I was expecting something along those lines, but Molière wrote a century earlier. He never would have thought of writing the scandalous subject matter taken on by Choderlos de Laclos who wrote the epistolary novel *Les Liaisons Dangereuses* on which Christopher Hampton's play is based. It is quite a study in changing mores foreshadowing the downfall of a depraved class. I come to this play with a particular advantage (or perhaps disadvantage) -- I've never seen the movie (or the play)!

The play depicts games of humiliation and deceit, waged by arrogant aristocrats who preen with a sense of invulnerability, using treachery, sexual perversion, and degradation as their weapons. Are these merely the games of the leisure class, a decadent society that is about to be destroyed in pre revolutionary France or is it a more universal theme? The fact that Choderlos de Laclos' novel has endured since 1782, and serves as the basis for a contemporary play, which was then reincarnated into a movie, seems to answer the latter question. Think of today's popular culture, the heartless "reality shows," the treachery played out every day in corporatocracy and government, and the Internet affording abundant opportunities for narcissism and voyeurism, as just some of the manifestations. Human nature is, well, human nature.

Two former lovers, aristocrats suffering from a severe case of ennui, Le Vicomte de Valmont (Jim Ballard) and La Marquise de Merteuil (Kate Hampton), for their own complicitous amusement set out to destroy some lives in their social circle. Merteuil wants Valmont to seduce a young girl straight out of a convent, Cécile Volanges (Kelly Gibson) to settle a score. *Too easy* responds Valmont who has his eyes on another more challenging target, the highly principled (and married) La Présidente de Tourvel (Katie Fabel). Merteuil finally promises Valmont that if he can produce "written proof" of seducing Tourvel, she would have sex with him. Meanwhile Cécile and her music teacher, Le Chevalier Danceny (Brian William Sheppard) have fallen in love. And Valmont has learned that Cécile's mother, Madame de Volanges (Maribeth Graham), has written to Tourvel calling him a "pervert." He now seeks revenge by bedding Cécile, Merteuil's original intended target. So the stage is set. Merteuil and Valmont devise a scheme to trick Danceny and Cécile into their confidence. From there the rest of the plot unfolds almost from its own internal energy, imbued with intrigue, deceit and sexual maneuverings. And the actions of our villains have consequences in the end, circling back to them. The guillotine awaits them all!

Central to the play is the sexual, competitive tension between Ballard and Hampton pulling the strings of the other players, frequently with soap-operatic overtones. Ballard plays his part with an arrogantly superior and disdainful demeanor but with a hint of humanity and, ultimately, vulnerability, while Hampton is the more malevolent predator. In fact, Hampton's Merteuil strikes me as a sociopath, whose verbal interactions can out maneuver any of the play's characters, including Valmont who excels in persuasive rhetoric when it comes to bedding a woman. Hampton comports herself with an untouchable imperiousness, and her power over the other characters is absolute. She also gives voice to feminist rage -- after all, this was a society that was male dominated, and Merteuil seeks revenge on that score as well. One tell-tale exchange between she and Valmont seems to sum up her entire being, after Valmont asks *I often wonder how you managed to invent yourself.* Merteuil replies *I had no choice, did I, I'm a woman. Women are obliged to be far more skilful than men, because who ever wastes time cultivating inessential skills? ... I've succeeded, because I always knew I was born to dominate your sex and avenge my own.*

The Dramaworks production is ambitious, twelve actors in a relatively small space with multiple scene changes, but the theatre company is up to the challenge. The Director (Lynnette Barkley), the costume designer (Brian O'Keefe), the scenic designer (Victor Becker), the lighting designer (Jerold R. Forsyth) and the sound designer (Steve Shapiro) bring this period piece to life.

Barkley has a specific vision and coming from an extensive background of musical theatre and choreography, this production benefits from that skill. (I loved the opening sequence of all the actors briefly posing "tableaux vivants" before the action begins, like a big production number of a musical.) There are eighteen scenes (too many, but that is what the play calls for) and Barkley tries to minimize interruptions of the action -- no blackouts and minimal moving of furniture -- so the many scene changes are as fluid as feasible, enhanced by Becker's clever scenic design, and Forsyth's lighting, moving from "sensual" to "cold and angry" and Shapiro's selection of musical interludes for those changes – "to keep the energy going."

The details of costumes and scenery are extraordinary. Ninety percent of the 18th century furniture on the stage is original, not replicas. The elaborate gold leaf railings and balusters were all welded in the Dramaworks shop. There are 26 costumes for 12 actors and as the play takes place over three months, the changes are designed to connote the passage of time. Brian O'Keefe's costumes are spectacular! (And kudos to the wig designer, Omayra Diaz Rodriguez.) Finally, there is a revolving staircase to assist with the multiple scenic changes. It is a formidable undertaking for a regional theatre.

But essentially *Les Liaisons Dangereuses* is a cerebral play – and a long one too, clocking in at almost three hours including intermission -- and although hearts are broken on stage, and there are several redeeming comic elements such as the scene where Valmont dictates a letter intended for his love, Tourvel, while he is having sex with his courtesan, Emilie (well played by Nanique Gheridian, a founding member of Dramaworks) with double entendres abounding, it is a play which may fail to capture the audience's heart. (Do we really care about these characters?) Nonetheless, *Les Liaisons Dangereuses* is well worth seeing for the costume pageantry and the script's barbed wit alone.

Thursday, March 26, 2015 '*Buried Child*' -- *a Spellbinding, Stark Production*

Dramaworks has returned to the kind of play that is right in the theatre company's wheelhouse, Sam Shepard's Pulitzer Prize winning, *Buried Child*. It fits perfectly with many of the family-focused plays the company has produced in the past, such as their 2007 revival of Frank D. Gilroy's *The Subject*

Was Roses also a Pulitzer Prize-winning play and its superb 2011 production of *All My Sons* by Arthur Miller, both of which involved sons returning to families that harbored secrets or strife.

Buried Child is an edge-of-your -seat riveting drama, the acting bringing you right into the work, the audience never knowing where the explosive anger of the unpredictable characters might lead. Throughout its three acts the audience is just waiting for something, well, unspeakable to happen.

We know Sam Shepard the actor, nominated for an Academy Award for his performance in *The Right Stuff*. But he is also the author of almost 50 plays, some of these going back to the 1960s. He is one of America's most important playwrights, and his works are difficult to categorize. In this play, there are hints of Edward Albee's *Who's Afraid of Virginia Woolf*, with its black humor, alcoholism, and imaginary child along with the grittiness of Steinbeck's *Of Mice and Men*.

The works of Eugene O'Neill and Tennessee Williams laid a path for Shepard's works as well. But in an interview with the *Paris Review* almost twenty years ago he said he mostly felt the influence of Pinter and Beckett on his work, saying, "the stuff that had the biggest influence on me was European drama in the sixties. That period brought theater into completely new territory—Beckett especially, who made American theater look like it was on crutches. I don't think Beckett gets enough credit for revolutionizing theater, for turning it upside down." Shepard brings an absurdist, surrealistic spin to his work and of all the playwrights I mentioned, his is the darkest view of the American family, and thus the American dream.

The drunken, damaged father of his plays comes from his own life experience. His relationship with his father was doomed when Shepard was young. He describes him as "boozed up, very violent and crazy." When asked whether his father ever saw *Buried Child*, Shepard said, "he went to the show smashed, just pickled, and in the middle of the play he began to identify with some character, though I'm not sure which one, since all those characters are kind of loosely structured around his family. In the second act he stood up and started to carry on with the actors, and then yelled, "What a bunch of shit this is!" The ushers tried to throw him out. He resisted, and in the end they allowed him to stay because he was the father of the playwright."

At the heart of *Buried Child* is the concept that you are only as sick as your secrets. In this case, a monstrous one – murder and incest -- one that corrupts the family although we're constantly reassured by the clueless Protestant minister, Father Dewis, that the family is well thought of by the community. The family consists of the helpless though extremely toxic alcoholic centerpiece, the father, Dodge, the psychologically damaged son, Tilden, the physically (and psychologically) maimed son, Bradley, and, finally, the prodigal grandson, absent for six years, Tilden's son, Vince. These impaired men have to deal with their mother, Dodge's wife, Halie, a hardened, embittered woman who hypocritically spouts piety holding on to her companionship with Father Dewis who tries, unsuccessfully, to keep the peace. Finally, there is the "outsider", Vince's girlfriend, Shelly, the person who is closest to being "normal" whatever that might mean in this play.

Shepard leans heavily on symbolism, juxtaposing the family's breakdown to the corruption of the American Dream itself. Here he further develops themes expounded by Arthur Miller and Edward Albee. The barren backyard in which the secret is harbored is also a surrealistic source of bountiful crops of corn and carrots. Perhaps it is Shepard's statement of what might have been: reality vs. illusion, one of the drama's leitmotifs.

The relatively brief first act establishes the setting, a run-down Illinois farmhouse in 1979 which is inhabited by Dodge, a wretched alcoholic, married to his flighty wife, Halie. They carry on a dialogue which sets the themes, and establishes the hopeless shambles of their lives. Dodge lies on the couch in disarray, watching TV, uncontrollably coughing, but mostly drinking and hiding the bottle. Halie, who speaks mostly unseen from upstairs, is getting ready to go out with Father Dewis, fleeing her feeble husband, and their two sons, the mentally challenged Tilden, who has returned from New Mexico after a long absence (with the implication of prison time) and who is now a dependent, and Bradley, who bullies Tilden and Dodge. Tilden wanders in – the spitting image of Lenny from *Of Mice and Men* – with corn from a field in back which is known to be barren – not having yielded crops since 1935. Tilden begins to husk the corn, leaving the shells on Dodge who has finally fallen deep asleep on the couch. Tilden exits as Bradley enters, limping, seeing the corn husks all over the place saying, *what the hell is this?* He pulls out hair clippers, takes Dodge's hat off, and cuts off his hair, leaving bloody scars. This leads to a brief intermission, necessary to clean the stage, but unfortunate as the audience is already being held in the grip of the play's tension.

The real dramatic action begins with the second act when Vince returns to see his family after such a long absence, Shelly in tow, only not to be recognized (or acknowledged) by his grandfather or even his own father, Tilden. It is a rude awakening given the idealized family that Vince wants to remember (and introduce his girl friend to). But when Shelly first sees the house, it is indeed the idealized image that fills her mind: *I don't believe it!....It's like a Norman Rockwell cover or something.*

Vince, played by the always reliable Cliff Burgess, is transformed, arriving with hopes and good intentions only to return later in the play just another angry alcoholic, the heir apparent to the throne of this dysfunctional family. Of all the characters in the play his character undergoes the most change with Burgess handling this admirably.

Rob Donohoe gives an inspired performance as Dodge, a breakout and well-deserved leading role. Dodge is perhaps the saddest, most reprehensible protagonist in contemporary American drama. He makes Joe Keller in Arthur Miller's *All My Sons* look like a saint. In fact I think of *Buried Child* as being a grotesque Arthur Miller version 2.0, ratcheting up the corruption of the American Dream to a new level. Dodge is a dying, drunken provocateur, lashing out at anyone in earshot. One senses that the "secret" he keeps has eaten at him from within, but he is nonetheless able to express the "truth," frequently with a kind of black humor which permeates the play.

Tilden, his son and Vince's father, has also been absent, gone for 20 mysterious years in New Mexico, but has recently returned to the family in a childlike state. He was an "All American" when young – a half back we're reminded by him twice, but without any enthusiasm. He now barely functions. Paul Tei who plays Tilden is a newcomer to Dramaworks, and he carries the heavy burden of his role with a solemnity befitting the secret of the play. He is the one who harvests the symbolic crops from a barren field which had once been fecund but now harbors something else altogether.

David Nail, another new face at Dramaworks, plays his brother, Bradley -- a difficult role because Bradley is not only immersed in a seething ugly anger, bullying anyone he can, but he is also physically non- functional, having cut off his leg with a chain saw, his artificial leg passed around like a hot potato, immobilizing him in the third act to the point of his having to drag his body around the stage like an injured reptile, the leg always just out of his reach. Until that point he is the most menacing of the characters in the play, one who the audience fears may commit some unspeakable act.

They once had another brother, Ansel, who died in a motel room on his honeymoon. Halie has idealized Ansel as their imaginary savior, if he had only lived. His greatness (to her) knows no bounds. And according to Halie, he was the only real man in the family, something that cuts deeply into Dodge, Tilden, and Bradle, saying *What's happened to the men of this family! Where are the men!* Indeed, where <u>are</u> the men?

Halie, however, is the quintessential hypocrite, trying to keep up the illusion of propriety, with the help (and perhaps more than that) of spindly Father Dewis, so convincingly played by Dan Leonard -- while keeping Dodge in check with the pretense of concern on the one hand, but constant criticism on the other. Everyone else is to blame, even the "Catholics" like the one who married Ansel. Angie Radosh is the consummate actress, well known to Dramaworks devotees. She carries a Blanche DuBois quality of imposing her own fantasy as reality. She has brushed aside that reality to imagine what might have been, constantly fantasizing about Ansel (who no doubt would have turned out to be just like the other men in the family).

Shelly is played by a rising young actress, New York based, the striking Olivia Gilliatt. She is like a ray of sunshine in the play, a sign of hopefulness. She has been duped coming along with Vince for this visit, and yet as the only authentic character in the play, cautions Vince about leaving her alone in the house, even for a moment: *I don't want to stay here in this house. I thought it was going to be turkey dinners and apple pie and all that kind of stuff....I just as soon not be here myself. I just as soon be a thousand miles from here. I'd rather be anywhere but here. You're the one who wants to stay. So I'll stay and I'll cut the carrots. And I'll cook the carrots. And I'll do whatever I have to do to survive. Just to make it through this.* Indeed, Shelly is a survivor.

As the tension mounts she has the temerity of confronting Dodge after seeing family photographs hanging upstairs, the clear juxtaposition of the idealized life of the past to the despair of the present.

As she makes her escape, leaving Vince and the rest of the family behind, she states the central theme in the play: *Don't you usually settle your affairs in private. Don't you usually take them out in the dark out in the back?..... I know you've got a secret. You've all got a secret. It's so secret in fact, you're all convinced it never happened.*

Although the title of the play is indicative of the ending, I will not go into details so they can unfold before you as they did before me, sitting on the edge of my seat. Note the short, staccato sentences, especially the monologues from some of the quotations I used. This moves the play along to a certain beat, almost like music.

Dramaworks veteran Resident Director, J. Barry Lewis, carefully balances the dramatic tension with the abundant black humor (yes, there is laughter in this play). There is not one dull moment, but only moments of anxious expectations.

The scenic design by Jeff Modereger captures the dilapidated farmhouse, so symbolic of the interior lives of its residents and the costume designs by Leslye Menshouse portray the characters in all their sordidness – except for the women, Halie, the belle of the ball, and Shelly, the sexy young woman who helps to stir up the lives of the family. I liked the "otherworldly" sound design during scene changes by Richard Szczublewski that captured the surrealistic nature of the play. Lighting Design is by Kirk Bookman, his first effort for Dramaworks although a veteran (the lighting of the fantastic New York Philharmonic version of the Sondheim's *Company* with Neil Patrick Harris was managed by him), is "spot on" in this production, capturing the somber mood of the play's content while illuminating the focal points and providing lightening during the outside rainstorm of the first two acts.

Buried Child may be one of the most unsettling but deeply satisfying plays you'll see in South Florida this season.

Saturday, May 16, 2015 **Lady Day Sings and Laments**

The Dramaworks season has ended but on a sad and powerfully striking note with the production of *Lady Day at Emerson's Bar and Grill* by Lanie Robertson. You're in that bar in Philly in 1959, a kind of seedy place, emblematic of the tail end of Billie Holiday's life. A lonely table is in front of the bar, her audience disappearing, along with her cabaret license consigning her to gigs outside of some of the famous places and large audiences she commanded in her past. This gig is at Dramaworks, the stage having been transformed into this south side Philly night club, the "small house" side of the club, where the locals perform, not the main stage. Satellite lights hang over the stage as well as the first few rows of the audience while red velour padded walls float behind the performers. Perhaps "Mad Men "came here when in Philly on business, downing a few during those late night performances. The only thing missing from the ambiance of this place are the cocktail waitresses serving the audience and cigarette smoke heavily hanging in the air.

But we've come here to see Billie Holiday, or more precisely a dramatic impression of her, not an impersonation. Tracey Conyer Lee channels Billie's story, pain, and songs during this 80 minute, intermissionless performance. She is an experienced actress, not a cabaret singer, although one would not know that from this evocative portrayal. She is true to a remark once made by Billie herself: "If you copy, it means you're working without any real feeling. No two people on earth are alike, and it's got to be that way in music or it isn't music." During this performance we are convinced it is Billie mournfully singing to us, truthfully talking to us. She follows what Billie says in the play: *I've got to sing what I feel.*

Tracey Conyer Lee's ability to pull off a legitimate gig must be credited in part to her highly experienced and extraordinarily talented piano accompanist, Brian P. Whitted who also plays the role of Billie's manager, Jimmy Powers. He is the musical director of the show, and is ably assisted by Phil McArthur on the bass. There is the easy give and take between Billie and Jimmy on stage – mostly by eye contact, so typical of the cabaret scene and perhaps more typical of Billie's routine at the end of her life. She needed to connect on all levels.

The playwright, Lanie Robertson, opens *Lady Day at Emerson's Bar & Grill* with a typical cabaret intro, a jazz piece played just by Whitted (Jimmie

Powers) and McArthur before Powers introduces Billie. You immediately know you are in the hands of a great jazz pianist and accompanist.

After being introduced, Billy sings a couple of straight up pieces before beginning to tell her story, addressing the audience, looking back at Powers from time to time, looking for his approbation as well. Once she begins her story between songs, she strolls over to the bar for a drink, or two, then more, until the show, her songs and conversation become darker, a little more rambling, when suddenly she desperately needs to take a break backstage, Powers covering for her with another solo. When she finally reappears, her left elbow length glove is rolled down, bruises and track marks visible.

At this point she dons her trademark gardenia, but she is now out of control, her songs disjointed, her accompanists trying to follow and fill in. It is simply a bravura performance by Tracey Conyer Lee, holding the audience spellbound. Yet at all times she manages to convey a dignity that comes from true art. As she says repeatedly in the show, even as she self destructs on stage, *singing is living to me.* And then summing up her life as a singer, *but they won't let me.*

There are 14 songs in the show, with the dirge like "Strange Fruit" commanding a hushed sadness. Her iconic "God Bless the Child" is included, as well as one of my favorites – one I play on the piano with some frequency – "Don't Explain," for which she wrote the music. ("God Bless the Child" was also written by her but "Strange Fruit" was not although she adopted it as her own – one does not think of the song without thinking of Billie Holiday.) But many of the songs are ones I've rarely heard her sing, such as "Crazy He Calls Me" which in part she sings, very appropriately, to Powers. She gives a tribute to Bessie Smith singing "Pig Foot (And a Bottle of Beer)." And believe me, Tracy Conyer Lee belts it out!

Small ensemble plays like this might seem simple to put together, especially with its reliance on primarily one character. But every element, the movements, the lighting, the stage design have to be just about perfect to make the play transparent, becoming a night back in the 1950s, one in which Billie Holiday reconciles herself to the consequences of both victimization and poor choices in her personal life. Jim Crow laws impacted her ability to perform in the south. And then there were her own personal tragedies, being raped as a child of 10, obsessed with her first husband, Jimmy Monroe, known as "Sonny" (sometimes addressing Powers as "Sonny" as the play devolves) who turned her on to heroin early in her career. After doing a year of jail time and losing her cabaret license, she was exiled from the big city night clubs, and ultimately consigned to gigs at out of the way places. As she says in the play, *I used to tell everybody when I die I don't care if I go to Heaven or Hell long's it ain't in Philly.*

We see her grateful to be performing anywhere, just months before the end of her life, standing there in her trademark white dress, a vision designed and created by Leslye Menshouse, with her signature gardenia, a light in the darkest days of her life. Particularly painful is when she laments about always wanting to have a little home, children, and to experience the simple joys of cooking. At the heart of it all she is an artist and the Dramaworks team captures the moment.

Director J. Barry Lewis is assisted by the rest of his able team of technicians. The lighting design by Kirk Bookman is especially important in this play, a spotlight on Lady Day as she sings, stage lighting changing colors to suit the song such as dappled blue when she sings the iconic "God Bless the Child." His focus spot on her and then diminishing in size to her face and then fade out at the end, the level of her voice in sync, is the perfect ending. The scenic design by Jeff Cowie captures that late 50's lounge feeling inside a large oval construct and the sound design by Richard Szczublewski completes the illusion.

As Billie once commented, "There's no damn business like show business - you have to smile to keep from throwing up." However, this is one performance not to be missed, a fitting end to Dramaworks' season.

Thursday, October 8, 2015 *'Picnic' – Youth, Dreams, and Disillusion Unfold*

In the context of the placid decade of the 50's, and its small town midwestern setting, *Picnic* by William Inge took on the daring theme of sexual repression. It also encapsulated classic literary themes of the American Dream and disillusionment. Inge was from Kansas and the characters he wrote about were emblazoned in his mind and empathetically translated to drama.

It is a Pulitzer Prize winning play, well worth seeing again, and it demands careful orchestration to bring a modern audience into yesteryear and make this still relevant. It doesn't help that burnished in one's mind is the movie version with the woefully inappropriate, over-aged William Holden playing Hal, the young man who energizes the action (as much as I admire Holden as a screen actor). But Bill Hayes, the play's director, has indeed avoided the overly theatrical approach and stereotypical characters, to create more "realistic and complex characters" with an ideal cast.

Inge prefaces his play with a Shakespearean quotation from Sonnet 94: *The summer's flower is to the summer sweet.* If you read the entire Sonnet, particularly what follows that quotation, it establishes one of the central themes of the play, a person is defined by his/her behavior, and there are a number of choices made by the characters in the play that carry significant consequences.

Picnic takes place in the shared yard – so often the gathering point in neighborhoods of the 1950s when people actually connected with one another-- of Flo Owens and Helen Potts. Upstage there is a fence that opens to an alley and beyond that is a panorama of the town buildings. The set is very important in this intricately arranged play, and scenic design has always been one of this company's many strong points.

Act I introduces the characters with only some mild hints of what is about to unfold later. Mrs. Potts, the elder stateswoman of the neighborhood, has given some work to a stranger in town, Hal Carter, a young down on his luck drifter, in exchange for something to eat. He has jumped a freight train to this small Kansas town to see his former college fraternity brother, who he considers his last friend in the world, Alan Seymour, hoping to find a job through Alan's wealthy father. Hal had flunked out of college (where he was a star athlete) and had tried unsuccessfully to make his way in Hollywood. Hal, his shirtless body on display for most of the first act, becomes a lightning rod for some of the lonely women in the play. At first he is only casually noticed by Madge Owens the high school homecoming queen who her mother, Flo, has been plotting for her to marry Alan for the secure life of a country club belle.

Hal is played by Merlin Huff, in his PBD debut, parading his manly presence around the stage like a badge, stomping and posturing, yet inwardly feeling totally insecure. It is a difficult role as Inge provides for little nuance and character development. He is a free spirit, who is yearning to become a "success" which nothing in his dysfunctional background has prepared him to achieve.

His friend, Alan, is convincingly played by Taylor Miller, also making his PBD debut, with his wholesomeness, and innate confidence from having grown up in the "right" family and following their expectations, only conscious of Madge's desirability as a beauty. He looks up to Hal as a rebel and admires his animal attraction to the women he encounters.

The key role of Flo, who is trying to orchestrate the lives of her two daughters, hoping that they will marry well, is outstandingly played by PBD veteran Patti Gardner, capturing her anxiety that her daughters should not have disappointing lives as she's had. Flo's husband had walked out on her after the birth of their second child so she is very wary of a man such as Hal. She is a strong mother lion guarding her cubs.

Alas, for Madge, she feels her beauty may be a detriment. She is played by the appropriately beautiful Kelly Gibson, who portrays the essence of a young woman tottering on the brink of full blown womanhood and what the future holds for her, trying to understand who she is other than what the mirror and people tell her she is. There are constant references to that power she holds over men, but in a sense she remains pure (a "summer flower" not tarnished by "base infection" as Shakespeare puts it), trying to break out to find something more relevant than her looks alone.

Flo's boarder, Rosemary Sydney, is a school teacher, who hangs out with two other unmarried teachers, and has a long-time beau, Howard Bevans. The story of Rosemary's and Howard's relationship is juxtaposed to the one which emerges between Hal and Madge, two middle aged people, who have let their years slip by vs. the story of youth and their expectations of the future.

Margery Lowe's performance as Rosemary is terrific. She is a woman who has had failed romances in the past and knows she is on the precipice of spinsterhood, especially after seeing the young people she is surrounded by, a desperation Lowe practically breathes from every pore. (And Lowe "cuts a mean rug" even after Rosemary becomes intoxicated.)

Another PBD familiar face, Michael McKeever, undertakes the role of the ambivalent Howard with an engaging homey affability. Fear of commitment shadows Howard who seems set in his ways.

Those are the basic ingredients for Inge's brew that boils over in Act II as the town's annual Labor Day picnic is about to take place. Madge's slightly younger, brainy, tom-boyish sister Millie has no date and Mrs. Potts (to Flo's horror) suggests that Hal becomes Millie's escort. Millie suddenly becomes obsessed with her looks as well (deeply jealous of the attention her sister commands) although throughout most of the play she remains true to her intellectual stand-offish self. In a sense she represents Inge's presence in the play. (She is reading Carson McCullers *The Ballad of the Sad Café*, which in some ways parallels the play.) Maren Searle, makes her PBD debut as a Millie and is on stage most of the time, maturing right before our eyes, and while she fights with her older sister, she deeply loves her as well. Searle brings an acting maturity to her role of a sixteen-year old.

Meanwhile, poor Hal, as much as he tries to "fit in" with everyone, he just seems to say the wrong thing and becomes self conscious about everything he's about to say. In a sense, he's an innocent, another "summer flower."It doesn't help that his friend Alan has indeed offered him a job, but as the lowest manual laborer which Alan does not let Hal forget. Still Hal wears his optimism, tempered by humiliation, on his shirtless sleeve.

Hal has Mrs. Potts, – so amiably and skillfully played by the seasoned PBD actress Elizabeth Dimon -- in stitches telling stories about his father – who he obviously loved in spite of his alcoholism and jail time. Mrs. Potts, her mother's caretaker who we only hear offstage, sees the inherent goodness in Hal and accepts his youthful, manly countenance without the criticism or jealousy of the other mature women. Perhaps that is because of her own impetuous love affair when she was very young resulted in a marriage that her own mother had annulled only 24 hours later. She understands the

urges of youth and acts as an observer, and a reconciler of some of the ensuing conflict.

Howard produces a bottle of liquor to share before the picnic, the truth
serum which particularly Rosemary has more than a swig of, erupting in a
vicious attack of Hal, and everything he represents – youth and freedom. –
culminating in her direct accusation:....*You're just a piece of Arkansas white
trash! And braggin about your father! And I'll bet he wasn't any better'n
you are! I'll bet you lose that job before your two weeks is up....You think
just 'cause you're young you can push the old folks aside. You'll end your life
in the gutter and it'll serve you right 'cause the gutter's where you belong.*
Howard puts a stop to the tirade.

Hal and Madge finally make an electrically charged connection at
the end of the second act and cannot take their hands off each other,
kissing passionately all over the yard, on the porch, in front of the shed.
However, they now have to face the headwinds of Flo's disapproval, not
to mention Alan who becomes insanely jealous and feels utterly betrayed
by both.

Act III takes place the morning after the picnic. Everything has changed.
Madge and Hal returned late in Alan's car. Alan has the police now looking
for Hal on the trumped up charge that his car was stolen. Flo is outraged.

Rosemary has seen her future and does not like the vision of old lady
spinster she knows she will become; she has begged Howard to marry her
and before Howard knows what has happened he has been railroaded into
a future he never thought would become real, although, deep down, he does
love Rosemary.

Hal plans to flee on the freight train that can be heard in the distance,
urging Madge to come with him, telling her where to look for him in Tulsa.
He sees in Madge "the only real thing I ever had," and he imagines a life
with her, settling down, perhaps buying a farm, a future. Their relationship is different than the others, based on strong sexual desire and the
unbounded optimism of youth. Hal is no longer the drifter.

In spite of Flo's disappointment and objections, Madge follows on the
next bus. Flo's neighbor, Helen Potts, has to restrain Flo who still can't
believe that her beautiful daughter could be throwing away her life, but
Madge has opted for HER life, as Rosemary did.

That freight train whistle is a constant leitmotiv in the play, a reminder
of a vast nation with sprawling opportunities, at the heart of the American
Dream. Hal arrives and departs via that beckoning train. From Inge's
description of the setting before the beginning of the play: *Far off, the whistle of a train is heard coming to town. It is a happy promising sound.*

Interesting that Dramaworks' season opens with this classic play, as it
did last year with *Our Town*, a play with which it shares many characteristics,

simple but direct fundamental themes unfolding in a small-town setting, superbly staged and acted.

It is a complicated production, even requiring a choreographer, Michelle Petrucci, for the sexy and disturbing dance number on the crowded stage in Act II.

There can never be enough praise for scenic design by Michael Amico, and the set for *Picnic* is exactly as Inge required, and even for the company's relatively new home and larger stage, must have been a challenge for Mr. Amico. Challenge accepted and achieved!

Costume design is by Brian O'Keefe who did not want to use stock dresses, hand crafting more than a dozen for the show, with Madge's blue dress requiring 60 hours of work!

More about the devil is in the detail: the lighting design by Donald Edmund Thomas, something the audience might take for granted, was carefully planned to be in sync with the costumes and as the play takes place within 24 hours, the morning sunrise light begins on stage left, moves overhead during the day, and "sets" stage right. There are a number of "wake up" changes of light and there are some eighty lighting cues in the production.

The music (all original scores) and sound design are by Steve Brush, perfectly setting the tone and mood of the production. I loved the opening which indeed captured the morning of a late summer day, the sun coming up; the whistle of a train in the distance, a barking dog, and then the play unfolds. At night the sound of crickets fill the theatre.

Although in minor roles, special mention should be made of Julie Rowe and Natalia Coego who play Rosemary's unmarried schoolteacher friends, a kind of Greek chorus, one younger than Rosemary who teaches, what else, feminine hygiene (sounds very 50s to me) and the other, an older woman who reminds Rosemary what she might easily become. And kudos to young Riley Anthony who plays Bomber, the newspaper boy who unmercifully teases Millie, and naturally is gaga over Madge (although even his opinion of Madge changes at the end).

This is a huge undertaking for a regional theatre, flawlessly directed by Bill Hayes who obviously has a great rapport with his actors and behind-the-scenes technicians – a promising start to Dramaworks' new season.

Friday, December 4, 2015 'The History Boys' – A Memorable Lesson Taught at Dramaworks

At first I thought this was a rendition of "Everything You Wanted to Know about the UK Educational System, but Were Afraid to Ask." Although knowledge of terms such as Oxbridge, Supply Teacher, A-levels, Sixth-Formers are helpful, the themes in this play transcend time and place. This is about how boys become men, how teachers affect our lives forever, about the randomness of history and the importance of art.

These weighty themes are examined along with an entertaining pastiche of comedy and popular songs, adding to the play's representation of English school life as it was in the 1980's (although heavily reliant on the playwright's personal experiences in the 1950s). There is just so much substance in the play I feel like I'm using a toy shovel to mine its depths in this review.

From personal experience I can count the teachers who really mattered in my life on one hand and in particular two, one from high school and the other from college, men who urged me on and to whom I owe my life as it is. Remarkably, to this day I am still in touch with both of them. These are the kind of teachers celebrated in Alan Bennett's erudite *The History Boys*.

Ironically, my college British Literature class of nearly 50 years ago would come in "handy" for seeing this play. There are so many references to British poets here, W.H. Auden, Rupert Brooke, Thomas Hardy (albeit primarily a novelist, his poem "Drummer Hodge" is quoted as part of a lesson) , A.E. Housman, Philip Larkin, Wilfred Owen, and Siegfried Sassoon, to name but a few. Many of those poets wrote about the young men of WW I, the loss of innocence of an entire generation, which is still another theme of *The History Boys*.

The plot is fairly straightforward. The headmaster of a boys' school in Northern England hires a "supply-teacher" (temporary teacher), Irwin, who is "results oriented" to help more students get high grades in the "A-level" exams and into the sacred "Oxbridge" circle, either Oxford University or Cambridge University. He joins the two other teachers of the school's "sixth-formers," the exuberant, impassioned, and somewhat theatrical Hector, who has sort of an avuncular relationship with his students, and Mrs. Lintott who employs more conventional teaching methods.

Unlike Mrs. Lintott and Hector, Irwin's focus is twofold: helping the students get high exam marks and teaching them how to comport themselves in oral exams and interviews – the polish needed to excel in Oxbridge. If you can't get in the front door of an historical inquiry, use the back door. The "truth" is sometimes less relevant than how it is told. At times this puts him in direct conflict with Hector, who at one point says *I count examinations, even for Oxford and Cambridge, as the enemy of education. Which is not to say that I don't regard education as the enemy of education, too.*

Early in the play Bennett stages a scene entirely in French, taught by Hector, and in spite of the play being put on in front of an English speaking audience, one can glean the essence of what Hector is trying to do using this idiosyncratic method: teaching the students about the subjective in

French grammar using an elaborate conversation about how one behaves (or "should" behave) in a brothel. He even involves the headmaster at the conclusion of the scene – passing it off at that point as a hospital scene (hilarious!) -- as the headmaster is trying to introduce Irwin. It turns out that this lesson has a larger meaning in the play: the subjective in history or what might have been.

The headmaster clearly backs Irwin; especially after Hector is caught "fiddling" with one of the boys while they are riding on Hector's motorcycle. This is accidentally witnessed, and as the play makes clear, not unlike many events in history. The headmaster says to Mrs. Lintott: *Shall I tell you what is wrong with Hector as a teacher? It isn't that he doesn't produce results. He does. But they are unpredictable and unquantifiable and in the current educational climate that is no use. He may well be doing his job, but there is no method that I know of that enables me to assess the job that he is doing. There is inspiration, certainly, but how do I quantify that? And he has no notion of boundaries....So the upshot is I am glad he handled his pupils' balls because that at least I can categorize.*

At one point Bennett has some fun at the expense of acting, further emphasizing the chasm between Hector and Irwin. Irwin suggests that a student should downplay his interest in the theatre: *Then soft pedal it, the acting side of it anyway. Dons...most dons anyway...think the theatre is a waste of time. In their view any undergraduate keen on acting forfeits all hope of a good degree.* Hector replies: *So much for Shakespeare.*

Mrs. Lintott has her special moment in the play too, a sudden feminist outburst that leaves the boys, Hector and Irwin momentarily silent: *I'll tell you why there are no women historians on TV, it's because they don't get carried away for a start, and they don't come bouncing up to you with every new historical notion they've come up with...the bow-wow school of history. History's not such frolic for women as it is for men. Why should it be? They never get round the conference table. In 1919, for instance, they just arranged the flowers then gracefully retired. History is a commentary on the various and continuing incapabilities of men. What is history? History is women following behind with the bucket.* Mind you, this play is set in the era of Margret Thatcher.

The "boys" are equally diverse and interesting, some turning out as we might imagine, and others a surprise. A follow up of them later in life concludes the play, with some touching moments.

Fittingly, the teachers in the play are all PBD alumni, consummate professionals in every way. If I were casting this play these are the very actors I'd seek for such pivotal roles. Colin McPhillamy plays Hector with flair, making his eccentricities more heartfelt than bizarre. One feels compassion for his unusual teaching methods and his relationship with "the boys." Cliff

Burgess is all business as Irwin who inveigles himself into a "co-teaching" role with Hector, or the "yin and yang" as one student describes the experience. And yet Burgess makes sure the audience has empathy for him as well, especially in his edgy "approach-avoidance" relationship with Dakin, one of the students. Angie Radosh plays Mrs. Lintott with the wisdom befitting a teacher who has taught at the same school for a long time. Rob Donohoe is the headmaster, performing a humorous counterpoint, easily frustrated and bewildered by anything Hector does. But he rises to dramatic moments too. Outstanding performances by all.

The students are all new to PBD, played by Jelani Alladin, Colin Asercion, Kristian Bikic, Kyle Branzel, Mike Magliocca, Matthew Minor, John Evans Reese, and Nathan Stark. All the "boys" are terrific actors and although there are eight of them on stage, each one's personality shines through. It was a casting coup to find such a talented group on the regional theatre level. Special callouts to Nathan Stark's rendering of Dakin, whose brimming testosterone level and talk of the sexual conquest of the headmaster's secretary lands him in the inner circle of the boys, envied. Loss of sexual innocence is yet another theme in the play. Contrast that to the sensitive portrayal by John Evans Reese as Posner, a boy who feels he is an outsider, desperately trying to connect, in spite of his being gay, Jewish, wanting Dakin to return his love. And kudos to Kyle Branzel who doubles as the musician, playing a number of popular pieces on the piano for sing-alongs, and to accompany Posner who is able to express himself in songs, including a touching rendition of Rodgers & Hart's classic "Bewitched, Bothered and Bewildered."

Once again, special accolades go to the Director, J. Barry Lewis. How does one put so many people on stage and in constantly changing scenes, the classroom, the hallway/locker room, the headmaster's office, the coffee room, without breaking stride and dramatic momentum? Lewis moves his characters at a pace which keeps the audience fully involved for its nearly three hours running time, including intermission.

Scenic design by Victor Becker and lighting design by Paul Black work together as those four scenes are revisited multiple times so in all there are more than 30 changes, the actors, mostly the students, moving the designs while lighting focuses on a character on a side of the stage so action is not broken. Once the scenery is in place, full lighting snaps on. Aside from the tunes of bygone years sung by the boys, and recordings of Edith Piaf, contemporary 80's music accompanies the scenery changes, thanks to the sound design by Tyler Kieffer. Costume design by Erin Amico cleverly captured that 80s feeling.

Alan Bennett's *The History Boys* is a rollicking intellectual feast, celebrating life-long learning and exploring the importance of art and the nature of history: is it merely a random series of events (or as one student espouses, *It's just one fucking thing after another*) or events that we impose meaning on after the fact, finding patterns where there are really none? The play's cadence of language, the quips, the acting out of famous movie scenes by the boys, the songs, and its stream of literary and popular cultural references make this a living, breathing experience. The staging of this play is a very ambitious and successful achievement by PBD – it gets an A+.

Thursday, February 4, 2016 **'Long Day's Journey into Night' –a Landmark Production**

Last night a hushed, frequently stunned audience witnessed Dramaworks' long anticipated production of *Long Day's Journey into Night* by Eugene O'Neill. It takes America's greatest playwright to reach the inner depths of his tortured soul, creating a virtual verisimilitude of his own family life (it is as autobiographical as any play ever written; he viewed writing it as an act of forgiveness). And it takes a great production company to nurture this spiraling inward play, sustaining the drama for more than three intense hours. All four of the actors portraying the Tyrone family deliver electrifying and physically exhausting performances. It was a master class of staging, directing and acting.

Long Day's Journey is but a day's journey although it encapsulates a lifetime. It unfolds one late summer's day in 1912 at the family's home by the Connecticut seashore, a place not unlike O'Neill's summer childhood in New London. The action unremittingly reveals well worn emotional paths to the present. Love transitions to hate and hate to anger and then to contrition and guilt and thus back to love. The Tyrone family knows how to love, but does not know how to be loving. It is a study of emotional ups and downs, the audience rising with the few crests and falling with the numerous troughs.

The play revolves around the life of James Tyrone, the family patriarch, an actor whose "good bad luck" was to "find the big money-maker," a romantic part in *Monte Cristo,* a play that became a box office success and had the Tyrone family on the road for most of their formative lives. It brought money, a considerable amount in those days. But Tyrone sold his soul, knowing he could have been a great Shakespearian actor. That shame shadows him and corrodes his family. He is obsessed with money, the wastefulness of leaving lights on, the imprudence of hiring expensive doctors for his wife, and his son, Edmund, and is continually derided by his family for being a tightwad.

The role of James Tyrone is among the most challenging in American Drama and veteran Dramaworks actor Dennis Creaghan embraces the alternating sadness, anger, regret, and even love. Alcohol is his refuge, its tentacles reaching out to his sons. It is a wrenching performance by Creaghan and although much of the family's pain can be traced to him, James had his own hardships as a child and one's heart goes out to him thanks to Creaghan's sensitive portrayal.

Mary, his wife, is played by Maureen Anderman, a last minute replacement for the original actress who had to leave the production for personal reasons. It is a difficult part to play with adequate preparation, but to perform this demanding role on short notice (although the opening was delayed six days) is simply remarkable, and Anderman being such a pro, a Broadway actress who we've seen before at Dramaworks, at the Maltz Theatre, and most recently at the Westport Country Playhouse this past summer, delivers a performance which theatre lovers will always remember and associate her with. She is achingly heartbreaking as Tyrone's wife. O'Neill has given us a window into Mary's subconscious with her suspicion of not being trusted, deep shame, and eventual disappearance into drugged somnambulism. Along with the believable gnarled hands and regal bearing, Anderman gives us a fully fleshed and real character that astounds with its perfection. She has complete command of every aspect of Mary's persona.

Mary had her dreams too. Before meeting her husband, she was in a convent school and had thoughts of being a concert pianist or even a nun. She was swept off her feet by James but increasingly her life became one of a secondary player to James, accompanying him while he was on the road which was most of the time. The only "home" she has known is their summer residence on the sea. And it is a permanent "home" she has longed for. *In a real home one is never lonely*, she says to James, reminding him that she gave up such a home – her father's – to marry him. *I knew from experience by then that children should have homes to be born in, if they are to be good children, and women need homes.* Also in the context of "home," she acknowledges that the men in her family have *barrooms where they feel at home.*

Her life as an appendage to James is bad enough. But O'Neill drills down further into her heartache where the rarely mentioned sorrow of their deceased child, notably named Eugene, resides. Eugene would have been the middle son had he not died when he was two, exposed to the disease by the older son, Jamie, before the youngest son, Edmund, was born. Thus Mary's accusation: *Oh, I know Jamie was only seven, but he was never stupid. He'd been warned it might kill the baby. He knew. I've never been able to forgive him for that.*

Following Edmund's birth (which she perceived as a duty to her husband, following the death of Eugene) and Mary's increasing feeling of isolation and blame, she turns to morphine as her chosen remorse-killer to which she becomes addicted for the rest of her life.

She worries about the health of her younger son, Edmund, and although she is in constant denial about the seriousness of his condition, he is finally diagnosed with tuberculosis. Edmund is played by a new Dramaworks face, Michael Stewart Allen. Edmund is O'Neill's alter ego and much of the playwright's tortured and poetic observations are expressed through him. Allen's portrayal of Edmund's drunken conversation with his father in Act IV is passionate and his final confrontation with his brother reveals a physical side which takes the audience by surprise. He is there to be pitied by the family, always a source of their guilt, and, yet, if anyone is "the sanest" in the family, Allen brings that out.

Jamie or James Jr. is played by another Dramaworks pro, John Leonard Thompson. Here is yet an additional dynamic for the family's dysfunctional gristmill: the failed older son who holds on to his "infinite sorrow of life." He is his father's greatest disappointment. Jamie's cynicism is his protection from the truth but when drunk (which is most of the time) his love-hate relationship with Edmund comes to the surface, jealous of his younger brother on the one hand and loving on the other. *You're all I've got left* he drunkenly confesses. Nonetheless he has introduced his younger brother to the same debauchery in which he has indulged; bars and prostitutes. Thompson's portrayal of Jamie's antagonism gathers momentum to the final drunken confrontation with his brother in the last scenes. It is a physically exhausting performance and, as I think O'Neill intended, one does feel pity and fear for the tragedy of being the first born in the Tyrone family. John Leonard Thompson, who has excelled in so many Dramaworks productions, will be remembered for this extraordinary portrayal of so many conflicting emotions.

Carey Urban, making her debut at Dramaworks, is Cathleen, a household servant, the only non-family member in the play. Although a minor character, she plays an important role, briefly imbibing with Mary, waiting for the men to return home, expressing rage at the druggist in filling Mary's morphine prescription (which Mary insists is for "rheumatism"). Urban provides what little comic relief there is in the play with aplomb.

And as the home is by the sea, there are numerous references to the fog. It is both a source of comfort and of sadness. It is a porous curtain into the past. Mary wonders *why is it fog makes everything sound so sad and lost?* Edmund, the younger son laments *Who wants to see life as it is, if they can help it?* It is a symbolic reminder of the kind of fog hanging in their lives, alcohol for the Tyrone men and the opiate for Mary to diminish the pain of their past histories. The fog actually enters the home in the last act, seemingly seeking out Mary in her final Ophelia-like scene.

Accusations and regret make up the "action." The Tyrones have to exhume the past to deal with the present and lie (to themselves as well as to each other) to exculpate their guilt. It is simply a masterpiece of painful writing and brilliant performances. The dark and personal content challenges the directors and the actors every step in the development and its execution. Performing *Long Day's Journey* has to take its toll day in and day out. It is emotionally exhausting.

Bill Hayes, the play's director, felt the Dramaworks' audience -- as well as the theatre's production team -- was ready for such a journey. He successfully merges the symbolic and literary elements of the play. And the play does read like a novel, O'Neill providing extensive, descriptive stage directions which must be interpreted by the director.

The technicians behind the actors and the director are top notch. Scenic design is by K. April Soroko, and lighting design is by Donald Edmund Thomas. The lighting evolves as morning passes into the afternoon, to twilight and finally to midnight connoting the dark denouement. Even the lighting of John Singer Sargent's paintings was studied to capture the time period and mood. At the conclusion of Act II, a dramatic bright white spotlight shines on Mary, dressed in white, as "she gives a little despairing laugh" [stage directions] saying, *Then Mother of God, why do I feel so lonely?* The spotlight fades and cuts to darkness. Intermission.

The Dramaworks stage has an upstairs and an outside where the fog comes and goes. It is a sea-side home of some substance by 1912 standards, wood-paneled, a book case, framed pictures of Shakespeare, and another of a *Monte Cristo* 19th century playbill, the play which made O'Neill's father rich playing the role more than 6,000 times. Costume design is by Brian O'Keefe with his usual careful attention to period dress. Sound design is by Matt Corey and along with the fog, there is the obligatory fog horn, timed to sound at some of the most dramatic moments.

In short, if you are ready to see the greatest American play, and perhaps one of its best productions, visit the Tyrone family at Dramaworks.

Friday, March 25, 2016 'Outside Mullingar' – A Lyrical Irish Love Story

Dramaworks turns to a moving romantic comedy, John Patrick Shanley's *Outside Mullingar*, a well chosen change of pace.

On the surface, it's a familiar formula of two star-crossed lovers who initially don't seem to like each other or can't get together because of some obstacle. All we have to do is to find out how love finally prevails. It worked well in one of John Patrick Shanley's best known works, a movie, *Moonstruck*. His Tony award-winning drama *Doubt: A Parable* was something quite different though, about possible sexual misconduct in the Priesthood leaving the audience in "doubt" about the resolution. An excellent production of that play was put on by the Maltz Jupiter Theatre three years ago, directed by none other than J. Barry Lewis, the director of *Outside Mullingar*.

This is a delicate but sometimes melodramatic tale of unrequited love. And what do we have in Ireland? Rain. Lots of it. As well as loneliness, isolation and repressed feelings. Plus we have old family farms in the Midlands, one owned by the Reilly's and the other by the Muldoon's. They are side by side, but there is frontage between the two which old man Reilly, Tony, sold to old man Chris Muldoon almost thirty years ago, Reilly considering it a loan and Muldoon considering it a sale. Reilly wanted the money at the time for a particular purpose which we later discover is an important turning point in the play.

Muldoon promptly deeded the frontage to his daughter, Rosemary. Why? Because she asked for it. It is where Tony's son, Anthony, pushed her over when she was seven and he was thirteen and she wanted the land to ultimately hold it out, seemingly as revenge (although we later find out it is for love). Very prescient for a young girl. Time has come to cash in her chip.

Her father's funeral was just held, and dreamy-eyed Anthony invites Chris Muldoon's widow Aoife and Rosemary over to the Reilly home afterwards, at the objection of his father who says, *Ah you're half woman.* Rosemary at first does not show, enjoying her cigarette outside in the rain. Instead there is a humorous but sometimes confrontational discussion between Tony and Aoife about their inevitable demise and how they will leave their farms.

Alex Wipf compellingly and comically plays Anthony's father, Tony, with a stubborn pride in the land and of his dominion over it. He's a cantankerous old man, hardly acknowledging he has not done most of the work on the farm for years and his days are numbered with breathing difficulties. Rosemary's mother, Aoife, is played by Patricia Kilgarriff who carries her role with a deadpan hilarity at times, hoping her pacemaker can keep up with the conflict. She is a perfect foil for Tony.

Rosemary is in line for the Muldoon farm but Tony does not feel Anthony is a true "Reilly," someone who loves the farm and land as he should. No, he thinks he takes after his deceased wife's family, the Kelly's - a little daft in the head (*John Kelly put his dog on trail for slander*). He has already thought of selling the farm to an American cousin (a Reilly of course), hoping to leave money to Anthony so he doesn't feel slighted. But he needs the frontage to sell the farm. And now Rosemary owns it!

But Anthony always seems to be out in the fields, either meditatively walking or working hard. One would think this is where he belongs. Except Anthony has a secret, which he once revealed to his one and only past love, Fiona, long ago. But when *I opened my heart to her she ran like the wind. She ran like fire."* What kind of a terrible secret could it be? Might he be a morphodite Rosemary wonders? It is yet another dramatic element that John Patrick Shanley holds out for the end.

Although Rosemary doesn't appear in the first scene, you already have the sense that she is feisty, a real Irish lass; but the flip side of her anger is romantic longings. She's loved Anthony all those years. Will they ever get together?

She furiously turns upon Tony in the third scene, castigating and shaming him to such a degree about his plan to turn over the farm to anyone but Anthony that he finally relents. It is just one of Rosemary's several intense moments in the play, which Kathy McCafferty portrays with a full range of emotions, passion, pain, humor, and prideful joy. McCafferty shines in the role.

It is several months later and Anthony is nursing his father in his bedroom. He is dying and his son now knows he is inheriting the farm (not aware of Rosemary's role in the decision). Nick Hetherington's Anthony has a hang-dog look most of the time but his sullen soulfulness reveals he's more poet than daft. It's a difficult role to play and Hetherington carries it with a certain amount of humorous naiveté, often puzzled by Rosemary's reactions to much of what he says.

Three years pass after the death of both Tony and Aoife, but Anthony still doesn't seem to have a clue about Rosemary's feelings – or be willing to follow his own in fact. They hardly see each other except across the frontage, until one day Rosemary spies Tony in the rain with a metal detector, something she's seen him with before. She insists he come into her house, out of the rain, and it is there that Shanley works his way towards a fiery denouement, when the "secret," along with a coincidence -- a "sign" so typical in Irish mythology – are both revealed. One could say it is a contrived ending but if you give yourself over to the play, it is amusing and satisfying, as "the pain of love" emerges. The sun shines. We all want happy endings and this one is wrapped in feel-good four leaf clover and delivered with the lyricism of the Irish theatre.

As a born and bred New Yorker, Shanley didn't want to be thought of as an "Irish writer" but lovingly wrote this play after having accompanied his father to the Irish Midlands on a visit, where his "Da" grew up and still has relatives. And while poetic, thematically Shanley's play has a hint of Sean O'Casey's strong women and clueless men. (Rosemary: ...*men are beasts and need height to balance the truth and goodness of women.*)

Shanley's deep affection for his flawed but real characters comes through in a very crisply crafted script. It is elegant, threadbare writing with the comedic elements woven in its romantic and dramatic undercurrent. The director, J. Barry Lewis, seamlessly orchestrates this delicate play so it can leap to life before our eyes.

We love Shanley's characters too. Our hearts go out to Anthony when he hears of his father's plan to leave the farm to a cousin: *Don't criticize me, Daddy. Some of us don't have joy. But we do what we must. Is a man who does what he must though he feels no pleasure less of a man than one who's happy?....Living as I do here with nothing but the rain and cold, and Mammy gone?....You know I'll tell ya. Sometimes lately I can't breathe in this house. You'd hold back the farm, would ya? You stun me.*

He confesses to Rosemary that *My life is fixed down with a rock on each corner.* She asks *by what?* He replies: *There's the green fields, and the animals living off them. And over that there's us, living off the animals. And over that there's that which tends to us and lives off us. Whatever that is, it holds me here. No. The voice I hear in the fields wants me in the fields.* It sums up hundreds of years of Irish misery and history. The lyricism of the language lives, and the wonderful cast makes this seem like a slice of real life.

In spite of this being only a four person play, it is complicated to stage as there is the passage of some four years during the play and there are five specific locations which challenges any production company. Dramaworks' rotating stage helps the play to maintain its pace, with well defined sets for each scene, and for a representational depiction of the three year interval before the last scene.

Scenic and lighting design by Paul Black takes full advantage of the Dramaworks' stage. The land and the sky are prominent and those are weighty themes in the play itself. Although this is a contemporary play, the props are straight out of the 1950s, conveying the multigenerational nature of the farms.

Sound design by Steve Shapiro is yet another element enhancing the art of presentation. There are the requisite occasional barking dogs and a train in the distance. But most noticeable is the omnipresent rain, in various pitches that add to the gloom and then with the rarely blazing sun, a residual rain falling off the trees or from gutters. Costume design is by Leslye Menshouse, reflecting what these contemporary working people of Ireland wear, and having to connote the passage of time from the beginning of the play to the end.

But not enough praise can be heaped upon one of South Florida's leading directors, J. Barry Lewis, and the cast, all professional actors from New York City, making their Dramaworks debuts. One can tell that his is a tight knit group, "singing" Shanley's vision of his Irish roots in perfect harmony. The last Irish play put on by Dramaworks was The *Beauty Queen of Leenane*, which was a straight forward tragedy. *Outside Mullingar* although arising out of Irish sadness is a successful romantic comedy and another high-quality achievement by Dramaworks.

Saturday, May 14, 2016 'Satchmo at the Waldorf' – An Intensely Moving Experience

Terry Teachout, the esteemed theatre critic of the *Wall Street Journal* has gone full circle, from Louis Armstrong's biographer, *Pops; A Life of Louis Armstrong*, to playwright, *Satchmo at the Waldorf*, and now director of his own play on the Dramaworks stage. His biography is a work of prodigious scholarship and intellect while the play is clearly written straight from the heart. His professional directorial debut is the confluence of his intimate knowledge and love of Louis Armstrong and years as a working critic. How can such erudition not result in a work of art to stir even the most casual theater-goer?

The play not only moves, but informs. Louis Armstrong, for many in the audience, was a figure from popular culture, holding a horn more than blowing it, usually singing a song in his gravelly voice, his handkerchief in hand, an overall good guy in movies and on TV. Teachout's work reclaims not only his jazz genius but documents his rise from lowly beginnings, so improbable for a poor illegitimate child born to a part-time prostitute in New Orleans (his baptismal card described him as "niger, illegitimus"), how he was used by his manager, Joe Glaser, and then reviled by the black community, as represented by Miles Davis in the play, into the public persona we all fondly remember. This is a testimony to his indomitable spirit.

One person plays are difficult. They're usually retrospective accounts of a life, with little or no interaction and in this case, a play about a musician who doesn't get to perform (other than hearing some brief recordings and a few bars of a song by the actor). But the absence of live music doesn't detract from the story of this great musical icon, as you will easily suspend disbelief and find that one actor, Barry Shabaka Henley, successfully captures the essence of these three people, each with a distinctive "take" on Louis Armstrong. His is a bravura performance which will leave you a good deal wiser and more emotionally connected to the great Satchmo.

There is of course Louis himself who tells his story in his own unique vernacular, expletives and all, told directly to the audience or into his tape recorder in an attempt to capture the story of his life. This is delivered in the dressing room at the Waldorf, his last gig in 1971, only months before his death. A lighting change announces the arrival of another character, Joe Glaser, his manager who Armstrong dutifully (and gratefully) obeyed (to keep him out of harm's way with the mob) and who made him the performer we most remember, the happy-go-lucky entertainer. But that is the very personality most despised by the third character (another change of lights), Miles Davis, who despised what he viewed as Satchmo's Uncle Tom demeanor. Armstrong was comfortable in his own skin, but besieged by these two opposing elements. It is a testimony to Barry Shabaka Henley that he pulls off this personality trifecta with such ease, allowing the audience to believe the unbelievable. This internal tension is why the drama excels.

There is so much revealed in the play about Armstrong, much of it contrary to his public image, lovingly written by Teachout, encapsulating his accepting, optimistic personality on the one hand, and his bewilderment as to how he was used by his manager, one who had ties and debts to the mob who upon his death left nothing to the very person who made him rich. As such the play is as much social commentary about race (Armstrong wore a Star of David to honor a Jewish couple who were exceedingly kind to him as a child) as it is about the world of a black jazz-man's life during those early years and what it was like to work hundreds of gigs a year while mobsters controlled many of the clubs. Imagine playing at hotel venues, not being allowed to stay there or even eat at its restaurant, having to grab food in the kitchen. Imagine the hours they endured and the drugs that were ubiquitous (Armstrong himself was a regular user of marijuana).

Nonetheless, it was a two way street, Glaser transforming him from a jazz figure to a world class entertainer. Perhaps no one song symbolized that transition more than *Hello Dolly*. As Armstrong laments in the play, *Now just between you and me, "Dolly" ain't much of a song. Tell you the truth, it's a piece of shit. Tune kinda go round in circles, words ain't so hot. But Mr. Glaser, he say, "Louie, you go make the song," and I say, "Yes, sir, Mr. Glaser" just like I always do. Got to do what the boss man say. So I cut the record, hit the road, forget about it.* Here the lights change as Glaser's character remerges, explaining that Louis was doing a gig somewhere in *East Jesus, Wyoming, or some shithole like that, and the audience was yelling, "Hey, Pops, do that 'Hello, Dolly!'"... Louis looks over at the piano player and says "What the fuck are they talking about?" So the piano player tells him they want him to sing this song he cut in New York a couple of months ago. And get this: Louie can't remember it! Can you believe it? Man cuts a fucking record, they're playing it on the radio a hundred times a day, and he still can't remember the goddamn thing. But that ain't the good part. He asks the guys in the band if they know how it goes...and none of them can remember it, either! Musicians. Whatta bunch of knuckleheads.* This wonderful dialog faithfully imagines their relationship and does so throughout the play.

But, then, there is the admonition of Miles Davis. If Armstrong was the black jazz innovator of the first half of the 20th century, Davis was the leading black jazz musician of the second half. Although both were trumpeters, they were as different in their styles of jazz as they were in their attitudes, Davis being an outspoken social critic. He was partially schooled in classical music at Juilliard, not on the streets of New Orleans like his predecessor. Armstrong was always sensitive – especially later in life – as to his standing in the black community.

But if anyone got Louis right, it was his mother on her death bed, her last words recalled by Armstrong: *You a good boy. You treat everybody right. Everybody loves you, white and colored, they all love you 'cause you gotta good heart.*

This was Teachout's professional directorial debut. He achieves an impressionistic sensibility, one that is felt as pure poetry, particularly given the wonderful script and the heart and soul of a great actor. It was especially revealing to see the hand of the director through Teachout's transparent Twitter feeds. As this was a learning experience for him, he kept his followers informed. One tweet in particular sums up his approach as a director, "Much of directing is observing. You search out found objects in the actor's improvisations, then make the accidental intentional."

The last production of the show in Chicago starred the same actor, Barry Shabaka Henley, so he came to his PBD debut well prepared with his lines, awaiting Teachout's take on his own play. He had some of his own interpretations, ones that appealed to Teachout, so he went with the flow.

Indeed, the play broadly succeeds on the astounding performance of Barry Shabaka Henley, a consummate professional who WILL have you believe he is Armstrong, Glaser, or Davis. It's an incredible accomplishment for one person on stage for about 90 minutes, having to deliver a 13,000 word monologue, convincingly playing three different characters. He doesn't have the advantage of having other actors to feed off (or even to rescue him if he loses his way). The pauses are as important as the words and their emphasis, and this is where the director and actor worked in close collaboration.

Lighting designer Kirk Bookman handles the delicate lighting changes as Henley segues from one character to another, but making these changes subtle (other than Davis who has his own unique muted red palette with a purple backlight), creating a lighting design which helps the audience <u>feel</u>, not only who's who or where to look.

Matt Corey's sound design includes parts of Armstrong's beloved songs, either hummed by Henley or heard over Armstrong's tape recorder, something he invested in midway through his career at the suggestion of Bing Crosby (with whom he was friends for many years but was never invited to his home – a sad commentary).

Scenic designer Michael Amico has built a perfect set, creating multiple focal points – his dressing table, his oxygen tank, the tape recorder station, a couple of places to sit, so there is always action. The dressing table doubles as Glaser's office. Miles Davis appears only stage left, always in the same spot, kind of a Greek chorus of criticism.

Teachout said that he approached his first directorial job as if he was not the playwright. This objectivity, with the remarkable performance of

Barry Shabaka Henley, freed his inner voice, his passionate hymn to Louis Armstrong, allowing it to soar.

Saturday, July 2, 2016 *A Rousing '1776' Musical as Reimagined by Dramaworks*

Talk about a timely show, given our prickly political season: *1776* has been staged by Dramaworks in a stirring, "reimagined" version with top notch acting and singing talent. It is THE musical of the year in South Florida. The show was written during its own contentious times, the Vietnam conflict, and also when the musical theatre was in a lengthy transition period, the days of Rodgers & Hammerstein in the past and at the dawning of the age of Sondheim, with *Hamilton* lying in the future. I mention these as there is a dotted line to all.

However *1776* stands on its own as an innovative musical and although it has some long dramatic stretches between musical numbers, its inspired songs fit perfectly with "the book." It is in the tradition of some of Broadway's best since Rodgers & Hammerstein changed the course of musical theater. And now Dramaworks has augmented it with several innovative concepts, including a clever opening, the cast in modern dress, clutched to their smart phones and iPads, images of MSNBC and FOX news and important moments of electioneering history projected in the background, wondering whether political acrimony has always been the norm in America. Costume changes on stage bring them into the Continental Congress and so begins the journey of discovering that the here and now is not that dissimilar to the then and there.

1776 portrays our founding fathers as real people. It was conceived by Sherman Edwards who at one time taught high school history and wrote the music and lyrics. The brilliant book was written by Peter Stone who chronicles the event with dazzling drama, tenderness, and abundant comic elements. There are the blue and red states, each with axes to grind, federalism vs. state's rights, but, debate, <u>commitment</u> and compromise inexorably drive the production's calendar pages to July 4, 1776 so we all know how it ends. The show is about how we get there. Suffice it to say, one wonders whether we would have a nation at all if today's dysfunctional congress was arguing the case.

It invites comparison to today's musical sensation, *Hamilton*, which we were fortunate enough to see last year. *Hamilton*'s "room where it happened" is about a grand compromise - the assumption of debt by a new national bank in exchange for placing the capitol on the Potomac whereas 1776's "room where it happened" is about another grand compromise, striking the slavery clause for unanimity on signing the Declaration of Independence: two monumental moments in American History, two outstanding musicals on the subject, both ageless in their own right.

1776 is the story of the events leading to the Declaration of Independence while *Hamilton* is more about the revolution and its aftermath. Hamilton himself does not figure at all in *1776* while Adams is not in the musical *Hamilton*, other than when Alexander Hamilton makes reference to off-stage John Adams, saying, "Sit down, John, you fat motherfucker!"

That was Lin-Manuel Miranda's hat tip to *1776* and its opening number "Sit Down, John," the lyrics which immediately grab you and bring you into the show, establishing its central character, an impassioned John Adams vs. the hot and tired Continental Congress and the themes of discord that run throughout the musical to its ultimate resolution.

John Adams is compellingly played by Gary Cadwallader, the only actor in the show who has a singular role. He is on stage almost during the entire show -- a bravura performance! Most of the other actors play characters from the liberal <u>and</u> conservative sides of the aisle. Necessity was the mother of a creative solution of staging this play with "only" 13 actors instead of the original show's 26 and even having some of the female cast members play male roles, seamlessly, convincingly – sort of the same way the audience of *Hamilton* adjusts immediately to its multicultural cast. This conceit of playing parts from both sides of the aisle also challenges the confirmation bias that tends to permeate political views.

Never shying from having to be "politically correct," the satirical song "Cool, Cool, Considerate Men" elegantly portrays the right-wing members of Congress doing a minuet around the lyric "never to the left ... forever to the right." It was originally cut from the film version of *1776* because of pressure from Richard Nixon through the producer, Jack Warner. The song is led by the conservative leader from South Carolina, John Dickinson, delectably played by Nicholas Richberg. His other part is Richard Henry Lee of Virginia, singing the "delicious<u>lee</u>," "compelling<u>lee</u>" memorable "Lees of Old Virginia" with "hilari<u>tee</u>." It is a show stopper and Richberg is a very talented young actor whose professional future is assured.

Allegedly Nixon also wanted to excise the song "Momma Look Sharp," a plea from a dying soldier to his mother. Again, it helps to put the musical in the context of the times: the Vietnam War. This song was not cut. It captures the heartbreak and misery of war on a very personal level and you can hear a pin drop when it is hauntingly sung by the courier played by Mallory Newbrough, yet another young rising star. She also plays the passionate wife of Thomas Jefferson singing "He Plays the Violin" with exuberance and joy, dancing with Adams and Franklin. Remarkably she also has the minor role of George Washington reciting some of his dispatches to Congress.

"Molasses to Rum" is a powerful piece about the struggle to include an antislavery clause in the Declaration of Independence which the northern states capitulated on to make the final compromise. The song incorporates auctioneer's sounds of slave markets, and links ties to the northern states in the practice of slavery thus encapsulating the hypocrisy. It has to be one of the most devastating songs ever written about slavery, and its economics and pain. We wondered who could bring the voice and emotion to this song like the great John Cullum did in the original stage and film version, and fortunately the show has the experienced Carbonell Award recipient Shane R. Tanner to play Edward Rutledge of South Carolina who is definitely up to the task and the comparison. He also plays Dr. Josiah Bartlett representing New Hampshire.

One of my favorite songs from the show is "Is Anybody There?" -- a lament sung by John Adams (Gary Cadwallader). While his sentiments come from the Adams' letters to his wife Abigail, the title is from the dispatches sent by the weary George Washington to the Congress without action or reply.

Although he is separated from his wife throughout the convening of the Congress in Philadelphia, she appears on stage for duets with Adams, always very dramatic and touching, their correspondence to song. Abigail Adams is wonderfully depicted by four-time Carbonell nominee Laura Hodos who has a Broadway-class voice and seems ideally paired with Cadwallader. Her duet with him "Yours, Yours, Yours," is heartbreakingly beautiful as they conclude the song with "Till then, till then/I am as I ever was and ever was/ And ever shall be/Yours, yours, yours, yours, yours." She also plays the critical role of John Hancock, the President of the Second Continental Congress, excelling in that role as well.

Special mention goes to Allan Baker who plays the sometimes cynical and often bawdy, but always pragmatic and influential Ben Franklin as well as Clay Cartland who convincingly plays the aristocratic Tom Jefferson, pining for his wife and suffering from writer's block until she appears. Mr. Cartland also plays Georgia's Dr. Lyman Hall. The rest of the cast, without exception is terrific: Kevin Healey, Sandi Stock, Troy J. Stanley, Matthew Korinko, James Berkley, and Michael Collins (providing much hilarity as New York State's Lewis Morris who repeats "New York abstains....respect-fully" to all motions).

The musical numbers remind me of Sondheim with their harmony and internal rhymes. There is a touch of Gilbert and Sullivan as well. These are not the songs one immediately remembers as so many of Rodgers and Hammerstein's, but they get under your skin and I find myself today while writing this review thinking about them and even singing (in my mind) Martha Jefferson's *I hear his violin/And I get that feeling within/And I sigh, oh I sigh/He draws near, very near/And it's hi-hi-hi-diddle diddle/And it's goodbye to the fiddle/My strings are unstrung/Hi-hi-hi-hi/I'm always undone.* Just brilliant lyrics set to a wonderful waltz melody.

Dramaworks' production is under the competent direction of Clive Cholerton who had his hands full with a crowded stage and multiple set changes that had to be choreographed to perfection. He demanded that the actors fully get into their characters although playing two different people, bringing to the show "creativity not from freedom but from restrictions."

As a fully formed musical, the set and the costumes were critical, especially with frequent costume changes and the limited space on the stage. Scenic designer Michael Amico emphasizes functionality above all because of the space and large cast. Brian O'Keefe's costumes were equally functional, period perfect, and numerous. In one scene there are actually 31 quick-change of costumes! Lighting design is by John Hall, and video design is by Sean Lawson. Michelle Petrucci is choreographer and assistant director. Sound design by Brad Pawlak adds an additional layer of drama to the production. James Danford, Dramaworks' always dependable stage manager, shows his expertise in keeping all these moving parts together.

The musical director Craig D. Ames, who doubles as an extraordinary keyboardist, brought out the best in this talented cast and his five piece combo sounded more like a full orchestra. *1776* is a must see, not only for its relevancy, but simply because it is one of the preeminent Tony Award-winning American musicals and "reimagined" and perfectly presented.

Saturday, October 15, 2016 'The Night of the Iguana' – Tennessee Williams' Poetic Drama

Dramaworks' opening season traditionally begins with a challenging masterwork, with a full scale cast, and *The Night of the Iguana*, perhaps one of Tennessee Williams' greatest plays, is no exception. This is their first Tennessee Williams play, something director Bill Hayes felt the company could not do until they were ready. Opening night occurred after one preview performance (delays in rehearsals courtesy of Hurricane Matthew), conceivably an obstacle in making this a totally flawless production.

Under the allegorical canopy of a tropical sky *The Night of the Iguana* unfolds as two improbable "kinsmen met a night" – the defrocked Reverend Lawrence Shannon and the persevering artist Hannah Jelkes. Williams' setting is an unforgiving universe where survival and endurance are requisite attributes.

As an epigram to the play, Williams quotes the last four lines of an Emily Dickinson poem, "I Died for Beauty." Shannon and Jelkes are indeed "brethren" in that they are out of place with the rest of the world on the Mexican coast at The Costa Verde Hotel in 1940 – an actual hotel where Williams himself stayed during that time, loosely basing the play on his own personal experience.

The play is heavily constructed around symbolism and metaphor, the most obvious being a captured Iguana which is tied at the end of a rope awaiting slaughter. It represents the human condition. Shannon exclaims that he *is going to go down there with a machete and cut the damn lizard loose so it can run back to the bushes because God won't do it and we are going to play God today.* The very difficult role of Rev. Shannon is played by Tim Altmeyer who endeavors to express the anguish of this tortured character, but at times he makes Shannon appear more pathetic than desperate. Unfortunately, not all of Altmeyer's dialogue could be easily heard (or understood) and therefore some of Williams' brilliant language was lost on the audience.

Although Shannon is "a man of the cloth," Hannah's own theology (her philosophy of living) gives her the power of redemption, Shannon admitting to her that he arrived, at this place in time, his voice choking, *to meet someone who wants to help me, Miss Jelkes.* Williams' stage direction describes Hannah as "remarkable looking – ethereal, almost ghostly. She suggests a Gothic cathedral image of a medieval saint, but animated. She could be thirty, she could be forty: she is totally feminine and yet androgynous-looking – almost timeless." Katie Cunningham masters the mysterious Hannah, capturing her delicacy on the one hand, and her steely strength on the other. Her performance is almost certainly what Williams had in mind when he originally wrote the part for Katharine Hepburn (who was unavailable at the time the play was staged).

Jelkes has traveled to Mexico with her 98 year old Grandfather, Nonno. He is a "minor" poet who hasn't written anything in decades, but is now working on what will be his last poem. Hannah and Nonno, in spite of their obvious education and Nantucket upbringing, are now reduced to a peripatetic life of "depending on the kindness of strangers" to borrow from another Tennessee Williams play, Hannah doing quick artistic sketches and Nonno reciting some of his poems for money and room and board. Dennis Creaghan, the seasoned professional, his ninth time on stage at Dramaworks, plays Nonno, deftly mines his character's aging angst trying to finish his first poem in 20 years.

A group of German tourists are also guests at the hotel. As it is the summer of 1940, they are closely following the Battle of Britain on the radio. Their demonic, bacchanalian behavior – and their sense of arrogance, knowing that they are "right"-- is juxtaposed to the inner struggles of Hannah and Shannon to find themselves.

If Hannah is a Freudian superego, the other key female character, Maxine, is clearly the id. She is sultrily played by another Dramaworks veteran, Kim Cozort Kay. Maxine was married to Fred, Shannon's friend, a Hemingwayesque character who, unknown to Shannon, had just recently died. Shannon detoured his tour group-- women from a Texas Baptist college -- to the Costa Verde Hotel in a last ditch effort to salvage his job with the third-rate Blake Tours, hoping that Fred would be able to rescue him.

The woman who engaged Blake Tours for the Mexican tour, Judith Fellowes, is enraged by misrepresentations made of the tour and by Shannon's one night sexual encounter with the youngest woman in the group, the 16 year old Charlotte Goodall, played by Alexandra Grunberg making her Dramaworks debut. Fellowes is a one-dimensional character (always angry) but a catalyst, off stage and on, for moving the action; she is played by long time south Florida actor, Irene Adjan.

With Fred deceased, Shannon is now desperately dependent on Maxine as she is on him. Prior to his unexpected arrival, she was a lonely widow being "serviced" by two young Mexican boys, her only source of intimate human contact after years of a celibate marriage. She needs Shannon, but he is on the verge of a nervous breakdown. He has suffered these episodes before ("the spook" as he refers to it), a condition Maxine is very familiar with.

Williams masterfully brings all of these themes together probing Hannah and Shannon's relationship and their recognition that they are both damaged creatures, at the end of their ropes. Ultimately Shannon has to be restrained in a hammock, much the same way as the Iguana is tied, while he is pursued by "the spook." Hannah rescues him as he ultimately rescues the Iguana.

The play culminates in Nonno's completion of his poem, one that embodies Williams' themes, man's relationship to nature, to God, to death and to a new kind of love that transcends "the earth's obscene corrupting love." Full circle back to Emily Dickinson's virtuous love of beauty and truth, the two main characters' "failures" ("he whispered softly for what I failed") being an intimate knowledge of one another, a kind of uncorrupted understanding. It is Williams' most hopeful play, or, as he put it "how to live with dignity after despair."

Executing this play is complicated. Hayes strives to walk that fine line of being trapped in symbolism and the melodramatic, so typical of the theatre in the early 1960s, seeking to attain a sense of heightened realism. His assistant director is Paula D'Alessandris. Hayes is skillfully supported by the incredibly talented Dramaworks technicians.

Scenic design by Michael Amico craftily captures the theatrical realism of a hotel in decay, the encroaching active jungle, alive with danger, and the symbolic isolation of the separate rooms on the verandah (I think of the tombs in Dickinson's poem). Paul Black's lighting design works in harmony with the set, characterizing a wide range of lighting challenges, late afternoon sun, sunset, a long night, and a severe storm.

Matt Corey's sound design serves up that storm, echoes from the hills, and appropriate guitar interludes, all in sync with the production. Brian

O'Keefe, PBD resident costume designer creatively captures the era and the sweltering heat, as well as Hannah's stealthy delicacy, as if she is indeed otherworldly.

Other members of the large cast are David Nail, Michael Collins, Brian Varela, Thomas Rivera, David Hyland, Becca McCoy, Rebecca Tucker, and Jordon Armstrong.

Dramaworks' *The Night of the Iguana* is an ambitious production by one of America's greatest playwrights.

Saturday, December 3, 2016 'TRU' – A Poignant "Holiday Play"

While he dishes the dirt with the audience, 'Tru' as Truman Capote was nicknamed as a youth, is inherently alone on stage. Alone. That's the essential message from Jay Presson Allen's play, which takes place during one holiday season (circa 1975), a time when his expectation of joy is displaced by a sense of estrangement from many of his closest friends. The play examines the place of the artist in society, drawn from the very words and works of Truman Capote. Dramaworks' lapidary craftsmanship and Ron Donohoe's outstanding performance make this a compelling production.

Capote is a flamboyant and proud homosexual, a person of acerbic wit with that lisp and unmistakable southern drawl, and that is part of the charm of this play. But Tru is also an author's author, as a sensitive boy drawn to writing, later launching a career predominately as a writer of short stories. However, his two best remembered works are his novella of a writer coming of age in *Breakfast at Tiffany's* (unlike the focus of the movie), and *In Cold Blood*, where he skillfully demonstrated his striking ability as a nonfiction journalist, written with the eye of a novelist.

Rob Donohoe's performance as an openly gay man is not an impersonation but a tribute. Donohoe is a Dramaworks veteran, having played a wide range of parts. Before Dramaworks' Producing Artistic Director Bill Hayes finalized arrangements for producing *Tru* this season, he wanted a commitment from Donohoe to play the part. That was a year ago and Donohoe has since immersed himself in Capote's work and life story, going to a voice coach to capture the high, nasal, southern accent of Capote and then modulating it for the stage.

Capote's angst becomes palpable as we first see him unraveling the day before Christmas Eve. Thanks to a recent publication in *Esquire* of a part of his unfinished novel *Answered Prayers*, in which he unflinchingly reveals unflattering portraits of his "friends", the super wealthy, idle rich, he has now been summarily abandoned by them, and most depressingly by his high society women friends with whom he shares a gossipy codependence. This is a very harsh blow. But here Tru responds to his critics, *Answered*

Prayers is the book I've been in training for my whole life.......I've written a lot of books, but basically I've always had this one book to justify.....everything. What's it about? Answered Prayers is about them. The Super Rich. As seen through the eyes of an outsider who for various reasons has privileged access. Hehehe. It's about sexual license and ethical squalor.

The artist's relationship to the wealthy is frequently a symbiotic one, the artist needing financial support while the uber rich need something to fill their relatively empty lives. Tru feels this deeply, saying, *Money, money, money! They're very nervous with you if you think you don't have any. That's why they hang together so desperately. It's not that they like each other...they don't. A yacht and five houses are what they have in common. And they get very bored with each other. So when they can, they try to take in amusing artists.*

So it is with some bewilderment that Tru is facing the holidays, wondering what in the world did they think he was doing with them, other than entertaining them; after all he is a writer and to him *Answered Prayers* is the culmination of his life's work. And as we learn, he has known EVEYONE in society. If they've ever been to Studio 54 they were under his scrutiny. He proudly states: *I am an artist. Artists belong to no class. And people like that who cozy up to artists do so at their own risk.* Nonetheless, this work becomes a path to self destruction, lubricated by alcohol and pills.

Conflicting Christmas emotions set the tone for the entire production. On the one hand he has fond Christmas memories, particularly of "Sook" who was his mother's oldest sister, a person some people considered retarded, and thus people thought her "funny." *Sookie and I were like forgotten people. Sook by her brothers and sisters and me by my parents.* These two misfits were close, particularly around the holidays, when they made fruit cakes together. His book *Christmas Memory* provides some of the narrative about their distinctive relationship. Nonetheless, Capote confesses -- and this is the essential sadness of this "Christmas play" -- *I'm very ambivalent about Christmas. I want it to be magic – warm and lavish with all your friends like a family. Which sets up terrible anxiety because I don't have a very good history with Christmases. And that's true with alcoholics, you know.*

Yet, in spite of the bravado, the cutting wit, and drunken cynicism, there is vulnerability about Rob Donohoe's performance, one we all have about our lives, whether we are "liked," and essentially the meaning of our existence, and the choices we have made, which brings Capote to this moment in time. For much of Capote's life he was a pop culture figure, "famous for being famous," but Rob Donohoe delves into that other place where the artist and the true human being reside. Although there is a sense of sadness and resignation it is not all gloom and doom as the play provides for plenty of laughs, such as when Tru receives *a veritable horse trough of unspeakable poinsettias.....[which] are the Bob Goulet of Botany.*

One person plays are not everyone's cup of tea, yet in many ways they are harder to produce than conventional plays and therefore more challenging to the small team of actor, director, and technical staff. *Tru* is skillfully directed by Lynnette Barkley, her third directorial stint at Dramaworks, and working closely with Paul Black, the scenic and lighting designer, they created other "characters" using the set --the bar, the Christmas tree, and the piano, points which relate to Capote's life and help create movement and modulate the mood as Tru moves from his highs to lows.

The set is gloriously breathtaking, capturing a sense of Capote's UN Plaza apartment, with its books, framed black and white photos on the wall of Capote and friends, ubiquitous parquet floors and view of NYC. You are a visitor in Capote's home and get to know the man and all the different layers of his life through his interaction with his environment. This is the magic of a one person play: you are in a one to one relationship with the character. This person is talking to you, even breaking the fourth wall at times, which can't help but create a special sense of intimacy.

Costume design is by Brian O'Keefe, and although only one person is on stage, he needed clothes that would enable him to perform the part believably, not to mention making him look shorter and heavier than Donohoe is himself. Sound design by Brad Pawlak captures voice overs from the answering machine, from Tru's memory, and an interesting musical selection Allen's play requires, concluding with the haunting lyrics of "Little Drummer Boy."

Tru is a little gem of a theatre piece.

Saturday, February 4, 2017 '*Collected Stories*' *– Literary Lives Diverge*

Donald Margulies' *Collected Stories* is a fascinating look into the creative process and the relationship between writers, compellingly brought to life by Dramaworks. For more than two hours an intense emotional struggle unfolds between two women, one ascending and the other descending, leaving us to wonder who "owns" the stories of our life?

Paul Stancato's PBD directorial debut is an auspicious endeavor, taking what is already an engaging play and transforming it into a mesmerizing evening. He not only had the Dramaworks' extraordinary technical team to assist his efforts, but the notable debut of the two fine actors who inhabited their roles, Anne-Marie Cusson as Ruth Steiner, the mature writer and teacher, and Keira Keeley her star struck, initially compliant student, Lisa Morrison. Cusson and Morrison are the consummate actors in this production, connecting with one another to the point of perfection.

Although emotionally turbulent, there are many subtle comic moments, not only in some of the dialogue, but pauses where even facial expressions allow a twitter to ripple through the audience. These are welcome interludes, carefully orchestrated by Stancato.

At the onset Lisa insinuates herself into Ruth's well ordered life. Ruth, an established writer, has published numerous short stories, collected as well as uncollected. Lisa, arriving at Ruth's apartment for her first out of the classroom session with her mentor, marvels *What I'm trying to tell you, Ms. Steiner, in my very clumsy stupid way... Being here?, studying with you ... ? It's like a religious experience for me. No, really, it is. I mean, your voice has been inside my head for so long, living in this secret place, having this secret dialogue with me for like years? I mean, ever since high school when I had to read The Business of Love ... ? I mean, from the opening lines of 'Jerry, Darling,' that was it for me, I was hooked, you had me. I knew what I wanted to do, I knew what I wanted to be.*

Lisa speaks in the vernacular of innocence and youth, one of the many layers in this play, the process of Lisa's maturing and Ruth's aging. This theme is as dominant as the teacher/student relationship and Margulies continuously weaves these leitmotifs. As with any great short story itself, Margulies moves the plot along within a structure which is ripe for complication, confrontation, and in this case an intentionally ambiguous resolution which is sure to keep the audience talking long after they have left the theatre.

Teaching writing is the ultimate paradox. As Ruth attempts to explain in her deprecating way that it really can't be taught: *Please. Never pay attention to what writers have to say. Particularly writers who teach. They don't have the answers, none of us do.* Cusson infuses this role with bravado, a self assuredness that comes from her many years of teaching experience and professional success.

The setting is Ruth's Greenwich Village apartment. Scenic designer K. April Soroko has faithfully imagined an apartment filled with the very publications, relics, and books that define her life, the view from her window which changes with the seasons, the sacred place of her writing desk, her selection of music and the prominent placement of Matisse's *The Dance*.

This setting of a writer's life combined with reminders of Ruth's cultural heritage are well mined in Cusson's performance and proves to be a source of Lisa's jealously, something she can admit to at the point in the play when she is no longer the star struck student and is coming into her own as a writer. Lisa complains to Ruth about her limited experience and one could look at this as a climatic part of the play from which the scales tip dramatically afterward: *LISA: You had all that rich, wonderful, Jewish stuff to draw on. RUTH: Why was that luck? That was what I knew; I started out writing what I knew, just like you and everybody else who writes.*

And there is the crux of it all. All writers draw from experience in some way. Short story writers aspire to the holy grail of novelist, something never achieved by Ruth. The line between fiction and memoir can be hair-thin. Philip Roth once said "I wouldn't want to live with a novelist. Writers are highly voyeuristic and indiscreet." Ruth, as Lisa's mentor and teacher, urges her to not censor herself: *You can't censor your creative impulses because of the danger of hurting someone's feelings...If you have a story to tell, tell it. Zero in on it and don't flinch, just do it.*

Early on in the play Lisa comes across a volume in Ruth's collection by the poet Delmore Schwartz and a letter slips out by him addressed to Ruth. She puts it back, embarrassed, as clearly this is something Ruth does not want to talk about. Later when Ruth and Lisa have more of a mother/daughter relationship, Ruth unburdens the story of her liaison with Schwartz to Lisa, with pride and regret. He of course was an older man; she the young (and she proudly exclaims, "pretty then") student, dazzled by meeting Schwartz in a pub and becoming a companion afterwards.

Ruth's story is mostly a long monologue and Cusson delivers it with such heart and vulnerability. Keira Keeley's Lisa listens with wide-eyed amazement, taking it all in.

The play moves to the next level. Lisa has had a short story published. They are now colleagues. Ruth, the teacher, had given Lisa a story of *hers* to critique. Lisa recognizes one of the characters, Emily, as resembling herself. In fact, this heartfelt moment in the play is almost a play within itself, the story line about a mother and a daughter without a clear resolution. Ruth defends the latter to Lisa saying: *But that's life, isn't it? What relationship is ever truly resolved? People, perfectly likable people, inexplicable, inconveniently, behave badly, or take a wrong turn...it happens.* This conceit is not lost on the audience, foreshadowing their own relationship. After hearing Lisa's criticisms of the story, Ruth has a sad epiphany: *I'm jealous that you have all of life ahead of you. I can't sit back and watch you do the dance that I danced long ago and not think about time. I can't....That's what it's about. Don't you see? Time.*

One can see where this remarkable play is taking us. The last scene in the second act is explosive, raw, and Cusson and Keeley plumb the depths of their characters at the climatic denouement. By then the scales have tipped the other way, Lisa appropriating the essence of the Delmore Schwartz story for her first novel, one she claims was written as a tribute to Ruth (was it or wasn't it?, the audience must decide for itself), but a story Ruth feels was purloined from her (contradicting her earlier advice that Lisa must write whatever story without regard for hurting anyone). Where does the moral compass point? Whose literary life is it anyway?

The costume design by award-winning Brian O'Keefe captures the passage of the six years beginning in the 1990s as well as the maturation of Lisa from girl student to published author in her stunning black outfit of the last scene. As this is not a period piece and the passage of time allows for only subtle changes in dress, O'Keefe's costumes appear to be designed more for the emotional moment.

Time passage was clearly the focus of lighting designer Ron Burns, both the realism of the time of day and the surrealistic feeling of its passage over years. The latter in particular was the fulcrum for sound designer Matt Corey, jazz interpretations of classics such as "Guess I'll Hang my Tears Out to Dry" and "In a Sentimental Mood" playing as seasons roll by. Music also distinguishes Ruth's listening habits which reflect the jazz of the 50s and 60s while Lisa listens to the urban rock of the time.

Regret and loss permeate the play; loss of time, loss of friendship, loss of loves. Yet there was real love between these two women. Ruth transitions from self assured, in control, to friend, and ultimately to feeling utterly betrayed by Lisa, who in essence has now become her mortal enemy. Margulies has created an extremely thought provoking, powerful story and the Dramaworks ensemble delivers it with high-intensity and top notch acting power.

Saturday, April 1, 2017 'Arcadia' – Stoppard's Intellectual Repartee Reigns

Tom Stoppard's masterpiece *Arcadia* is a play of ideas. Although the love of learning is a central theme, it explores the dangers of deducing history from tidbits of clues. Matters of the heart and sexual desire are laid bare, as well as the connectedness of all who have come before and those who will follow, questioning the very fate of the human species. Conflicting views of free will vs. determinism, chaos vs. predictability are among a dizzying array of concepts explored, and yet the play is basically a farce, laugh out loud at times. The language is elegant, poetic, and profound, even Shakespearian.

Arcadia is a challenging play to produce and equally challenging to watch, Stoppard asking the best from both sides of the 4th wall. If you are willing to let the ideas just flow and not get caught up in the myriad cerebral details, Dramaworks delivers the goods in a remarkable production.

The action takes place in the Coverly's country home in Derbyshire England, Sidley Park, alternating from scene to scene between the early 19th and the late 20th centuries. One is an age of change as Classical is giving way to Romanticism, only years after the American and French Revolutions. This part of the play is juxtaposed to the beat of today's scientific and exploratory pulse. The 20th century characters are trying to unravel what happened there nearly 200 years before from remnants of documents and some preconceived assumptions.

In 1809 a brilliant 13 year old mathematics and science student, Thomasina Coverly, is being tutored by a gifted young man, Septimus Hodge. She spurns his preference for Euclidean geometry, seeing instead – way before her time – a more complicated mathematical representation of nature itself. She also craves a more thorough knowledge of "carnal embrace" as she is cognizant of a number of sexual dalliances happening on the estate. Both roles are played by actors making their PBD debuts. Caitlin Cohn is the playful and mercurial young genius Thomasina, who hangs onto every word her tutor utters. Although Cohn is young, she is an experienced actor of exceptional talent, craftily mesmerizing the audience.

Ryan Zachary Ward's Septimus is an attentive teacher and scholar who never is at a loss for words. His performance is always riveting, whether he is toying with an adversary or discussing a tryst, and particularly when he delivers a consoling monologue which encapsulates the play's philosophical foundation, saying to Thomasina ...*your lesson book...will be lost when you are old. We shed as we pick up, like travelers who must carry everything in their arms, and what we let fall will be picked up by those behind. The procession is very long and life is very short. We die on the march. But there is nothing outside the march so nothing can be lost to it....Mathematical discoveries glimpsed and lost to view will have their time again.*

The estate's matriarch is Thomasina's mother, Lady Croom, whose libido as well as her nobility must be indulged. She is considering her landscape architect's recommendation to abandon the garden's classical motif in favor of the increasingly popular romantic, gothic design. The always dependable PBD veteran, Margery Lowe, plays Lady Croom with an imperiousness befitting the role.

Septimus and Thomasina have three academic counterparts in the 20th century, each tackling a scholarly endeavor. There is the caustic Hannah Jarvis, a published author, currently researching the transformation of the estate's garden, as well as attempting to unravel the mystery of the "hermit of Sidley Park." She is in a battle of wits with Bernard Nightingale, a don who has arrived to score what he thinks will be a major scholarly scoop, that the romantic and mystical poet, Lord Byron, was in a duel at the estate and killed a minor poet of the time, Ezra Chater, currently a guest of Lady Croom. We never see Byron on stage although he is an important part of the play.

Peter Simon Hilton who plays Nightingale and Vanessa Morosco as Hannah are also making their PBD debuts. They are husband and wife who have played opposite one another in many other productions, and they reveal that edge of familiarity, delivering Stoppard's barbed dialogue to perfection.

Their acerbic and competitive sparring is delectable and their performances outstanding.

The 20th century estate is still in the Coverly family. Valentine Coverly, generations removed from Thomasina, is the mathematical sleuth, frequently asked by Hannah to interpret the shreds of evidence from the past. He too is involved in research, centering on the estate's grouse population revealed in the records kept in the family Game books, "his true inheritance...two hundred years of real data on a plate." He views this data as fodder for chaos theory, another dominant theme of the play, life moving from order to disorder. Hannah asks to what end? "I publish," he says and Hannah amusingly replies, *Of course. Sorry, Jolly good.* Valentine is played by Britt Michael Gordon (his PBD debut as well) with a breathless enthusiasm as well as a deepening frustration explaining the complexity of the mathematical concepts, all the while hoping to seduce Hannah.

Dispassionate Hannah, while rejecting the romantic advances of both Valentine and Bernard, focuses on the garden of that era, calling it *the Gothic novel expressed in landscape. Everything but vampires.* As to the hermit, she says *He's my peg for the breakdown of the Romantic imagination... the whole Romantic sham....It's what happened to the Enlightenment, isn't it? A century of intellectual rigor turned in on itself. A mind in chaos suspected of genius. In a setting of cheap thrills and fake beauty... The decline from thinking to feeling, you see.*

Morosco emphatically delivers a key takeaway for the audience as Hannah says to Valentine, *It's all trivial – your grouse, my hermit, Bernard's Byron. Comparing what we're looking for misses the point. It's the wanting to know that makes us matter. Otherwise we're going out the way we came in.*

Among the farcical hilarity of the 19th century sexual dalliances are those of Charity Chater who we never see on stage. Veteran PBD actor Cliff Burgess plays the undistinguished poet, her dandy husband, Ezra, to perfection as he hopelessly and hilariously tries to defend his wife's "honor," challenging Septimus Hodge to a duel, demanding "satisfaction." This leads to an irresistibly quotable retort by Septimus, delivered by Ryan Zachary Ward with precise comic timing: *Mrs. Chater demanded satisfaction and now you are demanding satisfaction. I cannot spend my time day and night satisfying the demands of the Chater family.*

Captain Brice, Lady Croom's brother, is yet another paramour of Mrs. Chater who finally sweeps her off her feet and takes her, as well as her husband to the West Indies. Brice is haughtily played with righteous indignation by Gary Cadwallader.

Finally, the two halves of the play come together, with both the 19th century and the 20th century casts on stage at the same time, talking over one another, sometimes turning pages of books in tandem, but never interacting.

One thinks of Valentine's statement earlier in the play, *The unpredictable and the predetermined unfold together to make everything the way it is*, as two couples, one from each century, waltz on stage. After such an intellectual exercise, these are the tender, loving moments the audience has longed for. Stoppard saves the best for last.

Veteran PBD director, J. Barry Lewis, had a vision about human nature and love's unpredictability which prevails throughout the play and can be appreciated by his deft handling of his talented cast.

Lewis has been aided by an outstanding team of collaborators. The scenic design is by Ann Mundell, her PBD debut. Her ethereal set is a marvel to admire, representing both the classical and romantic elements. There are French glass doors to the garden and two solid doors on each side, perfect for slamming, fast entering and exiting, as in a traditional British farce. The monochromatic set has led veteran Brian O'Keefe's costume designs to showcase his creativity and skill, standing out but not disappearing into the set. They are of course period appropriate, easily taken for granted as they so perfectly match the characters' personalities.

Donald Edmund Thomas' lighting design shows no distinction between the two time periods, further reinforcing connectivity. Sound design by Steve Shapiro has incorporated the requisite barking dog, gun shots from the outdoors, and as piano music figures prominently in the play, some classical piano during the 19th century scenes, transitioning to more modern, yet still a classical feel for the 20th century. He even dramatically clues us into the first such change by a very conspicuous roar, presumably a jet plane.

It is a large cast. Stoppard knows how to draw distinctive, passionate characters and everyone is spot on. In addition to those already mentioned are Dan Leonard as Jellaby, the 19th century butler who facilitates gossip, James Andreassi as Richard Noakes (PBD debut), the dashing landscape architect who is always trying to placate Lady Croom's whims, Arielle Fishman, a flirtatious Chloë Coverly (PBD debut), Valentine's sister who thinks sex might impact chaos theory, and Casey Butler playing two roles, Augustus, Thomasina's bratty older brother as well as Valentine and Chloë's mute brother, Gus.

Widely acclaimed as one of the greatest intellectual plays of the 20th century, *Arcadia* is brought vividly to life by Dramaworks, characters dancing at the end *...till there's no time left. That's what time means."*

Saturday, May 20, 2017 *Martin McDonagh's 'The Cripple of Inishmaan' Beguiles*

The Cripple of Inishmaan is an extraordinary theatre experience, a very good play becoming great in the hands of superlative actors, the steady vision of the Director, and a technical staff that is at the top of its game. The play itself is Martin McDonagh's love song to Ireland and its people, distilling centuries of Irish misery, laughter, and story-telling. The characters he draws are as memorable and distinctive as the music from a Rodgers and Hammerstein musical.

Dramaworks last staged a Martin McDonagh play six years ago, *The Beauty Queen of Leenane*. Think of *The Cripple of Inishmaan* as "Beauty Queen Lite." Although tragedy and sadness abound (after all, this is Irish theatre), there is a hopefulness, a heartening instead of *Beauty Queen's* unrelenting mournfulness.

The play is McDonagh's hat tip to Sean O'Casey's play *Riders to the Sea* about Aran fisherman and their endurance. It is also linked to a 1934 fictional documentary film, *Man of Aran*, directed by Robert J. Flaherty about life on those craggy Aran Islands off the western coast of Ireland where people stubbornly cobble a life. The film itself plays a central part in the play.

McDonagh uses every dramatic trick in the book, the plot taking us down unexpected paths with a number of plot reversals which leave us wondering where the truth really lies. Little things in life matter on this desolate island where Johnnypateenmikes's mundane news makes life more endurable. In Inishmaan there are many cruel ironies, but one must go on living.

The author has the audience irresistibly empathetic to these idiosyncratic, endearing but fallible characters, even the most bizarre. They say outrageous things to and about each other. The truth hangs heavily in their banter and sarcasm.

One observes Kate talking to stones, Mammy drinking her Poteen, Bartley having his "sweetie" obsession and Helen exhibiting her sadistic streak. Each character is crippled or feckless, especially contrasted to Billy. Yet it is Billy, the literal cripple, who contrives to leave Inishmaan in pursuit of the dream of a better life. *Another day of sniggering, or the patting me on the head like a broken-brained fool. The village orphan. The village cripple, and nothing more. Well, there are plenty round here just as crippled as me, only it isn't on the outside it shows.*

Billy is imaginatively played by PBD newcomer, Adam Petherbridge. This demanding role requires a high degree of physicality, as well as serious acting skill. Both are on display here, Petherbridge walking with a twisted leg and foot and deformed arm along with constant coughing and wheezing while creating a sympathetic character with insurmountable challenges. Petherbridge strikes the fine balance of being submissive to the mockery of his fellow villagers, yet possessing the insight and intelligence to con his way to America for a screen test in a film. This is a scrupulously convincing actor who carries us achingly through his story.

Among his most devoted supporters are the eccentric and fussy sisters Kate and Eileen played respectively by Laura Turnbull and Elizabeth Dimon, two grand dames of the Florida stage. They are orphaned Billy's "pretend aunties" and as the story unfolds, we learn that they have been raising Billy since his parents drowned shortly after Billy was born. The circumstances surrounding this event is one of the great mysteries of the play, and that story evolves, changes, and has a great bearing on Billy's melancholy in addition to his physical disabilities.

The play opens with the aunties who tend the little town store. Their opening dialogue is funny, revealing: *KATE: Is Billy not yet home? EILEEN: Not yet is Billy home.* It is a harbinger of dialogue to come, where subjects and verbs are inverted, and repetition makes a humorous moment, and a reminder that if there is any difficulty the audience might have understanding the western Irish accent, listening to the whole statement will bring home the meaning.

If there was ever a vision of the kindly Irish grandma prototype, look no further than Kate and Eileen. However, if any two characters manifest a sort of helplessness, a disability of the psyche, again look no further. This is in sharp contrast to the boy they have cared for, who in spite of his physical limitations is a more fully realized person. The "aunties" manifest their dependence on Billy by falling apart in his absence. Both Turnbull and Dimon bring a wealth of acting experience to their roles, raising the humor bar with simply a look or gesture, popping the eyes or talking to a stone.

Dominating the play with his outrageous brio in a staggering performance is Colin McPhillamy who plays the pompous town crier, Johnnypateenmike O'Dougal. Larger than life, he intensifies an already hilarious role playing opposite his alcoholic "Mammy", whose care of her falls amazingly short of the dutiful son! He barters his exaggerated mundane news for food at the sisters' store and elsewhere to make himself feel important. The more scandalous the better. In fact there is a touch of Schadenfreude in his reports : *My news isn't shitey-arsed. My news is great news. Did you hear Jack Ellery's goose and Pat Brennan's cat have both been missing a week? I suspect something awful's happened to them, or I hope something awful's happened to them.* He puts down Billy constantly, but there is a back story to his relationship which is ultimately revealed along with our change of heart toward him.

And what would an Irish play be without a love interest and that person originating in the most unlikely form: shrewish Helen. Young and attractive, she can be foul-mouthed and vicious, an expert at humiliating anyone who crosses her path while she leads around her clueless young brother, Bartley who is fascinated by telescopes. Helen is played by Adelind Horan, another PBD newcomer, who saw this play when she was 10 years old and knew then that she wanted to become an actor and play Helen. Her wish is the audience's delight. "Slippy Helen" is hell on wheels yet Horan knows how to express a tender moment when needed, revealing her latent sensuousness. We are struck by her tomboyish behavior throwing her legs wide on any table surface and yet managing to reveal the blossoming woman waiting to be loved.

Wesley Slade's Bartley McCormick (PBD debut) is the perfect comic foil, especially enduring his sister's sadism, always hanging around the store looking for sweet Fripple-Frapples, or Mintios. Slade's body language and popping his cheeks when bored (which is most of the time) are priceless. His inexplicable fascination with telescopes is one of those many repetitive subjects that are ripe for humor. Slade captures these moments on stage in exaggerated and inartful poses slinging his body into absurdly awkward positions.

Babbybobby Bennett is played by the always dependable veteran of many PBD productions, Jim Ballard. He has the darkest role in the play and brings a frightening menace to his character. He provides the means of escape for Billy in a touching scene where you see him melt into compliance. Much later, Babbybobby discovers that he was seriously deceived and finds a violent way to repay his being taken advantage of. Babbybobby is yet another damaged person, his young wife having died from TB, leaving a permanent scar which Ballard's performance heightens. His is a fine portrayal of the hardships demanded by living on a stony remote island and being a dark force in the play.

The cast is rounded out by PBD veterans of many plays, Dennis Creaghan as the straight-talking, small-town Doctor McSharry who is in constant astonishment at Johnnypattenmike's complicity in providing liquor to his elderly mother, Mammy O'Dougal, alternately hilariously and cantankerously played by Harriet Oser. Doctor McSharry warns Johnny that when his Mammy dies he'll cut out her liver to show him the damage to which Johnny says: *You won't catch me looking at me mammy's liver. I can barely stomach the outside of her, let alone the inside.* But far from the good Doctor's assumption, Johnny's supply of Poteen for his Mammy, a highly alcoholic drink made from potatoes, is really an act of love.

Director J. Barry Lewis profoundly understands the challenges of Irish theatre, focusing on a text analysis of *The Cripple of Inishmaan* which draws on traditional and native customs, and establishes the characters foibles without them becoming stereotypes. He finds the "spine" of the work in Bartley's line: "It never hurts to be too kind." He capitalizes on the play's inconsequential acts which become heightened actions.

Lewis taps into McDonagh's mix of realism and humor. Timing is everything and Lewis plays along with McDonagh's poking fun at a negative national identity, a humorous leitmotif throughout the play, various characters making observations at different points in the play about why people would want to come to Ireland.

You will hear the term "dark comedy" bantered about when discussing a McDonagh play. As Billy says to Bartley: *You shouldn't laugh at other people's misfortunes.* Perhaps that is the essence of dark comedy. But this play is more of a character driven drama with comedy that is intrinsic to each of the characters. You laugh more at their eccentricities. It is satire, funny also because of careful timing and facial expressions. This can be experienced only in live theatre.

Costumes acquire a special importance in this production. Their design is by Franne Lee (PBD debut) who has Tony Awards for her Broadway productions of *Candide* and *Sweeney Todd,* and who even worked at "Saturday Night Live" (think iconic Cone Heads). While she had the historical footage of *Man of Aran* to work with, she used a creative approach to define the individuality of the characters through their costumes. Some are designed to inspire laughter, such as Johnnypateenmike's long coat with cavernous pockets and all the gewgaws hanging around his waist to draw attention to his role as the bombastic town crier and buffoon. Helen's costumes reflect her younger age set, flimsier and short, while the "aunties" clothes with multiple long wool skirts and layers of long sleeved blouses and long aprons clearly denote the older generation. Mammy's little bonnet is, well, precious. Babbybobby is attired to display his bludgeoning virility, first nearly shirtless with his yellow canvas pants and later with his long dark pea coat, Wellington boots and wool cap contrasting to Billy's cobbled together pants and suspenders, suggesting a fragile vulnerableness.

The scenic design by Victor Becker is modular in nature, six different transitional designs connoting isolation and desolation. As the set is monochromatic, Paul Black's lighting accentuates color palettes, valuing tone and mood over starkly lit realism.

Sound by Steve Shapiro conveys the unrelenting sea, the sound of seagulls at the opening while at the same time balancing those sounds of the hard life on the island with transitional, uplifting Irish folk music.

Friday, July 14, 2017 *A Stirring Production of Sondheim's 'Sweeney Todd'*

When one of the finest regional theatres presents the preeminent work of the greatest living Broadway lyricist and composer (arguably the best ever), we can expect to experience a performance work of art that will be long remembered. Such is Dramaworks' production of Stephen Sondheim's *Sweeney Todd.* It packs such an emotional wallop that the stunned audience left exiting, "wow," after a standing ovation.

Even though *Sweeney Todd* flopped on Broadway and the West End when it first opened in 1979 -- critics and the public were not prepared for the bizarre subject matter and Sondheim's treatment of it in a musical -- the show has become one of his most frequently performed on all levels ranging from expurgated school productions to full-scale professional theatres.

The story itself, which can be traced in various English publications going back to the mid 19th century, is based on "The Demon Barber of Fleet Street." Sondheim saw a retelling of the tale in a 1973 play by Christopher Bond in London and it immediately struck him as the basis of a musical horror story.

In Sondheim's version, Sweeney Todd, AKA as the barber Benjamin Barker, has been ruined by Judge Turpin who coveted his wife, Lucy and stole her away by banishing Barker to Botany Bay for life. But Barker, now under the cloak of a new name, Sweeney Todd, eventually returns to London with the help of Anthony Hope, a young, good natured sailor he befriends. Todd has one overwhelming yearning aside from escape: retribution.

He sets up a barbershop over Mrs. Lovett's pie shop -- known for making the worst pies in London. She is aware of Todd's past and tells him that his wife, Lucy, had taken poison and their daughter, Johanna, was adopted by the Judge, becoming his ward. His quest for retribution is intensified. Little does he know that Mrs. Lovett has her own designs on him, hoping they will ultimately become lovers and has twisted the truth to her own advantage.

Todd challenges Adolfo Pirelli who claims to be "the king of the barbers, the barber of kings" to a contest to inveigle the Judge into his shop. Ultimately, Pirelli becomes the first of Todd's victims and ingredient in one of Mrs. Lovett's new, much celebrated "meat pies."

Judge Turpin's attention to Johanna turns from regarding her as his ward to wanting her for his wife. Anthony, the young sailor, has developed an intense love interest in Johanna as well. Meanwhile, Mrs. Lovett and Todd are grinding people from all walks of life as their pie enterprise flourishes.

These story lines converge with the death of many of the major characters, sparing the young lovers, Anthony and Johanna, and Tobias Ragg, Pirelli's assistant who is devoted to Mrs. Lovett.

That's as brief as I can make it, but this musical is, oh, so much more. It is genius every step of the way demonstrating Sondheim's cardinal rules: *Content Dictates Form; Less Is More; God is in the Details – all in the service of – Clarity.*

The very opening line of the show's first number "The Ballard of Sweeney Todd" is "Attend the tale of Sweeney Todd." Simple enough? God is in the Details! It foreshadows that this is a period piece, a fable, and as the exacting Sondheim explains about that line, *the alliteration on the first, second and fourth accented beats of "Attend the tale of Sweeney Todd" is not only a microcosm of the AABA form of the song itself, but in its very formality gives the line a sinister feeling, especially with the sepulchral accompaniment that rumbles underneath it.*

Sondheim is the consummate artist, approaching every lyric, every note in this gorgeous "black operetta" with the same level of thought and detail. Interestingly, Sondheim's antipathy for opera led him to construct it mainly as *song forms, something between a musical and a ballad opera.* His love of background music in film, and he has scored several, became infused in the music. Lyrics were a challenge and he decided to invent some colloquialisms to go along with British ones he knew.

There are a number of chorus numbers, their role ranging from serving as a Greek Chorus and as provocateurs moving the action along. Sondheim rejects the notion that all people in a chorus will be singing the same thought in harmony. Thus, chorus and duet numbers in the work can have different overlapping lyrics but all in perfect sync with the music (although, alas, and this does not distract from the overall achievement, not every single word can be heard or assimilated).

Dramaworks' interpretation relies on the deft hand of the Director, Clive Cholerton, and the equally important musical director Manny Schvartzman, making his PBD debut. Cholerton directed the enormously successful *1776,* last year's musical offering from Dramaworks but by his own admission, *Sweeney Todd* is his favorite show. Thus, he found it a bit daunting to finally have the opportunity to direct it. Some previous versions had Sweeney as a crazed mass murderer at the onset, but his vision was to have Sweeney arrive bitter and angry from prison, but not a murderer out of the gate.

His take came more clearly into view working with the costume designer, Brian O'Keefe, whose idea was to make a strong costume statement -- a "steam punk" look, almost science fiction, a post apocalyptic world (although still strongly grounded in 19th century England). O'Keefe is also reaching to younger audiences with this gothic but futuristic feel to it -- or perhaps even a contemporary spin given the current political zeitgeist. The costumes are simply astonishing, from Mrs. Lovett's seductive lacy top with the tightly strung corset to Johanna's virginal gowns and nightdresses to Beadle Bamford's sinister black boots, menacing cudgel and flowing overcoats.

Schvartzman successfully works with the inherent complexity of Sondheim's music, blending the cast seamlessly with the score and wringing out every drop of color and emotion Sondheim has poured into the work. He is also the talented pianist and conductor of the show, along with an orchestra of five, including himself. He clearly achieves his objective of providing the same support as a larger orchestra, hitting every note Sondheim intended.

Shane Tanner returns to the Dramaworks' musical stage, having last appeared in *1776*, this time in the title role of Sweeney. Tanner is well known for a wide range of musicals, including Sondheim's *Into the Woods, A Little Night Music,* and *Assassins.* He makes a critical transition when he crosses the line from merely plotting one person's murder to becoming a mass murderer with ghoulish composure. Beware of the razor in his hand. It is the ultimate equalizer of classes. Tanner's performance starts with despair and lack of hope, gradually escalating to rage and the audience feels that steady spiral to its core. He is a Sweeney to be remembered.

Ruthie Stephens as Mrs. Lovett twists everything in her lust for Todd. We root in many ways for Lovett and Sweeney as they grind up aristocrats along with everyone else, *Those crunching noises pervading the air?.....It's man devouring man, my dear.* Stephens focus is on Mrs. Lovett's role as an opportunist and as Stephens is from the UK, she expertly capitalizes on the very Brit humor of the part. Her clarion voice and performance were stunning and when she is on the stage, your eyes never leave her.

The lovely Johanna is central to all the major characters in the work, the Judge lustily desiring her, Lovett wanting her out of the way, Todd trying to protect her, Anthony loving her. This key soprano role is played by Jennifer Molly Bell. She is as radiant as her namesake song in the show, "Johanna." Bell effectively communicates what it feels like to be a bird trapped in a cage, longing for escape.

Michael McKenzie, as Judge Turpin, makes a strong case for the Judge being "misunderstood" yet unable to tame his emotions – although by banishing Todd to seduce his wife and claim his child makes him decidedly villainous. His scene of self-flagellation singing a new verse of "Johanna" as he voyeuristically peers at his ward is unforgettable. By the time he finally succumbs under Todd's razor (the first such attempt going amiss), the audience is as ripe for revenge as Todd.

The good-natured, madly-in-love with Johanna, Anthony Hope, is performed by Paul Louis Lessard (PBD debut) whose tenor voice soars in his numbers. When Lessard first sings "Johanna" he demonstrates that Sondheim can write a genuinely beautiful love song. The song is sung in several iterations in the show. It was one of Sondheim's favorite's -- *writing songs like these not only appeals to my instinct for intricate plotting, it makes me feel like a playwright, even if the plays are only six or seven minutes long.* Lessard captures Anthony's sensitivity and determination to have his lovebird.

My own favorite songs from the show, aside from "Joanna," are "Pretty Women" sung by Todd and the Judge when the Judge is first in the barber's chair, and the ghoulishly hilarious "A Little Priest," sung by Mrs. Lovett and Todd which brings the curtain down on the first act. I might also add "Not

While I'm Around," a beautiful ballad sung by Evan Jones who plays Tobias Ragg (PBD debut) and then is joined by Mrs. Lovett. It's an unusual number as it mixes both warmth (Tobias' take) and evil (Mrs. Lovett's plotting as she sings).

PBD veteran of many shows, Jim Ballard plays Beadle Bamford, Judge Turpin's thug and partner in crime. Ballard's portrayal is the personification of evil and brutality and that characterization combined with his strong voice left an indelible impression.

Rounding out the cast are Alex Mansoori as Pirelli (PBD debut), Shelley Keelor as the Beggar Woman / Lucy, and the rest of the ensemble, Terry Hardcastle, Christopher Holloway (PBD debut), Hannah Richter (PBD debut), and Victoria Lauzun (PBD debut). All have fine, powerful, operetta quality voices which enhance this production.

Michael Amico's scenic design captures the drab factory-like industrial conceit with the worn paneling and the large overhead windows, for letting in light or the color red, symbolizing blood at the appropriate times. It functions perfectly for the action and atmosphere.

Lighting design is by Donald Edmund Thomas. The lighting has an appropriately grungy feel to it with shadows streaming across the stage.

Sound design is by Brad Pawlak who puts the focus on the music itself as well as a well -timed screeching whistle at emotional peaks.

This PBD production of Sondheim's masterpiece haunts, staged by a team of professionals worthy of Broadway. It is a powerful, stunning performance, not to be missed.

Sondheim's comments are from Stephen Sondheim: <u>Finishing the Hat; Collected Lyrics (1954-1981) with Attendant Comments, Principles, Heresies, Grudges, Whines and Anecdotes</u> (Alfred A. Knopf, New York, 2010

Sunday, October 22, 2017 'The Little Foxes' -- Avarice and Malice Erupt in a Skillful Production

Dramaworks opens its 2017/18 season with a masterpiece, *The Little Foxes*, reimagined with spellbinding staging, imaginative costumes, and impressive acting, It is an outstanding production, especially as the director, J. Barry Lewis was unexpectedly called away for personal reasons half way through rehearsals and Dramaworks' Producing Artistic Director Bill Hayes ably stepped in.

Although written in 1939 and set in 1900, *The Little Foxes* is as relevant today as when written by Lillian Hellman, among the greatest American playwrights of her time, foreshadowing the great family dramas of Tennessee Williams and Arthur Miller. It is set during the waning years of the Reconstruction, the gentility of southern aristocracy transitioning to the New South, and the advance of unrestrained, unscrupulous capitalism of the Gilded Age. Hellman's work was darkened by ten long years of a depression and the shadow of the Bolshevik Revolution.

The Little Foxes theme of unconscionable rapacity strongly resonates in our own time with essentially a plutocracy ruling our nation. The famous quote from the play is spoken by one of the black servants, Addie, *Well, there are people who eat the earth and eat all the people on it like in the Bible with the locusts. Then, there are people who stand around and watch them eat it. Sometimes I think it ain't right to stand and watch them do it.* This theme is omnipresent in this production, melodramatic in the contrasts it projects.

Two factions in the play represent those "who eat and those who are eaten." The former is depicted by the Hubbard family: Oscar, who married Birdie a member of the southern aristocracy for the sake of cotton and the plantation, his older, shrewder brother Ben, and Birdie's and Oscar's loathsome son, Leo. Oscar, Ben, and Leo form a triumvirate of venality, and are joined -- or even outdone -- by Regina Hubbard Giddens, their sister, who married -- with great expectations of wealth -- Horace Giddens, a banker.

The Hubbard clan is in sharp contrast to the rest of the characters: Horace himself, who in his dying days sees the immorality of his prior ways; the fragile and much abused Birdie, Oscar's wife; Alexandra, Regina and Horace's dutiful, young daughter; and the "downstairs" people, the black help Addie and Cal.

The Hubbards are ruthless in their dealings with the people in their small town, especially the poor whites and the blacks who have survived slavery. The brothers have an investment scheme with a Chicago manufacturer, William Marshall (well played by the veteran actor, Frank Converse, jovial, stalwart but vulnerable to Regina's flirtatious charms), to build a cotton mill in the area to take further advantage of cheap southern laborers.

However, the Hubbards need more money to invest and have to turn to Horace, who is ill and has been away at a hospital in Baltimore for months. Regina must get the money from her husband and will stop at nothing to get her share as well – and more -- knowing full well that he is a dying man. Regina inveigles their daughter Alexandra to bring her father home, under the pretense of making him more comfortable, but with only one thought in mind, to get the money.

Once home, Horace discovers that the brothers and his nephew have embezzled bonds from his safe deposit box for the investment, and tells Regina he will revise his will to virtually block her from profiting as well. Not one to be outsmarted, she uses her knowledge of the embezzlement to blackmail her brothers.

The Hubbard family is plagued by infighting, intrigue, and revenge. Their furtive looks on stage speak volumes. Hellman plays out their greedy machinations as naturally as a walk down the street, almost as products of natural selection, becoming what life intended for them. Indeed, as Lillian Hellman said in an interview, "I merely wanted, in essence, to say: 'Here I am representing for you the sort of person who ruins the world for us.'"

In so "representing," Hellman creates two of the preeminent female roles in a single American Drama. Birdie, is played by Denise Cormier, her PBD debut, capturing the character's vulnerability and sad innocence. This is in stark contrast to Regina, played by Kathy McCafferty who stalks the stage with calculating malevolence. As different as they are, they share the commonality of women trapped in a man's world at the turn of the century.

Birdie's "escape" is to dream of returning to her old family plantation, Lionnet, the way it once was, Denise Cormier channels Birdie's disconnection with reality. Yet she is also the innocent truth teller, expressing the ugly reality about her husband's love of shooting small animals for sport while the blacks go hungry and are begging at the door: *It's wicked to shoot food just because you like to shoot, when poor people need it so.* She is an alcoholic, something she admits so painfully to Horace, Alexandra, Cal and Addie, musing about her husband Oscar when she was first married, *he was kind to me, then. He used to smile at me. He hasn't smiled at me since. Everybody knows that's what he married me for. Everybody but me.* Cormier's performance is heartbreakingly ethereal and memorable, particularly her unconditional love for her niece, Alexandra.

The leading role of Regina is played by Kathy McCafferty who revels in Regina's venality while still leaving the audience feeling some empathy as she's an ambitious woman held prisoner in this male dominated world. She was victimized by her father leaving all the money to her brothers and then by the brothers themselves. No wonder she perceives her escape as having what the men have, power and money. McCafferty's performance walks that fine line, making Regina's actions plausible although reprehensible.

When Horace first comes home and learns why Regina really wanted him back, Regina's words to Horace wound, one of the several emotional peaks of the play. McCafferty dips her dialogue deep in cynicism explaining why she married him in the first place: *You were a small-town clerk then. You haven't changed....It took me a little while to find out I had made a mistake. As for you – I don't know. It was almost as if I couldn't stand the kind of man you were --- I used to lie there at night, praying you wouldn't come near.*

The Hubbard brothers are detestable in their own distinctive ways. James Andreassi portrays Oscar as a bully, abusive and dismissive of his fragile wife, and demeaning of his odious spoiled son, Leo, played by Taylor Anthony Miller with a hang-dog look, anxious to please with a phony smile (even his mother, Birdie, confesses that she does not like her own son).

But Oscar is also a tool of his older brother Ben. The PBD veteran actor, Dennis Creaghan, portrays the behind-the-scenes manipulator as if it is just intrinsic to his personality. In an environment where duplicity and suspicion reign, Oscar delivers a line which is central to the play, *It's every man's duty to think of himself.* Yet it is Ben who is prophetic: *The century's turning, the world is open. Open for people like you and me. Ready for us, waiting for us. After all, this is just the beginning. There are hundreds of Hubbards sitting in rooms like this throughout the country...and they will own this country some day.* It is pragmatically and chillingly delivered by Creaghan, prophesying today's world.

Horace Giddens is movingly played by Rob Donohoe, a man whose illness has given him new insight into the errors of his former ways. Donohoe shows the distress of knowing he is a dying man trapped in such a toxic environment but resolute and protective of his daughter. He delivers the crushing message to Regina explaining why he intends to redraft his will with all the repressed fury he can muster: *Not to keep you from getting what you want. Not even partly that I'm sick of you, sick of this house, sick of my life here. I'm sick of your brothers and their dirty tricks to make a dime..... Why should I give you the money? To pound the bones of this town to make dividends for you to spend? You wreck the town, you and your brothers, you wreck the town and live on it. Not me. Maybe it's easy for the dying to be honest. But it's not my fault I'm dying. I'll do no more harm now. I've done enough. I'll die my own way. And I'll do it without making the world any worse. I leave that to you.*

Their daughter Alexandra, also called Zan, is played by the young actress who helped make last year's *Arcadia* so memorable, Caitlin Cohn. She renders Zan as an innocent idealist, yet one striving to discover her own individuality, learning the shocking truth about her family which is rotten to the core. She has a joyful relationship with her Aunt Birdie and worships her father. At the end Hellman seems to point to Zan as having the options which Birdie and Regina did not: escaping the family altogether, a statement of female empowerment.

Also representing "goodness" are the two house servants, Avery Sommers playing Addie, who is Zan's nanny and Patric Robinson as Cal. Cal and Addie articulate a folk wisdom throughout the play like a Greek chorus. They have borne witness to the exploitation around them, and are victims of the Hubbard's dismissiveness. In spite of that, both Sommers and Robinson play their parts with an elevated dignity and supply some of the much needed humor in the play. Sommers' facial expressions reveal her character's knowledge of the family flaws and the basic humanity of Horace, Birdie, and Zan. There is love there in a basically loveless play.

Clearly it was Director J. Barry Lewis' vision to present the play with a high degree of realism. Even though the play is in three acts with two brief intermissions, time flies as we witness the winding and unwinding of the plot, a real-life story in another time but it could be our own.

Michael Amico's set is stately and is in neutral colors. This becomes a perfect palette for Brian O'Keefe's costume designs, supplying the color of the production. Those follow the changes in this character-driven play. Regina's in particular are striking, at times suggesting a seductress, a femme fatale, and of course, as her name implies, regal. Birdie's are designed to make her look refined, a southern belle, and as her name implies, flighty. Zan's bespeaks innocence and virtuousness. Paul Black's lighting design had to work with "windows" that allows daylight to come from the audience's side of the stage. The lighting of the lively first act is dramatically different from the high drama of the final scene. Brad Pawlak's sound design sets up moods mostly at the beginning and end of scenes, tapping into classical pieces by Amy Beach, a pioneering American female composer of that era.

It is not surprising that the play ends sadly, but acceptance and hopefulness are also in the mix. Dramaworks wisely leaves it open to the audience to interpret the "winners" in this unforgettable production.

Saturday, December 9, 2017 Poetic Truth-Telling Prevails in 'Billy and Me'

Blow out the candle of the present and imagine going back in time into Tennessee Williams' memory revealing his relationship with William Inge. That opportunity has been remarkably created by Terry Teachout in his latest play, *Billy and Me*, world premiering at Palm Beach Dramaworks. Williams and Inge were among the playwright elites, friends, and possibly even lovers. Teachout, a well known critic, playwright, and writer, is guided more by his knowledge of the two men and their plays than by historical record. He has created a provocative new drama of uncompromising art and imaginative truth, vividly executed under the direction of William Hayes, PBD Producing Artistic Director, who inspired the idea for the play. In fact, the play is a major collaborative effort between these two professionals.

It is a memory play like *The Glass Menagerie* which is a centripetal force throughout. Williams is the narrator and a character in *Billy and Me* as is Tom in *The Glass Menagerie*. Both plays even end with the same three words.

In the opening act, Williams is anxiously awaiting reviews of *The Glass Menagerie* after Chicago tryouts on New Year's Eve, 1944. The setting is a gay bar where he is also waiting for a relatively unknown critic he once met who has come to review the play, William Inge. Inge who is furtively gay, shows up in a faltering state, terrified of the bar scene and seeing Tennessee Williams again. He is stunned by his unpretentious way of living his life openly and particularly of his gift for poetic language. He is so staggered by the play's force and honesty that he timidly confesses he's thought of becoming a playwright himself. He is goaded on by Williams: *You've got to write about sissy little Billy Inge. You got to be him. Face it and tell it, starting right here in this dump. No more secrets! No more shame! Live your life! You hear me? It's all you've got! There isn't anything else!*

And it is <u>language</u> Teachout so perfectly captures, bringing his interpretation of both men to the stage, the repressed Inge, and the charismatic, poetic Williams. He incorporates special conceits, the audience being allowed behind the hallowed veil of backstage, the setting of the play's scenes and breaking the fourth wall to speak to the audience or visiting his inner self to address his mother and sister Rose.

It's a dizzying journey and the second act bursts upon the stage some 15 years later, with the unthinkable, Inge's first commercial failure, *A Loss of Roses* being panned by the critics after years of Broadway and film hits. In contrast to the sleazy bar scene of the first act we witness Inge's badge of prosperity, his Sutton Place apartment, replete with a Willem de Kooning painting and all the trappings of monetary success as the framed posters from the Broadway productions of *Come Back, Little Sheba, Picnic, Bus Stop, and The Dark at the Top of the Stairs* attest.

In contrast to Tennessee Williams' rise in the first act, is his apparent career stagnation in the second, which brings out his monstrous jealousy of Inge, in spite of his apparent attempts to console his friend. He reminds Inge that it was his encouragement and contacts – particularly Audrey Wood his agent -- which paved the way for his friend's success. The table is set for the play's gripping climax which begins with a contretemps between the two about their plays, the kind of argument no friend can win, gathering intensity to a near calamitous result.

As much as Tennessee Williams is the luminary of *Billy and Me*, the play's dramatic arc is about William Inge. But the story about how Inge became a playwright and the impact Williams had on his career, could not have been compellingly told without the bravura performance by Nicholas Richberg who strikingly captures Williams' flamboyant persona. His transformation in real time, on stage from the aged Tennessee Williams to his younger self, and then back again is heartbreakingly effective. His comic timing is carefully executed, inhabiting Williams' personal pathos and vitriolic embrace of the truth, frequently in an alcoholic daze. He carries the play's poetry, some quoted from *The Glass Menagerie* but most penned by Teachout. *Beauty is truth, truth beauty – start with the truth and then make it beautiful.*

In many ways Tom Wahl's challenge in portraying William Inge is the playwright himself. Teachout could take just so many liberties with a character who mostly eschewed the public spotlight, especially when held up to the brassy extroverted nature of his counterpart. Wahl stoically holds his own, courageously portraying a conflicted character, shy, insecure, secretly gay, and an alcoholic like Williams. His role as straight man is compellingly acted with self loathing and awkward pauses that successfully capture a deeply disturbed man.

There is a reference made in both acts that the two writers are "speckled eggs." As Inge relates it, his mother *called me...her 'speckled egg'.... I wonder how you ever got into my nest.* Wahl's character never is able to break through the shell. It is heartbreaking to watch, a metaphor for anyone who has ever felt like an outsider. It's a difficult part and Wahl emerges as that self-effacing, insecure writer, a character with whom the audience can easily empathize.

Cliff Burgess, a PBD veteran, effectively plays three different characters, the impassive stage manager, the flirtatious waiter, and a somewhat comical doctor. All three roles are integral to the drama, validating both playwrights. He creates needed pauses from the taut action on stage.

The skillful scenic design by Victor Becker effectively highlights the stark contrast between the dank and seedy bar room scene of the first act to Inge's affluent Sutton Place apartment in the second. Each part of the scenery is moved as Williams recalls it from memory. In fact, when the audience arrives, the stage is simply a backstage set creating an anticipation of the action to follow.

Paul Black, the lighting designer picks up on that with constructive lighting, carving out space where there may be a black wall in the background, casting light to make the abstract seem real. His lighting on the aged Tennessee Williams is particularly effective in achieving the suspension of disbelief.

David Thomas is the sound designer and there is an interesting backstory to his PBD debut. Three years ago Thomas was the sound designer for the off-Broadway revival of Inge's *A Loss of Roses* which is the subject of Act II of this play. Terry Teachout reviewed that revival, praised the play, and David Thomas' musical selections, and unknown to him, Bill Hayes hired him for *Billy and Me*. Clairvoyantly, Williams says to Inge: *Hell, maybe all those bastards are wrong about Roses. Who knows? Maybe in fifty years some hotshot producer will dig up the script and a new bunch of bastards will go see it and say, 'You know what? Those other bastards—they were wrong!'* Teachout is ironically one of the "new bunch."

Thomas has a lot to work with for sound, the singing of the drunken men in the unseen back room of the bar, the music on the jukebox, and magical elements that work with the memory aspects of the play. As quoted by both Williams and Inge (from The *Glass Menagerie*): *In memory everything happens to music* and the sounds are evocative.

Costume designer extraordinaire, Brian O'Keefe, who is PBD's Resident Designer, while needing a limited number of costumes for the five different characters plus stagehands in the play, imaginatively reinforces all the personalities and the different periods of the two acts with his usual creative touch.

William Hayes, the Director, has taken many dramatic inventions and put them seamlessly together into one flowing production, and we're caught up in the illusion. His inspired staging clearly conveys Teachout's structure and words and the underlying message: be true to ones' self and if you are a writer, write --- claim your artistic destiny!

As Williams said in the prologue to The Glass Menagerie, *Memory takes a lot of poetic license. It omits some details; others are exaggerated, according to the emotional value of the articles it touches, for memory is seated predominantly in the heart.* The same can be said for this superb production, worthy of this world premiere.

Saturday, February 3, 2018 **Aging and Redemption Resonate -- 'On Golden Pond'**

Dramaworks' version of *On Golden Pond* returns to what the playwright, Ernest Thompson, originally intended, a less sentimental, more honest rendering of what we all ultimately face: aging, and as with many families, disconnection and hopefully reconciliation. While this is the stuff of most great American drama, the playwright inextricably links humor and pathos, leading to the ultimate question: what does it mean to be? This is a tender rendition, performed by an interracial cast under the direction and inspiration of Paul Stancato.

Novelist and environmentalist Wallace Stegner once said "we live too shallowly in too many places." Not Norman and Ethel Thayer who for 48 years have made their summer home on Golden Pond in Maine the bulwark of their lives, raising their only child, Chelsea, during their summers away from Wilmington. Dramaworks' striking set characterizes the rusticity of lake side living as well as years of memories, both happy and hurtful. It is in some state of disrepair. Take that cranky screen door which is always falling down for instance, good for laughs but serving as a metaphor for aging and neglect.

Norman is a retired university literature professor on the eve of his 80th birthday. He has his routines in the cabin which mostly revolve around arranging his fishing hats, and curmudgeonly railing at the annoyance du jour, but now he's also having memory difficulties, perhaps the early signs of dementia. He's convinced that his impending status as an octogenarian will mark his last year at Golden Pond. *Oh shut up,* the ballast in his life, devoted wife Ethel says to all that death talk. And, then there is Chelsea, a chip off the old block of Norman. They've become ever more remote with Ethel as the reconciler.

A touching secondary story-line involves Chelsea's once-upon-a-time boyfriend when she was growing up --a "townie" -- who is now the mailman, delivering the mail by boat to the residents around the pond. Charlie Martin is still in love with Chelsea, but while that ship has sailed, he gives the play many nostalgic moments as we glimpse at those yesterdays.

The rising action of the play is a letter that declares Chelsea will be arriving from California with her fiancé, Bill Ray to celebrate Norman's 80th birthday. Unannounced is that they are bringing along Bill's 15 year old son, Billy. And as the first act ends, we learn that Billy will be left with Chelsea's parents for a month at Golden Pond as Bill and Chelsea travel through Europe. The clock is wound and the stage is set for change.

With the opening of Act II, we find that Norman and Billy have created interesting new lives for themselves during that stay. Then with Chelsea's return and at Ethel's urging, Norman and Chelsea finally have their moment of acquiescent truth. Bill and Chelsea were married while in Belgium. The screen door has apparently been fixed. And so life moves on in unexpected ways.

Director Paul Stancato makes the most of the play's many bittersweet comic opportunities, having the actors pause for a beat, simultaneously capturing those humorous and heartrending moments. He sets the play in 1988 before the ubiquity of cell phones and the associated diversions of the Internet. Stancato is an accomplished musical director as well and he finds rhythms in the play, almost pacing it as a piece of music with an Andante tempo.

John Felix excels as Norman, who persistently laments about how little time there is in his future. He wears "curmudgeon" as a badge of honor, and yet Felix's interpretation makes him likeable, even lovable, approaching the Aristotelian definition of a tragic hero, evoking a sense of pity and fear. After all, Norman's fate of physical and cognitive decline is one which awaits most who live long enough.

Felix seizes the opportunities to embellish his death obsession with laughs, the perfect tonic for his depression. He is particularly effective during those moments. He explains to Ethel that this summer he's been casually looking for a job because *I'm in the market for a last hurrah.* To which Ethel responds *why can't you just pick berries and catch fish and read books, and enjoy this sweet, sweet time?*

Here the dark comedy becomes serious, Felix's demeanor changing to a heartfelt confession: *Do you want to know why I came back so fast with my little bucket? I got to the end of our lane, and I...couldn't remember where the old town road was. I went a little way into the woods, and nothing looked familiar, not one tree. And it scared me half to death. So I came running back home here, to you, to see your pretty face, and to feel that I was safe. That I was still me.*

Pat Bowie's Ethel is the "great woman" behind her now declining man. She lovingly replies *Well, you're safe, you old poop. And you're definitely still you...* Bowie carries a heavy burden of Ethel's constant sacrifice and devotion to the love of her life, trying to keep his thoughts of death under control.

She is always listening for the loons, a metaphor for life and in her mind capable of speaking to her. While she is the positive to Norman's negative, Bowie's portrayal of Ethel shows vulnerability as the years and the estrangement between her husband and daughter have taken their toll on her as well.

Karen Stephens as Chelsea longs for love from her father but the chasm which has built over the years seems insurmountable. Stephens brings sublimated pain into her role, expecting so little from her father, accustomed now to call her mother, Mommy, and her father, Norman. She even sets up her fiancé so he is already on guard before meeting Norman: *Bill, you want to visit the men's room before you go through the shock of meeting my father?*

Chelsea still feels "like a little girl" whenever she returns to Golden Pond. Stephens channels that pent up anger saying to her mother, *I act like a big person everywhere else. I do. I'm in charge of Los Angeles. There's just something about coming back here that makes me feel like a little fat girl."* She goes on to accuse her mother: "Where were you all that time? You never bailed me out.... You don't know what it's like being reminded how worthless you are every time that old son of a bitch crosses your path.*

Ethel does not back down, even slapping her daughter: *That old son of a bitch happens to be my husband. I'm sorry, Chelsea. That he's not always kind. It's not...always easy for me either. You're such a nice person, can't you think of something nice to say?* With that she plants a seed for reconciliation between husband and daughter.

Jim Ballard comically plays Bill Ray, Chelsea's fiancé, nervously stumbling into the cabin with their suitcases, convinced he's seen a bear. His first encounter with Norman is especially amusing, Ballard playing the foil to Felix's Norman, clearly ill at ease, not only in meeting Norman but left alone while the others go down to see the lake. He tries to bring up the sleeping arrangements, his expecting to sleep with Chelsea while visiting though they are not yet married (after all, it was the times and these are two vastly different generations). This results in an awkward but funny give and take.

But as Bill has been forewarned about Norman, Ballard turns serious, even admitting to the similarities between Norman and his daughter. His monologue is in contrast to his initial unease. *Chelsea told me all about you, about how you like to have a good time with people's heads. She does it, too, sometimes, and sometimes I can get into it. Sometimes not. I just want you to know that I'm very good at recognizing crap when I hear it.*

This "speech" as Norman calls it begrudgingly commands Norman's respect. Ballard has appeared on the Dramaworks stage twelve times and shows his gift to deliver both dramatic as well as the comedic moments.

Paul Tei plays Charlie, a local who has long loved Chelsea, motoring around the lake in the summer to deliver the mail. Tei is perfect for the part, his infectious goofy laugh reaching out to the audience. He poignantly relates his memories to Chelsea about her camp years, when he used to help his Uncle deliver the mail, and when they came by the camp.

It's such a wistful memory exchange between Chelsea and Charlie, and so tenderly delivered by Tei. This leads to Chelsea and Ethel singing the camp song, which concludes with *but we'll remember our years, On Golden Pond.* Both mother and daughter attended Camp Koochakiyia as kids, another hat tip to the passage of time and continuity.

Young Casey Butler last appeared at Dramaworks in the challenging play *Acadia.* He is already a seasoned pro. Now as Billy Ray, Bill's fifteen year old son, he expresses the unbounded energy and innocence of youth.

When he and Norman first meet, it's as if two different species are in shock looking each other over, an antediluvian confronting a Marty McFly. Ultimately, both are redeemed by one another. He is the grandchild Norman never had, and Norman is the teacher who will make a difference in Billy's life. Norman is now a different man with a reason to live. Casey's portrayal of Billy as Norman's lifesaver is spot on.

Dramaworks' production is firmly grounded in spectacular scenic design by Bill Clark, his PBD debut. It evokes all the themes of the play, but in particular the Thayer's love of Golden Pond, its woods, and its wildlife. The wood pillars of the structure seem to reach for the sky, the forest in the background, the solid stone mantelpiece displaying the age of its construction, 1917, presumably the year Ethel's father built the cabin. Ethel's toy doll, Elmer, now 65 years old, sits on the mantle shelf along with photographs, and many others strewn about the living room. It's an award-winning set, a perfect backdrop for the action on stage.

Brad Pawlak's sound design reproduces the eerie calls of the Loons across the lake. Add the sounds of the forest, the fluttering of bird wings, even the insidious insects, Charlie's boat approaching, as well as the rising wind in September, all so evocative of a summer in Maine. Musical interludes such as "Moonglow" and "Sentimental Journey" during scene changes contribute to the ambiance.

Lighting design by Donald Edmund Thomas captures the time changes, from the deep dark of night to the blazing sun off the pond, as well as enhancing the changing emotions on stage.

Resident award-winning costume designer Brian O'Keefe emphasizes the casual dress of country living, as well as Bill's comical 1980's California style jacket and pants.

Dramaworks' production of *On Golden Pond* is a deeply satisfying play, perhaps the perfect tonic for our times and the theatre company's traditional audience.

Sunday, April 1, 2018 **Kinsmen Meet at the World Premiere of 'Edgar and Emily'**

On a snowy evening in 1864 the poet laureate of death, Emily Dickinson, is visited by the master of the macabre, Edgar Allan Poe in a world premiere play, Joseph McDonough's *Edgar and Emily* at Palm Beach Dramaworks. And indeed the play is shaped around the main theme of many of their poems (or stories): death (and its corollary, what it means to live), Emily taking a more transcendental view and Poe the ghoulish.

Although this may seem initially distressing, this delicate but insightful play is a work of art. Its universal truths lie between comedy and melancholy. Throughout the play there are pratfalls or physical comedic elements to give it an absurdist twist, giving the audience permission to laugh, even though the characters are two well known poets and the subject matter is one we all generally try to avoid thinking about.

Its brevity (one act packed into 1-1/4 hours) belies its profundity. It is like a Dickinson poem, a meaningful deliberation of what it means to live and die laid bare in but a few lines. I kept on thinking of one of my favorite Dickinson poems "I died for beauty" which has the phrase "as kinsmen met a night." In many respects, Dickinson and Poe are kinsmen. Words intensely mattered to them, and ultimately *Edgar and Emily* lead us there.

Those absurdist elements allow this unlikely meeting to suddenly occur fifteen years after Poe's death. But he is very much alive, stumbling into Dickinson's universe, her bedroom in her parent's house in Amherst. But wait, what is it he drags around with him? It's his coffin! Naturally Emily is indignant at this man visiting her in her room, claiming to be Edgar Allan Poe, and how can this be so many years after his death? Easy explanation, after being buried alive he was miraculously rescued by a woman in white, perhaps an angel (ironically, Dickinson is normally attired in white), with the condition he take his coffin wherever he goes. Unfortunately, he is being chased by his doppelganger who wants to make his rigor mortis permanent.

The play is a beautiful piece of writing by McDonough, smoothly flowing from comedy, to poetry to expectation of flight, to deep philosophical discussions of what it means to live with eternity before birth and after death. They reveal themselves to one another and in the process both are changed. The play ultimately leads to Poe suggesting that he and Emily go out into the world together. Her hesitation, whether she could bring her words, creates as much dramatic tension as the ominous voice of his pursuer crying out, "Poe!"

When Gregg Weiner as Edgar Allan Poe barges into Dickinson's bedroom, he is agitated and in great fear that he's being followed. He is totally indifferent to the woman in the room. When he tells her who he is, laughter erupts as he ends up defending his own work. The tables soon turn and he expresses a cynical dismissiveness about her claims of being a poet as well. Weiner's nuanced performance creates an aura of unpredictability. His gift for comedic sarcasm is much in evidence, such as his exchange with Emily when he first reads one of her poems: *I have survived poetry that is considerably more nauseating than yours* which Emily takes as a compliment, Edgar going on to say *In fact, I will admit....I detect in your poetics, a concise resignation to morbidity that I personally find exhilarating.*

It is a joy to watch Weiner dial up those comedic elements while at the same time expressing his terrified awe surrounding the mysteries of life, his fear of death, and his struggle to resolve his present dilemma. Here he has the help of Emily.

Margery Lowe is the veteran of fifteen appearances on the Dramaworks stage. Her versatility as an actress shines in the part of Emily Dickinson, with shades of some zaniness juxtaposed to the gravitas of the character of Emily Dickinson. Lowe's Dickinson ranges from being an uncertain, sheltered woman, entirely inexperienced in the ways of the world, unlike Poe, to being a poet of unmatched greatness, her inner world immeasurable. And if you're looking for verisimilitude, it also helps that Lowe is about the size of Dickinson and with similar hair coloring. Another doppelganger!

Lowe exhibits all the emotions from bewilderment, to fear, to being dismissive of Poe's work such as *The Raven* (*You rhymed 'lattice' with 'thereat is'? It's no wonder someone's trying to kill you*). She's coy about having Poe read some of her poems, and at last amazingly tempted to leave her universe (but asking plaintively *Will I be safe from the enormity of living?*). Lowe announces her decision as a central truth of Dickinson's art: *I am the queen of infinite space here in my room ....I fear the rest of the world might prove tiny.* It's a bravo performance to pull all of this off, particularly staying grounded in comedy of which Lowe is a master such as when she breathlessly says to Edgar, *You praised my morbidity! I am so happy!*

Avoiding spoilers, the play inexorably moves to a conclusion shaped by the two characters, one most audiences will find gratifying, even breathtaking, the climax eliciting an audible gasp from the audience, a touch of magical realism, enhanced by lighting and color.

Both must live their lives, for whatever the duration. For all of us, "Living is shockingly brief." And for Poe and Dickinson, in particular, "The words are the only living, lasting things we have." Since Lowe and Weiner have been on the stage opposite one another several times before, their chemistry has been honed to perfection.

PBD Producing Artistic Director William Hayes directs the play and has been involved since its gestation, purposely picking local actors, Margery Lowe and Gregg Weiner to go with him and the playwright on the journey from the Dramaworkshop to the Main Stage. He wisely concentrates on the comedic elements of the play, making sure the jokes and quirky dialogue are highlighted. Comedy is always an audience pleaser while the dark drama of the play, the tug of war between living and dying, is always disturbing.

Hayes also relies heavily on his technical crew to bring the play to fruition. Scenic design by Michael Amico is simply stunning, while realistically depicting what could pass as Emily Dickinson's 19th century bedroom, but symbolically casting that room through time and space, enveloping it in the wild world of Edgar Allan Poe. So, like the play, there are unconventional elements.

Lighting design by Paul Black is particularly critical to the play. Here is a room supposedly lit by candles. As they are extinguished or lit, lighting has to gradually anticipate each action, it being jarring to just turn the spots on and off. It all comes across so naturally, as does the shift from light to darkness during the more ominous moments in the play. Watch the lighting at the very beginning as Emily stands at her window, the snow falling, lit like a Rembrandt portrait.

Sound design by David Thomas heightens the suspenseful moments, the storm raging outside, the wind whirling when the window is blown open, the banging of the coffin as it is dragged up the stairs. There is the terrifying crying out of Poe's doppelganger, "Poe, Poe, Poe!" And here and there we hear a musical interlude, particularly at the beginning, classical violin and piano to (falsely) establish just another calm night in the life of Emily Dickinson. When Poe tells his tale of being rescued from the coffin, the sound effects of the story are like those used in movies, unusual on stage, but eerily appropriate for this production.

The one technical element which has little room for departure from reality is the magnificent costumes by Brian O'Keefe. Emily is known for being a "lady in white" especially later in life, so O'Keefe complies with a beautiful costume, ostensibly white under the lights but actually a shade of grey, with some gold thread to counteract the grey. The dress is slightly ethereal, as is her poetry. Poe meanwhile, known to be usually in black, is indeed dressed in a dark jacket, but with a ruby waistcoat and pinstripe pants, depicting his once outrageously profligate and debauched lifestyle.

As Emily says, *Words endure, Mr. Poe. They endure.* And so are those of playwright Joseph McDonough, who has already been commissioned for a new play during Dramaworks' 2019 season. *Edgar and Emily* is sure to provide gratification as well as enlightenment to those who are open to the experience of an absurdist drama about two of our most famous poets.

"I cannot tell how Eternity seems. It sweeps around me like a sea... Thank you for remembering me. Remembrance — mighty word" -- *Emily Dickinson*

Saturday, May 19, 2018 'Equus' Soars, Stuns, and Unsettles

Director J. Barry Lewis takes a metaphoric jig saw puzzle and puts it together in a flowing, mesmerizing, gut-wrenching production of Peter Shaffer's great late 20th century play, *Equus*. The actors are at the very top of their games, particularly the two leads, the skilled, seasoned Peter Simon Hilton as Martin Dysart, a child psychiatrist, and an upcoming actor whose brilliant performance portends an extraordinary acting future, Steven Maier as his patient, 17 year old Alan Strang.

Passion vs. the cerebral, paganism vs. Christianity, normal vs. abnormal, regret and hope: these are just a few of the layers of *Equus*. The abhorrent act of blinding five horses with a metal spike brings all these discordant themes together in an incomparable thought-provoking and passionate production.

It is a long play, sometimes difficult to watch as there is such self loathing on the part of the two major characters and as they reveal more, they change the other, but for better or for worse? The sparse Greek staging strips the story down to its bare essentials while the acting makes this so deeply affecting.

The play was written in the 1970s at a time when an anti-psychiatry movement was underway. In fact, Shaffer himself amusingly recalled that "in London *Equus* caused a sensation because it displayed cruelty to horses; in New York, because it allegedly displayed cruelty to psychiatrists." Nonetheless, Shaffer's ability to incorporate all the major themes in the play into a psychological "why he did it," has been dealt with by the vision of the production's director, the astute J. Barry Lewis, a combination that makes this great theatre. Some have even called the play dated, but Lewis' direction shapes the play so the ideas are still as relevant in today's world as it was nearly fifty years ago.

Lewis brings out the best of the playwright, and the actors, with the technical staff facilitating its implementation. The direction and the staging are like a skillfully solved Rubik's Cube. This is a Master Class in every respect.

Alan Strang is a disturbed inaccessible boy, the product of a stern atheistic father who also leads a secret life and his very piously religious wife who has fervently read passages from the Bible to her son all his life. Are they to blame for Alan's aberrant behavior of savagely blinding those horses at the stable where he worked?

The incident leads to Alan being admitted to a psychiatric hospital in southern England and into the care of its head psychiatrist Martin Dysart. Dysart at first objects to taking on still another patient but his friend, Hesther Salomon, a sympathetic magistrate who believes Alan would be better off in his care than in a prison, urges him on. Increasingly, for reasons Shaffer steadily feeds to the audience, the case fascinates Dysart. In fact, he becomes obsessively involved as his unhappy personal life is revealed and he begins to doubt the consequences of his life's work, "curing" people of their aberrations (passions?).

Alan Strang is grippingly played by Steven Maier. This is not only his PBD debut but, remarkably, his Regional Theatre debut. He is an amazingly gifted actor who portrays this tormented boy with complete abandon. Alan's repressed sexuality merges into a conflation of the agony of Christ with those of horses, their having to endure bridles, reins, and stirrups. And yet, Alan is moved by *the way they give themselves to us*. He replaces a portrait of Christ in his room, one of him in chains on the Road to Calvary, with a picture of a horse looking straight on, it's enormous eyes the most salient feature: *behold I give you Equus, my only begotten son*. Maier goes places you rarely see on a stage, a place where inner demons dominate.

At first he can only chant advertising jingoes as he enters therapy but as Dysart brings him closer in touch with the heinous act he has committed, Maier's performance builds and builds to an insistent crescendo. It's exhausting and exhilarating at the same time, Alan literally climaxing while on his favorite horse, Nugget (Equus), to which he is erotically attracted, the two becoming centauresque at that moment.

Peter Simon Hilton plays Dysart as a stern ringmaster, orchestrating, pressing, questioning, and controlling what happens in the present and making Alan play out what happened in the past. Frequently the past and the present are happening concurrently, actors talking across one another. As more is revealed in the abreaction process, Hilton effectively shows

Dysart's jealousy of his patient and his increasing doubt in his own life's work. Hilton holds the audience in his grip delivering Shaffer's simply brilliant analytical monologues which conclude with such introspection. He comments on his concern about taking away Alan's "worship" of horses to Hesther: *I only know it's the core of his life. What else has he got? Think about him. He can hardly read. He knows no physics or engineering to make the world real for him. No paintings to show him how others have enjoyed it. No music except television jingles. No history except tales from a desperate mother. No friends. Not one kid to give him a joke, or make him know himself more moderately. He's a modern citizen for whom society doesn't exist. He lives one hour every three weeks -- howling in a mist. And after the service kneels to a slave who stands over him obviously and unthrowably his master. With my body I thee worship! ...Many men have less vital with their wives.*

Indeed, such as Dysart's non-existent relationship with his off stage wife. More and more of Dysart's thoughts go to his own deferred passion, Greek mythology, particularly the dichotomy of Apollo and Dionysus, and thoughts of retiring to Greece (but with whom, not with a wife who fails to appreciate the mythology, or him). Frequently Dysart addresses the audience directly, Hilton staring into our faces, drawing us yet further into the heart of the play.

Dysart is one of the most conflicted cerebral characters in a 20th century play which Peter Simon Hilton conveys effortlessly, leaving us all to wonder, have we done what our hearts dictated or has society merely set us *on a metal scooter and sen[t]...puttering off into the concrete world?* Have we made a difference? Are we condemned too to wear a metaphoric horse's bit?

The major supporting roles are all played by experienced PBD actors. Julie Rowe as Dora Strang, Alan's semi-hysterical mother, candidly displays the emotions of a loving parent, but is understandably bewildered and horrified by her son's act, particularly because of her belief in the religious education she provided. Her husband, Frank, is played by John Leonard Thompson, darkly, uncomfortably -- being such a private person now thrown into the light of the courts and the institutional process of treating his son, their only child, of whom he's been critical all his life, (*son of a printer and you never open a book!*). His work ethic collides with his urge to visit adult films. Thompson shows a man racked by guilt and self defensiveness.

Dysart's friend, and magistrate, Hesther Salomon, is compassionately played by Anne-Marie Cusson, she being the only sounding board for Dysart other than the audience itself. Cusson is stalwart in bolstering him up at those very difficult times when he is expressing his greatest doubts, both as a man and a doctor. Her sensitive portrayal is deeply touching, especially when she expresses the constant reminder to him and us that "children before adults" must be humanity's mantra if we are to remain a civilized world.

Alan ends up working with the horses at a local stable thanks to a job offer from Jill Mason, skillfully played with a sexual free spirit and sang-froid by Mallory Newbrough, characteristics of the "new age" of the early 1970's. Her playful and persistent interest in Alan ultimately leads to an unsatisfactory sexual incident in the stables, which causes Alan's destructive anguish to surface, melding his shame and fear and derangement into an unfathomable crime.

Harry Dalton, the owner of the stable, is played by the accomplished Steve Carroll and the nurse who works for Dysart is professionally played by Meredith Bartmon.

Not enough accolades can be directed to the actors playing the horses. Sounds silly, I know, yet led by head horse, "Nugget" majestically as well as muscularly played by Domenic Servidio (he also plays "The Horseman," a man who takes Alan for a ride on a horse at a beach as a youngster), are the others skillfully and mesmerizingly played by Austin Carroll, Nicholas Lovalvo, Robert Richards, Jr., and Frank Vomero.

Talk about method acting, each of the horsemen, as well as Maier (Alan) spent time at a local stable – in fact Servidio went to a dude ranch for a long weekend – to have a better understanding of a horse's movement, particularly in a stable. They discovered horses' ticks, with their hoofs, their reactionary movements, their ubiquitous eyes. I truly believe this enhanced the performance, not to mention certain choreographed moments when the horses provide a ghoulish background for some of the action "in the ring."

And, indeed, the scenic design by PBD veteran Anne Mundell borrows both from the prize fighting ring and the Greek theatre. The play involves constant confrontation, between characters and with the inner self, so the stripped down representation of a boxing ring is a visual source for these pugilistic encounters. And as in Greek theatre of classical times, it's a simple space to tell a story, with minimal props, most of which are pantomimed, except for the horses' heads which are in keeping with the masks worn in Greek theatre. It's up to the audience to visualize the scenes from those outlines.

Both the horses and the actors who are not engaged in a particular scene play the role of a Greek chorus. The actors sit on seats slightly off stage, watching all the action, as Dysart urges Alan on into the depths of his soul, waiting for their turn to engage in the "fight" in the ring.

The lighting by Kirk Bookman enhances this sense of a pugilistic ring, a bright spotlight on the action from directly overhead, while other lighting is used to demark other settings, such as Alan's room at home, the stable which is Alan's sacred temple, or a scene at a beach. The lighting is particularly effective in the breathless scene when Alan mounts Nugget, PBD's turntable stage whirling counter-clockwise while the surrounding prism-like lighting turning clockwise outside to create a dizzying sense of movement.

Costumes of the 1970s by Franne Lee are the real deal, often having been "borrowed" straight out of her own time capsule closet, particularly for Jill in her bellbottoms and boots. Every character seems to have a warm or cool aspect to their clothing, but the boy has been clothed for comfort and simplicity since he is often falling or flailing or clutching at his well worn pullover. The horses, on the other hand, are dark forbidding masculine beasts all in skin tight black, either wearing or carrying their grotesque but compelling horse head masks, while mesmerizingly stamping the ground with their ingenious booted hoofs.

One cannot overstate the importance of the work by the sound designer, Steve Shapiro. It is an "otherworldly" sound, not the mood music associated with most theatrical productions. Think of electronically reproduced fragments of "Also sprach Zarathustra." Everything becomes electronically magnified by Shapiro, including the horses' "hum" when dramatic action is rising. There is some dissonant electronic music when necessary, especially when taking the audience into Alan's mind, making us all feel deeply unsettled.

Much has been made of the nudity in the play but it only serves as a metaphor for underscoring that when things are stripped down to the bare essence, there is no place to hide. And as Alan plaintively says, *a horse is the most naked thing you ever saw*. It is not gratuitous nudity but totally befitting the play's honesty.

This production of *Equus* is theatre which will haunt your thoughts, electrifying in every way live theatre can be, brilliantly written, conceived and sharply executed.

Saturday, July 14, 2018 **An Exuberant 'Woody Guthrie's American Song'**

A rollicking, moving songfest of fellowship bursts forth on stage inspired by the life, words and music of Woody Guthrie. This high-energy production of *Woody Guthrie's American Song*, as conceived by Peter Glazer, is particularly poignant and relevant to our times. Does history change to remain the same? Must there always be a disenfranchised faction of Americans?

Woody Guthrie was first and foremost a poet of the people; "people's songs" as he called them, the aggrieved and the downtrodden, migrant workers, busted union members, and victims of income inequality by birth. They were our farmers, our steel workers, our coal miners, one might say the very builders of our great country, but victimized by bankers, politicians, the Great Depression, and, then the final blow, a severe drought that hit the Southern and Midwestern plains creating hoards of "Dust Bowl refugees." It may be the dark side of the American Dream, but Woody had a dream of "A Better World" and the goodness of the man and his dream shines through.

Guthrie presages such "peoples" performers as Bob Dylan, Bruce Springsteen, and most recently receiving the Woody Guthrie Prize, the rocker John Mellencamp. His spirit endures and this show preserves it.

Peter Glazer's musical was adapted entirely from Guthrie's words and music. It features five gifted actors & singers who are backed by the musical ensemble of the three Lubben Brothers (local multi-talented musicians and singers), playing a number of instruments which amplify and elevate this memorable production. They serve as backup singers and musicians on most songs, giving this production a special inspirational quality at times and at others a downright knee slapping driving force.

The simplicity and the beauty of the music evoke those of gospel songs and hymns. It is astounding what Guthrie could do musically with just a few chords, songs sometimes just a variation on the others. His heart-rending words take flight in this production.

Glazer's work is not a mere hootenanny; it is musical theatre. The "book" in musical parlance is about Guthrie at different stages of his life, and the turbulent times in which he lived, the Gibson guitar being handed off as a baton from one actor/singer to another. He thematically ties all these pieces together into a chronological narrative, a Prologue, On the Plains – the Early 1930s, A Train Heading West, The California Line, The Jungle Camp, New York City, Middle 1940s, and then an Epilogue.

Director Bruce Linser is also obviously intent on making this a meaningful show, not just a concert, working with the actors and the technical crew to create an atmosphere of drama for each scene. He ensures that even though there are more than a score of songs, the ensemble group holds together as an honest to goodness musical, true to storytelling, making homogeneity out of a mosaic.

The actors start with the words of Woody, defining what it means to be a ballad singer: *The ballad singer is a mystery to everybody except maybe his own self.... What heart of the people has he found, what passport, what ticket, what philosophy, what religious faith has he found that takes him out to the roads and the trails again?*

The words morph into one of Woody's most famous ballads which summarize the travelogue basis of the show and the hardships of those years, the entire cast singing "Hard Travelin'" with exquisite harmony.

The stage is now set to trace Woody's life. Representing Guthrie earlier in life is Jeff Raab also known as "the Searcher," singing a lick of the touching dust bowl ballad / waltz " "So Long, It's Been Good to Know Yuh," and then a reprise of "Oklahoma Hills." This culminates in the song "Dust Bowl

Disaster." Later in the show he is "Cisco.". He has a fine voice and plays the guitar, banjo, and harmonica.

One of Guthrie's best known songs "Bound for Glory" is sung by the entire cast on a freight train with a hobo and "cripple Whitey." The train is bound for the "glory" of California and is amusingly choreographed as the actors are singing as the train is moving at 60 mph. At the California line the rousing and ironic "Do Re Mi" (what you had to have to get into California) is sung by the five actors with gusto.

Sean Powell plays the next stage in Guthrie's life with a jovial exuberance, now that he is established as a bona fide folksinger. Powell is also the Musical Director of the show and as such brings together the cast's wonderful harmonies. He plays seven different instruments in the show while having orchestrated it at the same time. His work is as important as the Director's and it is seamless throughout.

One of the two women in the show is Cat Greenfield who comes from a blue grass background and cabaret theatre, exhibiting a fine, commanding soprano voice, as well as playing the guitar, banjo, mandolin, and the spoons (yes, the spoons, a real hoot). PBD veteran Julie Rowe also triumphs in a number of roles, giving heart tugging renditions of some songs and comic turns in others (she makes a great saloon singer later in the show). They both add a harmonizing poignancy to other songs, "Ain't Gonna Be Treated This Way," "End of My Line," and "Grand Coulee Dam," culminating in the moving "Pastures of Plenty" at the end of Act I.

The second act brings the musical to another level. While "Grand Coulee Dam" was the employment they sought, Act II opens with the dark "Ludlow Massacre" which is about a miner's union strike during which 13 children were killed by National Guardsmen, Greenfield and Rowe carrying the leads with the imaginative and effective playing of the instruments in percussion, its military rhythm driving the song forward.

After that incident, the folksinger says *the months flew past and the people faster. The coast wind blew me out of San Francisco, over the hump to Los Angeles and all the way to New York.... I run onto a guitar playing partner standing on a bad corner. His name was Cisco Houston, and he called his self the Cisco Kid."*

The "kid" introduces him to New York, and its saloon halls, his next stop in his ramblin' life, amusingly singing "New York Town" together, vying with one another for sidewalk tips. They strike up a friendship with Cisco offering a line that could summarize the show: *As long as we've got wrecks, disasters, floods, trade union troubles, high prices and low pay and politicians, folk songs are on their way in.*

The talk turns political and Guthrie's "Union Maid," is sung with the catchy refrain, "Oh, you can't scare me, I'm sticking with the Union." This is a song for the entire cast but is enthusiastically led by Cat Greenfield and Julie Rowe. Here the audience is invited to sing along, and sing along we did with gusto.

Now we come to the tragic story of the Reuben James, the first military vessel sunk by the Germans in WW II (Guthrie served in the Merchant Marines). The folksinger explains that the sinking happened before Pearl Harbor by a German U-Boat. He goes on to say *I can't invent the news but I do my job, which is to fix the day's news up to where you can sing it.* A roar of laughter came forth from the audience, acknowledging that in this respect times have changed.

But not all that much. Here the show transitions to the mature Guthrie as "the writer" played by Don Noble. Noble is a veteran of Broadway with a commanding bass voice, and comes to the show with guitar and mandolin skills as well. Among other songs, he introduces what, to me is the show stopper, perhaps the most moving Guthrie folksong, "Deportee" and as explained, *A chartered Immigration Service plane crashed and burned in West Fresno County this morning, killing 28 Mexican deportees, the crew and an immigration guard.* The "deportees" were illegal immigrants and the song is about their stark anonymity to history and an indifference to them as human beings.

The song itself is sung primarily by Cat Greenfield, silhouetted by a spotlight, with the cast joining in. The parallels to our time are unmistakable with barely a dry eye in the audience. The song's Chorus, heartbreaking, devastating...*Goodbye to my Juan, goodbye, Rosalita, / Adios mis amigos, Jesus y Maria; / You won't have your names when you ride the big airplane, / All they will call you will be "deportees."*

The show gathers momentum to a happier conclusion, with "Better World", and the iconic "This Land Is Your Land." There are many comic moments too, one of which Director Linser has the cast singing a lick of song, lined in a row facing the audience with their steel stringed instruments, one hand working the frets and the other strumming the strings of the musician next to him or her! A crowd pleaser.

The technical support also makes this production such a success. Scenic design by Michael Amico was influenced by the American painter and muralist, Thomas Hart Benton whose work focused on the mid West. He was able to transfer the sense of Benton's color and movement to a barn siding, depicting Guthrie's "journey" from west to east.

This gave costume designer Brian O'Keefe colors to work with and as the journey takes place over a lifetime, multiple costumes for the characters, adding still another layer to the production. The costumes reflect the threadbare realism of the characters' hard times and their regionalism.

John D. Hall's lighting design is careful not to wash out the colors, but highlight the action. Brad Pawlak's sound design finds ways to provide depth to the sound, especially when the show reverts to narrative.

This is a feel-good musical, filled with both pain and joy. As the show ends with his most easily recognizable "This Land Is Your Land" you'll find yourself emerging from the theatre savoring the words or singing them out loud as the audience did last night, celebrating what it means to live here in this great land, even perhaps with a sense of optimism in the headwinds of history and our times.

Saturday, October 20, 2018 'Indecent' by Paula Vogel Hauntingly Opens Dramaworks' Season

Ashes to ashes, dust to dust....a theatre troupe comes back from the dead to tell its story. Let this superb production wash over you. Bask in its bittersweet intensity and breathe in its essence of purity. There is a tragic sadness juxtaposed to unadulterated joy, of living, of loving and of art. Dramaworks' production of Paula Vogel's *Indecent* is faultlessly potent.

While *Indecent* is a play about a very good play, Sholem Asch's 1907 *God of Vengeance*, it is more of an impressionistic work, capturing feelings about themes that are exposed in the actual production of *God of Vengeance:* gender discrimination, lesbian love, censorship and persecution, art and freedom, anti-Semitism and immigration. All of this is encapsulated in playwright Paula Vogel's love poem to theatre itself.

God of Vengeance is dated in its melodramatic approach to the subject of Jewish filial tradition and obligation, incorporating a lesbian love affair with the powerful retribution all being played out ironically above a Jewish brothel. As Asch's wife, Madje, says in *Indecent* of her young husband's play, *My God, Sholem. It's all in there. The roots of all evil: the money, the subjugation of women, the false piety ... the terrifying violence of that father ... and then, oh Sholem, the two girls in the rain scene! My God, the poetry in it—what is it about your writing that makes me hold my breath? You make me feel the desire between these two women is the purest, most chaste, most spiritual—.*

One of the central characters in *God of Vengeance* is father and husband Yekel, who lives with his family upstairs, while operating the brothel below. He has one purpose in life: to make his "perfect, innocent" daughter, Rifkele, into a marriageable candidate for a scholar from a fine family. He commissions the writing of a Torah which is to become part of his daughter's dowry. Instead, a prostitute from his brothel, Manke, and Rifkele have fallen in love which results in Yekel's rage and violence.

In *Indecent* Vogel chronologically takes the productions of *God of Vengeance* through different iterations, both real and imagined, over a swath of time to another level, focusing now on the two lovers and on the obscenity charges which were brought against it for its infamous lesbian scene (which played without incident before the Broadway production in the early 1920s). The play covers the sweep of history since Sholem Asch wrote the work, to the time he disowned it in the 1950's.

Indecent has a musical core in this robust production. Dramaworks' choreography, under the direction of Lynnette Barkley, working with its klezmer musical underpinning, is stirring, unforgettable, defining the emotion of the moment through dance, mostly to evoke the Jewish Horah circle dance but also including wonderfully arranged Berlin cabaret style numbers for dramatic effect.

Three very talented musicians weave Yiddish sound throughout the play. Glen Rovinelli is both the Musical Director and the Clarinet player. Anna Lise Jensen is the Violinist while Spiff Wiegand is the Accordion player. Music and dance were always important in Yiddish theatre and Paula Vogel incorporates these elements as a celebration of Jewish life and culture.

J Barry Lewis directs this *Gesamtkunstwerk* ("a total art work ...that synthesizes the elements of music, drama, spectacle, dance, etc.) with a multimedia mix of 155 slides projected on the wall in the background which make the story clearer, and scores of scenes (characterized as "blinks in time"), some as few as three or four lines, bringing clarity to the narrative. Plus he's working with seven actors playing forty different roles, telling multiple stories with subplots. It is a testament to his skill as a director to make it all seem natural and transparent.

He has the "help" of one character in the play, Lemml, played with such poignant conviction by Jay Russell, his PBD debut. Lemml is the only character played by one actor with no other parts in the play. He serves as the effective storyteller as does the narrator in *Our Town*.

Lemml stays with the play as its stage manager in each and every one of its performances over decades, to the point where he feels ownership but is ultimately betrayed by Sholem Asch who allows the play to be deleteriously edited for Broadway and refuses to defend it in court. All of this action is taking place while Europe's anti-Semitism is on the rise, and we suspect the fate awaiting Lemml and the troupe as they leave America to return to Europe.

Otherwise, this gifted ensemble cast plays multiple characters. When Lemml introduces the troupe, he divides them into three groups. First *the fathers, all of the mothers, the sagest of our characters, or the ones who remain fools at any age* played in this production by PBD veteran Laura Turnbull and by Mark Jacoby making his PBD debut. Both are seasoned performers who bring their long list of acting credits and accomplishments to their parts in this production. In addition to other characters, their main role in the play within a play is that of the father and owner of the brothel, Yekel, and his wife Sarah, who was formerly a prostitute.

Lemml continues: *And our members of the troupe who are in their prime!"* In this production there are two PBD newcomers. Making a stunning debut is Kathleen Wise who is Manke, the prostitute, among other characters. She sings and dances and acts flawlessly. Matthew Korinko makes his presence known with his rich voice, and convincing ability to play five roles, effortlessly changing from a NYC cop to the Rabbi Joseph Silverman, who brings legal action against the play.

Finally, Lemml says, *And our ingénues!...All the brides, all the grooms, the writers, the socialists. So ardent in their beliefs, so passionate in their lovemaking.* Here we have the seasoned PBD veteran Cliff Burgess who has the distinction of playing the younger Sholem Asch as well as Eugene O'Neill (briefly), not to mention three other characters. He always brings an ardent sensibility to every part. Finally, there is the PBD debut of multi talented Dani Marcus gorgeously playing Rifkele with six other brief roles. With her expressive face and exquisite singing voice, she adds a strong dimension to this incredibly talented cast.

When Marcus and Wise are on stage as Rifkele and Manke, their presence and chemistry is striking. They even play the roles of "The Bagelman Sisters" singing a rousing rendition of "Bei Mir Bist Du Schoen" which the Andrew Sisters would envy in a brief scene from Grossinger's in 1938. (I did mention that there were scores of scenes, didn't I?).

In most shows one can point to the star or co stars and evaluate their performance. *Indecent* is about an acting troupe and the entire Dramaworks cast becomes that troupe, feeling their pain and joy to such an extent that the audience is viscerally brought into this production. It must be an actor's dream to be in this troupe and it shows singing such songs as *What can you makh dis is America! Iz America, un vot ken you makh?* Or *What can you do? It's America! It's America, so what can you do?*

Michael Amico's scenic design is in keeping with the ghostly acting troupe on stage, so there is empty space, reminiscent of ruins, in which the actors can tell their story.

Lighting design by Paul Black includes light changes intended to provide a sense of the location rather than the reality of the location. The lighting is also suggestive of those dark dramatic moments with nightmarish shadows on the back wall, as well as a cabaret feeling of Berlin in the 20s.

With so many characters being played out over decades, costume designer Brian O'Keefe scores another triumph of period piece and ethnic identity verisimilitude including quick costume changes (many right on stage). Brad Pawlak's sound design focuses on the musicality of the production.

One cannot emerge from this production after its famous love scene in the rain without a sense of wonder. Perhaps it is also the intimacy of the PBD theatre itself. When you are so close to the action in this play, and it is in constant motion, you simply feel part of it. You may leave with the love scene in your heart, but Paula Vogel's imagined words of Sholem Asch which precedes that gut retching joyous scene sound a clarion warning call to the arts, immigration policy, and tolerance: *I no longer care what is done on the stages of this country. Theater companies are started by young men who have the luxury to care about where they live. Or the false belief that they will be allowed to live in the place they care about.*

A blink in time.

Saturday, December 8, 2018 Lyle Kessler's 'House on Fire' Rages

This World Premiere of Lyle Kessler's *House on Fire,* signifies a play destined for a sustained life in the theatre world. If Kessler's name doesn't spring to mind as quickly as a Sam Shepard, David Mamet, or Edward Albee, these are American dramatists with whom he has much in common. He has several new works in development. *House on Fire* is among his most recent, and it builds in many ways on his highly acclaimed *Orphans* (1983) which is still being performed throughout the world and was later made into a movie starring Albert Finney. Another new play of his, *Perp,* will open in New York next March.

House on Fire's setting is Fishtown, a working class neighborhood in Philadelphia, with its collection of row houses and bars, "on the edge of the Delaware River, home of killers and robbers and four flushers." The element of gritty living hangs heavily in the play as does the legacy of great family plays, with sons striving for acceptance by the father.

This is where the "Old Man" lives with his son, Dale, the brother who still lives at home. Together, they tend to a newsstand which garners a modest living. Dale is a loner who has been writing stories, carefully depositing them in a safe in his room far from prying eyes. This is the repository of real value, words. Writing or "extrapolating" is Dale's method of survival.

He is the sensitive twin brother to the vagabond son, Coleman, whose survival MO is flight. After a ten year self-imposed absence, Coleman rushes home upon learning his father has just died. He finds Dale standing by his father's body covered under a blanket on the couch. Already, things seem unreal, why wasn't the body moved for nearly two days?

Here the "fun" begins, Kessler revealing his gift for vivid, jousting dialogue, expletives galore, particularly the black comedy which runs throughout the play. The sons amusingly argue back and forth as to whether the father is really dead. Dale, gullible, insists he is. Coleman claims it's a ploy to get him back home. We later learn the Old Man has sorrowfully marked thousands of X's on his bedroom wall, one for each day since Coleman left home.

The itinerant Coleman has been followed by a one-armed misfit, Noah, and his sister, Lane, both of whom he befriended while he was on the road, Noah saying "We come across the Great Divide" (either literally from the West Coast or figuratively crossing over from another life). Noah is the product of his own dysfunctional family, a dominating mother who had but three words for her son: "Good for nothing." He becomes a petty thief, and a protector of his sister, who has magical powers of hearing and feeling. Coleman, who they've renamed "Tokie" had been "adopted" by the two of them, rescuing him from the gutter. All of them, sons and intruders alike, find the Old Man to be the center of gravity in this metaphorical and mystical universe of Fishtown.

Kessler walks a fine line between naturalism and absurdism, embedding parables, Aesop's Fables, baseball metaphors, and a form of magical realism into his play which is as funny as it is thought-provoking. Borrowing my own baseball metaphor, this is not a play which is a fast ball down the middle. Much of the action dances unpredictably like a knuckle ball, hard to hit unless one has patience and chokes up on the bat. If you wait out the pitch, there is a discernible arc to the play. Five characters in Fishtown attempt to become a real family, connecting them to the fish in a mythical lake of Dale's imagination, creatures not understanding a world beyond the lake, and beyond that a "great mysterious universe." Kessler zooms into each character with a granular clarity and zooms out placing this theatre experience in a transcendental perspective.

At the heart of Kessler's writing is his characters' need to connect no matter what the underlying vicissitudes of their upbringing or environment. He underscores this layer of reality by examining the fungibility of truth. The Old Man's take on the subject says much about his son's struggles to find themselves: *People who proclaim the truth are speaking a lie. A lie lurks under every truth. A lie is just sitting there biding its time waiting to emerge triumphant. I'll take a Liar every time over a Truth Teller.* Is it no wonder they feel the Old Man sucks all the oxygen out of the room?

World premieres are a director's and actor's joy as well as extraordinarily challenging, tasked with the responsibility to first interpret the playwright's intensions where none have gone before. Both William Hayes, the Director, along with Kessler, started the auditioning process together, looking for actors who had the right chemistry, ones who are quirky and can act with great heart. Check that objective off with this production!

In spite of a number of physical confrontations in the play, successfully orchestrated by the Fight Choreographer, Lee Soroko, for authenticity and safety, Director Bill Hayes leans heavily towards the interpretive light of hope for each character, for reconciliation of the family itself and a reconstituted family. His pacing of the play brings out the comedy, making the vulnerabilities of the characters as apparent as their volatility, the play taking on a fully realized life of its own.

The "Old Man" is mesmerizingly played by PBD veteran actor, Rob Donohoe, who also played Dodge in the PBD production of Shepard's *Buried Child* several seasons ago. The two characters couldn't be more different. Dodge was a wretched alcoholic, and the Old Man is animated, opinionated, and even lovable at times. It is a testimony to Rob Donohoe's acting abilities to portray the foul-mouthed Albanian newsstand owner and long time Phillies fan so naturally, clearly finding his character's humanity, and in so doing making him larger than life. Donohoe's interpretation is true to Noah's description of him, *he is a rugged individualist, maybe the last of the breed*. His performance is a tour de force.

His sensitive son, Dale, is also a PBD veteran, Taylor Anthony Miller, who has to balance his need to be heard while being the more passive sibling. It is a difficult role to play but Miller heartbreakingly captures the essence of a person whose very existence is dependent on his imagination, his ability to "extrapolate" or write, while secreting those writings in an actual safe. He must keep his writing 'safe' from exposure, particularly from his father, whose criticism he has endured his entire life. Miller is deeply moving in allowing us to see Dale's scars, brightening up once when the Old Man compliments his imagination by replying, *That is the nicest thing you've ever said to me*.

Dale's twin brother, Coleman ("Tokie") is explosively played by PBD newcomer, Hamish Allan-Headley, with an omnipresent level of anger and cynicism. Allan-Headley modulates this fury when he allows his guard down with his father, showing us his vulnerable side. In spite of being a damaged soul, he clearly loves his brother, uneasily bearing the guilt of having abandoned him for ten years without a word of communication.

This is a man desperate to find his own identify and not succeeding. Drifting and drinking to black out has been his way of alleviating pain. Allan-Headley captures the drunken Coleman so convincingly that you could almost smell the alcohol on his breath. He is tripped up by Lane, the girl he left behind who has followed him with a secret of her own. Headley keeps a tight rein on himself, totally convincing the audience that he has returned home unwillingly, only to be forced to confront his own demons.

Christopher Kelly, a PBD newcomer, is the peripatetic, menacing one-armed Noah, with a sinister disregard for the residents of this ramshackle house, except when he feels praised by the Old Man. His sister's welfare is always paramount as well. Kelly spellbindingly captures his character's constant struggle to be accepted as a person of worth and to be appreciated as a protector. His is an impressive achievement, playing with one arm and mining Noah's raw explosive emotions.

His chemistry with another PBD newcomer, Georgia Warner, who plays his sister, is perceptible. Warner's Lane is lyrical, mystical, and Warner is intensely aware of Lane's role as an oasis of kindness in a sea of damaged men. Warner's Lane has a big heart, 1960's hippie style. She channels life itself and helps to bring this family together suggesting better times ahead.

The sharp personality difference between brother and sister is beautifully captured in one of their exchanges, when Noah says that *Reality is a sorry business* to which Lane ultimately replies *I prefer flights of fancy.* Her performance adds just the right leveling influence, a beautiful creature, yearning for love and stability. She becomes the light that draws all these damaged men to her.

In addition to a perfect cast for director Bill Hayes to work with, his technical crew shines. Scenic design by Bill Clarke is reminiscent of the home of the hoarding Collyer Brothers. The past hangs heavily from every nook and cranny of the stage, old magazines, baseball books, posters, baseball cards, bats, stuff shoved here and there, including the soffits. It is the external chaos of the inner life of the man who inhabits the house. It's just a masterpiece of staging.

There is a bank of lights stage right to depict the one-way light into the row house, and to help define the different times of the day or night, one scene to the next. Lighting designer Donald Edmund Thomas also supports the magical realism of the play with dirty lighting (as opposed to clear lighting) and provides motivating lighting in sync with the character's emotional cues.

Brian O'Keefe's costume designs ingeniously depict the atmosphere of the play and an amorphous time period, but dress suggests anytime in the last couple decades. Coleman and Noah's apparel clearly reflect their knock about time on the road while Dale's is "working class casual." O'Keefe has imagined and executed the perfect outfits for the Old Man, the ubiquitous stained, off white undershirt and beloved baseball jersey. Lane naturally stands out from the men, with her fringed jeans, braided and beaded hair, billowy tops, reminiscent of the ethereal flower child of the 60s.

Sound designer David Thomas brings in some of the ambient outside sounds you'd hear on an urban street but these are unobtrusive and for atmosphere. The music played at scene changes are clearly to give the audience permission to smile, even inviting tapping one's toes, all mid century baseball music, some of which I've never heard. Naturally, "Take Me Out to the Ballgame" headlines these.

Kessler has something important to say about human nature, the family, and the existential nature of existence itself – whether the "balls and strikes" are being "adjudicated" by a "Deaf an' Dumb God." *House on Fire* is the work of a playwright of consequence and Dramaworks' spirited and affecting production of its World Premiere gives it wings.

Sunday, February 3, 2019 'The Spitfire Grill' Serves Up Hardy Fare

An exuberant production by topnotch professionals convincingly delivers *The Spitfire Grill*'s message of the redemptive power of forgiveness and second chances. This compelling effort by Palm Beach Dramaworks' cast enhances the play's many transformational high points, as satisfying as meat loaf with mashed potatoes and a helping of hot apple pie for dessert. American literature and theatre has always been susceptible to the wholesome yet troubled heartbeat of small town life, Thornton Wilder's *Our Town*, Meredith Willson's *The Music Man,* William Inge's *Picnic*, Sherwood Anderson's *Winesburg, Ohio*, and in film Frank Capra's *It's a Wonderful Life*. Add this production of *The Spitfire Grill* to the list, distinctive and deeply moving in its own way.

The music and lyrics by James Valcq with lyrics and book by Fred Alley is based upon the 1996 film by Lee David Zlotoff, but with an unabashedly (and in these times desperately needed) upbeat ending. While in prison our young protagonist, Percy Talbott, prepares for her life as a parolee by randomly cutting out a photograph of the fictional town of Gilead, Wisconsin in resplendent fall colors from a travel magazine. She chooses this as her serendipitous destination upon release. But she finds it a depressed community; people on guard about her, including the local Sheriff, Joe Sutter, who declares she's come to a place to leave (projecting his own feelings). There is no real employment other than at the centerpiece of the town, the now failing Spitfire Grill, a diner owned by cantankerous Hannah Ferguson who has been trying to sell it for years.

The townspeople come and go through this diner, ultimately revealing their own figurative prisons. Hannah's nephew, Caleb Thorpe, is still bitter that the stone quarry closed, losing his job as foreman. He's lost his self respect, dominating his timid wife Shelby who ultimately comes to help out at the diner. The postmistress, Effy Krayneck (names don't get much more vivid than that) carries the town gossip and supplies some much needed comic relief. There is also the mysterious stranger who never utters a word but stalks the action.

This incendiary mixture ignites a cathartic yet palliative plot for revealing secrets and allowing the town to see itself in a new light. The awakening begins with an idea Percy suggests – aided by her persuasively written contest copy -- to give the outside world an opportunity to enter an essay contest with a $100 fee "Why I want the Spitfire Grill." Those essays arrive in increasing numbers, and with heartrending content.

This dramatic musical is delivered with soul searching intensity by an outstanding cast and musical accompaniment. It is not a big Broadway production but is reminiscent of Sondheim's work where language and song seem to merge, and the inner thoughts and feelings of the characters are transported by the lyrics. Each performer in the PBD's production is ideally suited to his or her part, making one wonder whether they are exceptionally talented actors who can also sing, or professional singers who can also act.

Ashely Rose, her PBD debut, plays Percy, the parolee with a dark secret, a shocking past. Rose carries her character's deeply seated hurt and trust issues with a defensive jadedness; slowly opening up to the community as friends are made and ultimately secrets are shared. She once played the lead in *Always...Patsy Cline* and here she delivers her songs with that country sensibility, always reaching those notes of loneliness and powerful emotional truths that country music so often evokes. Rose's comedic talents are on full display in her number "Out of the Frying Pan" as she sings this country song while wrestling with the demands of cooking, frantically juggling pots and pans, reminiscent of a Lucille Ball. Her show-stopping song near the end, "Shine," is both musically heartrending and dramatically affecting. It is at this moment that she finds the light, the "shine" in herself and can cast off her past.

Amy Miller Brennan's performance as the initially introverted, browbeaten Shelby, is metamorphic as she blossoms into an independent woman right before our eyes. She and Percy bond at the Grill and it is there she sings her beautiful ballad to Percy "When Hope Goes" revealing the day the town's childhood hero went to war, Hannah's son, Eli, much admired by the town, never to return and changing the town forever. Brennan has an exceptional musical theatre voice, so ideally suited for pairing to Rose's as is evident in their duet, "The Colors of Paradise." Also a PBD newcomer, her passage from Caleb's often abused wife is heartening to witness, culminating with her song, "Wild Bird" consoling Percy in her arms.

This is also a play about three wildly different women miraculously bonding and the bedrock of that triumvirate is the veteran many PBD productions, Elizabeth Dimon. She's the prickly, hardened Hannah, the owner of the Spitfire, who through her interaction with Percy and Shelby finds a family and redemption. She, like Percy, has carried a sad secret and is ultimately able to cathartically expunge it. Her beautiful musical rendition of the dirge like ballad, "Way Back Home" displays her talents both as a singer and an actor.

Johnbarry Green makes his PBD debut a poignant success through playing the part of Caleb Thorpe, the nominal villain as he dominates his intimidated wife, Shelby. But at heart, and Green brings this out with such conviction, he is a man who has been emasculated by the loss of work, and changes brought on by the passing of time over which he has had no control, the audience feeling his pain while he sings "Digging Stone." Green showcases his character's loss of self respect with a heavy, mystified force. Ultimately he too finds release from the prison of his own making with his clear baritone voice adding conviction to his acting and depth to his songs.

It is also the PBD debut of Blake Price as the Sheriff, yet another character who has failed to see the beauty of his surroundings and yearns to leave this sagging town for greener pastures. Then he suddenly meets Percy and has a new insight on how his life could flourish right where he lives. Price's strong tenor voice and handsome face win the audience over to him, rooting for something positive to come from his relationship with recalcitrant Percy. Indeed, the outbound train that he had imagined being on now has "one less passenger," as he sings his moving solo ballad "Forest for the Trees."

PBD veteran of six productions, actress Patti Gardner, plays the busybody postmistress Effy Krayneck with comic ease and in perfect harmony with the cast. Gardner also imparts her character's inherent loneliness, and in the end finds her emotional place in the community, having "the thread" and "finding the needle."

David A. Hyland is the "The Visitor." Hyland is a PBD veteran and it is strange to see him in a non-speaking role, but his hulking pained figure on stage speaks volumes about the past and regret, and tears easily well up in his eyes about his life. Suffice it to say, the audience quickly surmises who the "Visitor" is and how he relates to the core of the story.

Director Bruce Linser has many musical credits on his resume, including last season's smash hit, *Woody Guthrie's American Song*. He knows how to manage a complicated musical, and, in spite of its outward simplicity, there are so many moving parts to this show, different scenes, and times of the day, seasons, and the evolution from depression to outright joy, all of this in a relatively small space. Scenes are changing on one side of the stage as another is underway on the other side. Linser brings out the best from his talented cast and musicians, not allowing the characters to become stereotypes. Each has his or her own story, becoming fully integrated as the plot evolves.

The incredibly talented Lubben Brothers, triplets Josh, Tom and Michael (who were such a hit in *Woody Guthrie's American Song*) now perform under the show's musical director, Joshua Lubben, along with his talented wife, Katie. They form the orchestra for this show and resoundingly back the company with mostly piano, guitar, accordion, violin, or bass, the latter instrument underscoring the mournful moments. Some of the music has almost a liturgical feeling, although deeply rooted in folk and country, with many elements of Celtic music. Phrases are frequently repeated in a song, driving home meaning and emotion. Even when the cast is not singing there are often musical riffs played in the background.

Paul Black had the unusual task of being both the scenic and lighting designer. Accordingly, he could conceive one knowing what he would do with the other so there is a harmonic effect. This is a complicated play to design, the same challenges that Linser had to deal with in the performance space, he addresses in the physical space. At first I thought the scenic design too intricate until the performance was underway, each scene flowing into the next, actors passing from the figurative outside, into the diner, through the back door and to the outside once again. There are stairways to a second level which serve different scenes, including the opening one of Percy leaving prison and her concluding one, reaching the top of her emotional mountain. Lighting had to denote seasons, times, moods, and highlight one side of the stage while another was preparing for the next scene.

Costume design by Brian O'Keefe was similarly challenged given the cinematic, scene to scene, month to month, changes over a full year. These are realistic costumes to identify everyday people in rural Wisconsin. Think plaid, jeans, and mukluks.

Brad Pawlak sound design captures all this great music, and sounds from the woods – birds, geese flying overhead, and I thought I heard a few Wisconsin crickets. In spite of a very busy sound design, the sound and the musical accompaniment never overwhelmed the lyrics.

Indeed, "Something's Cooking at the Spitfire Grill." Palm Beach Dramaworks serves up this heartwarming musical story with skill and enthusiasm.

Saturday, March 30, 2019 *An Inspired Rendering of August Wilson's 'Fences'*

It begins sweetly, the easy jousting of two old friends, Jim Bono and Troy Maxson, so innocently that the audience is quickly ushered into their lives. Although these are two garbage men returning at the end of a work week in 1957 Pittsburgh, a bottle of gin to share, and are African-Americans, we identify with the universality of their banter. Troy has dutifully brought his weekly pay to give to his wife, Rose, and enjoys spinning yarns to his appreciative listener, Bono. So begins August Wilson's Pulitzer Prize winning *Fences* and steadily builds to a cathartic climax.

Palm Beach Dramaworks' Producing Artistic Director, Bill Hayes, also the Director of *Fences,* has undertaken to make this production a signature piece in his company's long history of triumphs.

Here the cast are all accomplished actors dedicated to the works of August Wilson, among the greatest of American playwrights. Many have played in several Wilson plays, often in the same role. Although just beginning its run, *Fences'* cast has already come together as a "family." Their performances soar, unforgettable, mining the heart of Wilson's poetic dialogue and the African-American experience many of us can only imagine. Here we get to viscerally walk the walk. It is enlightening and heart-wrenching.

Hayes takes the play to the very edge of Wilson's intent, wanting Troy's vulnerabilities and his humanity to be on full display. There is an element of "every-man" in the universality of the themes. He underscores the many comedic aspects of Wilson's first act, disarming the audience, leaving us all the more susceptible to the dramatic fire kindling beneath that will blaze into full fury. Hayes saves his most emphatic directorial statement until the end with a touch of magical realism but throughout, the director's vision coupled with his love of the play and cast is tangible and affecting.

This is no easy task as the span of the play's eight years is panoramic and emotionally consuming. And its main character, Troy Maxson, is a conundrum of a character, full of tragic flaws and yet possessing traits of nobility along with a disarming honesty. He is larger than life, an inherently good man who has been seriously damaged by his father, poverty, and the disadvantages of his race, and deterministically visits the sins of the father upon his sons. In so doing he impacts the lives of all in his orbit. And like many of us, he is wrestling with his own mortality, symbolized by his imaginary encounters with death, building a fence to metaphorically keep the grim reaper out.

Making his PBD debut, Lester Purry's portrayal of Troy Maxson is seismic and when he is on stage it's as if all the oxygen is taken out of the room by his performance, his forceful voice reaching one's very solar plexus. He alternates between accepting his lot in life, assuming his responsibilities, and then helplessly allowing his subliminal rage of victimization to rise to the surface. He is intransigent about his beliefs and can be a terrifying bully, particularly toward his son, Cory.

It all starts with Troy's own father who was a failed sharecropper, tantamount to being a "free slave." His father had one mandate for his son: work. As Troy recalls, he had taken a 13 year old girl by a creek when he was supposed to be working. His father finds him and begins to whip Troy with the reins from a mule. He realizes that his father was chasing him *so he could have the gal for himself.* They fight but in the end, his father beats the 14 year old Troy senseless.

He has a "cutting down" period when he is incarcerated for 15 years, having unintentionally committed murder during a robbery, becomes a star baseball player in the Negro leagues afterwards, marries Rose, and becomes a garbage man in Pittsburgh. When Troy says *you got to take the crookeds with the straights*, it is a baseball metaphor which has grown into how he now looks at the world and becomes his advice to his sons. Yet there is always the resentment that he was denied the chance to play baseball in the major leagues, "born too early" to break the color line.

As one of the best plays of American theatre, each character has real depth and development. Troy's wife, Rose, is played by PBD veteran Karen Stephens. This part was Stephens' dream role. She displays her comically loving moments with a heartfelt admiration of Troy, and even when he humiliates her, she accepts her situation. From Wilson's stage notes, "She recognizes Troy's spirit as a fine and illuminating one and she either ignores or forgives his faults, only some of which she recognizes."

Her performance intensifies when Troy confesses that he's been having an affair. In fact he's going to be a father. He rationalizes that this relationship is separate from his love for Rose (implying that he's staying with Rose), saying this other woman makes him feel special, and that for 18 years (with Rose) he feels like he's *been standing in the same place.*

Stephens now agonizingly tells Rose's version of the truth: *....I've been standing with you! I've been right here with you Troy. I got a life too. I gave 18 years of my life to stand in the same spot with you. Don't you think I ever wanted other things? Don't you think I had dreams and hopes? What about my life? What about me.... You always talking about what you give... and what you don't have to give. But you take too. You take... and don't even know nobody's giving!"* Those words illustrate the poet in the playwright, some repetition to drive home themes, the rhythm sublime.

Other than Rose, nearest to him is his sidekick, Bono, worshiping Troy, and serving as a sounding board and Troy's conscience. PBD's veteran, John Archie, reprises his recent Florida Repertory Theatre role as Bono, the best friend who articulates the thematic heart of the play *some people build fences to keep people out and other people build fences to keep people in. Rose wants to hold on to all of you. She loves you.*

Archie wrings out all the emotion portraying Bono who, towards the end of the play, comes by one last time to give Troy a loving tip-of-the-hat to acknowledge that "[you] learned me." By this time, Troy is a very lonely man finding consolation in his gin.

Much of the play's drama focuses on Troy's relationship with his two sons. Troy bestows his own peculiar kind of love on the one hand and his ever present wrath on the other. Each is caught up in his own generational perspective, Troy's formative years being so different than his sons. His fatherly skills rise only to the point of wanting his sons to find "responsible work," expecting they abandon their own dreams. But in his heart he simply does not want them to turn out like he did.

Lyons is his older son from a previous relationship with a woman who left Troy while he was in prison. Warren Jackson in his PBD debut plays his part with a benign, arms-length acceptance of his father. There is some playful back and forth between Troy and Lyons, his son always borrowing some money from Troy, his father holding that over his head, admonishing him to get a real job, not as a part-time musician. Jackson conveys the absent father theme, like a leitmotif saying *hey Pop why don't you come on down to the grill and hear me play?* He knows the answer will always be an excuse and Jackson's expressions of regret are never lost on the audience.

Troy and Rose's biological son Cory is played by Jovon Jacobs, his PBD debut. Jacobs just finished a highly praised engagement as Walter Lee in New City Players' *A Raisin in the Sun*. He has an explosive relationship with his father, Jacobs showing his character's developing strength of conviction, distain for, and then willingness finally to challenge his alpha male father. His is another bravura performance, seething with heart hurt fury.

Cory is the depository of all his father's shattered dreams of sports glory, the generational violence, and Troy's denial of Cory possibly playing football on a college sports scholarship. No, Troy insists, he must find a trade to survive in a white man's world, not accepting that times have changed. He demands that Cory address him as "sir." They finally have a highly charged climactic confrontation.

Cory knows a secret about his father, his using some of the money Troy's brother, Gabriel, gets from the government. Upon revealing this knowledge to his father, their verbal combat escalates into a terrifying physical brawl, stunningly choreographed by Lee Soroko.

Uncle Gabriel, Troy's brother, is masterly played by Bryant Bentley, also his PBD debut although a veteran of several Wilson plays. Having suffered a mentally disabling head injury in WW II, he is now convinced that he will play his broken Gabriel's trumpet to open heaven's gates one day. Bentley plays up the role with a moral purity and a child-like innocence frequently foreshadowing the action.

He loves Rose, usually bringing her a rose when he visits during his many wanderings through the streets. Gabriel is a symbol of African-American pain, his screaming incantations at the end of the play a stake in the heart of American racism. Bentley's performance is stirring, cutting through to truths about how our society marginalizes people of color or those with disabilities.

There is still another half sibling in the play, Raynell. We first see her as an innocent baby in Troy's arms who Rose agrees to raise after Troy's other woman dies in childbirth, and then as a delightful young girl at the play's end. Raynell's youthful innocence has a pivotal role in helping Cory get past his blind anger as they plaintively share the refrains of a song their father used to sing:...*I had a dog his name was Blue/You know Blue was mighty true/You know Blue was a good old dog* .... Ultimately there is forgiveness and hope for the future. The part of Raynell is alternating played by two local elementary school actresses, Jayla Georges and Raegan Franklin.

Scenic design is by Michael Amico who has created a masterpiece set by capturing a slice of a downtrodden Pittsburgh neighborhood in the 1950s. It rises on the PBD stage as a monument to the lives that are so accurately portrayed by Wilson. There life stubbornly pushes forth from the ashes of the past. Little patches of grass can be seen beneath the porch, and although two buildings next to the Maxson house are abandoned during most of the play, at the end there is life in them and it is spring.

Resident costume designer Brian O'Keefe nostalgically recreates the working class outfits of the economic and social station of the characters. Rose, in particular, with her changing housedresses and church going costumes and glorious wig, recall with perfection those outfits that live in the memory of the PBD audience. His usual attention to detail enhances the realism of the play.

George Jackson's lighting design bathes most of the production in full light with an occasional dimming spot at scenes' end. His dramatic lighting at the conclusion enriches the dramatic effect envisioned by Director Hayes.

Sound design by David Thomas focuses on realistic street sounds stage right, a barking dog stage left, and swirling wind as the play transits six years at the end, enhanced by musical blues riffs between scenes as well as some traditional 1950s jazz. (Wilson himself said the blues influenced his writing more than the work of other playwrights.) Thomas' sound and Jackson's lighting effects join together to offer a consoling conclusion to this incredible piece of work.

With *Fences* Wilson has written an ode to his protagonist, befitting his literary beginnings as a poet. The language is rich, rhythmical, and through the prism of the African-American experience. This production ranks as one of PBD's very best in many seasons of consistent achievements.

Saturday, May 18, 2019 **A Comic and Heartbreaking Rendering of 'House of Blue Leaves'**

Palm Beach Dramaworks' season concludes with its production of John Guare's Obie Award-winning play, *The House of Blue Leaves*. On one level there is a manic zaniness, a laugh out loud plot, but below that there is the characters' inherent desperation. Their lives are out of control. PBD's production unpeels all these disparate layers achieving exactly what Guare must have envisioned, giving us a play completely relevant for our own time, and for all time, demonstrating the futility of equating happiness with fleeting fame.

The plot is an ingenious situation comedy about a zookeeper who lives in his own menagerie in a Sunnyside Queens apartment in 1965. Artie

Shaughnessy is also a mediocre songwriter which he and his girlfriend, his downstairs neighbor Bunny, see as a ticket to stardom if they could only ditch his "crazy" wife Bananas in a mental institution. They are hell-bent to go to Hollywood where his boyhood chum, Billy Einhorn, has become a famous director.

There, Artie presumably will become a famous writer of musical numbers for film, but just to make sure, Bunny insists they must get the Pope's blessing during his trip from the airport, past their apartment on Queens Blvd, ultimately on his way to Yankee Stadium for a speech in 1965. (Indeed, the Pope made such a trip then with the world hoping his visit would help end the Vietnam War). Everyone wants in the action with the Pope, three Nuns who wind up in the apartment and the Shaughnessy son, Ronnie, who has gone AWOL from the military to "take care of" the Pope (if you know what I mean). Also arriving is Billy's hard-of-hearing girlfriend, the movie star, Corrinna. Why? Because Billy too will soon arrive in NY as they are planning to go off to Australia for Corrinna's ear operation (*Australia's the place for ears!*) and to film Billy's Australian epic, entitled, what else, "Kangaroo." Did I miss anyone? So sets the stage for a dramatic denouement while many animals in the Central Park zoo are giving birth simultaneously.

Here are all the elements of farce superimposed on the tragedy of a world gone inexplicable, which encapsulates the entire play in an absurdist undertow. The cast frequently breaks the fourth wall, engaging the audience directly, yet another unusual technique employed by Guare. This works brilliantly because it feels so natural. And how many playwrights compose their own songs and lyrics for a non-musical drama, with Artie frequently and frantically compelled to perform a lick or two on the piano?

In full disclosure, I lived in Brooklyn and Manhattan in the 1960's and was born and bred not far from the same Queens Blvd in the play, near where the playwright himself grew up. It's very personal to me, the geography, but most of all the events transpiring just at that time; the horror of the Vietnam War, the assassinations of JFK, RFK, MLK, Malcolm X, the transformation from the placid decade of the fifties to one of upheaval and anxiety. These were assimilated in our popular culture, our theatres, our literature, our newspapers and airwaves. They lurk below the surface in Guare's idiosyncratic *The House of Blue Leaves*. It was not terribly unlike today's wacky world, but without the Internet and social media. Yet, celebrity worship, fame and the quest for notoriety are among the play's driving themes.

Director J. Barry Lewis punches up the hilarity level so the audience starts laughing at the first glimpse of Artie, but to make this play work, he walks that fine line between slapstick and poignancy. In particular, Artie and his wife Bananas are not one dimensional characters, but fully fleshed out vulnerable human beings we can all relate to. Lewis knows exactly how to engage the audience to feel for them as well as laugh at them. A frenetic chase scene through the Shaughnessy's cramped apartment demonstrates Lewis' mastery of split second timing to squeeze every ounce of hilarity from his characters. And at those moments where pathos is called for, he is at the top of his game in wringing all the emotion out of his players and audience alike. It is another J. Barry Lewis directorial success.

Bruce Linser is Artie Shaughnessy, the struggling songwriter who is a zookeeper by day and lounge piano player/singer on local amateur nights. Linser is well known locally as a musical director and an accomplished actor as well. This is a tour de force role for him. He not only successfully brings his musical training to this part, but as an actor he brilliantly displays the vulnerability of a man who is out of control in his life, manipulated by the demands of his girlfriend Bunny who has beguiled Artie to reach way beyond his abilities. He is also the victim of an American Dream of fame gone haywire. There is a deeply touching desperation in his portrayal of Artie, a man who more than once says *I'm too old to be a young talent* with such comic sadness.

Linser is especially effective in suddenly changing course, showing true love and care for his unstable wife, resisting attempts to institutionalize her on the one hand, but ultimately relenting to Bunny's demands and his own need to escape. He thus finds her a "home" which he describes to Bananas as one where there are beautiful blue leaves on the trees. He looks at her lovingly and at times holds her with the love of yesteryear. Linser makes Artie an everyman tragic figure, succumbing to the demands of his exterior world. Artie, who frantically sought a blue spotlight when we first meet him playing the piano at a Queens Blvd lounge, gets his blue spot at the end, the metaphor full circle.

Besides Artie, the most fully realized and developed character in the play is Bananas, played by Elena Maria Garcia, whose antics on stage are belied by sudden clarity of thinking, sometimes the only really sane person as the fool was in Elizabethan drama. As with her son, there is a shame based scar from her past, but in her case, her imaginary past. Garcia sits on the edge of the stage and tells the story to the audience which culminates in her being humiliated on TV, Garcia achingly relating *Thirty million people watch Johnny Carson and they all laugh. At me...I'm nobody... Why can't they love me?*

In some ways, the character of Bananas could be compared to Mary Tyrone or Blanche Dubois from conventional award-winning dramas. Although essentially a comedy, Garcia brings her character into the tragic realm with her acting and Guare's incredible script. Like Mary Tyrone, Bananas is a victim of drugs, not morphine but psychiatric drugs which deprive her of the ability to feel. Her fear of leaving the apartment for treatment relates to those drugs: *I don't mind feeling nothing as long as I'm in a place I remember feeling.* Shock treatments add to her disorientation and fear of institutionalization.

It is a role that cries out for an actress who can sustain detachment, looking blank and uncomprehending, yet grasping the significant moments. She is a woman fighting for her life. Garcia's performance is heartbreaking as she struggles to stay home and to help her son Ronnie as well. Her facial expressions while other actors are engaged speak volumes of pain and even insight.

The comic fulcrum of the play is Vanessa Morosco's performance as Bunny Flingus, Artie's downstairs neighbor and wife in waiting, as soon as they can get rid of Bananas. Morosco's portrayal of Bunny is primarily played for laughs which keep coming. She has a burning ambition for Artie (and therefore herself) to make it big in Hollywood with the help of Artie's friend, Billy. Morosco is a gifted physical comedian as she struts in her high heels and leopard tights or skin tight skirt. Guare gives Bunny some of the best comic dialogue in the play, but even when not delivering lines, the audience is primed to crack up by Morosco's gestures alone.

Bunny admits to being a bad lay and will sleep with Artie at the drop of a hat. But she is holding out something much more special for her marriage: *My cooking is the only thing I got to lure you on with and hold you with. Artie, we got to keep some magic for the honeymoon.* This comes up again and again and has a bearing on a twist in the plot later. It is hard to believe another actress could give this role that sexy, zany, eccentric punch that Morosco delivers so effortlessly.

Austin Carroll plays Artie and Bunny's son, Ronnie, who opens up Act II with an audience heart to heart about his damaging experience when he was a 12 year old boy. He had heard that Billy Einhorn, his father's best friend from Hollywood, would be visiting NYC to cast his movie, "Huckleberry Finn." He secretly prepared himself for an "audition" and Carroll then manically demonstrates the memory of that night, laughing and crying, wildly dancing across the stage concluding with a hilarious dying swan ballet gesture. Billy just assumed from his bizarre behavior that he was mentally challenged and that humiliation set Ronnie on a course for revenge, his objective to be on the cover of *Time* magazine. The Pope's arrival gives his delusions flight. More fodder for the absurdist tilt and the theme of seeking fame or in this case infamy.

As the Pope is parading by on Queens Blvd, Billy's girlfriend, Hollywood starlet, Corrinna Stroller arrives. PBD veteran of untold productions, Margery Lowe, dials up the laughter as her hearing aids give out and she pretends to understand people, perplexing other characters by her amusing inappropriate responses.

To add to this farce, suddenly three nuns show up, played by Elizabeth Dimon, Irene Adjan and Krystal Millie Valdes. If the first two names sound familiar it is because they have appeared in many South Florida productions, including PBD. It was fun to see them in cameo roles. It is Valdes' PBD debut as "the little nun." All three nuns seek their own moment of fame and surround the TV so they can have photos taken of them "with" Jackie Kennedy or Mayor Lindsay. As Adjan exclaims *Mayor Lindsay dreamboat! Mayor Wagner ugh!* But when they spy Corrinna, they really lose it. More celebrity worship, with the "A list" celebrity, the Pope himself appearing on the "sacred shrine:" a black and white TV with a rabbit ear antenna.

We finally meet Billy, the successful Hollywood director, played by PBD veteran Jim Ballard. Reclining on the couch he says, *Good to see you Artie* with teabags covering his weary eyes. Ballard is convincing as a Hollywood mogul, one who must surround himself with people and admiration, delivering the supremely ironical line to Artie: *You're my touch with reality.* And some foreshadowing: *Love is all Bananas needs.*

Pierre Tannous plays the Military Policeman who comes to round up Ronnie and throw him in the military brig and Tim Bowman the Institution Orderly who Artie called to pack up Bananas for the Funny Farm.

Palm Beach Dramaworks' technical crew work hard to bring off this absurdist comedy with a relatively large cast. Brian O'Keefe's costumes more than meet the challenge and I suspect the award-winning designer had a ball conceiving them, particularly Bunny's over the top 60's garb. Such a pastiche of leopard tights and pink sweater with plastic booties and later her gold speckled black high heels with a skin tight skirt and dazzling brocaded waist-cinched jacket take your breath away. You simply cannot imagine her looking any other way.

Bananas' outfits, by contrast, solidly reflect her broken mental state, particularly the old flannel nightgown and "shmata" blue sweater and frayed robe which reflect her disheveled personality, a sharp contrast to her one appearance in an elaborate dress with fake flowers and multiple crinoline petticoats doing a runway fashion walk saying *it's a shame it's 1965. I'm like the best dressed woman of 1954.* Billy's outfit screams Successful Movie Mogul, with his suede jacket, cream silk scarf, and huge gold chain hanging on his chest. And of course, unremarkable Artie is irresistible in his serviceable Zoo Keepers khaki shirt and other nondescript clothes of a typical hard working put-upon sixties man.

Scenic design by Victor Becker showcases the shabby apartment that might have seen better days when Bananas was well and could keep up with the housekeeping. Now it simply reflects the exhausted state of the tenants who are barely hanging on. Their apartment is oddly pressed up against another apartment house with Ronnie's bedroom seemingly built into that building, and has an outside fire escape at an odd angle neither going up or down – a hat tip to the absurdist sense of reality. The space allows just enough room for a hysterical chase around and over the furniture. Even the wall photos reflect a happier time when Bananas and Artie and Billy and his wife would frequent hot spots in the city.

Steve Shapiro's sound design is branded 1965 by music such as "Hard Day's Night" and sound clips of the Pope's speech in the background. Shapiro also "plays" Corrinna's hearing aid breaking down with an exaggerated piercing sound which early hearing aids made, all part of the hilarity.

Lighting by Kirk Bookman is mostly full on with characters bathed in light, with appropriate lighting for the opening lounge scene and then finally the blue spotlight turning into a stage bathed in blue for the dramatic conclusion.

Shows like this are rare with realism, absurdism, comedy, and tragedy coexisting, toggling from one to another and, equally rare, a theatre company that can find that exquisite delicate balance.

Saturday, October 12, 2019 **A Journey Like No Other – Dramaworks' 'A Streetcar Named Desire'**

Palm Beach Dramaworks has skillfully and compellingly taken on an American theatrical masterpiece, Tennessee Williams' *A Streetcar Named Desire*. With their capable staff, technical crew and resources but particularly in the indefatigable hands of Director J. Barry Lewis, the theatre company has brought together actors who deliver with every fiber of their being. The drama is high pitched and gut wrenching.

It is a play for all times but perhaps especially these times, when cultural warfare is underway. *Streetcar* is a battlefield where the weak are ravaged by the powerful, where ethereal aspirations are bludgeoned by the brute force of animal spirit and cultural ignorance. How Williams could be so prescient is the question I ask myself. Did he see the Norman Rockwell American Dream devolving after WW II and extrapolate into this new reality, perhaps his greatest play?

When Stanley Kowalski makes his appearance, he throws a blood-stained package of meat to his wife, Stella, like a hunter's "kill". It immediately establishes one half of the dramatic equation in the play. The other half is the arrival of Stella's sister, Blanche, who appears from a different era, the antebellum south, in shock and disbelief as she tries to negotiate the symbolic streetcar "Desire," which runs along Cemetery Road, to find Stella's home in "Elysian Fields," an ironic description of a place Blanche could never image as her sister's home. Ironic too that she comes as a faded shadow of her former self.

So the stage is set for the eventual confrontation between these two highly charged, but unequal forces. It is Stanley who says to Blanche at the climax *we've had this date from the beginning*. Williams seems to posit that the Meek will not inherit the Earth, but instead a dystopian world of carnal pleasure and poker will prevail, full of pain and alienation.

Williams' play is set apart from other American classics by its language. He was a poet at heart and to listen to the dialogue is akin to being at a free verse poetry reading, the language exquisite in its own right.

Emblazoned in our collective memory of the play is the film version with Marlon Brando reprising his Broadway role as Stanley and Vivian Leigh reprising her role as Blanche from the London production. But those memories quickly fade watching the PBD version; director J. Barry Lewis' textualist interpretation of Williams' work establishes a powerful, moving production, with superb acting.

Knowing Kathy McCafferty's outstanding performances in past at PBD I had expected her to take on the pivotal role of Blanche with a sense of ownership. And she does. Perhaps at first one might make mental comparisons to Vivian Leigh but McCafferty quickly dispels such thoughts and makes the case for why live theatre is so different than two dimensional movie depictions.

McCafferty's Blanche is the nucleus around which the other major roles orbit, Stanley, Stella, and Mitch. Their interactions become exceptional by McCafferty's catalytic performance. She walks a fine line between fantasy and reality, at times fighting to retain her dignity confronting Stanley but as the play evolves, hers is a losing battle, taking long baths "to calm her nerves" and slipping into dream-like reveries about her one husband of long ago, a teenage marriage, a boy who was denounced as a degenerate. She danced with him to the Varsouviana polka the night of his death and those reveries in her mind play fragments of the music, and the suicide shot that killed him. He was a poet; he was cultured; he was sensitive: all the qualities that modern life has increasingly marginalized. Blanche lives in expectation of finding those traits again in a man who will offer her love and protection, in spite of a past she wants to forget.

McCafferty leans on her character's flirtatious inclinations in her dealings with Mitch and even Stanley. She can turn on the charm and sees it as her last bastion of youth. That ability painfully reveals a window into her past though when a young man (John Campagnuolo, his PBD debut) comes to collect for the newspaper. Alone in the apartment, she toys with him but finally says to the bewildered young man: *Young man! Young, young, young man! Has anyone ever told you that you look like a young Prince out of the Arabian Nights? Well, you do honey lamb! Come here. I want to kiss you, just once, softly and sweetly on your mouth!* It is an act of remembrance of things past and highly effective in the overall drama, foreshadowing what is to come.

Williams increasingly turns from the early realism in the play to symbolism to make his statement about Blanche's deteriorating condition and obsession with death such as the figure of the Mexican seller of flowers for the dead. Williams even comments on his dramatic style through Blanche: *I don't want realism. I want magic.*

McCafferty has the difficult role of portraying Blanche already on the edge, her incredulity at having arrived at this place, at this moment of her life, and then devolving into complete fantasy. She moves between emotional levels, sensitive to sound, light, sadness, regret, but carrying some fantastical hopefulness. Her erratic persona is as if she is in a play of her own making. Director J. Barry Lewis choreographs her stage movements like a trapped animal while emphasizing her melodramatic tendencies. This is clearly a once in a lifetime role for an actress of unparalleled talent. The audience was clearly mesmerized by McCafferty's performance.

Blanche's first introduction to Stanley is through a photograph her sister, Stella, hands her of him in his army uniform, Stella cautioning her sister that she shouldn't expect him to be like boys they knew back home at Belle Reve which was the plantation where they grew up and was squandered by the family, leaving nothing. Stella comments that he is *a different species.*

Danny Gavigan, a PBD newcomer, has played Stanley Kowalski before and he brings with him that experience as well as the necessary physicality to play the role. He is a terrifying presence on stage, swallowing up the space and dwarfing everyone around him. Stanley is given to sudden bursts of rage, constantly feeling he's being conned by Blanche, and is intent on exposing and destroying her. Yet as much as he is the alpha male, Gavigan cries out "Stella!" while in a prostrate position. He is totally dependent on Stella loving him, although he is ruthless in his behavior toward her. It is hard to feel much sympathy toward him, but his acting is remarkable in portraying that sexually dominant male who refuses to let anyone best him, in bowling, at work and even when fighting in the war which perhaps affected his aggressiveness. But it is his nemesis Blanche who threatens him by stepping between him and his wife, lying about her past and weaving fantastical tales which literally brings out his savage side.

And it is on his terms that Annie Grier (PBD debut) playing Stella loves him. She's torn between supporting her sister, even in some of her fantasies, and placating Stanley. She is the go-between. Neither work in the end and Grier's performance of her failed attempt is sadly reflected in the arms of her neighbor, Eunice, as Blanche is led away to an institution. Fundamentally, Grier's Stella is captivated by Stanley's brutal sexuality. She gives a compelling performance steeped in joy of her impending motherhood and palpable pain in not resolving the hatred between the two people she loves most.

One character bridges both worlds of Stanley and Blanche. Brad Makarowski (PBD debut) plays Mitch, a well-meaning but flawed character, portraying him as "one of the boys." But he is more than that. He is devoted to his mother who is dying, and although having served with Stanley in the army and being a poker buddy, also has an artistic bent, carrying a silver cigarette case with an inscription by Elizabeth Barrett Browning, *And if God choose, / I shall but love thee better—after—death*. This deeply impresses Blanche, who was an English teacher who had to leave her town in disgrace.

Until Blanche's past is cruelly and crudely revealed by Stanley, Blanche and Mitch are drawn to each other, her seeing him as her last chance and he seeing her – with his mother dying – as a possible wife. Makarowski negotiates a delicate dance with Blanche, wanting to be a "gentleman" but having desires. He is in the climactic scene with Blanche when she tells him about the death of "the boy" – her husband.

Although the long monologue is Blanche's scene, Makarowski's pain in hearing the story culminates in his moving closer to her, drawing her into her arms, and saying *you need somebody. And I need somebody, too. Could it be – you and me, Blanche?* Finally he kisses her. Williams' stage notes say "Her breath is drawn and released in long, grateful sobs," Blanche says the last line of the 2nd act, *Sometimes – there's God – so quickly!*

The boom is lowered in Act 3. Mitch confronts her about her past after being a no-show for her birthday celebration. Stanley has told all the true gossip about Blanche to Stella, but Mitch in particular. At first Blanche fantasizes he has come back to apologize for being late for their date, but no, Mitch is there to utter the words that break Blanche forever: *You're not clean enough to bring in the house with my mother.*

At the conclusion Blanche is carted off in an enigmatic haze (here she delivers the iconic line, *I have always depended on the kindness of strangers*) past another poker game. While this scene plays out Mitch mostly stares down at the poker table in shame and anger until finally as Blanche passes by he takes a swing at Stanley and then returns to stare at the table. It is his tragedy too. Although a more secondary role, Makarowski makes it memorable.

What is played out between Stanley and Stella – a tempestuous, but devoted relationship -- is also reflected in a minor and sometimes humorous subplot between their upstairs neighbors, Eunice and Steve, played convincingly by PBD alumni, Julie Rowe and Gregg Weiner. The occasional violence of their relationship foreshadows the Kowalskis.

Rounding out the cast is Thomas Rivera; Suzanne Ankrum (PBD debut); Renee Elizabeth Turner; and Michael Collins.

Although this is a long, serious drama, with two brief intermissions, it flies by, a testament to J. Barry Lewis' direction. There is humor embedded in parts and Lewis is careful to allow a pregnant pause for the humor to sink in emitting some laughter from the audience. One of the sound effects is a sudden screeching cat. Blanche's nervous system is always on the edge and at one cat screech she even leaps into Stanley's arms. Such humor helps makes this masterpiece a true human tragedy.

The scenic design by Anne Mundell anchors the entire production. Most notably is the openness of the stage. There is no place for Blanche to hide, from people, sounds, and light. It is a cold hard set, not the Belle Reve of her youth. The set design literally takes your breath away when entering the theatre.

Costume design by Brian O'Keefe focused on colors to contrast to the set and while the working men of the play are dressed as they would be in post WW II New Orleans, either coming home from the factory, or for playing poker, or, for Mitch, a suit and bow tie going out on a date with Blanche. The big challenge is the number of dresses Blanche required, with several costume changes right on stage. The design and colors speak southern belle, and especially Blanche's white lace gloves.

Lighting by Kirk Bookman bathes the stage in dappled light, allowing the time and date to dictate colors and intensity. Festive lights dangle from the top of the stage. This is decidedly New Orleans.

As the Kowalskis live near a railroad, the rumble of a train is occasionally heard and this is just one of the many effects sound designer Abigail Nover (PBD debut) introduces. Mostly it is the sounds of the city, New Orleans music, at the time the jazz capitol of the world, and the haunting refrains of the Varsouviana that are heard during Blanche's reveries. J. Barry Lewis makes the most of these sounds during the most dramatic moments, particularly a train rumbling by.

There are not enough superlatives to commend this production. Take a theatrical ride of a lifetime on *A Streetcar Named Desire*, live theatre at its best.

Sunday, December 8, 2019 **"Yoo-Hoo, Mrs. Goldberg!" 'Ordinary Americans' has a Deeply Affecting World Premiere**

Palm Beach Dramaworks' co-production with GableStage of Joseph McDonough's *Ordinary Americans* made its triumphant World Premiere on the Dramaworks' stage. This new play peels away to the truth of what it means to be human and to be vulnerable to political polarization, demagoguery and anti-Semitism. Playwright Joseph McDonough's insightful script touches us all, especially today. The 1950s may have been "the placid decade," but underneath all the apparent innocence of the times American politics and ethnic relations were as fractious as they are now.

It is an ironic title as the characters in this play were anything but ordinary, especially our protagonist, Gertrude "Tillie" Berg who brilliantly and single handedly conceived, wrote, and starred in *The Goldbergs,* first on radio and then TV for more than two decades. Her extraordinary accomplishments, as a woman, and a Jew, particularly in a man's world echo throughout the play. Yet she, her colleagues, especially Philip Loeb, fell victim to McCarthyism. The play resonates with the feeling that the ghost of Roy Cohn still stalks the land.

Ordinary Americans is performed on a nearly barren stage, serving a multiplicity of scenes in different places, the audience basically having to fill in for Michael Amico's imaginary scenic design. It is the logical platform for those scene changes, fluidly balancing the play's highly dramatic moments and humor to underscore its serious themes.

It is a memory play, opening with a scene in a diner in Ohio (circa 1958), the *I Love Lucy* program on the diner's TV, quickly transitioning to the NBC studios in NYC in 1950. There stands the indefatigable Gertrude Berg, playing her spiritual doppelgänger, Molly Goldberg, surrounded by her TV cast in spotlighted tableau, her husband, "Jake Goldberg" (played by David Kwiat as Philip Loeb), and "Uncle David" (played by Rob Donohoe as Eli Mintz), as well as her lifetime assistant Fannie Merrill (played by Margery Lowe), and TV Production Manager for the show Walter Hart (played by Tom Wahl). All are PBD veterans except David Kwiat who is making his PBD debut. This dramatic "snapshot" of the major characters truly sets the stage for the story they will tell.

Elizabeth Dimon's performance as Gertrude Berg is so graceful that we forget we are watching a consummate artist at work. While radiating genuine warmth as *The Goldbergs'* creator and star, Dimon's "Tillie" does not suffer fools when crossed. Yet, like her creation Molly, she too has a heart of gold. Her TV family is her family. In fact, at times she wonders "what would Molly do in this situation?" Or "sometimes I think Molly is a better me than me." It is a difficult role to execute, a bifurcated person, yet Dimon believably conjures both Tillie and Molly's kindness and humor. If one wonders how Dimon can play this part with such heart and soul, it's because the play was originally her idea as well as her dream role. She's been with the play since its inception and a couple of years of workshopping it at PBD. A perfect fit for such a seasoned actor.

Dimon shows the other side of her character, an increasing frustration, especially in a maddening chaotic scene in her imagination of her being surrounded by potential advertisers or networks, screaming at her, multiple voices simultaneously. Dimon slowly comes to the conclusion that her Tillie is at the end of her rope yelling *PLEASE LISTEN TO ME!* And then finally having to admit to herself that it's *the first time in my life I feel helpless.*

While Tillie is the creative engine of the *The Goldbergs* program, and clearly the master of her fate, she is surrounded by people dependent on her for their employment. At the top of the list is Philip Loeb, who David

Kwiat deftly portrays as the perpetual optimist, an advocate for just causes, such as Actors Equity. It is he who has to cope with the consequences of being on the infamous John Birch Society sponsored pamphlet of 151 artists and broadcasters entitled "Red Fascists and their Sympathizers," otherwise known as "the Red Channels list." (Tillie observes that the way they define "communist" is *anyone they don't agree with, union organizers, activists, artists* and especially Jews.)

Kwiat is the ideal Philip, always hoping for the best, for himself, his colleagues and his son who needs institutional help. He skillfully portrays Philip as a man suffering increasing desperation; his world falling apart under appalling injustice. Kwiat's final scene in front of the House Un-American Activities Committee is powerful as well as heartbreakingly pitiful, as he finally cries out, *Leave me alone...I'm a citizen and a human being. You can't take these away from me.* It is a brave performance. You will not forget his exit near the play's end.

Tillie's right hand gal, Fannie, is effectively played by the PBD veteran Margery Lowe, along with another minor role as "Mrs. Kramer" in *The Goldbergs* show itself. Lowe, who is the accomplished professional having appeared in a number of PBD productions over the past, again comes through in these important supporting two roles, the efficient, buoyantly supporting Fannie, and her brief moments at a window as Mrs. Kramer, bellowing out *Yoo-Hoo, Mrs. Goldberg!*

Another long-time PBD veteran, Rob Donohoe, plays a number of roles, showcasing his versatility. As Eli Mintz he is "Uncle David" in the show, adding humor and Greek chorus support in the background, Yiddish accent and all. Eli Mintz is the play's Cassandra; always thinking the "Red List" will metastasize into something serious for the show (he was right of course). His interaction with Philip in particular is filled with much needed humor and affection for his colleague.

His portrayal of Cardinal Spellman is purposely pedantic, which speaks to Tillie's private admonishment of the man, *All politician, no clergy.* He's also the voice of the grand inquisitor, a Senator from the House Un-American Activities Committee bellowing out at Philip with eerie "witch hunt" hysteria assisted by David Thomas' sound design

Donohoe has a brief hilarious role as the diner owner in Dayton Ohio, fumbling his words, touting chicken salad as his special, and pretending to know the play, *The Matchmaker* by Thornton Wilder, which Tillie has come to Dayton late in her career to play, her television show now an apparition of the past.

PBD veteran Tom Wahl is a jack of all trades in this show, playing a number of roles, not an easy task to differentiate them all, but succeeds amazingly. First and foremost, he is Walter Hart, *The Goldbergs* Production

Manager on the set, played with exasperation on making deadlines, clip-board in hand. He also plays other key roles: as Roger Addington, the General Foods executive who first brings the "Red Channels List" to Tillie's attention, requesting that Philip Loeb, whose name is on the list, be removed from the show, but backing down as Tillie responds: *no one tells Gertrude Berg to fire anyone.* While Addington takes her no as a temporary answer, he warns Tillie worse is to come.

As Frank Stanton, the President of CBS, Wahl expresses empathy yet the firmness which earned Stanton's reputation at CBS as being a "son of a bitch." It is an affecting scene, Stanton and Tillie, Stanton demanding that Tillie fire Philip Loeb, and Tillie refusing, yet again. Wahl walks that fine line evoking some audience sympathy for the character trying to cajole Tillie (*We're survivors in this business.*). The stalemate ends in the cancellation of the show.

Wahl plays still another "one of those men in suits". a young ad execu-tive, who Molly hopes will help find a sponsor for her reconstituted show which has been off the air for a year (now without Philip as her husband and set in the suburbs of all places). Wahl's ad man recounts the facts: *It's 1955. Nobody has ethnicity anymore...Celebrate the Unity....People want to see ordinary Americans...Molly Goldberg had a good run. Let her rest in peace.* And while sensitively delivered by Wahl, Tillie now stands alone finally mouthing the plaintive line, so achingly delivered by Dimon, *Molly, Goodbye Molly.*

There are many seamless scene transitions in this memory play and this is where the excellence of Director Bill Hayes and his technical crew shine. Where actors need to be with split second timing is a key to the play's success and this work is generally invisible to the audience, without cur-tains being drawn. It leads to lively pacing, and Hayes knows when actors should slow their pace, or even pause, to let the play's funny moments land securely.

PBD newcomer Christina Watanabe's lighting design is critical in this play, such as, the subtle flickering of lights when a TV showing *The Milton Berle* or *I Love Lucy* shows is on the restaurant or bar, or the sudden burst of full lighting when cutting to the studio scenes. Or most effectively (and affecting) the lighting during the Hearings, Philip Loeb in a solitary spot, alone on stage except for Tillie watching from her memory in the shadows, and then during the news report of Philip Loeb's suicide, the lights slowing coming up in muted yellow bathing the audience itself, as if we're part of the same story today.

Sound design is usually important for mood and background, but takes on another level of importance in this show. It of course has the req-uisite musical interludes, especially different takes on the music that was associated with *The Goldbergs*, Toselli's gentle waltz, "Italian Serenade." Sound designer David Thomas also had the challenge of delivering lines from the play, electronically enhanced echoed questions being thrown to Philip Loeb during the Hearings, and the cacophony of news headlines crying out about McCarthy's accusations, teletype clacking in the background, and haunting sounds in Tillie's mind.

PBD resident costume designer, Brian O'Keefe, cleverly decided to go with red, white and blue palettes against the barren stage, in particular Tillie's red dress with a wide satin collar and pearls, a jacket to delineate important meetings. Of course, TV Molly became easily identifiable with her added white apron as a "typical" housewife of her time. Fannie was normally dressed in dark blue while the men wore subdued grays, all outfits mid fifties perfect.

This is an important play, constantly underscoring themes that are so significant and germane to our current, often stressful, times. Joseph McDonough's *Ordinary Americans* joins the canon of classic plays honorably based on aspects of our own dark American history, ones that remind us to heed our past.

CHAPTER III

OTHER THEATRE AND
MUSICAL RIFFS

This is the most eclectic portion of this work, but it is not intended as simply a catch all of everything else I've written in Lacunaemusing.blogspot.com. If it was, it would be many times longer. Living first in New York City and later in Fairfield County, Connecticut for a good portion of our adult lives, and frequently traveling to London where the West End beckoned, and participating in other meaningful cultural events in Palm Beach County in more recent years led to yet other opportunities to broaden our cultural education. One of these opportunities for me has been to give performances as a pianist, focusing on the Great American Songbook. Music is part of the larger picture of what makes us human.

I've taken liberties with this chapter. Some books are reviewed here as they relate to music. And as the Table of Contents indicates multiple topics might be covered in some entries. Many of the reviews are of plays or musical performances we have seen at the Eissey Campus Theatre, Maltz Jupiter Theatre, Florida Stage, or the Westport Country Playhouse, but these are highly selective. I also cover some performances in London and New York City.

These productions have a commonality: the reasons why I sought them out and then finally decided to review them, toggling back and forth between music and theatre as it is chronologically arranged.

A symbiotic relationship exists between music and the times we live in. We can trace such a relationship back to the era of the emerging classical pieces of a Hayden, to the groundbreaking music of Beethoven at the time of the French Revolution, to the later Romantic Movement, to the abstraction of Shostakovich and the modernists, and so on. This relationship exists in our popular music as well.

Two of the many musicals I review in this chapter make this very point: the recent "re-imagined" *Oklahoma* and the new *Moulin Rouge*. As I commented on them: "these are our times, brutish and violent, frequently unfair, sometimes steeped in narcissism and eroticism, a kind of dystopian landscape captured by the remake of one of our most innocent musicals (*Oklahoma*), and a movie (*Moulin Rouge*) brought to stage. But bravo to both as art marks the way and records our moment in time."

Joanne Lipman's article "A Musical Fix for American Schools" *Wall Street Journal*, Oct. 10, 2014, is especially pertinent for our times. It hit me as an epiphany when I read it. Perhaps you too have long lamented the state of our educational system, particularly the wide gap between the schools attended by the haves and the have-nots, and the little regard our current value system has for our educators. Especially deplorable is the fact that we pay our teachers a mere fraction of what we pay other professionals, lawyers, doctors, business people, not to mention entertainers and sports figures whose disproportionate salaries are offensive by comparison.

The issue here is not only about paying our educators more, and holding them at least on the same plane as we do other professionals; it's about radically revamping our educational system. Music democratizes education, allowing every child to participate on an equal footing, and teaches cooperation. According to Lipman, "research shows that lessons with an instrument boosts IQ, focus and persistence."

Why shouldn't our educational system incorporate extensive music education (and by that I don't mean only music history, but musical theory and practice, classical music, as well as jazz for its improvisational characteristics) into its curriculum?

Our music and our theatres have much to teach us about how we live our lives, and what it means to be part of a society whose very survival may depend on how we live with others. We need the arts not only as a diversion but also for instruction.

Sunday, January 27, 2008 **The Great American Songbook**

Kate Watson (the vocalist who I accompany on the piano) and I are preparing our next concert program, which will be devoted to Irving Berlin, Cole Porter, and George Gershwin, indisputably among the artists at the heart of the Great American Songbook (*GAS*).We have worked together for the past three years giving benefit concerts, paying tribute to the music of that tradition. I met Kate by answering her ad in the *Palm Beach Post* for a piano accompanist who is familiar with Broadway and cabaret style music. She has used her soprano voice and clear phrasing to entertain audiences for more than twenty years, performing in a variety of community events. I feel honored to work with someone with such experience and have learned much about the art of being an accompanist from this collaboration. It's about listening while one is playing, trying to stay out of the singer's way on the one hand, and filling in while she is not singing.

While I am not a naturally gifted pianist or have had much formal training, I continue to try to improve my skills by listening to a number of pianists I greatly admire such as the late Oscar Peterson and Bill Evans.

It was perplexing to read some obituaries of Oscar Peterson who died just last month. A few critics said Peterson's work was derivative or unemotional. While I was in college I had the privilege of seeing him at Birdland and ever since I have been in awe of his incredible keyboard abilities and followed his recordings. More than forty years later in 2006 he made his final appearance at Birdland to celebrate his 81st birthday. This is after he had had a stroke in 1993, underwent extensive rehabilitation, and learned to play again with his left hand partially impaired.

All artists build upon the base of the past and if Peterson "sounded like" other jazz pianists at times, he also advanced the art to another level. I think he could play more notes within a measure than any other pianist, classical or jazz. And his light touch never strayed too far from the melody and the intention of the composer, perhaps a shortcoming of some later avant-garde jazz styles. Goodbye Oscar Peterson.

Like Oscar Peterson, Bill Evans had extensive classical training and that was certainly evident in his interpretations and compositions. At times one can hear the spare, minimalist approach of an Erik Satie in his music, such as his rendition of "My Foolish Heart."

Evans was the consummate introspective artist, hunched over the piano as if he and it were one. His phrasing and chord voicing were innovative and unique. His numerous recordings, in my favorite jazz form, the trio, preserve his genius.

I was mindful of these two artists when I made two CDs at a professional studio last year. Not that my skills can be compared in any way to theirs. If you think of music as a language, they speak at a level I can only fleetingly understand, but I chose some of the pieces they've recorded and a few that they wrote. This was intended as an archival effort for private distribution to friends and relatives. The first album, *Smile*, was followed a few months later by *Sentimental Mood*.

The recording studio experience was intimidating, having about two hours to record the songs I selected for each CD and then an hour with the sound technician deciding what cuts to use and in some cases rerecording a song. I was given the option of wearing a headset to listen to what I recorded, and then merging different sections by picking up the song at a certain point. As I read chords and melody lines, and then improvise everything else, I rarely play a composition exactly the same way. Therefore, I opted to play each piece entirely through and then redoing it if I was not happy with the results. The six total hours in the studio were finally winnowed to two forty-five minute CDs. One of the pieces was an original composition I wrote to my wife, Ann. My CD selections are simply my favorites, an eclectic group as evidenced by the list at the end of this entry.

I suppose every older generation has a level of intolerance of the music of the younger generation. My parents did not understand the Rock & Roll music of my youth, which we now refer to as the "oldies." I am now guilty of not understanding today's music ranging from rap to the fare served on American Idol. At least the oldies are memorable and singable. Will that apply to today's popular music forty years from now?

A *GAS* melody is but one of the elements that makes the genre so timeless. Ultimately it is the perfect marriage of the melody and the lyrics, songs that carry meaning and drama, and can be interpreted by the performing artist. Thanks to the pioneers of the genre and their successors and performers, it will endure as long as people listen to music.

From *Smile*

Annie's Waltz Music by Robert Hagelstein; *Once Upon a Summertime* Lyric by Johnny Mercer, Music by Eddie Barclay and Michel Legrand; *A Day in the Life of a Fool* Words by Carol Sigman, Music by Luiz Bonfa; *Dindi* Music by Antonio Carlos Jobim; *How Insensitive Music* by Antonio Carlos Jobim; *Waltz for Debby* Music by Bill Evans; *Quiet Now* Music by Denny Zeitlin; *Someone to Watch Over Me* Music by George Gershwin, Lyrics by Ira Gershwin; *Love is Here to Stay* Music by George Gershwin, Lyrics by Ira Gershwin; *Can't Help Lovin' Dat Man* Music by Jerome Kern, Lyrics by Oscar Hammerstein II; *Ol' Man River* Music by Jerome Kern, Lyrics by Oscar Hammerstein II; *I've Grown Accustomed to Her Face* Words by Alan Jay Lerner, Music by Frederick Loewe; *Losing My Mind* Music and Lyrics by Stephen Sondheim; *Anyone Can Whistle* Words and Music by Stephen Sondheim; *Not While I'm Around* Lyric and Music by Stephen Sondheim; *I Won't Send Roses* Music & Lyric by Jerry Herman; *Look for Small Pleasures* Music by Mark Sandrich, Jr., Lyrics by Sidney Michaels; *Oh, What a Beautiful Mornin'* Music by Richard Rodgers, Lyrics by Oscar Hammerstein II; *That's All* Words and Music by Alan Brandt and Bob Haymes; *Blame it On My Youth* Words by Edward Heyman, Music by Oscar Levant; *Love Changes Everything* Music by Andrew Lloyd Webber, Lyrics by Don Black and Charles Hart; *Wishing You Were Somehow Here Again* Music by Andrew Lloyd Webber, Lyrics by Charles Hart; *The Point of No*

Return Music by Andrew Lloyd Webber, Lyrics by Charles Hart; *Memory* Music by Andrew Lloyd Webber, Text by Trevor Nunn after T.S. Eliot; *Someone Like You* and *This Is The Moment* Lyrics by Leslie Bricusse, Music by Frank Wildhorn; *Smile* Words by John Turner and Geoffrey Parsons, Music by Charlie Chaplin

From *Sentimental Mood*

In a Sentimental Mood by Duke Ellington, Irving Mills and Manny Kurtz; *Time After Time* Lyric by Sammy Cahn; Music by Jule Styne; *Moon River* Words by Johnny Mercer; Music by Henry Mancini; *How My Heart Sings* by Earl Zindars; *Once I Loved* Music by Antonio Carlos Jobim; English Lyrics by Ray Gilbert; *Nobody's Heart* Words by Lorenz Hart; Music by Richard Rodgers; *Old Cape Cod* by Claire Rothrock, Milt Yakus and Allan Jeffrey; *Charlie Brown Christmas* by Lee Medelson and Vince Guaraldi; *Take Five* by Paul Desmond; *Fortuitous* by Bill Oliver; *Laurentide Waltz* by Oscar Peterson; *Spring Can Really Hang You Up The Most* Lyric by Fran Landesman; Music by Tommy Wolf; *A Cottage for Sale* Words by Larry Conley; Music by Willard Robison; *Bewitched* Words by Lorenz Hart, Music by Richard Rodgers; *Where Your Lover Has Gone* by E.A. Swan; *Mona Lisa* by Jay Livingston and Ray Evans; *Isn't It a Pity?* Lyrics by Ira Gershwin, Music by George Gershwin; *What's the Use of Wond'rin'* Lyrics by Oscar Hammerstein II, Music by Richard Rodgers; *Another Suitcase in Another Hall* and *Don't Cry for Me Argentina* Words by Tim Rice, Music by Andrew Lloyd Webber; *Tell Me On a Sunday* Lyrics by Don Black, Music by Andrew Lloyd Webber; *Not a Day Goes By* Words and Music by Stephen Sondheim; *They Say It's Wonderful* by Irving Berlin; *Like Someone in Love* By Johnny Burke and Jimmy Van Heusen; *My One and Only Love* Words by Robert Mellin, Music by Guy Wood; *Solitude* by Duke Ellington, Eddie DeLange, and Irving Mills; *Look for the Silver Lining* Words by Buddy DeSylva, Music by Jerome Kern

Thursday, February 28, 2008 **How His Heart Sung**

My favorite gifts -- to give or to receive – are books and music. This past holiday Ann, and her best friend, Maria, who was visiting us from Sicily, gave me Peter Pettinger's biography *Bill Evans, How My Heart Sings* (Paperback; Yale University Press, 2002) and a collection of sheet music and books on theory, including the *Bill Evans Fake Book*, transcribed and edited by Pascal Wetzel from Evans' recordings. (A "fake book" gives the melody line and the basic chords, without arrangement, which the musician then has to improvise.)

Between the biography and the fake book I have a greater apprecia-tion of Evans' musical genius and can understand why he has been called the Chopin of jazz. I highly recommend the biography to anyone who has admired Evans, although you should be aware that as Pettinger was a concert pianist, the biography delves as much into the intricacies and structure of Evans' music as it does his life.

His life was tragic as he began a heroin habit in an effort to "fit in" when he first played with Miles Davis' group. This ultimately contributed to his early death at 51. But, oh, his music, the extent of which I was not fully aware until reading the biography and working on the fake book. His compositions are melancholy and ethereal, frequently changing keys and tempo, with unique chord voicings abandoning the root note. This leaves the listener with a feeling about the sound rather than a musical denotation, almost like comparing poetry to a short story. His classical training clearly comes through and one gets a sense of his Slavic heritage as well. As Evans said, "I have always hoped to visit Russia, to feel at first hand the roots of this part of myself."

Before the gift of *Bill Evans Fake Book* I was already familiar with his "Peri's Scope" and "Waltz for Debbie," probably among his best known compositions.

Delving into the fake book I discovered other gems and my favorite piece now is "Bill's Hit Tune," which Evans described as having "a quality of a French movie theme if played slow."

Then there is "Comrade Conrad," with its changing keys and alternating sections of 4/4 and 3/4 time. The soaring "Turn out the Stars" seems to evolve almost on its own accord and as abstract as it might be, it all makes sense. I think this piece reflects his deep classical roots and it might be his masterpiece. I also love his plaintive "Funny Man" and fragile "Time Remembered."

"Letter to Evan" is one of the few Evans pieces for which he also wrote lyrics. I think of it as a tone poem, beautiful in its simplicity. It was written for his son's 4th birthday; tragically Bill Evans would be dead only one year later. His son is a musician as well, writing for films.

Finally, I love playing the mournful, haunting "We Will Meet Again," which Evans wrote soon after his beloved older brother, Harry, committed suicide.

For the amateur pianist, playing Evans' work and trying to understand the structure of the music can be intimidating. I take encouragement from Evans' own definition of jazz: *It's performing without any really set basis for the lines and the content as such emotionally or, specifically, musically. And to me anybody that makes music using the process that we are used to using in jazz, is playing jazz.* So, I'll keep trying to play jazz, "music of the moment" as defined by Evans, and hopefully learning with the inspiration of these two gifts, Pettinger's biography and Wetzel's transcriptions of Evans' music.

Monday, April 7, 2008 **Hunger Artist Redux**

Last Friday we went to the Maltz Jupiter Theatre, where we have had a season subscription since the theatre opened five years ago, to see *Master Class*, Terrence McNally's Tony prize-winning play about the great soprano, Maria Callas. The play was based on classes she gave at Julliard at the end of her illustrious career.

The productions at Maltz have been inconsistent. Some are chosen to appeal to its diverse, mostly retirement age, audience and as such they are merely a pleasant way to pass the evening. But *Master Class* was unlike anything else this season or in prior ones, with a soaring performance by Gordana Rashovich who plays the iconoclastic diva.

We knew we were watching an extraordinary performance, one that vaulted a very good play into greatness. During intermission I stepped out into the breezy, balmy Florida night and was surprised to see a number of people leaving the theatre, overhearing objections such as they felt they were being lectured to, the play was too confrontational, or, even, disappointment there was not more music. These criticisms of course missed the whole point of what this play is about. It **was** a lecture; the audience is attending a "master class" which by the very definition is a place where students come to be taught, but the play is a conceit for us to see into the very soul of a true artist, the remarkable opera soprano, Maria Callas. And we <u>are</u> confronted by Callas' caustic observations about art and life, and her inner musings about her rivalries and her love affair with Aristotle Onassis.

The comment about not being "enough music" jogged a memory, while standing there in the Florida night, of the Franz Kafka's short story I read so many years ago, *A Hunger Artist*. Those details came flooding back as I watched a few people getting into their cars, driving off. Kafka's allegorical work portrays a "hunger artist" – a man in a circus sideshow who is a fasting artist, one who is literally starving himself to death for his art and for the spectacle of the masses. They ignore him, streaming past his cage, going off to see the lions being fed instead.

And similarly *Master Class* is about the artist's relationship to society and the sacrifice required to attain a level of perfection, one that Callas achieved in her career, and now Gordana Rashovich finds in portraying Callas.

All art is a solitary journey, for the creators and the performers, although in the performing arts it is a symbiotic relationship, somewhat of a contradiction for the performer who on the one hand must be a vessel for the creative artist's intention, and this was at the heart of Callas' performances (*listen to the music!* Callas demands of her students in the play), but on the other hand feeds on the approbation of the audience. McNally says, and Rashovich states with such conviction, that the performer must <u>dominate</u> the audience, in a sense to bring the audience to a level that the artistic creator intended. McNally and Rashovich make you actually feel the gut–wrenching sacrifices and demons that possess a great artist such as Callas and the art which she served.

Rashovich's performance prompted my wife to write her first ever "fan letter." It says volumes about this extraordinary performance...

Dear Ms. Rashovich:

I've been a devoted theatre lover since I was 16 and spent a summer visiting NY from my hometown of Atlanta, Ga. and saw a string of fantastic plays on Broadway that left an indelible mark. I moved to NY on my own in 1959 and saw every conceivable play I could afford and have been an insatiable devotee of live performance all my life, both in this country and abroad.

But last night, I felt privileged and blessed to witness what I can only say was such a tour de force as to leave me breathless. Your performance was so outstanding, nuanced and powerful, that it reincarnated Diva Callas before my eyes. I had seen this play years before in NY, but the actress was completely lacking in your ability to possess the role, body and soul.

I just want to say thank you, for all your hard work, years of dedication to your craft and for giving my husband and me such a thrilling evening, which we will never forget.

Saturday, April 26, 2008 *Stacey and Nicole*

Kudos to Rob Russell and his vision for the Colony Hotel's Royal Room. What used to be a storage room at the famous Palm Beach boutique hotel has been transformed into what the Oak Room is at the Algonquin, or Feinstein's at the Regency, or call it the Great American Songbook South. Last week we were fortunate enough to see Stacey Kent there. She may well be regarded as the new first lady of the genre. Very talented musicians back her up, in particular her husband, Jim Tomlinson, a superb saxophonist who produces her albums and is her business manager. He and novelist Kazuo Ishiguro wrote several new pieces for Stacey's recent album, *Breakfast on the Morning Tram*, four of which she performed.

What catapults an artist like Stacey Kent to the top of her field? First, she is completely dedicated to the genre, living the music. When she says that her very favorite lyric is from "People Will Say We're In Love," *Don't keep your hand in mine; Your hand feels so grand in mine* you feel it deeply when she sings those words as she did the other night.

Then, she articulates the lyrics while singing them, and when listening to the Great American Songbook selections, the words are as important as the music itself. Every nuance intended by the songwriter surfaces in her performance.

Stacey came to her art somewhat by accident, studying for a Masters degree in comparative literature in Europe where she met her husband who also arrived on the music scene via an academic labyrinth.. Her perfect phrasing is reminiscent of Sinatra's who was the master. But she is one-of-a-kind. Just listening to her rendition of "The Boy Next Door" underscores that observation.

After her performance at the Royal Room we chatted with her and Ann gave her a big hug, which was reciprocated. It's as if we've known her forever.

She reminds us of another great jazz singer, Nicole Pasternak, whom we've befriended and regularly see perform when we're in Connecticut, as the Northeast is her home base.

In some ways Nicole is a more versatile performer, belting out a Patsy Cline song as readily as an Irving Berlin classic. Stacey by contrast has honed a distinctive style, restricting her performances to the very songs and style she can make immortal.

It is hard for a regional performer such as Nicole to bring her talents to the national scene. I've been trying to find the right gig for her in South Florida without success. I'm more disheartened by this than Nicole who mostly sings just for her love of this unique musical treasure we call the Great American Songbook. Thanks to her dedication and to artists such as Stacey Kent this distinctively American cultural experience lives on for future generations.

Wednesday, November 26, 2008 *Coming to America*

It took a local concert to briefly snap me out of a funk.

We live near a local theatre, the Eissey Campus Theatre, of the Palm Beach Community College. Over the years we've seen some wonderful performers and concerts there, subscribing to series featuring The Florida Sunshine Pops, a 65 piece orchestra under the direction of the venerable Richard Hayman who at the age of 18 started as a harmonica virtuoso in the Harmonica Rascals and became a leading arranger and conductor. And he is still conducting an orchestra at the age of 88!

The series always includes some of the finest singers – light opera and Broadway voices – and the genre is generally the Great American Songbook, my favorite.

The first concert of the season, last night, was *Coming to America -- Celebrating The American People, Armed Forces and the individuals who chose America.* It was a night filled with memorable patriotic songs and marches. One of the very talented singers was Teri Hansen, a soprano, who has that something extra for the stage – a great presence, a performer who gives her all to an appreciative audience. One of her numbers was a rousing rendition of "Boogie Woogie Bugle Boy of Company B" and during the orchestral interlude she boogied down to the front of the stage and grabbed me out of my seat and we did a Jitterbug, one of the two dances I've mastered (the other equally complicated one being the Twist). I think Teri was a little surprised.

But the surprise was mine, walking to our car afterwards, remarking to Ann that the night had a special meaning to me because the outcome of the election made the patriotic theme all the more poignant. Where else but in the United States of America can a Barack Obama rise to the highest office?

The greatness of this nation is its ability to constantly reinvent itself. I wonder what Washington, Adams, Jefferson, and Franklin would think of their masterpiece that has managed to survive wars, both internal and external, slavery and reconstruction, depression, assassinations, and the constant ebb and flow of the political tides and, now, more than 200 years later, faces an epic economic crisis. Looking back at some of my prior writing, I lost sight of this underlying strength, our best hope of avoiding the fate of other great nations throughout history. It took a refrain from the "Boogie Woogie Bugle Boy of Company B" to remind me of our capacity to rise to such challenges.

Saturday, February 7, 2009 **West Palm Beach Hosts Sondheim**

As Stephen Sondheim would say, "life is Company!" A few days ago we saw the great man himself at the Kravis Center in *A Conversation with Stephen Sondheim* with musical examples. As Updike is to contemporary American literature, Sondheim is to contemporary American music. When he walked onto the stage, Ann and I held our breath: a living legend before us. We've seen many Sondheim shows and revivals and even have a small "connection" with him through our old hometown of Westport, Ct. where Sondheim served as an apprentice at the Westport Country Playhouse in 1950. But this was such a different experience.

I wasn't sure what such an evening might be like, although I suspected the venue would be a discussion prompted by a moderator, in this case Sean Patrick Flahaven the Associate Editor of *The Sondheim Review* with musical illustrations by Kate Baldwin who apparently was a last minute replacement for Christine Ebersole. Kate is a quintessential Sondheim singer, someone with a wonderful voice who articulates every word with the emotive intent of the song. The pianist, Scott Cady, was equally up to the task of communicating the subtleties and rhythms of the master's music.

In fact, that is what Sondheim's work is all about, the perfect marriage of lyric and music. As he explained in his "Conversation," "I write for actors." I watched him watch Kate sing the examples, wondering, exactly what was he thinking. Was he remembering how and when he wrote those pieces, or was he subliminally critiquing her performance, or was he just taking in the evening, as we were, a tribute to a legend?

I had hoped to hear more about the music itself, his comments on the particular pieces that were sung during the evening, but most of the night was about his reminiscences of his fabulous career. Having followed Sondheim, I was familiar with most of his musical works but was amused by some of the "inside information" he shared such as, in addition to *Sweeny Todd*, his musical *Into the Woods* had been prepared for film, although it never made it to the screen. This version was created with Jim Henson puppets alongside such luminaries as Robin Williams, Roseanne Barr and Steve Martin. With Henson's death, this project ended.

I also learned he wrote a musical, *Saturday Night*, in 1954 when he was only 23, but it was not produced until about ten years ago. I think of it as a precursor to his portrayal of urban life in his breakthrough musical *Company* (the first Sondheim musical we saw when we lived in Manhattan in 1970). *Saturday Night* has a breathtakingly beautiful piece "What More do I Need?" which Kate Baldwin sung as the opening example. I was so taken with it I immediately bought an mp3 copy on Amazon (very competently sung by Dawn Upshaw but I like Kate's version which is only accompanied by the piano) and then downloaded the sheet music from FreeHandMusic.com using the Solero Music Viewer (great service for musicians – allows you to buy just one piece, download it, even transpose it, and then print it). I've been sort of "consumed" playing the song since then. It can be seen on YouTube, sung by Anne Hathaway of all people (never knew she could sing so well).

Rodgers and Hammerstein brought the musical art to a new plane making the songs intrinsic to the plot. (Hammerstein in fact was Sondheim's mentor.) With *Company* Sondheim took the Broadway musical to the next level, and he has elevated it ever since. Sondheim is in a class of his own. As he explained in "Conversations" *Company* is not a plot driven musical. He thinks of it as it as a work of art you can look at from different perspectives and find different meanings.

Before seeing "Conversations" we rented the brilliant 2007 revival of the show, filmed for PBS and now available on DVD, staring Raul Esparza. Esparza's interview on the DVD is worth the price alone – how it feels to play in a Sondheim musical. *Company* is chock full of Sondheim's trademark conversational songs, works of art in their own right, looking at the foibles of relationships and what life means without them. Baldwin sang "Another Hundred People" from the show.

Most of my piano repertoire is focused on the great American Songbook, including the music of Stephen Sondheim. I regularly play his pieces; they are intricate, and while some are not necessarily melodic, many are beautiful, and all are memorable. His lyrics and music are so closely intertwined that just hearing the music is like looking at an impressionist painting without the brush stokes or reflections of light. But, I hear the lyrics in my mind as I play, and I am continually drawn to his work.

"Not a Day Goes By" is one of Sondheim's more poignant ballads which is sung twice in his 1981 musical *Merrily We Roll Along*, first as a statement of a husband's unequivocal love for a wife who now wants to divorce him, and then as a reprisal (in this musical time goes backward) on the day they were married.

Life is *Company*. Thank you Stephen Sondheim!

Tuesday, March 10, 2009 **Music For Our Times**

Maybe it is merely a coincidence that directly or indirectly through professional musicians I recently received emails with the text of Karl Paulnack's welcome address that was given to entering freshmen at the Boston Conservatory. Although this was made last September it is just making the rounds via email.

The timing of this address, at least the timing of it becoming well known at this particular moment in our economic malaise, is noteworthy. For the past decade we have "mortgaged" the country's future for fast, easy gains, and government, corporate America, and consumers alike have been complicit in this unprecedented moral breakdown, perhaps similar to the roaring 20's, resulting in the depressed 30's which only WW II could rescind. Today we are left with the consequences of failing financial institutions, declining residential and commercial property, and other gathering storms, bad consumer loans and ultimately failing municipalities as their taxing power is dependent on a strong labor market and real estate values, and finally inflation. And the global nature of the crisis just makes it more frightening. This collapse is building a crescendo of anxiety.

It is easy to think of the arts being irrelevant in such an atmosphere. This is the very idea that Paulnack's address contradicts. In fact, music is not only relevant but also essential to our survival. This address by the director of the Boston Conservatory music division who is also an accomplished pianist should be required reading during these tumultuous times.

Paulnack reminds us that even in WWII's concentration camps there was music. *Art is part of survival; art is part of the human spirit, an unquenchable expression of who we are. Art is one of the ways in which we say, "I am alive, and my life has meaning."*

Or after 9/11 the author remembers, *people sang around fire houses, people sang "We Shall Overcome." Lots of people sang "America the Beautiful." The first organized public event...was the Brahms Requiem, later that week, at Lincoln Center, with the New York Philharmonic. The first organized public expression of grief, our first communal response to that historic event, was a concert. That was the beginning of a sense that life might go on. The US Military secured the airspace, but recovery was led by the arts, and by music in particular, that very night.*

The essence of his message is *music is one of the ways we make sense of our lives, one of the ways in which we express feelings when we have no words, a way for us to understand things with our hearts when we cannot with our minds.* He therefore charges the incoming freshman: *I expect you not only to master music; I expect you to save the planet. If there is a future wave of wellness on this planet, of harmony, of peace, of an end to war, of mutual understanding, of equality, of fairness, I don't expect it will come from a government, a military force or a corporation. I no longer even expect it to come from the religions of the world, which together seem to have brought us as much war as they have peace. If there is a future of peace for humankind, if there is to be an understanding of how these invisible, internal things should fit together, I expect it will come from the artists, because that's what we do. As in the concentration camp and the evening of 9/11, the artists are the ones who might be able to help us with our internal, invisible lives.*

Perhaps this is one of those times when music *is needed to make sense of our lives.* Music is among the oldest of human activity (certainly predating economics!) and as Daniel Levitin states in his innovative work *This is Your Brain on Music,* an argument *in favor of music's primacy in human (and proto-human) evolution is that music evolved because it promoted cognitive development. Music may be the activity that prepared our pre-human ancestors for speech communication and for the very cognitive, representational flexibility necessary to become humans.*

One of my favorite melodies is from the depression years, the plaintive, ironical song, "Smile," written by Charlie Chaplin, for the 1936 film *Modern Times,* in which he starred. In the film, Chaplin's Little Tramp struggles to survive the Great Depression and the indifference of the modern industrialized world. The song's melody captures the sadness of the times while the lyrics remind us to *smile and maybe tomorrow, you'll see the sun come shining through.*

Tuesday, March 31, 2009 **He jes' keeps rollin' along**

Last night we had the pleasure of seeing the last of the season's Florida Sunshine Pops series of concerts, with its gifted, octogenarian conductor, Richard Hayman.

This was a special concert devoted to Rodgers and Hammerstein, the undisputed Broadway innovators who, with *Oklahoma!,* changed everything about the Broadway musical.

So yesterday's concert was a "grand night for singing" and that is what makes this series so special: the level of the talent and professionalism that accompanies the orchestra. Last night's featured performers were William Michaels, Lisa Vroman, and Stephen Buntrock all leading players on Broadway. They were joined by the Fort Lauderdale Gay Men's Chorus, giving a truly inspirational dimension to those particular songs that so readily lend themselves to choral accompaniment such as "Climb Every Mountain" or "Oklahoma!" (the title song of which we learned, last night, was written by Rodgers and Hammerstein in a half hour while the show was being previewed in New Haven).

Another highpoint was the Florida Pop's rendition of the beautiful "Carousel Waltz," no doubt orchestrated by the maestro himself, Richard Hayman. If it were not for Johann Strauss, Jr, I think Richard Rodgers would be known at the "waltz king" as so many of his greatest pieces were in three quarter tempo.

But for me, the solos by Michaels, Vroman, and Buntrock, were especially remarkable, not only for the quality of their voices but as Broadway trained actors, by their ability to communicate the emotion of the song as they comport themselves on the stage.

Naturally, I had my favorites, Lisa Vroman has a Julie Andrews voice and in fact sang "The Lonely Goatherd," the yodeling ditty so closely identified with Andrews from *The Sound of Music.*

William Michaels is currently appearing in the landmark revival *South Pacific* at Lincoln Center. His rich baritone voice lends itself to the role of Emile de Becque but last night he sang what some have called the greatest song from the American musical theatre, *"Ol' Man River"* from *Showboat* (artistic license: music by Jerome Kern, but lyrics by Oscar Hammerstein). Hammerstein described it as "a song of resignation with protest implied." Perhaps it is a song for our times.

Stephen Buntrock's rendition of "Oh, What a Beautiful Mornin'" the opening song from *Oklahoma!,* sung by the cowboy, Curly. In fact, Buntrock recently appeared as Curly in the Broadway revival of *Oklahoma!* so he follows in the tradition of Alfred Drake, Howard Keel, and Gordon MacRae. It's a delicate, beautiful song, an uncharacteristic opening song for a Broadway musical, but after all, this was the musical that established a new direction for the musical theatre.

Sunday, May 3, 2009 *Cagney!*

One of the admirable qualities about local theatre in South Florida, aside from the usual touring revivals of classic musicals and plays, is that some will take chances on innovative new productions. I'm referring in particular to original productions offered by The Florida Stage in Manalapan over the years. Yesterday we saw such a work -- *CAGNEY!* -- a world premiere at Florida Stage.

I was wondering how the life story of the famed Jimmy Cagney could be carried off as a musical and the answer is the passion and commitment of one man, Robert Creighton, the lead actor, who conceived the work, and wrote the music and lyrics along with Christopher McGovern. Creighton is also a dead ringer for Cagney and Ann and I were taken in by the play and his inspired performance. In fact we felt as if Creighton was channeling Cagney himself.

It is the rare creative genius who can bring it all together – the vision, the ability to write music and lyrics, and then to act, sing, and dance as well. Creighton is one of a handful of unique actors able to create such a work as CAGNEY! He joins Hershey Felder who was brilliant in bringing *George Gershwin Alone* to life, which we were fortunate to see at The Cuillo Centre for the Arts in West Palm Beach several years ago. It ultimately made its way to Broadway, and Felder was actor, pianist, playwright and arranger. (Believe me, as an amateur pianist I have a special appreciation for Gershwin and the skill needed to do justice to his music which embodies elements of jazz, ragtime, and classical.) No one could have accomplished that better than Felder, as no one could have created such a successful, moving musical on Cagney other than Creighton.

My Uncle Phil had a summer home in Stanfordville, New York where I used to spend time as a kid. Cagney bought a farm there in the mid 1950's, one that we frequently drove by, usually trying to catch a glimpse of the great actor, but Cagney kept to himself and was rarely seen in the area. *CAGNEY!* reminded me of those days and raised my interest in learning more about his life. The musical's level of detail and accuracy is remarkable.

But most impressive is *CAGNEY!* as a musical itself. This is not a little revue with some nice song and dance numbers. On a smaller stage it follows the principles of the great musicals of our times. The story line, songs and the chorography are woven together with one element advancing the other. We never felt that we were being "performed to" but, instead, brought into the action and moved every step along the way. The entire cast was outstanding, obviously being inspired by Creighton as well.

It also follows the traditions of excellence from the Great American Songbook with witty lyrics sometimes reminiscent of Cole Porter or Ira Gershwin, seamlessly woven into the music, appropriate for the era and the major themes. They brought out the tensions between Cagney and Jack Warner, Cagney's bulldog convictions, his devotion to his mother and his wife, and the accusation of his being a Communist sympathizer, an irony not lost by Creighton's depiction of Cagney as George M. Cohan in *Yankee Doodle Dandy*.

I hope that, as with Felder's work, *CAGNEY!* will find its way to a larger audience perhaps on Broadway. But my concern, after my generation dies away, is that there will be succeeding generations who care enough to preserve the memory of people such as James Cagney and, equally important, dedicated to carrying on the traditions of the Great American Songbook. Creighton's musical, not to mention his performance, accomplishes just that and I can think of no greater compliment.

Wednesday, July 14, 2010 **Happy Days**

What a cynical title for Samuel Beckett's brilliant play, courageously presented by the Westport Country Playhouse to celebrate its 80th anniversary. It is not the kind of light fare one might expect on a languid summer's night at a country theatre far off Broadway, and it was a brave choice by the Theatre's Artistic Director, Mark Lamos. But this is Westport, Ct - a bedroom community of NYC where we lived for so many years. In fact, we were there during the celebration of the Playhouse's 40th anniversary – half of its lifetime ago -- so although we are now only summertime visitors, its byways are subliminally imprinted on us.

Edward Albee, one of the many playwrights indebted to Beckett's trailblazing works, once said "I am not interested in living in a city where there isn't a production by Samuel Beckett running." So we've been lucky enough to live first in New York City, and then Westport and now the West Palm Beach, Fl area as well, the latter with its Dramaworks Theatre, producing plays "to think about."

And indeed *Happy Days* is the kind of theatre that one thinks about as much in retrospect as when one experiences it. In fact, I would have been happy to have had a Samuel French edition in my lap with a tiny flashlight to follow what is mostly an uninterrupted monologue. It is so rich in meaning and innuendo. Such a performance requires an exceptional actress and the Playhouse engaged the veteran actor Dana Ivey for the task.

My wife, Ann, had a personal connection with Ivey as they were two of the lead females in their senior high school play in Atlanta, Ga. something Dana Ivey either failed to remember or would like to forget. Ann saw Dana Ivey perform on Broadway with Morgan Freeman in *Driving Miss Daisy* and after the performance went backstage to say hello and praise Dana for an unforgettable performance. Ann was with two friends. Morgan Freeman first greeted them, said Dana was busy, but would be with them shortly. When she came out, she completely failed to recognize or remember Ann (an unforgettable person), and only vaguely remembered the extraordinary play they performed in or anything else relating to their high school experience. It was a shocking moment for Ann who minutes later laughed it off. I guess when one becomes a Broadway star you can afford to remember the past in any way you choose.

But credit is due Dana Ivy for successfully bringing the audience into Beckett's abstract world where days begin and end with a school bell and where we are all earth bound in an earth mound. Winnie in the first act sits waist up, at the top of her earth mound, carrying on mostly a conversation with herself, trying to read what is inscribed on her tooth brush and, finally reading the smallest print with the help of a magnifying glass, proclaiming it is another *happy day* as she has learned something new. Talking validates her existence as does the large black handbag at her side filled with her possessions. These are symbolic of our own possessions we tote around during our lifetimes, things that really own us than we them. She reminds us that these things *have a life of their own*. She arranges and rearranges the contents of her bag during the play which prophetically includes a pistol, carefully declaring a new place for the pistol which will no longer reside in her bag but by her side.

At one point, the earthbound Winnie ebulliently declares that she feels it is such a *happy day* that she should be able to ethereally rise into the sky, holding her parasol above her, one that mysteriously burns up and is tossed aside by her. Also, interestingly, except for Willie, her husband, the only other character who "makes an appearance" in the play is an ant, one that Winnie spies with her magnifying glass and carefully follows until it disappears under a rock. We are but ants in Beckett's universe, but with the ability to talk and, unfortunately, be aware of our own brief, inexplicable existence on this mound called earth.

Meanwhile she directs questions, demands, and criticism of her husband Willy played mostly off stage by Jack Wetherall. Unlike Winnie who is at the top of the mound, Willy mostly lives in a cave and has to be reminded by Winnie, as if he is a child, that if he enters the cave head first he might have difficulty backing out. There is humor in all of this, very dark humor, which takes a darker turn in the briefer second act when the bell rings and Winnie is now buried up to her neck in her earth mound, unable to move anything at all, including her head. (In fact, Beckett in his correspondence with the play's American director, Alan Schneider, when the play premiered at NYC's Cherry Lane Theatre in 1961, said of Winnie: "She simply can't move, that's all. Times when she can't speak, times where she can't move. Her problem is how to eke out, each 'day' and organize economy of these two orders of resources, body and speech."

It is at this point that Willie finally makes an on stage appearance, a disheveled and shaking old man, formally dressed in spats and tie who grunts and claws his way up towards Winnie, something that pleases her at first, falling back, being egged on by Winnie to try again. Is Willie reaching for Winnie or is it the gun, as the play and their marriage and perhaps their lives devolve to their abrupt end? Lights out. Curtain.

It was a night of powerful theatre. We exited to the parking lot. It had just rained and the humidity hung in the air, also rising off the steaming macadam and fogging our glasses. So we drove the back roads of Westport, returning to our boat, passing landmarks indelibly imprinted and always remembered such as the location of the old Westport National Bank (gone) turning left onto the only road that runs west and parallel to Riverside Avenue, along the southern side of the Saugatuck River, passing homes where we had partied in our youth (including one Christmas eve where guests in an alcoholic induced stupor set a couch on fire and it had to be dragged out to the snow to extinguish the flames), the building our first Internist once occupied (who later died in the same nursing home as Ann's mother), the Westport Women's Club where my publishing company held our annual Xmas party for so many years, my old office itself across the river where I worked for the first ten years in Westport, now the Westport Arts Center, past the street where Ann and I went for Lamaze classes when she was pregnant, over the old bridge crossing the Saugatuck, turning left then right under the Turnpike past the structure which used to be The Arrow Restaurant (long gone) where Ann reminded me they made her favorite dinner, crispy fried chicken, and then further west to Norwalk, all fragments of our own earth mound, being earth bound, trying to understand. Theatre to think about. Oh, happy days!

Saturday, July 24, 2010 **I Had a Session With Freud**

Thursday night we boarded a time machine which began on the ancient New Haven Railroad, the same cars I rode on decades before, still shuffling their way to Grand Central Station, laboring in the heavy July humidity and heat. The seats are worn thin with the years and most riders seem to be worn as well, with the exception of a sprinkling of younger people, their ears dangling with all the attendant cords from their iPods.

We were on our way to a New York premiere of a play that had been highly acclaimed when it was first performed at the Barrington Stage Company where it became the longest running play in the company's history, *Freud's Last Session* by Mark St. Germain. Our unlikely attendance at the NY opening was prompted by Bill Hayes and his wife Sue Ellen Beryl, the Producing Artistic Director and Managing Director of Dramaworks, our favorite theatre in West Palm Beach. They will be producing the Florida premiere of the same play in December and had planned to see the NY production. It was over a recent dinner in Florida that they offered to secure tickets for us as well.

There is a time machine portion of this story: The NY premiere was at The Marjorie S. Deane Little Theater at the West Side YMCA which is right next door to where we lived at 33 West 63rd Street. Since we lived there forty years ago, the West Side has dramatically changed, losing much of its original character. Our little apartment house is surprisingly still standing, dwarfed by behemoth high-rises on all sides, making it stick out like a sore thumb in its old fashioned hardiness.

As we were to meet Bill and Sue Ellen at the theatre and later, by invitation, at a gathering after the performance, we booked a table at a nearby restaurant, Gabriel's, to have a pre theatre dinner with a long-time friend from my high school days, Ed. This provided our "once a year" opportunity to look back over the last 50 years and as we always do, laugh at ourselves, and then fill in the news from the last year.

Freud's Last Session has all the ingredients that make for an evening of great theatre, some eighty minutes without an intermission that seemed to pass in eight minutes. The play is set in Freud's study in London, as WW II is breaking out, only weeks before his death, and portrays a fictitious meeting between Freud and C.S. Lewis, the renowned author and Christian apologist, where they discuss their polarized positions concerning the existence of God and the nature of man. It is a weighty discussion but much of the genius of the play is in the many moments of humor. Comedy brings out the best in serious drama.

Furthermore, the staging made it feel like we were indeed in Freud's study, and that WW II was just underway. Brian Prather is the scenic designer and Mark Mariani the costume designer. Martin Rayner IS Freud and Mark H. Dold a credible C.S. Lewis. Tyler Marchant's direction paces the production perfectly.

I could go into greater detail, but I confess, I saw the *New York Times* review which appeared as I was writing this. It covers most of the facts, although the review is inexplicably lukewarm, criticizing the play for having a "lack of tension" or lack of "suspense." There is plenty of tension, perhaps not in the traditional dramatic sense, but certainly of a cerebral nature. It is so well written, requiring thought and careful listening as well as an appreciation of the myriad subtleties, something the *Times* refers to as "clever talk." It is more than that.

I love the quiet ending, Freud left alone in his study to contemplate his discussion with his now departed guest, his own mortality, and the carnage that is about to begin, wondering how one reconciles WW II with religion, listening to the very music C.S. Lewis had admonished him for turning off after the news broadcasts. To me this was a logical resolution to the play, a sign that these opposites had indeed struck a chord in one another, even though their respective positions, Freud's atheism, and C.S. Lewis' theism, were left uncompromised.

It will be fascinating to see how this production migrates to the stage in West Palm Beach.

Tuesday, December 14, 2010 **Finishing The Hat**

This is one of the most remarkable documents of the theater that I've ever read, so exceptional in fact that I'm having trouble breezing through it, instead savoring every word. So even though I'm only half-way through, I'm writing a "first installment review," a respite from the political and economic shenanigans I've been held hostage to over the last few weeks. I prefer to think about great literature, music, or theater and *Finishing The Hat; Collected Lyrics (1954-1981) with Attendant Comments, Principles, Heresies, Grudges, Whines and Anecdotes* (Alfred A. Knopf, 2010) is a perfect tonic.

This is a detailed account of the American Broadway theater (1954-1981) written by our greatest living Broadway composer and lyricist, Stephen Sondheim, arguably the greatest ever.

As the subtitle hints, it is not only an erudite, introspective, and sometimes self deprecating account of his own works with the complete lyrics, both those retained and discarded for the shows he wrote during the period, it is also a frank discussion of the "major players" of his time, most of whom he of course knew or knows, and some of whom he did not but nonetheless influenced him in some way. I call this book "a document" as only a first-hand participant of Sondheim's stature could make his reminiscences a treasure-trove which will be studied by students of Broadway for years to come. We can eagerly await Sondheim's next installment covering the musicals after 1981.

Although as a young man Sondheim struggled to become known as a composer, *Finishing The Hat* understandably focuses on his lyrics as visiting his music in the same detail would require technical knowledge few of us mere mortals possess. He sets out his mantra for lyrics -- for which he gives attribution to Oscar Hammerstein, his mentor, and Strunk and White's *The Elements in Style* -- as follows:

1. *Content Dictates Form*
2. *Less is More*
3. *God is in the Details*

As an example of the latter he quotes his lyrics "Losing My Mind" from *Follies*, one of my many favorite Sondheim pieces, one that is in my own piano repertoire. Funny, I've played this song hundreds of times and never made the connection that as Sondheim puts it, *musically, this was less an homage to, than a theft of, Gershwin's "The Man I Love," with near-stenciled rhythms and harmonies* (although the lyrics are more along the lines of Dorothy Fields, a lyricist Sondheim holds in higher esteem than Ira Gershwin). Now I can clearly see the similarities, never noticing them in my many renditions of both songs. But the "God is in the Details" issue is from the last stanza of that song where Sondheim uses the word "To" in the fourth line from the end rather than the more prosaic "And."

No doubt Sondheim's best work begins when he is both lyricist and composer, finding the perfect marriage of the subtleties of the English language with the progressions and rhythms of music. But before establishing himself as a composer (although he was both lyricist and composer for his rarely performed earliest work, *Saturday Night*, in 1954), his friend, Oscar Hammerstein, persuaded him first to take on the role of lyricist for *West Side Story* with the renowned composer, Leonard Bernstein, who according to Sondheim, thought himself "poetic," which set up a continuing battle, Sondheim trying to write lyrics within the characters and Bernstein wanting an unrealistic poetic lyric. Sondheim then was too young and inexperienced and frequently had to accede to Bernstein's demands, something he is still not happy about. I love Sondheim's comments regarding the song "America": *Some lines of this lyric are respectable - sharp and crisp, but some melt in the mouth as gracelessly as peanut butter....*

While things went better when he collaborated with Jule Styne for *Gypsy*, he felt he was ready to write both the music and lyrics but the show's star, Ethel Merman, insisted on a "name" composer for the show. Nonetheless, Sondheim had respect for Styne, thought he captured the right atmosphere in the music for the show, and undoubtedly learned a trick or two from that collaboration.

His disaster collaboration was with none other than the great Richard Rodgers in the writing of *Do I hear a Waltz?* in 1964. This came on the heels of "two successful" musicals for which Sondheim wrote both lyrics and music, the commercially successful *A Funny Thing Happened on the Way to the Forum* in 1962 and the artistically successful (but commercial failure) *Anyone Can Whistle* in 1964 which, although it closed after only nine performances, was another great learning experience for the young artist, preparing him for greater successes in the future. The title song from *Anyone Can Whistle* is also one of my own personal favorites and when I play it on the piano I almost feel is if I am practicing a yoga exercise, "It's all so simple: / Relax, let go, let fly. / So someone tell me why / Can't I?"

Some, according to Sondheim, thought this particular song was autobiographical, to which Sondheim replies, *To believe [this song] is my credo is to believe that I'm the prototypical Repressed Intellectual and that explains everything about me. Perhaps being tagged with a cliché shouldn't bother me, but it does, and to my chagrin I realize it means that I care more about how I'm perceived than I wish I did. I'd like to think this concern hasn't affected my work, but I wouldn't be surprised if it has.* How's that for frankness?

In any case, back to his collaboration with Richard Rodgers, something he took on at the request of the, then, dying Oscar Hammerstein, and as a means to make a "ton of money" after the flop of *Anyone Can Whistle*. It was, as he admits, an act of self-deception, it made him *feel noble to sublimate my need to write music in order to support his [Hammerstein's] forlornly abandoned partner...Warmed by the personal aspects of the venture and rationalizing the right and left, I agreed to write the lyrics, as wrongheaded a decision as I've ever made.* Sondheim found Rodger's creative abilities were failing him and once he wrote music for a piece he refused to alter any of it for the lyrics. It was a spiritless collaboration and as Sondheim says it *was not a bad show, merely a dead one.* So with the failure of a work he loved, *Anyone Can Whistle*, and the failed collaboration of *Do I Hear a Waltz*, Sondheim began his voyage into a brilliant career as *I learned the only reason to write a show is for love -- just not too much of it.*

His musical *Company*, which is about marriage, or perhaps more aptly, about the potential misery of marriage, is one of my favorites and I have a coincidental personal connection with it as well as it opened on the same day as my second marriage. Also, the main character's name is Robert, and I play most of the music from *Company* on the piano, with the notable exception of "Getting Married Today" which is technically demanding and is best heard sung. Sondheim points out the irony that all his training under Hammerstein to write an integrated book musical had to be rethought for this show as it is an ensemble production, with the music having to comment on the subject, and not necessarily advancing the plot. Also, it required Sondheim to interpret the intricacies of a subject he had not personally experienced: marriage. He had to interview Richard Rodgers' daughter, Mary, to acquire "secondhand experience" on the subject.

What emerged is a brilliant collection of characters and songs, perfect for the subject and the cynical 70s. I was happy to learn that Sondheim's favorite version of the musical is the same one as ours, the 2006 production staring Raul Esparza. All the characters play musical instruments in this production and Esparza as I recall had to learn to play the piano to accompany himself when singing my favorite piece from the show, "Being Alive." Again, in a self-effacing mood, Sondheim confesses the following about the show: *Chekhov wrote, 'If you're afraid of loneliness, don't marry.' Luckily, I didn't come across that quote till long after Company had been produced. Chekhov said in seven words what it took George [Furth, the writer of "The Book"] and me two years and two and a half hours to say less profoundly. If*

I'd read that sentence, I'm not sure we would have dared to write the show, and we might have been denied the exhilarating experience of exploring what he said for ourselves. (Disclaimer: I don't agree with Chekhov!)

In 1971 he followed up *Company* with another musical with a loose plot, *Follies*. It is Sondheim's tribute to the subject he loves the most, Broadway history and *Follies* allowed him *to imitate the reigning composers and lyricists from the era between the World Wars....What made these songwriters imitable was that most of them had a style independent of whatever show they were writing. Just as you can listen to almost any piece by Chopin without ever having heard it before and still know that it's Chopin, so it is with Arlen, or Gershwin, as well as with a lyric by W.S. Gilbert or Harburg or Porter or Hart, at least the lyrics they wrote once they'd found their voices. Follies* has that great show-stopper, "I'm Still Here" as well as one of the most cynical pieces ever written on the subject of marriage: "Could I Leave You?"

But so much of the value of *Finishing the Hat* is Sondheim's observations about his contemporaries. Of course he pays homage to his "unsung collaborators" over the years, people such as Arthur Laurents and George Furth just to name a few, and then there are his accolades and criticisms of the composers and lyricists, and he frequently doesn't hold any punches.

His observations are but a few of Sondheim's *attendant comments.. heresies, grudges, whines and anecdotes..* He frequently devotes whole sections to his predecessors and contemporaries in *Finishing The Hat* and of course there will be others to follow in the succeeding pages.

If that in itself is not worth the "price of admission," *Finishing The Hat* is also a fine example of the art of the book, and why a Kindle cannot replicate the look and feel of good book craftsmanship. It is an oversize format so the lyrics and text can occupy three columns and to accommodate numerous illustrations, musical handwritten scores by Sondheim, lyrics both typed and handwritten and edited with the author's notes, and photographs from the productions of his shows. I was intrigued by his thought process, working out lyrics as shown on facsimiles of his yellow legal pad notes. He even goes into detail regarding his writing habits (in a footnote) about how he bought a lifetime supply of a special pencil with reversible erasers, ones which are flat and can't roll off a table, as well as a 32 line yellow legal pad (*allowing alternate words to be written above one another without crowding or wasting space*). Sondheim's eye for detail is omniscient.

The book is beautifully designed, printed on a high opacity stock that reminds me of the Warren Patina paper I used in my production days in publishing, when the esthetics of the book were paramount. My one minor criticism of the design is the lyrics are not as easy to read as they are juxtaposed to Sondheim's commentary text which is in bold.

Sondheim ends *Finishing The Hat* with "Intermission" and likewise, this entry ends on the same note.

Friday, January 7, 2011 **Senseless to the Sublime**

The last two nights make me think of how artists sacrifice themselves for their art and the general public's ignorance of what great artistry demands and preference for sensational pursuits.

One of the reasons we live in this area of Florida is for the cultural diversity it has to offer. True, it does not have the advantages of a London or a New York in its breadth or consistently high quality, but knowing where to go can uncover some wonderful cultural events. Case in point, our favorite small theatre where we never miss a production, Palm Beach Dramaworks. But the largest theatre in the area is West Palm Beach's Kravis Center for the Performing Arts and we've seen some fine musical revivals there over the last several years, *South Pacific* standing out in my mind, and some special programs such as when Sondheim visited for an evening discussion of his works.

Admittedly, it was with some trepidation that we got tickets for the Kravis' production of *Beauty and the Beast* but Ann had tried to see the Broadway version, liked some of the music, and never could get tickets so we were hoping that this touring production would at least be on par. Tuesday night we saw the opening and it was so dreadful that we left at intermission. This review gives some of the details although it is actually very restrained in its criticism.

It is a Disney dumb-down production presumably for the kiddies, with one dimensional slapstick characters, but, amazingly, most of the adult audience seemed to be laughing at the childish humor which at best rose to the level of a sitcom. The fact that a *Beauty and the Beast* could flourish for so long on the Great White Way says much about the public's taste in musicals. We should have known better!

The following evening we sought redemption, having long ago booked tickets for a series we have followed for years, *Keyboard Conversations* ® *with Jeffrey Siegel* at The Society of the Four Arts in Palm Beach. These are "unique concert-plus-commentary format in which he speaks to the audience about the music before performing each work" in their entirety. Wednesday night was one of the most demanding programs we've ever heard this highly-acclaimed American pianist perform, tackling three of the most difficult pieces written for the piano by Johann Sebastian Bach (Chromatic Fantasia and Fugue, BWV 903), Samuel Barber (Fugue from Piano Sonata, Op. 26), and Ludwig Van Beethoven (Sonata No. 23 in F minor, Op. 57 --- the

"Appassionata"). Mr. Siegel playfully calls the program *Three Great B's Bach, Beethoven and Barber* (the latter B normally reserved for Brahms, but this is the 100th birthday celebration of Barber, one of America's leading composers, a contemporary of Bernstein and Copeland). In addition he played two of Barber's "Excursions" which I had never heard and reminded me so much of some of Gershwin and Copeland.

The physicality of the performance was astounding. As a pianist, I have a special appreciation for what Siegel accomplished last night, performing the entire program without sheet music, keeping up with the tremendous technical demands of these pieces. Indeed at the end of the night, when he conducted his traditional audience question and answer portion of the program, he seemed, justifiably, physically spent. But this audience was brought to a standing ovation in appreciation.

Wednesday, January 19, 2011 *Finishing the Hat Redux*
I finally reached the conclusion of Sondheim's book *Finishing the Hat* but his melody lingers on.

The title of the book is a song title he wrote for *Sunday in the Park With George* (George Seurat, the Pointillist painter) and although that musical is after the cut off for this first volume of his "Collected Lyrics with Attendant Comments, Principles, Heresies, Grudges, Whines and Anecdotes," he says it is *the only song I've written which is an immediate expression of a personal internal experience.* And that experience is about what it means to create a work of art, "That, however you live, / There's a part of you always standing by, / Mapping out the sky, / Finishing a hat... / Starting on a hat../ Finishing a hat... / Look, I made a hat.../ Where there never was a hat."

Although now eighty years old, Sondheim still seems to be blazing new trails, with this book and the eagerly anticipated sequel which will cover the balance of his career and his continuing observations on Broadway colleagues and collaborators. (One of his criticisms of his mentor, Oscar Hammerstein -- and Richard Rodgers as well --- is that at a certain point in their careers, they no longer progressed, writing their musicals with a certain formula. Sondheim allows no grass to grow under his feet!)

I began this "review" (on a very personal level) before completing this first published volume, unable to contain my enthusiasm. So I now pick up with *Little Night Music* "suggested" by Ingmar Bergman's *Smiles of a Summer Night*. Sondheim says it gave him the opportunity to organize a musical around his favorite musical form, theme and variations, in which a theme is presented, and then follows various changes to that theme, either in key, harmony, orchestration or a more complicated musical variation to the theme which might even be unrecognizable, with a coda which usually repeats the theme in some way. His description of his meeting with Ingmar Bergman a year after *Little Night Music* opened, to discuss a possible collaboration on another project is priceless.

Sondheim's most recorded song (over five hundred) is from this show, "Send in the Clowns." Paraphrasing Sondheim, it used to be the song, not the singer that made a song, but in this pop generation, it's now the singer (or song group) not the song. It was amazing to him that the song won the Grammy Award of the Song of the Year in 1975, the last song to do so from a musical. Per Sondheim, *the success of 'Send in the Clowns' is still a mystery to me.*

The Frogs, with which I was completely unfamiliar, is an experimental piece he was asked to write for the Yale Repertory Theater, *one of the most deeply unpleasant professional experiences I've ever had.* The producer was one of the worst kind: *the academic amateur.* But he admits *it offered me a chance to harangue an audience, to use a chorus a cappella to make sound effects, to write massed choral music, and to indulge in vulgarity, adolescent humor and moral preachment, just like Aristophanes.*

With his *Pacific Overtures* Sondheim moved to a new level in his fusion of music and lyric, using the structure of Haiku poetry in his lyrics, his dedication to the principle that "less is more." I've never seen *Pacific Overtures* although Ann had when it first opened on Broadway and when I asked her what she thought, she said that at the time it was so different from anything else she had seen, she didn't know what to think other than she knew it was a work of genius.

It is all part of Sondheim's quest to "finish the hat." In this musical Sondheim has the opportunity, however, to "thumb his nose" at Gilbert (of Gilbert and Sullivan) with a piece from the show "Please Hello."

Ann & I were at a dinner party and we were talking about Sondheim's next work he covers in the book, *Sweeny Todd*, and I was surprised by their unanimous abhorrence of the musical. Although I understand an aversion to some of the gruesome scenes, I think they were simply not getting it, lyrics and music perfectly synchronized, one existing for the other. Perhaps it is because unlike the classic musicals of Rodgers and Hammerstein, some Sondheim musicals do not let you merrily exit afterwards humming the melodies. But Sondheim haunts and certainly his love of suspense music, the macabre, and his less than sympathetic view of mankind (Rodgers and Hammerstein's musicals always ending on an uplifting note in spite of any darkness that might inhabit part of their musicals), comes through in *Sweeny Todd*, off-putting to the audience in its graphic violence, "blood" even spurting as far as the orchestra pit in some performances. How can an audience which loves a Rodgers and Hammerstein's buoyantly optimistic "there's a bright golden haze on the meadow" reconcile itself to Sondheim's bleak "There's a hole in the world / Like a great black pit / And it's filled with people / Who are filled with shit"?

Sondheim describes the work as a "dark operetta" and really a "movie set for a stage" so it is no wonder that Tim Burton's translation of the musical to screen starring Johnny Depp and Helena Bonham Carter is considered (by Sondheim) to be the most successful adaptation of one of his works for the silver screen. The movie is remarkable as neither Depp or Carter had ever sung before. Singing Sondheim is difficult enough for trained singers as his lyrics come fast and furious in many songs with few spells for breathing. In fact, the DVD edition of the movie is the perfect way to see *Sweeny Todd*, turning on English subtitles, sort of like reading the libretto of an opera while the performance is underway. It's the best method of fully appreciating what Sondheim accomplishes with this and his other opera-like musicals.

Finishing the Hat concludes with his *Merrily We Roll Along*, which reminds me a little of *Company*, as it is a contemporary urban piece, also about friendships, and somewhat autobiographical as it concerns a song-writer. *(In my heyday as a young songwriter, I played many requests at many parties through the short attention span of the requesters and suffered many opinions of producers and directors who felt that their credentials demanded that they have something critical to say.)* Although there are memorable pieces in the musical, it closed after only a handful of performances, but with subsequent revivals, Sondheim tweaked it over the years.

The time line of the play is in reverse as our songwriter (Frank) devolves from being a rich Hollywood type to his beginnings on Broadway. It has one of my favorite Sondheim songs, "Not a Day Goes By" sung with two different meanings, first as Frank's final plea of love when his wife wants to divorce him and then in a reprise as a love song on their wedding day. Because of the reverse time line, it is the complete opposite of the usual reprise (think of Rodgers and Hammerstein's "People Will Say We're in Love" or "If I Loved You").

Although his music is best appreciated with his lyrics, "Not a Day Goes By" reminds me of the other wonderful, frequently melodic, pieces by him that I enjoy playing as piano solos. True, there are others that do not work as solos, but I think Sondheim gets a bad rap for not being melodic. Sondheim confesses a penchant for "list songs" (as do many other lyricists, think again of Rodgers and Hammerstein's "My Favorite Things" from Sound of Music which we just saw brilliantly performed at the Maltz Jupiter Theatre) and so, I am concluding with my own list, those Sondheim songs that I like to perform: "Anyone Can Whistle" (*Anyone Can Whistle*); "Being Alive" (*Company*); "Broadway Baby" *(Follies)*; "Company" (*Company*); "Good

Thing Going" (*Merrily We Roll Along*); "I'm Still Here" *(Follies)*: "In Buddy's Eyes" *(Follies)*; "Johanna" *(Sweeny Todd)*; "Little Night Music" (*Little Night Music*): "The Little Things We Do Together" *(Company)*; "Losing My Mind" *(Follies)*: "Not a Day Goes By" *(Merrily We Roll Along)*; "Not While I'm Around" *(Sweeny Todd)*; "Pretty Women" *(Sweeny Todd)*; "Remember?" (*Little Night Music*); "Send in the Clowns" (*Little Night Music*); "Side By Side By Side" *(Company)*; "Someone is Waiting" *(Company)*: "Sorry-Grateful" *(Company)*: "Waiting for the Girls Upstairs" *(Follies)*; "Who's That Woman?" *(Follies)*; "You Could Drive A Person Crazy" *(Company)*.

Friday, March 4, 2011 'Ghost-Writer' Haunts

Florida Stage is the "other" serious theater in the West Palm Beach area and although I've written often about the consistently fine productions of Dramaworks, I've only occasionally touched upon those of Florida Stage. This season is a significant one as they have now moved to the Kravis Center's Rinker Playhouse. Unlike Dramaworks, Florida Stage is bravely dedicated to new or relatively new plays, so that is an added risk, as if presenting serious theatre is not enough.

They opened the season with *Cane* which was followed by *Goldie, Max & Milk*. But with *Ghost-Writer* by Michael Hollinger, Florida Stage will have its first big hit of the season, drama at its best. Of course, it doesn't hurt that the play is by a well-established playwright, and even though this is the southeast premiere, it was vetted on the stage in Philadelphia at the end of last year.

Ghost-Writer apparently is not for everyone as a few people inexplicably left the performance right in the middle (there is no intermission). But if you cherish the nuances of language and how great staging and performing can turn little moments and glances into profound occurrences, Florida Stage has the play for you. As Louis Tyrrell, Florida Stage's innovative Producing Director said before the play, "it is an elegant play performed eloquently by the actors."

The play takes place in 1919, set in a studio apartment of a well-known writer, Mr. Woolsey, who hires an amanuensis, fresh out of typing school, Myra Babbage. She is obviously enamored of working for a renowned author. Their relationship gradually becomes more than just employer and employee, both developing affection for one another. It also progresses to the point where Myra can anticipate what Mr. Woolsey will dictate and will even interject her own opinion as to choice or word or punctuation. Stirring the dramatic pot is Mr. Woolsey's wife, Vivian, who is jealous of Myra, and displeased that her husband has set up this apartment (away from their home) for his work.

Every play needs a change catalyst, and in this one it is Mr. Woolsey's death before he has finished what might be his masterpiece. But after his death, Myra feels she can still channel his muse. Is it a ghost? Or is she simply looking to make a name for herself (as Vivian suspects)? Or did their relationship evolve to the point where the voice in the novel is really a collaborative one? Myra puts it to the audience to decide (or not to decide).

One thing that does not change is the role of the typewriter which, sphinx-like, sits in the middle of the stage, almost the fourth character in the play. At one point, when Mr. Woolsey is suffering from writer's block, he has Myra type "anything" just so he could hear the clatter of the Remington. Type it again he says as he stares out the window. And, again. Finally, the words spring to him, just as the final words of the unfinished novel come to Myra after days of not feeling the muse (or hearing the ghost?), but not until she, too, has typed the "catch phrase" -- which Mr. Woolsey had entreated her not to reveal to him (and, therefore, not to us). What could it be?

The play slides back and forth from the present to the past, effortlessly, almost imperceptibly. The staging is like a delicate dance, the characters taking a position on stage (as Mr. Woolsey at the window) or gracefully gliding about each other to the point where Myra and her employer actually dance (ostensibly to familiarize Mr. Woolsey with a subject he needs to write about but clearly is unfamiliar with). The early 20th century set was developed with period piece precision and the three quarter round seating puts the audience in the action.

But to succeed with a play which is about language and understated emotions also requires fine acting. Considerable measures of the play are monologues given by Myra, played by New York City based regional actor, Kate Eastwood Norris, who deserves accolades for her carefully articulated and poignant performance. J. Fred Shiffman plays the restrained, somewhat bland but meticulous, Mr. Woolsey to a tee. Lourelene Snedeker does a fine job displaying Vivian's jealously and even conjures up our sympathy. Woolsey had once portrayed her as a vivacious, desirable woman in his first novel but he now shares his muse with another, younger, woman.

What is a ghost, in any case, but vivid memory, visiting when one least expects it? And aren't we all subject to haunting?

So was it a ghost? The beautiful language of the play itself provides a key, as spoken by Myra: *What is a ghost, in any case, but vivid memory, visiting when one least expects it? And aren't we all subject to haunting? The smell of liniment conjuring Mother at the bedside; the pair of shoes recalling a son or brother fallen in the fields of France? Surely memory is ghost enough...*

Monday, August 8, 2011 **Summer Endeavors**

One of the benefits of living on our boat in the summer is being able to finally get to some postponed reading and catch up on local theatre either in Westport or NY and the last few weeks reminds me that so much of what we read or see in the theatre often serves as historical guideposts, snapshots of different periods of cultural change. I recently picked up John Irving's *The World According to Garp,* which I first read when it was published in the late 1970's. I'm not sure why I felt compelled to reread the novel other than I had forgotten much of it and always liked Irving's quirky self-reflective story-telling, so much about the process of writing itself. I had forgotten how much the role of women's rights plays in *Garp,* such a major issue in the 1970s. Irving playfully toys with the issue, satirizing it to a great degree, reminding me of my first business trip to Australia in the 1970's when a Sydney taxi driver lectured me about the evils of women's rights and, in particular, the role that Americans had in exporting those dangerous thoughts to Australia. I wonder whether Garp (or Irving) might have agreed with the accusation at the time.

Then a few weeks ago we saw Terrence McNally's *Lips Together, Teeth Apart* at the Westport Country Playhouse, portraying two heterosexual couples vacationing at a home on Fire Island, in the middle of a gay community. It is a play that is constantly on an uneasy edge, the problems of the two couples acting out their aberrant behavior contrasted to the high-spirited, better adjusted gay community, off stage. But central to the play is the paranoia of how AIDS was thought to be transmitted at the time, symbolized by the couples' dramatic fear of going into the pool (on stage) -- an obsession of twenty years ago when the play was written. Nonetheless, the play is still a compelling tragicomic drama and wonderfully staged at the beautifully restored Westport Country Playhouse.

A twenty year leap forward brings me to reading Jonathan Tropper's *Everything Changes.* Here is a very contemporary novel by a thirty-something author about relationships between fathers and sons, and male female relationships. Tropper's idiosyncratic characters (in particular, the protagonist's father) at times reminds me a little of Richard Russo's and Anne Tyler's. Trooper's writing can be very funny but sensitive at the same time. His writing immediately pulls you into the novel:

Life, for the most part, inevitably becomes routine, the random confluence of timing and fortune that configures its components all but forgotten. But every so often, I catch a glimpse of my life out of the corner of my eye, and am rendered breathless by it. This is no accident. I made this happen. I had a plan. I am about to fuck it all up in a spectacular fashion.

It was quite a contrast reading Anita Brookner's *Strangers,* perhaps the most interior novel I've read in some time, most of it taking place in the mind of the 72 year old protagonist, a retired banker and confirmed bachelor, who feels he may be missing something not sharing his life with a woman. By chance he meets one of his old lovers (he hasn't had many), now aged and frail, but one for whom he thinks he still has feelings. He also meets a woman on a flight to Venice, younger than he. Much of the novel is a debate (in his mind) of the advantages or disadvantages of being with one or the other or neither. Brookner's writing is timeless, meticulously exacting, set mostly in London, but a London that seems to exist merely in some recent time. It is also about aging and finding meaning in life after a lifetime of work.

Finally, yesterday, we saw the NYC preview performance of Stephen Sondheim's great musical, *Follies*. This is a show I failed to see when it opened in 1971 or any of the revivals and have been waiting, waiting for the opportunity. Sondheim is the last surviving composer of another era. Talk about historical markers. This is Sondheim's tribute to various eras of Broadway's past and it has some of his best known songs, too many to mention, including one of my own very favorite, "Losing My Mind."

This new Broadway production, coming via the Kennedy Center, is spectacular, the kind of show no longer written for Broadway. It was Sondheim's first musical as both composer and lyricist and every line, every word is delicious. The Broadway production includes some of Broadway's luminaries, Bernadette Peters, Danny Burstein, Jan Maxwell, Ron Raines, and Elaine Page. Each brings the house down with some of Sondheim's most iconic numbers. The juxtaposition of their ghosts from eras past is particularly evocative. Here is a two and half hour production which seems to pass in minutes, portraying innocent and happier times past, lost loves, regrets and heartbreak.

Saturday, February 18, 2012 **RED at Jupiter's Maltz Theatre**

I didn't expect to write this, hoping for merely an enjoyable Friday night at Jupiter's Maltz Theater to see one of our subscription plays, in this case *Red*, by John Logan. I knew something about the play, that it is about art, the same general subject as portrayed two nights earlier at Dramaworks, in their fine production of *The Pitmen Painters*.

So I suspected the plays might invite comparison, but I was determined to take a break from "reviewing." But here I am at 5.00AM getting down my thoughts without the benefit of any notes which I usually take during the evenings we're at Dramaworks. Such is the burden of an obsessive compulsive.

Not only do the plays invite comparison, the theaters do as well. We've been subscribers to the Maltz since the first day it opened ten years ago, having been awed by it's opening play, one that we thought "set the stage" for what would follow in their future seasons, *Anna in the Tropics* by Nilo Cruz. Consequently we eagerly bought season tickets that night and have done so every year. If I was writing reviews then, I would have posted something extensive about that Pulitzer Prize winning play, a true story of a cigar factory in Tampa in the late 20s (also based on historical fact) that employed lecturers to read classic literature to the workers who were mostly illiterate but came to appreciate great literature while they were working. Their emotional transformation while listening to Tolstoy's *Anna Karenina* is nothing short of electric, mesmerizing theatre. And it is a very sensual play with passionate interaction between characters.

Although always impressed by the level of professionalism exhibited by the Maltz since then, we have at times been disappointed by their choice of shows. Each season there would be a plum of a play, such as their production of *Master Class*, Terrence McNally's Tony prize-winning play about the great soprano, Maria Callas or *The Tin Pan Alley Rag*, a dramatic depiction of a fictionalized meeting between Irving Berlin and Scott Joplin, or last year's production of the classic *Twelve Angry Men*. But interspersed are productions that pander to Florida demographics.

Until seeing *Red*, we were actually thinking of reluctantly cancelling our season's tickets and just going to the few plays we think worth the time to see. But *Red* reminds us of an obligation to support serious theatre in South Florida, especially after the demise of Florida Stage where our prepaid subscriptions turned into those of an "unsecured creditor "and the recent financial difficulties of the Caldwell (to which we do not have season's tickets but occasionally go).

But as I said, *Red* invites comparisons to *The Pitmen Painters* which we had seen just two nights before. The Ashington artists were uneducated, neophytes to art, their artistic egos as fragile as butterflies whereas the ego of the artist in *Red*, Mark Rothko, fills the stage and the entire auditorium, with some left over for the parking lot. The nature of art is also discussed in *The Pitmen Painters* but on an elementary level, reflecting the nature of their primitive or folk art while art is discussed in its most intellectual and symbolic form in *Red* befitting the modern impressionistic works of the highly experienced Rothko. It's not that one art is better than the other (and personally, I like the more traditional art of the Ashington group, although appreciate abstraction as well), but it is interesting how these two plays approach a related subject and how the dramatic experience affects us. They challenge us to think about what art means, to us as individuals and to society.

Red is about the real life abstract impressionist Mark Rothko (played by Mark Zeisler), and the drama springs from his relationship with his young assistant Ken (JD Taylor), fictionalized by the play's author, John Logan. What happens between the time Ken is hired by Rothko who emphasizes that he is an employee only, not his student, not his son, not his patient, to the moment when Ken is finally fired by Rothko is 90 minutes of uninterrupted highly charged drama. *Red* leaves us stunned and even tearful at the end, a dramatic transformation of two men, the artist and his young assistant. Yes, only a two character play with such power.

And "red" is discussed in its many manifestations, as in different shades of that color, and black overtaking red, Rothko's metaphor of death overtaking life. Meanwhile it connotes something entirely different to Ken who, as a seven year old, witnessed the aftermath of his own parents' murders, saw the dark blood, still sees it and imagines (in his own paintings) what the murderers might have looked like. A perfect element for Rothko to connect with Ken on a human level, but can he, does he?

Rothko is a depressive misanthrope, railing out at others who fail to recognize his greatness and who fail to understand what art really is about while Ken has the buoyant innocence of an aspiring artist, secretly hoping to learn from the master, and to be appreciated by him. Rothko has been engaged by the architect of the Seagram's building, which houses the Four Seasons restaurant to paint their murals. And there is the conflict, art vs. commerce, something Ken the student sees, argues with Rothko to see, but it is not until Rothko himself goes to the Four Seasons for dinner that the realization that he is prostituting his soul sets in. He describes his visit with a misanthropic distain for the other diners, their wealth, their dress, their judgments, their small talk, all the vacuousness we have come to despise about modern society itself.

It is a stunning turn of events on stage, and after two years (in 90 minutes) Ken is fired, hurt, bewildered, demanding to know of the master, why, why, why. At first Rothko stays within his curmudgeonly demeanor, but finally looks at his assistant and painfully says, *I am setting you free, to be with people your own age, to experience your own art.* Ann and I knew we had just shared one of those special theatrical moments.

The quality of the acting, the stark staging of an industrial warehouse, the lighting which seamlessly highlighted the paintings or the action, was executed with such expertise that the audience could just dwell in the production, experiencing what only live theater can provide. The two roles were so very different, with such diverse demands, that they are hard to compare. JD Taylor perfectly plays the starry-eyed, eager-to-learn, but ultimately disillusioned Ken. Mark Zeisler has the task of playing the Herculean Rothko and has to modulate an almost stream of conscious intellectual banter about the nature of art while screaming invectives about his competitors (cubism before abstract expressionism and then the drip painting of Jackson Pollock and the pop art of Andy Warhol) and his distain about the art "public." Art and the character are almost inseparable, one inhabiting the other. The role's difficulty and how it is portrayed lead to a few discernible moments of hesitation on Zeisler's part, something I find rare on the professional stage, but understandable given the nature of the role and how people really talk.

We usually like to arrive at a theater early enough to read the program, and this was the other odd thing about the evening. The program had no information about the play's author, John Logan (or did I miss it?). This is a brilliant and passionate piece of writing, one that precisely reflects Rothko's inspired work, so I thought this apparent omission very bizarre. *Wikipedia* to the rescue. Logan is primarily a screenwriter, with such credits as *The Aviator*, *The Gladiator*, and *Hugo*, among others. Not surprising, *Red* was the 2010 Tony Award winner for Best Play. One hopes he returns to play-writing again.

As I noted, Andrew Cato, Maltz's Artistic Director, is trying to walk a fine line between appealing to everyman (what he calls family theater) and serious theatre. Maltz has the advantage of having a stage suitable for musical productions as well and there, too, it waivers between adult musicals such as its past exceptional productions of *Cabaret*, *Man of La Mancha* and *Evita*, and frothy "fun" musicals, pabulum some South Floridians apparently crave. We wish they would stick more with the former. While tempted to choose only the plays we want to see, live theater needs support, so we will renew again, hoping for thoughtful productions in the future. Such as *Red*.

Saturday, May 5, 2012 **He Made a Hat**

It's a wrap, a life of joy and genius, the second volume of Stephen Sondheim's biographical and encyclopedic collection of his lyrics and recollections, *Look, I Made a Hat; Collected Lyrics (1981-2011) with Attendant Comments, Amplifications, Dogmas, Harangues, Digressions, Anecdotes and Miscellany* (Alfred A. Knopf, 2011). My enthusiasm for the first volume, *Finishing the Hat*, led to writing about it before I was finished reading it and then again upon completion more than a year ago.

The amusing subtitles of the two volumes at first glance look similar, but there are subtle differences. Both have "Attendant Comments" and "Anecdotes" in their subtitles, but *Finishing The Hat's* "Principles, Heresies, Grudges, Whines" have been replaced by "Dogmas, Harangues, Digressions," and the all encompassing, "Miscellany" and "Amplifications" in *Look, I Made a Hat's* subtitle. Sondheim is too precise a thinker to imagine these changes were made only because of his playful, almost sardonic sense of humor. This second volume is less about others in his profession (although it is still that to a degree), than it is about himself, the process of creating, an attempt to tie everything together, the dominant figure of the NY Stage coming to grips with the process of aging and looking back at what defines his work.

This second volume covers his more mature works, 1981 to the present. It also reviews a wide range of "miscellaneous" works, ones I've never heard of, some incomplete or unproduced pieces. The "big four" here are his well-known *Sunday in the Park with George, Into the Woods, Assassins*, and *Passion*.

Sunday in the Park with George is about the life of George Seurat and, in particular, the two years he took creating his "A Sunday Afternoon on the Island of La Grande Jatte." Of significance to Sondheim is this musical united him with the author of the book, James Lapine, with whom he would frequently collaborate afterwards. The song "Finishing the Hat" is from *Sunday* and as he uses the title as the general metaphor for both these volumes, it bears some closer examination. He says it *reflects an emotional experience shared by everybody to some degree or other, but more keenly and more often by creative artists: trancing out -- that phenomenon of losing the world while you're writing....*

He continues with an anecdote. One of his pleasures is "inventing games" and he was once playfully challenged by his friend, Phyllis Newman, the actress and singer, wife of Adolph Green, to create "a game of murder" (a more interesting one than the card game of the same name that already existed) and once Sondheim started to work on the game, he labored continually through the night, saying *I hadn't moved for eleven hours. I must have, of course, if for nothing else than to go to the bathroom, much less get a drink or a snack. But I had no memory of it....As befits the creative act, 'Finishing the Hat' is a stream-of-consciousness lyric. There is no complete sentence."...That, however you live, / There's a part of you always standing by, / Mapping out the sky, / Finishing a hat... / Starting on a hat../ Finishing a hat... / Look, I made a hat.../ Where there never was a hat."*

Into the Woods came right on the heels of *Sunday in the Park with George*, Sondheim wanting to collaborate with James Lapine again. It started off as a *quest musical along the lines of The Wizard of Oz*, one of Sondheim's favorites as the songs help define the characters and convey the story. *Into the Woods* became a potpourri of famous fairy tale characters going into the woods, *the all-purpose symbol of the unconscious, the womb, the past, the dark place where we face our trials and emerge wiser or destroyed...* Sondheim says of the two main characters, the baker and his wife, *their concerns are quotidian, their attitudes prototypically urban: impatient, sarcastic, bickering, resigned -- prototypical, except that they speak in stilted fairy-tale language and are surrounded by witches and princesses and eventually giants. This makes them funny and actable characters, and their contemporaneity makes them people the audience can recognize.*

Sondheim thought the work would be producible by a wide range of theatre companies, from schools (with an absence of obscenities) to professional theatres, and the musical works on two levels, one for just entertainment and the other as a sophisticated adult parable. *I predicted that Into the Woods could be a modest annuity for us [he and Lapine], and I'm surprised to say I was right.*

I've "feared" seeing *Assassins* as having lived through so many of them in my lifetime, I just did not want to have it in my face on the stage, pretty much the same reason Ann and I don't see violent movies. But, after reading Sondheim's description of the musical, it's on our list to see if it should ever be revived. Leave it to Sondheim (and his collaborator, John Weidman, based on an idea by Charles Gilbert, Jr.) to make a musical out of nine of the thirteen attempted presidential assassinations.

In describing how he came to *Assassins*, Sondheim reveals much about the process and writing lyrics in particular. It also shows his own level of enthusiasm for this work, not to mention the level of reflection and his prose: *Writing lyrics is an exasperating job, but there are occasional moments which compensate, such as finding the right word that sits exactly on the right phrase of music or stumbling on the surprising but appropriate rhyme....Because of the quality of my collaborators, I have experienced that moment often, but the most exhilarating of those highs was the evening I read the first pages of John Weidman's script for 'Assassins'.*

Passion is another collaboration with James Lapine, although the idea itself was conceived by Sondheim after he had seen an Ettore Scola film *Passione d'Amore* which struck him *as a story worth singing.* He was concerned about making it into a musical as *the characters were so outsized.* It might have demanded an opera, not a musical, and that is an art form that Sondheim (I am happy to learn) does not enjoy. I say "happy" as I too have carried around the scarlet letter of "OP" (opera-phobic) even though I enjoy both music and theatre. Sondheim has exonerated the tinge of guilt I feel about opera, even though I briefly studied it in college when I used to go to the Met, sitting at the student's desk which had a very limited view of the stage in my day where I followed the score of the opera. Maybe I simply don't go in for pageantry.

Passion is an epistolary musical, with the songs, as Sondheim puts it, *somewhere between aria and recitative...[and] there's enough dialogue so that no one could mistake Passion for an opera. I hope.*

Then, some one hundred plus pages of the book are dedicated to the on and off again fourteen year affair of creating a musical based on the Florida resort architect, Addison Mizner and his raconteur brother, Wilson

Mizner, perfect models of picaresque lives. *Wise Guys/Bounce/Road Show* went through four different incarnations, finally ending up pretty much as it began as far as the main theme is concerned, the relationship between two brothers. The show had *four distinct scripts; three distinct directors; nine leading actors.* Sondheim had written thirty songs, most of which did not survive all four versions. Among the directors who impacted the show was, ironically, Sam Mendes in London who was also the director of the film *Revolutionary Road*, based on the novel by Richard Yates which I republished when the first edition had gone out of print.

But the director who had the most impact was John Doyle, who put the work on the course of becoming *Road Show*, after its previous variations over its ponderous life as *Wise Guys* and then *Bounce*

Then, Sondheim covers his "Other Musicals," "Movies" and "Television" (following college he wrote for the TV shows *Topper*, and *Kukla, Fran and Ollie* an amusing aside to his career).

In the mix of his lyrics and reminiscences are some of the "attendant comments." Although Oscar Hammerstein was his mentor, and Sondheim thinks of himself as a lyricist, he is also a first rate composer. When Sondheim graduated from Williams, he won a coveted prize for music which allowed him to study composition with the composer and music theorist Milton Babbitt. Sondheim explains why he focused on lyrics in his two books: .... *the technique of composition is impossible to be precise and articulate about without using jargon. The inner workings of lyrics can be communicated easily without resorting to arcane terms; understanding what a perfect rhyme is requires no special knowledge. But understanding what a perfect cadence is requires knowing something about harmony and the diatonic scale. Music is a foreign language which everyone knows but only musicians can speak. The effect is describable in everyday language; how to achieve it is not.* Those last two sentences are profound in their content and succinctness.

Sondheim has had a love-hate affair with critics and while he takes some head on in these volumes, he writes generally about the art of criticism and the impact of this Internet age.

I think of Broadway as having several fairly distinct periods. Before Rodgers and Hammerstein, the American musical was primarily revues with a loose plot to introduce song or dance, mostly light musical fantasies and comedies without much serious meaning to simply amuse and entertain. R&H changed all this with the introduction of the "book" -- a play in which music, dance, and plot were all integrated. And musicals became more serious, introducing themes that were largely ignored before. It became the most emulated form for the Broadway musical since.

But the fermentation of social change in the 60s and 70s brought a new period to Broadway. Sondheim was part of that but so was the so called "rock musical" starting with *Hair* and *Tommy*, coming into full bloom with musicals by Andrew Lloyd Webber, beginning with contemporary rock pieces such as *Joseph and the Amazing Technicolor Dreamcoat* and *Jesus Christ Superstar*, morphing into operetta type musicals such as *The Phantom of the Opera*. Broadway came full circle with some of those works, operettas having flourished before Broadway's golden age. Of those works, Sondheim says, *Rock and contemporary pop are not part of my DNA; worse, I find them unsatisfying when applied to the kind of musicals I like to write because of the limited range of their colors. Perhaps someday (maybe even by the time this book is published) someone will write a rock score that will have suppleness and variety, but the ones I've heard seem to me rhythmically and emotionally restricted, earnest to a fault and, above all, humorless except when they're being 'satirical' (that is, sarcastic). This lends them a pretension which rivals the British pop operas that briefly conquered the world during the 1990s.*

Sondheim, meanwhile, blazed new trails, the "urban musical" such as *Company*, in addition to pushing musical limits in areas normally reserved for drama, *Pacific Overtures, Sweeny Todd, Assassins*, to name but a few. He also sought vehicles for his love of panache and paying homage to those that made the Broadway theatre, most clearly celebrated in *Follies*.

Who will now carry on the tradition of Broadway innovation? Instead, revivals seem to be sweeping contemporary theatre (maybe just a deficit of good stuff being written?). They of course have their place. It is the lifeblood of good regional theatre. Sondheim's thoughts on revivals? .....*I suspect that every writer who has had the pleasure of seeing his shows revived, whether on Broadway or in a community theater, has also suffered the chagrin of seeing it distorted almost beyond recognition-if it were truly unrecognizable, it would be a relief. The problem is that a great many directors, not just the academics or the amateurs, reconceive for the sake of reconception, usually in the name of "relevance" or of "fixing" the show's flaws. They want to be considered creators so desperately that they think nothing of rewriting the authors' work. Good directors shine a new light on a piece; the others shine a light on themselves.*

Irreverent or outspoken? Perhaps. But, if Sondheim isn't entitled, who is? If you decide to read the book, read the "Epilogue" closely. It reveals as much about the man as it does the artist. He says that one would think writing songs for the theater, after so much experience, would become easier but "invention" does not.

Here is a man who knows he has climbed most of the mountains of his life, and is looking back, trying to bring it altogether and make some sense of the inexplicable and iniquitous process of aging. (Fitzgerald had it right with his short story "The Curious Case of Benjamin Button," but T.S. Eliot best summarized the process in his poem "Little Gidding" -- "Having rehearsed the bitter gifts reserved for age / the end of all our exploring / Will be to arrive where we started / And know the place for the first time.")

About this universal truth, Sondheim laments, *The diminution of energy and the fear of superannuation are unpleasant enough, but you learn to put up with the first and ignore the second; the loss of memory is worse, and dangerous. The thing that bothers me the most is not forgetting faces or names, but forgetting trivia....As time goes on, I watch old movies and listen to old songs more and more; when asked my place of residence on a customs form, I always want to write 'The Past.'*

Sunday, July 1, 2012 *Plaintive Melodies*

As much as we enjoy returning to live on our boat in Connecticut, the worst thing about summer is leaving my piano behind. If I was a professional, or played nearly at that level, it would be intolerable. But I remember having once worked with the great harpsichordist, Ralph Kirkpatrick (in the capacity of publishing and cataloging the works of Scarlatti), visiting him at his home in Guilford CT which was populated by harpsichords and grand pianos. He had made lunch for us, with some wine, and before we got back to work I timidly asked him whether he might like to play a piece. He looked at me as if I had lost my mind, saying he never gives private audiences and especially not after a glass of wine. I wondered, doesn't the love of music transcend everything else?

Contrast that experience to the one I had with Henry Steele Commager, who was the dean of American intellectual historians. I used to visit him in Amherst and we would work in his study on the second floor. On the first floor he had a baby grand piano and one day, again after lunch, I asked him whether he played. He raced to the piano and I quietly sat listening to him play a Beethoven sonata, and very competently. For Commager, playing the piano was his creative outlet and during that moment historian took second place. I understand that.

My piano has been good to me this past year and in fact we've been partners, preparing programs that I performed at the Hanley Center in West Palm Beach, a rehab facility, and at The Waterford in Juno Beach, a retirement home. Actually, most of the music I played at the Hanley Center was impromptu from fake books but at the Waterford I gave musical presentations with some commentary (Ann frequently helping me with the latter), something I really enjoyed doing, and now have programs for the music of Rodgers and Hammerstein, George Gershwin, Andrew Lloyd Webber and Claude-Michel Schönberg, and songs of the Great American Songbook as immortalized by Frank Sinatra.

Next season, I'll do others and perhaps record another CD at a professional studio. Of course I have no illusions about the enduring value of such recordings, other than having goals keeps one young, and it is a joy to be able to play. Luckily for me, my kind of piano playing -- reading the melody line and improvising with chords -- is sort of like riding a bicycle; once you know how to ride, you can do it anytime without frequently practicing. So, a summer away from my friend doesn't really set me back in terms of my ability to play – or at least much until I get back on the bike.

Nonetheless, as we prepare to leave, I look at my piano with a melancholy regret and I tend to play pieces that reflect that mood. Recently, I found myself playing some Bill Evans songs, constantly reverting to his "Time Remembered" -- a piece with abstract, floating harmonies, not exactly melodic. It reminds me a little of Debussy, but in a more abstract form, so I found myself fiddling around with some classical music, not one of my musical strengths, but what better piece to play than Debussy's "Reveries" as a bookend for the Bill Evans piece. From there I turned to one of Stephen Sondheim's most beautiful ballads, "Johanna" from *Sweeny Todd*, much more structured than the Evans piece, but all three musical compositions share this sense of the plaintive. But "Johanna" most accurately captures my mood. Whoever said Sondheim can't write a beautiful melody is crazy as this is one of the most haunting songs I know. It is also one of his few outright love songs.

Friday, July 13, 2012 *'Clybourne Park' Downer*

Ann and I boarded the Metro North at South Norwalk station anticipating a wonderful night of good theater and dinner. We had purchased tickets to see *Clybourne Park* by Bruce Norris, well before it received the Tony Award for Best Play. It is now near the end of its run on Broadway. The play had opened off Broadway a couple of years before, played London, and had toured some of the top regional theaters before returning to the Great White Way. Besides winning the Tony, it had won the Pulitzer, but our other reason for seeing the play is that next season Dramaworks is reviving Lorraine Hansberry's classic *A Raisin in the Sun*.

Clybourne Park is both sort of a prequel and sequel to Hansberry's groundbreaking work about racism in, ironically, a suburban neighborhood in Chicago, the environs where Barack Obama rose in his political career.

Unfortunately, *Clybourne Park* was disappointing, although the mostly out of town audience was captivated by its in-your-face racial invectives and humor. Maybe we were just expecting something more, to feel engaged in the production, but I wasn't and felt emotionally duped.

It takes place in two acts, the first in 1959 and the second fifty years later, in the same house in the fictionalized "Clybourne Park." The first act depicts the sale of the house to a black family, the same one Hansberry wrote about, the Youngers (who we never see). The lily-white neighborhood association is up in arms about the sale, but that same act carries the revelation that the current owners had lost their son in that house, his having committed suicide after returning from the Korean War under a cloud of possible war crimes. The second act puts the shoe on the other foot. It is now a middle class black family selling the house to a white couple who are in the vanguard of gentrifying the neighborhood. (Whole Foods is right down the road!)

There is some very clever dialogue, much of it delivered with such breakneck rapidity that we had trouble hearing all of it. Maybe we're at the age of needing one of those assistive listening devices given out at theaters, but I don't think so. Of course the Walter Kerr Theatre, a venerable institution, perhaps has outlived its useful lifespan. The seats certainly have. The configuration was designed for a much earlier generation, when, indeed, the average weight of an adult was 150 pounds. Those were the days when people dressed up for the theatre, not arriving in their shorts, their arms and the rest of their bodies spilling over into their neighbor's seats. Half of the audience looked like they were about to get on an airline and we all know what that now looks like. The space between rows is mere inches. No leg crossing here, assuming you can fit your legs in the row at all. If I was not at the end of the row, I would have fled the theatre in a claustrophobic angst.

Throughout the play I was aware of something I'm never conscious of while watching a great play: that indeed I am watching a play. Here are competent actors going through the motion of delivering lines, traversing the stage as competently directed. I suppose all of this was convincingly done judging by the audience's reactions, but I never felt engaged, although Norris had his opportunities for some real drama, particularly with the death of the son. He touches on that issue, but never really explores it. He could have gone to emotional places where Arthur Miller has gone in his work, but as quickly as it arose, its development was abandoned, the symbolic trunk of the son left behind, buried, but unearthed fifty years later, just like the racial issues.

Consequently, the play is more a device for delivering Norris' justifiably misanthropic view of the "progress" we've made on race in America. Could it be the paucity of great theater that renders merely an interesting play, with edgy humor, a prize winner?

I also felt that I was watching a bunch of stereotypes, stick figures, no one really drawn out in any engaging way although Russ' character, the father of the boy who committed suicide, played by Frank Wood, comes closest to one I can empathize with. But sometimes his lines were delivered with such briskness they were not decipherable from the mezzanine.

The dialogue at times, with its edgy racial humor, was well timed, and I suppose that is the glue that holds the play together, but much of it was well telegraphed, and in its poor taste meant to be tolerated by what we would like to think is a post racial world. But is it? At times I thought of the 1970's sitcom *All in the Family*, which implied much of the same humor decades before. The difference here is the humor is now explicit. Norris is clearly an equal opportunity insulter, with ne'er a good word for any ethnic group of people, including the WASPS howling in the audience.

I tried to take notes while watching the play, which is my general practice, but as I lost interest. I put down my pen (usually I can't read half of what I write in the dark anyhow). However, I did get one quote near the beginning of the play which I think resonates right to the end, one of the characters in the 1959 first act saying *we all have our place*.

And I think that is Norris' point. Nothing has really changed in the intervening fifty years, in spite of having a President of mixed racial heritage. One of the characters at the end of the play, after all the confrontational humor says something to the effect, *instead of doing this elaborate dance, what we're really saying, it's about race, isn't it?* Indeed, we're still battling out the shame of the heritage of slavery, whether it is the beer summit involving Henry Louis Gates, Jr.'s arrest, or the Trayvon Martin incident, Norris makes it clear that while some things are for the better (we can at least laugh and talk about it), the "change" we have long hoped for remains elusive. Racism is still alive and well in America. And the latent racial tentacles could still impact the coming presidential election, although it miraculously eluded its grasp last time around. Great theater? No. But as a philosophical statement, right on the mark.

Saturday, September 1, 2012 **'Harbor' Lights up Westport Country Playhouse**

Mark Lamos, Westport Country Playhouse's Artistic Director has done it once again. A couple of years ago he bravely produced and directed Samuel Beckett's *Happy Days*, a daring choice I thought to celebrate the Theatre's 80th anniversary.

And now he has chosen to produce and direct a new play by a new playwright, Chad Beguelin, always a risky endeavor for a theater. Our beloved Florida Stage took that route, and it paid the price during the recession, having to close its doors after so many years. Unlike the Westport Country Playhouse, the Florida Stage made the production of new works its specialty, rendering it even more vulnerable. Excellent new plays are hard to find and harder to produce.

So, kudos to Mark Lamos in choosing Chad Beguelin's first play (although he has been successful as a musical book writer and lyricist). Lamos put the play and playwright through a workshop process to improve the script and what has emerged, as directed by Lamos, is a play which is Neil Simonesque in its dialogue, pacing, and mix of pathos and humor.

Although a harbor is "a sheltered part of a body of water deep enough to provide anchorage for ships," it is also "a place of shelter; a refuge,' the kind of place when one thinks of "family." But the definition of family is drastically changing, as has the area in which the play takes place, modern day Sag Harbor, once a whaling town and now one of the hot spots of the Hamptons. Coincidentally, it is also where my own dysfunctional family vacationed during the summer months when I was a kid and years later, where Ann and I would often take our boat for a nostalgic weekend, thus occupying a special place in my memory.

Neil Simon was once asked what he would advise new playwrights about writing comedy, and he said they should *not to try to make it funny. Tell them to try and make it real and then the comedy will come.* This is precisely what Chad Beguelin has done in *Harbor,* a modern day tale of a gay couple, together ten years, and living in Sag Harbor. Ted, is the successful architect, and his partner is Kevin, the perpetually aspiring writer (the same novel ten years in the making), whom Ted supports and enables.

In the great tradition of American comic-drama, the dysfunctional family is at heart of this play. Kevin is from an alcoholic family of "poor white trash," the first from his family to go to college. A catalyst is needed for the play. Guess who is coming to visit? Kevin's sister, Donna, who he hasn't seen since their mother's death, and dragging her very reluctant 15 year old daughter, Lottie, with her. They live in a VW Camper, Donna being a knock off of the family from which she emerged while the precociously mature Lottie, through literature, is making every attempt to save herself from a similar fate.

Kevin and Ted of course do not know of the visit until Donna calls from a gas station some three blocks away. Kevin, stunned, tries to derail the visit, knowing that something dreadful is about to happen, but there would be no play without this visit! And from there, the action really begins.

Sister Donna has an ulterior motive for the visit, and if I begin to go into detail at this point, this commentary on the play will become a spoiler, so I will simply say that plays about gays has moved into the next phase – they have their own biological clocks ticking, pressures to become parents either through adoption or surrogate birthing.

Kevin has strong 'mothering' instincts but Ted is set in his ways, envisioning a life of travel and freedom after work, certainly not parenting, although, ironically, he is in a sense Kevin's caretaker, and those feelings begin to transfer to Lottie who also needs protecting. In fact, all the characters in the play need saving and the ebb and flow of their interaction makes for engaging and at times hilarious theater-going.

I can't say enough about the actors, all at the top of their form, delivering some very funny dialogue and facial expressions where timing is everything.

Donna is played by Kate Nowlin who delivers caustic wisecracks that has the audience laughing. Any time she's on the stage, she is a presence. Special accolades to Alexis Molnar, a high school senior, who plays Lottie with such poise you would think she's been around theatre since she was born.

Both Bobby Steggert who plays Kevin and Paul Anthony Stewart as Ted were flawless in their role as a gay couple trying to adapt to the intrusion of these two women into their lives and the truth they are forced to face about their own relationship.

I think of this play as a beginning of a new phase in American theatre, finding its roots perhaps in the works of Neil Simon, or A.J. Gurney (who, coincidentally was in the audience last night and whose works we have enjoyed over the years) but blazing new trails to reflect the changing mores of the times. We hope this play will make it to other enlightened regional theatres throughout the country. Congratulations to the Westport Country Playhouse for having the foresight to stage a 'world premiere comedy' and to Mark Lamos for his encouragement and expert direction. And may we enjoy other new plays by Mr. Beguelin.

Friday, May 3, 2013 *Music Makes Us*

David Byrne made a profound observation in his recently published *How Music Works*: *We don't make music; it makes us.* So naturally we are partially defined by the music we listen to. For myself, it is the Great American Songbook, music we sometimes refer to as "The Standards," many coming from the theatre and films or just pieces performed by some of our favorite recording artists.

I've made two CDs in the past several years. Since I made those CDs I've taken some piano lessons, pretty much my first block of lessons since grade school years. Those lessons were abruptly brought to an end by my open heart surgery and although I would have liked to resume them, it is a huge commitment of time. Sigh, if I was only younger! Still, the interim lessons have helped my skills, and I decided to test them with a new CD, and selected some more challenging pieces, diverse ones, from "The Songbook." Appropriately, this album is named *Music Makes Us*.

Some of the songs in this album are close to my heart for mostly idiosyncratic reasons, which I will explain. But first here is the complete list:

"My Man's Gone Now," "Bess You Is My Woman Now," "I Loves You Porgy" (from *Porgy and Bess*, music by George Gershwin); "The Rainbow Connection" (from the *Muppet Movie* by Paul Williams and Kenneth Ascher); "Never Never Land" (from *Peter Pan*, music by Jule Styne); "Alice in Wonderland" (from the Disney animated film, music by Sammy Fain); "Over the Rainbow" (from *The Wizard of Oz*, music by Harold Arlen); "Johanna," "Pretty Women" (from *Sweeney Todd* by Stephen Sondheim); "No One is

Alone" (from *Into the Woods* by Stephen Sondheim); "Till There Was You" (from *The Music Man* by Meredith Willson); "Getting Tall" (from *Nine* by Maury Yeston); "Why God Why" (from *Miss Saigon* music by Claude-Michel Schönberg); "If We Only Have Love" (from *Jacques Brel Is Alive and Well and Living in Paris* by Jacques Brel); "It's Love - It's Christmas," "Letter to Evan" (by Bill Evans); "Seems Like Old Times" (by Carmen Lombardo); "Laura" (by David Raksin); "Here's to My Lady" (by Rube Bloom; lyrics by Johnny Mercer); "Two Sleepy People" (by Hoagy Carmichael; lyrics by Frank Loesser); "What is There to Say?" (by Vernon Duke and Yip Harburg); "I See Your Face Before Me" (by Arthur Schwartz; lyrics by Howard Dietz); "Time To Say Goodbye" (or "Con te partirò" by Francesco Sartori)

The first three are from *Porgy and Bess* by George Gershwin. There are many other Gershwin pieces I love to play but *Porgy and Bess* stands alone as a folk opera. What can one say about such a consummate musical genius other than he was a prodigy who died too early but nonetheless flourished in all musical genres, from popular songs, to Broadway, to opera, to the concert halls.

Then I play four songs that are whimsically fairy-tale focused -- think rainbows and wonderlands.

From there, I move towards Broadway, the first three pieces by the reigning king of the Broadway Musical, Stephen Sondheim, all favorites of mine, two from *Sweeney Todd* and the breathtakingly haunting "No One is Alone" from *Into the Woods*.

A few months ago we saw an inspired revival of *The Music Man* at the Maltz Jupiter Theatre. I had forgotten that the beautiful ballad "Till There Was You" was from the show, and I couldn't get it out of my head until I decided to include it here. I found the song "Getting Tall" from *Nine*, based on Federico Fellini's film *8½* to be very poignant and although I never saw the musical (Ann did on Broadway in 1982) I included it here. On the other hand, we both saw *Miss Saigon* in London, and thought "Why God Why" was a show stopper -- certainly as moving as some of Claude-Michel Schönberg's other pieces in his more famous *Les Misérables* – and thus I felt compelled to record it. That section concludes with "If We Only Have Love" from *Jacques Brel is Alive and Well and Living in Paris* which is the first Broadway (actually off Broadway) show that Ann and I saw together when we were first dating -- in 1969. As such, it has special meaning to me. That song is the concluding piece from the revue.

A brief shift, then, to two pieces by Bill Evans, his one and only (to my knowledge) "Christmas piece" – "It's Love - It's Christmas" -- and the other a musical "letter" to his only son, Evan, written soon after he was born. If I could be reincarnated as a professional pianist, it would be in the Bill Evans mold, as he was truly one of a kind.

Then a group of songs, classic standards, such as "Two Sleepy People" by Hoagy Carmichael, which is my little hat tip to the late and great Oscar Peterson whose rendition of this song is the best I've ever heard.

Finally, and appropriately, I conclude with the now well known (thanks to Sarah Brightman and Andrea Bocelli) "Time to Say Goodbye," which is also the last piece I recorded at my session at Echo Beach Studios in Jupiter, Florida, a recording studio that is mostly utilized by professional musicians.

That brings up the difficulty of the process itself. I had one three-hour block to get everything recorded, to get it right as best I could. Three hours to make a 45 plus minute CD. Not only is it imposing, sitting alone in the recording studio before a concert grand piano with microphones all around, with the control room behind a glass in which my technician (the very competent and understanding Ray) is monitoring events, but it is exhausting as well. The fatigue factor took its toll, especially with the longer, more complicated pieces, when I had to flip pages of music quickly while also trying to avoid that sound being recorded.

The other difficult issue is simply being able to translate what I "feel" when playing the pieces and the recording studio is not the most conducive place for that. It becomes a technical performance which if one is a professional, perhaps that is good enough, but for me, I need that feeling factor. It is sort of like having to make love in a public place. Nonetheless, I had established big goals for this CD, worked towards them, and I'm happy I did it, even if those results may not be the same as in the privacy of my living room playing my own piano (certainly the quality of the sound is).

I'm not sure whether I'll do another CD again. Between my three, I've recorded about 75 songs. I'm somewhat content with that. The piano has been and will continue to be a big part of my life. I've been lucky enough to have a little talent, and a big love for the Great American Songbook genre, and the time to play for pure enjoyment. But never say never again!

Thursday, February 13, 2014 **Cultural Miscellany**

I don't comment on or review every cultural event we go to in our area, but one I should have covered was the Maltz Theatre's spectacular production of *A Chorus Line*, which has now closed, after a very successful run. We saw the original 1975 Broadway production and I came away with the same feeling from the Maltz production, one mixed with pathos and joy for the performers, each with their own individual story to tell. Maltz intelligently used Michael Bennett's innovative choreography, preserving it like a classic ship in a bottle, executed with the same degree of professionalism as in the original show.

We're hoping for more productions such as *Chorus Line* at the Maltz, and looking forward to their forthcoming production of the highly acclaimed

Other Desert Cities (hooray, serious theatre!), and their concluding production of *The King and I*. Any Rodgers and Hammerstein show is worth seeing in my estimation.

No sense "reviewing" their production of *A Chorus Line* in more detail. It even captured the attention of *Wall Street Journal's* Terry Teachout, his first visit to the Maltz and undoubtedly not his last. I agree wholeheartedly with his praise.

I rarely touch upon movies here. We don't see many, cherry picking the best when they come out on DVD (why put up with cell phones, texting, long lines, people talking, the endless previews and selling in the movie theatre merely to say you saw the film immediately upon its release -- does it make the film any better?) but I can't leave this cultural odds and ends entry without mentioning what I think is a Woody Allen masterpiece, *Blue Jasmine*, and a bravura, Academy Award deserving performance by Cate Blanchett. Regrettably the sturm und drang over child molestation accusations made by Dylan Farrow might overshadow what Allen (and Blanchett) have achieved in the film, a loose tale about lives of the Bernie Madoff crowd and the little people he destroyed. In fact, the film is a classic portrayal of the "upstairs" and the "downstairs" people, so skillfully portrayed and exactingly written by Allen -- the despicable rich, the admirable working class! Much of the success of the film is due to the casting by Juliet Taylor, who has cast all of Allen's films since the mid 1970's.

Cate Blanchett portrays a kind of fragility as "Jasmine" Francis, a Blanche DuBois character, while her sister's boyfriend, Bobby Cannavale, reminded me of Stanley Kowalski. The film, indeed, seems to be almost a tribute to *A Streetcar Named Desire*. It was strange to see Sally Hawkins playing Ginger, Jasmine's sister, as we have seen her so often playing Anne Elliot in the BBC production of Jane Austen's *Persuasion* (a DVD we dutifully watch once a year, it is that good). Hawkins is English and to hear and see her play a bag packer in a San Francisco supermarket was somewhat startling, but a real tribute to how brilliant casting makes all the difference. Woody Allen gave full attribution to Taylor for so much of his success in a recent open letter to the Hollywood Reporter.

Finally, last weekend we attended the yearly American International Fine Art Fair, an eclectic collection ranging from classic art pieces to contemporary ones capturing the comedy of modern absurdism.

For Ann's delectation, sprinkled here and there are magnificent pieces of antique jewelry to be admired and as for me, rare books, a potpourri of interesting cultural experiences, all on one manageable floor of the Palm Beach Convention Center.

In my fantasy life, the one where we win the lottery (and I don't mean merely a $1 million one -- a lot more is needed to haul some of the exhibit home, including a new penthouse apartment overlooking the intracoastal and ocean -- you have to put the stash someplace appropriate), I'd snap up some of my favorites from the show.

First, as one "needs" something to view the water and the boating activities from the new penthouse; clearly an obligatory purchase would be the Kollmorgen U.S. 20 x 120 Battleship Binoculars for a mere $110,000.

It's a modern penthouse so it would be nice to have something very contemporary such as David Datuna's *Eye to Eye Marilyn* which will set you back $180,000.

Offsetting the modern, we have to add one of Edouard-Léon Cortès' paintings, his style so unusual, the light crying out from the city of Paris in the late 19th century in *Après la Pluie, St Denis, Paris* for $165,000

Finally, putting some real life perspective on fantasies of penthouses, expensive art, were the *Robben Island Sketches* by Nelson Mandela. Perhaps seeing his work, reading his words, and knowing what he endured and achieved was the best wakeup call from the fantasy. His work, priceless.

Sunday, February 23, 2014 'Other Desert Cities,' A Classic American Drama at the Maltz

As we drove up to the Maltz Jupiter Theatre Friday night there was a storm north, probably over Jensen Beach, and the night sky was crackling with constant cloud to cloud lightning in the distance. We seemed to be headed into its vortex which, in a way, I would describe the essence of Jon Robin Baitz' play, *Other Desert Cities*.

It was a pleasant surprise to see such a stimulating play at the Maltz Theatre. This one included two actors who frequent the Palm Beach Dramaworks stage, the always dependable Cliff Burgess and the fabulous Angie Radosh. Add the other very competent actors, the set and staging, and the result is an evening of fine theatre.

I'd almost call the play "Arthur Miller Lite" as it has many of the tragic elements of some of his plays -- families in weighty conflict -- but with comic elements as well, a tragicomedy of sorts. It is a Christmas get-together, which is supposed to be a wonderful time of the year, right? Yeah, "right" -- a perfect time for discord, especially when you put a dysfunctional family under the microscope.

Here we watch the Wyeth family in their home in the desert city of Palm Springs "welcoming" back one of their own who has strayed from the flock, Brooke, Lyman and Polly Wyeth's daughter. She's been away for six years. During that time she wrote and published a novel, but since has been in and out of mental hospitals. After her "recovery" and a dissolving marriage, she wrote a memoir that is about to be published, one that paints her parents in a very unfavorable light. Her parents live in a power-broker world, a well connected family, former friends of Nancy and Ronald Reagan, extremely wealthy and very conservative, set in their ways, and never expecting their only daughter to publicly expose family wounds.

Brooke's arrival and her project are the catalysts to begin the pot stirring on stage, and joining her parents (who were involved in television, she as a writer and he as an actor) are her brother Trip who produces reality television shows and Brooke's Aunt Silda, Polly's alcoholic sister, who is staying with the Wyeths now that she is out of rehab. Silda used to collaborate with Polly writing for TV as well.

So we have a bunch of writers getting together. What could be more fun with the potential for sharp, cutting dialogue than that? And in spite of Brooke's hope that the family will approve of her memoir -- her real purpose for visiting -- what hope is there for that as she blames them for one of the family secrets, her brother Henry's suicide? Henry had spent his teenage years rebelling against the family values, joining an anti-Vietnam war underground movement which culminated in the bombing (and a death) at an army recruiting center. Presumably, he jumped off a Seattle ferry, leaving suicide notes and for that Brooke intensely blames her parents. But there is much that Brooke does not know. This family, in fact, is shrouded in secrets.

As the play evolves, these other secrets are peeled away leaving the exposed, corrupted core of the family. Add to that the divergent political views, opposite polarities of the daughter and mother, and the action taking place during the time of the Iraq War -- the microcosm of the family war in "one desert city" against the macrocosm of carnage in "another desert city" -- and you have a play with lots of moving parts and things to think about.

It's also a play about writing itself. How much can a writer step over the line of fiction into non-fiction, writing about characters who are close family? It reminds me a little of when Thomas Wolfe published *Look Homeward Angel*, a thinly disguised novel of his family and town folk in Asheville, NC, which enraged the town and left him an outsider. It is one of my own constraints when writing, especially when I attempt any fiction as I always seem to circle back to childhood memories that are not too dissimilar from those Jon Robin Baitz writes about. At a certain point should I abandon self-censorship? These were thoughts that went through my mind watching this play. And I think Baitz is as concerned about the issue of writing truths from one's experience fully conscious of the pain that might elicit.

So I take this play very personally and therefore why shouldn't I think it exceptional, especially as you often hear the question: where are the great new playwrights? My one regret is not having read this play first, as I think it is one of those plays which may be as good (or better?) in the reading.

However, while on an intellectual level I profoundly connected -- so many elements of my childhood were stirred up -- emotionally that connection was not as robust and I'm not sure this was the play itself, the acting, or the direction.

But before making some comments on those elements, I must say a few words about the set, the first one designed at the Maltz by Anne Mundell, a highly accomplished set designer. If verisimilitude is the objective of a set, this one is over the top. It IS a desert home and one feels as if real people live there. It is also somewhat monochromatic, like the desert, with people living out their secrets there. Outstanding. And Cory Pattak took full advantage of lighting the extraordinary stage and capturing changing emotional moments.

The mother (Polly played by Susan Cella) and her daughter (Brooke played by Andrea Conte) perhaps have the most difficult roles in the play. Polly comes from Jewish roots, now transformed into a waspy, right wing wife of a former Ambassador, after a stint in Hollywood, a woman who now revels in her wealth and connections. Painfully she is also now saddled by an emotionally distraught daughter with whom she is so congenitally at odds. She has to deliver some of the more caustic lines in the play such as: *You can die from too much sensitivity. So much pressure to be fair. I hate being fair.* Or when asked whether she is acting or not she replies: *acting is real -- the two are hardly mutually exclusive in this family.* Cella plays Polly professionally but uninspired. Perhaps it is the role itself, a complex one of the controlling mother when juxtaposed to the other complicated roles on stage.

Andrea Conte's Brooke begins her role as an anxious, depressed, physically agitated young woman and then elevates it to an angry depressed person, with a certain shrillness about her portrait that was at times jarring, frightening. I don't know how she could have played the role any differently -- it was her yoke as written by Baitz -- and she was certainly credible, transforming herself into a "different Brooke" in the play's coda, an act of resignation and acceptance.

Angie Radosh who plays Polly's sister, Silda, inhabited a similar role as Claire in Edward Albee's *A Delicate Balance.* (In fact, I would be remiss in not noting the subtle tip of the hat by the playwright to Albee's play. When the father wants to send Brooke a check, support her in some way, Brooke protests having seen friends ruined by monetary interference from parents saying, "The balance is so delicate."). The two plays are eerily similar as is Radosh's role in each (although in Albee's play she is a drunk and here she is a rehabilitated drunk) but she is a consummate pro, having antipathy for Polly's values, leading her to prod her niece to take on the family in her memoir (secretly providing information for her). Silda, though, has a part in the family secrets as well, and when it is revealed, the look on Radosh's face is one of horror. Another outstanding performance by Angie Radosh.

Cliff Burgess is really coming into his own as one of the more versatile actors in South Florida. We've seen him play many roles, with his portrayal of Brooke's brother, Trip, and his unique relationship in the family dynamics (he was only five when his brother's suicide occurred, so of all the characters in the play he is the most "blameless") he comes across as the voice of reason in the play, a truth speaker, to his parents and to his sister. Not surprisingly, as he was a "privileged kid" his interests seem superficial, producing a TV show where real life people are "put on trial" and the jurors are celebrities. The perfect cynicism, carried off by Burgess depicting the way we live today along with his constant texting, even while speaking -- the modern day multitasker. But he's had his own secrets as well, revealed later in the play to his sister. A bravura performance by Burgess.

Richard Kline's performance as the patriarch of the family, Lyman, is spot on. He is a man of financial substance and conservative social connections, but truly supportive of his children (in surprising ways as well but no spoilers here), who bears the burden of the multiple layers of secrets, with a pleasantry in sync with his former profession of actor. He is the peacemaker in the family (as was my own father), always trying to use his skills as a former Ambassador (having been appointed to the position by his old buddy, Ronald Reagan), to reconcile differences between his daughter and his wife, and to get his daughter to accept the ways of the privileged, even offering to buy the home next door so she can leave Long Island for Palm Springs (failing to see the depth of Brooke's rebellion). Kline, who once had a regular role in the sitcom *Three's Company*, rises to the occasion in this serious drama.

I think this play is a director's nightmare. The play is long -- 2 hours plus an intermission -- and there is a lot of dialogue and raw emotion, and although only five characters, it is a crowded stage, so, unavoidably, there are times when actor's backs are to some part of the audience (especially ours as we were seated far stage left). The first act all seems to be about establishing the characters, not the explosive emotion of the second act, a fault of the play or the director? It's hard to tell. Still, Peter Flynn, who directed the Maltz's award-winning *Man of La Mancha*, keeps focused on the playwright's intention, so accurately summed up by a line from the play that Flynn quotes in his playbill commentary: *Everything in life is about being seen, or not seen, and eventually, everything IS seen.*

Indeed, the Maltz has done a very credible job with a very interesting play. Although upon exiting I heard someone say, "I wish they just did all musicals," for me, keep a fine play or two in the mix each season!

Wednesday, April 2, 2014 *Author! Author! Indeed!*

"Dramalogues" is a special program of Dramaworks where they delve more deeply into an aspect of theatre. Last night's program was *Author, Author:*

Israel Horovitz. This was a live intimate interview with Horovitz himself, one of our most prolific playwrights, very capably moderated by Sheryl Flatow.

In the 1960s I occasionally went to Café La MaMa and there I might have seen the play that launched his career, *Line.* This had an off Broadway revival beginning in 1974 and still runs to this day, the longest running NYC play ever!

What struck us about the interview was how engaging and personable he was, not remote like the interview with Stephen Sondheim we attended a few years ago. Perhaps Sondheim has some disdain for anyone less then genius level and outside the world of the creative arts (not that he isn't entitled to his perspective!).

Horovitz is a remarkable man at the age of 75. He looks and speaks like a man in his early 60's and has the demeanor, a bounce to his step, of a much younger man. He has a great sense of humor as well, offering that he was born in 1939, *not a good year for Jews!*

He just seems like an average guy, although he was best friends with Samuel Beckett! Born in Wakefield, Massachusetts, a town of just six Jewish families, he hardly thought of himself as a Jew. He joked that the Jewish families there all sounded like Jack Kennedy. However, his first trip to Germany made him more sensitive to his own heritage.

His father was a trucker who became a lawyer at age 50. Some of the anger issues in his plays are derived from his father's frustrated and abusive behavior during his trucking years while the humor and tenderness come from his mother. Today, Horovitz makes Gloucester, Massachusetts one of his homes where he founded The Gloucester Stage Company -- still going strong after 35 years.

Horovitz has also been active in the world of films, perhaps his best known being the somewhat autobiographical *Author! Author!* starring his old friend Al Pacino. That was until now -- as he's just returned from Paris where he directed *My Old Lady* based on his own play, not too coincidentally the second play of Dramaworks' next season. The film will be released sometime this fall.

The three main characters are none other than film icons, Maggie Smith, Kevin Kline and Kristin Scott Thomas. Nothing needs to be said about Dame Smith especially given her recent notoriety in the continuing series, *Downton Abbey* (our favorite "TV show"). Kevin Kline and Kristin Scott Thomas have also been in scores of films but my favorite Kline movie is the idiosyncratic *Dave,* and I thought Thomas' role in *Four Weddings and a Funeral* memorable.

Recently I've been trying my hand at some short stories, and maybe that's the most important take away I had from this extraordinary interview with Horovitz. He emphasized that you need not write about the world, but, instead, write about the world you uniquely know. If you do it right, the world will come to you. Certain truths are universal. Actually, he was given that advice by Thornton Wilder. Ironically, Dramaworks' first play of next season is Wilder's *Our Town*, a play that we've seen in many venues, and one that we could watch again and again.

Thank you Israel Horovitz, for your plays and for the very good advice that you passed along!

Saturday, May 10, 2014 **Masters**

I was going to call this entry "Finale" as the title of the last CD piano album I will record, my fourth one over the years. However, on the good advice of an old friend who warned me never to say "never" (as I had said when I wrote about my penultimate CD, *Music Makes Us*) I've changed the title to *Masters*. Also, "Finale" sounds maudlin – and I don't intend it as such whereas "Masters" is a better description of the composers I showcase in this latest CD.

Nonetheless, I am fairly certain that this is my last recording as I've now covered most of my favorites as well as the different kinds of music I enjoy playing (although all fall under the "Great American Songbook" rubric). *Masters* is intended to "fill in" some of the blanks in my Broadway repertoire, having already included thirty four songs that were performed on Broadway in my previous CDs.

The "missing" songs are by the composers I feel dwarf all, George Gershwin (with his lyricist, his brother Ira) Richard Rodgers (with Oscar Hammerstein) and Stephen Sondheim. *Masters* addresses that lacuna by including twenty-three other songs by these celebrated Broadway innovators.

In an interview by PBS' Great Performances the daughter of Richard Rodgers, Mary Rodgers, related that *Noël Coward once said that Daddy just 'pissed melody.' She also revealed that Gershwin was a close friend. If he was ever jealous of anyone — and I don't mean 'jealous' in any nasty or competitive way — it was Gershwin.* No wonder, Gershwin wrote in all musical genres, Broadway being just one. (And some of the Gershwin songs in this CD were actually written for Hollywood, but written in the Broadway vein.) Who knows where he might have moved music if he hadn't suddenly died so young. So there is continuity here -- Gershwin knew Rodgers & Hammerstein, and Hammerstein, the lyricist, was a mentor to Sondheim – who naturally began as one as well, but would go on to become a composer of intricate, urbane songs, as well as writing the lyrics. George Gershwin and Richard Rodgers always had a lyricist to rely on (although after Hammerstein died, Rodgers wrote his own lyrics for the show *No Strings*).

I should footnote that the music for the last song in the program, *Maria*, was written by Leonard Bernstein, although I include it here as Sondheim wrote the lyrics and his collaboration with Bernstein helped launch his long-time career. Sondheim is now the senior statesman of Broadway and I can't imagine anyone touching his legacy.

There is another reason I decided to work on this album. This is the first year I've been without a regular "gig," normally performing at retirement homes during the season. My contacts at previous intuitions had changed and my season started with adverse health news. I had other things on my mind. So, instead, I turned more inward, playing these songs and others, writing some fiction.

It is restricting, just so much time to play the piano, and having a studio recording session one has a tendency to practice these songs more, to the detriment of other piano music. I'm looking forward to no such responsibilities in the future (other than my "senior circuit" engagements) so I feel this will indeed be my last such recording.

Here are the contents of *Masters*:

George and Ira Gershwin *Summertime / I'll Build a Stairway to Paradise / Somebody Loves Me / The Man I Love / Embraceable You / Who Cares? / Love Walked In*

Richard Rodgers and Oscar Hammerstein *People Will Say We're in Love / The Carousel Waltz / What's the Use of Wond'Rin' / If I Loved You / You'll Never Walk Alone / Bali Ha'i / Some Enchanted Evening / Hello Young Lovers / We Kiss in a Shadow / The Sound of Music / It Might as Well Be Spring*

Stephen Sondheim *Send in the Clowns / Sorry – Grateful / Being Alive / I Remember / Maria*

Friday, August 15, 2014 **Maelstrom**

It was a night to remember on the boat. Islip, NY, only some 25 miles away as the crow flies, had more rain than they have in an entire summer, 13 inches, in the early morning hours of Wednesday night. Here we had only about two inches, but the wind was unrelenting out of the east and southeast, the most vulnerable direction in the Norwalk Harbor. Plus it was an astronomical high tide. Our boat is half way out into the Norwalk River so at about 1.30 AM around high tide, with the wind roaring and the rain horizontal, our boat began to pitch and roll. Anticipating this weather, I had tied redundant spring and bow lines but within a short time, those stretched and we found ourselves occasionally banging into the piling on our port side. Go out and put more lines on or tighten the existing ones a part of me said – no way; nothing would help, said the other. Try to sleep I told myself, although it felt as if we were underway.

Sleeplessness was aided by anticipation. The weather forecast for most of Wednesday was for more wind and rain, here and in NYC, the day we were going in for lunch and the theatre, something we had planned for months. By the time we could get off the boat and dock, and onto the train, we'd be like a couple of drowned rats, not to mention the difficulty of getting to the theatre, walking from Grand Central Station to the New York City Center between 6th and 7th on 55th Street. We're veteran New Yorkers and know how to book it to time the lights, but rain and wind would make that impossible, not to mention getting a cab.

Months ago, as soon as I heard it would be appearing as part of the Lincoln Center Festival, I had booked tickets – 3rd row orchestra, practically center, to see the Sydney Theatre Company's production of Jean Genet's *The Maids* starring Cate Blanchett. We've long admired this hugely talented actress, who has not only appeared in scores of films, but has been supportive of live theatre, particularly the Sydney Theatre Company which she and her husband helped to make known internationally after taking over the reins from Robyn Nevin. An added bonus in this production included two other highly acclaimed movie and stage actors, Isabelle Huppert and Elizabeth Debicki. Having never seen Genet's masterpiece, and always being a "fan" of the Theatre of the Absurd, and given the cast, how could we go wrong seeing this production?

Well, the weather and forecast Tuesday night / early Wednesday morning almost made us regret the obligation to go into the city, if we arrived at all, given the reports of flooding. But miraculously, the skies cleared as we got off the train at Grand Central Station and we had a leisurely walk to a restaurant, Milos, near the theatre. As it was recommended by our son, Jonathan, we met him there for lunch.

It is "restaurant week" in New York City so we were able to order a delicious Mediterranean meal at "reasonable" prices, compared to the typical astronomical ones. NYC restaurants of that distinction are frequented by executives seeking a power lunch and by "ladies who lunch" (as Sondheim put it).

As we entered the theatre we learned that our tickets were being scalped for $700 apiece, ironic I thought, people going to see a play by Genet who clearly despised the class of people who could afford to pay that price. I suppose the movie star cast, and the very limited engagement led to those prices – supply and demand!

The stage set looked placid enough, but within only minutes into the play we knew that it would be our second maelstrom in 24 hours. Crude gutter language, bodily fluids (spit and drool galore), and raw sexuality with the help of readily available props on stage unfolded. Voyeuristic views of what went on in the off stage bathroom shot live with hand held cameras and projected on a huge screen on stage, and close ups, sometimes of flowers (there were hundreds of them in vases all over the stage), but frequently of the actresses faces slapping on powder and lipstick at the "mistress'" make up table, or close ups of humping or physical abuse on the bed or floor, accosted us for almost the next two hours, with no intermission. And then there is the "plot" – really the imaginary murder of the "mistress" by the two maids, one pretending to be the mistress (Cate Blanchett) and the other the maid (Isabelle Huppert), fantasizing the murder, in anticipation of the arrival of the "mistress." Genet's play was loosely based on a real life incident, but of course he extrapolates it to its most outrageous and sordid extreme.

This production puts a 21st century spin on Genet's work, not only with the innovative use of viewing the characters using two video cameras and projecting those emotions close up, but casting a much younger woman, Elizabeth Debicki, as the "mistress." She not only has the class advantage over her imprisoned Maids, but she has youth and indeed, she struts it – all six feet three inches of her gorgeous young body. And when she finally arrives about half way through the play, one can appreciate Blanchett's impersonation even more.

Above all, there is an high energy level that is poured into this production – all three of them playing their roles on the borders of frenetic madness. How, we thought, would it be possible for these same actors to do an evening performance? After all, we, the audience, left exhausted, and can only imagine what they would have to do to recover.

Afterwards I wondered to myself why any actor – especially well-established screen actors – would take the risks of these roles on stage, in front of a live audience. Film acting must be so much easier. But I think it says something about these particular actors, accepting a gauntlet thrown, the challenge to excel overwhelming the perceived risk. They are just that good.

The philosophical merits of what Genet has to say are clear from 30,000 feet, but I'd have to read the play to have a better, detailed understanding. My one criticism concerns the maid Solange played by Isabelle Huppert, a French actress of renown, and perhaps selected for the role as homage to the French playwright, Genet, but her strong French accent sometimes caused many missed words. We all were desperately trying to make sense of her complete dialog, so important, I think, in understanding Genet – and particularly the impassioned monologue at the end of the play.

That comment, however, is not to detract from the overall production, with a standing ovation at the end and multiple curtain calls.

Wednesday, February 25, 2015 *Glengarry Glen Ross*

The Maltz Jupiter Theatre scores another artistic hit with their current production of *Glengarry Glen Ross* by David Mamet. It was even singled out and highly praised by the *Wall Street Journal*'s Terry Teachout.

Having loved Dramaworks' production of Mamet's *American Buffalo* (hard to believe that was five years ago now), we saw the Maltz production with high expectations and what a play Mamet has written! It is sort of the other side of the coin of Arthur Miller's *Death of a Salesman* – the American Dream corrupted by greed.

Teachout not only praised the production, but justifiably focused on Rob Donohoe's performance as Shelly, who is the central character in the play. For those of us who saw the film, who could forget Jack Lemmon's Shelly? Donohoe is up to the task of creating his own unforgettable portrayal. We've seen Donohoe in several local productions in the past, but never in such a leading role.

Peter Allas who plays Ricky (played by Al Pacino in the film version) is one of only two actors in the production who has never played on the Dramaworks stage (this production being under the skillful direction of another Dramaworks' veteran, J. Barry Lewis). We last saw Allas ten years ago in the Maltz Theatre's opening production, *Anna in the Tropics*. It was that play that persuaded us to become season subscribers ever since.

Maltz usually gravitates toward revivals of Broadway musicals and lighter dramatic fare aimed at the mature South Florida audience. It always takes on those challenges professionally and does not depend on touring companies. Once in a while, it will produce some superb serious theatre such as this Mamet play.

Saturday, April 25, 2015 *He Had That Certain Feeling*

Earlier this week I gave a concert at the Brookdale Senior Living Center of Palm Beach Gardens, a special experience as it was an all Gershwin program, the composer I most admire for his versatility and genius. He wrote some of the greatest songs for the American Songbook, as well as concert and operatic works. He singlehandedly removed the barrier between jazz and classical music.

Also, of all the composers I play on the piano, my style is most suitable for his works. I can't imagine where Gershwin would have taken American music if his life wasn't extinguished by a brain tumor at the age of 38. But his output during his short life was remarkable, from Tin Pan Alley, Broadway to classical and operatic, to Hollywood. He could write in all venues and he was a consummate pianist himself.

George Gershwin once said that *true music must repeat the thought and inspirations of the people and the time. My people are Americans and my time is today.* Indeed, he had that "certain feeling."

My audience at Brookdale was more than appreciative. This is the longest of my prepared concerts, lasting a little more than an hour without a break, a medley of 24 songs, including some from *Porgy and Bess*, and concluding with the theme from *Rhapsody in Blue*. The sheet music for all pieces was *from The New York Times Gershwin Years in Song* (published by Quadrangle Press which was then owned by the *NYT*). It was presented to me in my publishing days by one of our printers in 1973 and it is a prized possession as the songs include all the introduction sections which, in a George and Ira Gershwin song, can be as interesting as the song itself. I'm grateful to still be playing from this treasure some 42 years later -- and so the circle closes.

Tuesday, August 4, 2015 Summer Comings and Goings

We returned again to the Westport Country Playhouse to see A. R. Gurney's *Love and Money*, a world premiere. Just one look at some of the old billboards and memorabilia in the lobby evokes deep and fond memories. We've been going there for some 45 years now, and while it has changed, it has changed to stay the same, to present plays of meaning to the community.

For many years Paul Newman's restaurant, The Changing Room, stood adjacent to the playhouse (both Paul Newman and Joanne Woodward were active in the theater's success). Now Positano -- which had been near the beach -- moved into that space and Ann and I had dinner there before the show.

What better place to premiere Gurney's *Love and Money* than the Westport Country Playhouse, near the epicenter of the play's subject, the enigma of the WASP. Cheever had defined the very species and Gurney has now attempted to dramatize its fading years of glory.

Gurney has been heavily influenced by Cheever and in fact as a tribute to the great short story writer he created a dramatization of some of his stories some twenty years ago, *A Cheever Evening*. Gurney used more than a dozen Cheever short stories to create his vision of what Cheever might have composed himself if he were a dramatist. I've read that play but have not seen it performed but maybe it will be revived on the heels of Gurney's new play. Cheever and Gurney are students of this privileged, melancholic, frequently inebriated class, one to which it is time to say goodbye.

Unfortunately Gurney's play is not primetime ready yet and although the cast includes the consummate actress Maureen Anderman, who not long ago we had seen at Dramaworks in *A Delicate Balance*, her presence is not enough to save what we thought was a very contrived plot intended to mark the passing of the WASP species. Unlike Cheever, whose characters mostly aspired to money or had the pretense of money, this is about real money and how it alters relationships.

Cornelia Cunningham (Maureen Anderman) feels tainted with loads of WASP money from her deceased husband. Her two children had directly or indirectly been destroyed by their wealth and/or alcoholism, and she is determined to leave most of her money to charity. Against the advice of her attorney, Harvey Abel ("ably" played by Joe Paulik), she has no intent to leave the money to her two "zombie" grandchildren and then, suddenly -- a young black man arrives on her doorstep claiming to be the child of her deceased daughter – and thus another grandchild has been added to the mix. Let the drama and comedy begin! – or at least attempt to begin. From there a series of non sequiturs – ones that don't seem to be organic to the plot -- are thrown at the audience, F. Scott Fitzgerald, Cole Porter, and a number of zingers at the encroaching political oligarchy and foibles of modern day life.

Cole Porter of course is emblematic of the WASP culture and a couple of his songs are suddenly introduced as a young Julliard student, Jessica Worth (Kahyun Kim), comes to inspect Cornelia's player piano which is programmed to play only Porter, Jessica bursting into song. The young black man, Walter Williams (played by Gabriel Brown) who is after his own fortune, claims he is nicknamed "Scott" because of his love of Fitzgerald (who ironically lived in Westport briefly with Zelda) and in particular his affection for *The Great Gatsby*.

While *Love and Money* is billed as a world premiere production, it is a play in development, gearing up for an off-Broadway run at the Signature Theatre. It needs work -- an organic fluidity that seems to be lacking and a more believable plot.

In the program notes Gurney says *at the age of 84, I assumed this play would probably be my last. As its various characters leave the stage at the end, I felt I was figuratively going with them. But now that the excitement of an actual production is taking place, I am reminded of an adage from the Jewish culture... "Wasps go without saying goodbye. Jews say goodbye and won't leave." So now, in my golden years, with perhaps another play or two already churning around in my head, I've decided to be Jewish.* Let us hope one of our great social-comedic playwrights has a few more plays up his sleeve, and improves the present work. Perhaps he should reread his own *A Cheever Evening*?

Tuesday, August 11, 2015 **An American in Paris in NYC**
Last Sunday we ventured into the city to see *An American in Paris*. Our son saw the preview in Paris of all places and gave us ample advance notice

of how spectacular the production was and therefore we were able to buy tickets in the third row center many months ago, perfect seats for the most stirring Broadway musical we've seen in recent memory.

Alone on the stage before the performance began is an older grand piano, perhaps much like the one George Gershwin might have composed on. And that is the conceit of the play – a composer being central to the action, Adam Hochberg (a.k.a Oscar Levant) movingly played by Brandon Uranowitz. He composes a ballet for a woman he has fallen in love with, Lise Dassin, luminously performed by Leanne Cope. Unfortunately for him, two other men are in love with her too, Jerry Mulligan (Robert Fairchild) and Henri Baurel (Max von Essen). Because Lise and her family were harbored by Henri's family during the Nazi occupation of Paris, she feels honor bound to accept his proposal although her heart has clearly been lost to the artist, Jerry, who fell in love with her at first glance. All the action takes place in post WW II Paris and of course the "book" heavily relies on the movie version of *An American in Paris*.

In fact, the two leads could easily pass for the two movie leads. Robert Fairchild, the principal dancer with NYC Ballet, credits the physicality of his dancing to his idol, Gene Kelly, and Leanne Cope is highly reminiscent of Leslie Caron. As both Fairchild and Cope are luminaries in the world of ballet, not Broadway theatre, it is remarkable to witness the transition – even their singing roles were of Broadway caliber. Of course the dancing was superlative, breathtaking and from our vantage we could see every drop of sweat, and could feel the incredible energy that went into the play. As for the astounding performance by Fairchild, Ann, my ballet expert, could not stop raving about the perfection of his dancing, his grand jetes, his jazz movements and energy.

Ann was particularly interested in seeing Sara Esty, a talented young dancer she has enjoyed watching from her first performance with the Miami City Ballet when she joined the company several years ago along with her twin sister. She auditioned and won a part in the Ensemble of this show enjoying the time spent in Paris and blogging about it. Well to our surprise, we noticed in the *Playbill* that in addition to this being her Broadway debut; she has been chosen to dance the lead in place of Leanne Cope on the Wednesday matinees, surely an indication of how far along her career has progressed. Robert Fairchild has substitutes as well for the Wednesday evening and Saturday matinee performances, so we were fortunate to see the leads at our Sunday matinee.

But for me, the heart, the very soul of the production is the music of George Gershwin. I feel I have a special affinity for his music -- much of it is the bulk of my more confident piano repertoire. After hearing this production I'm tempted to play only Gershwin in the future!

Unlike the film, the Broadway production is more musically far ranging, including pieces I don't remember in the movie, such as parts of the "Cuban Overture" and many other Gershwin songs.

An American in Paris is a massive undertaking, even on Broadway, a full orchestra, a large cast and striking, multiple sets. The pace was intense under the brilliant direction and choreography of Christopher Wheeldon. During intermission while Ann went to the ladies room, I texted our son, Jonathan, my thanks for pushing us to get tickets early, beginning my text with just two words. "Intermission. Fabulous." When Ann returned to her seat she said that she texted Jonathan. I said I did too. She said, here, look at what I wrote and it began with two words: "Intermission. Fabulous."

Sunday, August 23, 2015 **Hamilton Hip Hops into Broadway History**

Ann and I once again boarded the New Haven train to NYC, this time to see *Hamilton*.

We had secured tickets way before the opening as I had heard an interview with Stephen Sondheim who praised this show as a quantum step in the evolution of the Broadway musical. That was good enough for me and lucky we acted as by the time we went, our tickets were going for five times what we paid.

It's everything that has been written and said about the show, probably the most talked about Broadway musical prior to its opening in history. No sense repeating the story here about Lin-Manuel Miranda's genius in putting together the most original Broadway musical since, perhaps, *Oklahoma*. As with *Oklahoma*, *Hamilton* breaks all the rules, but similar to its predecessor, it uses dance, music, acting, and a fine "book" to move the action along. The action is explosive, a constant pulse measuring the beginning of our nation, the meaning of compromise, and the contributions of immigrants, particularly the Caribbean born Hamilton.

This nation's historical founders are played by people of color in period customs, singing history through the medium of rap and hip hop, where the copious dialogue springs to life. There are very few speaking parts, and that factor as well as the staging, the subject of revolution, and some of the love songs hearken back to a previous transforming musical, *Les Misérables*. The reminder of the latter in Lin-Manuel Miranda's work is omnipresent. And like "Master of the House" there is a change of pace humorous song embedded in *Hamilton* as well, one sung by a foppish King George entitled "You'll Be Back," which contrasts with the hip hop in the show. It was sung with such a recognizable Beatles' beat that the audience erupted into instant laughter. Nevertheless, the other music, even for old Rodgers and Hammerstein and Stephen Sondheim fans, was memorable. Rap songs such as "My Shot" and "The Room Where it Happens" run like leitmotifs throughout the show and get under your skin (not that I could sing them or even play them on the piano).

If I had to sum up the musical in one word, it's pure raw <u>energy</u>. Never a dull moment, with many emotional ones, particularly if one has an understanding of the beginnings of this nation, as well as cautionary inferences pertaining to our own times, it is the must see show of this season, and probably many to come.

Tuesday, December 1, 2015 **This Funny World**

Before Rodgers and Hammerstein there was Rodgers and Hart. They wrote so many great standards such as "Manhattan," "My Funny Valentine," "The Lady Is a Tramp," "I Could Write a Book," "Bewitched," to name just a few of my favorites, but sometimes their songs became conflated with the other great standards of the era, those by George Gershwin and Cole Porter in particular. Yet Rodgers and Hart were trailblazers in their own right.

They met as young students at Columbia University and they seemed destined for one another. Rodgers of course could write a melody as us mere mortals can compose post cards. He was the consummate composer and partner, productive and businesslike. One could always count on Richard Rodgers. Larry Hart on the other hand was a troubled person. Unlike the "beautiful" people he wrote about and consorted with – first on Broadway and then in Hollywood -- he felt himself to be an outsider, he was gay, Jewish, and diminutive (always photographed standing while Rodgers was sitting at the piano).

His lyrics could be dark and cynical. But I've been so accustomed to playing their well known pieces, and as I do not have a singing voice, Hart's lyrics became submerged in the deep pool of their music. Furthermore, I've played most of their music from fake books, the melody line or verse only without the introductions. Their songs without the intros are like birds without feet, homes without foundations. I have a Gershwin songbook with the intros and I needed one for Rodgers and Hart. To the rescue: *Rodgers and Heart; A Musical Anthology.*

Alas, my songbook arrived but I should have known that in this profit driven world the publisher (Hal Leonard) would chose the less expensive "perfect bound" alternative to spiral binding (such as my 40 year old collection of Gershwin's songs). Very sensible for the publisher but a nightmare for the pianist as most songs with the intros are at least 4 pages and turning the pages of a perfect bound book is difficult if not impossible while performing.

Ah, for the want of a nail. I knew there would ultimately be an iPad in my life and this was the final straw to tip the scale. I'd photograph select songs with the iPad (still difficult to hold down certain sections of the book for photographing and having to accept some partially distorted pages, albeit legible). Then do the same for my Gershwin songs and other beloved standards, put them in albums, and then play the music from my iPad, merely swiping pages to "turn" them.

Voila it works! A couple of negatives though. If your finger resides too long on the page you are swiping, you are returned to the pervious menu of all pages, so I've "perfected" the technique of quickly swiping while playing. Furthermore, the page is about half the size of the printed book. Good reading glasses to the rescue for that drawback.

This commitment to the iPad for my sheet music repertoire in turn has led to a certain acceptance about my piano technique. I've gone into jazz, contemporary, some classical even, but I find the most satisfaction from the standards, particularly the music of the thirties and forties. I was born too late to live in that moment, but today I find the themes to be as relevant to today as when they were written. So I'm making my iPad music albums all standards focused when playing in public venues, mostly local retirement homes. To date I've performed at The Inn at LaPosada, the Hanley Center, The Waterford, Mangrove Bay and most recently a monthly "gig" at Brookdale Senior Living.

And now I can incorporate the introductions to many of the standards which so beautifully set up the songs, sometimes acting as a counterpoint and foreshadowing the content. Finally, playing the *Rodgers and Hart Songbook* yielded a double bonus, finding songs that are absent from my fake books, such as their hilarious "To Keep my Love Alive," and some songs I've rarely heard. One such song is "This Funny World." Here is where you see the genius of Larry Hart: the lyrics are so achingly cynical -- one can imagine Hart wearing his own heart on his sleeve.

Richard Rodgers' magnificent melody populates the introduction with minor chords, underpinning the dark lyrics by Hart. (Although, when working with Hart, Rodgers would normally first write the melody. When collaborating with Hammerstein, the lyrics would normally precede Rodgers' composition.) Rodgers writes the chorus in a major key. Such sad lyrics to such a beautiful melody and the chorus which is also the title of the song is repeated four times just to make sure you don't forget it!

I received a comment on my recording of "This Funny World" which I'll share here. I don't get many comments as my videos are not heavily trafficked as are so many of the professional ones, but it's always pleasing to learn that the tree is not falling in a silent forest and there are some people who come forth to express their feelings. This one is particularly appreciated for the reasons I expressed in my reply:

From "Tom"

I was looking around for the song "This Funny World" by Rodgers and Hart; I had remembered the song from the past and thought how poignant and in many ways also how true the words seem to be. These words as well as the music begins a chain of events causing a sharp sense of sadness, pity, and regret, and still a realization that life's journey for everyone,-- to one degree or the other,-- have to say that this funny world has been making fun of them. But I wanted to learn the song and of course put into you-to-bee "How to play (This funny World) and this wonderful looking keyboard came up with a pair of hands on it, I thought to myself -- ok let's see how bad this guy messes up the song, but to my surprise and delight I could sit through the entire song and drink in every beautiful note and expression, nothing added nothing subtracted it actually was what I was looking for, you have an extraordinary ear and the ability to present the song just as the writers intended. Thank you.

My Reply:

Thank you, Tom, for your kind comments. You touched upon both my strength and weakness as a pianist. I do try to focus on a literal interpretation and play the song as I feel it. I lack the musical education to render these songs with the kind of profes-sional voicing and interpretation one normally hears. But over the years I tried to commit some of my favorites to YouTube. I laughed when you said that you found a pair of hands and a keyboard in your search for the song. My recording device is a digital camera which I've learned that when I record a distance from the piano to get my body and all into the video, my living room becomes an echo chamber. Better be close, very close to the piano for the best sound and, even then, it has noticeable limitations. I've recorded 4 CDs in a studio and these sound better, but they are not available commercially.

(My YouTube recordings can be accessed by Google: "YouTube lacunaemusing.")

Wednesday, December 16, 2015 **Sinatra**

I gave a belated 100th birthday piano concert in honor of Frank Sinatra – only a few days late, my regular Brookdale Senior Living home monthly per-formance, ironically on my own birthday. I listened to Sinatra all day on

Dec. 12, his 100th and I wondered how different my life would have been if there had not been a Frank Sinatra. He permeated our culture.

The Great American Songbook would not exist in its present form if there was no Sinatra. I remember in high school I was just getting over my fascination with Elvis Presley, and abandoning my guitar lessons, when a new kid moved into my neighborhood. Ed was unlike any of my other friends. When we hung out in his room he had two albums he played over and over again, Frank Sinatra's *Come Fly With Me*, and Ahmad Jamal's *At the Pershing: But Not for Me*, both released in 1958 on the eve of my senior HS year. My parents never listened to such music. Those albums brought me back to the piano.

So, thanks to that accidental connection, and Frank and Ahmad, I've had a musical life of joy playing the songs of the Great American Songbook during my entire adult life. And I've had all those decades of enjoying Sinatra but it wasn't until he was in his mid-70's, the age I'm now approaching myself, that I had an opportunity to see him in person. It was June of 1991 and we had ventured to Las Vegas for a long weekend to see our dear friend, Peter and his wife Marge, who lived there.

Peter had been diagnosed with cancer but he was still mobile and relatively pain free and our mutual wish was to see Sinatra who was then appearing at the Riviera Hotel. We had practically front row seats, slightly off to the left, and he sang many of his signature pieces, some of the same ones I played at my concert such as "The Lady Is a Tramp," "I've Got you Under My Skin," "New York, New York" and the piece I naturally concluded my own piano tribute to him, "My Way." That June 1991 appearance turned out to be among his last concerts in Vegas. His orchestra was enthusiastically conducted by his son, Frank Sinatra Jr.

Although one could tell that age had taken its toll on Sinatra's voice by then, his phrasing, which made him so distinctive, as well as his personality, came through. He had the ability to convince the audience members that he was singing directly to and for you.

I had one tangential connection with The Chairman of the Board. In 1998 my publishing company published *Ol' Blue Eyes; A Frank Sinatra Encyclopedia*, chronicling every song he ever sang, every movie he ever appeared in. I gave a copy to a transient boater who was docked next to me at our marina as he was Sinatra's drummer for many of his concerts over a twenty year period (forgot his name). So I was regaled about several personal incidents and it was enjoyable to hear from someone who worked closely with him. Bottom line, Sinatra was a perfectionist when it came to music and how he sang a song.

He was also an outspoken person all his life. I found his 1963 Playboy interview fascinating. Then, of course, the threat was communism and the cold war. I'm pretty sure if he were around today, he'd have a thing or two to say about the present world tumult and the breakdown of our political process.

Wednesday, March 30, 2016 *Theatre Roundtable: Directly Speaking*

Last night's "Dramalogue" at Dramaworks was one of their season's best *Theatre Roundtable, Directly Speaking*. It was, for me, particularly fascinating and relevant.

This was a live question and answer session about directing, trying to answer the question "what, exactly, does a director do?" The participants were among the leading directors in South Florida, Joseph Adler the producing artistic director of the Gable Stage, David Arisco, the artistic director of the Actors' Playhouse at the Miracle Theatre, William Hayes a founding member of Palm Beach Dramaworks as well as its Producing Artistic Director, and J. Barry Lewis, Dramaworks' resident director and who also directs plays at other area theatres. Hayes and Lewis were the moderators of this spellbinding discussion. Between the four directors on the panel, they estimate having some 400 plays under their directorial belts!

What impressed me was not only the content of their discussion, but their passion as well. These directors are devoted to their craft; it is both an art and a process. I was also struck by how closely directing relates to the role I fulfilled during my career. To be a publisher for nearly forty years required the same degree of passion.

Joseph Adler likened his directorial career to pushing that absurd rock of Sisyphus up the hill, trying to reach the peak, but always being condemned to not reach it and having to do it all over again. To him, it has always been the attempt to achieve perfection, but having to settle for the act of directing as being an ongoing learning experience. I can relate. During my career as a publisher; the more I learned, the more I discovered there was to learn.

The director's role is to present the play as the author intended and to get all the artistic aspects of a production in alignment to achieve that purpose, stage design, lighting, costuming, blocking and movement of the actors, not to mention the auditioning process as actor selection is as critical as getting the actors to understand the director's vision and to act in harmony.

Amusingly, someone said when a play is good they commend the actors but when it is bad it's entirely the director's fault! It was also said that a leading actor's off night is always much worse than an average actor's average night, especially if an actor goes "rogue," changing interpretation after a play opens. The production will then most likely stray from the director's vision of the play. And, once a play opens (and in the South Florida regional theatre scene that occurs in most cases less than a month from when they first start to work on a play!), the play is no longer in the director's control; it is handed off to the stage manager. So the director has precious few weeks to get everything working together.

While there are overlapping choices of types of plays presented at the three theatres represented in the discussion, each has its specialization as well. David Arisco's background in musical theatre, as well as the size of Actor's Playhouse's 600 seat main stage has resulted in more musicals while Joseph Adler's intimate 150-seat theater in Coral Gables' Biltmore Hotel has gravitated to more experimental productions. Dramaworks' 218-seat theatre is also intimate but Hayes and company have focused more on well-established contemporary dramatic works, with some musical theatre during their summer programs. And next week it is opening its new 35 seat Diane & Mark Perlberg Studio Theatre on the second floor for its new endeavor, the Dramaworkshop, a lab for developing new plays.

There are so many similarities to my publishing days. We too would have overlapping publishing programs, particularly in academic publishing, but we also forged our way into unique reference programs and even occasionally a competitive trade book (one published for a general audience). Each press would generally be known for a particular specialty.

Unlike many commercial enterprises, book publishing is different as each book is a "unique product." Plays are similarly unique, each needing a creative team to produce it. The director of a play is its CEO, very often involved in the selection process itself, and then heading up his creative technical team, and the actors, to present the author's vision and to please his audience.

As in theatre, we had to do justice to our authors. In publishing, our team was comprised of advisory editors (to help select the publishable material or to develop new works from scratch), copy editors, production editors, marketing specialists to make sure the book reaches its intended audience, designers for promotion and for the book itself, and then the back office business -- royalties, sales receipts, customer service, etc. And there are similar business requirements to run a successful theatre, including fund raising as ticket sales themselves usually cover only about half of a regional theatre's expenses.

I make these observations as those were the thoughts running through my mind listening to these great directors speak. They were talking about a creative process I identify with although I neither have the knowledge or translatable experience to direct a play. Ask me to produce a book, no problem! Dramalogue helped bring out the sense of parallelism to my working life. The "invisible hand" of the director is not so dissimilar to working with a creative publishing team.

Tuesday, May 3, 2016 **The Great American Songbook Inhabits the Palm Beaches**

Some recent events bear witness to the title of this entry. A focal point, though, is Palm Beach's The Colony Hotel which has its very own version of Manhattan's Cafe Carlyle, or any of the well known NYC cabarets, only more intimate. The Colony's Royal Room attracts some topnotch American Songbook talent. Also, the Colony's Polo Lounge Sunday brunch this season featured one of our best jazz pianists, Bill Mays. Sometime ago we heard Mays accompany diva Ann Hampton Callaway (a composer and a great jazz-cabaret singer) at the Eissey Campus Theatre of Palm Beach State College and made it a point to seek him out at the Colony's Polo Lounge a couple of weeks ago.

I asked him to play Bill Evans' "Turn Out the Stars," not very frequently performed, a work of beautiful voicing and emotion. After a break, Mays played it solo, without the bass, effortlessly as if he plays it daily. To me, it was heartrending. Then we were treated to an impromptu performance by the then featured performer at the Royal Room -- Karen Oberlin. Amazing how an unrehearsed number by three professionals can be so natural. Bill Mays' CD *Front Row Seat* is exactly as titled – it's as if he is playing in your living room.

Last month we also caught Jane Monheit at the Royal Room who we saw years ago and who has matured into such a great stylist, with phenomenal range, her latest album, *The Songbook Sessions*, a tribute to the great Ella Fitzgerald. She performed pieces from her album and other numbers with her trio, husband Rick Montalbano on drums, Neal Miner on bass and Michael Kanin on piano, just the perfect combo for classic jazz. What a sultry performer, one of our leading jazz first ladies, along with Stacey Kent, two completely different styles but both at the top of their games.

Last Saturday our close friend and neighbor, Nina who is an artist, a cellist and a singer (do her talents have no bounds?), performed in the Choral Society of the Palm Beaches which is under the direction of S. Mark Aliapoulios – at Jupiter's Florida Atlantic University auditorium. This was one of the most diverse programs we've seen in a long time, culminating in a partially acted out version of Frank Loesser's *The Most Happy Fella*, a Broadway show which was recently performed at the New York City Opera.

The program's featured performers made it especially enjoyable, vocalists Lisa Vroman, a soprano with extensive Broadway experience (who played Rosabella in that New York City Opera presentation) and Mark Sanders, a baritone who frequently performs with the Gulf Coast Symphony. They had the perfect chemistry for performing one of the most beautiful Broadway duets ever written, Loesser's "My Heart Is So Full of You."

But for me the highlight was the appearance and performance of Paul Posnak, who arranged *Four Songs By George Gershwin* for two pianos, which he played with the Choral Society's pianist Dr. Anita Castiglione. The songs reminded me so much of Earl Wild's arrangement, *Fantasy on Porgy and Bess* and after the concert I told him so. He was delighted by the comparison, and it was apt.

Not enough praise can be directed to Dr. Catiglione for her nearly non-stop performance during the 2-1/2 hour program, easily transitioning to soloing, to accompanying, from Gershwin, to Irving Berlin, to Rogers and Hammerstein, then to Frank Loesser and finally to classical, accompanying songs beautifully sung by the 2016 Young Artist Vocal Competition Winners, Mr. Julian Frias and Ms. Celene Perez, both high school seniors with great artistic careers ahead of them. Our friend, Nina, was instrumental in organizing this competition.

Judging by these events, the American Songbook thrives and its future seems assured in the Palm Beaches.

Tuesday, June 7, 2016 **Jazz is Alive and Well in Jupiter**

I am very fortunate to have a new friend in my life, Nina's (see last entry) brother, David.

They were raised in a musical family and David Einhorn has established himself as a leading bassist. Although he lived in Martinique for the past several years, he has recently returned to South Florida to resume his jazz career here as well as continue his other vocation as a journalist.

David has played with some of the great musicians of our time, and was bassist with jazz pianist Dick Morgan for some 20 years, with several CD recordings. He's also played with Anita O'Day, Kai Winding, Nat Adderly, Woody Herman, among others. While in the Caribbean he recorded and toured with jazz pianist Reginald Policard.

Knowing that I play the piano he suggested we get together once a week and play some standards as well jazz classics. I am not a jazz musician, so I wondered why he would want to invest the effort, but as he explained it was all part of getting back in the grove, particularly with songs from The Great American Songbook, which given a lead sheet, I can play almost anything written. Meanwhile I dabble still at jazz compositions, particularly ones by Bill Evans, a great enigma to me as a pianist, beautiful melodies with harmonic and dissonance challenges.

After soloing all my life, other than accompanying a singer at one time, playing with a bassist has issues for me. Suddenly, timing became paramount. Alone, I'll add or delete beats here and there, where I "feel" the music. It's difficult for anyone trying to accompany a musical maverick. So David has been a taskmaster as well and I look forward to our usual Tuesday sessions as learning moments. But that will soon end for the summer when we depart for our boat in Connecticut, but hopefully our sessions will resume in the fall.

As David eases back into the South Florida jazz scene, I asked him to keep us apprised of any local gigs he might have and he told me that he would be performing at the Jupiter Jazz Society's 2nd anniversary Jazz Jam session at the Double Roads Tavern in Jupiter. Little did we know about this Society and the fabulous stage at Double Roads Tavern in Jupiter. This jam session is every Sunday from 5 – 9 and anyone with serious talent can sit in, but on this special occasion they started off with a professional jazz gig, Jérôme-Degey on guitar, John D. Beers III on trumpet, David Einhorn on bass, Goetz Kujack on drums and Rick Moore on keys (Cherie and Rick Moore are co-founders of the Jupiter Jazz Society).

David even inveigled Rick's group to play a Bill Evans piece in our honor, an embarrassing pleasure. For an hour this group improvised some of the great jazz classics. Where have we been Ann and I wondered? We'll now be at the Double Roads on Sunday nights when we can.

Once their set was over, and "Dr. Bob" an ophthalmologist had sat in at the keyboards, it was time to hand over the event to the "Jupiter Jazz Youth Ensemble." If this is the future of jazz it is in good hands. These kids were fabulous.

David goes into another world when he plays. He's as intense as I've ever seen a bassist and we asked David during the break, just exactly what he is experiencing at those moments. He replied that the music must come through you, almost from another place. He's found that sacred piece of real estate.

We'll be back. Maybe next year I'll pick out a lead sheet and try to do something myself with the group. Although an electronic keyboard is not my thing, and playing with a group would test my skills, one never knows

Wednesday, September 28, 2016 *Home at Last!*

Ann and I just returned from an overseas trip, a long overdue stay in one of our favorite cities, London, for a full week and then our fifth (and probably last) transatlantic crossing on a cruise ship, with numerous stops along the way.

The objectives in London were to see old friends, theatre, and museums, not to mention sampling some of London's fine restaurants. I was also looking forward to getting around on the underground. Having grown up in New York City, I know a thing or two about traveling subways, but London's underground is incomparable: it's clean, well organized, orderly (just cue up, no cutting in), and London's Visitor Oyster card makes it a pleasure.

That's how we travelled around London most of the time, although we also engaged a few Uber cars and traditional London cabs as well.

Theatre is always special there. We were able to see *In The Heights*, an early very successful musical experimentation by Lin-Manuel Miranda about the immigrant experience, his precursor to *Hamilton* with moving pastiches reminiscent of *West Side Story* and Sondheimian lyrics. We had seats on the stage, the theatre being set in traverse with seating banks on either side. Like *Hamilton*, the production is intoxicating high energy.

The following night we saw *The Go Between* based on the novel by L. P. Hartley, adapted by David Wood with music by Richard Taylor. This is a memory musical, a vehicle for Michael Crawford, beloved British star of the musical theatre. But when we arrived, the theatre was abuzz – and refunds or exchanges were being offered as Crawford could not perform and his understudy Julian Forsyth was filling in. Ironically this was the second time we had tickets to see a Michael Crawford musical in London when he couldn't sing. The first time some 25 or more years ago he stepped out onto the stage for a performance of *Barnum*, and announced he had bad news and good news. He said he had laryngitis and therefore could not sing, but, happily, his understudy would sing off stage and he would perform, Crawford mouthing the songs in sync, which he did successfully. This worked well and his understudy in *The Go Between* had a very fine voice and was an excellent actor and therefore I felt sorry for those who turned in their tickets. This is a haunting, albeit dark musical, strangely (to me) a little reminiscent of *A Little Night Music*. Doubtful it would ever come to Broadway, but well worth seeing if it does.

Another night we saw *The Truth* by Florian Zeller. This is very much in the style of Alan Ayckbourn in its conceit, a hoot with verity. One of the leads was played by a very sultry Frances O'Conner who also played Mrs. Selfridge in the British TV drama, *Mr. Selfridge*. With a little tweaking for a US audience, *The Truth* could be successfully brought here.

The following day we spent the late morning and afternoon at the Victoria and Albert Museum being enthralled as ever by the massive collections and wonderful art as well as enjoying a typical English Scones and Tea break.

That night we had tickets (which I booked well before leaving) to see *The Entertainer* produced by The Kenneth Branagh Theatre Company, starring none other than Kenneth Branagh, who plays the iconic, self-loathing, Archie Rice, a Brit comedian, singer, dancer, raconteur in the dying tradition of the old Music Hall, a metaphor for the post imperial British Empire. Among the other actors were John Hurt who had been absent from the London stage for a decade playing the legendary patriarch Billy Rice and Sophie McShera as Jean Rice – McShera played Daisy in our all time favorite *Downton Abbey*. This is a powerful almost absurdist drama by John Osborne, well known for *Look Back in Anger*.

I was intrigued by this play and its premise, my only problem being the very British accents that I found myself trying to piece together what was being said. Consequently, I bought the play on my way out of the theatre and read it. Now I understand and can recognize this as a great play. Would love to see it produced here with a more moderate accent and a guide to British Popular culture.

Saturday we decided to go to Oxford Street, visit one of Ann's long time favorite stores for nightgowns, Marks and Spencer, and walk through Selfridges, the latter being very impressive: Harry would be proud. That Saturday night we had tickets for the BIG theatre event, one very much anticipated by us both, the Open Air Theatre's production of Jane Austen's *Pride and Prejudice*, adapted by Simon Reade, in the famous Regent's Park. This is outdoors and preceded by dinner on the grounds with candlelight. The web site made it so inviting.

The one big variable for an outdoor dinner and show in London is weather of course. Well after a week of downright hot weather in London, and sunny each day, the forecast for that evening was threatening – a chilly drizzle and wind. After emerging from the underground, thinking the theatre was right nearby, we couldn't find the Regents Park entrance for the theatre and there was no indication where that might be. Well a few English ladies emerged from the underground and one had been to the theatre so we followed them. It began to rain and we walked and walked. Miles!!! We finally arrived and the rain abated (they do not cancel shows in advance no matter what the weather).

We had our dinner with the occasional pitter patter of rain on the tin roof covering our table. Ann had multiple layers and a genuine raincoat on. I had my windbreaker and a light jacket, nothing to cover my legs so I bought a thin plastic poncho just in case. The performance began in light mist and about midway it began to rain. Hard. The stage manager finally emerged with the news that they were taking a break to see whether the rain would stop. What a disappointment. While most locals were content to hang around in the bar, waiting, we looked at each other, happy that we at least saw a portion of the play, all the principals, and of course we knew where the story was going, so we left and got an Uber back to the hotel without having to fight crowds. As it was, Uber was doing surge pricing because of the rain. Thus our fifth and final theatre performance ended with a whimper.

Sunday, December 18, 2016 **Me and My Girl**

Many of the musicals produced at the Maltz are classic ones, such as *Man of La Mancha*, perhaps the best production of that show we've ever seen. Then there are the others, bordering on the silly side, such as *Me and My Girl*. But even then you can count on The Maltz to deliver a high energy professional production, so you forgive the selection and just sit back and enjoy the nonsensical. *Me and My Girl's* music is by Noel Gay and the book and lyrics are by Douglas Furber and L. Arthur Rose. It is a very British musical first performed in the West End in 1937, but you can't help but be impressed by the Maltz production in spite of the very thin plot.

Bill, a cockney Londoner learns that he is an heir to the Earl of Hareford. However, he will not receive his inheritance until he becomes a little more "civilized" and earns the approval of the Dutchess. Approval is withheld of course until he agrees to ditch his girlfriend, another cockney, Sally. True to his heart, he can't do that and is prepared to go back to his old life until, voila, as fast as you can say "Eliza Doolittle," Sally is transformed into a proper lady and all live happily ever after. The songs are mostly unmemorable (best known one is the "The Lambeth Walk") so you would think there is nothing to retain interest in such light-hearted fare. However it is the perfect plot for lots of shtick!

It is the production itself, the performers, the energy level and comic timing that made this an enjoyable evening. The cast has 26 talented people, probably the largest ensemble on any Florida stage (other than some touring companies) but this production has a secret entertainment weapon named Matt Loehr, who we've seen before at the Maltz in *The Music Man, Hello Dolly, Crazy For You* and *The Will Rogers Follies*. Not only can Loehr sing and dance with the best of them, he has that special athletic comedic gift, one similar to those skills Donald O'Conner demonstrated in the song "Make 'Em Laugh" from the film *Singin' in the Rain* One could not help but think of that number while Bill wrestles with his kingly robe. Loehr can do it all.

He's joined on stage by his leading lady Julie Kleiner who undergoes the transformation from cockney gal to proper lady as Sally, Lauren Blackman as the lovely Lady Jacqueline who has designs on Bill herself, and Mary Stout who plays the terrifying Dutchess Maria who finally relents when confronted by "true love." There are so many in the cast I could cite, too many, but I would be remiss in not mentioning one of our favorite South Florida actors, Elizabeth Dimon, who plays a supporting role as Lady Battersby. Dimon is a consummate pro, whether playing demanding dramatic parts, as we've seen her play in numerous productions at Dramaworks, or musicals (she has a glorious singing voice).

The direction of so many actors, dancers, and singers on the stage at one time is brilliantly accomplished by the very experienced James Brennan and kudos to the choreographer, Dan Knechtges, and to the scenic designer Paul Tate Depoo III. There are some very clever scene changes (such as several of Bill's ancestors coming to life from portraits on the wall during the "Song of Hareford"). All the behind the scenes technical people do a first rate job.

So, The Maltz Jupiter Theatre hits another one out of the park with this full-of-fun musical.

Monday, February 27, 2017 *Fake News in La La Land*

As they say, you can't make this stuff up. I speak of the Academy Awards' embarrassing mistake of naming *La La Land* Best Picture, only to have to retract that in the middle of *La La's* acceptance speech, naming *Moonlight*. This is all because Price Waterhouse Coopers gave the presenters the wrong envelope. Perhaps the Academy is shopping for a new accounting firm? In this era of "fake news" the mistake only feeds the Zeitgeist. Maybe it was Russian hacking? It's one thing to tamper with the election and it's quite another to mess with the Academy!

I have not seen *Moonlight*, but it does sound like award-winning material, adapted from a play. However, I loved *La La Land*, particularly Emma Stone's rendition of the song "The Audition" which I have made part of my piano repertoire. I also admired the film as a throwback to filmed musicals of the past, albeit updated for our times.

Our friends Betty and Claudia were visiting this weekend, both movie buffs, and neither they nor we had seen *Fences* (although Ann saw it on stage with James Earl Jones on Broadway when it opened) and I was surprised to find the film already being offered on pay-per-view so we watched it before the Academy Awards yesterday. I was stunned. August Wilson stands among the greatest American playwrights. Although the movie rights to the Pulitzer Prize winning play were bought soon after the play opened in 1987, it was only recently produced as Wilson had insisted that the film have a black director. His wishes continued to be honored after his death in 2005. It was Denzel Washington, one of our finest actors, who finally was chosen to direct and star in the play – he was in the 2010 revival of the play on Broadway with Viola Davis as well. I was surprised that Washington was not even nominated for best director, although he was up for best actor. Until I see *Moonlight,* which won for the "best" film, I can't comment, but what Washington accomplished as a director and as an actor has to be greatly admired. Viola Davis was spectacular as well. I will not easily forget this film, Wilson's writing, or the performances.

When you think about it, how does one chose between a *La La Land*, *Fences*, or *Moonlight* – all award deserving in their own right? It's one of the reasons why the Academy Awards doesn't resonate with me. I watched part of it, but did not see the controversial ending; both *Moonlight* and *La La Land* deserved better. But so did *Fences* and Denzel Washington.

I mentioned this before, but never went into any detail. We attended the 1980 Academy Awards as a guest of the Academy. Their "Annual Motion Picture Credits Database" was published by my firm at the time. In those days, such information was in reference book form. I used to visit the Academy and the American Film Institute searching for publishable material.

When I received an invitation to attend the Awards, I was able to combine the trip to LA with one of my editorial efforts, and, of course, Ann wanted to join me so I accepted. Unfortunately, this is way before cell phone cameras and I thought it a little tacky to arrive with my full-size Nikon hanging from my shoulder, so I have no photographs to record the experience.

I had a rented car (not very fancy) and wore just a plain suit. Ann was dressed nicely but no designer dress or even borrowed jewels. A valet took our car and in spite of being unknowns (and looking the part), we walked down the red carpet to some applause. Talk about imposters.

That was Johnny Carson's second year as host and the big film, winning most of the awards was *Kramer vs. Kramer.* I remember standing next to Gregory Peck during one of the brief breaks, I wanted to say something, but felt it would be intrusive. So we just stood there, admiring all the screen actors I recognized and he knew well. It was a lot of fun to attend this major Hollywood event, but Ann and I were outsiders, looking in.

Saturday, February 18, 2017 '*Disgraced*' *At the Maltz – Lives Come Apart at the Seams*

How does a Pulitzer Prize winning play written several years ago simply become more and more relevant since it was first produced? Is it a case of life imitating art? Here is a play about an upcoming corporate lawyer, Amir, attempting to become fully assimilated into the cultural circle of professionals, to distance himself from his Muslim heritage through marriage and lifestyle, only to watch that façade implode.

The unseen element in the play is the current political environment, the result of a campaign full of invectives directed at, among others, Muslims, and the resulting highly contested "Muslim travel ban" and reports of illegal Immigration and Customs Enforcement roundups and deportations. Playwright Ayad Akhtar might not have fully foreseen these extreme events when he wrote *Disgraced,* but after 9/11 he knew the xenophobic direction it was taking us and its impact on a man of Islamic heritage.

Amir (Fajer Kaisi) and his wife Emily (Vanessa Morosco) are pursuing the classic American Dream, living in a sophisticated Upper East

Side apartment, obviously possessing the resources to enjoy their professional lives. The set by Anne Mundell and lighting by Paul Black telegraph Manhattan power couple. It is a crisp, contemporary setting with a view of the Manhattan skyline from their balcony.

As a mergers and acquisition lawyer, Amir has acquired all the trappings of master of his craft. Fajer Kaisi revels in his alpha male role, one which takes him from brash overconfidence to a stunning reversal of fortune. He powerfully delivers this plunge with steely skill. We first see him stridently berating his paralegal for missing three words in a contract, screaming into the phone *that's why we pay you six figures!*

Emily, an artist, accepts this behavior as perfectly normal in her volatile husband who in turn is amused by and tolerates her latest passionate love for Islamic Art, something acquired during their travels in Moorish inspired Spain. While he mildly encourages her latest works, it is also clear that he is not happy about this obsession. Vanessa Morosco as Emily is a highly accomplished actress who portrays a striving artist waiting for her first big show, a wife devotedly in love who never fully grasps her husband's deepest insecurities and secrets.

Amir's nephew, Abe, sensitively played by Eddie Morales with wide-eyed adoration of his uncle is disturbed that a local Imam has been falsely imprisoned. He feels this is politically motivated, and the manifestation of growing Muslimophobia. He comes to his Aunt and Uncle for their help. Emily urges her husband to lend his professional legal advice. He loves his wife and reluctantly agrees. Eventually there is a trial. However Amir's name is mentioned in a newspaper article about the case although he wasn't acting on behalf of the defendant, but suddenly his firm is aware of his Islamic background, something he has conspicuously hidden.

The stage is set for a developing train wreck of a "dinner with friends," one Emily gives for Isaac (Joel Reuben Ganz) an art gallery owner who wants to exhibit her work (and has more than a professional interest in her), and his wife, Jory (Chantal Jean-Pierre), who coincidentally works with Amir in the same law firm. The evening devolves into an increasingly revelatory and combative conversation between a Muslim (albeit assimilated), a Jew, the African-American attorney and a WASP, where Amir has to confront himself and his apostate views.

Both Joel Reuben Ganz and Chantal Jean-Pierre as the interracial couple give outstanding, persuasive performances, Ganz a credible foil to Kaisi's Amir and Jean-Pierre's Jory providing some well timed comic lines. She comports herself with the precision of another professional on the move to corporate greatness. The pot is stirred with a boiling brew of high voltage issues, religion, the clash of cultures and civilizations; Christian, Judaic, and Islamic, as well as the volatility and infidelity of both marriages.

With the help of the ubiquitous truth-teller, alcohol, Amir, who is already feeling deeply abased by his law firm is steadily driven into the recesses of his ancestry to the point of uttering the unutterable, that the crucible of 9/11 gave him some secret satisfaction; it is a pin-dropping game changer in the play. Although he defends the revelation as being "tribal" and "in his bones," he has become radioactive, meant to be shunned by the ultimate fall from grace. The contrast is striking. He is a broken man -- and the audience is left to deliberate whether there is any hope for the millennium old conflict of religious indoctrination and bias.

It is stunning, powerful theatre. As J. Barry Lewis, the seasoned director of some 200 shows including many others at The Maltz as well as Dramaworks said "*Disgraced* focuses on the various ways each of us secretly continue to hold on to our tribal identities – our identities from birth, of our education – in spite of our various and ongoing attempts to enlighten our lives. We are products of the world we create, often finding safety in those tribal identities. The play has been called 'an evening of cocktails and confessions,' and it is certain to spark dialogue about our own contradictions." Lewis skillfully brings those observations front and center utilizing a talented group of actors and technical professionals.

In addition to Paul Black's lighting, Lewis had Marty Mets' skillful sound design, the opening scene overlaying Middle Eastern music with the sounds of the city below, segueing to the music alone during scene changes and then, again, the unmistakable sounds of the city when Amir angrily opens the door to their balcony, a reminder of the world from which he is suddenly ostracized. Leslye Menshouse's costume design is chic, in keeping with the sophisticated early 21st century Manhattan professional environment, replete with Amir's expensive dress shirts.

The Maltz Theatre's *Disgraced* is superb drama.

Saturday, March 25, 2017 **Vicki Lewis Triumphs in 'Gypsy'**

We all know the story and most have seen both the play and the movie *Gypsy* about the struggle of an obsessed stage mother driving her youngest daughter's rise to fame during the fading years of vaudeville. For me, there were three reasons to see this show yet again: the music of Jule Styne, the lyrics of Stephen Sondheim, and the character driven roles created by Arthur Laurents who mined the memoirs of Gypsy Rose Lee when creating the story.

Even with these attributes, how does one breathe new life into the well known story? There is of course the Maltz theatre's reliable skill of handling musicals, but in the case of this *Gypsy* there is also the powerhouse of a performer, Vicki Lewis, who plays Rose on steroids. Her portrayal alone is worth revisiting *Gypsy*, along with an exceptional supporting cast. But when Lewis is on stage, she is a force of nature, self deluded by her unrealistic ambition for her daughters, only to rise out of the ashes of self destruction with the colossal closing number "Rose's Turn." On the other hand she keeps the audience feeling distressed by her constant manipulations only to have our hearts go out to her, again and again.

This is a woman with many losses in her life, her own mother and several husbands, then June, the daughter she grooms for stardom, played with wide-eyed innocence by Jillian Van Niel, and then the man who stood by her, Herbie, flawlessly performed by John Scherer (seen previously at the Theatre in *La Cage aux Folles, Annie* and *They're Playing Our Song,* as well as on Broadway). Ultimately, we grieve as much for Herbie, another casualty of Rose's delusions.

We watch the transformation of talented Emma Stratton as Louise (whose national tour credits include *Bullets Over Broadway* and *Anything Goes*), from the ungraceful neglected child into the great Gypsy Rose Lee, an accident of Herbie booking the troupe at a burlesque theater. There we meet three of the most unlikely caricatures of burlesque performers, who belt out one of my favorite songs, so typical Sondheim in its word play, "You Gotta Get a Gimmick."

There are so many people to mention, but a special call out to Brett Thiele who plays Tulsa, whose dance and song solo with Louise looking on in an alley behind a theatre is reminiscent of a Gene Kelly routine, singing one of my other favorites, "All I Need is the Girl." It is at this moment that a "performance gene" is awakened in Louise, not to mention the spark of love. But Tulsa eventually takes June for his own now leaving Rose with her overlooked daughter, Louise, a new project to mold into stardom.

Marcia Milgrom Dodge, whose work on revivals, new musicals, and plays has been seen throughout the world, directed and choreographed the Maltz production. There is a very effective, moving scene where Rose's troupe of child performers meld into adults in an instant, still singing and performing the same old routines. Be prepared to be wowed by the conceit. She said the following about *Gypsy*: "I'm drawn to stories that illuminate the human condition: stories about families; flawed characters with strong ambitions and giant dreams." And, indeed, that is what the show is all about.

Gypsy is the show where Sondheim felt he finally came into his own and experienced a liberating freedom in writing the lyrics. He further acknowledged that the music by Jule Styne "supplied the atmosphere of both the milieu and of the musical theatre itself." It was one of the last musicals for which Sondheim was merely the lyricist but you get the sense he was learning the musical treatment from a master, saying "Jule's score was redolent of not only vaudeville and burlesque but of the old fashioned, straightforward, character-driven musical play...of which *Gypsy* was one of the last examples and probably the best."

The list of memorable songs is endless from this musical. In addition to the ones I already mentioned, "Let Me Entertain You." "Some People," "Small World," "You'll Never Get Away from Me," "If Momma Was Married" (another personal favorite, so vintage Sondheim), "Everything is Coming Up Roses," and "Let Me Entertain You," plus others!

Although frequently performed, and indelibly etched in our memories from the film, here is a refreshing revisit, made particularly memorable by Vicki Lewis' performance.

Saturday, June 24, 2017 **The Regency Era invades Boca with Sense and Sensibility**

Calling all Janeites! Calling all Janeites! Mr. Henry Dashwood has died, leaving his home to John, son from his first marriage, and John's scheming wife, Fanny, who has convinced her husband to banish his father's second wife and her three daughters from their home, relegating them to Barton Cottage in Devonshire. The shock of it all! A mere cottage! And the three young women, two of marriageable age, Elinor and Marianne, have no attachments and the bereft Dashwood women have but a very small inherited income.

If you are an inveterate Jane Austen enthusiast, you of course recognize this as the beginning of *Sense and Sensibility*, her first novel published in 1811. It is a whirlwind novel of scandal, gossip, attachments made and attachments broken, the manners and mores of Regency England, and of course love.

Here is a wonderful adaptation written by Kate Hamill for the stage which opened last night, and a high energy production by FAU's Department of Theatre and Dance. Ultimately, the affections of the steadfast Edward Ferrars, and the stalwart Colonel Brandon win over the sensible Elinor and the mercurial Marianne, respectively, but before that much anticipated denouement, we are treated to a dizzying array of plot complications and impediments to love conquering all.

The cast made up mostly of MFA Graduate Students and two equity actors are all equally professional. If this is the future of South Florida Theater, it will flourish. It is a large cast including several members of "gossip groups," sort of a Greek Chorus which brings the audience into the temper of the times. Hilariously, they also function as dogs and horses in the play, just adding more action to what is already a lot of moving parts on stage as the minimalist scenery is on wheels and the cast is constantly moving them into new places. Comedic elements emerge throughout the production.

Although it is impossible to comment on each and every performer, they are all very convincing, but I'll signal out Jessica Eaton who plays Fanny, her malice giving no grounds, and Traven Call who captures the essence of dog, horse, and finally the foppish brother of Edward, Robert Ferris. Amanda Corbett plays Elinor and Gabriela Tortoledo is Marianne, both performing flawlessly in these two demanding major roles.

What makes this production so enjoyable is the period Regency costumes (Dawn Shamburger), the music of the times (Sound Design by Rich Szczublewski), the fast moving choreography (kudos to Jean-Louis Baldet the Director and Suzanne Clement Jones, Stage Manager), and, again, a cast thoroughly committed to their craft. Technical and Lighting Design is by Thomas M. Shorrock, and K. April Soroko is Scenic Designer. A special mention goes to the Dialect Coach Jenna Wyatt -- getting that right is half the battle in such a production.

If there is one minor quibble (not to me personally, but it might be to some) it is the length, more than 2-1 / 2 hours including intermission. Of course a familiarity with the novel would be helpful. If you haven't read it, there is always Wikipedia. But after you've seen it, maybe you will want to read it as well as all of Jane Austen and become a Janeite like my wife Ann!

Tuesday, July 25, 2017 *We'll Take Manhattan*

We recently returned from a week in NYC, a whirlwind revisit of our old stomping grounds, cramming in too much for a single entry. Thus, this one focuses on the five Broadway shows we saw while there. I could write detailed reviews of each, but Broadway is well reviewed and doesn't need my help. So these are some personal comments on the shows we booked many months before the Tony Awards and even before three of them actually opened. In other words, we took a chance on those – although we knew something about them in advance. Call this write up an impressionistic review.

Before getting into the shows themselves, I must confess we were not fully prepared for the theatre district in the summer, although we're both ex-New Yorkers and should know better. The week before we left, every long term weather forecast had promised a week of ideal conditions, temperatures in the mid 80's, moderate humidity. Ah, we said in confidence as we packed to catch a Jet Blue flight to LaGuardia, lucky us. But that following week morphed from idyllic into a scorching heat wave, one day reaching the mid 90s with high humidity. And we left "cool" Florida for this?

As anyone who has lived in the city knows, if the air temperature is in the mid 90's, the buildings and the macadam, the traffic, and the hordes of people, just magnifies the heat. We were staying at 54th between Broadway and 8th Avenue and thought we'd be able to walk or Uber wherever we needed between the hotel, the shows, and restaurants. More unrealistic thinking. Traffic was at a standstill most of the time. The only way to get to your destination was to walk. Subways were impossible too. And we walked mostly on 8th Avenue, frequently in the street as the sidewalks were so congested. Because of the heat, the sidewalk vendors, the mobs of tourists and trash all over the place, the stench sometimes was insufferable. But as ex New Yorkers we beat on to our destinations.

I'll start with the least appealing show, although it was entertaining, *War Paint* adapted by Doug Wright, music by Scott Frankel, and lyrics by Michael Korie. We bought front row tickets way before it opened and were showered by the spit of Patti LuPone and Christine Ebersole, whose presence alone was worth the price of admission. When their contracts are up, *War Paint* will recede into Broadway history. The music was agreeable but not memorable. However, the costumes were fantastic as well as the scenic design by David Korins who designed *Hamilton* and two other shows running on Broadway now, *Dear Evan Hansen*, and *Bandstand*. We were disappointed that there was little dance, unusual for a big Broadway show. Personally, I also found the subject frivolous. Do I care about cosmetics, although I get the point that these were two women battling in a man's world? Nonetheless it was a privilege to see two divas at work.

Dear Evan Hansen lived up to its hype, Ben Platt a unique performer who can sing beautifully while crying at the same time. In fact, the audience was crammed with Ben Platt groupies. A young lady sitting in front of us (her friend sitting two rows behind us so we were privileged to be in on some of their conversation before the show and during the intermission), was seeing the show for the 6th time, seats to this particular performance being a present from her mother on this, her 21st birthday. She was at the edge of her seat whenever Platt was on stage and singing, which is most of the time. The music moved the plot along and some beautiful songs, "Waving Through a Window," sung by Evan and Company, "So Big/So Small" sung by Evan's mother Heidi (Rachel Bay Jones) to name just two. Both Jones and Platt won Tonys for their performances. Steven Levenson wrote the book and the Music and Lyrics were by Benj Pasek and Justin Paul (who is from our old home town, Westport, CT).

As moving as the show was, it's the first time Ann and I felt that this was a show for another generation (didn't feel that way when we saw Lin-Manuel Miranda's pre-*Hamilton* show, *In the Heights* in London which is hip hop multiculturalism). It's not that we didn't feel moved but the reality of how millennial families connect or are torn apart by social media is a major theme. We understand but it's not our world.

The Great Comet of 1812 was spectacular. The Imperial Theatre was gutted for the staging, some of the audience sitting at tables, the action taking place all around. Josh Grobin had just left the show. Okierite Onaodowan who we saw in *Hamilton* was his replacement. He did a credible job but I think Grobin's voice might have worked better in the role. But that is not to detract from the overall impression of the show, great music, phenomenal choreography – constant movement, and the kind of show only Broadway could put on in that form. It leaves an indelible impression, in the same way *Hamilton* and *Les Mis* does.

So much has been written about Josh Grobin that one would think his role playing Pierre was the primary one in the show. It is not – it is more of a fulcrum. The two dominant characters revolving around him are Natasha played by Denée Benton in her Broadway debut, who was nominated for a Tony, and Lucas Steele who plays the dashing womanizer, Anatole. It is a large cast, with many outstanding performances.

The music is infectious, rock at times, lyrical at other times (usually with a Cossack aspect), with an interesting back story as to how Dave Malloy who wrote the book, the music, and the lyrics came to envision the show: "I first read *War and Peace* while working on a cruise ship, playing piano in the show band, as a way for my landlocked girlfriend and I to stay connected. I remember being so enthralled by the scope of Tolstoy's vision; the book was a trashy romance novel, a family drama, a hilarious farce, a military thriller, a philosophical scripture, a treatise on history, all wrapped into one giant, messy, nearly unmanageable tome. And then there was that section. Volume 2, Book 5. I think I read the whole 70-page slice in one sitting, staying up til 5 a.m. with the delirious obsession I usually reserved for Stephen King or Harry Potter. Up to this point, Natasha had been so mirthful and pure that her downfall seemed to come screaming out of nowhere . . . and then Pierre, his sudden righteous action, his heart finally alive, his simple kindness, the comet . . . it all happened so quickly. At the end of it, as I read the last words "into a new life" with tears streaming down my face, I had the weirdest and clearest epiphany: that this was the perfect story for a musical." His epiphany was our delight.

Groundhog Day with the book by Danny Rubin and music and lyrics by Tim Minchin was enjoyable, surprisingly faithful to the movie. Very clever set designs and the infectiously likeable and talented Andy Karl who performed in spite of a torn ACL made the show. Great dancing too and the music was more than incidental. I just didn't see how that film could be turned into a musical, but it worked wonderfully. *Groundhog Day* will become a traveling show one day, and worth seeing.

One disappointment was not being able see an equal number of dramas as well, but we took a chance on one of The Roundabout's new plays which they developed with the Long Wharf in CT: *Napoli, Brooklyn*. Long after we got tix it opened and the *NYT* had a so-so review. It deserved a much better one. Rarely have we seen characters so sharply drawn, memorable, except in some of the classic American plays.

It is set in Brooklyn in 1960. I was living there then and there is a horrific incident that takes place at the time (no further detail to avoid a spoiler). It becomes a catalyst. The play is about Italian immigrants, a man who arrives as a stowaway with his wife, and how they try to make a life in Brooklyn. He's a manual laborer and his wife bears him three daughters. That's strike one in the family, the father frustrated he has no sons. His disappointment with life in the New World and his family is clear: *If we stayed in Italy we would have had a son.*

He's not an O'Neill alcoholic father, but he is a workaholic and expects the same from his family. He demands absolute obedience and is baffled by the way things devolved in his life. This leads to the conflict and the resolution. The mother is trying to please everyone, her husband in particular, with her food and peacemaking efforts, the older daughter has sacrificed her youth for the benefit of the family, the middle daughter has to retreat to a Catholic convent after being attacked by the father, while the youngest, 16 years old, is trying to stowaway to Paris with another girl, daughter of an Irish immigrant, with whom she's in love. There is much more to the play than that -- it was riveting, a feminist spin on American family drama , written by Meghan Kennedy. Remember that name. Fantastic acting.

In addition to the 5 plays we caught our favorite jazz pianist at Dizzy's Club Coca Cola, Monty Alexander (and his "Junkanoo Swing"), who takes swinging jazz and combines it with the rhythms of Jamaica. His original composition, *Hope* reminded me of Oscar Peterson's *Canadian Suite*, jazz compositions which have classical underpinnings, not improvisational jazz. It was an ideal setting on the 5th Floor of the Time Warner building at 60th St, overlooking Columbus Circle, nearby our first apartment. The view is as breathtaking as the music.

All in all, it was a magical week of theatre in Manhattan.

Saturday, August 5, 2017 **Life is COMPANY, Sondheim's Classic**

Bobby.../ Bobby.../ Bobby baby.../ Bobby bubi.../ Robby.../ Robert darling.../ Bobby, we've been trying to call you...

This is my favorite Sondheim musical. Yes, it's dated, but it's been updated. Yes, it doesn't measure up in some ways to some of his later works, but it stands on its own.

So, why do I feel this way? I think it is THE breakout musical for Sondheim, for which he wrote both the lyrics and music (not his first time, but his most successful first time). It set the stage for everything that followed in American musical theatre. His intricate scoring, the deep emotional, dramatic and comic connections, his ability to merge words and music, anoint him as our very own Shakespeare of the American musical stage. And it doesn't hurt that the main character is Bobby!

So we set off to see the MNM Production at the Rinker Playhouse which is part of the Kravis Center for the Performing Arts, albeit late in the production run. Therefore I was able to see what some other critics had to say about the show, which I would characterize as being lukewarm, one even unfairly comparing it to the Dramaworks' *Sweeney Todd* production which is concurrently playing nearby. Such a comparison is apples to oranges (although Dramaworks' production is the best *Sweeney Todd* that we've ever seen). One is more like opera and the other is like a cabaret revue.

This is a high, high energy production and MNM Production's mission is to bring Florida's own reservoir of considerable talent to the stage. These are all local professionals and we who live in South Florida have to applaud and support such an effort. Many of the cast we've seen before at different area venues. They are highly experienced and most of the cast have great voices and terrific comic timing.

Company is also squarely set in New York City in 1970, the year Ann and I married and we were still living there. In fact, the musical opened the day we were married. It speaks very directly to me. It rose out of a number of one act plays written by George Firth and was brought together by Sondheim, morphing the main character – outsiders in each -- into one person, "Bobby." It utilizes a series of connected songs that underscore the main theme: the foibles of marriage. For its time it was revolutionary as so many of Sondheim musicals have continued to be.

Bobby the bachelor is conflicted about being married versus the stories of his friends who have problematic marriages as well as his girlfriends who have issues of their own. He is plainly confused. It hangs out there like unresolved anxiety, right to the end.

As it was based on a series of plays that spoke for themselves, the music Sondheim wrote is not in the classic move-the-plot-along variety.

This groundbreaking musical explores the loneliness of love relationships, and the importance of friends, in the most vibrant metropolis of our time. We move through the "approach-avoidance" complex of marriage through a series of songs, so many of them now classics, and several incorporated in the widely performed Sondheim revue, *Side by Side by Sondheim.*

As some of the critical reviews pointed out, Robert William Johnston who plays Bobby does not have an exceptional singing voice, and he has to sing some of the more moving songs, "Someone Is Waiting," "Marry Me a Little," and "Being Alive," but he carries these on the shoulders of his acting abilities and we enjoyed his performance. He is also supported by some of the finest singers in South Florida and so much of the show is ensemble singing and then solos or duets by Bobby's friends and girlfriends.

The four couples in the play (Joanne and Larry. Peter and Susan, Jenny and David, and Harry and Sarah) knock it out of the park with "The Little Things You Do Together," an acerbic rebuke about marital relationships. The husbands meanwhile leeringly hover over Bobby, singing "Have I Got A Girl for You" in the first and second acts.

There are several real show-stopping moments in this production: Amy's (Leah Sessa) riotous, "Getting Married Today," Marta's (Mallory Newbrough) "Another Hundred People," capturing the city's sense of alienation with gusto, and Joanne's (Erika Scotti) stinging, cynical piece about the empty lives of affluent women in the city, "The Ladies Who Lunch." His girlfriends, Marta, April, and Kathy, critique his non-committal ways in a hilarious pastiche of a sister act song in "You Could Drive a Person Crazy."

One of my favorite songs from the show is "Sorry – Grateful," expressing the ambivalence of marriage, sung by Bobby's friends, Harry, David, and Larry when Bobby asks Harry whether he was ever sorry he got married. It's a perfectly measured argument, lyrically, and expressed in a waltz like rhythm, classic Sondheim: "You're sorry-grateful / Regretful-happy / Why look for answers / Where none occur?"

Every song in the show is timeless and every performer brings his / her best to the stage in their delivery. It is an extraordinary cast.

Bruce Linser demonstrates his considerable directing skills in this production, accentuating the comedic elements (e.g. Sarah's karate exhibition and her secret food addiction) and, with Kimberly Dawn Smith's choreography, brings out the best of the energetic, ensemble pieces such as "Side By Side By Side" in the second act.

Set design by Tim Bennett gives the director and cast a main stage to work on and five different platforms, sometimes all of them being utilized at the same time. The set suggests the isolated nature of city life and the 70's, although it is creatively brought into the present by Linser having his cast use the ubiquitous cell phone, replacing the answering machine.

The musical accompaniment is first rate, Paul Reekie directing four other musicians while playing the piano. This is the kind of theatre that merits our appreciation and support in the future.

Saturday, September 2, 2017 **Appropriate**

A return to our Connecticut roots would not be complete without attending a play produced by the Westport Country Playhouse. The playhouse retains its essential "country" character although the old wooden bench seats are gone (thankfully) and air conditioning has been introduced (in fact too air conditioned), but the essential mission of presenting the highest caliber theatre has been retained. The play we saw – *Appropriate* -- just finished its run. Even without having seen the play when it opened Off Broadway in 2014, I imagine the Westport Country Playhouse's production is every bit as successful,

The play was, as the author admits, "appropriated" in some way from a number of the finest American family dramas of our times. In particular there is attribution to Sam Shepard's *Buried Child*, Horton Foote's *Dividing the Estate*, and Tracy Letts' *"August: Osage County"*. And to say the play is derivative of such works, to me, is not a criticism but a compliment. Branden Jacob-Jenkins' dialogue is a new voice in American theatre and even though every family may be unhappy in its own way, eventually it all boils down to dreams deferred or unrealized and the blame that hangs heavily in rare family reunions. When that reunion is over the death of a patriarch, and there is a dark secret that explodes on the family, as it does on the adult children, Toni, Bo, and Franz, the stage is literally set for conflict. And when you take your seat, the chaos of the gloomy stage foreshadows what will unfold.

I was amazed at Jenkins' ability to draw such well defined characters and to write such potent dialogue. There is even a "fight director" for the play as verbal accusations, not only become loud, but physical as well. And the three siblings are not the only ones caught in the fray; there is an aggrieved spouse, a new age girlfriend, and children of the spouses. The dysfunction is multi-generational. No one escapes the tragedy, which is eerily heightened by a decaying ancestral Arkansas family home (think Tennessee Williams), the increasing intensity of the sound of cicadas, and the suggestion of ghosts haunting the property. And of course, the secret, the inexplicable discovery of a photo album containing pictures of lynching's among their father's property (in addition to the home being on the border of a white graveyard with stones, and unmarked graves of blacks on the other side): the original American sin and their father's potential complicity confounds and divides the family further.

The Westport Country Playhouse has spared no expense in scenic design, lighting, and sound. They recognize Jacobs-Jenkins as an astute dramatist who is at the beginning of an important, noteworthy playwriting career. We were fortunate to catch this production. This is what great theatre is all about and we will be watching for future works by this talented and gifted writer.

Saturday, February 10, 2018 *A Gripping Production of 'An Inspector Calls' at Maltz Jupiter Theatre*

J.B. Priestley's *An Inspector Calls*, a cautionary moral tale encapsulated in a mystery, is successfully portrayed by accomplished actors under the fast-paced direction of J. Barry Lewis at the Maltz Jupiter Theatre. It is a period piece reminiscent of *Downton Abbey* or *Upstairs, Downstairs*, with the "downstairs" staff silently bearing witness to the conscienceless actions of their "superiors."

Although written at the end of WW II, the play is set in 1912. As Europe emerged from WW II, J. B. Priestley saw the irony of calling WW I "a war to end all wars", and realized the dangers of relying on the privileged aristocracy to ameliorate the travails of the masses. This play remains relevant for today's audience. No doubt J. B. Priestley would have seen parallels to the present with a plutocracy now permeating our government.

The entire play takes place on one evening in 1912 at the home of the wealthy Birling family who are celebrating the engagement of their daughter Sheila to Gerald Croft, who is the son of one of Birling's competitors in the mill business. The family patriarch, Arthur Birling (Rob Donohoe) is particularly pleased by the union as it will probably be good for future profits. He is the quintessential capitalist, in his ineffable aristocratic way pontificating that "a man has to look after himself and his own."

It is all very jovial but that initial scene takes place behind Dadaesque style suspended windows which convey a sense of unreality. The "downstairs" help sit stoically listening while the festivities are underway.

Suddenly an Inspector Goole (James Andreassi) arrives to question the Birling family about the apparent suicide of a young girl, Eva Smith. The abstract windows have been lifted from the scene and the proceedings are now realistic. Goole is arrogant in his demeanor, relentless in his interrogation, insisting that he question each family member in a particular order (all part of the mystery). Andreassi recently finished a successful run in *The Little Foxes* at Dramaworks where he was one of the greedy businessmen. The two plays are jarringly similar in their meaning and are set almost in the same time period. Andreassi's performance is mesmerizing and compelling as he had an expectant audience waiting for him to turn on the next family member.

His first victim is Arthur Birling imperiously played by Rob Donohoe. His character shifts from high handedness to reluctant admission that he did know the girl, having fired her two years before as she asked for a small raise. He was also concerned about union activity. So what's the crime in that, he wonders? No, in fact he had an obligation to fire her to keep his costs under control (and his profits high, of course). Donohoe gives a shimmering depiction of a desperate man trying to hold on to his position in society (perhaps a Knighthood?) and keep himself and his family from defamation.

Next, the Inspector turns his attention to the Birling's eldest child Sheila (Charlotte Bydwell), who confesses that she recognized the photo of Eva as a person who waited on her at a dress shop where Sheila had felt slighted, complained to the shop owner resulting in Eva being fired (once again). Sheila's actions are culpable but not criminal. Bydwell gives a brilliant performance, expressing remorse and guilt for her actions, righteous fury at her fiancé when she learns of his involvement and stunningly becomes the conscience that her family members lack.

Her fiancé, Gerald (Jeremy Webb) is next on the docket. Here matters escalate as we learn that Eva had changed her name and ultimately became Gerald's mistress. At this point the family is collapsing upon itself. Webb plays the consummate aristocrat now humiliated in front of his fiancé and her family. He is full of contrition while attempting to maintain his aristocratic demeanor, making us feel sympathy and loathing simultaneously.

Enter the matriarch Sybil (Angie Radosh) who is the head of a women's charity. She had recently rejected Eva Smith's plea for charitable help although she knew Smith was pregnant. Smith called herself Mrs. Birling, which infuriated Sybil even further. Radosh is the classic condescending grand dame, scoffing at the Inspector, rejecting any fault of her own or her family members. She is a consummate actress and when she speaks, the audience is captivated. Her mood swings from arrogance to stricken conscience to haughty elation when she believes it all a hoax is a master class in acting.

Finally, attention is paid to the young adult son of the Birlings, Eric (Cliff Burgess), who is also connected with the young woman, but it would be a spoiler to reveal more. Eric is an alcoholic and by the time he is questioned, the moral culpability of all has been well established. Burgess is a very versatile actor and portrays the troubled scion of a wealthy family with the physical skill and emotional clout of a spoiled unprincipled young man.

Interestingly, most of the characters briefly break the fourth wall to plead their case directly to the audience. This brings the audience into the play as we all ultimately have a stake in our own conduct and the outcome of our actions. We have just witnessed a multitude of societal misdeeds that unfold every day in thousands of ways.

With the finishing of the questioning, the family implodes upon itself culminating in an explosion, as if a bomb has been dropped on the house. The mysterious Inspector departs with the admonishment *each of you helped to kill her.*

Gerald, who went for a walk to cool off and to reconsider his broken engagement, returns to the shambles of the house, and finds everyone in utter abasement. But he brings a theory which seems to exonerate the family, giving them, especially Arthur, false hope that it was all fabricated (although what they confessed to actually took place) by this unverified Inspector Goole, for what reasons, unknown.

The content of a phone call at the play's end is like a sledge hammer dropping. And suddenly, bathed in stark bright light is Edna (the incomparable Elizabeth Dimon), the head of housekeeping in a silent but disapproving role, and behind, a handful of refugee, hungry and poor onlookers, the silent jury. It is an absolutely riveting production, without intermission, that gathers momentum until the mystifying conclusion.

Priestly is an indirect literary descendant of Charles Dickens whose focus on social conditions and the bleak prospects for the masses were endemic to his work -- although, Dickens was not thought of as a socialist, more as a humanitarian. His works were not political. J.B. Priestly was a socialist, but *An Inspector Calls* is not a polemic. It merely cries out that no man is an island. We are a society and even our slightest actions have ramifications. If we are to reject "the dreamers" we, as a society, bear responsibility.

As the play's multiple Carbonell Award-winning director J. Barry Lewis commented "Such plays remain relevant because they portray everyday people – you and me – often at our worst. While as an audience we are voyeurs to the story, we may see ourselves in the choices and mistakes that each of the characters make. *An Inspector Calls* explores the capitalistic nature of society, the hypocrisy of the Victorian and Edwardian eras and examines the role of the individual and their responsibility to their fellow man."

In fact the staging endeavors to make the audience feel somewhat complicit as well. Kirk Bookman's lighting design bathes the stage, and sometimes the audience, in an eerie bright light. That combined with resident sound designer Marty Mets' rumbling sound, piercing at times, heightens the tension and the culpability of all. Tracy Dorman's costumes are stunning, period perfect.

Victor Becker's imaginative scenic design captures both the surrealism and the realism of the production. It is one of Maltz Theatre's most successful plays of the season. No wonder when we entered the theatre for last night's production a sign read "this performance sold out."

Monday, February 19, 2018 *A Cultural Capitol in the Winter*

This is "high season" in Palm Beach County for countless opportunities to enjoy theatre of all genres, dance, music and art exhibitions. To try to take them all in would leave little time for anything else. While I love the theatre in general, I share Stephen Sondheim's general aversion to the opera, probably because, for me, it's too much of a hybrid, theatre, music, sometimes dance and high drama all rolled into one, and while I appreciate a fine voice, my sensibilities draw me to the Great American Songbook.

It's not as if I've never been exposed to opera, although my parents never went to one or listened to them on their "Victrola." In college, when I minored in music, I was able to get a ticket once in a while to the nosebleed section of the Metropolitan Opera House where there were students' desks, and I would endeavor to follow the score. I was impressed by the pageantry, but the music left me rather indifferent. So I grew away from opera which I'm sure is my loss.

Ann on the other hand loves the opera so we've gone our separate ways, she subscribing to the Palm Beach Opera season (after having enjoyed the Metropolitan Opera in NYC while we lived there or nearby) with a friend. One of the features of the PB Opera is a "lunch-and-learn" a couple of weeks before each performance and recently one of her friends was unable to go and offered the ticket to me. Normally I'd decline, but the program focused on *Candide* by Leonard Bernstein, one of my musical "heroes" who could write for all different musical genres.

Remarkably, and luckily for us all, Nina Bernstein Simmons, the youngest daughter of the great Leonard Bernstein, was the main speaker, lovingly guiding the audience through the humor and genius of her father's operetta. *Candide* is to be performed at the Kravis Center in West Palm Beach at the end of this month. Parts of the program are brief performances, accompanied by piano, by the Benenson Young Artists, all opera students ready to graduate to the main stage.

Their voices soared, and in particular, the best known piece, "Glitter and Be Gay," sung by Chelsea Bonagura. None other than the great Barbara Cook who one normally associates with the Great American Songbook can be heard singing this on You Tube.

David Stern, the conductor for the Palm Beach Opera and the son of Isaac Stern joined Nina Bernstein to reminiscence about his father's friendship with Bernstein. It was moving to see their two adult children sharing those memories.

Before that, again I was lucky enough to be the recipient of a subscription ticket from another one of Ann's friends, this time to the Miami City Ballet. Ah, the ballet. *Everything was beautiful at the ballet, / Raise your arms and someone's always there. /Yes, everything was beautiful at the ballet, /At the ballet, /At the ballet!!!* With a few exceptions, that song from *The Chorus Line* is as close as I've been to a ballet as well.

But a couple of weeks ago I did a grand jeté to the Miami City Ballet centennial celebration of Jerome Robbins. Like Bernstein, Robbins is a cross over artist, probably best known for his work on *West Side Story*, which he directed and choreographed, with Leonard Bernstein the composer and Stephen Sondheim the lyricist. Here are all the musical artists I most admire.

And, the second part of the program was dedicated to the *West Side Story Suite*, including, a "Prologue," "Something's Coming," "Dance at the Gym," "Cool, America," "Rumble," concluding with the "Somewhere Ballet."

Ironically, it was a company premiere in the first part of the program which stole the show, *The Cage*. When it first premiered in NYC in 1986 the *New York Times* remarked: "Once seen, *The Cage* tends not to be forgotten. Jerome Robbins's depiction of life in a covey of female insects is gruesome. These are females who consider males of the species their prey, and two males are killed with brutal dispatch during the ballet, with Stravinsky's String Concerto in D somberly accompanying the murders." Indeed, not to be forgotten. It was spectacularly fascinating.

Thursday, March 8, 2018 *I Didn't Know About You*

The longer I live the more I'm astounded by the cornucopia of beautiful music from the Great American Songbook. You think you've heard all those classic songs, ones which will endure and transcend what passes as popular music today, and suddenly you hear a "new" one (at least to me), either at a jazz jam or even on the old fashioned radio.

One would think radio is a thing of the past, all the FM stations mostly devoted to contemporary "music" until Legends Radio 100.3 FM was founded in the Palm Beaches by professional broadcaster Dick Robinson, who is also the founder of the *Society for the Preservation of the Great American Songbook*. Even though local, it's available world-wide at LegendsRadio.com.

I remember pulling out of our driveway one day, listening to 100.3 and hearing "I Didn't Know About You." I said to Ann that song sounds like one by Duke Ellington. His "In a Sentimental Mood" is one of my favorites. I made a mental note of the song and looked it up in one of my Jazz fake books when we returned home and sure enough, it's by Duke Ellington, with beautiful lyrics written by Bob Russell.

The version we heard on the radio was performed by one of our jazz favorites, Jane Monheit who we saw a couple of years ago at the Colony on Palm Beach. Her rendition of "I Didn't Know About You" on YouTube is priceless. What a singer and performer.

I've incorporated "I Didn't Know About You" in my own piano repertoire. I posted it on YouTube so there is some documentation of my profound gratitude to the great musical artists who created this body of music, loosely referred to as The Great American Songbook. It enriches our lives. May it endure!

Saturday, March 10, 2018 *There Is Nothin' Like 'South Pacific' at the Maltz*

Nothin' in the world.

To paraphrase Samuel Johnson, when a person is tired of Rodgers and Hammerstein's *South Pacific*, one is tired of life. How many times have we seen this glorious musical, from Broadway to regional productions? Many. And how many times have I played its captivating music on the piano? Thousands.

So what does the Maltz Jupiter Theatre's production have to offer? Plenty.

First and foremost is a full professional cast of 28 that would rival any Broadway assemblage. Then, the show plays to the Maltz's strength:

classic musicals that are not road shows, but original from the bottom up, casting, scenic design, costumes, musical arrangements, and expert directing. Finally, the secret ingredient: an intimacy which is unusual for a big production. We saw *South Pacific* at the Kravis years ago. Although excellent, we're talking about a theatre which seats more than 2,000 and seeing a full-size Broadway-designed musical is not the same as enjoying the intimacy of a 600 seat Maltz. The music, the performances, the sheer energy simply reaches out and envelops the audience. In fact, the performers are up and down the aisles, often interacting with the audience.

Then of course it is the greatness of Rodgers and Hammerstein, and their place in transforming the musical genre from merely a series of songs loosely tied together. Their groundbreaking *Oklahoma!* solidified the importance of "the book" in the Broadway musical, with music, songs, dance all integral to the plot. Plots became more complex such as in *South Pacific*, two main story lines interwoven, each tackling a subject which was taboo before, interracial relations, all of this against the backdrop of WW II in the South Pacific.

It was based on a series of interrelated short stories, the *Tales of the South Pacific* by James Michener, with the book for the musical by Oscar Hammerstein II and Joshua Logan. The importance of the themes was underscored by its winning The Pulitzer Prize for Drama in 1950, a rare distinction for a musical. Its relevancy today is undiminished. Its place as a classic among American musicals has been assured by the glorious melodies of Richard Rodgers and Oscar Hammerstein's lyrics, irrefutably one of the best musicals of the twentieth century.

When Erin Davie as Nellie belts out "A Cockeyed Optimist" at the beginning of the show Hammerstein's lyrics and Rodgers bouncy melody announces her typically apple pie American attitude towards life. In spite of the war surrounding her, Davie gives her introductory song a special cheery oomph. Davie's voice is a sweet soprano, but what she might lack in vocal power is more than compensated for by how spellbindingly she sells a song with her irresistible stage presence.

Segue to the other co-star, Nicholas Rodriguez as Emile, whose duet with Nellie in "Twin Soliloquies" establishes his character and showcases Rodriquez's rich baritone while alternating with Nellie's dreamy lyrics. This is an ardent falling-in-love duet. Then Rodriquez tenderly delivers what is perhaps Rodgers and Hammerstein's most famous love song, "Some Enchanted Evening" recalling how he and Nellie met.

The stage is set for a more upbeat number sung by the talented Sailors, Seabees and Marines, "Bloody Mary" followed by the rousingly iconic "There Is Nothing Like a Dame." We're talking pure testosterone-high- energy in these production numbers with impressive choreography by Connor Gallagher.

Bloody Mary, played by Jodi Kimura sings the ballad "Bali Ha'i" with an exotic dreamy quality. Kimura knows how to play to the audience and she's the center of attention when on stage. The moment she sees the other major character Lieutenant Cable played by Stephen Mark Lukas, Kimura articulates what the audience sees, telling a Seabee that *you not sexy like Lieutenant.* Lukas' rendition of the beautiful ballad, "Younger than Springtime" sung to Liat, Bloody Mary's daughter, is especially memorable.

His other major song "You've Got to Be Carefully Taught" is the one which cuts to the core of *South Pacific*, a world torn apart by war and more thematically in this show, racism. It was like no other song before in a Broadway musical. Lukas performs the song with anger and self loathing, not being able to shake his inbred prejudices.

Christian Marriner who plays seaman Luther Billis, "a sailor who bullies, bribes, and charms his way," offers a show stopping performance in "Honey Bun." He performed this role in the national touring company of *South Pacific* which explains his owning this part with such assurance and bravado, bringing forth rousing applause from the audience.

The concluding scene, Emile returning from a dangerous mission and discovers Nellie singing "Dites-Moi" with his children, Ngana and Jerome (played by Hana Roberts and Ray Zurawin), is a guaranteed tearjerker as Emile completes the song. He and Nellie rush into each other's arms. She has made the transition from being "as corny as Kansas in August" to knowing "I have found me a wonderful guy" (in spite of his being previously married to a Polynesian). Love conquers all, even ingrained prejudice.

The show is performed under the award-winning director Gordon Greenberg's extraordinary expertise, whose credits include Broadway and PBS Great Performances' show, Irving Berlin's *Holiday Inn* and London's acclaimed West End revival of *Guys and Dolls*. He directed the Maltz Theatre's critically-acclaimed hit production of *Barnum* in 2009. With so many performers on stage it is a feat to direct *South Pacific*.

The Maltz *South Pacific* production especially succeeds in stunning scenic designs by Paul Tate dePoo III, with scene changes on the fly and little interruption. Costume designer Tristan Raines reveals a creative and colorful imagination, yet period perfect. Lighting designer Rob Denton bathes the stage in exotic Island colors. And the 13 piece live orchestra under the musical direction of Eric Alsford delivers the exceptional accompaniment that a musical of this caliber deserves.

Friday, April 20, 2018 Emmet Cahill--- Remember that Name

The applause was thunderous, the audience in raptures, a young man singing his heart out, so much talent and personality wrapped up in a dimpled package. Here is a young singer on a solo tour with hundreds of ardent fans making their way to see and hear Emmet Cahill. He is an Irish tenor who has performed with the renowned Irish singing group, Celtic Thunder, all over the world. On Thursday night, he made his second appearance in the West Palm Beach area, again accompanied on several numbers by the Robert Sharon Chorale, the 84-voice-strong local community chorale.

Cahill is from Mullingar, County Westmeath, the same setting of John Patrick Shanley's play *Outside Mullingar*. Irish theatre is one of my favorite theatre experiences so I was particularly intrigued by the opportunity to see the performer whose debut album, *Emmet Cahill's Ireland*, went to number one on the Billboard World Music chart.

He made his Carnegie Hall debut in New York City recently and this fall he will sing in 75 cities across North America with Celtic Thunder on their 10th anniversary "X" tour. But for now he is embarking on a multi city tour as a soloist which will take him to nearly a score of other US cities during the next two months. So expect to see him somewhere! He promises to return to the West Palm Beach area sometime in the future as well.

Cahill played to a packed house and it's no wonder. He is one of the most dynamic and personable, not to mention immensely talented, singers I've seen. His program on Thursday naturally included several Irish classics such as "Danny Boy", "When Irish Eyes Are Smiling", "An Irish Lullaby" and "Wild Mountain Thyme." "I am very proud to be Irish," explains Cahill. "I want people to feel a real connection to the songs, as well as the people and the stories that they represent. There has always been a special relationship between the Irish and American people and I want to further enrich that friendship."

As his performance was in a religious setting, the Holy Name of Jesus Catholic Church in West Palm Beach, and he has strong religious roots beginning his singing career at his own local church in Mullingar, he sang several moving hymns including a tearful, heartfelt performance of "Amazing Grace."

His tenor voice is strong and clear. He manages to bring forth so much emotion and clarity with his voice, an instrument onto itself, with never an inaudible word. Cahill can deconstruct a song to certain simplicity so not one emotive moment is lost on the audience. It doesn't hurt that his accompanist, Seamus Brett, is an extraordinarily gifted pianist who knows how to showcase this rising 27 year old star.

They even challenged the audience to suggest six or seven songs which they would perform as unrehearsed requests and then extemporaneously they strung together a medley of those songs. One such request was "O Sole Mio." Enrico Caruso and Mario Lanza would have been proud, maybe envious, of Cahill's rendition which demonstrated his classical vocal training at the Royal Irish Academy of Music in Dublin.

But Irish folk songs and liturgical hymns are not Cahill's only strengths. He is equally comfortable with the Great American Songbook and Broadway. In fact he said that Rodgers and Hammerstein's work is among his favorites and to illustrate, he delivered a rendition of "Some Enchanted Evening," wringing out all the emotion and depth from that song. His rendition of "This is the Moment" from *Jekyll and Hyde* was thrilling. The nostalgic favorite "Moon River" was as beautiful as those Irish folk songs.

He said that among the songs he first sang on stage as a professional was "Bring Him Home" from *Les Miserables*. He is much too young to play Jean Valjean, but you wouldn't know it from his masterly performance. I've never been able to hear that song – or play it on the piano – without a tear in my eye, and his performance, with so much emotion, brought the house down with yet another standing ovation. Clearly, so much of this young man's future might be directed into the oeuvre of Broadway and the Great American Songbook. He has the presence and that rare emotive gift for those songs, while never having to desert his unique Irish folk roots.

Monday, May 7, 2018 *Under the Radar*

When we think of the great body of work which constitutes the Great American Songbook, there is a tendency to forget the great composers who never wrote a Broadway show but whose songs are as much part of our musical heritage. I'm reminded of this while reading William Zinsser's *Easy to Remember; The Great American Songwriters and Their Songs*. Zinsser's passion for the music is evident on every page, it's encyclopedic, and finally, he frequently discusses the songs' construction, both musically and lyrically. This is my kind of tribute to the music I love.

And, yet, there are omissions. A composer such as Henry Mancini gets but a passing mention, only because of working with the "vernacular poet" of lyricism, Johnny Mercer, on the song "Moon River." But a glaring total omission is the work of Johnny Mandel, perhaps not a household name, unless you hear one of his songs which you would swear was written by someone else. He's written a wide range of idiosyncratic songs and teamed up with some interesting lyricists. He has, most notably, worked extensively as an arranger for well known singers of his time as well as playing with some of the big bands of the 40s such as Jimmy Dorsey and Count Basie.

Mandel too worked with Johnny Mercer the lyricist on perhaps one of his best known songs, written for a movie, "Emily." Tony Bennett, Sinatra, and a host of others have recorded it. The jazz community has adopted this work as their own, particularly the superb interpretation by Bill Evans, a version of which can be heard and seen on YouTube, Bill Evans in an intimate setting, Helsinki, 1969.

My mother's favorite song was "The Shadow of Your Smile," another film song he composed. Whenever I visited her at my boyhood home from which I had long moved she'd ask me to sit at our old piano, by then partly out of tune, and play what I didn't realize was a Mandel piece.

And talk about unusual, he composed the "Song from M*A*S*H (Suicide Is Painless)", which is also now played in jazz venues.

His work with lyricists Alan and Marilyn Bergman produced two classic pieces, the mystically evocative "A Waltz from Somewhere" which reaches back to another era and one of my other favorites, "Where Do You Start?" about how does one disentangle one's life from another's?...."So many habits that we'll have to break and yesterdays we'll have to take apart."

Yet the song which landed me in the sea of Johnny Mandel songs, never tying them altogether until I bought the composer's *Songbook,* was "You Are There" as sung by today's first lady of song, Stacey Kent

Her rendition of "You Are There" really elevates the composer's intention: "To be done in a rubato feeling throughout."

Dave Frishberg, a musician who is sometimes best known for his satirical lyrics, wrote the words to this moving ballad and his collaboration with Mandel produced a classic, the story of a lover who is not just absent but is dead. The ethereal quality of Mandel's music works perfectly with the lyrics.

Thursday, August 2, 2018 A Whirlwind Theatre Week

From classic farce, to Shakespearean comedy, to a tragic love story, from the Westport Country Playhouse, to the Hudson Valley Shakespeare Festival on the grounds of Boscobel, to the Imperial Theatre in NYC, it has been a whirlwind week of theatre, the commonality being relationships of men and women and some of the most glorious acting and staging we've seen in such a concentrated time period.

Last week we saw *A Flea in Her Ear,* a new version of Georges Feydeau's classic early 20th century farce at the Westport Country Playhouse. Although the old playhouse has been renovated, it still retains its old time charm as their collection of playbills of yesteryear attest. And, under the artistic direction of Mark Lamos who also directed this particular production, the old WCP is in good hands.

A Flea in Her Ear is such an ambitious, interesting selection, made possible by a co-production with the Resident Ensemble Players from the University of Delaware, 14 actors in perfect harmony, choreographed with such precision, that the laughter was non-stop. It's been a long time since I laughed so hard at a show which, at its heart, is nothing more than intended to do just that.

The acting made it something special. How often have you been at a three act play with two intermissions, which seemed to pass in a flash? Michael Gotch played an unforgettable Don Carlos de Histangua and whenever he was on stage, laughter was uncontrollable. That does not mean to distract from any of the other players, as well as the technical staff of the Westport Country Playhouse. We're so grateful for our summer visits to Connecticut, and to our old home town of Westport which continues to keep this jewel of a theatre in mint condition.

Three days later we went up to the Hudson Valley Shakespeare Festival at Boscobel in Garrison, NY. This outdoor theatre is in a large, well appointed tent, a sand floor for a stage and some of the most breathtaking views. Before the show begins, the grounds make an ideal setting for a picnic. As the production begins, the sun fades to twilight setting just to the right of West Point on the other side of the Hudson in the distance. In fact the players emerge over the lawn and some of the action takes place there, although the play unfolds in the tent.

From farce to comedy. *The Taming of the Shrew* must be close to the way the bard intended except for all the modern references, including even some music of the Village People. Once again theatre magic emerges from some clever choreography and a group of ensemble players who are deeply immersed in Shakespeare's intent.

These are not easy tickets to get. Plan in advance. In fact, Ann and I could not get good seats together but fortunately the people sitting in back of me saw us chatting and as Ann went to her seat, they offered us the two front row seats as their friends had booked them and last minute had to cancel out. But as the show began we learned why they preferred the second row, as the actors frequently interact with those in the front row, so it was not unusual for one to sit next to Ann, take her bottle of water, look through her program, even commenting on it, all in fun of course and it just added to the immeasurable pleasure of seeing Shakespeare performed in this setting.

Liz Wisan played Kate with a fiery demeanor, but Biko Eisen-Martin who played Petruchio, usually in torn jeans and an undershirt, had the cunning and patience to wear her down. Comedy is different from farce, the latter designed for belly laughs while *Taming's* comedic elements brought out some of Shakespeare 's more serious observations regarding male - female relations of his times (the "Me Too" movement might not wholeheartedly approve of Kate's final relenting to her taskmaster's Pavlovian training, but all is in fun).

Like the Westport Country Playhouse's presentation, this show is performed by a talented ensemble that performs four other plays in rotating repertory. Everyone in the cast is perfectly fitted into the director's take on the show. It was more than theatre; it is an experience when performed in the open air, in a tent, after an early evening picnic.

Last year we were part of the picnic festivities, but we're getting a little too old to spread out a blanket or to cart chairs so we had an early evening dinner at the nearby Bird and Bottle, an inn which has operated since 1751 and used to be a stage coach stop between New York and Albany. The ambiance was special.

But the highlight of "our theatre week" was going into New York City yesterday to the revival of Rodgers and Hammerstein's *Carousel*. As soon as we heard of the serendipity that it was going to be performed while we would be in the area we booked tickets, front row, as we did not want to miss a word or even a mannerism of the performers. It is the kind of show that one would like to see on a Broadway stage, although there have been good scaled down or concert versions.

It's hard to say that one has a "favorite" R&H show, sort of like saying of your children, one is the favorite. But when I play their music on the piano, I seem to gravitate to *Carousel* or *The King and I,* although *South Pacific* and *Oklahoma* are in the mix too. Maybe my preference for *Carousel* is partially because it takes place in New England, or the "Carousel Waltz", a rousing piece of musical composition, or the incredible comic/moving piece, "Mr. Snow." All the songs fit perfectly in the book but the one weak song, and I think it is simply our times, verses when the musical was written, is the (now) somewhat schmaltzy "You'll Never Walk Alone," which is the emotional finale. Still, it works.

"Soliloquy" which concludes the first act is perhaps the longest solo in all Broadway repertoires. Joshua Henry, who plays the wayward Billy Bigelow in this production and sings his parts with powerful gusto, performs this song a little too quickly. I simply feel it needs to be finessed in all its normally allocated time. Perhaps this is his take or Jack O'Brien's direction, I don't know, but I missed the pauses, or even the phrasing which some have brought to the song, including Frank Sinatra, who's voice cannot hold a candle to Henry's, but he knew how to sell the emotional content.

There. The end of picky criticism as one has to judge a performance of *Carousel* by its gestalt. The orchestration is per Richard Rogers' intent by Jonathan Tunick and a 30 piece orchestra under the solid Musical

Supervision of David Chase brings out the highs and the lows. The singing is splendid, the voices soaring, and how could they not with Renee Fleming among the leads?

I've heard some criticism that the dance portions of the play were not the Agnes de Mille's original. Given what Justin Peck accomplished with his award-winning choreography, transparent and perfect, it is hard to accept that criticism. After all, every artist has his/her take. Look at the liberties the Hudson Valley players took with Shakespeare, only to arrive at the same destination. Maybe I'm not being impartial as Peck once worked with the Miami City Ballet and one of the performers in the *Carousel* ensemble is Leigh-Ann Esty who Ann actually watched "grow up" in the Miami City Ballet over the last decade.

An outstanding cast, a classic musical, a full orchestra, and many of the best technical people in the business, make this production so memorable, even if I have to leave the theatre humming "You'll Never Walk Alone," after wiping away the requisite tears.

Saturday, February 9, 2019 **A Diva Blessing**

A couple of months ago our friends Karen and Bob suggested we join them at Del Ray's Arts Garage where Ann Hampton Callaway was performing selections from the Great American Songbook.

The Arts Garage performance venue has been configured into a cabaret, six to a table, bring your own food and drink. Karen supplied a delicious cream and fruit tart for dessert and Ann brought the wine (coffee for me).

My seat was ideal with a full view of the piano, a Kawai Grand. You rarely see a Kawai being used professionally, the instrument of choice usually being a Steinway or a Yamaha. I have a Yamaha baby grand which I love, but I almost bought a Kawai as I think it has a brighter sound, so ideally suited for playing The Great American Songbook.

As I said, we were seated at a table for six and our two other table-mates turned out to be a man who we used to watch on NYC TV years ago, Bill Boggs, who had an interview show with some of the entertainment greats, and to this day does a professional speaking tour discussing those people, so watching the Diva perform with Bill and his partner, Jane, was serendipitous.

We've seen other great Divas in a cabaret setting before, and three special ones spring to mind, including a rare US appearance at the Colony by perhaps the greatest living female jazz singer, Stacey Kent.

We also saw another fabulous Diva at the Colony, Jane Monheit, who has a distinctive style and great range with her voice. She too performs with a back up group headed by her husband on drums.

When we lived in New York we were lucky enough to go over to a small Supper Club on the Upper East Side and there we sat right at a front table, mesmerized by the jazz legend, the late, great Carmen McCrea. I think we have all her CDs. Jazz doesn't get any better than that. She too was backed by a combo she probably worked with for years.

Of course we've seen other singers, Keely Smith at the Colony once, but usually on stage in an auditorium, as we once saw Ann Hampton Callaway at the Eissey Campus Theatre of Palm Beach State College many years ago. She was accompanied there by, arguably, one of the most original jazz pianist today, Bill Mays. There is a world of difference, however, between a stage performance and cabaret.

The obvious difference is the intimacy created, resulting in the give and take between the performer and the audience. One feeds on the other. You get the sense that we're all part of the Great American Songbook "family." And it is a family that loves its progenitors, the composers, the lyricists, the performers who have stylized this great body of music.

Ann Hampton Callaway preserves and has become part of this wonderful tradition in her program "Jazz Goes to the Movies." Her program fully realizes the breadth of the great songs which emerged from film. In addition to the obvious ones, there are endless streams of classics that have come from lesser watched films, such as "This Time the Dream's on Me" by Harold Arlen, and lyrics by Johnny Mercer for the 1941 film "Blues in the Night," just one of the many songs sung by Callaway during her two part performance.

Her song selection was extensive. I wrote them all down, but I'll only mention a few of the 18 (yes, 18!) songs she sang. Naturally, I'm going to focus on some I love to play on the piano myself.

This has to be at the top of the list, the not often performed song by Henry Mancini with lyrics by Leslie Bricusse, "Two for the Road." Undoubtedly she chose to perform this wonderful song, I think Mancini's best, because the co star of the film of the same title, the actor so many of us watched "grow up" on film from his first performance in "Tom Jones," Albert Finney had just passed away. This is the same song which Ann (my Ann) and I chose to "perform" at our son's wedding last August, me at the piano and Ann reading (as, unfortunately, my Ann can't sing – and neither can I) the evocative lyrics, so appropriate for Jonathan and his bride, Tracie.

We hung onto every word as Callaway lovingly performed this number.

I interject an important observation here regarding her performance, unique among the cabaret divas I mentioned above, and that is she accompanied herself on the piano. I guess I simply expected a pianist and a bass player to come out to accompany her. Oh, it is so, so much better when a great singer and pianist are one. Her piano chops may not be in the league of a Bill Mays, but in accompanying herself, she is able to ring out every drop of emotion from The Great American Songbook. It's as if her piano and voice are but one instrument, in perfect harmony and symmetry.

Her opening number, "From this Moment On" demonstrated her remarkable range, her smoky voice, and her ability to scat. During another number, again one of the strengths of a cabaret setting, was taking the audience through a scat lesson and we found ourselves scatting along with her. Really fun stuff.

She incorporates all styles in her piano accompaniment, from a bluesy feeling playing and singing "As Time Goes By" and some bouncing boogie-woogie in her tribute to Fred Astaire (she knows his sister) in "Let's Face the Music and Dance."

Her jazz sensibility on the piano came out in "This Can't be Love," again demonstrating her incredible voice range.

One of my favorites when I play the piano is "Folks Who Live on the Hill," by Jerome Kern, and lyrics by Oscar Hammerstein II from the 1937 film "High, Wide, and Handsome." But, oh, my heart be still listening to Callaway play and sing this song, channeling Peggy Lee with whom the song is closely associated.

Her rendition of "At Last" Etta James's signature song but more recently Beyoncé Knowles' "big song" demonstrated the power of Callaway's voice. Rarely does a singer have the gift of the subtle and power as well. It was breathtaking.

Callaway is not only a performer, but a composer as well, and those skills were put on full display in a playful impromptu performance she composed and sung on the spot taking silly suggestions from the audience; a blind man, a pizza maker, meets a woman who makes burrata, they make love on the beach in Del Ray, a one night stand, where they lose their clothes while swimming, the details not being important other than her ability to compose in real time. She also jokingly "tuned" her voice to the piano, easily singing a half step below or above a note to display her voice control and musical sensibilities.

At one point, she gave a "diva blessing" to the audience. In sum, it was an exhilarating night. There is nothing in the world like the joy from hearing the Great American Songbook, performed by a woman completely in command of her musical gifts. In fact, her warm personality, eager to be with her audience in every way, happy to greet them on the way out, made it a perfect evening of "being with family."

Saturday, March 2, 2019 *Maltz Theatre Stages a Cutting-Edge Production of 'A Doll's House Part II'*

Knock. Knock. No answer. Bang. Bang! Hello, is anybody there? You bet.

The family you left behind 15 years ago, Nora, slamming the door heard around the world. They have it in for you. And you in turn have to deal with some of the same issues, being an independent woman living in a man's world and now new ones of your own making. You didn't think you could come back to ask for a favor without consequences, did you?

Nominated for eight Tony Awards, Lucas Hnath's *A Doll's House, Part II* is the most produced play throughout the country this season. Maltz Theatre's production is a welcome addition to the bandwagon, and for South Florida Theatre goers in particular.

The play's Director J. Barry Lewis commented, "While A Doll's House was written nearly 140 years ago, it has a contemporary flair that speaks to today's audiences. It is at its heart a very modern story that deals with self-ishness, selflessness, growth and compromise. *A Doll's House, Part II* is not a sequel to the original work, but more of a thought experiment of 'what if.' It presents a very sophisticated argument about what we owe to ourselves and to each other."

J. Barry Lewis has taken this highly-charged intellectual tour de force and framed it in period dress but with a contemporary off kilter set. The stage itself reflects that theme, the soaring white stucco walls, the minimalism of furniture, the stage floor sloping downwards into the audience's lap and scene changes electrified by cringing amplification and visual identification. The audience has entered Nora's nightmare world.

Carol Halstead as Nora returns "home" on a self-serving mission. She boasts to her former maid/confidant, Anne Marie, about becoming a highly successful author, with all the connections and money anyone could desire. Nora writes books about women, their bondage in and the superfluous nature of marriage.

Halstead stalks about the stage, highly satisfied with herself as Nora, while explaining (or bragging about) the last 15 years to the maid who not only raised her as a child, but has raised Nora's three children as well.

Anne Marie is hilariously played by Mary Stout, who welcomes Nora on the one hand, but has her own reservoir of anger for everything she's sacrificed for Nora and Torvald (including giving up her own child to keep that job), and Stout begins to wear that on her sleeve. It is she who explosively uses the F word, quite a few times in fact, indicating that although this sequel is supposedly taking place in late 19th century Norway, the dialogue is strictly contemporary. It is in perfect harmony with the surrealistic staging and the plays' theme.

Nora has returned to her marital home for a simple request: to ask Torvald to properly file their divorce papers. She had naturally assumed that had been done when she left as she went about her life as a single woman, signing contracts, having lovers (which Nora proudly enumerates), until one of her anti-marriage books led to a Judge's wife leaving him. Once the Judge discovered her true identity, that in essence she was still a married woman and as such could be incarcerated for signing contracts, not to mention having affairs, he made demands that she refute her work or be exposed. In essence, blackmail. Thus, Nora has to become once more a supplicant to her husband.

Not so simple Anne Marie explains, *A lot of people thought you were dead.* In effect, it's awfully hard to get a divorce from a dead person and for Torvald to do that would expose him to the fact that the assumption which he never publicly denied, could even threaten his high level banking position.

Indeed, a complication. What would a drama be without one or in this case several which keeps the audience guessing?

Suddenly Torvald unexpectedly returns home for some papers. Nora wasn't prepared to make the request at that very moment, but after his stunned realization that the person standing before him is really Nora, he forces her to explain why she's returned. Torvald is played by Paul Carlin, with the confidence befitting his position as a highly respected member of society, as well as the very perplexed disheartened husband of a wife who inexplicably walked out on him 15 years ago, and with no explanation, no discussion. Now she has some 'splainin' to do.

So the fencing match begins. He refuses to grant her request for the reason Anne Marie has explained.

What is Nora to do? The thought of agreeing to the Judge's demands is an anathema to her. In another tete-a-tete with Anne Marie, who is scheming for her own benefit, perhaps to retire or at least not lose her job, she suggests that Nora approach her daughter, Emmy, to intercede on her behalf in asking her father to grant the divorce. Apparently Emmy has clout with Torvald.

No, Nora, says, I didn't come to meet or involve Emmy but then her seemingly lack of alternatives make her relent.

There is a one-on-one scene with Emmy who we soon learn is a chip off the old block. She could be Nora in her youth. She's in love and wants to marry! -- a young man from Torvald's bank. Emmy is deliciously played by Mikayla Bartholomew, who radiates that confident bloom of youth with the smarts of the mother she never really knew. She is standoffish but civil, genuinely trying to help her mother as she has her OWN agenda. This is yet another ingredient in the bubbling broth. She knows that if Torvald is taken down at the bank, her impending marriage might be in jeopardy.

First, though, mother and daughter have to debate the merits of marriage (or demerits according to Nora). Nora is confident that marriage is not only not needed in society but that in 20 or 30 years from now (the late 19th century being the "now") all these issues of marriage and women's inequality will have been settled. Sure, Nora. Emmy on the other hand, to her mother's horror, "wants to be possessed."

So, there you have it, another stalemate, although Emmy gives Nora yet a third alternative. Forge the death records at city hall (Emmy conveniently knows someone there, one of the many stretches of plot Lucas Hnath uses to move the story and the complications forward). After you are "dead" disappear for a while as you did 15 years ago, going to your own fortress of solitude. Nora had confessed that when she first left she lived alone "up north" until the "voices in her head" dissipated.

Eureka! Saved by the bell, Torvald stumbles home, bloodied, holding a piece of paper which he reveals is the divorce. He's a good guy after all! Why he is bloodied and the choice Nora now has to make I'll leave for when you see this audacious play. The author has us all guessing until the very end.

This production has it all, comedy, suspense, empathy, and some of the finest acting you'll see this season. In fact, what may make this play especially distinctive, besides the pedigree it attempts to follow, is how all four characters come across as likeable. There is no one who you can call a hero or a villain. They are all believable and engaging.

Acting accolades have to go to Carol Halstead as Nora. She's on stage full time in this intermission-less fast paced production and Halstead IS the Nora we have imagined, beautiful and brash. Mary Stout as the maid, Anne Marie, is the perfect comic foil, mesmerizing to watch on stage. Paul Carlin as Torvald personifies the man we'd expect for this part, knowing the hurt he harbors, while Carlin mightily tries to keep his dignity. His anguish in learning that one of Nora's novels is about their very own marriage and how he doesn't come out too well is affecting (although laughingly Nora had to "kill off" the heroine to make it acceptable – a bit of foreshadowing for one of her own alternatives). Mikayla Bartholomew is self-assured as Emmy, passionate in her own beliefs, but always under careful control of her emotions, the perfect foil for the very arguments that Nora has lived and written, not hesitating to say to Nora *I'm better at life because you were gone.* Ouch.

J. Barry Lewis directs this parlor drama for the comedy and the messaging. He moves his characters into interesting positions among the sparsely decorated stage to bring out both their character and the "debate."

The play moves steadily, like the second hand of a clock, striking a strident note as scenes change, the characters we're about to see in that scene briefly stenciled in lights on the back wall across the door. And when I say "strident" I mean electrifying, like the dialogue. Yet Lewis knows when his characters must pause to give the audience time to take in a look or a pained response of a character.

His technical crew, particularly lighting designer Kirk Bookman and sound designer Marty Mets play a significant role in those scene changes. Scenic designer Anne Mundell has created the perfect space and feeling for this contemporary play based in the 19th century. Costume designer Tracy Dorman and wig designer Gerard Kelly provide that touch of verisimilitude against the backdrop of the surrealistic set.

A Doll's House Part II is a reminder why live theatre is so, so, much better than the ubiquitous streamed entertainment to which we are now subjected. This play and production is intellectually engrossing and comedic as well.

Friday, March 15, 2019 **Two Different Musical Eras**

We attended concerts two nights in a row. As it turns out, they are like the bookends in my life.

I began my love of music in my early teens, the music of rock 'n roll. In college my musical allegiance morphed to classical. My adult years have been consumed by the Great American Songbook, and Jazz. As I've matured I've come to appreciate some opera and in particular the potent instrument of the human voice.

Last night we revisited a performance of one of the world's great tenors, Emmet Cahill, who returned to the Holy Name of Jesus Catholic Church in West Palm Beach. Last year when I reviewed Cahill's concert I had thought that his titanic talent warranted "a bigger boat" but nonetheless he returned to this same church and I understand why. He began singing as a child in his home church in Ireland with his family and besides being a proud Irishman from the town of Mullingar; he is a religious young man as well. Interestingly his love of these essential elements of his life transcends the ambition of many of his contemporaries. Thus, he is content to allow his career to develop rather than rocketing overnight which perhaps it could if he pursued it at the expense of other values. I have profound respect for him as a human being, not to mention as an astonishing artist.

He is also loyal to the Robert Sharon Chorale, the 84-voice-strong local community chorale which appears with him at the church, usually performing as an opening to Emmet's solo appearance but sometimes backing him up as well. His voice, though, needs no backup, other than his very talented accompanist, Seamus Brett, an extraordinarily gifted pianist.

The format of last night's concert was similar to last year's with perhaps more emphasis on liturgical and Irish pieces, but still a number of Broadway pieces so suitable for his voice such as "This is the Moment" and "Bring Him Home." Of course, with St. Patrick's Day around the corner, his Irish upbringing impacted his musical selections this time around.

Many of the pieces he sang were from his new CD *Blessings of Music* which includes "Be Thou My Vision, "Galway Bay," "The Gaelic Blessing," "Amazing Grace," "Ag Criost An Siol" (Christ is the Seed"), "Panis Angelicus,", "The Last Rose of Summer," "Moon River," "Danny Boy" and "How Great Thou Art."

As with last year, the audience was invited to shout out some pieces for him to sing and Seamus Brett would arrange them on the fly and Cahill performed them as if having rehearsed them for that particular concert. I asked him to sing "Children will Listen" which he knew was by Sondheim, but said he'd better practice that. And so I wait for Cahill to take that next step in his career.

And as he said, he would not be let out of the auditorium on the eve of St. Patrick's Day without performing "Danny Boy."

Emmet, you had us at the words "glad to be back" and we gladly look forward to your next appearance here and will watch your career with interest and amazement. You are a unique talent, a captivating personality, and are truly blessed with a golden voice.

It's hard to segue from Emmet to the dynamic denizens of Rock 'N Roll, so apologies to Emmet's fans, but welcome to those who remember the 50's. The night before seeing Emmet I experienced that other end of the "book-end" and that is seeing *One Night in Memphis* at the Maltz Jupiter Theatre. This included the original cast members of the Broadway hit *Million Dollar Quartet*. In effect it's a concert rendition of the show which was about a legendary one night session in Memphis at the birth of Sun Records, a jam session featuring Carl Perkins, Johnny Cash, Jerry Lee Lewis and Elvis Presley.

Carl Perkins was my first favorite as a kid, a cross over performer of rockabilly and country. His big hits were the original rendition of "Blue Suede Shoes" (before Elvis' version), "Honey Don't," "Everybody's Trying to be My Baby" and he was quickly followed by Jerry Lee Lewis ("Whole Lot of Shakin' Goin' On," "Great Balls of Fire"), Johnny Cash ("Folsom Prison Blues," "Ring of Fire") and of course the most famous of them all, Elvis Presley ("Don't Be Cruel," "All Shook Up"). These are but a FEW of the songs performed by the four talented guys in the show.

Normally, I don't seek out performers who are imitators of famous entertainers, but will make an exception for this show as with every passing moment they seemed to become the originals. This particularly applied to the performer who played Elvis, as he was under the most scrutiny and at first your senses reject him as Elvis, but quickly he won over the audience. I still have Elvis' first 33-1/3 record he recorded for RCA. My wife, Ann, actually saw him in person in 1956 at the Fox Theatre in Atlanta as an Elvis crazed teen!

John Mueller who played Carl Perkins was particularly effective as his guitar playing accompanied all the performers throughout the show. Blair Carman as "the Killer" is a very talented pianist, convincing as Jerry Lee Lewis, even "tickling" the ivories with the heel of his shoe. Shawn Barker plays the "Man in Black," Johnny Cash and in one song manages to sing a lick an octave below bass. Truly, a crowd-pleaser. Finally, Brandon Bennett as Elvis undergoes that transformation before our eyes. And boy can he twist and shake!

Heartfelt thanks to all the many talented artists in this world who bring the joy of music into our lives, so desperately needed in these times.

Sunday, April 14, 2019 **A Musical Week**

It's our universal language and while the political discourse is discordant, music seems to bring out our commonalities such as the music a show at the Delray Beach Playhouse, *I Believe in You! – The Songs of Frank Loesser.*

Ann arranged a preshow dinner at Racks Fish House off Delray's famous (and congested) Atlantic Avenue, a happening place. It was a balmy early April evening, with a nice breeze so we dined al fresco. Imagine our surprise reading the appetizer menu which included Copps Island, CT oysters! Copps Island is connected at low tide to Crow Island, where we have taken our boat for the last 35 years during the summers, anchoring there on weekends. So here we were, some 1,250 miles away dining on wild oysters from those very waters. These are bottom planted as opposed to cage or floating trays and the oysters are known for "sweet briny flavor and plump meats." It was a nice and nostalgic start to the evening.

Delray Beach Playhouse which opened in 1947 is a community theatre featuring everything from one person acts to full scale plays. They have a dedicated audience, we now among them. But who knew, the playhouse is on Lake Ida, a fresh water lake right off of I95, comprising 121 acres, but seeming much larger than that as it is long and narrow. Looking at it is reminiscent of our days on Lake George in NY and Candlewood Lake in CT as one can see similar boat houses and lake front homes.

I Believe in You! – The Songs of Frank Loesser was narrated by Randolph DelLago who has been the Resident Artistic Director of the Playhouse since 1982. He also sings in this production. When one thinks of Frank Loesser, one recalls the iconic *Guys and Dolls*, a great classic musical of Broadway's Golden Era. It perhaps has more recognizable songs than any other musical, including those of Rogers and Hammerstein. He only wrote four other musicals, *The Most Happy Fella* and *How to Succeed in Business Without Really Trying*, being the most notable. Songs were performed from all of these with original still scenes projected on a backdrop. *The Most Happy Fella* has one of the most moving rhapsodic opera style songs ever written for the Great White Way, "My Heart is So Full of You," one of my favorites for the piano, with an exotic bridge section of eight bars.

But Loesser, who was cast out by his family as they thought "song-writing" was beneath their dignity (his father was a piano teacher and his brother was a classical piano prodigy), found his roots in popular song in Hollywood before migrating to Broadway. There are many memorable songs he wrote for The Great American Songbook and this show had many, such as "I Don't Want to Walk Without You," "Heart and Soul," "On a Slow Boat to China," "Two Sleepy People,""Baby, It's Cold Outside,""No Two People," and "Spring Will Be a Little Late This Year" (the latter being another personal piano favorite of mine). Along with DelLago, performances were given by Alicia Branch-Stafford, a soprano, baritone William Stafford, and Hanz Eneart who added a little cabaret dancing to the show as well as joining the ensemble in song with a comedic rendition of" Once in Love with Amy."

A few days later we were off to the Maltz Jupiter Theatre. There we saw *West Side Story* towards the end of its run. Although this is what the Maltz Theatre does best, still we were a little concerned about seeing this yet again. Could it still possibly be fresh (although the music by Bernstein and lyrics by Sondheim are immortal)?

The short answer is a resounding yes! I think some of the classic musicals are being looked at in a new light, due to the times and the influence of *Hamilton*. Most recently this is apparent with the Circle in the Square's current production of *Oklahoma* which some have criticized as a travesty, irreverent to Rogers and Hammerstein's intent. I'm not too sure, although that was my knee jerk reaction. Now, thinking about it, and reading more about it, I'm willing to be persuaded and therefore we're going to see it sometime in August. I'll be lining up for the chili and corn bread!

There is a dark side to *Oklahoma*, as in all of the R&H plays. Just think of Billy Bigalow's corruptibility in *Carousel*, or the racial tensions of *South Pacific* and *The King and I*, the lurking Nazi shadows in *The Sound of Music*. These musicals were played out for the audiences of their times with relatively happy resolutions (just what was expected then). One could cast them now in an entirely different light and why not?

In a sense, the Maltz's interpretation of *West Side Story* has been so influenced. A framing device of Hurricane Maria has been introduced. How ironic is that, the Maria of the story picking up after Hurricane Maria, alone with her memories of Tony? This scene reprises at the end of the show. It was a lovely, moving touch, particularly in the light of how this terrible storm has been politicized.

And with Puerto Rican born Marcos Santana's direction and musical staging, we have more of a take on the Sharks rather than the Jets. The hell-bent fury of xenophobic victimization is explosively probed by Angel Lozada who plays Bernardo. Michelle Alves performance as Anita is more than up to the easily remembered performance of Chita Rivera in that part. Alves is every bit as dynamic as a dancer and is a very talented vocalist as well.

Not enough praise can be directed toward Jim Schubin who plays Tony and Evy Ortiz as Maria. Schubin brings a strong sense of constant optimism and wonder to the role as well as a clear tenor voice. Ortiz is the ideal Maria, a soprano and coloratura who is radiant in the role of Maria (she was recently on the *West Side Story* national tour). They had the perfect chemistry as Tony and Maria and their duets soared.

The choreography by Al Blackstone (with additional choreography by the director), gives a hat tip to Jerome Robbins' choreography but is original and pulsating on the Maltz stage. It's a smaller cast than the original musical, but one would not know it.

With the refugee crisis of our times, it was time to look at *West Side Story* through a different lens, and the Maltz comes through.

And last night we attended the 1st Palm Beach International Jazz Festival, the first, we hope, of many in the future. It is the idea of one of South Florida's premier jazz singers, Yvette Norwood-Tiger, who has traveled the world with her interpretations of jazz classics, particularly songs sung by Ella Fitzgerald and Billie Holiday. She performs in six languages including English, French, Italian, Portuguese, Spanish, and Xhosa.

She created an afternoon and evening performance with different groups and singers. We attended the evening performance and thus my comments are confined to that.

First up was Marlow Rosado, a Latin Jazz pianist from Puerto Rico, and his group. Rasado is a salsero, and is imposing at the piano with his driving salsa rhythms, somewhat reminiscent of Monte Alexander. I said to Ann that I've never seen a pianist who could pass as a football tight end and the physicality of his performance spoke wonders.

Next up was Eric & The Jazzers, a South Florida group of professional musicians that play swing/bebop from the great era of Duke Ellington. Eric Trouillot also served as MC for the night's performances, a guy from the Bronx who brought out the best of the very well represented NYC crowd (including us).

His group's trumpet player, Yamin Mustafa, is one of the best we've heard and pianist, Chad Michaels, obviously has studied Oscar Peterson's technique closely. As Mustafa said, the group's musical selections are eclectic.

But the star of the night was clearly the evening's organizer, Yvette Norwood-Tiger. Yvette is a survivor of a benign yet life-threatening brain tumor because of its size and position, but had a successful operation some seven years ago. Every time we've seen her she encourages the audience to "find that door opening" and for her it is singing Horace Silver's jazz classic "Song for My Father." Naturally, Yvette means it quite literally, thanking God for the opportunity to continue on with her unique gifts, a powerful yet sometimes subtle interpreter of the Great American Songbook.

Backing her up musically were all the "old gang" we see almost every Sunday night at Double Roads in Jupiter, her musical director for the evening and oh-so talented pianist, also the co founder of the Jupiter Jazz Society, Rick Moore. Along with Rick were Marty Gilman, on sax and flute, Joshua Ewers on bass and Michael Mackey on trumpet. Marty is a multitalented musician who can play a large number of instruments at the professional level and we watched Joshua and Michael while they were still in high school, and have now grown into professional musicians in their own right.

And to bring this entry back to where it began (remember, Copps Island, in the Norwalk CT chain of islands), I learned that Horace Silver (Yvette's tribute composer), was born in Norwalk, CT so it seems that all roads lead back to our years there.

Monday, May 13, 2019 *There Will Never Be Anyone Like Her*

Doris Day is dead. Ann and I have been dreading this moment and no sense repeating all the accolades that will be posted and written, all deserved.

But to me, a piece of me has died. The only way I can put it is I loved her public persona. I felt the same way when John Updike passed away, one who occupied my reading life and made sense of the changes in America, decade by decade. Can it be he has been gone ten years now?

Doris Day occupied my idealized fantasies of the girl next door during the same period, fresh, wholesome, shorn of pretense. This is something that cannot be faked. She was radiant, buoyant, and whenever I needed a pick me up, all I needed was to watch, yet again, one of her films as her inherent goodness was infectious.

Her talent was peerless. I don't think anyone in film could match her for her ability to act, sing, and dance, especially in the comic realm. She was the whole package, and projected a special kind of lovable personality.

One theatre/film critic, who will remain nameless, has criticized her as being merely an average singer. Perhaps her voice was not exceptional.

Nor was Sinatra's. But there was that something else that made their singing extraordinary. Sinatra's phrasing and ability to capture his audience as if he was singing to you might be the best way to describe his gift. Doris' was to project her golden personality in song. Just listening to one of her recordings, I see her radiant smile in my mind.

We've usually heard her with big bands but she would have made it as a cabaret singer if movie land did not appropriate her for their own in some 40 films. One of those was a biopic where she played cabaret singer, Ruth Etting, with Jimmy Cagney, demonstrating both her acting ability and cabaret style in *Love Me or Leave Me* (1955). Or one can hear her with pianist André Previn on the 1962 album *Duet* and appreciate her gift for singing without the silver screen prop, that sparkling personality still shining through.

In a world sorely in need of rectitude and hope, another "companion" of ours has passed, but at least we have her films and recordings to remind us of what can be. RIP Doris Day.

Tuesday, July 16, 2019 **Have I Stayed Too Long at the Fair?**

Billy Barnes is not exactly a household name in the annals of the Great American songbook but he had a successful career as a composer and lyricist. Maybe his relative anonymity is because so much of his work was for TV rather than the stage, but one recognizable hit alone catapulted him into the company of some of the greats, "(Have I Stayed) Too Long at the Fair." My attraction to the song is similar to the one I have for Jerry Herman's romantic ballad, "I Won't Send Roses," both bittersweet, haunting, regretful.

It takes an exceptional lyricist to make a great song so memorable. Barnes' song crafting created a certain kind of poignancy in this one, rendering it a classic. One can listen to two completely different versions on YouTube, Barbra Streisand's highly stylized rendition recorded early in her career and Rosemary Clooney's recorded late in hers. Clooney brings the perspective of an older woman with life's experience to the song. After all, it is more about a mature, "successful" woman, now alone "in a carnival city."

The melody itself, although memorable, can't do the song justice without the words. The song is written in 4/4 time, but the lyrics cry out for it to be played in a waltz tempo so frequently associated with the merry-go-round of the lyrics and I'm constantly drawn in and then out of that tempo so when I play the song on the piano I simply play the way I feel it, wrong timing and all: I added it to my YouTube library of some of my favorites.

The lyrics are poignant as the last few lines illustrate: *I wanted to live in a carnival city / With laughter everywhere / I wanted my friends to be thrilling and witty / I wanted somebody to care / I found my blue ribbons all shiny and new / But now I discover them no longer blue /The merry-go-round is beginning to taunt me / Have I stayed too long at the fair? / There's nothing to win / And there's no one to want me / Have I stayed too long at the fair.*

Sunday, August 4, 2019 *Hershey Felder BECOMES Irving Berlin in this One Man Tour de Force*

Westport Country Playhouse's production of *Hershey Felder as Irving Berlin* is a poignant and persuasive reminder that this nation is a nation of immigrants.

It took a Jewish immigrant from Russia to write such classics as "God bless America" and "White Christmas" two of the top selling pieces of music of all time.

Felder traces Irving Berlin's life having written not only the Book for this production, but acting, singing, and as an accomplished concert pianist, accompanying himself. It is a one man theatrical triumph with a beautiful set (a representation of Berlin's New York City Beekman Place apartment) and lighting by the Westport Country Playhouse.

In addition to those two classics previously mentioned, Felder's bio-musical tells Berlin's story in a score of songs, including "Alexander's Ragtime Band," "My Wife's Gone to the Country - Hooray! Hooray!" (seriously, Berlin could make up a song just about anything and Felder engages the audience with this one, allowing us to sing the "Hooray! Horray!" refrain), "Oh, How I Hate to Get Up in the Morning", "A Pretty Girl is Like a Melody," "What'll I Do?," "Blue Skies," "Say It Isn't So," "Puttin' On the Ritz," "Supper Time" (a song about racial violence, sung by Ethel Waters) and "There's No Business Like Show Business" from one of his most memorable and enduring Broadway hit musicals, *Annie Get Your Gun* (which he was enlisted to write at the last moment by the Gershwin Brothers as the intended composer, Jerome Kern, had died). Incidentally, Felder does a great Ethel Merman imitation!

Felder traces Irving Berlin's life in chronological order starting with his birth somewhere in the Russian empire, his family's escape from the Russian pogroms and their arrival at Ellis Island when he was only five years old, and his beginnings in music as a singing waiter.

He had two marriages, his first wife dying soon after their marriage, and his second from one of the wealthiest families in America -- a marriage to which her family of course strongly objected. He lost his only son in his infancy and had three daughters. These facts are woven into the incredible musical accomplishments of his life.

The evening is further enhanced thanks to the astute direction of Trevor Hay who cleverly embeds scenes from movies, still photographs and other emotionally relevant images and sounds on a large "mirror" and wall behind Felder.

But foremost is Felder's spirited and talented portrayal of Berlin – in song, in piano performance, and acting, capturing the essence of the man and an era, underscoring the importance of Berlin to the Great American Songbook. Indeed, as Jerome Kern said "he IS American music."

Remarkably, his composition and performance abilities were all self-taught. He wrote all his songs in F Sharp and they had to be transposed for most performances. It is a most unlikely story, the immigrant songwriter who couldn't read music and ultimately wrote some of the most iconic American songs. Felder's story emphasizes his contributions to both the WW I and WW II war efforts. Simply put, he loved America.

Berlin's times, of course, had its own societal afflictions and horrors, and except for a few brief moments here and there, referring to the depression, and racial segregation and prejudice, and a little about anti-Semitism from his father in law, Felder mostly avoids those issues. But this is meant to be more of a "feel good" bio-musical, and the author/performer sticks to his mission.

Felder's ability to tell this story as an integrated musical performance has, I think, matured over the years. About 15 years ago we saw him perform his first bio-musical *Gershwin Alone* at The Cuillo Centre for the Arts in West Palm Beach which ironically has now been transformed into the home that Dramaworks now occupies. We loved that show as well, but I recall it was not as much of a biographically integrated theatre piece as this one of Berlin. Instead, it was more reliant on Felder's considerable talent as a concert pianist. His *Irving Berlin* show tells the life story seamlessly through his acting, singing, and playing. In other words, it meets the test of the modern Broadway musical although only one person, but, oh, what a remarkably talented person he is.

The thousands of songs Berlin wrote during his long career, which included more than a score of Broadway shows and Hollywood musicals tapped into feelings and tunes that appealed to his generation and succeeding ones, and Felder frequently engages the audience to sing along. As he said after the show in a casual Q & A, there are basically three players in his piece, he, the piano and the audience.

After more than 1-1/2 hours without intermission and a standing ovation, he still had the enthusiasm and energy to spend another half hour with the audience amusingly fielding questions. It was like talking to your best friend, but one with exceptional gifts.

We look forward to his future works, including a new play featuring the music of Sergei Rachmaninoff. Sign us up!

And so after such a satisfying evening we followed the winding roads of Westport back to our boat as a thunderstorm was gathering in the west. Luckily, we beat it "home."

Thursday, August 15, 2019 'Moulin Rouge!' and 'Oklahoma!' Seismically Shake Broadway

This summer we saw only two Broadway shows but what a change of pace from many of those we've seen in summers past. One would think *Moulin Rouge!* and *Oklahoma!* would be "traditional" musicals but they felt as "revolutionary" as *Hamilton* was when we saw that when it originally opened. Hearing so much about these two shows, some negativity from a critic we highly respect, we were determined to experience these with a tabula rasa mentality.

We're glad we did. Had we approached these with our built in biases, ones that are due to our age and previous theatre experiences, there would be a lot that we could seize upon for criticism. First and foremost as traditionalists, if we had to see *Oklahoma!* over and over again, it would probably be some of the previous stage versions we've seen or even the movie version with Gordon MacRae and Shirley Jones. They come closer to Rodgers &Hammerstein's original.

This version of *Oklahoma* is darkly different. Last April we saw Ted Chapin, chief creative officer of the Rodgers & Hammerstein Organization, interviewed at Dramaworks' "Dramalogue – Talking Theatre!" Much of the discussion was about the decision making process that went into his giving the green light to this 'dark-side-of-the-moon' version of this fabled musical. Clearly, had there been no *Hamilton*, perhaps this adaptation would never have been approved. It is indeed reimagined, taking such an innocent story (albeit with a sinister side) and turns it topsy-turvy; utterly stripped down to its essentials.

You know the second you enter the Circle in the Square Theatre, Winchester Rifles decorating the walls, a brightly lit stage made up of picnic benches and plywood floors, a small area for an equally small on stage orchestra, multicolored metallic fringe hanging from the ceiling, crock pots lining bench tables on stage left and right at which some audience members are sitting that the goal is to involve the audience members in a very contemporary rendering. This isn't why the farmer and the cowmen can't be friends. The essence of this production is Laurey having to choose between Curley and Jud Fry. Yes, having to choose! In all versions we have ever seen, this choice was made for us right at the burst of "Oh, What a Beautiful Morning." It's Curley, hands down.

While Jud is clearly a loner in those early days when Oklahoma was emerging from a small territory to statehood, today our Jud would be one of the 21st century misfits who 'merely' needs understanding to bring him into "society." So, in this adaptation Laurey, heavenly played by Rebecca Naomi Jones, is attracted to the brooding quiet Jud. She actually waivers in her choice!

When we sat down and opened our Playbill, we were disappointed to learn that Curley, the male lead, usually played by Damon Daunno, was to be played by his understudy Denver Milord. He more than rose to the occasion as not only did he exude that sexy American as apple pie good looks but he could belt out his songs with his guitar, finally winning over Laurey. But Laurey's infatuation with Jud is a hurdle for him, constantly perplexing and the end of the play is something unexpected. It is a road we have seen walked so many times in contemporary society, quick to judgment to exonerate the "good guy," which, as the last moving refrains of "O-K-L-A-H-O-M-A" ring out, leaves one bewildered.

Everything in the production is atypical, including the audience being served some delicious chili and cornbread during the intermission. The cast is small but the essential story lines are there, Will Parker played with wide-eyed innocence and gullibility by James Davis, declaring his love for Ado Annie, played by the exceptionally talented Ali Stroker with such hilarity and an ethereal voice that one hardly notices she is wheel chair bound, another hat tip to contemporary society. 'Ole Aunt Eller played by Mary Testa is the peacekeeper and Will Brill plays the flirtatious Ali Hakim, the peddler who will take what he can from Ado Annie as long as it doesn't involve marriage. Jud Fry is quietly, but achingly played by Patrick Vail. He originated the role of Jud while a student at Bard College.

Most emblematic of the departure of this *Oklahoma!* from the original is the dream ballet. The original, choreographed by Agnes DeMille is ethereal. Now it is one of boldness, parts of it performed in darkness, music dissonant and other parts filmed in real time as cinema verite and projected on the rear wall. Its vivid content was brilliantly translated by anther understudy in this particular production, Coral Dolphin, whose physicality, including cartwheels, took precedence over ballet. It is a modern dance of the 21st century.

And as far as *Moulin Rouge!* is concerned, the pastiche of seventy or so songs is not of our generation for the most part, except for "Diamonds are A Girl's Best Friend" and "Nature Boy." The songs of younger generations predominate, but the swatches of them are seamlessly woven into the production, picking out the right lyrics and musical riff for the moment, so that they move the production right along.

We found ourselves enjoying them in spite of our ingrained aversion to ultra contemporary music. Our son and daughter-in-law sat in the row in front of us, their heads bobbing along to the music with which they're totally familiar, enhancing our enjoyment as well.

Moulin Rouge! is intended as an over the top extravaganza, another criticism which could be leveled at it from the vantage of the highbrow. It is that, especially sitting in the third row as we were fortunate enough to be. It is a love story as anyone familiar with the movie or *La Boheme* knows, but the dazzling staging and sensuality trump the love story. Or, one could consider it the strength of this production, one that shares some aspects of *Cirque du Soleil*, replete with the female lead, Satine, gloriously played by Karen Olivo, descending from the ceiling of the Al Hirschfield Theatre. It is the type of gimmickry we would normally decry but in the context of this musical, it works, as do the songs and the erotic nature of the presentation, the costumes and the movement on the stage. Only a great Broadway company could pull this off.

Satine's love interest, Christian, played by Aaron Tveit, is yet another star in the diamond of a cast as is Tam Mutu playing Christian's adversary, The Duke of Monroth. Danny Burstein plays the MC Harold Zidler, reminiscent of the demonic MC of *Cabaret*. The ensemble is sexy and vibrant. The chorography of moving all these players around ramps, and platforms stage left and right is breathtaking. When we saw *Hamilton*, now years ago, we knew we were seeing something for the ages. In its own way *Moulin Rouge!* will be that memorable.

In fact, that is what we came away with after these two groundbreaking musicals. These are our times, brutish and violent, frequently unfair, sometimes steeped in narcissism and eroticism, a kind of dystopian landscape captured by the remake of one of our most innocent musicals, and a movie brought to stage. But bravo to both as art marks the way and records our moment in time.

Saturday, November 23, 2019 **A Riotous Production of 'A Funny Thing...' Erupts at the Rinker Playhouse**

Something for students of Sondheim. Something for lovers of shtick. Something for supporters of South Florida theatre. "Something for everyone – a comedy tonight!" MNM theatre company knocks A *Funny Thing Happened on the Way to the Forum* out of the Coliseum at the Rinker Playhouse, part of the Kravis complex.

It is thought of as Sondheim's first musical for which he wrote both the lyrics and the music. It is and it isn't. His first such attempt, *Saturday Night*, was written eight years earlier, but it never made it to Broadway at the time (although that was where it was headed) as the Producer suddenly died and the bankroll evaporated. It reflected his youth of being only 22, a traditional musical, so unlike his later innovative works. Still, the unproduced musical put him on the radar scope and he was soon sought out as a lyricist, with such shows as *West Side Story* and *Gypsy*.

Sondheim however wanted to be a composer-lyricist; thus, indeed, *A Funny Thing Happened on the Way to the Forum* IS his first Broadway credit in both capacities. For any Sondheim fan, it is a must see musical for that reason alone. It clearly reflects his genius as a wordsmith, although one can also detect his unique musical gift incubating, particularly in the duets. And it is the lyrics and "the book" by Burt Shevelove and Larry Gelbart (of M*A*S*H fame) that made, and continues to make this early Sondheim work a success. It unfolds at a hilarious frenetic pace and it immediately grabs the audience's attention with "Comedy Tonight."

The mad cap farce involves a conniving Roman slave (Pseudolus) who wants his freedom while his master (Hero) wants the virginal girl next door (Philia), and so the slave concocts a plan to achieve his master's desire IF he will give him his freedom. Sounds pretty straightforward except every complication known to vaudevillian theatre is thrown in the way.

So, kudos to MNM Productions for bringing Sondheim's vintage, formative work to the Rinker Playhouse. MNM's mission is to "showcase talented Florida-based actors, Equity and non-Equity alike, live musicians and a top-notch crew of designers and technicians." With this show, mission accomplished! It is a professional production in every way, particularly due to the talented cast whose voices soared in the ensemble musical numbers.

Johnbarry Green who we have seen perform locally at the Maltz and at Palm Beach Dramaworks, plays the iconic part of Pseudolus (Sondheim originally thought of the fast talking Phil Silvers when he was writing it, but it was Zero Mostel who first played the part on stage and in the movie so it is he who is traditionally identified as Pseudolus). It's a tall order and the entire production depends on Green's ability to successfully pull off this buffoonish role and sing and dance and basically knock himself out for 2-1/2 hours. Within minutes he has the audience laughing so that possible hurdle is comfortably cleared. In fact, throughout the performance Green shows his comic physicality and even had to ad lib on stage when he almost fell off a bench, turning to the audience who drew in its breath in anticipation, saying "It's OK, don't worry!!" not missing a beat. Only live theatre can convey such a special moment.

Green is all over the stage throughout the production, just one of the many details of the show's complex choreography so seamlessly arranged by Laura Plyler. But in Johnbarry Green's performance, "a star is born." He has all the acting and comic chops and a rousing voice that enhances his performance.

J Savage plays Hero the young master who is so naively induced into Pseudolus' increasingly complicated scheme with wide eyed wonder of innocence, his heart set on having the virginal Philia who was entrancingly played by the beautiful Meg Frost.

Hero's father, the lecherous Senex, is skillfully performed by Troy Stanley who is clearly carrying the burden of being the henpecked husband of Domina, who Aaron Bower plays up as a shrew to be feared. The pivotal role Hysterium is truly hysterically acted by Michael Scott Ross. He is not on the stage for a moment without a laugh. Terry Hardcastle plays the owner of the house of courtesans, Marcus Lycus, who is willing to agree to any of Pseudolus' plans as long as he is not in jeopardy. The character Erronius is condemned to wander around the stage most of the night looking for his children who were stolen as infants by pirates. Paul Thompson's portrayal of the old man received greater laughs after each turn around the 7 hills surrounding Rome. And his plight is part of the show's resolution.

Another star in the show bursts forth near the end of the first act, the arrival of Miles Gloriosus, a Roman Captain who has a claim on Phila (part of the plot's complication). Miles is indeed gloriously played by Sean William Davis. (Think of the bravado of Lancelot singing "C'est Moi" in *Camelot*.). Davis just oozes Majesty and sex appeal on stage, while his voice is clear and powerful. Yet he, too, is duped by Pseudolus.

The courtesans – "Tintinabula, Panacea, Geminae Twins, Vibrata, and Gymnasia" – are so amusingly and seductively played as their namesakes by Meredith Pughe, Alexandra Van Hasselt. Victoria Joleen Anderson, Alexandra Dow, Lauren Cluett, and Ashley Rubin respectively, while "The Proteans" who are called upon by the characters to play different roles to move the comedic plot along are entertainingly and sometimes acrobatically played by Stephen Eisenwasser, Frank Francisco, and Elijah Pearson-Martinez.

This classic production is under the capable directorial hand of Jonathan Van Dyke who also coordinated the costumes and a special mention should be made of the original set design by Cindi Taylor and superb wigs by Justin Lore. Lighting Designer is Rachel Weis. Sound Engineer Vincent Bryant's work excelled: rarely have we been at a performance where every word can be clearly heard, whether said or sung, so important in this production. Even James Danford came out of retirement briefly to serve as Stage Manager, no small feat in this show. Paul Reekie serves as a musical director of a band of six which in the intimate Rinker Playhouse sounds almost like a full Broadway orchestra.

I mention all these names as they are South Florida actors and theatre technicians who deserve our support, especially as together they created a "pretty little masterpiece" (Green sings the memorable song "Pretty Little Picture").

EPILOGUE

COVID-19 engulfed the world while I was doing the final proofing of this work. Ann and I had been self quarantining even before it finally became a mandate, that coming too late to save even more lives. Our unpreparedness comes at a terrible cost, upending all our lives, causing unbearable economic hardship for many, and putting our health professionals in the line of fire as well as people who have been sadly marginalized before, our truck drivers, grocery workers, postal and delivery workers.

Our own early embrace of isolation was due to our age and health condition, particularly mine having both lung and heart issues. Some think that everyone should "tough this out." This disease unfortunately is not a one size fits all issue. Until there are effective therapeutics and better still a proven vaccination, as a society we are going to have to carefully weigh the meaning of our "Unalienable Rights to Life, Liberty and the Pursuit of Happiness." Concessions will have to be made while our best minds (and I do not mean anyone remotely connected to politics) tackle the scientific data, therapeutics, and vaccines.

Our most vulnerable members of society -- I personally think of the many residents of assisted living facilities I've entertained with my piano concerts over the years – will depend on reasonable social distancing to be practiced by all until we can treat this disease. It is not an issue of "liberating" society. It is one of following scientifically based best practices for the greater good. On the other hand there is the economy, unemployment which is cruelly borne by people most unable to suffer that consequence, and the massive debt to consider, as well as the animus of youth: a "delicate balance," indeed.

While editing this work, the horror of COVID-19 seemed, on the one hand, to minimize its meaning and, on the other, validate its contents. Human beings are social animals. I think of what I reviewed in this book as being evidence of that, the culmination of extensive interaction and intensive creative thought and emotion. Surely the collective energy that went into the works and performances described in these pages could move mountains, find solutions to the current crisis, and continue to nourish our souls.

So, ultimately, *Explaining It To Someone* is dedicated to all involved in finding valid scientific solutions, those in the front lines allowing society to function, and to the artists who help us find our humanity.